Brecht damals und heute

Das Brecht-Jahrbuch 20

Redaktion des Bandes
John Willett

Geschäftsführende Herausgeber:
Marc Silberman und Maarten van Dijk

Mitherausgeber:
Roswitha Mueller, Antony Tatlow, Carl Weber

Redaktionelle Hilfe: **Susan Spruell**

Die Internationale Brecht-Gesellschaft
Vertrieb: University of Wisconsin Press

Brecht Then and Now

The Brecht Yearbook 20

Guest Editor
John Willett

Managing Editors:
Marc Silberman and Maarten van Dijk

Editorial Board:
Roswitha Mueller, Antony Tatlow, Carl Weber

Editorial Assistant: **Susan Spruell**

The International Brecht Society
Distribution: University of Wisconsin Press

Printed by Graphic Services, at the University of Waterloo, Ontario,
Canada. Distributed by the University of Wisconsin Press, 114 N.
Murray, Madison, WI 53715

ISSN 0734-8665
ISBN 0-9623206-7-6

Special acknowledgement to Barbara Hochstedt (University of
Waterloo) and Thomas Jung (University of Wisconsin-Madison) for
assisting in the translation of abstracts, Sigfrid Hoefert for assistance,
to Carl Hennig (University of Waterloo) for work on graphics, as
well as to the Department of German at the University of Wisconsin-Madison for generous financial support of the Yearbook.

Officers of the International Brecht Society:

Michael Morley, President, School of Humanities, Flinders University, Bedford Park, South Australia 5042

Siegfried Mews, Vice-President, Department of Germanic Languages, 438 Dey Hall, University of North Carolina, Chapel Hill, NC 27599-3160, USA

Ward B. Lewis, Secretary/Treasurer, Department of Germanic and Slavic Languages, University of Georgia, Athens, GA 30602, USA

Vera Stegmann, Department of Modern Foreign Languages, Lehigh University, Bethlehem, PA 18015, USA

* * * * *

Membership:

Members receive *The Brecht Yearbook* and the biannual journal *Communications of the International Brecht Society*. Dues should be sent in US$ to the Secretary/Treasurer or in DM to the Deutsche Bank Düsseldorf (BLZ 300 702 00, Konto-Nr. 76-74146):

Student Member (up to three years)	$15.00	DM 24,-
Regular Member,		
annual income under $20,000	$20.00	DM 32,-
annual income over $20,000	$25.00	DM 40,-
Sustaining Member	$30.00	DM 48,-
Institutional Member	$30.00	DM 48,-

* * * * *

Submissions:

Manuscripts submitted to *The Brecht Yearbook* should be typed and double spaced throughout, addressed to the Managing Editor:

Maarten van Dijk, Drama Department, University of Waterloo, 200 University Ave. West, Waterloo, Ontario, Canada, N2L 3G1

Submit manuscripts prepared on computer with a hard copy and diskette (ASCII, WordPerfect, or Microsoft Word). Endnote format should be internally consistent, following the MLA or Chicago style manuals.

Inquiries concerning book reviews should be addressed to:

Marc Silberman, Department of German, 818 Van Hise Hall, University of Wisconsin, Madison, WI 53706, USA

The International Brecht Society

The International Brecht Society has been formed as a corresponding society on the model of Brecht's own unrealized plan for the Diderot Society. Through its publications and regular international symposia, the society encourages the discussion of any and all views on the relationship of the arts and the contemporary world. The society is open to new members in any field and in any country and welcomes suggestions and/or contributions in German, English, Spanish or French to future symposia and for the published volumes of its deliberations.

Die Internationale Brecht-Gesellschaft

Die Internationale Brecht-Gesellschaft ist nach dem Modell von Brechts nicht verwirklichtem Plan für die Diderot-Gesellschaft gegründet worden. Durch Veröffentlichungen und regelmäßige internationale Tagungen fördert die Gesellschaft freie und öffentliche Diskussionen über die Beziehungen aller Künste zur heutigen Welt. Die Gesellschaft steht neuen Mitgliedern in jedem Fachgebiet und Land offen und begrüßt Vorschläge für zukünftige Tagungen und Aufsätze in deutscher, englischer, spanischer oder französischer Sprache für *Das Brecht-Jahrbuch*.

La Société Internationale Brecht

La Société Internationale Brecht a été formée pour correspondre à la société rêvée par Brecht, "Diderot-Gesellschaft." Par ses publications et congrès internationaux à intervalles réguliers, la S.I.B. encourage la discussion libre des toutes les idées sur les rapports entre les arts et le monde contemporain. Bien entendu, les nouveaux membres dans toutes les disciplines et tous les pays sont accueillis avec plaisir, et la Société sera heureuse d'accepter des suggestions et des contributions en français, allemand, espagnol ou anglais pour les congrès futurs et les volumes des communications qui en résulteront.

La Sociedad Internacional Brecht

La Sociedad Internacional Brecht fué creada para servir como sociedad corresponsal. Dicha sociedad se basa en el modelo que el mismo autor nunca pudo realizar, el plan "Diderot-Gesellschaft." A través de sus publicaciones y los simposios internacionales que se llevan a cabo regularmente, la Sociedad estimula la discusión libre y abierta de cualquier punto de vista sobre la relación entre las artes y el mundo contemporáneo. La Sociedad desea, por supuesto, la participación de nuevos miembros de cualquier área, de cualquier país, y acepta sugerencias y colaboraciones en alemán, inglés, francés y español para los congresos futuros y para las publicaciones de sus discusiones.

Contents

Editorial

Plans were laid for establishing the International Brecht Society in December 1968 at the Modern Language Association Conference in New York City, and the Society's first Yearbook appeared in Germany in 1971. The Yearbook has changed its title, editors, and publisher several times since then. An index at the end of this Yearbook lists all twenty volumes, indicating the various changes. This volume, the twentieth, marks twenty-five years of IBS publication and scholarly activities. John Willett, the guest editor and a former editorial board member of the *Brecht Yearbook*, has brought together a rich selection of material from international contributors that we, the managing editors, have grouped together with the usual scholarly essays and book reviews. The stunning variety and vigor reflected in this writing are, we feel, an appropriate way to celebrate the occasion.

An editorial oversight in volume 19 (1994) led Dr. Erdmut Wizisla, director of the Bertolt Brecht Archive in Berlin, to grant permission subsequently for the publication of the two poems by Margarete Steffin on page 113 and for the previously unpublished play *Die Geisteranna* on pages 1-43. For future reference scholars should note that, to quote material held in the Bertolt Brecht Archive, permission is necessary from the Archive *as well as* from the respective estate; the Weigel and Hauptmann archives are part of the "Stiftung Archiv der Akademie der Künste" in Berlin, as is the Bertolt Brecht Archive, and the Stiftung grants permission for quoting from these archive materials.

At this time volume 21 of the *Brecht Yearbook* is being planned as an open volume, and scholarly submissions are welcome on all topics "around" Brecht as well as essays on broader issues of contemporary theater practice. Selected proceedings from the Ninth IBS Symposium, held in Augsburg (Germany) on March 10-11, 1995, will constitute one section of the volume. With volume 21 managing responsibility for the Yearbook shifts entirely to Maarten van Dijk in Toronto.

Marc Silberman
University of Wisconsin

Maarten van Dijk
University of Waterloo

Thirteen Poets Look at Brecht

John Willett

It occurred to us while planning this volume of the *Yearbook* that it would be interesting to find out how some of today's poets react to Brecht's poetry, which even now is less widely known than his theatrical work. So we consulted a very mixed set of writers to see what they might have to say. Most of them write in English even when it is not their native language; one or two in German; some are known to have translated Brecht or adapted him; some read him in translation. Their knowledge of the original varies. Some have a deep understanding of the material; others are drawn to Brecht by much simpler, more superficial considerations. All, however, seem to reflect from their own approach some aspect of this polymorphous artist, who left his unmistakable imprint on everything he touched. Reading through their remarks and their poems it is as if something in these had flown off a single brightly spinning nucleus — a nucleus composed of many different elements, old and new, aesthetic and political, individual and collective. In the theater there are recognizable characteristics and mannerisms that are still called "Brechtian." Among the poets the effects are not so neat.[*]

* * * * * * * *

Naomi Replansky, now living in New York, whose responses open our inquiry, was the translator of "The Swamp," set to music by Eisler as one of the Hollywood Elegies. It was only after Brecht's death and her translation's inclusion in *Poems 1913-1956* that the original German text came to light among papers left by Peter Lorre, the actor whom Brecht had cast in *Happy End* and *Die Pioniere von Ingolstadt* even before Fritz Lang's *M* made him famous. Lorre was

Brecht Then and Now / Brecht damals und heute
Eds. Marc Silberman et al. *The Brecht Yearbook / Das Brecht-Jahrbuch*
Volume 20 (Madison: The International Brecht Society, 1995)

[*] *All poems are used with permission of the writers*

a good friend to the Brechts in the US, and the poem is concerned with his drug habit and the dealers supplying him. Her recollection of work with Brecht leads into some examples of her own poems from the collections *Ring Song* (Scribner, 1952) and *The Dangerous World* (Another Chicago Press, 1994, distributed by the Talman Company).

How Does One Distinguish Literary Influence?

How does one disentangle literary influence? In my early twenties, I first encountered Brecht's work through the songs in *The Three-penny Opera* and a translation of that great poem, "An die Nach-geborenen." I was already imprinted: by Shakespeare; English and Scottish songs and ballads; spirituals and blues; Chinese and Japanese poetry in translation (in my youth mostly by Arthur Waley); Villon; the Greek Anthology (in the Loeb edition). So there was already an affinity of influence.

In 1946 I was 28; had published poems but no book as yet; and had just arrived in Santa Monica, California. Brecht and Charles Laughton were then collaborating on *Galileo*. In the course of that year I worked with Brecht on translating some of the poems that were later published in Switzerland under the title *Kriegsfibel*. He had accumulated clippings of World War II photographs from European and American magazines and had written four-line rhymed epigrams in comment upon each. Many of these quatrains — ironic, or angry, or deeply moving — had a concentrated power. I translated only those that appealed to me.

Here is how I recall the translation sessions. I had only high-school German. Brecht read English subtly and well, I thought. We would go through the original word by word, making sure I got the exact meaning. We digressed; Brecht walked up and down the narrow workroom, gesturing with his cigar, open to criticism and disputation.

I would then take the original home and try (often obsessively) to carry over its poetic strength into English and to keep at least two of the rhymes. A few came easily into rhyme, a few only after long struggle, others defeated me, and I would compromise with an un-rhymed poem.

A couple of examples — under a photograph of defeated German soldiers in the Russian winter:

Seht unsre Söhne, taub und blutbefleckt

Vom eingefrornen Tank hier losgeschnallt;
Ach selbst der Wolf braucht, der die Zähne bleckt
Ein Schlupfloch! Wärmt sie, es ist ihnen kalt.

[Our sons, deaf and bloodspattered, here behold
Pried from the frozen tank. Ah, even the wolf
Who bares his fangs, at last must find himself
A hole to hide in. Warm them, they are cold.]

Another — beneath the photo of the execution of a blindfolded
Frenchman by German soldiers:

So haben wir ihn an die Wand gestellt:
Mensch unsresgleichen, einer Mutter Sohn
Ihn umzubringen. Und damit die Welt
Es wisse, machten wir ein Bild davon.

[And so we put him up against the wall
A man like us, a mother's son like us
To murder him. And then we took
A picture of it, that the world might know.]

I had long been intrigued by the epigrammatic form and had written
some epigrams (mostly epitaphs) in the past. But a poem I wrote at
the time was I think a direct outcome of my immersion in the work
on *Kriegsfibel*.

EPITAPH 1945

My spoon was lifted when the bomb came down
That left no face, no hand, no spoon to hold.
A hundred thousand died in my home town.
This came to pass before my soup was cold.

A lyric that Brecht wrote, I believe that same year, was "Der
Sumpf," which I translated from his handwritten copy. It is a
beautiful poem. (Hanns Eisler set it to music. He used my translation, but rewrote some of the lines in quite fractured English. To my
chagrin he left my name on as translator of *his* version.)

    Another group of earlier poems, *Aus einem Lesebuch für
Städtebewohner*, which I translated in part, exerted a definite
influence on me, with their direct, stripped, almost conversational

3

diction; their use of homely metaphor. The following poem of mine is a product of that influence and that time:

HOUSING SHORTAGE

I tried to live small
I took a narrow bed.
I held my elbows to my sides.
I tried to step carefully
And to think softly
And to breathe shallowly
In my portion of air
And to disturb no one.

Yet see how I spread out and I cannot help it.
I take to myself more and more, and I take nothing
That I do not need, but my needs grow like weeds,
All over and invading; I clutter this place
With all the apparatus of living.
You stumble over it daily.

And then my lungs take their fill
And then you gasp for air.

Excuse me for living,
But, since I am living,
Given inches, I take yards,
Taking yards, dream of miles,
And a landscape, unbounded
And vast in abandon.

And you dreaming the same.

Brecht's voice still echoes in my head. The other day, I saw in a newspaper a photograph from World War I: a file of British soldiers, blinded by poison gas, each with his hand on the shoulder of the man in front. I looked at it with shock. Then, almost as a reflex, I thought I could hear Brecht comment on the scene in another bitter and compassionate epigram.

Naomi Replansky

Loss in Los Angeles

Outside, unmoving smog.
How can there be a hurricane in your head?
Around you, gardens too sweetly scented.
How can you contain wilderness?
The rainy season is over.
What is that wet on your cheeks?

Factory Poem

The tool-bit cut, the metal curled,
The oil soaked through her clothing.
She made six hundred parts a day
And timed herself by breathing.

And what she made and where it went
She did not ask or wonder:
Gone to rust, or to machines
Of pleasure or of murder.

She dared not quit; she had seen those
Who fought like jackals over
The carcass of a rotting job
In cold Depression weather.

As if each payday would repay,
As if she'd live forever,
She wished away the newborn week
And wished the daylight over:

> *Evening bell, you I long for*
> *With such restless longing,*
> *Come, straighten my shoulders*
> *And deliver my hands.*

Night Prayer for Various Trades

Machinist in the pillow's grip,
Be clumsy and be blind
And let the gears spin free, and turn
No metal in your mind.

Long, long may the actress lie
In slumber like a stone,
The helpless words that rise from sleep
Be no words but her own.

Laborer, drift through a dark
Remote from clay and lime.
O do not tunnel through the night
In unpaid overtime.

You out-of-work, walk into sleep.
It will not ask to see
Your proof of skill or strength or youth
And shows its movies free.

And may the streetcleaner float down
A spotless avenue.
  Who red-eyed wake at morning break
  All have enough to do.

Enough to do. Now let the day
Its own accountings keep.
But may our dreams keep other time
Throughout our sprawling sleep.

(1957)

IN THE BROKEN CITY

The small ghost
stood on the roof
and cried.

In the broken places
mother was searching
father was searching
both were crying
ghost was crying

in that thin voice
from the last roof.

(1992)

* * * * * * *

Christopher Logue is a poet living in London and widely respected for his translations of Homer (broadcast several times on BBC radio). For some years he wrote the "True Stories" column for the satirical fortnightly *Private Eye*. Already in 1957 he was using Brechtian lines in his original poems, while his songs for the musical *The Lily White Boys* (1959) at the Royal Court Theater were evidently inspired by *The Threepenny Opera*. In Paris he worked for Girodias at the Olympia Press (writing a pornovel under the name Count Palmiro Vicarion); in Berlin he sat in on rehearsals at the Theater am Schiffbauerdamm and watched Brecht at work. His translation of *The Seven Deadly Sins* was published by Ambit Books in 1986. Following his "Note on Brecht," we cite sections IV and V of his "version" of the "Rat an die bildenden Künstler, das Schicksal ihrer Kunstwerke in den kommenden Kriegen betreffend" from Brecht's *Svendborger Gedichte*: "To My Fellow Artists," from Ode to the Dodo (Cape, 1993).

Note on Brecht

I first heard of Brecht as a writer whose work expressed political thoughts from a left-wing point of view in Paris in 1952. Not long after I was over at Simon Vinkenoog's studio near the Invalides. Knowing I was keen on Brecht, he read off from a newspaper (German?) a poem Brecht had sent to a South American magazine "about the use of atomic weapons," me copying out his oral translation. In the 1970s the National Theater held a Brecht exhibition in their foyer. The young scholar who was responsible for the catalogue [Nicholas Jacobs, founder and publisher of Libris books] came to me, and I told him about this poem's supposed source. Some time after this he wrote to me, saying "I can find no trace of the Brecht poem."

Wishing to express such ideas in my own work but being without an English model, I began to read Brecht's plays. I love *Courage*, *Ui* and *Galileo*, but it was not until I began to read his poems — again in translation — that I saw what a wonderful poet the man was. "Evelyn Roe," the "Nasty Fellow," the "Ballad of Friendship" — how unusual this man's mind is, I thought, at once analytical, intellectual, ironic, and at the same time lyrical, and so friendly, so confiding...superb. A master. I shall always be in his debt.

Christopher Logue

From **TO MY FELLOW ARTISTS**

IV

Listen, I beg you. Six days ago
a paper called *The Sunday Times*
revealed, with witless candour,
their dead thoughts:

You are confused about destruction, yes?
they said. And then — recommending the death of the country
in the name of the country: *We shall bomb,*
if bomb we must, bomb like King Billy,
for the British have something to die for.
No mention was made of something to live for.
Saying (in the names of loyalty, faith, integrity):
How vile they are who wish to live here
minus the local notion of democracy.
Not speaking of those who wish to die here.

The death before dishonour, boys;
the death before gestapo, boys;
the death before a tyrant, boys;
the death before *The Sunday Times.*

But where is the dishonour, gestapo, or tyrant?
And who wants to dishonour or govern a cinder?
My friends,
How difficult it is for those who speak
out of anger to answer those who speak
out of complacency.

And yet, imagine a horror
and perpetrate horrors because of it,
is called mad.

Think desolation
and create desolation because of it,
is called mad.

Thus the Ripper and Christie
thought of whores.
Thus they think of our country.

V

So do you agree with them
Spender, and Barker, and Auden?
And you, my newly married master, Eliot —
will you adopt their lie by silence,
and having sold our flesh to war
bequeath our bones to God?
Or are there two sides to *this* question?

But I fear we are easily beaten.
So where shall we hide them, our treasures?
Uncertain the disused chalk pit;
uncertain the bank's steel vault;
and the holds of ships are uncertain.

We must beg for permission
to hang our paintings underground,
to store our books and stones in mines;
but the rents will be high underground,
and I doubt if we can afford them.

Perhaps they will let a few of us hide
in the negative silos, 1000 feet down,
where, beside telephones, uniformed men
await fatal words.
We must not be afraid to ask;
for works concerning the private heart
will not alter devoted experts.

But let us remember to leave behind
permanent signs. Signs that are easily read.
Signs that say: So deep,
beneath so many feet of stone,
is a poem expressing refinement of taste,
a book about logic, a tape of quartets,
and a picture of the painter's wife.

Then can our six-handed grandsons,
our unborn consolation,
discover that we too, had art.
And those who dare look
over the crater's jagged rim,

may, in the evening, climb down
into the mauve bowl of London,
and dig.
While their guards watch out
for tyrants, and food, and sun.

Think, men of no future,
but with a name to come.

* * * * * * * *

Andy Croft lectures on English literature and creative writing for
Leeds University's Department of Adult Continuing Education in the
Yorkshire industrial city of Middlesbrough, Cleveland. He also
broadcasts for BBC Radio 4. He is author of a critical study of
English literature in the 1930s entitled *Red Letter Days* (Lawrence
and Wishart, 1990) and is now preparing a biography of the English
Communist poet Randall Swingler.

Poetry in a Bitter Wind

I came to Brecht's poetry late. This is not difficult in British literary
culture, which long ago learned to inoculate itself against writing
like Brecht's — too ideological, too propagandist, too much like
hard work. The end of the Cold War has of course only legitimized
prejudice against Brecht's writings, easy to dismiss now as period-
pieces, dated, dull, and so *obvious*.

It was not until I was at performance of *Die Dreigroschenoper*
by the Berliner Ensemble at the Schiffbauerdamm Theater in 1989,
that I realized — with some shock — how much I had underestimated Brecht as a poet. Waking the following morning in a flat in the
Tiergarten "Die Moritat von Mackie Messer" still on my mind, I
switched on the radio to find an American Forces station playing
Frank Sinatra singing "Mack the Knife" and suddenly understood the
sheer *scale* of the writing, the extraordinary force of such simple,
brutal, unironic verse, undiminished by translation across that
divided city.

Despite all the invigorating developments of recent years,
English poetry is still terribly constricted by irony, unable to say
things directly, embarrassed by plain-speaking. The welcome
interest in provincial, vernacular, conversational speech patterns has
done little to erode this; if anything it has simply introduced another

layer of street-wise double meanings. Much of the liveliness of contemporary poetry may be said to derive from its intimacy with film, short-story, cabaret, and rock music. But as a consequence, much of even the best new writing is more interested in the surface pleasures of language and cultural reference than in ethical or political questions. There is, to be sure, a new kind of "political" poetry in Britain; poets like Ian Duhig, Simon Armitage, Sean O'Brien, Carol Ann Duffy, Mark Robinson, Ken Smith, Linda France, and Peter Sansom are writing a "sassy," knowing, tongue-in-cheek poetry which I enjoy, but which is rarely adequate for addressing the historical ironies of our time.

Following the coup-d'état in the Soviet Union and the subsequent fall of Mikhail Gorbachov, I knew I needed to try to write about the tragi-farcical end of whatever it was that had died. The Soviet Union, certainly. "Actually-Existing-Socialism" forms of Leninist organization, and of course "Stalinism." But much more than this — *perestroika* and *glasnost*. Dubček's hope for a "Communism with a Human Face," the Eurocommunist project, the dream of a reforming, popular, democratizing Marxism, and the hopes of my friends in the SED in the GDR. And beyond that, five thousand years of oppositional, critical, utopian thought and poetry. I don't suggest, of course, that the Soviet Union was any kind of utopia, but it clearly did exert a sort of millenarian pull on the imaginations of several generations of Socialists (including Brecht) and millions of people around the world. As a Eurocommunist, I was surprised how badly the collapse of the Soviet Union affected me, how implicated I was, how much I had invested in Gorbachov's reforms.

But trying to address this kind of large subject directly is not easy on this island, where ambivalence is hard to distinguish from ambiguity, seeing two sides of a question soon turns into a very English "plague on both your houses," and despair and confusion are a literary manner. The poetry of Tony Harrison and Douglas Dunn is a great encouragement for anyone wishing to engage with political events without sounding either shrill or sentimental, but it was Brecht's poetry, especially the poems and songs written after Brecht left Germany in 1933, that encouraged me to try.

The *Svendborg Poems* in particular struck me with their extraordinary simplicity of diction and clarity of expression, Brecht's ability to express complex ideas in bald, flat, unadorned phrases. Irony here lies *outside* the poem, in the changed meanings forced upon words by historical events, rather than in a knowing, tongue-in-cheek speaking voice. Brecht's easy use of meter and rhyme, particularly his familiarity with the sonnet form, seems to me an important expression of the need to impose some kind of form upon terrible and overwhelming experience. Above all, the powerful elegiac sense of these poems is never once confused with nostalgia for the past, always leaning forwards into the bitter winds of History.

The resulting sequence of poems falls a long way short of my hopes for it. And it is not at all "Brechtian" but it does owe a great deal to my desire to catch the plain, unironic form of address of the *Svendborg Poems*, private and public at the same time.

One of these is written in memory of Margot Heinemann, English Communist, critic, novelist, poet and Brecht scholar. The poem tries to draw on Brecht's 1938 "An Die Nachgeborenen," not only for the epigraph (which took me back to Enzensberger's *The Sinking of the Titanic*) but for the sensibility of apocalyptic defeat:

AFTER THE DELUGE

You who will emerge from the flood
In which we have gone under
Remember when you speak of our failings
The dark time too
Which you have escaped

                    (Brecht)

Margot is dead, and the sun is out,
And the wet London streets from the train
Are lovely, dazzling rivers of brass
Bursting their banks in the rain —
A submarine city, a mirage, a drought,
An ocean of sand in this hour's empty glass.

History's an iceberg, a desert of snow,
And the future's a hole in the ice,
The cities of sand are all raining down,
And glaciers float in the skies,
And swimming in sand, down we all go,
Still dreaming of water, together we drown.

Nothing is constant but change, but this weather,
But sinks to the bottom one day.
The nearest we get to the Land of Cockaigne
Is a vision of clouds, up, up and away
And over the mountains, still wheeling for ever
Like ashes and dust, still falling like rain.

Among the *Svendborg Poems* I was especially struck by Brecht's 1938 poem "Bericht über einen Gescheiterten" about a Viennese doctor, an anti-Fascist exile whom Brecht met in Denmark. The following is a kind of "re-tread" of this poem, using the original sense of "gescheitert" with its other sense of failure, where the castaway becomes Brecht himself (and to a lesser extent Prospero) — an attempt to recall my sense of wonder and gratitude when I first met his poetry:

DESERT ISLAND DISCS

(After reading BB)

Only those who, waking, ran down to the sand,
Now ship-shape and scrubbed by last night's gales,
Leaping through surf at low tide like castaways
Beached on a dirty little island
Littered with sea-wrack, sun-bathers and dead whales,
Who kept the bonfires dry for clear days
Like this — know how it felt to see a man
Swimming towards them, to feel like Caliban.

Only those who listened to the stranger's speech
While the sea looked the other way,
Saw fabulous cities fall, sacked by the sand.
Who smelt diesel rumors creep up the beach,
And pitied the pity of the castaway,
Whose silence hath cheated us of this island —
Know the cost of Empire, buying and selling
Ourselves for cargo-cults, which first was mine own king.

Only those who breasted the tide and could not swim
And made a religion of the sea
Knew why he spoke of water with such respect,
And how it had almost defeated him,
Embraced the nakedness of the refugee,
And watched all hope of rescue wrecked
In sight of land, the last hopeless chance for years,
Whom he taught language — know now how to curse.

And only those of us who can't say whether
This black tide will fall back at last,
If thunder still blows hoarse or continents will wait

Or if the Flood won't last for ever —
Know the ruin floating past
Is fuel for fires we must create
Again, to keep the world's one hope still burning,
Above high-water. Thus may we too die learning.

The poem's title is taken from the long-running BBC Radio program where "castaways" are invited to choose eight records and one book to take with them on an imaginary desert island. I don't know what music I would take, but I can't think of a better book for those of us cast away on this poor island in the closing decade of the twentieth century than Brecht's *Collected Poems*.

Andy Croft

* * * * * * * *

Darko R. Suvin, a Professor in the Department of English at McGill University, Montreal, is a leading member of the International Brecht Society. A Slovene by birth, he is a Fellow of the Royal Society of Canada, concerned broadly with intercultural studies; he is also a keen student of science fiction. His poetry, greatly influenced by that of China and Japan, is primarily (perhaps even exclusively) written in English.

Note on Brecht's Influence

I think of BB — i.e., the authorial and largely also the civic persona — as my "guru" or "sensei" (without the religiously dogmatic connotations), so his influence is pervasive rather than point-like and very difficult to pin down. I have translated *Galileo* and *Jasager/ Neinsager* and written about these; I've also written about *Kreide- kreis* and *Heilige Johanna der Schlachthöfe*, so it might be assumed these had an effect on me; yet I find some stuff from *Szechwan* or *Courage* recurring just as frequently under my pen. I've also translated a lot of poetry and short prose (*Me-Ti, Keuner*), which clearly feeds into my parables.

I read the Chinese poets before I read Brecht, i.e. I liked him because he liked the Chinese and not vice versa, though I was certainly strengthened in my chinoiseries and japonaiseries by his example. The basic factor is that I largely share what Raymond Williams would have called the Brechtian "structure of feeling" or *Haltung* of an unsentimental yet passionate anti-capitalism etc. I did so before and without knowing him, I therefore glommed on to him; I was then in feedback strengthened and inflected by his variant of it. Finally, living in another epoch ("and the wench is dead": Marlowe), I had to face problems different from BB's and therefore adopt situations different from his, though one hopes in his spirit, by and large.

A similar argument would apply to BB's basic proceeding, the allegorical exemplum or parable. This was present in me before I knew BB (my BA work for L.C. Knights in 1954/55 was on English medieval drama etc.) and it is now so deeply etched — in that I took for the motto of my collection *The Long March* Baudelaire's "Tout pour moi devient allégorie." Seeing the general in the particular, and especially seeing a possible new and better generality instead of the automatically accepted and current one today, seems to me the basis for the *Haltung* of *Verfremdung* — a poetic *Haltung* par excellence.

Darko Suvin

MARCHING THROUGH THE BB MOUNTAIN RANGE

The pleasure of dazzling peach and sweet plum is quick
And simple, the pleasure of the great pine stretching tall
Deep and complex. Blossom-time is beautiful but soon gone,
Petals revert to brown earth and fade in, the pine grows
Needles all the time, eventually cones, goes on branching,
Slow and sure like sexual congress on the morning
Of the fifth night.

I love the textual melody of old Bert for he memorably
Mingles the deep and quick rhythms grasping the palpably
        present
Things and relations of our unrepeatable but alternative worlds
How they are and also could be, altered. From his youth he
        was
Wholly a passion for the just gesture, a serious jester exiled by
The scary witless theater of power. With him went always
The scroll of the Skeptic, the cloth cap of finest material
And plebeian cut

And the nodding model donkey who had to understand too.
    Shifting
Clockwise he ran hoops around the fascists in three world
Theaters of deadly power, his own Pale Mother, imperial
Muscovy like the banks of the Styx, onto the Dream Factory
    where
Lies are sold extricably mixed with truth, always typing
Without caps for the once and future Berlin workers of the
    world
Stories of wily
Swabian peasants, a classical Chinese-style poet, public
Intellectual impatient of dominating hierarchies if domineering
Himself: a high range we can however not only lift eyes
Toward and see but also tread upon, going up.
                Yet by now
Mountain grave has grown a marble monument and we must
    remember
How he said progressing is better than being progressive
And leave to go

Further through wild grass, following the present star of
    pleasure,
The breeze playful in our hair, nevertheless bearing along,
As we traverse new rocky passes, seedlings planted
On BB Mountain Range; many of them still growing, tight
Blind scale-work cones, as with passion and regret we move
Pleasurably on.

THE GOOD BEAR THE BRUNT

A wooden statue of the Emperor of Heavens was guarding the road.
A passerby in the rainy season, finding himself blocked by a ditch
full of water, took the statue and laid it across the ditch for use as
a plank. The next passerby took pity on the statue and carried it
back into its shelter. The god reproached him for lack of reverence:
he had not reconsecrated the effigy by prayers and incense
offerings. He was sent a violent headache.

The good passerby cried out against such injustice: "Why didn't
you punish the blasphemer who had trod on you?"

"First of all, his need was great," replied the Emperor of
Heavens. "And more important, only good people are worth
bothering about. It is the duty of pious people like you to see that
ditches are properly dredged and blasphemers punished — having

first taken away any excuse they might derive from material circumstances."

AN OBITUARY TO ONE SELF

Coniugi Incomparabili bene de se
meritae (To the peerless partner
of whom I deserved well).
Ex Imp[erio] Ips[orum], L[ibens]
(At their behest; Willingly)
Memorial inscriptions, German-Roman
Museum, Cologne

He died too soon, as we all do for sure,
Moderately useful in the few persons he touched,
Some terms he taught arresting tho obscure.

Like the Good Person, he tried to balance too much
(Goodness to others & self in this strong storm),
So that, crippled, he had to lean on the crutch.

He had deserved well of either side, had performed
Willingly as best he could at their imperious behest;
Taken all in all, that he had Socratically formed

A shapely sense for others, met the peerless request,
All the while slyly adjusting his regardant reason
From others' bearing; so he could go to a friendly rest.

His regret: the few deep loves, their too brief season.

* * * * * * *

Michael Hamburger, former Reader in German at Reading University, is at one and the same time poet, translator and critical authority on such writers as Hölderlin, Hofmannsthal, Rilke, Huchel and Celan. German by birth, English by education and residence, he made many of the Brecht translations in *Poems 1913-1956*, and is generally regarded as the outstanding German poetry interpreter and translator of our time. Our extracts are taken from *After the Second Flood*, his critical account of modern German poetry and his own *Collected Poems 1941-1983* (Carcanet, 1984) which established him above all else as a very fine English poet. A new, extended edition of the latter is due in 1995. The examples given here come from his writing over some thirty-five years and both sides of the Atlantic, handled with compressed wisdom and touching on one or two themes akin to those found in Brecht.

Brecht's Development Towards Classicism

For two hundred years or so the progress of European and American poetry was one towards autonomy. The more "advanced" the poet, the more his or her language differed from the language of discourse, exposition and plain talk. Not only meter, rhyme and metaphor — still regarded as "ornament" by Dryden — served to remove poetry from those prosaic media of communication; more significantly still, the very syntax of poetry evolved in such a way that ambiguity or multiplicity of meaning came to be regarded as a distinguishing and essential feature of poetic utterance. The language of poetry, its practitioners and exegetes assumed, is unlike any other language. Far from being only a fine or memorable vehicle for thoughts, feelings, or assertions that could be conveyed by other media, true poetry is at once the vehicle and substance of its utterances; not a different way of putting things, but the only way of putting things that could not be said at all in any language but the language of poetry.

Non-specialists continued to complain of the peculiar difficulty or obscurity of modern poetry. Specialists continued to relish it, accepting Archibald MacLeish's dictum that "a poem should not mean but be," while devoting long books and articles to the analysis of difficult poems and their dubious or multiple meanings. Among sophisticated poets with a middle-class background and education, Brecht was virtually alone in writing a large and varied body of poetry that was clearly intended to convey a single meaning in a language as plain and unfigurative as the best prose. (That Brecht could also write quite differently, if he chose, is evident in early poems like his "Psalms.") Quite deliberately, Brecht set himself the aim of reversing the two-century-old development in question. Since believers in the aesthetic self-sufficiency of poetry — beyond the autonomy of all art he himself insisted on in the teeth of agit-prop and crude notions of "socialist realism" — found it impossible to deny that Brecht was both a modern and a good poet, though his theory and practice alike contradicted their basic tenets, most of them found it prudent to ignore Brecht's poetry.

Whether we see it as a revolution or as a counter-revolution, Brecht's achievement in poetry was not only remarkable in itself but inseparable from the survival of poetry after the Second World War, at least in those parts of the world in which the very foundations of aesthetically self-sufficient poetry had been demolished by moral, social and political upheavals. If Brecht's later poetry is a kind of anti-poetry or minimal poetry by Romantic-Symbolist standards, no other kind of poetry could withstand the anti-poetic fury of those who had seen European civilization reduced to a heap of rubble. It was Brecht's anticipation of this crisis that prompted him to "wash" the language of poetry, as he put it, long before the crisis occurred; and what he washed out of poetry was nothing less than the sediment of the whole Romantic-Symbolist era, with its aesthetic of self-sufficiency.

...In the later poems the toughness has become more than a gesture, so that Brecht can also admit tenderness and gentleness, just as he could admit that love of nature about which he tended to feel uneasy, suspecting that it might be a residue of bourgeois self-indulgence, escapism and idyllicism. (In the self-portrait ["Of Poor BB"] in the 1920s, pine-trees are said to "piss" in the early morning, and the birds in them become their "vermin.") Above all, in the later poems he has ceased to care about his image, or about himself at all as an individual. Though he draws freely on his own experience, even on his dreams, and has no qualms about using the first person singular, he can do so just because he is not writing autobiography, but availing himself of useful material for reflections on the complexities of human motives and behavior.

...Brecht's art has come to lie in the concealment of art, as Horace wrote that it should; in a manner as seemingly casual, throw-away, undemonstrative as possible. What distinguishes such poems [as "Fahrend in einem bequemen Wagen"] from prose is a rhythmic organization inconspicuous precisely because it is right, perfectly accordant with what the poem says and does; and an economy of means, a tautness and conciseness that are rarely attained in a prose narrative. (The tautness begins with the very first word; the present participle construction unusual in German, but adopted by Brecht before English had become his second language. Latin is his more likely model here.) By renouncing emotive effects and that vagueness which Baudelaire considered an essential element in Romantic art, Brecht was able to create a didactic poetry that seems innocent of any design on the reader, but all the more persuasive and convincing for that. Brecht's language here is anyone's language, if anyone were capable of putting the right word in the right place, of saying neither more nor less than what he wants to say. Brecht's ability to do so consistently, in hundreds of poems written in this later manner, amounted to the establishment of an art at once modern and classical. To read Brecht's later verse is an experience akin to the reading of Horace — whom Brecht repeatedly read in his later years — the Catullus of the social epigrams, or any Latin poet at home not only in his art but in his world.

This does not mean that Brecht accepted his world uncritically, any more than the Latin poets accepted theirs uncritically, either before or after his residence in a Communist country. It means that in Brecht's later poems personal and public concerns are inseparable. The sequence of short poems which he called *Buckower Elegien* — though by modern criteria they are much closer to epigram than to elegy — was written after Brecht's return from Germany, yet its dominant tone is one of satirical or self-questioning unease, as in the opening poem, "Der Radwechsel" "Changing the Wheel":

Ich sitze am Straßenrand
Der Fahrer wechselt das Rad.
Ich bin nicht gern, wo ich herkomme.
Ich bin nicht gern, wo ich hinfahre.
Warum sehe ich den Radwechsel
Mit Ungeduld?

I sit on the roadside verge
The driver changes the wheel.
I do not like the place I have come from.
I do not like the place I am going to.
Why with impatience do I
Watch him changing the wheel?

I have written that Brecht's later manner dispenses with metaphor and simile, and so it does, except in so far as idiomatic usage is intrinsically figurative. Yet the very reduction of means in this short poem — more Chinese or Japanese than Latin, one would suppose — its extreme spareness and plainness of diction, invite us to read more into the poem than it says, to read it as an allegory. Since self-projection and self-expression are not what we look for in Brecht's later poems, the extension of meaning we are likely to provide in this instance is of a political or historical order; and, however we interpret them, the implications of the poem are very far from the optimism encouraged, if not positively enforced, under Communist régimes. Several other poems in the sequence quite unambiguously disparage or censure this official optimism.

...Historically, the whole phenomenon of minimal language in poetry, whether in East or West Germany, was never a purely literary one. Poetry has always tended towards compression, so much so that Ezra Pound wanted the German word "dichten" — to make poetry — to be derived from the adjective "dicht" (dense), though etymologically it is not. Brecht's language, though, was not particularly dense or condensed. Except where he was cryptic, deliberately so, for good and cunning reasons, his plain language was logical and relaxed, minimal only in its avoidance of ornament, emotive devices, and the subjective associations cultivated by Romantics and Symbolists. What Brecht wanted, and would have achieved if political developments had allowed it, was a social poetry of dialogue about matters of interest to everyone. This eminently classical relationship between writer and reader had long been made impossible by the individualism of writers and readers alike, and nowhere more so than in serious and "advanced" poetry, with its need to escape from vulgar norms of communication in every conceivable direction. It was to put poetry and poets back where he thought they belonged, in society and in history, that Brecht undertook his drastic and rigorous revision of the functions and practice of the art.

Michael Hamburger

LINES ON BREUGHEL'S "ICARUS"

The ploughman ploughs, the fisherman dreams of fish;
Aloft, the sailor through a world of ropes
Guides tangled meditations, feverish
With memories of girls forsaken, hopes
Of brief reunions, new discoveries,
Past rum consumed, rum promised, rum potential.
Sheep crop the grass, lift up their heads and gaze
Into a sheepish present: the essential,
Illimitable juiciness of things,
Greens, yellows, browns are what they see.
Churlish and slow, the shepherd, hearing wings —
Perhaps an eagle's — gapes uncertainly;

Too late. The worst had happened: lost to man,
The angel, Icarus, for ever failed,

Fallen with melted wings when, near the sun
He scorned the ordering planet, which prevailed
And jeering, now slinks off, to rise once more.
But he — his damaged purpose drags him down —
Too far from his half-brothers on the shore,
Hardly conceivable, is left to drown.

BIG DEAL

The smartest, greatest and most American
Of all those great Presidents
Had this brainwave: a package deal.
Why not simplify, putting the whole great country
From Maine to California, Alaska to Florida,
On the market. Right. Put it up for sale.
Not only her natural and unnatural resources,
Grand Canyon, Pentagon, Howard Johnson, Niagara Falls
And the rest, but the know-how and ethos,
The secret of making folks want what they do not need.

Strange, though the moon was thrown in,
And the means of getting there, it was not
That nobody could afford it —
Long-term credit was offered,
With no down-payment at all —
But that nobody wanted to buy.

YEW

Too slowly for us it amasses
Its dense dark bulk.
Even without our blood
For food, where mature one stands
It's beyond us, putting on
Half-inches towards its millennium,
Reaching down farther
Than our memories, our machines.
Its fertile berries can kill.
Its dead wood even, still harsh,
In gate-post or bedstead
Outlasts many users
Of gates, of beds.

Woodworm, bedbug avoid it,
Those who used it said.

If one tree stands, black,
Where many trees were
And they whose counter-nature
For all things had a use
Till unburied their flesh littered
The used, the flayed earth,
A yew it will be, split,
Thrusting down slow roots,
Millennial, still to where
Soil remains whole.

THE SOUL OF MAN UNDER CAPITALISM

Looks for its body among
The skyscrapers, tenement blocks
Where a white man's unwise to walk.
At the thought of revolution
Sends kites, balloons into air opaque
With excremental vapors of produce
And sees them vanish, glad
That where they've gone they'll be free.
Meanwhile it feeds refrigerators
With bags of lobster tails, whole sides of prime beef,
Homogenized milk by the gallon; and, hailed by Donuts,
By Steak or Chicken Dinner it glides
Down Main Street emptily, starving
For the smell of newly baked bread.

TWO PHOTOGRAPHS

1
At an outdoor table of the Café Heck
In the Munich Hofgarten
Six gentlemen in suits
And stiff white collars
Are sitting over coffee,
Earnestly talking.
The one with a half-moustache
Wears a trilby hat.

The others have hung up theirs,
With their overcoats, on hooks
Clamped to a tree.
The season looks like spring.
The year could be '26.

On a hook otherwise bare
Hangs a dogwhip.

No dog appears in the picture —

An ordinary scene.
Of all the clients
At adjoining tables
None bothers to stare.

2
The year is '33.
The gentleman in a trilby
Is about to board a train.
Behind him stand
Four men in black uniforms.
"For his personal protection"
The Chancellor of the Reich
Carries a dogwhip.

No dog appears in the picture.

* * * * * * * *

Michael Hofmann is a (formerly East) German poet based in London but currently with the Department of English at Ann Arbor. Not yet thirty, he translated *Der gute Mensch von Sezuan* for Deborah Warner's production at the National Theater. "On Fanø," with its implied reference to "Ein Ruder liegt auf dem Dach" from the *Svendborg Poems*, comes from his collection *Acrimony* (Faber and Faber, 1986).

Michael Hofmann

On Fanø

Acid rain from the Ruhr strips one pine in three...
To supplement their living, the neutral Danes
let out their houses during the summer months —
exposure, convexity, clouds and the shadows of clouds.
Wild grass grows on the manure of their thatch.

There are concrete bunkers among the sand dunes —
bomb shelters, or part of Heligoland and the V2s...?
German hippies have taken them over, painted them
with their acid peace dreams; a cave art of
giant people, jungles, a plague of dragonflies.

* * * * * * * *

Marianne Rossi is a German actress living in California with her director-husband. She has been writing poetry in German and English for a number of years. "As to Brecht's influence," she says, "certainly Brecht isn't on my mind when I'm writing. And certainly I am not tempted to copy a model, as great as it may be."

A Memory

Since you asked me about Brecht's influence — in any one of the many possible ways — I thought about it very carefully. When I was still very young, during a cold post-war winter in East Berlin, all we hungry little school kids were crowded into icy busses to be driven to a "Kino" house in Lichtenberg, at ten in the morning. We were herded into the building and told to get seated. The children were agitated and really wanted to go home to find a warm spot and some food, maybe. Then a small woman entered the small stage. I noticed she was freezing herself, wearing a long black winter coat. She seemed as cold as we were. To keep warm we were shouting and jumping around. She just stood there and, in a loud voice, tried to get us quiet. There wasn't very much response from us. So she stopped and was silent. We couldn't care less. But this woman had a job to do. She started talking, first loud again and then, when no one paid attention, she spoke in a softer voice. She recited Brecht's *Children's Crusade*, she lowered her voice even further and continued in the pace of the poem's natural rhythm. And it was like a miracle, the children first became quiet and then they started to listen. I felt suddenly warm, and she was still talking slowly in a very soft voice. I started to cry and then I noticed that the poem was very clear and that it told a story that was very plain. And I didn't have to cry. When she had finished the poem, she went right on to the next one, and there was no hunger, no cold, and we listened and listened for two hours and didn't think of anything else. When she finally had ended, I wanted to kiss her and didn't know why. It was Helene Weigel, who often recited Brecht's poetry to East Berlin school children in those days. That is all I wanted to tell.

Marianne Rossi

ZWEI STROPHEN

1

Gott zu den Sternen
Und wer rät auf Erden
Den Wenigen
Die wissen
Worum es sich handelt?
Gott zu den Sternen
Und wer beugt auf Erden
Die Ängste der Vielen
Die ahnen
Und können nichts tun?

2

Wer ist willens
Und folgt dem Gesetz
Das niemand ergründet
Und keiner besitzt?
Mutmaßung?
Anmaßung?
Zweifeln?
Borniertheit?
Oder ist es
Die Angst.

BEING IN LOVE

Ich will Dich —
Ist das schlimm?

Kann nichts dafür
Soll man es ändern?
I want you —
Is that bad?
Should we change
Arrangements?
And who then
Would be happy?
Maybe the ghost
Of twenty-five years
Could explain
His mucking about.
Or is love
Just a normal matter?

ANGELA

Ich sehe
Nur was mir gefällt
Ich höre kaum
Ich bin fast taub
Ich sitze gern auf weichen Sesseln
Wenn niemand da ist
Keiner lauscht.
Spanisch sprechen
Ist mir eigen
Ich kann es jubeln.
Ich entkomme allem Argen
Das ich nicht kannte als
Ich mich entschloß
Zu dienen.
Ich lerne viel
Auch English
Von Jehovas Zeugen.

KINDERREIME

Es gibt einen Gral
Da tunkt man sich ein
Dann steigst Du heraus
Und bist herrlich und rein
Golden die Haut, unsäglich reich

Niemand ist nötig, kein Lehrer, kein Freund
Kannst Dir alles erdenken
Bleibst immer allein
Die Liebe? Die Treue?
Da fehlt mir der Laut
Du spürst keine Reue
In goldner Haut.

Eiapopeia
Wo ist nur der Reim
Es raschelt im Stroh
Ich lass' lieber sein
Herr B. konnt es besser
Die Gänslein schneeweiß
Und manchmal ein schwarzes
Vielleicht ist das froh.

Ta Deus Ta Dum
Was macht denn das Schaf
Ich wollte es weiß
De Dum Es ist schwarz
Kann ich nicht zaubern
Das geht mir nicht ein
Ta Deus Ta Dum
Krieg soll jetzt sein
"I push the button"
Gesummse und Brumm
Schwarzes Schäflein ist traurig
Das weiße ist dumm.
Ta Deus Ta Dum
Was soll es nur werden
Wir hatten auf Erden
Soviele Beschwerden
Ta Deus Ta Dum
Das Märchen ist eckig
Schwarz ist das Schäflein
Weiß wird schnell dreckig.

* * * * * * *

Günter Kunert, now living in Schleswig-Holstein, is probably the best known of the poets in Germany to have been influenced not only by Brecht's writings but also by personal contact with him. He has won a number of literary awards in the Federal Republic and has written in various media. He sends us two recent poems reflecting on Brecht's death, with two "Marginalien," of which the first sheds new light on the difficulties involved in publishing the *Kriegsfibel* epigrams discussed with Naomi Replansky in Santa Monica in 1946. Here is Brecht, following his return to East Berlin.

Ein Nachwort zur Herausgabe der *Kriegsfiebel*

Während einem meiner Besuche bei Brecht in der Chausseestraße zog er unvermittelt das schmale Fach eines Schrankes auf, der vermutlich einst für Graphiken oder Landkarten gedacht wesen war und entnahm diesem Fach eine mit Bändern verschnürte Mappe. Ein spannungsvoller Moment, den er auch entsprechend zu inszenieren verstand. Die Mappe enthielt schwarze Kartonbögen, etwa im Format DIN A, in deren Mitte Zeitungsbilder aufgeklebt waren und unter diesen Vierzeiler. Das war die *Kriegsfiebel* im Urzustand.

"Meinen Sie, Kunert, daß man sowas veröffentlichen kann?" hieß die Frage, die ich — nach Betrachten der Blätter — ziemlich enthusiastisch bejahte. Über das "wie" wurde noch eine Weile debattiert, und ich versprach, dem Eulenspiegel Verlag das Projekt vorzuschlagen. Ich würde die Übersetzungen der englischen Zeitungstexte vornehmen und so etwas wie "historische Hinweise" verfassen. Doch bevor dieses Stadium erreicht war, ergaben sich mit dem Manuskript einige Probleme. Eines war ein sachliches: Zwei Bilder ähnelten einander zu stark, da sie nur Stahlhelme zeigten, und auch der jeweilige Text auf die Helme anspielte. Brecht entfernte das Blatt mit dem folgende Text:

> Dies sind die Hüte, die wir Armen trugen
> Und findst du einen, der im Bachkies liegt
> Oh Mann aus Narvik, wisse du, der klugen
> Kommenden Zeiten Sohn: hier ward mit uns gesiegt.

Das andere Zeitungsfoto hingegen bot etwas wie eine Scheunenwand dar, an der sich französische Stahlhelme stapelten, vermutlich eine Aufnahme nach der Kapitulation Frankreichs. "Das geht nicht, Brecht," meinte ich, "denn die Franzosen waren ja nicht besiegt, als sie gegen Hitler die Helme aufsetzten, sondern als sie sie, verraten von der eigenen Führung, abnehmen mußten." Ganz offenkundig hatte noch die alte Komintern-parole vom Krieg zwischen imperialistischen Mächten bei dem Text durch Brechts Gehirn gespukt. Da Brecht aber das Blatt beibehalten wollte, wurde durch einen Fotografen ein neues Foto angefertigt. Aus dem Fundus des "Berliner Ensembles" dienten ein paar deutsche Stahlhelme und das Pflaster vor dem Theater als "ideologische Korrekturobjekte." Es ist das einzige nachgestellte Foto im Band.

Als nächste Probleme erwiesen sich zwei andere Bilder. Die ordensgeschmückte Jane Wyman wurde wegen der volkstümlichen, noch dazu falsch geschriebenen Bezeichnung für ihr Geschlechtsteil erbarmungslos eliminiert. Ein weiteres Bild fiel aus ideologischen Gründen der Schere anheim. Das Foto "Famine" (Hungersnot), unter dem es heißt:

Viel muß bestehn und viel muß untergehn
Viel Weisheit brauchst wo so viel Hunger ist
Viel muß geschehen und viel darf nicht geschehn
Daß diese da ihr schönes Pferd vergißt.

In der originalen Bildunterschrift wird die Auseinandersetzung zwischen der Pferdeeigentümerin und einem deutschen Offizier im Osten beschrieben. Es ging nicht an, die offenkundige Tatsache vorzuführen, daß zwischen der deutschen Besatzungsmacht in Rußland und Teilen der Bevölkerung im Zuge von Beschlagnahmen und Enteignungen sich Diskussionen, wenn auch nutzlose, ergeben haben könnten. Das paßte nicht zum Negativ-Image der Deutschen.

Aber selbst nach dieser "Reinigung" des Bandes waren die Schwierigkeiten noch nicht beendet. Denn nun verlangte das Amt für Druckgenehmigungen, über die Köpfe von Hitler, Göring und Goebbels sollten Hakenkreuze gedruckt werden. Warum? Damit Käufer des Buches, so das "Argument," nicht Porträts ihrer einstigen Führer ausschnitten und sich ins Zimmer hängten.

Ob dieses schwachsinnige Verlangen ernst gemeint war, weiß ich nicht. Es könnte sich auch um reine Schikane gegen Brecht gehandelt haben, den das Kulturfunktionärspack haßte. Wahrscheinlich hat Brecht hinter den Kulissen interveniert, so daß die *Kriegsfibel*, wenn auch mit Verzögerung, doch noch erschien. Ich vermute, er hat die idee einer "Friedensfibel," die ja folgen sollte, nur ins Spiel mit der Kulturbürokratie gebracht, um die Druckgenehmigung zu erlangen. Und die hat er dann ja auch bekommen.

B.B.'S SPÄT GEDENKEND

Der große Dichter
im Stahlsarg unter dem Stein
und im Nirgendwo. Kein
lesender Arbeiter stellt noch
eine Frage: Es gibt ja
keine Antworten mehr.
Der arme reiche Dichter
in enger Erde
aufersteht täglich zum Dienst
als Objekt.
Umgeben von lauter Verrätern
aus Liebe oder
sonstiger Bedürftigkeit
hast du deine Wahl
getroffen: Keine Nachrichten
mehr an Nachgeborene.

30.1.92

DES TOTEN DICHTERS GEDENKEND

Später Gesandter von Zeiten,
die ich nicht erfuhr.
Sein Beglaubigungsschreiben füllt Bände.
Sein Land aber welkte indessen dahin
und verstarb ihm. Er hat seinen letzten Irrtum
gut vorbereitet: Die Unsterblichkeit
im Blechsarg in Berlinischer Erde.
Aber manchmal auferstehen
die Toten erneut
mit fremder Miene und falscher Stimme
wie jede Wiederkehr
wie zu Lebzeiten
sich gewöhnlich vollzieht.

14.5.94

Versagen der Gedichte

Die Leser Brechts, eine wachsende Minorität, um mit einem Paradoxon die Abnahme des Publikums für diesen Autor zu bezeichnen,
belasten ihn unbewußt mit dem "Versagen" seiner Gedichte:
Dadurch, daß die Zeit und die Zeitläufte die politische Intention
dieser Poesie widerlegen, sinkt das Image des Autors, wobei selbst
das ästhetische Moment der Nichtachtung anheimfällt. "Wir beziehen unsere Ästhetik aus den Erfordernissen unserer Kämpfe": so
was sagt man nicht ungestraft; die Geschichte, wenn sie schon
keine letzte Instanz bildet, die Gerechtigkeit zu üben imstande ist,
negiert doch wenigstens irgendwann einmal solche Überheblichkei-
ten, wie wir sie nur aus dem Mund des Kambyses gewohnt waren.
   Kunst ist wahrer als Wissenschaft: Eine alte Weisheit. Das Bild,
und alle Kunst, auch die Literatur, ist Bild, wird stets, wenn auch
unbewußt, als Symbol, als Gleichnis verstanden, und das symbol ist
anpassungsfähig, interpretierbar, ausdeutbar auf jene Wahrheit hin,
derer die Leser bedürfen. Insofern ist natürlich der Vergleich von
Wissenschaft und Kunst unsinnig, da Kunst nicht falsifizierbar oder
verifizierbar ist und durch kein Experiment widerlegt noch bewiesen
werden kann. Darum müssen alle Deklarationen des sogenannten
"Sozialistischen Realismus," welcher auf Grundlage einer "Wissenschaft," des Marxismus nämlich, geschöpft werden, grotesk erscheinen, da das absolut Unvereinbare zur Synthese gebracht werden
soll, aber schon der Versuch solcher Synthese läßt den Verdacht zu,
es sei möglicherweise mit der Wissenschaftlichkeit dieser Wissenschaft nicht so weit her, wenn sie als geistige Grundlage für den
individuellen Ausdruck höchst persönlicher und höchst wenig wis-
senschaftlicher Lebenserfahrung gedacht werden kann.

Günter Kunert

* * * * * * *

Keith Armstrong is an English poet from Newcastle-Upon-Tyne,
formerly one of Europe's great shipbuilding centers. He has been
several times to Berlin, where he first went to attend a jazz festival
as a reader of the *Melody Maker*. His interest in Kenya originates in
a visit which he paid to that country in the 1970s; he does not
know Swahili, but was struck by the kind of phrases used (in lieu
of, say, "la plume de ma tante") in teaching the language. Northern

Voices, the arts organization for which he works in North Shields, is one of a federation of Worker Writers and Community Publishers. He helped to publish the poems of Jack Davitt, the retired shipyard worker, who writes under the suggestive pseudonym "Ripyard Cuddling."

A Line or Two About Brecht.

It is as a poet that Brecht has been of most influence on my own writing. It is the crafted simplicity, directness, and accessibility of his political verse which appeals to me. The concept of the engaged writer active on the page and in everyday life is important to my own life and I learnt a lot in this respect from Brecht and writers such as Erich Fried, who succeeded him.

Keith Armstrong

SENEFELDERSTRAßE 19, EAST BERLIN

In the oven of a Berlin heatwave,
this crumbling block bakes
and all the bullet-holed walls
flake.
Tenements skinned bare,
they burn with anxiety, death-wishes,
frustrated hopes.

From a cracked and peeling courtyard window,
a Beach-Boys' track
clashes against an old woman's ears
as she carries a bagful of bruises home.
In this rundown, sunful flat,
I am tuned in to the BBC World Service —
a cricket season just beginning,
and East Berlin sizzling
in a panful of history.

Senefelderstraße 19, crawling with flies.
On top of the wardrobe, some volumes of Lenin slump,
there is dust everywhere, dust.
And all we are saying in all the sweltering

is "Give me a piece of the Wall."
just "Give me a piece of the Wall."

Look down onto the street —
the cobbles still stare,
the cracks in the pavement leer.
And, like every day, Frau Flugge traipses gamely along,
trying hard not to trip,
shabbily overdressed and hanging on
to the shrapnel of her past affections,
to the snapshots of her dreams.

From corner-bars,
the gossip
snatches from doorways at passers-by.
Inside, it is dark
and the money changes hands
slowly,
burning holes in the shabby pockets
of the dour Prenzlauer Berg folk:

"The People are strong."
"They can't sit more than 4 to a table here."
"THEY say it's illegal."
"Let's sing!"

Amongst the clenched blossom of Ernst-Thälmann Park,
"a Workers' Paradise,"
this glassy Planetarium gleams
under an ancient East German sky
shining huge shell of a dome,
it traps stars and opens up Planets:
it is far-reaching, transcending walls.
It can stir the imaginings of all the World's children.
It is the light at the end of Senefelderstraße.
It beckons,
beacons.

And Me?
I am walking in blistered hours,
sick of the sight of money
and what it does
to all the people I love.
"A tip for your trip!

Instead of a brick from the Wall to take home,
bring back a Bertolt Brecht poem":

"And I always thought; the very simplest words
Must be enough. When I say what things are like
Everyone's heart must be torn to shreds
That you'll go down if you don't stand up for yourself
Surely you see that."

Through the letterbox of Senefelderstraße 19,
I push this poem.
And, for the last time, leave
through Checkpoint Charlie.
"Goodbye Frau Flugge, Herr Brecht,
the trams.
My friends, I wish you
sunny days."

* * * * * * *

Jack Davitt is a former welder at Swan Hunter's Wallsend Shipyard, whose 1993 volume *Shipyard Muddling and More Muddling, by Ripyard Cuddling* brings together two booklets "which sold 5000 copies in 1980." His model (also one of Brecht's) is Kipling, and among his readers is Tony Benn, a minister in the Wilson and Callaghan governments. Swan Hunter of Newcastle-Upon-Tyne was one of the most famous British shipbuilders; it worked for the Royal Navy and the big shipping lines. It was nationalized, but is now virtually at a standstill. Sir John Hunter, I gather, was the chairman, McIver a principal manager.

THE END OF THE GAME

My name is Ripyard Cuddling
And writing is my game;
I write of shipyard muddling;
I've won some mild acclaim.

I work for Swan and Hunter,
A welder second grade;
I've never shone at welding
'Cause writing is my trade.

I've worked in Docks and Shipyards
On both sides of the Tyne;
I've toiled on super tankers
And the dreaded "Panel Line."

Ships' managers and foremen
Have fell beneath my pen;
Sir John and Tom McIver
Have felt it now and then.

But everything is changing
And time is running out,
The hanging sword of Damocles
Will fall I have no doubt.

For the berths are lying empty;
The orders running down,
And the time is fast approaching
When Swan Hunter "Go to town."

When the drag chains have been fitted
And they launch the final boat,
There'll be scores of jobless welders
And one redundant poet.

* * * * * * * *

Adrian Henri is a Liverpool-based poet and painter, a regional cosmopolitan or cosmopolitan Scouser unconfined by boundaries between genres or between countries. Starting with staged Events in the basement of Liverpool's Hope Hall, he developed through Pop painting and his own Batman/Père Ubu mythology into an evocative artist and poet, an amusing writer for children and a generous presenter of other people's work. Why he calls Brecht "Dr." is puzzling: Brecht has been the subject of many doctorates in our well-doctored world of academe, but he was never one himself.

Henri's reflections on Brecht are followed by one or two typically pithy fragments from the *America* dossier (Turret Books, 1972). Brecht's long poem was of course dedicated to another of the artist's heroes, George Grosz.

B.B. and Me

I was brought up on, or, rather, brought myself up on, Modernism: Eliot, Pound, Jarry, Apollinaire. In amongst this I found the Auden of "Roman Wall Blues" and "Miss Gee," McNeice's "Bagpipe Music" and, later, the songs of Georges Brassens. French was my other language; there were few easily available Brecht translations around in the fifties; so I only became aware of his example gradually. In the early sixties, as I became more involved with poetry — I had trained as a painter, was teaching in art colleges — it seemed the problem was to keep the advances of Modernism, but to replace its elitism with something more popular and accessible, something that reflected the world we lived in, rather than the view from the Ivory Tower. It was there that Brecht's example was crucial: in particular the songs, the setting of poems to music, the use of songs in the theater. Instead of using the pre-Modern poetic forms, I explored the use of blues, ballad, and popular song conventions. One such was the Country and Western "Talking Blues," spoken rather than sung to guitar music: I wrote "Adrian Henri's Talking After Christmas Blues" in the early sixties; after the riots in Liverpool in 1981 I went back to the form in "Adrian Henri's Talking Toxteth Blues":

> Well, I saw the Chief Constable on TV
> And the Superintendents, but they never saw me,
> Saw the Home Secretary and the Minister for Riots,
> And all them social workers who just never keep quiet.
> ...never met one of them...
> ...neither did the coppers....

When I toured America with the poetry/rock group Liverpool Scene in 1969, I had a book of Brecht poems with me; later I put together a sequence of notebook pieces, interspersed with quotes from Brecht's "Vanished Glory of New York the Giant City," and called it *AMERICA: A Confidential Report to Dr. Bertolt Brecht on the Present Condition of the United States of America.* When Turret

Books published it in 1972, they gave it a cover suggesting a "Top Secret" dossier.

In 1987 I was commissioned to produce a modern-language version of the medieval Wakefield cycle of Mystery Plays: it seemed natural to write songs to highlight the main dramatic points of the Bible story — Creation, Annunciation, Crucifixion. Most recently, Altered States Theater Company proposed staging Brecht's *Fear and Misery of the Third Reich* in tandem with a piece about Mrs. Thatcher's Britain, using the Brecht work as a model, called *Fear and Misery of the Third Term*. Eleven younger playwrights contributed material: I was asked to write short narrative poems to link the episodes, from a single mother who throws her baby from a high-rise flat:

> Rockabye baby on the tenth floor
> Mummy will hold you nice and secure
> When Mummy breaks the cradle will fall
> Down will come baby, Mummy and all

to unemployed youths in Leicester Square dreaming of New York, and one of the unjustly imprisoned "Bedford Six":

> She stands, proud as Britannia,
> Rules the way we judge, and are judged.
> She weighs us in her cold scales;
> her ways mysterious, we do not see
> what she weights against us...

> ("Shadowland," *Wish You Were Here*, Cape 1990)

It is no accident that, writing about an unjust and divisive regime, it is again necessary to report to Dr. Bertolt Brecht.

Adrian Henri

From AMERICA

The Dixie Restaurant: Closed for Jewish New Year

Television: hideous quizgames

day	Batman
and	The Addams family
night	stockmarket quotations

CASTLE FOR MALCOLM MORLEY

man in a sailboat
placed there by the invisible hand
motionless for ever
not wondering why
stones as real as painted clouds
at the hard edges the dream fades
in the hard white empty studio

IMAGES FOR MIKE EVANS

AMERICAN WIG CO
COVERS THE WORLD

WORLD
HOUSEWRECKING CO

The Venus Brassiere Co

"what a shame they don't have Jurgens lotion in Russia"
— think of all those Red hands they could have avoided

DANTE'S INFERNO
STEAK TONIGHT

Also
Sprach Zarathustra
dawn spacemusic
for frozen breakfasts

FOR ALLEN GINSBERG

Allen stumbling walk guide to the nightworld
buying egg creams at the allnight Gem Spa
dirty faded sign FIVE-SPOT
trashcans car engines mattresses
meeting a man carrying a skining bikewheel
in dark wiremesh Tomkins Square
strange beautiful cracked voice
autoharp dulcimer songs of Innocence and Experience

lambs dancing on the hillsides
poet burying his face in rainsoaked grass
dark streets distant glass breaking
home in a yellow taxi

* * * * * * * *

Adrian Mitchell was the translator/adapter of Peter Weiss's *Marat/Sade*, as staged for the Royal Shakespeare Company by Peter Brook, with Glenda Jackson in the lead (she is now a Labour MP). Among his several other works for the theater are translations of *Fuente Ovejuna* and *The Magic Flute*, a piece about Satie, *Day/Night* and an adaptation of *Peer Gynt*. His TV plays include one on William Blake. He has also written often for children; sometimes under such pseudonyms as Volcano Jones and Apeman Bludgeon. Kenneth Tynan is said to have called him "the British Mayakovsky'. He has been a visiting poet or lecturer at several universities in Britain and the US, and is much in demand as a reader/performer. His poem "The Oxford Hysteria of English Poetry" suggests a rich literary-historical background.

Note on "Saw It in The Papers."

Brecht. He gave me courage. I wouldn't have dared to tackle such a bleak documentary subject if I hadn't read Brecht's poem about Marie Farrar, the infanticide. It's a great poem which I've read aloud often.

Mine was written in reaction to a horrific story I read in the news pages of *The Guardian*. I was working on a short-lived TV arts program called *Full House*. I was supposed to be writing sketches about the arts, but after I read this story I asked if I could write a reaction to it as my contribution to the week's program. Because the story shocked me so much and so many people so much and I wanted to try and understand the woman in the center of it through writing about her. I tried — I wrote it, I broadcast it, and *The Guardian* published it, together with my explanatory note. My friend Gaie Houston contributed to it after the first draft, helping me to find the key line about unlocking locked-up love.

More than a hundred letters arrived as a result, most of them sympathetic, many from people who wanted to help people in prison. I answered their letters, giving them addresses of organizations, etc. With my wife, I visited the woman concerned in prison and we helped her as much as we could.

I try to read poems in prisons when I'm invited. There's no hungrier audience, no more rewarding audience. I read this poem in Gloucester prison. In Victorian times each man had one cell for the night and another for the day. When I visited it they had three men in the day cell and three in the night — that is six men where the Victorians had one. The two verses beginning *There is love in prisons* were written in direct response to a speech made by a member of that audience. It's a piece which I've rewritten many times since it was published. Poetry doesn't have to be a one-man band.

Adrian Mitchell

SAW IT IN THE PAPERS

Her baby was two years old.
She left him, strapped in his pram, in the kitchen.
She went out.
She stayed with friends.
She went out drinking.

The baby was hungry.
Nobody came.
The baby cried.
Nobody came.
The baby tore at the upholstery of his pram.
Nobody came.

She told the police:
"I thought the neighbors would hear him *crying*
and report it to someone who would come
and take him away."

Nobody came.

The baby died of hunger.

She said she'd arranged for a girl,
whose name she couldn't remember,
to come and look after the baby

while she stayed with friends
Nobody saw the girl.
Nobody came.

Her lawyer said there was no evidence
of mental instability.
But the man who promised to marry her
went off with another woman.

And when he went off, this mother changed
from a mother who cared for her two-year-old baby
into a mother who did not seem to care at all.
There was no evidence of mental instability.

The Welfare Department spokesman said:
"I do not know of any plans for an inquiry.
We never become deeply involved."
Nobody came.
There was no evidence of mental instability.

When she was given love
She gave love freely to her baby.
When love was torn away from her
she locked her love away.
It seemed that no one cared for her.
She seemed to stop caring.
Nobody came.
There was no evidence of mental instability.

Only love can unlock locked-up-love.

Manslaughter: She pleaded Guilty.
She was sentenced to be locked up
in prison for four years.

Is there any love in prisons?

She must have been in great pain.

There is love in prisons.
There is great love in prisons.
A man in Gloucester Prison told me:
"Some of us care for each other.
Some of us don't.

Christopher Middleton

Some of us are gentle,
Some are brutal.
All kinds."

I said: "Just the same as people outside."
He nodded twice.
And stared me in the eyes.

What she did to him was terrible.
There was no evidence of mental instability.
What was done to her was terrible.
There is no evidence of mental instability.

Millions of children starve, but not in England.
What we do not do for them is terrible.

Is England's love locked up in England?
There is no evidence of mental instability.

Only love can unlock locked-up love.

Unlock all of your love.
You have enough for this woman.
Unlock all of your love.
You have enough to feed all those millions of children.

Cry if you like.
Do something if you can. You can.

* * * * * * *

Christopher Middleton, the English-born Professor of German at Austin, Texas, has published some six or eight books of his own poetry and has made many translations from German and, more recently, Spanish-language poets. He has written critical-historical accounts of Dadaism from its origin in 1916, as well as of the English Futurists and Imagists, and is a member of the Berlin Academy of Arts. He translated the first novel by Christa Wolf to appear in the US. He was also one of the principal translators represented in Brecht's *Poems 1913-1956*, making notable versions, inter alia, of the early "Psalms." His gift of linguistic imagination can

be seen in his long poem "Woden Dog," written in a very successful mixture of Anglo-Saxon with some Black American lingo. In
responding to our invitation he has left aside his own original
poems and written an in-depth analysis of two by Brecht. These can
be found in *GW* 740 and 743, or *Poems 1913-1956* (in translations
by other hands) and were written on the eve of the Second World
War.

On Two Poems by Brecht

I would like to start this brief essay with two references, one to
Rilke, the other to Brecht. These references relate to two polarized
fields of the lyric *parole*. To both fields I was being drawn when I
first read Brecht in the mid 1950s. In my experience, they clashed,
interfered with one another, or else could be dovetailed, though
seldom fused. Brecht himself, I believe, had it in him to activate
both, but historical circumstances drove him to cultivate just one of
them. In the other, Rilke reigns supreme.

First Rilke (from a letter to Gräfin Sizzo, March 17, 1922):

> The ability to write is, God knows, equally "difficult handi-
> work," even more so because the materials of the other arts are
> intrinsically separate from everyday use, whereas the poet's task
> crescendos (*steigert sich*) around the peculiar duty of distin-
> guishing *his* word, essentially and thoroughly, from words of
> mere usage (*Umgang*) and communication. No word in a poem
> (I mean every "und" or "der," "die," "das") is identifiable with
> its phonic equivalent in usage and conversation; a more pure
> principle (*Gesetzmäßigkeit*), the relationship, the pattern (*Kon-
> stellation*) it occupies in verse or artistic prose, change it, right
> down into the very core of its nature, make it useless, unfit for
> mere usage, untouchable and permanent..."

Brecht (piecemeal from "Über reimlose Lyrik mit unregelmäßigen
Rhythmen," c.1938):

> "I needed elevated (*gehobene*) language, but the unctuous
> smoothness of the usual five-stress iambic line was against
> me...I was working on the presentation of certain interferences,
> asymmetrical developments in human destinies...it was an
> attempt to present (*zeigen*) processes going on between human
> beings as contradictory beings, saturated with conflict, vio-

lent...I have already mentioned that the perception of social dissonance was the premise for the new gestic rhythmiciza-tion...The cadence of direct, moment-to-moment speech was needed....

In time, around 1960, I was coming to construe these positions not as opposites or complementaries, but as "distincts." This was my hunch: only later did I find the passages cited, which spelled out what I was at that time intuiting. Rilke might view the poetic word as a hearth interior to language as the "house of being" (Heidegger); Brecht, working up ideas provoked by his staging of *Edward II*, was viewing a possibility: dissonant, gestic poetry as a campfire out-doors, language as a tent of historical becoming. Propositionally, house and tent might seem incompatible. Yet evidence out of practices and times past supported either view. Neither compro-mised with stereotypes of lyrical convention or common usage. As regards the aliases for "language," I suspect that Rilke would often have been inclined to quit the Heideggerian house and opt for a tent, while Brecht, involuntarily nomadic, might well have fancied a permanent barricade.

It must have been around 1970 that I detected in two of Brecht's poems of the 1930s grammatical (and syntactical) patterns. Here I was having to walk, as a non-native speaker, on eggshells. For a German reader these patterns might be so self-evident as to go unnoticed, or else so simple that they might not seem, as they were seeming to me, precisely the "principle" that Rilke invoked, the "large relationship," the "pattern it (the word) occupies." Wasn't it the pattern that positioned the phrase and profiled it? The pattern, though repeated, passed through a limited set of transformations — it was moving through the text, a magnet in whose force field the lexematic filings constellated. In each poem, too, the pattern consti-tuted, or else the wording articulated, a negative-positive tension, a dialectic moving toward resolution. The poems are "Die Literatur wird durchforscht werden" and "Schlechte Zeit für Lyrik." Other investigators may have long since detected such patterns and briefly fussed over them — for me they were revelations.

What occurs in the first of the poems? Abstractly formulated, there are antitheses and parallelisms, there is semantic contrast mounted on grammatical equivalence, and (of interest or not) a light crossweaving between passive and future senses of the verb *werden*. I can best exhibit details by lining up in English the phrases that provide the armature of the text:

(I)
1. Those who are placed on the golden thrones to write
   Will be asked...
   Not for...
   Will their books be scrutinized, but...
   Will be read with interest, for here...

2. Whole literatures...
   Will be searched through for signs
   That agitators...
   Imploring invocations...
   Will prove...
   Delicious music...will only tell
   That...

(II)
3. But in that age will be praised
   Those who...
   Who...
   Who...
   Who...
   Who...

4. Their description...
   Will still carry...
              For to these
   They were transmitted, these
   Carried them...

5. Yes, there will come a time when
   These...
   Who...
   Who...
   Will openly be praised.

To flesh out this skeleton: Counterpointing the "plain" wording are "rich" phrases — in the first line, "placed on the golden thrones"; in lines 8-9, "traits of the famous ancestors"; in line 14, "superterrestrial beings"; in line 16, "delicious music of words"; in line 26, "For the glorification of kings." The intervals at which rich phrases occur are not constant. But their contrast with the plainer wording (an ironic contrast), is such that the absence itself of any such phrasing in the last thirteen lines points up a concluding contrast. It might be anticipated that the rich phrasing would recur; instead, just where it might have recurred, comes a reversal of it — "these/Carried them further beneath their *sweat-soaked shirts*/Through the *cordons of police*" (my italics). The overarching contrast between the sets of "Those who..." does indeed resonate in contrastive (dialectical) features throughout the text, at one point turned into a reiteration, in lines 20-23 — "lowly/combatants/lowly/combatants." The past paragraph seems to comprise, as a kind of grammatico-orchestral coda, most or all of the structures distributed serially through the poem: future tense, passive mood, anaphora, demonstrative and relative pronominal structures having grammatical equivalence and framing semantic contrast or antithesis (e.g., "the bare ground/surrounded by..." counterposes plain starkness and rich fullness). The emphatically quasi-logical bonding, too, achieved by the co-ordinating conjunction *denn* ("for") at pivotal points in each of the two sections of the poem, resolves into the concluding "Ja," which inaugurates the coda.

The pervasive patterning, reiterative with variations, gives the text every mark of internal necessity — inevitability. Random wording is, if not eliminated, certainly not allowed to interfere. Nothing arbitrary erupts through or across the economy of the patterning. The percolation of pattern through every phrase group also provides that the text be read as a poem, not as an utterance of opinion. Writers who think they are being "Brechtian" because they raise political voices, might think again. In Plato's nomenclature, "Die Literatur wird durchforscht werden" is much closer to *ikon* than it is to *doxa*.

"Schlechte Zeit für Lyrik" has comparable features. What intrigued me most was the variegation of verb forms (transitive and intransitive), the elegant designing and serial redesigning of work-order (no dulling reiteration of the same, but a quietly delightful elasticity of movement), and the reserving, for the closure, of wording that translates meditation into action. An interior conflict moves through sets of antitheses, finally to present (*zeigen*) the external combatants: the speaker and the "Anstreicher." Succinctly, too, their idioms are presented — both wield language, but the "speeches" of the latter drive the speaker of the poem to his *desk*. The core of the dilemma is manifest: those inflammatory speeches have an instantaneity, which has to be coolly challenged, but by a writer who, for all his being outraged, settles at his desk to *write*, against the odds.

Another feature that struck me was the start of the poem. It begins abruptly, as if breaking out of a soliloquy, or, perhaps, interrupting a dialogue: "Yes I know, but...." Casual and profane as the wording is, this abruptness is entirely in character with the old "lyric abandon" (*Ergriffenheit* — what Friedrich Theodor Vischer called "das plötzliche Zünden der Welt im Subjekte"): the ecstatic utterance when the god or muse prompts the poet to give voice. Recalling the start of Goethe's "Auf dem See" — "Und frische Nahrung, neues Blut/Saug ich aus freier Welt..." — , one even wonders if, albeit "unconsciously" or drawing on his mental library of models, Brecht might be re-writing, so as to gainsay, Goethe: the aquatic scene is there, with boats, fruitfulness — but here deprivation instead, for the tree is *verkrüppelt*, the soil is bad. The abrupt start gives rise to perceptions of an immediate scene, and the conflict in the speaker's mind is legible in terms of concrete singularities — the tree, the tattered net, the forty-year-old woman already stooped by penury and labor, then the girls' breasts warm as ever. There is even a sly concession to listeners: "A rhyme would be sheer extravagance here." Finally, following the deployment of variegated verb forms, inversions of word-order, statements, and a leading question ("Why do I attend to the pain and not the pleasure?"), you notice that transitive verbs have disappeared since line 10. In the "constellation" or pattern, the ensuing verbs are, for ten lines to come, three intransitives and one reflexive. This suspension surely gives the transitive *drängt*, in its position as first word in the last line, without any least flourish a punch that it might otherwise have lacked.

Looking back now over the text, I felt that the concluding accusative personal pronoun *mich* stood out in a special way — a last singularization? The only other personal pronoun object in the poem is *ihn* in the lines about the tree — "Die Vorübergehenden schimpfen ihn einen Krüppel." Didn't this appear to be a grammatical echo carried across the text from line 6 to the sixth line in the last paragraph? First I decided, aha, here a grammatical relation implies, on the thematic level, a kinship between the speaker and the tree-in-bad-soil. But soon I backed away from this pedantic idea. Like all sorts of prosodic (harmonic) patternings, grammatical ones sometimes do and sometimes don't articulate "meaning." When they don't, moreover, it can be a mistake to consider them mechanistically as "supports" or "reinforcements" of meaning on the semantic level.

The unemphatic, prosaic, but still "gestic" character of Brecht's voice in "Schlechte Zeit für Lyrik" entails an elegant, beautifully balanced grammatico-syntactical organization, which is appropriate for the "message" it carries, but is to a large extent there for its own sake, like the geometrical design distributing colors, volumes, lines in a Cézanne still-life. It is a "handle" which enabled the artist's conception to grip intractable objects crossing, thwarting, energizing his contestatory imagination. The grammar stabilizes the *ikon* dynamically; its patterned elegance refreshes ordinary words, makes them behave as if they belonged to the morning of the world; the radiance of the word is sustained by the "constellation" that arms it against any lapse toward *doxa,* toward "opinion."

Who knows whether or not Brecht (or Pushkin for that matter) consciously chiselled away at his grammatico-syntactical statuary. Quite possibly reiterative pattern and elegant variation come with the trade. You certainly have to allow for a poet's having trained his wits through trial and error, practiced and polished his instruments, got by heart his navigational maps. This is not to discount the hours of mumbling and erasing that may precede the nativity of the *mot juste.*

In conclusion, let me suppose that some of Brecht's practices may have been beacons for me. Yet I wouldn't say that, with all his amazing versatility, his lapses into *doxa* too, his balladeering and popularity, his empathetic narrative voices (the secret of "Marie Farrar"), he has ever exercised a direct influence on my sporadic bursts of writing. I invert the word. I make forays into ludic and intimate provinces of tone, pulverizing stereotypes. I have precious little public, even less a sense of one. Generally too I abide by two principles which, though not contrary to Brecht's lyrical practice, must usually exclude his sense of political history, the great theater of events, the clash of arms and of ideologies. The first principle is expressed concisely by Samuel Beckett (in his *Proust*): "The quality of language is more important than any system of ethics or aesthetics..." The second (a very long story) is no less concisely expressed by Zulfikar Ghose (in his *The Fiction of Reality*): "The more a writer tries to perfect his work the more he is engaged in the possibilities of language and less with the idea with which he began." That in certain moods Brecht would, with reservations, have nodded at least in assent, is demonstrated by the exquisite dovetailing he achieved by crossing grammar and *ikon* in his poem about libraries and stockyards:

Aus den Bücherhallen
Treten die Schlächter
Die Kinder an sich drückend
Stehen die Mütter und durchforschen entgeistert
Den Himmel nach den Erfindungen der Gelehrten.

[Out of the bookyards
Walk the butchers.
Holding their children close
The mothers stand in line and search aghast
The sky for the inventions of scholars.]

Christopher Middleton

Brechts "Straßenszene" - ausgerechnet am Broadway? Ein Gespräch mit Anna Deavere Smith

Die afroamerikanische Schauspielerin und Dramatikerin Anna Deavere Smith trat mit ihren Ein-Frau-Stücken über Rassenunruhen in Brooklyn und Los Angeles ins Rampenlicht des Broadway, ein ungewöhnliches Beispiel politischer Intervention auf den Bühnen des Mainstream-Theaters. In ihren Vorstellungen spielt Smith selbst beinahe dreißig Zeugen rassistischer Übergriffe. Die Texte dafür sammelt sie in Gesprächen mit authentischen Zeugen. Auf diese Weise hat sie ein einzigartiges dramaturgisches Modell geschaffen. Seit über zehn Jahren interviewt sie Zeitgenossen, um ihre Solo-Vorstellungen aus diesem Material aufzubauen. Smith kommt dem Schauspielmodell für das epische Theater sehr nahe, das Brecht in seinem Essay "Die Straßenszene" entwickelt hat. In unserem Gespräch kommentiert sie die Methode hinter ihrem Modell, ihre wenigen Begegnungen mit Brechts Werk und den "Brechtischen" Stil, den sie entwickelt hat.

"La Scène de la Rue" de Brecht - Entre toutes, la scène de Broadway? Conversation avec Anna Deavere Smith

L' Actrice et auteur de théâtre noire américaine Anna Deavere Smith tint la vedette à Broadway avec ses représentations en solo sur les émeutes raciales de Brooklyn et de Los Angeles - un exemple inhabituel d'intervention de la politique sur la scène d'un théâtre grand public. Au cours de la représentation, Smith elle-même joue le rôle de plus de trente témoins des événements dont elle a recueilli les propos au cours d'entretiens avec eux. Elle a ainsi créé un modèle dramaturgique unique. Pendant plus de dix ans, elle a interrogé des contemporains pour constituer ses représentations en solo à partir de leurs témoignages. Smith se rapproche étroitement du modèle de jeu pour le théâtre épique que Brecht élabora dans son essai "La Scène de la Rue". Durant notre conversation, elle évoque la méthode sur laquelle repose son modèle, ses rares rencontres avec le travail de Brecht, et le style très "brechtien" qu'elle a développé.

"Street Scene" de Brecht — En Broadway, ¿de todos los lugares? Una conversación con Anna Deavere Smith

La actriz y dramaturga afro-americana Anna Deavere Smith llegó a ser el centro de atención en Broadway por de sus representaciones individuales de piezas teatrales basadas en las manifestaciones raciales en Brooklyn y los Ángeles, un ejemplo poco corriente de la influencia política en los escenarios teatrales de hoy en día. En sus actuaciones la misma Smith interpreta a treinta testigos de los acontecimientos, así establece los respectivos textos a partir de entrevistas directas con esos testigos. De esta forma ella ha creado un modelo único de hacer dramaturgia. Durante más de diez años ella ha entrevistado a contemporáneos suyos con el fin de utilizarlo como material para crear sus actuaciones individuales. Smith se acerca mucho al modelo de representación que Brecht elaboró para el Teatro Epico en su ensayo "The Street Scene." En nuestra conversación ella comenta sobre el método que se percibe tras su modelo, sobre sus pocos encuentros con la obra de Brecht y sobre el estilo muy "brechtiano" que ella ha desarrollado.

Brecht's "Street Scene" — On Broadway, of all Places? A Conversation with Anna Deavere Smith

Carl Weber

Anna Deavere Smith is the African-American actress, playwright, and professor at Stanford University who, two years ago, quite unexpectedly, soared to national fame in the United States. Her solo performance *Fires in the Mirror: Crown Heights, Brooklyn and other Identities* received enthusiastic reviews in national newspapers and weeklies; her picture appeared on the front page of *Newsweek, American Theater,* and other publications; and roles in two major Hollywood films quickly followed. Smith's highly charged performance broke through all the barriers which usually contain or domesticate efforts at politically relevant art in the United States.

The work consists of a sequence of enacted excerpts from interviews the actress/playwright conducted with individuals directly or indirectly involved in the Crown Heights race riots of August 1991 in Brooklyn, New York City. The violent events were triggered by the accidental killing of a nine-year-old black boy who was struck by a car belonging to the motorcade of the spiritual leader of the Hasidic Lubavitcher sect. The boy's death provoked that same evening the fatal stabbing of a Talmudic scholar visiting from Australia who was attacked by a group of young blacks on a street not far from the site of the accident. In fast-paced acceleration these fatalities led to three days of rioting in Crown Heights among black and Jewish residents as well as a large contingent of the New York City police force. When the street battles stopped, the community was left reeling from the experience of violence and groggily tried to find answers to why and how all this came to happen.

Anna Deavere Smith interviewed many persons on both sides of the racial divide; twenty-nine carefully selected and edited interviews became the material she used to script her one-woman show. The performance at New York's Public Theater won her an Obie, a "Woman of the Year" award, and a place on the Pulitzer Prize short list. Later it was seen on stages in Los Angeles, Berkeley, and other American cities and, eventually, at London's Royal Court Theater.[1]

The amazing response to, and success of, *Fires in the Mirror* led

Brecht Then and Now / Brecht damals und heute
Eds. Marc Silberman et al. *The Brecht Yearbook / Das Brecht-Jahrbuch,*
Volume 20 (Madison: The International Brecht Society, 1995)

to an invitation by the Los Angeles Mark Taper Forum to create a similar performance based on another tragic chain of events that began in Spring 1991 with the brutal mauling of Rodney King by Los Angeles police officers, leading to the officers' acquittal by an all-white jury in 1992, and then to the subsequent explosion of interracial violence which, during three days of burning, looting, and killing, laid to waste large parts of South-Central Los Angeles. Smith taped more than two hundred interviews with participants in these events, from the city's Mayor and the Commissioner of Police to Korean shop owners and black gang members in East Los Angeles. During a long and intricate process of rehearsal, rewrites, and preview performances, twenty-five texts derived from these interviews were selected to construct the performance piece, *Twilight: Los Angeles, 1992,* which she enacted in Los Angeles and later at New York's Public Theater and on Broadway. The performance was nominated for a Tony Award. New York critics called her "the most exciting individual in American theater right now" (Jack Kroll, *Newsweek*) and "that rare actor who actually should be encouraged to run for public office" (Frank Rich, *The New York Times*). The performance was recognized as going "...some way toward reclaiming for the stage its crucial role as a leader in defining and acting out that ongoing experiment called the United States" (John Lahr, *The New Yorker*).

On the surface, Smith's work appears to emulate a model that has been very successful and widely appropriated on the contemporary American stage: the solo piece presented by a charismatic performer, such as Spalding Gray, Eric Bogosian, or Karen Finley, to name only a few of the many who are currently active in various venues of the American theater. These artists have developed a personal, often highly sophisticated and theatrically efficient mode to recount and enact experiences from their personal life and/or to present general comments on contemporary society, mores, culture, and politics in the United States. Smith is profoundly different because she does not draw on her personal life and opinions to create the performance texts but rather makes herself the medium through which voices of her contemporaries appear before the audience, voices that express their own views, recount their sufferings, and pass their individual judgment on the events. The performer Smith steps back behind the persons she performs, yet she still is clearly present in her own persona, with her own "gestus," as Brecht would have put it, while presenting with striking precision the specific gestus of the characters she is portraying on stage.

Smith's approach to enacting events and characters cannot but make anyone familiar with Brecht's writings immediately think of his essay "The Street Scene." There is probably no other contemporary performance that has come as close to the "Basic Model for an Epic Theater" Brecht proposed here as Smith's *On the Road* shows.

On the Road: A Search for American Character — the title borrowed from Jack Kerouac's seminal book of the fifties — is an ongoing project Smith began eleven years ago, interviewing people in the context of a specific event or agenda and then constructing her multi-character, one-person performances from those interviews:

> In developing the *On the Road* project, it was my goal to develop a kind of theater that could be more sensitive to the events of my own time than traditional theater could.... The challenge of creating *On the Road* works is to select the voices that best represent the event I hope to portray.[2]

Only with the thirteenth installment of the series on the Crown Heights events did she successfully reach a wide, general audience. She obviously had touched a highly sensitive nerve in the American collective subconscious. Smith belongs to the rarest species in the American theater: an artist who achieved national recognition and media celebrity not only through her talent and skills but also because of a deliberately outspoken piece of political art.

From my own experience of working with Brecht in Berlin and as a director of Brecht's plays in Europe and America, I would claim that Smith's work comes closer to the concept of performance Brecht had in mind when he wrote "The Street Scene" than that of any other actor I have seen, with the exception perhaps of Helene Weigel. I was therefore all the more surprised that Smith has had few encounters with Brecht's work and certainly had never read the essay until I brought it to her attention at the time of our interview. Here we have the unique example of an artist who truly is a performer according to Brecht's postulates, yet who discovered his project independently, in her own practice of creating a performance from critically selected fragments of carefully observed real events and behavior. The result is a lucid, enlightening presentation, a performance that transcends the literal and naturalistic and invites each spectator to assess the depicted reality and its political ramifications. Smith the actress never totally disappears behind the characters she is en-acting. Throughout the performance her personal gestus is as clearly and visibly present as the performed characters' gestus. As she herself described it: "My work is both political and personal. I'm trying to resolve this problem of strangeness and closeness in our world that's getting closer and closer. I'm interested in telling every side of the story."[3]

These aspects of the *On the Road* project inspired me to talk with Anna Deavere Smith about her work for *The Brecht Yearbook*, an invitation she gladly accepted. Her ideas on acting, her working methods, and her future plans made the affinity to Brecht's thinking as evident as her performance had led me to expect.

* * * * * * * *

Carl Weber: What would you regard as the most important stations in your career as an artist, as an actress as well as a playwright?

Anna Deavere Smith: Well, I always think of my first Shakespeare class as an actress as an extremely important moment. I had studied Shakespeare in English classes in college as an undergraduate but when I went to acting school it was the first time I ever paid any real attention to the speaking of Shakespeare. My Shakespeare teacher said to us on the first day to take fourteen lines of Shakespeare and repeat them over and over again and see what happened. And so I took her at her word and, not knowing very much about acting at all, I picked Queen Margaret from *Richard III*, speaking what was a curse almost: "That dog that had its teeth before his eyes" — very intense, dark imagery. I really felt it during that evening of doing it over and over again. I sort of visited another world and another person, and I was absolutely clear that this person was not me. But I felt that I had experienced that person, that I had in fact experienced another imagination than mine. Of course, it couldn't have been anybody's imagination but my imagination, but maybe we could say that parts of my imagination had been shaken, or opened, or lit. So, that was a very important experience, and nothing in my training in, well, psychological realism ever gave me the opportunity to have such a clear experience again. By clear, I mean the clear experience of seeing another world, another person, and therefore knowing how to enter it. So, that was a very important point.

Weber: And what would have been the next important point?

Smith: I guess... After that I always tell the story of seeing a Johnny Carson show with Sophia Loren and Joan Rivers, and taping it and having actors re-enact it, and just being really fascinated with how talk shows are making the illusion of being about revealing a personality. But it's more about the host. And I just got interested in what would happen if I had non-adversarial conversations with people. What would happen, what would come forward as their "personality?" And so I started doing my own interviews as a result of having seen that show.

Weber: What gave you the idea to begin the *On the Road* project, with that particular agenda you have pursued over the years? What was the first impulse to do that?

Smith: That Johnny Carson show was the first impulse. But I should say, to put this in context, that I had been in this big pursuit ever since that Shakespeare class. By the time I saw that Johnny Carson show, I was teaching acting myself. I had been in a pursuit to understand more about the relationship of language to character. When I saw that Johnny Carson show I was directing a production of *A Movie Star Has to Star in Black and White* by Adrienne Kennedy, and I was really interested in the difficulty I was having with young actors in terms of getting them to really inhabit somebody else. And [Kennedy's] characters are very complex, because they [the students] had a persona — a movie star or no movie star — but they had a script, a text that had nothing to do with that. So, it was with a very particular ear that I was watching the talk show and listening and watching for the places where text cooperates with persona and the places where it doesn't, where it has nothing to do with it. So, I would say that around the time I'm directing *A Movie Star Has to Star in Black and White* I'm becoming interested, for reasons of how to deal with the actors in [the play], in real interviews.

Weber: So, the actual stimulating impulse for the *On the Road* project was the Johnny Carson Show and your experience with students?

Smith: Yes.

Weber: In the meantime you have done a lot of work, and *Fires in the Mirror* became this enormous success and obviously hit a nerve of the country or the nation, a very sensitive nerve, and consequently had its great impact. What do you think — from what you intended at least — should be the...let's call it: the "mission" of the piece?

Smith: The mission of the piece? Well, I think it has different missions. One is that, because I play people who are clearly not me, who I could never be and would never portray in a realistic drama, that usually in the beginning people laugh a lot. Because I guess it's very funny to have that juxtaposition, and the people that I do perform, particularly in the first twenty minutes of the show, have really idiosyncratic behavior. And one mission is that by the end, I hope, perceptions of the audience have changed so that they're no longer laughing at such external things, and if they're laughing, they are laughing for more complicated reasons. Because I think that way the audience has to respond to the difficulty that they are having, imagining *me* instead of a person, [which] is not unrelated to how racism works. It is impossible for us, almost ever, to see beyond what we see in front of us. So, in a way, I'm trying to evoke from the audience a different relationship than [their] accepting things on the surface. The other part of the mission is: I'm really trying to create community. I'm trying to bring together on the stage, trying to display on the stage, people who aren't normally portrayed in the American theater or in the media, in trying to make the audience *see* those people, people who don't normally come to the theater. To use the theater — to go back to what we talked about today — to use the fact of physical presence to create a way that strangers can come close [to each other].

Weber: Would you define that as something we should call "political theater?"

Smith: Oh, I think it is political.

Weber: What fascinates me aside from this aspect is the way you go about it as a performer. You define a particular personal gestus or "persona," as you called it, of a specific individual whom you have observed and then present it to an audience. It reminds me, more than anything I have seen on stage, of what Brecht wrote in his famous essay "The Street Scene." So, I would like to ask you what impact Brecht had on your work over the years? What did you know about his ideas? How much did you know when you started on your project *On the Road*, and to what extent do you believe you've been influenced by him?

Smith: My experience with Brecht was as a spectator and as a person acting in, well, just two of his plays...

Weber: And which were those?

Smith: *Threepenny Opera* and *Caucasian Chalk Circle* when I played Ludovika.

Weber: Where was that, by the way?

Smith: Ludovika was in a small theater in Brooklyn, in a production directed by Gitta Honegger. And I also played in, well, it was Brecht, although it was *Mother Courage* in the version by Ntozake Shange at the New York Public Theater.[4] I just played a very small role as one of the ensemble, and I was understudying Kattrin, which is a role I always wanted to play. The very first time I saw any Brecht was when I was in my late teens, I saw *Arturo Ui* in London. There is a vigor to his imagination that I had never seen before in my life. I mean, I didn't know anything about the theater but I felt that it was the vigor...it is the only word I can think of, it was more concrete, more vigorous. I'm sure it had a lot to do with the staging but it had a lot to do with Brecht, too, there was more distinction. And it was quite a season that year in London, I saw *Hair* at the time, and *Boys in the Band*. But nothing had this type of distinction, and I really liked it because I felt that it stimulated my imagination, not unlike the type of stimulation I was trying to describe [when talking] about Queen Margaret. And I think that's the vigor and the genius of the author that can transcend everything in making a connection with the spectator. So, after having seen that, I wanted to see more things like it but I didn't really know how to go about that. Of course, working on *Mother Courage* was just fascinating to me, especially since I was an understudy and had a lot of time.

Weber: That was Wilford Leach's production?

Smith: Right, with Gloria Foster playing Mother Courage. It was that vigor, again, which was fascinating to me. And for some reason in every experience [during those rehearsals] I had been very engaged intellectually. It was just the kind of rehearsals I couldn't take my eyes off, always fascinated by the text, always entertained by the twists and the turns in the language. What also comes to mind is my having directed *Tales from Hollywood* by Christopher Hampton. And in the play the H.U.A.C. tape of Brecht is used, and that is just a phenomenal piece of theater... Just thinking what an active and disciplined mind he must have had. I'm not a Brecht scholar but I am fascinated by that man and that imagination.

Weber: *Fires in the Mirror* is, in my opinion, quite a demonstration of Brechtian principles in defining the personal gestus of a person who is obviously not you, the actress. While I see the person fully, at the same time I still see you as the actress presenting the person and having an opinion about it. Which is exactly what Brecht was writing about in the essay I mentioned. Now, what became the most important aspect of the project for you as a performer, being on stage in relation to your audience?

Smith: Well, I think the most important aspect in relation to the audience is that it changes all the time, although I performed it many, many times. JoAnne Akalaitis actually said two things which are very interesting, [things] I constantly think about. I think about them at least once or twice in a performance week. One was that I have to play every character, or every scene, as if it's the whole play. So that there is a real clarity to the beginning and the end of each thing, and everything has its world. Once again, this distinction which I think is wonderful when I see it elsewhere. And the other thing she said to me was to have independence from the audience, never to play for them. To some extent I do play for them. But I'm always learning the importance of playing for them but of having my separate space. And I think, again, that's about creating the distinct worlds these people live in. But, you know, the thing that is the motor for all my performance is the spoken word. So, audience members say things like "How do you remember all those things that people do? Do you videotape those things?" And it's a complete illusion, because I remember a few things only. I've really made it all up over the course of the performance, bringing to these people a physical life. It's highly unlikely that it's accurate. But there is a connection that I don't understand intellectually, between the spoken word and what the body does physically.

Weber: That reminds me of what Brecht kept telling actors while rehearsing scenes: "Each scene for its own sake. Don't play the whole play in one scene, or the future of the character in one scene. Play each scene fully for its own sake." Which is very close to what you were describing about what you do with your characters. And secondly, the kind of space that you talk about, that you occupy as a performer in front of your audience, which you retain as something independent nearly of the audience...this is again very close to what Brecht demanded of his actors in performance. Playing for an audience but not playing to an audience, not pandering.

Smith: Right. It takes a lot of discipline. But what I've been learning is it doesn't always work because an audience is so moody, and you may feel that you have them and then you don't, you don't know where they are at all. And I realize how much energy one could waste trying to pander to them.

Weber: The other thing which was fascinating in what you just said was that the characters you create on stage are not a kind of photocopy of the people you actually interviewed. But that you create them by way of the language you have on tape and some specific idiosyncratic items of their behavior, maybe.

Smith: Exactly.

Weber: You actually create a new character which, on the other hand, obviously contains a kernel, or the basic gestus, of the character you're portraying. I think here of the [Reverend] Al Sharpton piece, for instance, or Angela Davis, because these two people I have seen myself and can judge what you are doing against the way they really behave. And the stunning thing was that you seem to have distilled the essence of their behavior pattern, of their personal gestus, and brought that on stage, which made me think of a statement in Brecht's "Street Scene" essay. I quote: "Our demonstrator need not imitate every aspect of his characters' behavior, but only so much as gives a picture."

Smith: Well, in both the cases of Sharpton and Angela Davis, and with others, if I do have access to video tape, I do watch the video tape. But even if I remember — because I don't have a photographic memory — if I remember one gesture or one posture, then that one thing has to become the kernel for a system of movement. And sometimes, with some characters, as with Leonard Jeffries, for example, I only remembered a few things about his behavior. But over the process of performing him some things came back into memory, suddenly I remembered something else. In performance this usually happens. Something else will come to me in a physical way...a physical memory of it.

But I just want to tell you one thing I've been thinking about a lot lately during performance. It goes back to what my desire was when I was doing my initial experimentation. I was a little bit disturbed, for social and political and spiritual reasons, by the idea that as actors we must identify with character. Even when an audience says "All right, I identified with this character or identified with that character." It bothers me a bit that that's the limit people feel they had in terms of experience. Of course, they do much more than identify. And so, something I have been thinking a lot about lately is not identification but illumination. That is to say, a person gave me the words on tape, I kept the words, and then it isn't that I even try to act like the person. I try to present what they did, to take care of what they did, but the creative part of me is trying to illuminate what they did.

Weber: The Los Angeles project was a continuation, in some ways, of *Fires in the Mirror*. On the other hand, it posed a different set of problems you encountered, I suppose, when trying to put it all together. To what extent do you think it became similar to the Brooklyn project and to what extent did it greatly differ from it?

Smith: Well, it's changing even again, working now with Tony Kushner [as a dramaturg] and George C. Wolfe [as the director], and it will be very different from what I did in the Los Angeles performance. The process of creating the piece was much different from that in Brooklyn, for the simple reason that Los Angeles is so huge in terms of physical space. And also, I think many, many people who come to the theater to see *Fires in the Mirror* know something about Jews and they know something about blacks, even if they're not Jewish and they're not black. They have an emotional relationship to black people and to Jewish people, and they have very strong feelings. In L.A. it's much more complicated than that. And I think the average audience doesn't bring as much, for example, in terms of an attitude towards Korean Americans, who are a big part of this. And many people don't even know how to react to, say, the black people in it. Particularly the young people who are really unknown, even to the average black audience member. It's a whole different generation, it doesn't have the same history, the same roots. For example, in *Fires in the Mirror* many of the people are clergy. I don't think I represent the clergy at all [in the L.A. piece], there is no apparent leadership. It's much harder to find than it was in *Fires*.

Weber: I would like to bring up once more the idea of gestus as Brecht understood it. It seems so much present in what you are doing on stage, namely creating a specific gestus for each individual character, and at the same time retaining something of your own personal gestus, underneath, shining through to a degree. Which makes the performance much more fascinating than impersonation which, of course, is the usual route actors try to go when they play living, contemporary people. Did the idea of gestus come into play at all for you, or is it just something which you discover in retrospect?

Smith: To tell you the truth, I was trying to make an accurate document, which is impossible. And I didn't want to impersonate, that would be me, adding things. I was trying to make an accurate document. So, in a way, what you see is as much as I could remember, as much as I could do in the time. I think of it as very unfinished, what I'm doing. The people are only in half their clothes, I never finished making their dresses.

Weber: That's exactly what Brecht writes about in the essay "The Street Scene." That's the way people on the street, who have seen an accident, would describe it to others because they don't remember every detail, just what they regard — subconsciously, maybe — as the most essential details.

Smith: In a way, I think, in any hour that I talk to a person when I'm interviewing, they actually say very few essential things in that regard. When you talked to me about "Street Scene," I remembered something that influenced the way I did interviews when I first started interviewing people, way back ten, twelve years ago. I wanted to get people to say those few essential things. And I knew if I talked to somebody an hour, they would only say a few of these things which I would call essential things. In other words: repeatable things, things which are quite distinct, nobody could have said it like they said it. Then I'd take that and use that, because it's a very clear structure.

A linguist told me these three questions I could ask to get people to do this type of talking. They were: Have you ever come close to death? Do you remember the circumstances of your birth? Have you been accused of something that you did not do? And the thing that was interesting to me when people answered those questions is that they did begin to act, usually, that is to say, the language became more demonstrative. When you tell me that story by Brecht about the street, it is quite like, for example, the young boy in *Fires in the Mirror* who talks about watching the accident. He is breaking away from his own narrative to "act out." And certain people — usually, as this linguist told me, less educated people — tend to do that type of talking. Of course, more educated people begin to cloak their narrative with a longer explanation. So it takes questions which really bring back to them either very pleasurable or traumatic experiences to get them to leave the cloak of language and come to the real expression. And it is that real or essential expression I'm trying for, cutting away the rest of the scraps in there to get that. Even though somebody may have said something which is a much more eloquent narrative and would help me tell my story more quickly, it won't be of use. What's of more use are the bits and pieces of disconnected language with a peculiar syntax which seems to have nothing to do with the rest of the interview.

Weber: Which are, of course, the clearest expressions of the personal gestus of a character.

Smith: In that there is something quite resonant about that person. And then my acting is usually a journey. Because there is still "fat," probably you see more of me in the journey towards those actual twenty seconds.

Weber: So, what happens is that the performer Anna merges with the playwright Anna, who edits and selects and structures the raw material?

Smith: Right.

Weber: Which brings me to a question for the playwright: What avenues would you like to explore in the future?

Smith: Well, I have a lot of concern about theater, American theater, right now, and its difficulty with becoming more a part of the heart of America and being more responsible to its community. There are many institutional road blocks I face in that regard because I'm very dependent on the [given] venue to take me closer to that community. For example, with *Fires in the Mirror* the ideal audience is a mixed audience with very strong attitudes who would applaud a person that others would be offended by.

Weber: An audience that takes sides.

Smith: I want the audience to take sides. I want it to be a civic event. And I have been to only a few theaters where they were able to attract such an audience. So, I have this question about where I should work next. I don't know if I'm suited to the media. But it is very, very tempting for that reason of really wanting to meet a larger community, a more diverse community, a younger community, a community that is not as fortunate as subscribers are.

Weber: On the other hand, when you work in the media, on television or film, a very essential part of what you are doing gets lost.

Smith: An essential part of me is getting lost?

Weber: Yes, of what you do as a performer on stage. Comparing, for instance, your television presentation of *Fires in the Mirror* with the actual performance I have seen.

Smith: Because the gestus must get lost by this attempt to bring the audience closer, by giving them more, and not doing a document of a stage piece. No, I'm not that eager to act in television.

Weber: One of the very persuasive aspects of your stage performance is that you play all these characters in quick succession within one and a half or two hours. An important part of what makes us take sides, I think, is the observation of the power of the performer who can do this kind of a performance and is bringing it off. Now, I had a question about the present state and the future of the American theater, and to some extent you already answered it by what you've said about the venues you'd like to explore. I was not only thinking about the venues you would like to use as a performer but, as well, what kind of forms you'd like to explore as a writer now?

Smith: I don't think I want to necessarily create another one-person show. Part of that is just having a desire to create roles for other people and to be able to watch other people becoming those people. I've been interested in doing something about incarceration for a long, long time. I don't know what kind of form that would take.

Weber: Do you have any particular dramaturgic ideas?

Smith: Structurally?

Weber: For instance, would you like to work in a very "realistic" vein, like most American drama is written these days, or more in what you might call an epic mode?

Smith: I don't know. I don't think in a realistic way, I think it suits me to create things that are short — short, choppy things in quick succession.

Weber: Which is, of course, precisely the form you have developed in the process of creating your *On the Road* project.
 I'd like to thank you for a very instructive and stimulating conversation.

(The interview was conducted in Spring 1994.)

NOTES

[1] Anna Deavere Smith, *Fires in the Mirror* (New York: Anchor Books/Doubleday, 1993) includes the complete text and an instructive introduction.

[2] Anna Deavere Smith, *Twilight: Los Angeles, 1992* (New York: Anchor Books/Doubleday, 1994), xxii. This volume contains a large selection of interviews not used in performance as well as a chronology of the events and an introduction that illuminates Smith's creative process.

[3] *Time*, October 10, 1994.

[4] Ntozake Shange wrote an adaptation of *Mother Courage* for the New York Shakespeare Festival. Her version situates the play's fable in the American West at the end and after the Civil War between the Union and the Confederate Southern States. Mother Courage and her children are African Americans, like several other characters in the play.

Brecht Then and Now / Brecht damals und heute

Ich greife immer wieder auf Brecht zurück: Ein Gespräch mit dem Dramatiker Tony Kushner

Kushner hatte mit seinem zweiteiligen Stück *Angels in America* einen internationalen Erfolg, dem auf der Seite amerikanischer Dramatiker nur der Erfolg von Edward Albees *Wer hat Angst vor Virginia Woolf?* in den frühen sechziger Jahren gleichkommt. Brecht spielte eine entscheidende Rolle in Kushners Entwicklung als Dramatiker und Regisseur. Er betrachtet dialektisches Denken und die epische Form als charakteristisch für sein Werk. In unserem Gespräch schildert er seine immer noch andauernde Auseinandersetzung mit Brecht und legt seine Ansichten über Brechts Theater und Theorien dar. In diesem Zusammenhang nennt er auch John Fuegis neue Brechtbiographie und kritisiert deren Motivation und Vorgehensweise. Kushner spricht über seine Produktionen *Das Badener Lehrstück* und *Der gute Mensch von Sezuan* (letztere in seiner eigenen neuen englischen Übersetzung). Ferner diskutiert er die zeitgenössische amerikanische Theaterpraxis sowie die sozialen und politischen Veränderungen im vergangenen Jahr und deren zu erwartende Konsequenzen für die darstellenden und bildenden Künste in den USA.

J'en reviens toujours à Brecht: Conversation avec l'auteur Tony Kushner

Tony Kushner a remporté un succès international avec sa pièce en deux volets *Angels in America*, qui, pour un auteur américain, n'est concurrencé que par la pièce d' Edward Albee *Qui a peur de Virginia Woolf?* au début des années soixante. Brecht a joué un rôle décisif dans l' évolution de Kushner comme auteur et metteur en scène. Il considère que le mode de pensée dialectique et la forme épique sont des caractéristiques de son propre travail. Au cours de notre conversation, il décrit son dialogue continuel avec Brecht et explique sa conception du théâtre et des théories de Brecht. Dans ce contexte, il mentionne également la nouvelle biographie de Brecht de Fuegi et critique à la fois l'approche et la motivation sur laquelle elle repose. Kushner parle de sa mise en scène du *Badener Lehrstück* et de *La bonne âme de Setchouan* (cette dernière dans sa propre adaptation en anglais). Par ailleurs, il discute les pratiques contemporaines du théâtre américain, ainsi que les changements politiques et sociaux survenus l'année dernière et leurs conséquences prévisibles sur l'art aux Etats-Unis.

Siempre vuelvo a Brecht: Una conversación con el dramaturgo Tony Kushner

Con su obra teatral titulada *Angels in America*, Kushner disfrutó de un éxito internacional sólo comparable para un dramaturgo americano con la obra de Albee titulada *Who's Afraid of Virginia Woolf* de los sesenta. Brecht ha jugado un papel decisivo en el desarrollo de Kushner como escritor y director de teatro. El considera que el pensar dialéctico y la forma épica caracterizan su obra. Kushner describe su interacción constante con Brecht a la vez que explica su propia perspectiva sobre el teatro de Brecht y la visión teoríca de este. En este contexto, también menciona la nueva biografía sobre Brecht escrita por John Fuegi y critica el punto de vista y la motivación existente tras esta biografía. Kushner habla sobre sus producciones *The Baden Learning Play* y *The Good Person of Sezuan* (esta última en su adaptación al inglés). Además Kushner opina sobre la práctica del teatro contemporáneo americano y sobre los cambios políticos ocurridos en el último año y las consecuencias para el mundo artístico en los EEUU.

I Always Go Back to Brecht:
A Conversation with the Playwright Tony Kushner

Carl Weber

Tony Kushner's epic play in two parts, *Angels in America*, became during 1994 the internationally most acclaimed and most widely performed play by an American writer since the success of Edward Albee's *Who's Afraid of Virginia Wolfe* thirty years earlier. The first part, *Millennium Approaches*, received a Pulitzer Prize and a Tony Award; the second part, *Perestroika*, was given another Tony Award as "Best play of the 1993/94 Season." Kushner's adaptation of Corneille's *The Illusion* has been frequently performed by regional theaters and by drama departments at American universities, while his play about a circle of artists and intellectuals in Berlin during the final days of the Weimar Republic, *A Bright Room Called Day*, was produced by the New York Shakespeare Festival at the Public Theater and in London and San Francisco. He also has adapted Goethe's play *Stella* for a production at the New York Theatre Workshop. Kushner has successfully worked as a stage director in New York, New Haven, St. Louis, and other cities. He has a Bachelor's degree from Columbia University and an M.F.A. in Directing from New York University's Tisch School of the Arts, where he studied with me. He since has taught writing and theater at NYU, the Julliard School, Princeton University, and other schools. Among Kushner's most recent work has been a new English-language version of Brecht's *The Good Person of Szechwan*, which premiered at the La Jolla Playhouse, California, in the Summer of 1994, and the play *Slavs!*, in which he tackles some of the complex problems of post-Socialist Russia.

The following conversation was conducted in November 1994. It is a free-wheeling exploration of Kushner's views on Brecht, the art of the playwright, the American theater in the nineties, and the impact which the recent historical/political shifts might have on the reception of Brecht's work in the United States.

* * * * * * * *

Brecht Then and Now / Brecht damals und heute
Eds. Marc Silberman et al. *The Brecht Yearbook / Das Brecht-Jahrbuch*,
Volume 20 (Madison: The International Brecht Society, 1995)

Brecht Then and Now / Brecht damals und heute

Carl Weber: Tony, in articles and interviews you have frequently commented on the impact which Brecht's theater has had on your own work. When did your first encounter with Brecht's work actually happen, and what brought it about?

Tony Kushner: It was in the second semester of my freshman year at Columbia University. I took a Modern Drama survey course. We read Duerrenmatt and everybody else, Ionesco, Beckett, etc. And I believe, if I remember correctly, we read *The Good Person of Szechwan* and *Threepenny Opera*. I was intrigued by *Threepenny Opera*, although not terribly impressed with it. I thought that *Szechwan* was complicated and interesting but I don't remember having much more of a reaction than that. If I'm remembering correctly, two things happened simultaneously the next semester when I was a sophomore. I had a professor who was teaching my Western Humanities class, a sort of survey course in classics of Western political, ethical, and philosophical thought. He was a Latin American Marxist, and he gave me Ernst Fischer's *The Necessity of Art* to read. I was very disturbed and upset, challenged and excited by Fischer. That started me reading Marx. At the same time, Richard Foreman was doing *The Threepenny Opera* at the Public Theater at Lincoln Center. I was seeing a great deal of theater in New York at the time, almost all of it on Broadway, and Foreman's *Threepenny Opera*...I was absolutely devastated by it. I thought it was the most exciting theater I had ever seen. I went back to see it six or seven times and I became very interested in Brecht from that point on.

I took another Modern Drama course that had a heavier amount of Brecht in it and I read the *Short Organum*, which is the point at which I fell completely in love with Brecht. I read all of *Brecht on Theater*. The *Short Organum* was a kind of revelation for me. It was the first time I believed that people who are seriously committed political intellectuals could have a home in the theater, the first time that I believed theater, really good theater, had the potential for radical intervention, for effectual analysis. The things that were exciting me about Marx, specifically dialectics, I discovered in Brecht, in a wonderful witty and provocative form. I became very, very excited about doing theater as a result of reading Brecht.

Weber: What was it that immediately captured you in Brecht's writings?

Kushner: I think in all of German literature there is, for Jewish people, a certain recognition. The history of Jewish literature and the history of German literature are fairly inextricable. Even in translation there is a kind of a diction and sensibility that is recognizable. I've always felt myself very deeply drawn to German literature.

Weber: What do you actually mean when you talk of a certain kind of diction?

Kushner: It probably is the Latinate structure of the sentences. Also, the folk idioms that are very similar to the idioms of Yiddish.

Weber: Of course, a lot of Yiddish idioms crept into the German over the centuries. A lot of German sayings are Yiddish sayings, and vice versa.

Kushner: German-Jewish culture is sort of the *Hoch* culture of Jewish society. It is — what's the term? — *plumpes Denken*, it's a kind of "fat" thinking. It is Benjamin's term, I think.

Weber: *Plumpes Denken?*

Kushner: Yes, the idea of "fat" thought. It is a very cause-and-effect kind of thinking, a very grainy sort of thinking. It isn't French...I'm doing a bad job of describing it.

Weber: You mean a specifically dialectical kind of thinking?

Kushner: Well, it is very dialectical and firmly rooted in the Enlightenment and in a kind of rationality, a belief in the recoverability of ultimate causes. It is ethical and not obfuscating or obscurantist.

Weber: If you think of Heidegger, for instance, there is lot of obscurantist German thinking.

Kushner: There is certainly also a great deal of obscurantist writing in Jewish mystical traditions. But this is another sort of thinking, like Spinoza, or Bloch, or Hannah Arendt, or Goethe. There is a very domestic sort of clarity about it.

Weber: And you found that in Brecht?

Kushner: Yes, I did. I think of it as a diction that is also intrinsic and rather grim, and that I find in Brecht. I think there is a Jewish-German connection.

Weber: Absolutely, a connection and a long tradition that started with Lessing and Moses Mendelssohn, and maybe even earlier.

Kushner: Yes, I guess that's it.

Weber: Now, when was it that you decided to study directing? And at what time did you begin to think about becoming a playwright?

Kushner: Well, I didn't really think about becoming a playwright. I mean, being a playwright is what I always wanted to be. But I was too intimidated by it, and I felt that, if I couldn't write *Mother Courage*, I shouldn't write any play at all. Also, when I studied Brecht, I studied Shakespeare, and I studied Shakespeare with a man named Edward Taylor. I don't think I remember that he actually spoke about dialectics, but his approach to analyzing Shakespeare was entirely a matter of analyzing the dialectics and paradoxes in Shakespeare. Reading Brecht and Shakespeare at the same time was wonderful because I was discovering what a dialectical method was and finding it was a critical tool for understanding the two playwrights whose work I admired the most. I was also very much drawn in Brecht to the epic form, to the chronicle play. It was almost immediately as soon as I read *Mother Courage* that it became my favorite Brecht. I loved the multi-focal, the multiple perspective of it. You know, Brecht talks about it when he writes about Breughel and the lack of a single point of perspective, the complexity of signs, and the physical conflict in a terribly grandiose prism. I liked this sort of sprawl of the big epic plays in Brecht.

Weber: That essay on Breughel reflects very much Brecht's directorial approach. When did you decide to explore directing?

Kushner: I think that I wanted to be a playwright, and I think that I wanted to be a playwright very much like Brecht. But I was afraid to try that, so I thought, well, maybe I could be a person who directed Brecht. It felt to me that it was a reasonably good way at least to start to explore how to make theater. And that if writing was going to happen, it would happen alongside it, which is pretty much exactly what happened. I had read an article in *Yale Theater* about you and R. G. Davis. In the absolutely most violent flash of my Brecht fixation I was just reading everything about him that I could find. And I think *Yale Theater* published in one of its first issues...

Weber: Yes, they published a piece about Epic West in Berkeley.

Kushner: Right. And you were working on *Calendar Tales...*

Weber: No, Ronnie was. I was working on *The Baden Play of Learning* and on *Messingkauf*.

Kushner: Right. I read it and I thought you sounded great. I wanted to fly right out to San Francisco and work with you. It seemed this was the kind of stuff that I should be doing. I had also read Ronnie Davis's book about the San Francisco Mime Troupe, which is a really wonderful book.

Weber: It is, I agree.

Kushner: And he talks about Brecht with a very strong American sensibility. Also, one thing I've never really mentioned is that I did study to be an artist for a brief while. I mean, not exclusively to be an artist, but I took painting and drawing.

Weber: You are actually very talented in that way, as I know from all the drawings you did while you were at NYU. I remember especially a New Year's card you made and gave me after Brezhnev's death, a cartoon-like drawing that somehow seemed to anticipate *Perestroika* and its results, at least in retrospect.

Kushner: I also used to make masks, and the idea that Brecht's was a theater that had room for things like half-masks, that it incorporated popular forms of theater like *Commedia* felt exciting to me. In fact, one of the very first experiences that I had at NYU when I was thinking about applying there...maybe I called you and asked about meeting you, and you didn't have time to meet with me but you said that I should come and see one of the projects. Someone had just finished directing the first half of *We Won't Pay We Won't Pay*, and I had never even heard of Dario Fo before. As I remember it, it was presented in one of the studios on Seventh Street, and it was a rather good, lively performance, and I loved the play. I believe it was directed by Bob Bresnick.

Weber: Yes, I think it was.

Kushner: He was supposed to do the whole thing and felt they only had enough time to do the first half, and that was all they were going to present. But it was actually very good, as I remember it, and it introduced me to Dario Fo. At any rate, that's how I think I decided I would direct instead of simply writing. I already had written a couple of things that were heavily influenced by Brecht. A children's play, based on a Grimm fairy tale and in twenty-four scenes, that was completely epic, though I had no idea what I was doing.

Weber: That was before Columbia or while you were there?

Kushner: That was in my last year at Columbia. And then I went to NYU.

Weber: Why did you pick that particular Brecht one-act play that you auditioned with?

Kushner: Well, I had read the Methuen volume with the Brecht one acts. I needed something short, and I thought I'd like to do Brecht. *The Beggar, or the Dead Dog* was small. It was a very strange little play, and I was kind of moved by it. I also liked some of the visual ideas that I had had about it. And I thought that it had the possibility of using masks, which I was determined to do.

Weber: I also remember very well the backdrop you had painted for it.

Kushner: Yes, it was based on an Inigo Jones drawing. It was sort of black, and it had a lot of death imagery which was very important to me at the time [laughs]. And I think that I had absolutely no idea what I was doing and I had absolutely no idea what the play meant.

Weber: During your time with our program and the further work on Brecht that you did when you were at NYU, and while we worked together on *Happy End* and other things, did your earlier perception of Brecht change, or not? And if so, in what way?

Kushner: Well, it's weird to be talking to you about this directly because it has so much to do with you. You know, from that first interview with you, I felt that getting the chance to work with you was going to be a chance to work with a live connection to the Brechtian tradition. I didn't really know very much about you when I showed up at NYU, I didn't know that you were also someone who had worked with Handke, and with Heiner Müller, and Ed Bullins, and people like that. So, I was unprepared for the extent to which you had been a figure in the American avant-garde. And as I told you, I think, when we were all graduating, and you were leaving NYU, that was an incredibly important part of our work together, establishing the connection between two key radical traditions in the theater.

Your main pedagogical tool, the fable, taught me a great deal about the way in which content, narrative, and meaning function together, and the kind of rigorousness that is necessary to make a successful play. That forced me to reconsider the Brecht that I had read and to look at it more thoroughly, and it gave me a new appreciation of how intricately and carefully worked the texts are, and how incredibly economical they are. Especially the scripts where Brecht had a chance to hone them through rehearsal, there is nothing wasted at all. Even in *Szechwan*, which he didn't really have the chance to trim, everything is in the service of the fable and everything is important. I don't know if I'm making myself clear, but there is a sort of marriage of the narrative drive, the emotional life of the play, the psychological life of the play, and the political meaning, the *Inhalt*. I mean, it's all so beautifully and intricately interwoven. And also the necessity of having a deep understanding of history, a political understanding of history. And having an overtly ideological historical narrative that one uses in a sophisticated way, I think that was something I got from working with you. Also, I think of an instance of when you were demonstrating. Somebody had brought in a scene from the *White Devil* or *Duchess of Malfi* to the directing seminar, and you were sort of acting for us. You did it again when we were doing *Happy End*. And I felt that I was watching a way of doing things, and a way of rehearsing, that was a direct example of the way that...I mean, it made something clear to me about what Brecht means. I don't think Brecht is actually very good in describing what he expects actors to do.

Weber: When writing about the theater, he never concerned himself very much with what particular method an actor would employ and how an actor should work. He basically wrote about the results, the results he wanted to see in performance.

Kushner: Right. And it was fascinating to watch you perform. I think I understood something about what Brecht wanted in acting from watching you, in terms of creating moments that are deeply invested and also clearly observed by the performer.

Weber: Isn't it actually Brecht's concept of gestus that you are talking about now?

Kushner: Yes. But gestus is one of those promiscuous terms, I think. I understand it as having several possible applications.

Weber: Brecht was never very consistent in writing about it and in defining it clearly.

Kushner: Particularly in what it meant.

Weber: Probably, in his own mind, he was at times also quite ambiguous about it, about what it was supposed to be. When you saw him at work, however, you really understood it.

Kushner: I think when you work on one of his plays, you understand the usefulness of finding the visual motif that will help to string ideas together for an audience that run through the play and appear at various points, a visual motif that will privilege those moments.

Weber: Did your directing experience — at NYU as well as during the various Off-off-Broadway productions that you directed while you were still a student and shortly after — did these experiences change your way of appropriating Brecht's methods? In my memory, your production of *The Heavenly Theater* was a striking example of a young director who is writing plays and who is beginning to bring both things together.

Kushner: Yes, I think I was. Although your critique of *Heavenly Theater* — that it was in a sense too rational, that what I was trying to describe, which is this extraordinary historical phenomenon of a revolution that takes place during a carnival, that it was too mired in a kind of "Marxist-Leninist" or even Brechtian dramaturgy, and that the carnivalesque was not really happening — I think that this was absolutely true.

Weber: But it was probably a necessary phase to go through for you.

Kushner: Right. In many ways that was really my first play. And I didn't have the tools or the skills to take it where you suggested that I should take it. It was a lesson in terms of finding the right model for the subject at hand. The real, deliberate attempt to write a "Brecht play" was *A Bright Room Called Day*. You and I had a discussion about Brecht writing various plays as answers to other plays that he was impressed or disturbed by, and about the way in which Brecht or Shakespeare incorporated or used previous material and tried to write a dialectical response to it. I took a Brecht play that I have very little respect for, which is *Fear and Misery of the*

Third Reich, and attempted when I started out to write *Bright Room* to do a sort of Reagan-era version of it.

Weber: Did you say you have little respect for it?

Kushner: I have very little respect for it. The scenes are fairly mediocre. They have a lot of interesting moments because they are Brecht's but they are not terribly impressive. The whole thing, when it is strung together, has certainly never been one of my favorite Brecht plays, especially not for its dramaturgy.

Weber: Well, that is an opinion you share with Heiner Müller.

Kushner: In terms of its response to what was going on in Germany at the time it simply failed. The play that really impresses in that regard is *Mother Courage*, which I think is very much Brecht's response to Hitler, and then of course *Arturo Ui*, which I have gained a great deal of respect for in recent years. I still think of *Mother Courage* as a sort of a Trotskyite piece. It is consonant with Trotsky's analysis of what was going on in Germany in the years before, which allowed Trotsky to prophesy the rise of Hitler. The petty bourgeois run amuck. The perilous socio-economic position of the petty bourgeois in Germany resulted in their manipulability and turning to Hitler. And I think *Mother Courage* still is a tragedy which is appropriate to the history that Brecht had been watching.

Weber: You said that *Bright Room* was kind of an answer to *Fear and Misery*.

Kushner: It was a necessary thing to do for me. It was an attempt to deal with Brecht, with German subject matter, with Germany... probably with you. I think, in fact, definitely with you, which is why I wrote in the introduction that the play is about exile. I don't want to get "bloomy" (as in Harold Bloom) about it, but there is something to the idea that, when one is a writer, one is profoundly influenced by a very great writer the way I was profoundly influenced by Brecht. That one does have to engage in a struggle, you may call it an Oedipal struggle or not, depending on your views of Oedipus and Freud, but it is certainly a struggle of someone who is fighting to find his or her own voice and persona as a writer, and to wrest an independent persona from a progenitor. There was a way in which I used *A Bright Room Called Day* to do that with Brecht. I did many other things for myself with that play but I think I made an attempt in direct imitation, to — in a certain sense — get it out of my system. And also to find a way in which I was indebted to and also diverged from Brecht in terms of handling political material, in terms of a style and a diction, while recognizing the impact that other writers, including writers who were not necessarily dramatic writers, like Wallace Stevens and Pound, had had on my sense of how to use language. I think that I was working on all of that, and with Brecht. And I was also dealing directly with German subject matter, dealing with you as another father figure and, struggling with that, using a kind of a fable. *Bright Room* was the first play that I basically outlined and wrote a fable for, doing the fable scene by scene by scene.

Weber: You didn't do that for *Angels*, did you?

Kushner: No, I didn't. I tried very hard, but in *Angels* something else happened. The play took over and went off in a direction I had never foreseen. When I was plotting the play, I started with a fable that I had to discard because the play went off in a direction I didn't anticipate, including being seven hours long. Then I returned, by the time I was working on *Perestroika*, to a fable, just because the plot was so complicated that I needed to lay it all out or I wouldn't have known what the hell I was doing. And I still do use outline in form but I discovered that sometimes a play just has to take off and run on its own.

Weber: Well, that could happen to Brecht too. Look at his journals, for instance, when he writes about wrestling with certain plays.

Kushner: In *Szechwan* his characters certainly took him by surprise.

Weber: You wrote a couple of years ago an article for *American Theater* where you argued for an "American" Brecht, an Americanization of Brecht, so to speak. Do you still see things the way you wrote about them at the time or have you changed your mind?

Kushner: What I was writing about in that article, if I remember it correctly, was what I'm describing now. Which is the necessity of making any writer one's own, or one's country's own, if the writer is not of one's own country.

Weber: Or one's culture, if one is living in a country with a multitude of cultures, like the U.S.

Kushner: Yes. I have become very depressed about the way Brecht is done in this country. And I also think the failure that the theater practice in this country has had in coming to terms with Brecht points to all the things that are deeply problematical with our theater practice in general.

Weber: Nevertheless, he still is one of the four most frequently performed playwrights in translation in the country.

Kushner: I am sure that is true. But what depresses me about the way he is done is the complete lack of intellectual rigor. People simply don't have the intellectual tools to understand him.

Weber: Sometimes they don't even seem to care.

Kushner: That is completely true. They are steeped in a set of images and of notions about what Brecht is supposed to be. And there is a desire to be apostate about a tradition about which one knows nothing, and apostasy by uninformed heretics is really uninteresting. It is senseless to stand Brecht on his head if it is done by people who don't understand whose head it is.

Weber: And who don't even know where his feet are.

Kushner: [laughs] Right. Basically, what one winds up with is a kind of carnival, an unintelligent, bourgeois production. The best productions of Brecht that I have seen — not surprisingly — have been by a Rumanian.

Weber: By Andrei Serban?

Kushner: Serban's *Good Person of Szechwan*, and by Foreman. I have not seen a lot else, but most of the stuff I have seen was just gruesome.

Weber: How was the production of your version of *Good Person of Szechwan*?

Kushner: The problem is, first of all, that the American theater allows for four weeks of rehearsal. I am convinced that it is absolutely impossible to do a play of the length and complexity of any of the great Brecht plays in that amount of time. It is especially impossible with Brecht because you must learn something before you approach him. I don't think you can understand *The Good*

Person of Szechwan without understanding the historical process that the play is describing, in terms of the beginning of modernization in a country that is pre-modern but becoming modern in a very ugly and a rapid fashion, and the devouring of the country by the city. You really have to understand the sort of disintegration or, rather, the destruction of the craftsmen and the family, the cottage industry, by the factory, to know what is happening to these people in the play. People have to understand it, and they also have to care about it. I mean you can't do *Szechwan*, you can't do *Mother Courage*, unless you care about money and where the money goes. American actors don't care about those things, and American directors don't, and American designers don't. They don't want to bother with them too much. Economics seems unworthy as a subject.

Weber: Which is particularly absurd in a country where money really is the most important thing in most people's mind.

Kushner: Yes, absolutely. And of course it is always the way that the people most obsessed with money are the people who, like the British, go on and on and on, in their sort of mildly anti-semitic way, about Jews and money. But there are no people on earth, except maybe Americans, who are more obsessed with money.

Weber: Well, meanwhile the Germans are also obsessed with money, I dare say. And the Chinese, I'm afraid.

Kushner: There is, maybe, another German-Jewish similarity. I find that Germans and Jews are at least willing to talk about money, and willing to talk about haggling, which is after all an activity in which most human beings spend an outrageous proportion of their life. I mean, people haggle, that is how you get through.

Weber: Well, many Germans actually don't like to hear about haggling and think that it is bad manners.

Kushner: Yes, but there is a lot of it. Look at *Faust*. It is all haggling about money and about contracts.

Weber: Of course, it is going on all over the place. But they ignore it, they suppress it. They don't want to know about it, or they pretend, at least, that they don't know about it.

Let's go on to another topic, a very timely topic: The recent historical changes, and also some scholarly investigations into Brecht's private life, have caused a sharply critical re-evaluation of

Brecht's achievement. What do you think about this phenomenon? Is it valid? Is it just a fad? Is it overblown or is there some justification?

Kushner: Well, my friend Brian Kulick said, and I think he is right, that one of the manifestations of the poverty of American intellectual life is that we frequently only turn our attention to important writers and thinkers and artists when we discover a scandal or ostensible scandal about them that will enable us to justify the fact that we don't know anything about them. So, we become interested in Freud at the point at which Jeffrey Masson has shown up to tell us that Freud, you know, covered up important information about the extent to which his female patients were being sexually abused and not just hysterically fantasizing sexual abuse. And even though Masson's discoveries in that regard, if they are actually discoveries, are incredibly important, it has enabled a new generation of lefty-type intellectuals to decide that Freud is not worth coming to terms with. Or the discovery that Marx had illegitimate children means that we don't have to bother with Marx any more. Or the discovery that Paul de Man was a Nazi sympathizer or that Heidegger was a Nazi means we don't have to bother with Heidegger anymore. Or if Hitler gave Elisabeth Forster-Nietzsche a bouquet of roses, that means that we don't have to worry about Nietzsche any more. John Fuegi's book on Brecht is, it seems to me, an appropriation of feminism for the purpose of commie bashing, and really tremendously unimportant. The great tragedy of it is that it is the only major biography of Brecht that has come out in a very long time, and there desperately needs to be a good, responsible, serious, in-depth biography of Brecht in English, a new one.

Weber: There isn't one even in German.

Kushner: Yes, and it is appalling. This is definitely not it. It seems to be sensationalistic, and the parts of it that I have read at least seem to be kind of nuts. I mean, it is just an outrageous overstatement that I find deeply offensive. The man is all but saying that Brecht is a villain equivalent to Adolf Hitler or Joseph Stalin. That is insane, completely insane. And this endless carping after the issue of ownership of ideas and the actual authorship of the plays and poems is suspect in the extreme, although a great deal needs to be written about Brecht's collaborators, especially the women. And it is unquestionably the case that were he not someone who had this penchant to work with really brilliant women collaborators, he probably wouldn't have written such great female characters. I simply think that he was a very, very great writer. I don't know if Margarete Steffin was as great a writer, I don't really know.

Weber: Well, you have occasion to read about Steffin's collaboration with Brecht, and also some of her writings, in the last issue of *The Brecht Yearbook*.

Kushner: Oh, that is great.

Weber: There is a play of hers, a children's play which is quite nice, but it is miles away from the level of Brecht's own writing.

Kushner: I don't think that even Fuegi claims that the journals were written by someone other than Brecht.

Weber: I don't think so, no.

Kushner: There are passages in the journals that, in the case that everything else that Brecht had ever written were lost, would certainly make you sit up and take note and say this was some kind of writer. And the *Organum* and a lot of the theoretical writings and a great deal of the poetry will certainly secure for him one of the most prominent seats in the pantheon of twentieth-century literature. Even if you want to believe that Steffin wrote *Mother Courage*, and I don't believe it...

Weber: But Fuegi doesn't claim that, only that she had a part in it.

Kushner: Well, that she a had part in it. And that, after she died, he didn't write any more great plays.

Weber: That is especially stupid, of course.

Kushner: I think it is a shame. It is an offensive book by somebody, as you pointed out, who really doesn't know the first thing about creating theater. He also is somebody who has absolutely no idea of what Brecht was trying to do theatrically.

Weber: Now, what about the recent historical changes, the collapse of Socialism and all that. Does that, do you think, necessitate a reviewing of Brecht and a re-evaluation of what he did? I think I know the answer but I'd like to hear it from you.

Kushner: The answer is yes. I think that, simply because of the collapse of the Soviet empire, the necessity is there to examine what the passage of time and history has done to any writer's understanding of his trade. You know, at this point it is wonderful to have Heiner Müller as well as Brecht because I think that Müller has already done a great deal in terms of considering Brecht in the light of the passage of the last fifty years. Müller points us back to the *Lehrstück*, which I think is very important.

Weber: Why do you think that?

Kushner: Well, in my reading of it — which may be idiosyncratic or completely insupportable in terms of scholarship — it really does seem to me that Brecht is in the *Lehrstück* wrestling with a phenomenon that Fuegi never admits Brecht wrestled with, which is the question of the individual ego and the question how one marries a historical, social construct like the individual ego to a theory, and what is the practice of that. What is the way in which the individual, which is a sort of glorious and immensely destructive creation of hundreds and hundreds of years of Western civilization, how does the individual become a socialist subject? How are we to remake ourselves into people who are fit to remake the world? And what becomes of the individual when the individual encounters the necessity to collectivize, in the sort of struggles unto death that the protagonists or antagonists in the *Lehrstück* suffer? I think of the construction/de-construction of the flyer, or the young student on the road, or the revolutionary. The capacity for collectivity is profoundly interesting.

Weber: You are talking of the Young Comrade?

Kushner: Right, in *The Measures Taken*. It is a form of death and it leads Brecht into some very interesting poetry and some very powerful writing.

Weber: But it is actual death, of course.

Kushner: It is actually death, although it is death with a kind of resurrection. Although, in some cases there is not a resurrection, in some cases it is death and oblivion. But look at the *Baden Play of Learning* and the use of Chinese poetry, not just in terms of the sound of it but also quite literally in the use of Buddhism and Confucianism, of Lao-tse. It is fascinating, and I think he asks very important questions. The plays are extraordinarily radical, both in terms of their content and also in terms of their problems. I am very excited by them, and many of the questions raised by a play like the *Baden Play of Learning* are of immense applicability to the examination of the ruins of the Soviet system and the socialist experiment in Russia. Was it Peymann or was it Wolfgang Bauer? Who was it who said you may carp and criticize about Brecht but in times of crisis you'll reach for him?

Weber: That was Claus Peymann, in the late seventies.

Kushner: And it is true.

Weber: Actually Dan Sullivan, the artistic director of the Seattle Repertory Theater, said something quite similar to me once: "In times of political crisis you either play Brecht or Shakespeare, that is, certain plays by Shakespeare."

Kushner: Well, there you go.

Weber: You already answered to some extent the next question I jotted down: which of Brecht's works do you believe are today the most timely ones? Certainly the *Lehrstücke*, in your opinion, are among them.

Kushner: Yes. I had a wonderful time staging the *Baden Play* and would love to do it again. I think that *Mother Courage* is always going to be first and foremost for me, because I think it is simply the greatest play written in the twentieth century.

Weber: How about *Good Person of Szechwan*, which you just recently translated and adapted?

Kushner: I think *Szechwan* is almost as good. It simply moves me less strongly than *Courage*. I really do believe that in *Courage* we see the influence of Benjamin or, at least, the ground on which Brecht and Benjamin really understood one another. *Courage* is really a Benjaminian vision of history. *Szechwan* is to an extent, although...

Weber: Of course, *Courage* was begun at a time when he saw a lot of Benjamin, they did spend quite some time together in Denmark.

Kushner: Exactly. It is truly history as the accumulation of catastrophes and calamity. It is so tremendously dark and incredibly powerful in a way that, I have to admit, I personally don't find in *Szechwan*. *Szechwan* is a purer thing in a way, it is very much what pure epic theater is supposed to be. In *Courage*, as in *Galileo*, he strays a bit here and there from the absolute template to create the most powerful work that he can. But there is something very pure about *Szechwan* that is enormously challenging. Although, I don't know what the goodness of Shen Te is. That is the mystery for me, and I would like to crack that. We talked about it a great deal when we were working on it in La Jolla. I don't know what her goodness is. One should be careful that it doesn't become a kind of Forrest Gump-ism. It must not be essentialism, she must not be "essentially" good. She has a very strange poem in the trial scene that ends with something like "For your great deeds, oh Gods, this poor mortal...."

Weber: It is the long apologetic speech to the Gods when she tries to defend her invention of Shui Ta.

Kushner: Yes, it goes all over the place and it is very, very odd. I suspect it needs badly to be newly translated, because I didn't trust it in the process of working on my adaptation of *Szechwan* from a literal translation. I was also looking very closely at every other translation which I could get my hands on in terms of finding out how to understand that speech. No one translated it satisfactorily. It has got some very strange things about it as, for instance, "My mother washed me with gutter water...." It almost seems to be heading towards a kind of psychological explanation. Why is this person a "good person?" We get the point that good people in general don't succeed. But what is it about Shen Te that is different from, let's say, the water seller Wang? It is an odd thing in the play that I am not entirely clear about. I don't have any such problems with *Mother Courage*.

Weber: How do you feel about the early plays, like *Baal* and *In the Jungle of the Cities*?

Kushner: They are incredibly beautiful because they are written by a genius. Despite what I guess Mr. Fuegi says, that Bie Banholzer wrote *Baal*. They are very powerful and very disturbing, and they would be wonderful to stage. I have never been terribly interested in them beyond that because they are too close to Expressionism.

Weber: They are actually not, they are really a response to Expressionism. They refute nearly everything that Expressionism believed in or postulated. I just have directed *In the Jungle of the Cities*, and it worked extremely well, it is a wonderful play. It worked much better, frankly, than I expected when I started exploring it.

Kushner: It was the first time you did it?

Weber: Yes, the first time that I did it and that I did a real analysis of it. It is an incredibly demanding play and very timely, I think, in its harsh view of a market-based society. My feeling is that several of Brecht's plays that describe or comment on capitalist society might become very interesting again, plays that for a long time were thought of as old hat and that appeared to be obsolete. But I don't think they are now.

Kushner: Certainly, with the kind of freedom he had before he became, how shall I say, more responsible. The freedom to explore issues of sexuality, which to a certain extent he edges away from or homogenizes in the epic plays. *Baal* is fascinating in that respect. Sexuality is just an anarchic principle in *Baal* and it is dangerous. I think that the visitation of various kinds of political discipline that Marxism brought to Brecht made the difference between him being a very interesting, early twentieth-century writer and the writer of transcending importance that he became. He would always have been inasmuch more interesting than Stefan Zweig. But it is important, that, had it not been for Marxism and his commitment to a political movement, he might very easily have gotten lost in the same thickets of psychology and sexuality that others did. But still, I agree with you, those are very interesting plays.

Weber: In this context, to what extent do you expect the recent changes in American politics, and specifically their consequences for the arts, will influence the American reception of Brecht?

Kushner: Of course, since there won't be an NEA [National Endowment for the Arts] in the next year, nobody will be able to afford to do Brecht plays, they are all too big, except for *The Beggar or The Dead Dog.*

Weber: Yes, you were very prophetic way back in 1981.

Kushner: [laughs] Well, I think that is going to be a big problem. It seems to me that the successes of the Right frequently happen in periods when nobody wants to hear of any kind of oppositional thinking or art, which are then followed by a worsening of circumstances, which are then followed by an interest in oppositional or alternative vision. But it may be slow in coming, I am feeling very, very nervous for my own skin, respectively speaking.

Weber: I was just going to ask, how do you feel about your own position right now?

Kushner: Well, I really don't know.

Weber: Did this change your interest in certain topics? Have certain topics become more important to your mind than they were before, or not?

Kushner: I don't know what last Tuesday means [the elections on November 8, 1994]. I am confused by it in a way that I have never been confused by any political phenomenon in my own life time. I don't get why it happened, exactly. There are some subjects that are becoming extremely interesting to me, for instance the question of labor.

The *New York Times* had an interesting article on the front page of Sunday's *The Week in Review* asking: why isn't there class conflict, why aren't all these people recognizing they have class interests that are being betrayed, lethally betrayed, by Big Business, and why now do people blame government instead of blaming business, and why is the boss never really seen as being the enemy and is rather being seen as a fellow victim? The article laid out in political and sociological terms how much the Right has won and how much the elimination not even so much of the Soviet system as an alternative — because it never really has been an alternative for us — but of an ideological space marked "alternative," how the elimination of that has absolutely forced people into simply accepting as a given all the things that are contrary to their own self interest. You won't blame the boss because blaming the boss means developing a critique of capitalism as a system and, of course, we all know now that capitalism is the only conceivable system. Look at the destruction of the trade unions, the idea that everybody is downscaling and everybody is being put out of work. No one is getting angry at these corporations any more because it is simply assumed they will maximize profits at the expense of human beings, and that this is the way that it has to be. There is no notion of any sort of redistribution of wealth. The only thing currently acceptable with respect to redistributing wealth is the capital gains tax so that we can send more money to the people who already have enough of it.

Weber: Do you think that Brecht's work, in whatever shape, plays or whatever, could have any impact on this situation at all? If it would be performed, that is.

Kushner: I think there is one thing. It is like the hope of the desperate and the weak and the perilous. It is incredibly important, especially now, to state publicly that socialism once existed and is still being thought of, and thought enough of to be mentioned. In other words, there are times so reactionary that the best one can do is to serve as a marker for the possibility of alternatives. As a marker for the antithesis, and I think that Brecht serves that function. In doing *The Good Person of Szechwan* at La Jolla, California, for incredibly wealthy people who finished eating their toasted brie with almonds and come to their seats, you know, the audience is completely white...

Weber: How did they react?

Kushner: With a certain amount of condescension, and a certain amount of subdued enjoyment, and a certain amount of discomfort and dismissal, and all the things that one would expect. I have nothing astonishing to report. Except that I felt that it was enormously important that this important cultural institution was devoting this kind of money and human energy and space to the statement that the play makes. When Shen Te says: "You miserable people, look at what you're doing!", it is in some way the most obvious, corny thing in the world, and it is also immensely powerful. She takes the child and she says: "Look at this dirty mouth. Are you so debased that you can't even take care of your own children?" I mean, nothing could be more relevant. When I staged *Mother Courage* at the University of New Hampshire, in the shadow of a giant nuclear power plant out there, the whole town of Hanover worked in that plant. And the whole time that we were doing *Courage* — this was in the dark years of Reagan — there was a radio ad running which we actually used during the intermission where an engineer says — and you hear children playing in the background — and the engineer says: "People are always saying they are afraid of the nuclear reactor, but I am a safety engineer and I know that this reactor is safe." And then he says: "I have to know because my children and I live a mile from the reactor." You know, this man *is* Mother Courage. And so, on one level, it seems like a corny little bromide when she says "If you want the war to work for you...." But on the other hand, it is the simple truth, it is the great motto: "The very simplest words must be enough...." And so, I think it is incredibly important to keep doing it, to remind people that reality is to be interpreted and is not just what it seems. Which is a radical concept in these days.

Weber: We have covered a lot of ground. Just one final thing: In what way do you feel Brecht is important for your work in this particular historical moment? It is a sort of corny question, I know, but also a kind of capping question.

Kushner: Important in terms of my work? I guess that there is a personal as well as an aesthetic answer to that. Personally, when I go back to Brecht, which I do constantly and I just did it in a very extensive way for *Szechwan* and also reading the journals, there is an issue of re-doing one's commitment. Look at those wonderful little nips he takes at those who he is talking about in the journal when he refers to the kind of writers who — and he is talking about some of the emigré writers in Hollywood — writers who didn't like capitalism because, unlike themselves, capitalism isn't harmless. He also talked about a writer who is a petty bourgeois and who has acquired the propensity for ethical thinking. Brecht had a great contempt for a certain kind of writer who sounds politically engaged and yet really isn't, who is essentially content with things remaining as they are. Through everything in Brecht there is an absolutely serious desire to see the world change *now*, as they say in *Szechwan*: "Now, Now, Now." The urgency of that "Now" is something that I go back to Brecht for. So I remind and then I chastize myself if I feel that I am slipping because it is very hard to maintain the commitment. I think he is incredibly important to me as an origin and also as a goal. In terms of the specifics, after having written a different kind of epic with *Angels*, where I went off in new directions for me in terms of creating an epic play, I am interested in going back and in re-examining in the next play that I am writing the epic form in a more traditional way, a more classically Brechtian sense.

Weber: Which play is that?

Kushner: It is a play about the relationship between the textile industry in Britain and American slavery that has a more conventionally epic form. And then *Dutch Masters*, a play about Vermeer, which is huge and sprawling. I have been thinking a great deal recently about epic theater and what the epic actually is, what the large form is, since it seems to be the form I am going to spend my life with. I mean, even *Slavs!*, a one-act play, became three acts and an epilogue. It seems to be the form that I am wedded to. So, I am thinking about what it means and if it is something that I should simply accept. Is it a form that I am suited to, or is it something that I should try and wean myself from.

Weber: And how is your present production going? After all, it is your first foray into directing in a long time.

Kushner: I find I am directing like a writer now. I stage a little of it, and I go back and I re-stage it, and I do a little bit more and then I re-stage the whole thing.

Weber: That is the way Brecht worked as a director.

Kushner: Because he was a writer, I think. That is the way most writers write. The problem is you need to give the actors more space. What is frustrating is that I have put the whole thing up now, and I like the flow of it and the look of it, I'd just wish I now had two or three weeks to really let the actors take it over and run with it. But I don't, it is frustrating. Remembering how hard it is for actors to get to perform it is staggering. I usually come to the first reading and then I go away.

Weber: It's been a long time since you have directed.

Kushner: Yes, it really is.

Weber: It's good for you, believe me. It will help you a lot as a writer.

Kushner: Yes, I think it does, it's very good to do it, at least once in a while.

Weber: For Brecht, writing and directing were always two sides of the same coin. Tony, I thank you for a most inspiring conversation.

Internationales Brecht-Kolloquium in Bourges

Die 1992 von John Willett initiierte und unter der Schirmherrschaft des iti und der UNESCO abgehaltene Brecht-Konferenz in Bourges widmete sich dem weitgefaßten Thema: Brecht im Licht der Ereignisse von 1989. Theaterleute sowohl im akademischen Bereich wie auch aus der Theaterpraxis nahmen daran teil. Die hier gehaltenen Vorträge und Erwiderungen (einige sind überarbeitet worden) verweisen auf die Vielfalt der Reaktionen aus der Perspektive verschiedenster Nationen (Senegal, Bangladesch, Frankreich, Finnland, Niederlande, Australien, England): die Nützlichkeit der Lehrstücke und anderer Techniken beim Verständnis der Gegenwart, jenes "schwindelerregenden" Moments (Binnerts, Ivernel); die Notwendigkeit neuer Versöhnungen, z.B. zwischen Brecht und Stanislawski (Benedetti); Probleme der Übersetzung und des Zugänglichmachens durch Text und Musik (Chowdhury, Archer, Langbaka); sowie die universelle Bedeutung Brechts trotz aller sich verändernden politischen Verhältnisse (Diakhate, Willett).

Le Colloque International Brecht à Bourges.

Tenue en octobre 1992 sous l'auspice de l'iti et de l'UNESCO, la conférence fut "animée" par John Willet, et aborda le thème général de Brecht à la lumière des changements intervenus dans le monde depuis 1989. Des représentants de nombreux pays et de nombreuses disciplines théâtrales, à la fois pratiques et académiques, y participèrent. Les écrits et les déclarations présentés (révisés dans certains cas), donnent une indication, à partir des multiples points de vues nationaux (Sénégal, Bangladesh, France, Finlande, Pays-Bas, Australie, Angleterre), de la vaste gamme de réactions des participants: l'importance permanente des *Lehrstücke* et d'autres techniques brechtiennes pour favoriser la compréhension des moments historiques "vertigineux" du présent (Binnerts, Ivernel); la nécéssité de nouvelles réconciliations - entre Brecht et Stanislavsky par exemple (Benedetti), l'importance et les problèmes posés par la traduction pour rendre Brecht accessible par le texte et la musique (Chowdhury, Archer, Langbacka); et l'universalité permanente de Brecht en dépit de circonstances politiques et sociales fluctuantes (Diakhate, Willett).

El coloquio brechtiano internacional en Bourges

Celebrada en Octubre de 1992 en Bourges bajo los auspicios del iti y de la UNESCO, la conferencia sobre Brecht fue "animada" por John Willett y se enfocó sobre el tema general de Brecht a la luz de los eventos de 1989. Participaron representantes de muchos paises y disciplinas teatrales, tanto prácticas como académicas. Los trabajos y ponencias presentados aquí (en algunos casos revisados) indican una amplia gama de reacciones surgidas de varias perspectivas nacionales (Senegal, Bangladesh, Francia, Finlandia, los Paises Bajos, Australia, Inglaterra): la utilidad del Lehrstücke y otras técnicas brechtianas para comprender el momento "vertiginoso" del presente (Binnerts, Ivernel); la necesidad de una nueva reconciliación — entre Brecht y Stanislavsky, por ejemplo (Benedetti); problemas de traducción así como de hacer accesible a Brecht a través del texto y de la música (Chowdhury, Archer, Langbacka); y la universalidad de Brecht a pesar de las variables circunstancias políticas (Diakhate, Willett).

The International Brecht Colloquium at Bourges: Introduction

John Willett

At the beginning of 1992 I was asked to "animate" an international Brecht conference at Bourges, plumb in the middle of France, which was to be held in the autumn of that year. This was part of the celebration of the "twinning" of the two historic mercantile and religious centers of Bourges and Augsburg in accordance with the policy of Franco-German rapprochement associated with the names of Konrad Adenauer and Robert Schumann — though not hitherto with that of Bertolt Brecht.

Bourges however had played an important part in the French cultural decentralization to which the theater in that country owes so much including its assimilation of Brecht's plays and other notable German works. Its Maison de la Culture was the first to be founded in accordance with the ideas of André Malraux, whose name it bears, and it has an excellent one-man museum devoted to the work of Maurice Estève. It belongs therefore in the 1960s tradition of Planchon and Dasté, the subsidized theaters of the Paris suburbs, the Avignon festival and before that, the Paris International festival where the Berliner Ensemble's *Mother Courage* first established Brecht's fame in 1954.

It was Bernard Dort — teacher, critic, and theater advisor to Jack Lang, the then Minister of Culture — who was to preside over the conference and who roped me in to help plan it and chair its discussions. From the Augsburg end, Helmut Gier would provide an exhibition of related art works; at Bourges itself Pierre Sallet of the Maison de la Culture made all the arrangements, including simultaneous translation, theater performances, a song recital and a showing of *Kuhle Wampe*. The Moroccan Albert Botbol, formerly of the Paris Theater festival, was our channel to UNESCO; André Perinetti of that body our link with the International Theater Institute who invited nearly all the foreign and overseas participants. It was to those people accordingly that I addressed my suggestions about the nature and composition of our "Colloque," starting too optimistically with a core of three hour-long demonstrations devoted first to

Brecht Then and Now / Brecht damals und heute
Eds. Marc Silberman et al. *The Brecht Yearbook / Das Brecht-Jahrbuch*
Volume 20 (Madison: The International Brecht Society, 1995)

Brecht's variegated interpretations in the cinema (from Pabst to Broccoli), the second to song settings and their articulation, and the third to valid types of staging and acting techniques in different societies. One problem that I hoped to see addressed was: is faithfulness or freedom the most effective approach to the Brechtian model?

This was soon reduced to a more modest proposal for a handful of themes that could be freely discussed by the conference, and towards the middle of the summer, as the answers to the invitations came in, the project had been cut down to something much less ambitious. I drafted a press release which spoke of Brecht's wide appeal in many countries and the reasons for it. "But," I went on

> the alternative system which he supported has now very largely collapsed; many of the values which he upheld are being called in question; and his private relationships are being used to divert attention from his work. What we hope to do at Bourges therefore is to take a fresh look at that work in the light of the changes that have taken place in our world since the summer of 1989, and see how much it still has to say to us.
>
> To this end we are inviting people from a number of countries — people concerned with theater, cinema, music and literature — to join in a discussion about all aspects of the matter. It will not be like an academic meeting where each speaker talks about his/her specialty, but an open re-examination which moves from point to point without being tied down to a predetermined order.

We met for three days at the end of October, when some 45 participants from 24 different countries gathered in the Maison de la Culture for wide-ranging talks, mainly in French and English, with only one demonstration-type session of the sort first envisaged, when Robyn Archer and Michael Morley spoke of the poems, their settings and their reception in two hemispheres, while Maurice Regnaut read French translations. Otherwise the general pattern adopted was that of a series of statements about the approaches to Brecht followed in the various countries, interspersed with some longer papers about particular aspects. It is these — revised in some cases by their writers — that are included in the present *Yearbook*, though the original intention of the conference was to transcribe and publish the entire proceedings.*

---

* *Several of the authors wish to make it clear that their submissions are edited transcriptions of discussions which were not intended as formal papers. Ed.*

This is much more easily said than done, as I found when trying to identify the different speakers on the incomplete set of tapes sent me, which give some impression of the cheerful give and take of the debate and the topics covered. Part of the trouble was that some of the ITI guests from Central and Eastern Europe represented a cultural reaction against the former communist-led regimes with which they associated Brecht, so that they were not really interested in him; it was a pity that there was no transcript of Ernst Schumacher's remarks about the situation in Berlin and the former GDR, along with the prospects for the newly-reconstituted Berliner Ensemble. Eighteen months later, when asked for a text, he found that the situation had so changed that he no longer felt able to write about it. More recently, Dr. Günter Berg of Suhrkamp Verlag, who had also been a lively contributor, had likewise felt inhibited by this problem.

Besides Dort, Regnaut and Ivernel, and Henri Massadau as director of the Maison de la Culture, the French participants included the Germanist Ursula Meyer-Lapuyade from Aix-en-Provence University and Pierre-Etienne Heymann who directed *Le Debit de pain (Der Brotladen)*. Neither the USA nor the UK now being members of UNESCO, their representatives were mainly French and German speakers suggested by me, such as Stuart Hood, Susan Engel, the cinéaste Pascale Lamche and the conductor Robert Ziegler. Archer and Morley came from Australia. And among others on the ITI list who contributed usefully, though we have no adequate record of their interventions, were Robert Branco (Cuba), Haikara (Finland), Levent (Turkey), Hagerup (Norway) and Monterde (Spain). There was nobody from the former USSR, Italy, India, China, or Japan. As a cross-section of world interest in Brecht it was eccentric, to say the least. But at least the participants loosened up and talked increasingly freely. I saw no evidence of boredom except during one marginal but over-extended paper.

At the end of the third day we discussed some of the obstacles placed in the way of the performance of Brecht's works and agreed on a unanimous resolution for submission to the ITI in Paris. "We feel," it said, "that Brecht's future demands the removal of a number of constraints on the performance of his plays and songs." Notably

1. His objections of the 1950s to the performance of *Die Maßnahme* with Hanns Eisler's music cannot be seen as relevant today.

2. It must be recognized that no holders of the musical rights to settings of Brecht's plays and poems have any right to demand cuts and changes in the spoken text.

3. Amateur companies must not normally be refused the right to perform whatever Brecht work they wish.

To which we added a comment that "we are not denying the rights of the copyright owners, merely saying that these must not be exercised unreasonably and against the interests of the work, its performers, and the audience." This went to the ITI executive, and was included in the Secretary-General's report of May 1993 to the various national centers. (See page 148 for "Bourges Resolution.")

Historically — or *kulturgeschichtlich gesehen* — our attempt at stocktaking came at the end of an era. The national and regional elections of 1993 brought the defeat of the French Socialist Party; Jack Lang gave way as Minister of Culture to Jacques Toubon; dissemination of the arts via the suburban and provincial art center network seemed less urgent than the protection of the "heritage" and the French language. On the inter-European level too the prospect of a Socialist-influenced Eurocracy imposing its standards and social regulations became less alarming to friends of the free market. The enemies of Brussels began to take heart, the cultural rehabilitation of the Third Reich gained ground. More immediately, some of the figures connected with the French theatrical revival of the 1960s and 70s left the scene. Bernard Dort died, one of the last links with *Théâtre Populaire* and the French discovery of Brecht; so did Denis Bablet, whose work on Kantor and Peter Brook and avant-garde stage design was one of the triumphs of the CNRS; so did Albert Botbol, who was a solid and intelligent backroom influence from the earliest stages of my own involvement.

Down in Bourges we had been meeting and arguing, of course, at a time when Brecht stood for a great deal in different parts of the world. That the background was constantly changing was a central concern for us, and it has changed further since we met. We saw the need to re-evaluate his contribution in the light of those changes. For others, more concerned with publishing and public relations, they offered a new challenge to dismantle the writer's reputation. This was something that was already in the air. We could hardly have foreseen the unworthiness of its expression or the unconvincing form which it would take.

Brecht Reviewed

At the end of the Third Reich in 1945 Bertolt Brecht was banned, out of print, unperformable, and almost entirely forgotten in his own country. Elsewhere he was known, at least by reputation, among the anti-Nazi exiles and to a lesser extent among those of their foreign friends who were interested in literature and the theater. Published and (above all) translated texts of his writings were difficult to get. Academic Germanists in Europe and America had little use for him, and he had not been favored in the USSR since the mid-1930s. In the rest of the world he was as good as unknown.

The story of Brecht's enforced obscurity and his triumph over it is unique. No German writer is now so widely known, read and performed, cutting through the great barriers that still divide humanity, rich/poor, north/south, black/white, skeptical/religious, industrial/peasant — and much of this transformation took place in the eleven years between the defeat of the Nazis and Brecht's own death. It was during the first two-thirds of the 1950s that the greater part of his plays were published and produced in German and properly performed, in some notable instances under his own direction and by his own company the Berliner Ensemble — twice as part of the Paris Théâtre des Nations. In the English-speaking countries it was over the same period that he became famous, thanks mainly to the record-breaking success of *The Threepenny Opera* in New York. Yet when he died in 1956, great parts of his work outside the theater were still unpublished even in German — most of his poetry, for instance, was unknown — and even now discoveries are still being made.

This growth of Brecht as a world figure has worried many of his enemies, and ever since some ideological cold warrior of the 1940s put forward the notion of a "battle for men's minds," Brecht has been part of the battlefield. The choice of weapons has varied. To start with he was attacked as a Stalinist who chose to settle in the Soviet Zone instead of remaining in the United States or at least under Western rule. It was suggested he had been bribed by comfortable living conditions and the setting up of his Ensemble. Evidence was sought that he was not a serious communist after all; this was the time when the polemicists of the Congress for Cultural Freedom made so much of his Austrian passport and Swiss bank account, now complaining that he had never wanted to live in the USSR. The snide term "survivor" was borrowed from one of his poems and applied to him, as if it was somehow regrettable that he had remained alive. Then for a time the two separate Germanies tried to share him — exemplified by the parallel East-West editions of the years 1953-69 — despite the odd hiccup at controversial moments.

It became clear after 1953 that Brecht had at times been bitterly critical of Stalin and the Stalinists of him; and at least by Soviet and East German standards his work was incompatible with their doctrine of Socialist Realism. Meanwhile the relative "thaw" that followed Stalin's death was affecting his status elsewhere in Eastern Europe, while the new Left in the Federal Republic and the conciliatory policies of the SPD gave him a fresh lease of life in his old country. By the late 1970s there was a growing international interest in Brecht and his work. He began to be seen in relation to many other aspects of Weimar culture which were then being sought out, revived and re-evaluated; young musicians in Europe, America and Australia were learning from the work of his collaborators Hanns Eisler and Kurt Weill; there was a new awareness of the designs of Caspar Neher. In December 1986 the International Brecht Society's Hong Kong conference brought home to the old Brechtian community how acutely and resourcefully the plays were now being interpreted and applied in India, China, Japan, the Philippines, and South Africa, as well as Latin America and the Middle-Eastern countries where they had already been assimilated. A month or two earlier in Toronto a declining Berliner Ensemble had performed in North America for the first time.

Up to this point the Ensemble was liable to be criticized as a matriarchy whose politically conformist leaders had been able to keep Brecht in line. Brecht for his part was widely praised for the stature and vitality of his women characters — Courage, Vlassova, Begbick, Joan Dark, Shen Teh, Grusha — who could be associated with that matriarchy and also with the communist view of women. Then suddenly, starting in the United States, a quite different view of "Brecht's women" took over, mainly grounded in the tragic case of his Danish mistress Ruth Berlau, who had been with him for over twenty years and eventually drank herself to death. Brecht, in this interpretation, which spread internationally through the feminist movement, was a chauvinist exploiter of women, recruiting them to do the donkey work on his plays — to type, adapt, and translate — failing to acknowledge their contribution and using them arrogantly in bed. Propagated by people without much feeling for his work, this duly became the main tactic for discrediting him. The earlier allegations had worn too thin.

Today we have the radically changed political climate of the post-Gorbachev era. Nearly everywhere the communist system has broken down; the Federal Republic has taken over the GDR, and the United States appears to be leading a campaign to seek out and destroy the remnants of that "specter of socialism" which once haunted Europe. So what about Brecht, who did so much to express, dramatize, and poeticize the great socialist ideals along with his own skeptical attitude of mind? Does he too now go into the dustbin of history, or does socialism still have something to offer after all?

What we need, then, is to look at Brecht afresh in the light of our present confused societies and see whether he still stands for something useful and positive that may help guide us through today's unforeseen mess. For the Bourges meeting we (that is, Bernard Dort, Albert Botbol, myself, Pierre Sallet, with André Perinetti and UNESCO) have provisionally identified certain areas where this could be the case and are inviting a number of distinguished guests to help in the new task of defining the great Augsburger's moral, political, theatrical, literary, musical, and artistic contribution to the modern world.

Area One: Politics and the Theater

How far is a political message or lesson still a viable element of theater today? Viable in what kind of society, and to what end? Where, in Brecht's case, is it most effectively conveyed? In the story itself and the class analysis which it embodies? In the persuasiveness and abrasiveness of his characters? In the language and the poetry? In the production methods which he specifies? In the theories which underlie them? How far may any of these elements now turn out to be counter-productive, alienating in the wrong sense, off-putting — and to what kind of audience? Who are the plays addressed to? In what way do they need reinterpretation and readjustment to make the impact he wanted? Or is there a better and more useful impact which they may make in a changed context?

Could they not be politically effective in a much wider sense? For instance through their embodiment of ethical values, their commitment to the socially and economically disadvantaged, their particular concept of goodness? Or on the artistic/intellectual level, i.e. through Brecht's harnessing and balancing of the different stage elements, his way of seeing, his dry humor, his sense of irony? Or again theoretically, through his insistence on clarity and detachment, his epic structure and montage? And what about the attitudes conveyed, almost subconsciously, by the mixture of power, originality, and imagination in his language? And can this mixture be expressed in translation?

Area Two: The media

Arising out of area one is the question of Brecht's role in film, TV, radio, and recording. Again, the same problems arise of the political message or lesson, the ethical values, and the artistic/intellectual level. In this area, of course, the size and nature of the audience are entirely different, the impact of Brecht's contribution (for better or worse) far more important politically, and the likelihood of governments and great production companies wanting to control it correspondingly greater. So how far does Brecht in fact have an influence? How far is his work really suited to today's mass media? Are his own ventures in film and radio (*Kuhle Wampe*, *Lindberghflug*, the contributions to the German Freedom Radio of the 1930s, and so on) a usable model? Why does he seem to be a name to conjure with in film theory? How far is he indirectly influential in the documentary movement and, through that, in modern TV news and features? In which countries? What about the impact of his musical collaborators — Eisler, Weill et al. — in Hollywood and elsewhere? Musical clarity instead of mush? Does this apply outside the realm of Euro-American music?

Area Three: Brecht and Music

Arising out of areas one and two, the place of Brecht in the "new music" of the Weimar Republic. The requirements of his theater (and its language) and the accident of his finding musical collaborators who could meet them. What did this mean above all to Weill and Eisler; the examples of *The Threepenny Opera* and *The Measures Taken*? How persistent are these examples today? Can they be taken further? The relevance of new techniques, new instruments and new outlets? The restoration of Grand Opera as the ideal of social-musical "excellence" and establishment-friendly sponsorship: how far can the Brechtian examples be reconciled with it? The new demands on the singer: does his/her training help or hinder the clarity of the words? Which is the better equipped for worthwhile texts: the actor or the singer? How far has the traditional attitude to the "librettist" and the poet been changed? How different is that attitude in non-European societies?

Once again, what is it that composers have found in Brecht's songs and poems that makes his words particularly settable, and is this something that can be retained in translation? How about his debt to the cabaret songs of Wedekind, which in turn originated in the example of the Paris literary cabaret of the 1880s, Le Chat Noir (with Verlaine and Bruant)? Is Brecht to be seen in the context of *The Blue Angel* and *Cabaret*? If not, how is he different?

Area Four: Brecht as a Poet

Following Frank Wedekind, Brecht began as a poet inventing or borrowing tunes to which he sang his own words, and this activity was the backbone of his first play, *Baal*. The different ways in which his poetic gift contributed to his theater: the role of songs, most conspicuously in *The Threepenny Opera*, the collage of poems in *Mahagonny* and the *Berlin Requiem*, the idea of the "city" poems as texts for gramophone records, the cantata-like *Lehrstücke*, the interruptions and changes of level in *Mother Courage*, the quasi-oriental epic of *The Caucasian Chalk Circle*. And of course the non-naturalistic language. What does all this demand of the performer? How are the spoken texts — for instance the "arias" of *The Good Person of Szechwan* — to be delivered? The caesuras? The end-stopping and punctuation?

Which aspect of his work came more naturally to him? Play writing and construction? The directing of his own plays? Or the writing and delivery of his poems? Which did he see as the more important? The less natural one? Why? And why is the great bulk of his poetry not better known? Is this once again entirely a matter of translation, or do its qualities get across even so? What are these that distinguish it from the poems of his contemporaries, and what other leading poets share his characteristics? Who has notably been influenced by him? In East and West Germany? Elsewhere? Once again, is this of interest to non-Europeans, and if so why?

Our examination of these areas is complicated by the fact that Brecht is all of a piece. The areas overlap, they merge into one another. One cannot for instance discuss his musical ideas without reference to his politics, nor his theatrical principles in isolation from his language. This was one of his great strengths, and it went with his very "dialectical" willingness to appear inconsistent.But for a discussion like ours it means that we cannot stick to a neatly planned program where the main theme is divided under separate headings and carved up between appropriate specialists. Any of our speakers must be able to touch on any point, and consider him- or herself entitled to do so. What is more, there will clearly be further points of relevance to be discussed, and we hope that our meeting will be able to deal with them as and when they arise. The four areas interlock. None can be seen as secondary.

This may be the secret of Brecht's stature and the reason why his work is of continuing significance in our changing times. As he said in a poem written in America around 1944:

Alles wandelt sich. Neu beginnen
Kannst du mit dem letzten Atemzug.
Aber was geschehen, ist geschehen. Und das Wasser
Das du in den Wein gossest, kannst du
Nicht mehr herausschütten.

Was geschehen, ist geschehen. Das Wasser
Das du in den Wein gossest, kannst du
Nicht mehr herausschütten, aber
Alles wandelt sich. Neu beginnen
Kannst du mit dem letzten Atemzug.

[Everything changes. You can make
a fresh start with your final breath.
But what has happened has happened. And the water
You once poured into the wine cannot be
Drained off again.

What has happened has happened. The water
You once poured into the wine cannot be
Drained off again, but
Everything changes. you can make
A fresh start with your final breath.]

For there is a combination of flexibility and compactness in Brecht's whole approach to life and art, and this is what gives it its power. True enough, those who wish to dance on the tomb of communism may choose Brecht's cemetery in which to do so, and those who are intolerant of his private conduct may feel moved to reject everything about him, particularly if they are ignorant of his public achievements. Perhaps that is what the "battle for men's minds" has degenerated to. Yet his work is still exceptional and no less universal in its accessibility than before.

Is there now any quantitative falling-off in Brecht productions, performances, or publications? If so it would be interesting to know and to see which countries and peoples were most subject to it. Whether such evidence would mean all that much is another matter. Whatever may be the political changes of front, the core of his creativity, once located, is likely to remain the same. Despite new parties and alliances, new looks and new sounds, shifting critical schools and changed academic fashions, it must continue to be a force in the life of mankind.

* * * * * * * *

Brecht, Stanislavsky, and the Art of Acting*

Jean Benedetti

The cliché is a danger for the academic no less than for the actor. There are ready-made histories as there are ready-made characters. Slogans and stereotypes are easy to use, difficult to question. They go unchallenged because they correspond to an established, comfortable (and comforting) world view; they are part of a consensus.

But we no longer live in an age of consensus. Ideologies, like walls, have collapsed; political dogmas have crumbled but the full implications of the new uncertainty have still not been fully worked out, least of all in our universities and conservatoires. Does the prevailing version of the complex, changing relationship between Brecht and Stanislavsky now being taught correspond to reality, or are we perpetuating simplistic Cold-War myths? Have we begun to understand the political and ideological manipulation to which both men were subjected during and after their lifetime?

After the creation of the Berliner Ensemble, Brecht was transformed, in the West at least, into the standard-bearer of a certain "left-wing" theater. His writings and productions were used as a pretext for classes in politics that were often stronger on vehemence than insight. The subtle, penetrating analyses which Roland Barthes published after the Ensemble's first visit to Paris were replaced by the pedantic outpourings of the intellectuals Jean Vilar trenchantly described as pseudo-Marxist pedants, who wanted to out-Lenin Lenin and only succeeded in being a "pain in the balls."[1]

A copy of the *Kleines Organon* (half-digested) in hand, they declared a holy war on Stanislavsky and all his works. The battle-lines were established on the flimsiest of foundations. Quotes were taken from such of Brecht's writings as were available and from poor, inadequate, truncated versions of Stanislavsky's one available book on acting, *An Actor Prepares,* so as to present an insurmountable opposition between "bourgeois" Naturalism and the Epic. It was the Cold War in microcosm. Students, in acting academies in particular, have been caught in a perpetual tug of war between two "theories" for the past forty years. They have either had to commit

---

* *This paper was originally given in French. The English translation is by the author.*

themselves to one or try to commute uncomfortably between both. But they have never been left in any doubt as to which theory was "right on," or perhaps we should now say PC.

It was, and is, a situation rich in irony. It was the "bourgeois naturalist" Stanislavsky who was presented as the perfect representative of theater in the Soviet Union, the "home of Socialism," while the "Marxist" Brecht was practically never played. He was a Formalist — hence "bourgeois" — and regarded with equal suspicion by Walter Ulbricht and his apparatchiks in the GDR. Western commentators were either unaware or affected to be unaware of these paradoxes.

How are we to extricate ourselves from this mish-mash of half-truths, fake ideologies, and legends? Should we perhaps apply a Brechtian technique and ask naive questions? First, what Brecht knew, what he was in a position to know about Stanislavsky and his ideas at any given moment; second, how Brecht's understanding of the Stanislavsky "system" developed between 1935 and 1955. Third, let us think the unthinkable and admit what has been for some an impossible notion: that Brecht might, at times, have been wrong.

Brecht and the Russian Avant-garde

If Brecht heard anything of Stanislavsky early in his career it would have been from the Soviet actors and directors he met in Berlin in 1924, when travel was freer than under Stalin. He derived most of his knowledge about developments in Russian theater from his friend Bernhard Reich and Asja Lacis. Reich was closely connected with Tretjakov (later to translate three of Brecht's plays) and Eisenstein, both of whom worked under the shadow of the all-dominant Meyerhold. Lacis was engaged as assistant director for the 1924 Munich production of *Edward II* and brought with her an intimate knowledge of the methods of Constructivist theater. All the essential features of Brecht's production vocabulary stem from the Russian avant-garde.

Brecht went to Moscow in 1931 to attend Taïrov's less than adequate premiere of *The Threepenny Opera*. He was in Moscow once again in 1935, where he was present at a performance given by Mei Lan-Fang at the Theater Worker's Club. According to Bernhard Reich, it was on that occasion that he heard the word "estrangement" (*Verfremdung*) for the first time.[2] His companions, including Tretjakov and Eisenstein, were long-standing opponents of Stanislavsky and the Moscow Art Theater (MXAT). Only Meyerhold, who was also present, continued to declare himself Stanislavky's pupil, although he was by no means an uncritical one.

Only Meyerhold was also aware of the long battle dating from as early as 1905 that Stanislavsky had waged against the artistic inertia of the MXAT and its theater's decline into dead naturalism and "literary" theater. Stanislavsky always used "naturalism" pejoratively. It denoted superficiality, a failure to analyze deeply and carefully enough. His major productions from 1908 onwards, such as the *Hamlet* which he staged with Gordon Craig, were mounted practically despite the Art Theater management. This bitter conflict was kept secret initially to avoid adverse publicity and later by Stalin, who for propaganda reasons wanted to present an image of the ideal Soviet theater, led by the ideal partnership, Stanislavsky and Nemirovich-Danchenko. The truth did not come to light until the 1960s, and even then attempts were made to suppress it.

One unfortunate consequence of this cover-up is that Stanislavsky has been identified with everything he disliked about the MXAT and its "style." It must be remembered, too, that apart from *My Life in Art* Stanislavsky had published nothing. Not a word about the "system," which everybody talked about, but few understood. Various "pupils" peddled their own versions, while Stanislavsky was still struggling to put difficult ideas on paper. He was judged *in absentia* and on hearsay evidence.

Stanislavsky American Style

In 1935, like so many refugees from the Nazis, Brecht turned to the USA as a possible new home. The Theater Union, a so-called "leftwing" group, was planning to present *Die Mutter*. Doubtless he expected to find people who would share his ideas on acting and staging. What he found was a group of actors who claimed to use the Stanislavsky "system" but saw his play merely as an excuse to explore their own feelings. His words had to be cut where necessary and changed to suit their "personality." Brecht fought hard to keep the text he had written intact and won, but was barred from the theater. It must be admitted that his usual method of directing which consisted of yelling "Das ist Scheiße!" at the top of his voice did not help matters. The play was a flop, and Brecht's first apparent encounter with the "system" left a bad taste in his mouth. He could not know, any more than the members of his cast, that Stanislavsky detested, and in his writings condemned, a narcissistic concern with what he called "actors' emotion."

In 1936 Brecht attended a number of rehearsals at the Group Theater with Lee Strasberg as director. They were working according to Strasberg on an unspecified *Lehrstück* (in fact *Die Maßnahme*). Strasberg claims that Brecht approved his explanation of "alienation" as a question of the level of emotional intensity the actor uses and was, as he later learned, influenced by the "narrative technique" that he used.[3]

After leaving the USA, Brecht asked his friend, the designer Mordechai (Max) Gorelik to bring him up to date with developments in the American theater. Gorelik sent him copies of the magazine *Theater Workshop*, which contained a number of articles, although none by Stanislavsky himself, on the "system." Brecht's reaction was hostile. Writing to Gorelik in highly sarcastic terms, he condemned the "system" as a quasi-religious act in which the actor, without reference to the world and political and economic events, "creates" like a god and is transformed like the bread and wine in the Mass.[4] He serves eternal "truth." The audience is, as it were, hypnotized by what it sees. It becomes a total victim of identification (*Einfühlung*). Where, Brecht asks, is there any discussion of class struggle?

It is difficult to see on re-reading them why the articles by Rapaport and Sudakov, which are very concrete in their approach, should have provoked the reaction they did. He could have found Giatsintova's contribution, written in the adulatory style of the period, irritating, but it is not religious.

Brecht also took issue with the term "justification," which he misunderstood. He assumed that actors were invited to justify the actions of their characters morally. In fact, all Stanislavsky meant was that actions should have a concrete, specific reason behind them, that they should not be done "in general." It was a question of probability not morality. It was, in fact the First Studio of the MXAT under the leadership of Leopold Sulerzhitsky, a disciple of Tolstoy, which saw the purpose of the theater as the Justification of Man, and it was former members of that Studio, such as Richard Boleslavsky, who exerted such a strong influence in the United States, particularly on the Group Theater and Lee Strasberg. While Strasberg was perfectly aware of the major differences between his Method and the Stanislavsky "system," the rest of the world confused, and continues to confuse, the two — as did Brecht.

Brecht's English at the time was very elementary and remained so. How much would he have really understood of the *Theater Workshop* articles? The likelihood is that he read such as he could with formalist eyes, seizing on an offending word here and there.

What he did not know, what was never discussed at the time, was the social and educational aspect of Stanislavsky's theater. When the MXAT opened, it was regarded as subversive. If, however, Stanislavsky never spoke openly of the class struggle, it was for good historical reasons. In Tsarist society all overt ideological, philosophical and political debate was strictly forbidden. Literature and the theater became the vehicle for social thought. Faced with draconian censorship, writers learned to be oblique; readers and audiences learned to read and see between the lines. How many of us nowadays are conscious of the political content of Chekhov's plays? Yet MXAT audiences were made aware of it, thanks to Stanislavsky's careful staging plans, as letters sent to the theater attest. Social and historical analysis were pioneered by Stanislavsky as an essential part of his production method, even before the "system" came into being.

And how was he to speak of class conflict after the Revolution, when classes no longer existed? In 1934, Zhdanov decreed a policy of "absence of conflict" (*bezkonfliktnost'*) in the theater. In his speech to the Writers' Congress Zhdanov proclaimed the triumph of communism, the collapse of capitalism, and the new doctrine of Socialist Realism. The theater's task was to expose the iniquities of the past, and present positive modern heroes, the New Communist Man. In 1935, as in 1835, coded messages had to be exchanged. A production which openly challenged the audience as Brecht advocated in his anti-Fascist campaign would have been considered "anti-Communist."

If Stanislavsky remained true to the traditions of the nineteenth-century intelligentsia and to the notions of critical realism, it was out of conviction. He believed it was more effective socially. The intellectual demonstration of a truth touches the mind only. An audience sees, registers coldly, and forgets. But if they are "hooked," if they enter into lived experience of the characters, they have much to think about. But they think *afterwards*. They go back again and again to problems which have become their problems. They are not so hypnotized that they lose all critical judgement. If there is identification, it is a clear-minded identification. If the production reveals the social dilemmas of the characters, if it presents the world in all its contradictions, audiences are led to reflect on their own situation. Stanislavsky always relied on the capacity of a Russian audience to pick up the slightest hint and allusion. His approach also had a certain Marxist respectability. After seeing a performance of Ostrovsky's *Enough Stupidity in Every Wise Man* just after the Revolution, Lenin remarked that Stanislavsky's characterization of General Krutitsky was so detailed the audience did not need to be told what a fool the man was, adding: "In my opinion that is the direction the theater should take." Engels had also expressed a preference for implicit rather than explicit criticism.[5]

Brecht in Hollywood

When Brecht returned to the United States in 1941, his isolation was almost complete. Not only had he lost his country, he had lost his artistic allies as well. A bleak entry in his *Arbeitsjournal* in January 1939 lists the Russian friends who had fallen foul of the Stalinist regime.[6] Reich would shortly join their number. Brecht himself, according to some, barely escaped arrest during his last visit to Moscow in 1941, shortly before Hitler invaded Russia.

The war years were a period of intense reflection. Brecht continued to define and refine his ideas, as can be seen from the *Arbeitsjournal*. Two preoccupations were empathy (*Einfühlung*) and emotion. He rejected the notion that his theater was cold, intellectual, and without feeling. The problem was one of balance between what he called *Emotio* and *Ratio*. When and how was it legitimate to use empathy or identification? To what extent should an audience be "drawn in" before it was "distanced"?

Of all the work Brecht did in the United States perhaps the most rewarding was his collaboration with Charles Laughton on *The Life of Galileo*. For the first time he was working with an actor of outstanding talent, not to say genius, capable both of subtle ideas and strong emotion. Laughton was an actor in the British "classical" tradition. Significantly, however, Laughton did insist on "justification" and Brecht appears not to have objected, nor when working on the adaptation, or in rehearsal, did he breath a word of theory.

Brecht in the GDR

With the creation of the GDR, Brecht for the first time had a permanent home. The Berliner Ensemble became, with the MXAT, the most pampered theater in the world with almost unlimited money and resources. Brecht had the perfect instrument with which to stage his plays just as he wanted them. His days were spent making theater. He wrote, translated, and directed. The one thing he did not do was train actors. His company learned and mastered their craft elsewhere. Like Laughton, they adapted to Brechtian methods. Problems were mostly resolved on the rehearsal floor, and it is there, in a working theater space, that the real encounter between Brecht and Stanislavsky finally took place.

The government, to some extent, engineered this encounter. Famous as the Ensemble was, heavily subsidized as it was, it did not enjoy full government favor. Indeed, the hard-line Stalinist, Walter Ulbricht, first Secretary of the Socialist Unity Party, had initially opposed its creation. In 1953, the GDR organized a Stanislavsky Conference in Berlin. Brecht knew that he was being targeted. The Conference was intended to bring everyone, himself included, into line. "Formalism" was out. The party line was Stanislavsky, official Soviet-style. A special production of *Egmont* was mounted at the Deutsches Theater to demonstrate the right approach. It was only remarkable for its mediocrity.

Brecht prepared his response. In 1953 he had read a translation of Gorchakov's *Stanislavsky Directs* in typescript.[7] It revealed a Stanislavsky he had not found in the German-language texts he had read so far. The first, ominously titled *The Secret of An Actor's Success*, had been published in Zurich in 1938. The second, *Das Deutsches Stanislawskibuch*, appeared in Berlin in 1946. Brecht read it while still in Los Angeles, and his reaction was the same as to his earlier reading.[8] He inveighed against the "Loyolaesque exercises," the "justification," and the "homespun moral tone." It is true that Stanislavsky can, at times, sound very "high-minded," particularly in certain translations, but the tone was of his time and generation, and was shared by other artists such as Chaliapin. The greater danger was the impression of total subjectivity which Brecht found so objectionable. Stanislavsky had foreseen this danger. Writing to his secretary on 25 December 1930, he expressed the fear that if people only read the first half of his book, *An Actor's Work on Himself* (known as *An Actor Prepares*), they would get an impression of "ultra-Naturalism" which was quite false. Later events amply justified his fears.

Gorchakov's book revealed Stanislavsky's emphasis on *action* not *emotion*, his insistence that everything should serve the "supertask" (the reason why the play was written). The actor's task was not to unleash a flood of highly personal emotions for his own benefit, but to use his own human resources to transmit the author's ideas; the "system" helped the actor serve the writer. Brecht discovered the "system" was *useful*.

He began to explore the Method of Physical Action. He was particularly drawn to the notion of "the line of the day," "the line of life," whereby the actor knows in detail what happens when he is not on stage. Another fundamental principle of the "system" would have interested him: that actors should base their characterization on contradictions, looking for the light side of a dark character and vice-versa. This would have gone some way at least to meeting his objection that Stanislavsky was "undialectical."[9]

He was now convinced that his knowledge of Stanislavsky's thought was totally inadequate. He decided first, to create a Workshop during the rehearsals for *Katzgraben* and, second, to refuse to enter into any useless polemic. Accordingly he only attended the Conference once and spoke very briefly. What he said was not recorded verbatim, but his Notes have now been published.[10] Weigel was the spokeswoman for the Ensemble. She, too, was very guarded, refusing to take up any fixed theoretical position on the grounds that insufficient hard facts were available. Meanwhile, Brecht demanded that Stanislavsky's complete works be published. He used the *Katzgraben* rehearsals to test out some of the techniques of the "system" and kept a careful record of the results, sometimes imitating the dialogue form which Stanislavsky preferred.[11] The recently published material in Volume 23 of the new critical edition confirms the seriousness of Brecht's intentions and calls into serious question the assertion made by some commentators that his notes, "Some of the Things That Can Be Learned from Stanislavsky," were a kind of lip service. Brecht adopted a position of scientific agnosticism.[12]

In 1955 Brecht read Toporkov's *Stanislavsky in Rehearsal,* which made such an impression on him that he wrote a letter of thanks to the author.[13] Toporkov was one of the rare actors to have been admitted to the MXAT from outside, rather than from the Art Theater school. His book has the advantage of being a practical record of Stanislavsky's rehearsal method, without any theorizing.

Even a cursory comparison of Toporkov's account with Angelika Hurwicz's and Hans Bunge's descriptions of Brecht's *Kreidekreis* rehearsals reveals many parallels of working method: the same rejection of the classical psychology of fixed character-types, of the "in general," the same breaking down of the text into a concrete series of actions, the same careful analysis of the characters' social and historical backgrounds.[14] It is worth noting that, as when working with Laughton, there was no jargon. The word *Verfremdung* did not pass Brecht's lips.

The Final Manipulation

While Brecht was exploring the "system" as a useful tool in staging plays — and for Stanislavsky it was never anything else; it was his "disciples" who "got religion" — the party ideologues were trying to cope with the implications of what was happening. How were they to explain this sudden reconciliation? Brecht's earlier views on Stanislavsky were a matter of public record. Fortunately for them, a solution lay at hand. The Soviet authorities had already come to grips with the same problem. How were they to explain the enthronement of Stanislavsky, the "bourgeois idealist," in the Soviet Pantheon? Simple: under the influence of Soviet behavioral psychology Stanislavsky had abandoned his subjective search for emotion and developed a more scientific method based on action. Crass but convenient, and eagerly seized upon by academics in the GDR.[15]

Two early accounts of the "system," however, by Michael Chekhov and Stanislavsky's former secretary, Vladimir Volkenstein published shortly after the Revolution, clearly indicate that the Method of Physical Action was already in operation.[16] In fact, Stanislavsky's preoccupation with emotion and Ribot's theory of Affective Memory only lasted briefly, between 1907-1914. It was the First Studio of MXAT which developed the technique further and, once again, members of that Studio who took the idea to the United States, where it became the cornerstone of Strasberg's Method.

If only Brecht had met Stella Adler instead of Lee Strasberg, history might have been different. Adler worked with Stanislavsky in Paris in June 1934, when he demonstrated the Method of Physical Action to her. On her return to the United States she told Strasberg that he was mistaken in his emphasis on Emotion Memory. He was unmoved.

Last Visit to Moscow

In 1955 Brecht paid his last visit to Moscow. Although rarely performed in the Soviet Union and still under a Formalist cloud, he had been awarded the Lenin Peace Prize. During his stay he attended a performance of Ostrovsky's *Burning Heart* in Stanislavsky's production. He noted in his *Journal*: "all Stanislavsky's greatness made apparent."[17]

Talking to his old friend Bernhard Reich, whose "rehabilitation" he had helped engineer, he wondered whether Gribov, who had played the role of Khlinov so well, would play Puntila. Reich praised Moskvin, a founder member of MXAT, who had played the same role but suggested that his success might not have had anything to do with Stanislavsky's methods. Brecht replied that they needed to study Stanislavsky "closely and without prejudice." Brecht's attitude, Reich notes, was truly "scientific."[18]

Our attitude should be no less rational. There is now no excuse for further ideological shadow-boxing. We now have a wealth of information which needs careful consideration and analysis. The new critical Suhrkamp edition of Brecht's works fills in the gaps in previously published statements on Stanislavsky; the new edition of Stanislavsky's works being published in Moscow and soon to be issued in English translation, restores the cuts and editorial changes which marred earlier publications. These, together with the accounts of rehearsals referred to earlier provide ample opportunity for a scholarly study of the Brecht/Stanislavsky relationship that may advance our knowledge of the process by which performances are created.

The first, essential step is to abandon what we thought we knew. Perhaps we should recall a moment in the *Flüchtlingsgespräche*:

> Someone who had not seen Herr K. for a long time greeted him with the words: "You haven't changed." "Oh!" said Herr K, and went deathly pale.[19]

NOTES

1. Jean Vilar, *Mémento*, early December 1954.

2. Bernhard Reich, *Im Wettlauf mit der Zeit* (Henschel 1970) 372. It should be noted that Reich does not use the usual term, *ostranenie*, made famous by Viktor Shklovskij, but *otčuždemie* which has the more legal sense of sequestration.

3. Lee Strasberg, *A Dream of Passion* (Bloomsbury 1988) 193-195. Strasberg's claims are uncorroborated.

4. Brecht, *Briefe* (Suhrkamp 1981), letter no. 310, 307-8.

5. Lenin's remarks were reported in Komoravskaja's *Videnoe i Perezhitoe* (Moscow 1965). See Engels' letters to Minna Kautsky (November 26, 1885) and Margaret Harkness (end of April 1888).

6. Brecht, *Journals 1934-1955*, trans. Hugh Rorrison, ed. John Willett (Methuen 1993) 20.

7. Nikolai Gorchakov, *Rezhissjorskij Uroki Stanislavkogo* (Moscow 1951). Trans. as *Regie. Unterricht bei Stanislavski* (Henschel 1959).

8. *Journals* 369, 383.

9. *Journals* 371.

10. Brecht, *Schriften 3*, Große kommentierte Berliner und Frankfurter Ausgabe, (Suhrkamp 1993) 232-38.

11. Brecht, *Schriften zum Theater 7* (Suhrkamp 1964).

12. *Große kommentierte Ausgabe, Schriften 3*

13. *Briefe*, no. 814. V. Toporkov, *Stanislabskij na Repetitisii* (Moscow 1950). English trans. *Stanislavsky in Rehearsal* (Theater Arts Books, 1979).

14. Angelika Hurwicz, *Brecht Inszeniert: Der kaukasische Kreidekreis* (Velber bei Hanover: Friedrich, 1964); Hans Bunge, "Brecht Probiert — Notizen und Gedanken zu Proben an Brechts Stück *Der kaukasische Kreidekreis*", in *Wer war Brecht?*, 1977. Bunge also kept a journal which is unpublished but extensively quoted by John Fuegi in *Bertolt Brecht, Chaos According to Plan* (CUP, 1987).

15. See Käthe Rülicke-Weiler, *Die Dramaturgie Brechts*, (Henschel 1968).

16. Mixail Čexov, *O Sisteme Stanislavskogo*, originally published in the magazine *Gorn* in 1919; Vladimir Volkenstein, *Stanislavskij* (Moscow 1922).

17. *Journals* 460.

18. Reich, 382.

19. *Prosa* 2 (Suhrkamp 1965): 114.

* * * * * * * *

Brecht in Bangladesh

Kabir Chowdhury

About the position in Bangladesh of Brecht, it is interesting to observe that in the course of about twenty years or so, after the liberation of Bangladesh, after its emergence as a free country in 1972, Brecht has received considerable attention from our theater workers, from our academicians, and from our playwrights. In our universities Brecht is now a text in the English literature course in drama. The specific prescribed text this year in the University of Dhaka in the Master Degree course is *Mother Courage and Her Children*, but references are constantly made to his other plays. And there are writings on Brecht, on his theater techniques, on his political ideology, on the ambiguities in Brecht's attitudes, but most importantly on the theoretical aspects of Brechtian dramaturgy, his distancing technique, his use of slides and music and newspaper headings. All this has a great impact on our drama. And Brecht is being performed an amazing number of times. I believe no other non-Bengali playwright, no other foreign playwright has been performed as extensively as Brecht has been. Interestingly Molière is another playwright who is widely played in Bengali translation. Shakespeare, of course, and some other foreign playwrights, too, but Brecht has been played on the stage so frequently that it amazes me. Some of the plays that have been performed in Bangladesh in Bengali are: *The Mother, The Caucasian Chalk Circle, The Measures Taken, Arturo Ui, Mahagonny, The Exception and the Rule, Galileo, Puntila and his Man Matti* (with great success), *The Good Person of Szechwan, Mother Courage,* and *The Threepenny Opera.* Eleven plays of Brecht have been performed in Bangladesh over the last 10-15 years.

Brecht incidentally is performed with great success in West Bengal (in India) too, where the language is the same. In Bangladesh we have now had all the above-mentioned plays of Brecht performed in Bengali. Two or three of them were direct translations, like *Galileo* and *Mother Courage,* without any change or adaptation. It was just a linguistic change, the transference from one language to another, but other plays have been adapted, changed into local characters and scenes. And the adaptations have gone better than the translations understandably because they establish better rapport with the audience. The costumes are different, changed to Bengali culture. So that is now the position of Brecht performance in Bangladesh. I would like to add that Brecht has greatly influenced our playwrights and our producers too, on the technical side as well. For example, in the use of song, the use of the narrator, breaking up the traditional format of story-telling in the sequential manner: all these things have undergone a change after Brecht. However, there has been a disadvantage, or not such a good effect, in my own opinion, in some cases. The use of songs and the use of group acting have sometimes altered the real intent of Brecht. For example, in the Bangladeshi version of *Puntila and his Man Matti* the element of humor was so over-emphasized, the drunken scenes were presented with such vigor that they vastly diluted Brecht's real intention. That has happened. But there were other cases where all those involved were conscious of this and tried to avoid all imbalances.

The position of songs in our plays has considerably improved as a result of Brecht's influence. For many years songs had little significance in our plays. In the nineteenth century they had great importance but in the twentieth, after the influence of Ibsen and Shaw, songs were neglected; but with Brecht's influence songs have again come to the fore.

About translations, I think much has already been said. In many countries of the world Brecht is known through translations to those who do not have access to the original German. I heard yesterday about the poor translation in certain Latin American countries, Argentina, and other places. Fortunately in Bangladesh, though the Brecht translations we have are from English, it has been said by competent and knowledgeable people that they have been faithful and tolerably good translations. We are now embarking on a very ambitious program of translation from German into Bengali in my country which will include plays by Hofmansthal, Schnitzler, Wedekind, Kaiser, Zuckmayer, Dürrenmatt. The interesting point is of all these playwrights only one play of each will be translated but Brecht will be translated whole. All of Brecht's works will be translated into Bengali in Bangladesh, and it will be a collaborative translation. A German who knows good German and fairly good English and a Bangladeshi author who knows good Bengali and good English will sit together and at first they will make a literal translation and then there will be a creative translation with the help of a Bangladeshi dramatist. Brecht's importance can obviously be felt through this kind of stature that we accord to him.

Now if I may briefly comment on our main topic: "the relevance of Brecht in today's world": relevance for whom? I should say it is not the same thing for the entire world. In the third-world countries Brecht has a special kind of relevance. In countries where there is still large-scale exploitation, where there are still remnants of authoritarianism, Brecht has a special relevance. Brecht's relevance can be seen there in the skilful adaptation of his plays. And this happens all the time. Take Brecht's own example. When he wrote *Señora Carrar's Rifles*, he took the story from Synge but there he thought it more appropriate in the context of those times to link it with the Spanish Revolution, against the Franco regime. In Bangladesh when we were groaning under military dictatorship, Zuckmayer's *Captain of Köpenick* was performed most effectively. It would not have been permitted if it was an original play by a Bangladeshi playwright. But when it was put forward as a foreign play by an eminent writer with a world reputation, it was simply translated and presented, and there was no censorship. But then the message to the audience was quite loud and clear. The importance of the uniform, that it controlled everything, the ruthlessness and stupidity — those of you who know the play know that. So it is the context, the period, that determines the relevance.

During our liberation war in 1972 Lady Gregory's *The Rising of the Moon* was adapted and performed with considerable success, again a play which emphasized liberty and patriotic feelings. Molière's *Tartuffe* has a relevance today in Bangladesh when there is an upsurge of religious hypocrisy. So the question of relevance is relative. It shifts from time to time and from situation to situation. Beckett's *Waiting for Godot* has a particular relevance in Bangladesh now, when we feel that things are stagnant, that nothing is happening and that the whole world is enmeshed in an atmosphere of uncertainty. These things determine the atmosphere of relevance. When Sartre wrote *The Flies* or Anouilh *Antigone*, though they were classics, they made them relevant in the context of occupied France and Marshal Pétain's role. In Bangladesh when we do a Brecht play, we try to introduce these shifts through our mode of production. We try to emphasize those aspects of Brecht which will make the play not only a good play but also socio-politically relevant and important.

I should say that more and more, as in many other countries in Bangladesh too, Brecht is being admired for his artistic role rather than for his political role. However, I should very emphatically like to say that there is a danger in de-emphasizing the political role of Brecht, because that is important, that is at the heart of things. If we forget about Brecht's fight against authoritarianism, against religious hypocrisy, against fascism, against the exploitation of the underprivileged, against militarism, we shall do a great harm to our appreciation of him. And I do not see any fundamental opposition between the two approaches. As some of you have said, Brecht is all of one piece. His songs, his techniques, his ideology, they are not different from or antagonistic to each other. In *Mother Courage*, for example, when a soldier talks about anger, the mother says, "My boy, make sure that your anger is big enough. Only then go ahead and rise up. If your anger is a small one, don't be foolish to pursue that path." Now I think this is universal. This would remain valid for all times, not for just today or tomorrow, valid for the oppressed and the downtrodden. If the anger is great, go ahead and you will have a revolution. If the anger is little, you will be sent to jail, and nothing will come out of your stand.

Finally, with respect to the controversy over the Stanislavsky and Brecht systems and other issues, Brecht himself always stood against a dogmatic position. I believe that more is made of the difference between the Stanislavsky system and the Brecht system of acting than there actually is. Brecht was certainly aware of the importance of Stanislavsky and of the utility of his approach. But I believe he felt that people were getting wrapped up in only one approach, that of Stanislavsky, that the actor had to feel empathy if he was to create a character properly. Brecht felt differently and from that stand he evolved his own attitude that it was not empathy or identification which helped an actor to present his role better. Rather, a sense of detachment, a sense of distancing enabled him to perform better. I would not say that Brecht anywhere came to negating Stanislavsky's influence. And it is in harmony with Brecht's total approach: "Don't go for absolutes, don't go for only one way of thinking. Think of alternatives, think of oppositions, the dialectics and probably you can arrive at the truth better that way." He was always for an admission of opposites, for dialectics. This goes also for his theories of alienation and epic theater. Much has been made of these things unnecessarily, where people have quoted something from his book but have left out important footnotes provided by him.

I believe Brecht's influence in Bangladesh is great. He has influenced our playwrights, our producers. I saw a production in Bangladesh of *The Caucasian Chalk Circle* where a very large sprawling area was used as the stage: rooftop, part of a swimming pool and things like that, taking the play out of the proscenium stage, trying to present it in the epic way and, of course, with songs, many folk elements, and earthy humor. All these are not necessarily directly from Brecht, but the influence of Brecht has definitely gone into the writing of some of our plays and in their production. I think Brecht is very relevant in today's world and will probably be more so in tomorrow's.

A few more words on the eternal problem of translation. What do you translate? Do you translate just the words, just the content, or the emotion and the atmosphere? And how much liberty do you take without distorting the original? You do take certain liberties, otherwise it will not go well in the language you are translating. So faithfulness is not the absolute and ultimate criterion in a creative translation. You translate, you do not distort, but you make it acceptable to your audience. To give just a little example. In *Mother Courage* in the last but one song: the dumb daughter is dead and the mother croons a lullaby-type of song, she does not want to accept her death and she says — I'll read out just two lines in Bengali:

Ak chhele morechhe Poland-e,
Ar ak chhele kothai ke jane
Ghumao shonamoni, ghumao.

"One son has died in Poland, I don't know what happened to the other son — sleep my darling, sleep." So there is a rhythm of the popular song here and you integrate that tune, it goes very well. You do not distort and you convey the sense. I believe if we are aware of these things we can do justice to Brecht translations and presentation.

* * * * * * * *

Vertiges de Brecht

Philippe Ivernel

Incapable de résumer cette première série d'échanges (comme m'y invite John Willett), je me bornerai à reprendre la question majeure que chacun se pose forcément, celle de l'actualité du théâtre brechtien, de son efficace aujourd'hui. Question d'autant plus obligée que ce théâtre se donne pour but de travailler à la transformation des rapports sociaux. Or, la faillite maintenant consommée du "socialisme réellement existant" (comme on disait dans l'ex-R-DA, par dérision autant que par conviction) accentue le recul des utopies révolutionnaires, déjà bien discrédités dans cette fin de siècle, à tel point que la catégorie du politique elle même en sort compromise.

Cela dit, la fin du siècle n'annonce pas pour autant une fin de l'histoire, un apaisement de celle-ci, comme d'aucuns nous le chantent à intervalles plus ou moins réguliers, sans doute à des fins intéressées. Les contradictions sur lesquelles Brecht a toujours bâti sa conception du mouvement, ne se sont pas résorbées: elles se sont tout au plus déplacées dans l'espace géographique et sociologique, et provoquent un sentiment de cahot grandissant.

C'est de ce sentiment de cahot que Brecht, en son temps, est parti. Son théâtre en est nourri, et la situation actuelle, à certains égards, le ramène à ses commencements, à son origine. On sait aussi que l'auteur fut amené à voir en Marx, dans le cours des années vingt, un lecteur idéal de ce théâtre; et que lui-même, Brecht, a pu passer parfois pour un "léniniste de la scène," par exemple aux yeux d'Ernst Bloch qui sous ce titre, dans un article de 1938, donc à un moment tournant de l'histoire européenne, commentait ses *Lehrstücke* ou pièces didactiques.

L'effondrement récent des Partis-États bureaucratiques se réclamant du marxisme porte-t-il un coup au théâtre épique, ou lève-t-il au contraire une hypothèque pesant lourdement sur lui? Quoi qu'il en soit, il convient plus que jamais de dissocier le théâtre brechtien de ce marxisme étatique, ainsi que de son esthétique dominante, le "réalisme socialiste,"qui a toujours davantage menacé le théâtre épique par ses tentatives d'enveloppement que par sa volonté affirmée d'exclusion. Opérer en toute netteté cette dissociation ne revient nullement, bien entendu, à "sauver" Brecht en distinguant sa poésie de sa politique, pour mieux congédier la seconde comme s'il s'agissait d'un accident regrettable de la première. Procéder de la sorte serait au contraire priver le théâtre épique de sa tension constitutive, émousser sa pointe qui, pour utiliser une image empruntée, fait épine dans l'œil du spectateur.

Politique, le marxisme de Brecht n'équivaut pas, en tout état de cause, à une *Weltanschauung*, à une conception intuitive et globalisante du monde, qui prétendrait savoir comment tout se déroule et concorderait finalement avec un idéal d'harmonie. La "doctrine," comme dit parfois Brecht en parlant des leçons de Marx et de ses successeurs avec une sorte d'emphase insolente, sinon ironique, se rapprocherait plutôt du modèle d'une science expérimentale et critique. Dès lors, le marxisme fournit tout au plus des critères et des méthodes d'où découlent des "points de vue" qu'il y a lieu de mettre à l'épreuve des faits. C'est par là qu'il devient à la fois un facteur et un objet de distanciation théâtrale. La "doctrine" ne peut critiquer la pratique humaine, dont la scène donne une image, que dans la mesure où elle se laisse aussi critiquer par elle. "A l'idéalisme, il faut demander d'où il sort; au matérialisme, ce qui en sort," écrit Brecht un jour. Et un autre jour: "Tous les éléments de la doctrine sont là, mais lequel s'ajuste à l'instant?" Dans un troisième fragment, il nomme "brechtisation" telle inflexion spécifique apportée par lui à l'héritage de Marx afin de satisfaire aux exigences de la situation historique.

A quoi il faut ajouter qu'en rapprochant le marxisme d'un certain modèle scientifique, Brecht ne manque pas de souligner les insuffisances de la démarche ainsi entreprise, et il en éloigne simultanément le théâtre. Quand donc il préconise, dans *l'Achat du cuivre*, un théâtre de l'ère scientifique, ce n'est pas pour l'assimiler à un théâtre lui-même scientifique. Nous touchons là un point de complication maximale, qui permet d'approfondir la modernité de Brecht. Le marxisme, explique l'auteur dans un passage trop peu remarqué de *l'Achat du cuivre*, traite surtout du comportement de grandes masses d'hommes: "les lois que cette science a établies permettent de rendre compte des mouvements de très grandes unités; elles ne traitent d'ordinaire, justement, que de la position de l'individu par rapport à ces masses. En revanche, dans nos démonstrations, nous aurions plutôt à traiter du comportement des individus entre eux." Doit-on supposer que les comportements des individus entre eux (individus qui ne sont jamais que des fragments de masse divisés, voire contradictoires) ne se soumettent pas mécaniquement aux lois statistiques, et favorisent l'exploration théâtrale du singulier, de l'insolite, des possibles en tous genres qui ne sont pas dans la ligne de l'attente? Et si c'est possible, objectera-t-on, relèvent du détail, et non des grandes masses, n'est-ce pas le détail, justement, qui fait événement et rompt avec le cours prévisible des choses? Autant de questions qui peuvent aider à relire Brecht autrement.

Non seulement Brecht n'est pas d'un bloc (en quoi il se révèle bien notre contemporain), mais encore tout se joue, chez lui, dans les écarts. De l'auteur, la meilleure photographie à retenir pourrait être celle où il essaie son propre masque moulé en plâtre: il le tient devant lui à hauteur de visage, comme s'il testait la bonne distance, variable sans doute selon les cas de figure, qu'il s'agit d'entretenir de soi à soi. Sur telle autre photographie, Brecht manie ses lunettes pour mieux accommoder (ce qui ne mène en rien à s'accommoder de quoi que ce soit). Dans ces deux gestes, la stratégie de la distanciation, qui n'est pas faite d'un simple recul, mais d'un va-et-vient entre le proche et le lointain, qui permette à la fois l'observation et l'intervention.

Adepte de la pensée pratique, Brecht ne peut être d'un bloc; son œuvre non plus (ni le marxisme auquel elle fait référence). Pour rendre cette justice à l'œuvre, il ne suffit pas de la périodiser en distinguant, comme on fait couramment, les pièces de la jeunesse, anarchisantes, puis les *Lehrstücke*, disciplinantes par leur didactisme, et enfin les pièces dites de la maturité, obligatoirement "dialectiques" (c'est à dire offrant la synthèse des deux premières phases). Ce type de traitement, implicite, ressemble à celui qu'une certaine tradition académique, en Allemagne, applique à Goethe: après le préromantique révolté, le classique sévère, et enfin le dépassement, faustien, de l'un et de l'autre, comme une *Aufhebung* hégélienne. Quitte à rappeler Goethe, ne vaut-il pas mieux avancer que l'œuvre de Brecht est de circonstance, au sens fort de ce terme: moins régie par un développement intrinsèque, auto-suffisant, que par des contraintes de l'intervention dans des champs historiques variables d'où, par conséquent, des changements de régime, dus à des changements de contextes?

Dès lors, il n'est pas vain de chercher à mieux comprendre le Brecht d'hier pour construire celui d'aujourd'hui ou de demain. Des correspondances inattendues viendraient peut-être à surgir. Si par exemple le vide ambiant de nos jours — la perte des repères dont plusieurs générations vécurent depuis la libération — ne va pas sans créer un certain vertige, il y a un vertige certain chez le Brecht de l'exil: son travail d'écrivain lui parait maintes fois excentré par rapport au cours des choses. L'auteur ne peut que durement ressentir la défaite de la classe ouvrière allemande écrasée par le fascisme, celle du prolétariat mondial livré à lui-même par le pacte germano-soviétique, puis engagé dans la guerre sous la direction des bourgeoisies nationales. De ce prolétariat il arrive à Brecht de se demander ce qui en reste; du communisme, ce qui en advient, à l'heure où l'URSS évoque à ses yeux — s'il faut en croire les conversations menées à Svendborg avec Walter Benjamin — un monstrueux frisson, une monarchie ouvrière.

Ce n'est pas un hasard si dans le théâtre épique de Brecht, soupçonneux comme on sait à l'égard des héros dits positifs, n'existe guère de sujet historique au sens plein du terme: celui-ci — individu, classe ou peuple — se caractérise plutôt par une sorte de présence-absence, à la limite du représentable: il demeure toujours à reconstruire, dans une "foutue époque" où la dialectique fonctionne comme un "sac à malices" (cf. *Journal de travail*, le 6-1-1948). Fixer le théâtre de Brecht dans ce vertige, n'est-ce pas loger son *Verfremdungseffekt*; sa faculté [de distanciation] au creux de notre propre actualité.

J'aimerais ici accrocher un mot en faveur du *Lehrstück*, de la pièce didactique, qu'on ferait mieux de nommer pièce d'apprentissage ou même d'auto-apprentissage. Faite pour être jouée plutôt que pour être vue, elle ne véhicule aucunement, comme on le lui reproche à tort, de véhiculer un "message" préfabriqué, à caractère autoritaire. Au contraire, elle sollicite des participants leur investissement productif dans le jeu théâtral, un investissement élargi par des scénarios conséquents mais renversables (*Celui qui dit oui, Celui qui dit non*), ou, à tout le moins, modulables. Ce type de théâtre, en incitant à varier les comportements en fonction des situations, peut justement participer très activement à la reconstruction du sujet historique. Des essais tentés à l'Université avec des groupes étudiants montrent que ceux-ci peuvent très vite s'emparer de ces "machines à jouer" pour y investir leur propre expérience et, du même coup, réfléchir celle-ci en variant les conditions de son déploiement.

Enfin, c'est en revenant sur la langue de Brecht que je terminerai cette intervention, pour répéter que le poétique, en l'occurrence, ne saurait se dissocier du politique, comme le rappelle mieux que tout la "gestualité" que l'auteur imprime à son discours aussi bien qu'à ceux de ses personnages. Le geste inscrit la parole dans l'espace physique, donc social. La difficulté de traduire Brecht vient de là: question de rythme. Quand celui-ci n'est pas codifié par la convention, il traduit le passage dans la langue de ce sujet historique en train de se frayer une voie.

* * * * * * * *

Bertolt Brecht et l'Afrique Noire

Ousmane Diakhate

Ma communication ne porte pas sur les options théâtrales de Bertolt Brecht de façon profonde, encore moins sur une analyse rigoureuse de l'histoire et de l'esthétique du théâtre négro-africain. Je voudrais simplement d'abord essayer de donner quelques exemples de tendances majeures dans l'utilisation qu'on a pu faire de la pensée et du travail de l'Allemand en Afrique, et, ensuite, m'interroger sur les points communs entre les procédés spectaculaires propres à l'identité artistique africaine et les conceptions dramaturgiques brechtiennes.

I. A quel niveau de la pratique théâtrale Brecht intervient-il en Afrique?

L'œuvre de Brecht trouve place dans le théâtre négro-africain. Ceux qui suivent l'évolution de ce théâtre et qui connaissent Brecht peuvent s'en convaincre facilement. Mais il faut admettre que cette place est relativement réduite et date de quelques années seulement. En effet, les premiers Africains à prendre contact avec Brecht, l'ont fait en Europe, de manière fragmentaire et tardive. Cela ne pouvait se passer autrement, quand on sait, par exemple, que cette œuvre était particulièrement inconnue en France avant la dernière guerre mondiale. Jean-Marie Serreau, un des metteurs en scène français qui s'est le plus intéressé au théâtre de Brecht en France avant le déclic provoqué par la venue du Berliner Ensemble à Paris avec *Mère Courage* en 1954, fut à l'origine de la rencontre entre Brecht et l'Afrique noire. La "Compagnie Jean-Marie Serreau," fondée en 1949, crée la même année *L'Exception et la règle* au "Théâtre des Noctambules." C'est la deuxième fois qu'une pièce de

Brecht est montée en France. Gaston Baty avait déjà mis en scène *L'Opéra de quat'sous* en 1930. Brecht fut l'auteur le plus monté par Jean-Marie Serreau que la tradition théâtrale retient comme un metteur en scène découvreur d'auteurs. En effet, c'est grâce à lui que nous avons découvert Eugène Ionesco, Aimé Césaire et Kateb Yacine, par exemple. Mais Jean-Marie Serreau a aussi permis à beaucoup de comédiens africains et maghrébins de se découvrir. Nous savons que la rencontre avec Jean-Marie Serreau fut un tournant important dans la vie et dans la carrière du grand comédien sénégalais Douta Seck. Dès 1949, le jeune acteur sénégalais d'alors se trouve à ses côtés pour *L'Exception et la règle* dont nous parlions plus haut. Douta Seck incarnait le rôle du Coolie dans la pièce de Brecht ouvrant ainsi pour la première fois, le contact Brecht et l'Afrique noire. Douta suit Serreau au "Babylone" (théâtre parisien) où il joue dans *Homme pour homme* de Brecht toujours avant de reprendre *L'Exception et la règle* en 1954 dans le rôle du Marchand.

Il faut signaler que la troupe de comédiens noirs créée par Jean-Marie Serreau, la "Compagnie du Toucan," dans l'aventure de ses tournées, a séjourné à Berlin-Est en 1964 à l'invitation de la veuve de Brecht, Hélène Weigel. Les comédiens ont eu ainsi l'occasion de prendre contact avec Brecht à travers le travail du Berliner Ensemble. Ils ont tous été émerveillés. Lucien Lemoine, qui a fait cette tournée, parle du Berliner avec admiration:

> Quel ensemble et en même temps quel soin du détail, quelle minutie! Jamais, jamais je n'oublierai cela. Plus de trente personnes en scène et l'impression très nette que chaque geste, chaque déplacement de chacun de ces trente comédiens est subordonné au geste ou au déplacement de chacun des vingt-neuf autres en même temps! Et tout cela naturellement, sans qu'on puisse y déceler la moindre intention ou velléité de chorégraphie.
>
> (*Douta Seck ou La Tragédie du roi Christophe*," Paris: Présence Africaine, 1993, 60.)

Ces quelques exemples nous montrent le rôle déterminant que Jean-Marie Serreau a joué dans le rapprochement entre Brecht et l'Afrique noire. Nous y ajouterons, toujours en Europe, l'exemple des Africains ayant séjourné en Allemagne, en apprentissage auprès du Berliner Ensemble, comme le dramaturge, metteur en scène, malien Gaoussou Diawara, qui a fait en 1985 un stage de quelques mois à Berlin dans cet Ensemble.

Mais, en vérité, la diffusion de Brecht, en Afrique même, reste surtout intellectuelle. Elle est avant tout livresque et idéologique. En effet, c'est dans l'enseignement dispensé dans les rares écoles dramatiques et dans les travaux de recherches des universitaires qui s'intéressent au théâtre, que l'on trouve le plus fréquemment les traces de la pensée de Brecht. Cependant, un certain nombre de ses pièces ont été montées au Mali où Gaoussou Diawara et son épouse ont fait jouer deux pièces de Brecht: *L'Exception et la règle* et *L'Opéra des quat'sous* dans le cadre de l'Institut National des Arts au Congo où la troupe nationale a joué *L'Exception et la règle* au Sénégal dans le cadre des travaux d'élèves au Conservatoire National d'Art Dramatique.

L'Africain qui s'est le plus illustré dans l'utilisation des pièces de Brecht est le Nigérien Wole Soyinka. En mai 1960, à peine est-il de retour au Nigéria que Soyinka joue deux pièces de Brecht: *Le Cercle de craie caucasien* et *La Bonne Âme de Szechwan*. A Ifé, en décembre 1977, il crée *L'Opéra de Wonyosi*, très librement adapté de *L'Opéra de quat'sous* de Brecht. La pièce fut remaniée selon les besoins de la représentation et de l'inspiration de l'auteur africain. De la pièce de Brecht, Soyinka ne retiendra que les grands traits de l'intrigue, c'est-à- dire le mariage d'un chef de bande captain Macheath avec Polly, la fille du roi des mendiants, la contre-attaque du beau-père indigné, qui aboutit à l'emprisonnement de Macheath, et l'amnistie in extremis du condamné. Les principaux personnages de Macheath dit Mack the Knife, Anikura le cynique exploiteur des mendiants, sa femme et sa fille, restent proches de leurs équivalents européens, mais Soyinka situe sa pièce dans un contexte africain bien précis à la fois dans le temps et dans l'espace. Le pays en question est la République Centrafricaine à la veille de l'instauration de l'Empire puisque les événements se passent avant le couronnement de Bokassa. Les protagonistes sont des Nigériens exilés en Centrafrique. L'auteur se moque principalement de Bokassa dit Boky et tourne en dérision sa cruauté. Le titre de la pièce est en relation directe avec le "wonyosi" (tissu de dentelle très couteux, recherché au Nigéria mais introuvable en RCA). Polly, grâce à ce tissu, espère impressionner les partenaires de ses futures transactions commerciales. Nous dit Michèle Lurdos:

> La satire de l'auteur ne fait donc grâce à personne, mais c'est la forme adaptée qui retiendra le plus notre attention. S'il fallait trouver un point de convergence entre le théâtre africain dans cette pièce, le plus évident serait probablement un rythme volontairement ralenti, hérité tout à la fois du modèle brechtien et de l'Opéra Yoruba.

(*Coté cour, Coté savane, le théâtre de Wole Soyinka*, Presse Universitaire de Nancy, 1990, 118.)

La pièce, en effet, comporte de nombreux chants soit en solo, soit en chœur destinés à commenter l'action en cours ou à énoncer une opinion générale. Le disc-jockey introduit six scènes sur les neuf que compte la pièce, par de longs commentaires qui permettent, par leurs remarques faites dans un style décontracté, de prendre le recul nécessaire vis-à-vis de l'action. Soyinka reprend entièrement à son compte le modèle brechtien.

Dans *La Danse de la forêt* (Honfleur: P.J. Oswald, 1971), les personnages sont des rappels tirés de l'histoire. La pièce évoque par sa structure la parabole dramatique d'*Arturo Ui* où Brecht explique en partie l'ascension d'Hitler au pouvoir et analyse la satire historique du nazisme. Dans la pièce de Soyinka, des transpositions analogues se rencontrent avec l'émergence au pouvoir de Madame Tortue dominant son mari et désireuse de posséder un guerrier rebel qui l'a séduite par sa bravoure et sa témérité.

L'influence du brechtisme en Afrique se remarque aussi dans les techniques de mise en scène et les théories qui les soutendent. Plusieurs metteurs en scène africains contemporains recourent aux panneaux pour annoncer l'action, pour préciser le lieu et le moment historique. Seyba Lamine Traoré (metteur en scène, Secrétaire Général du Théâtre National Daniel Sorano, Dakar) utilise ce procédé dans sa mise en scène de la *La République* (Ibrahima Sall, Dakar-Abidjan-Lomé NEA, 1985). Son confrère Jean-Pierre Leurs (metteur en scène, Sociétaire du Théâtre National Daniel Sorano, Dakar), comble la fosse d'orchestre dans sa mise en scène des *Battu cassé* (adaptation théâtrale du roman d'Aminata Sow Fall, *La Grève des battu*, Dakar, NEA,1979), faisant ainsi du théâtre un podium qui annule la discontinuité scène/salle. Il est enfin un moyen d'expression que la scène africaine utilise fréquemment: l'insertion dans le spectacle de projection de film ou de diapositives documentaires qui élargissent l'action dramatique afin de mieux aider le spectateur à la réflexion comme le faisait Brecht.

II. Idéologies, Artistiques Différentes, Esthétiques Voisines

Des idéologies artistiques différentes peuvent-elles avoir des esthétiques voisines? La réponse semble être positive quand on sait que le modèle pratique, source d'inspiration de la théorie des effets "V," Brecht l'a trouvé dans la dramaturgie ancestrale chinoise. Celui-ci part donc d'une culture qui, de par ses données, réfute le projet idéologique dont il est partisan avec ses visées révolutionnaires. Le système de pensée de l'Orient traditionnel est, pour autant qu'on puisse en juger, tout à fait étranger à l'Europe. Brecht est allé chercher un allié tout à fait différent dans son combat contre la dramaturgie traditionnelle occidentale même si aujourd'hui, parler de distanciation fait penser à Brecht seul.

Le Brechtisme considère l'art du théâtre comme une sorte de microcosme de la société à laquelle appartiennent les spectateurs. Il s'agit de faire collectivement le théâtre, de briser la différence qui existe entre acteurs et spectateurs.

De son côté, le théâtre africain, quand il était encore partie intégrante des cérémonies traditionnelles, était une production populaire. Tout le monde était concerné. Les spectacles rituels étaient destinés à assurer la cohésion des croyances, et au-delà, la continuité de l'ordre social. De même la dramaturgie moderne est soucieuse des réalités sociales et politiques. Elle présente au public des thèmes répondant à ses préoccupations, elle se veut un facteur de prise de conscience, un moyen d'éducation et une force mobilisatrice. Brecht n'attend pas autre chose du théâtre. Le théâtre épique, tel qu'il le conçoit est un théâtre didactique; il cherche à instruire, à éduquer. Le comédien africain traditionnel, comme le comédien épique est au centre de la tourmente sociale. Tous les deux reproduisent la vie avec ses contradictions et ils appellent le spectateur à intervenir dans cette vie. L'un et l'autre essaient de fournir une sorte de documentaire qui puisse aider les spectateurs à maîtriser et à transformer la réalité. Les spectacles qu'ils produisent sont des occasions de prise de conscience qui doivent se traduire par une action sociale.

Le jeu dans le théâtre épique exige du comédien une maîtrise socio-critique du personnage vis-à-vis duquel il prendra ses distances pour mieux en souligner les contradictions. Cette technique de jeu était déjà le comportement du conteur dans la tradition africaine. Le conte est présent dans toute la littérature orale ancestrale. Ses caractéristiques dramatiques sont nombreuses et variées. Il procure toujours un énorme plaisir par sa fable, ses personnages, ses thèmes, ses émotions et ses espaces imaginaires. Il s'appuie fondamentalement sur la narration qui est, avant tout, une performance théâtrale. Le conte est un théâtre de narration: un comédien, à partir de ses propres ressources, joue en tirant toutes les possibilités dramatiques du dire et en incarnant, seul, une multitude de rôles, tant humains qu'animaliers. A ce sujet Peter Brook affirme: "Nous avons toujours considéré une troupe de théâtre comme un conteur à plusieurs têtes." (*Points de suspension*, Paris: Seuil, 1992, 217). De la parole d'un seul surgissent des personnages attachants, des images marquantes et des histoires révélatrices. En somme le conteur est appelé à faire ressortir les multiples possibilités de jeu qui s'offrent à l'homme. Le conteur assume le récit par sa voix, son geste. La physionomie et la diction changent conformément aux différents personnages qu'il joue en établissant entre eux, parfois, de vives oppositions que seul un maître dans l'art du jeu peut respecter. Passant avec allégresse du monologue à la scène animée à plusieurs personnages, du registre tragique au registre comique avec la même habileté.

Mais le conteur ne s'emploie pas seulement à faire parler différents personnages qu'il incarne tour à tour: par intervalles, il reprend la parole pour son compte et expose les faits. D'acteur jouant plusieurs rôles, il redevient simple narrateur et, forcément, son ton change. Ici il s'adresse directement à son auditoire et en quelque sorte se démasque. La distanciation se produit. Le fait que le conteur interrompt le jeu dramatique pour commenter brise tout effet d'illusion. Se détachant du personnage pour redevenir conteur, l'acteur rappelle qu'il n'est pas le personnage mais qu'il le montre à la manière d'un montreur de marionnettes. Il s'y ajoute que, dans une séance, l'auditeur est co-créateur. On ne conte bien qu'en face d'un bon public. L'auditoire n'est pas seulement réceptif. Les spectateurs jugent le conteur et contrôlent la représentation en permanence. La prestation du conteur n'échappe à aucun moment au contrôle des auditeurs. Nous sommes loin d'une contamination émotionnelle entre production et réception. Le rapport entre conteur et auditoire est un rapport aussi lucide que celui que demande Brecht. On le voit, les techniques brechtiennes sont souvent et naturellement utilisées par des acteurs africains car le théâtre est en Afrique une activité communautaire, sociale et critique en même temps qu'il est un moment de plaisir. Il y a équivalence entre art et fonction sociale; le théâtre est une affaire collective et participative.

L'acteur africain se définit, selon Wole Soyinka, comme le maître de la "transition." L'importance de la mythologie yorouba dans la conception dramatique du Nigérien est connue. Selon lui, le créateur du théâtre africain serait Ogun, dieu du fer et de la forge. Ce dieu est l'emblème de l'acteur parce qu'il est le conquérant de la "transition" nécessaire entre les rituels, la danse et l'art dramatique. Ogun serait ainsi le premier comédien. Aux trois grandes zones d'existence retenues dans la religion yorouba: le monde des vivants, celui des morts, et celui de ceux qui ne sont pas encore nés, Soyinka ajoute un quatrième: le monde intermédiaire qu'il appelle la zone de la "transition." Le passage d'une existence à l'autre comporte le risque de la dissolution. C'est grâce au rite d'Ogun que l'homme arrive à franchir sans danger la zone de la transition. Le dieu, par une acte courageux de la volonté, a sacrifié son individuation pour organiser les forces mythiques et techniques de la terre et du cosmos pour en faire un pont destiné à traverser le chaos. Cet acte d'Ogun a une valeur métaphysique dans la pensée de Soyinka, mais il a aussi une valeur esthétique. Le dieu doit être perçu comme la synthèse entre Dionysos et Apollon. Ogun a traversé le chaos pour atteindre la joie esthétique; possédé comme Dionysos, il trouve le contrôle nécessaire à la maîtrise de l'œuvre d'art. La possession devient un état d'exaltation créatrice et l'art du comédien une maîtrise de la possession. C'est du passage de l'enthousiasme au contrôle, que naît le jeu dramatique. Le théâtre commence justement quand les techniques de la possession, de la transe sont mises au service du jeu.

Homme de maîtrise, l'acteur de théâtre est celui qui impose un ordre au désordre. La mission de l'acteur rituel est d'aider le spectateur à maîtriser son angoisse. Le théâtre rituel, comme le théâtre épique, est un lieu d'initiation en vue d'une prise de conscience sociale. Bien sûr dans certains rites africains, surtout les rites identificatoires, l'émotion occupe une place centrale. Le possédé s'identifie au dieu et extériose sa transe. La technique du jeu distancié que veut Brecht exige du comédien qu'il se trouve à distance du personnage qui demeure ainsi sous contrôle. Mais que l'on comprenne bien Brecht, il ne rejette pas, en effet, catégorique-ment le sentiment, il ne demande pas d'éliminer tout sentiment. Dans *L'Achat du cuivre* il dit: "Il ne faut entraver ni participation affective du public ni celle du comédien. Il ne faut pas empêcher non plus la représentation des sentiments, ni leur emploi par les comédiens" (Paris: l'Arche, 102). On le voit, Brecht ne réfute pas catégoriquement la sensibilité, il ne la considère pas comme étrangère à son système.

3. La Musique

En Afrique noire, peu de représentations ignorent la cadence, les chants et les danses. Dans les sociétés négro-africaines, les images sonores, le rythme, ont leur vie, leur charge d'émotion. La musique flatte les sentiments, elle évoque des histoires, des légendes, des mythes qui entraînent une série de transferts chez les Nègres et invoque des puissances qui les déchaînent. Les temps forts des spectacles africains sont ainsi mis en valeur par le rythme et la danse qui leur donnent une plus grande intensité. La musique est un trait d'union entre l'espace scénique et l'espace des spectateurs. Elle renforce les paroles, appuie l'action et offre aux spectateurs plus de lisibilité et plus de facilité d'accès à ce qui se fait. Les chants ajoutent à la valeur théâtrale du jeu. Les instrumentistes sont présent sur l'aire de jeu et participent à l'action comme acteurs au besoin. Les instruments de musique participent au décor et sont en harmonie, par leur plasticité, avec l'ensemble du tableau scénique. La manière dont la musique doit se définir par rapport à l'action soit pour l'approuver soit pour la contredire, la parodier, ou la situer à un niveau déterminé du jeu, est fonction du spectacle.

Nous savons que l'introduction des "songs" (chansons) sur la scène européenne marque une rupture entre le théâtre épique et le théâtre dramatique. En plus de la détente, les chants brechtiens ont une valeur didactique, elles sont une réflexion sur la société. En Afrique les chants ont la même fonction dramatique, il arrive qu'ils séparent les différentes parties du spectacle comme les "songs" chez Brecht. Le monde africain possède une longue tradition culturelle qui confère une place de choix à la chanson dont la mission, entre autres, est d'inciter le spectateur à la réflexion.

4. Conclusion

Ainsi, des idéologies artistiques différentes peuvent susciter des esthétiques voisines. Brecht n'a pas personnellement pris contact avec la culture africaine et son théâtre évoque la société européenne capitaliste de l'entre-deux-guerres. Il la critique du point de vue de la révolution socialiste idéale.

La société africaine contemporaine ne vit pas la même situation ni le même contexte culturel. La dramaturgie brechtienne suppose un consensus préalable entre le spectateur et la scène. Le public initié des rites antiques africains connaissait, peut-être, une harmonie comparable, mais celui du théâtre moderne est caractérisé, d'une manière générale, par une hétérogénéité socio-professionnelle et idéologique. Nous sommes aujourd'hui dans un climat politique radicalement différent de l'époque de Brecht, marqué par la crise du système communiste presque un peu partout dans le monde. Il serait intéressant de s'interroger sur les conséquences de cette situation sur le brechtisme.

Nous constatons en tout cas que la théorie du "théâtre épique" recoupe sur plusieurs points les préoccupations de la dramaturgie négro-africaine et que certaines vues de Brecht ne sont pas étrangères à l'horizon d'attente du public africain. Le brechtisme est une réflexion globale et pertinente sur l'art dans son universalité quelles que puissent être la culture de création et les fluctuations politiques.

* * * * * * * *

Brecht in Finland

Ralf Långbacka

I have to start by saying that in Finland, as in many other countries in the 1920s, the only known play of Brecht was *The Threepenny Opera*, which was mounted directly after the Berlin performance, in 1929, and really as a "model performance" (well before Brecht had started to use the idea of the *Modell*). That was a time when theater people went out to Europe looking at performances and came back doing a little of the same, and that was how *The Threepenny Opera* was put on in Finland in 1929. It was a big success and played in many theaters. When Brecht came to Finland in 1940 I think that no one knew him — or to say no one is too much — but almost no one knew him as anything other than the writer of *The Threepenny Opera*. Our gift to Brecht and the world is the year he spent in Finland 1940-41, because he wrote a great deal and was greatly inspired. He finished *The Good Person of Szechwan*. Then *Puntila*, naturally, because it was based on a cooperation with a Finnish playwright, Hella Wuolijoki. He wrote *Arturo Ui*, which he thought could be an introduction to the United States. It was a perhaps a wrong idea, but as an idea still quite good. Further, he wrote *Refugee Conversations*, which takes place at the railway station of Helsinki, parts of *The Messingkauf Dialogues*, and a lot of poems are influenced by his impression of Finnish nature. That's what I think Finland gave Brecht.

But we were not able to accept his theater. He tried to have *Mother Courage* staged at many theaters, but not one took it. He tried to interest people in his *Galileo*, but no one was interested in this either. Naturally, the political situation in Finland in 1940, after the first war with the Soviet Union and before the next one, which started in 1941, was in many ways difficult. I think that at that time he had no chance to be performed in Finland. No one could understand his type of theater, and politically he was a problem. He gave a lecture for members of a students' theater on his methods ("Über experimentelles Theater") and I think that most of the participants didn't understand a word of what he was talking about. When he saw Finnish theater he thought — and I think he was right — that it was very old-fashioned and naturalistic.

Though he had no influence at all on the Finnish theater I still think that this year in Finland was quite important. Not even *Puntila*, the most "Finnish" of his plays, was performed at that time.

It had to be altered into a naturalistic direction by his Finnish co-writer, Hella Wuolijoki, before it was accepted on a Finnish stage. That happened in 1945, after the war.

The first period of playing Brecht in Finland came in the beginning of the 1950s, when some of his big plays were performed — *Mother Courage, The Caucasian Chalk Circle* among others. The real breakthrough came in the middle of the 1960s. From 1965 to 1980 the influence of Brecht on Finnish theatrical life was important on many different levels:

1. His plays were performed in many theaters. Young Finnish theater practitioners went to Berlin, saw his performances and tried to realize their experiences in the Finnish theater. Finland had a lot of cooperation with the German Democratic Republic; we had many guest directors from the GDR. In this period almost all of Brecht's plays were performed, from *Mahagonny* and the plays of the 1920s to *Galileo* and *Turandot*.

2. The second level of Brecht's influence was in theater education. he cooperation with the GDR was important because we had many teachers with experience of the Brechtian methods working in the Finnish theater schools. Finnish acting instruction was at this time strongly influenced by Brecht.

3. The third level was the introduction of Brechtian methods — in many ways as important as the introduction of his plays. I myself was introduced to the Brechtian theater for the first time when I was studying in Germany in 1956-57 and I was so impressed by the quality of the performances in the Berliner Ensemble that when I started directing in 1958, I couldn't think of directing a Brecht play, because I found the models I had seen so outstanding, so marvelous. It was 1965 before I felt ready, but like many others I used the Brechtian methods on other playwrights, on Chekhov, Büchner, Shakespeare, and others. The method of reading, of analyzing plays, even the method of analyzing reality, was probably the most important thing we learned from Brecht, and I think that has remained the situation, when the plays of Brecht are not so frequently performed, as is the case today, for example. There are still people making Brechtian theater because they use his methods.

Brecht had less influence on the work of Finnish playwrights. The most significant "Brechtian" Finnish play is perhaps the *Lapualaisooppera* (*The Lapua Opera*), a play dealing with the Finnish Fascist movement in the 1930s and partly modelled after *The Threepenny Opera*. It had its first performance in 1968 and became one of the biggest theater successes in postwar Finland. That is one of a few examples where Brecht has influenced play writing in Finland. But Finland is in no exceptional situation in this case. It is obvious how little playwrights all over the world have been able to use the working methods of the playwright Brecht and go further with his advances. I think that is a topic we should discuss later on in this seminar.

4. One more important level in Brecht's influence was the Brechtian "song." The "song movement," that of the political song, was very popular, and the use of Brecht for this concept was very important. Few young people in our country had not sung some of the Brecht songs by the end of the 1960s and the beginning of the 1970s. They were like folk songs of our own. Mainly political songs, like the "Solidarity Song", but not only political songs. A lot of his poems were translated and the music used was not always the original music of the Brecht songs. We had many composers writing in the manner of Eisler and Weill — the most important of them probably was Kaj Chydenius, the composer of *The Lapua Opera*. I think he has written hundreds of songs in a Brechtian manner, and he and the KOM theater, where he worked, played a central part in the whole song movement.

And now I turn the situation today. In the period 1965-80 the political theater had a strong position and Brecht was its main inspiration. Then came a new situation with a clear regression. The political theater lost its position, new political ideas came in, the interest of the theater was not in society any more, but in the individual. Brecht almost disappeared from the theatrical repertory. From 1985 on I can remember only five Brecht performances in Finnish theaters — one *Baal*, *Mother Courage*, *Happy End* (for which Brecht only wrote the songs), one *Galileo*, and last summer (1991) a performance of *The Caucasian Chalk Circle*. I cannot state that this list is complete, but it is a fact that Brecht has been played very little in the last ten years in a country where he used to be one of the big names on the repertory lists.

It is rather surprising then, that in the last years we have produced two important books on Brecht. In 1991 came a great volume of Brecht's theoretical writings on the theater — a translation of *Schriften zum Theater* — fifteen years too late; I wrote the foreword. And this year came the first Brecht biography written in Finnish, by Kalevi Haikara. Perhaps this is a sign of change. It seems that we now have a chance to start using Brecht again, but we probably have to learn to use him in a new way. We have to read him in a new way, we have to change the "too-classical" Brecht tradition. But with today's economical and political situation in Europe it seems that it is not going to be difficult to play Brecht in a few years.

Outside Europe, in Asia, in Africa, in Latin America Brecht's influence has been constantly growing. In these parts of the world he is still an active playwright. Why? Because they have a situation, where they can use the themes of Brecht, that's the reason. In Europe we today have to put the question: How should we start to use him again? I do not know if Brecht would pretend to being a universal playwright, like Shakespeare, Molière, Chekhov. I think he has been universal in a special way, a very controversial universality. And he cannot be used without being controversial. There are people who are suggesting that a way to make Brecht usable again is to make him non-political. I think that is nonsense. We must do him as a political playwright, but we do not have to do him in an orthodox political way, as if he is still in the situation of the 1950s. We must see him with today's eyes, use him for today. But how? I think there have been several attempts. One has been to go to his youthful plays, saying they provide the answer. I think it is one way, but it is not the only way.

Another attempt is to make Brecht "poetic," to say that he is not political, but just poetic. I think it is a big mistake. He is always poetic, but it is always connected to content; he is not poetic for its own sake. Another idea is to go back to his *Lehrstücke*, his didactic plays. I do not believe this is a solution for Brecht as a whole. If we cannot apply our methods to his "big plays" we cannot use Brecht at all. We cannot just take one part or another and say: *this* is Brecht. We must see him as a totality. If we cannot use the big plays, for example, we do not have the solution for using him.

I think we must always accept that after 1926 Brecht, in his writing, his theories and in his theatrical praxis, worked with Marxist theories as a starting point for his work. Can that be taken away? No. I do not believe that we can find a Brecht for the future without accepting the methods he introduced. It means that if we state that Marxism is dead and we cannot use Marxist analysis at all, then Brecht is dead, too. That does not mean that we should blame Brecht for all "Marxist mistakes," for Ceaucescu, for what happened in the Soviet Union or the GDR; he was very critical of most of orthodox communism. We should not blame him for all that happened, but go back to his starting point — criticism of a society with a method based on the use of Marxist dialectics. If we leave this out, we are killing Brecht. But we have to avoid political and

Marxist orthodoxy: a Brecht used as a religion, a wrong religion, even in aesthetics.

For those who like me had their first experiences of Brecht's theater in the 1950s and the 1960s, the most striking thing was its "total" theater aspect, where all parts — text, acting, staging, music — formed a totality. We are in a new situation today. We have to ask: what of this can still be used? We cannot go back, we cannot be progressive by staging *The Threepenny Opera* in the way Brecht did it in 1928 or by trying to stage *The Caucasian Chalk Circle* as a copy of the Berliner Ensemble performance of 1953. We must apply to Brecht the method he used on other playwrights, namely to see how and where we can use him as raw material, as he proposes in *The Messingkauf Dialogues*. His method of using materials and reorganizing them must be used on Brecht himself.

I would now like to turn to the problem of using text for music. It is not only a question of what the audience is hearing, it is a question of what the actors, the singers are understanding. If an actor finds the gestus through the language, an audience can understand the acting without hearing a text fully. But if even the actor or singer does not understand what he is singing — if it is in a foreign language for him — where he cannot find the gestus, the audience will understand nothing. I think that in the Brecht songs you really have to find the gestus of the texts to be able to sing them.

I would like to give a practical example. Working on *The Good Person of Szechwan* with the song of "St. Nimmerleinstag," the actor playing Sun could not understand the reality of the text. The title was already a problem — it is very difficult to translate. To find a gestus we had to go to the original German text. After working with that, we could go back to the translation. The gestus was not translated, only the words.

In opera the situation is frequently the same. The singers sing in Italian or other foreign languages, but they do not really "understand" what they are singing, they are only singing words and vowels, high notes and low notes: they have no body in their singing. There cannot be body if you have no meaning. For singing Brecht songs this is terrible, just words and notes.

The Berliner Ensemble mounted a production of *Mahagonny*, I think at the end of the sixties, "The Little Mahagonny," which is not the same as the *Mahagonny Songspiel*. It is a version made exclusively for the Ensemble, and no one got the permission to perform it after that. It was a wonderful production, using the cabaret side of the Weill music, one of the best performances I ever saw by the Berliner Ensemble. That was an example of using the text and music in quite another way. I have myself directed the work in Helsinki and I really think that it is a mixture of two styles, which are very difficult to combine. You cannot do it with actors, the music as a whole is too difficult, and you cannot do it with opera singers, because they cannot sing the songs. To speak frankly, there is a lot of dreadful music in between. I think that the concentrated version made by the Berliner Ensemble at that time was marvelous. I think here we touch on one of the problems we have already been discussing in connection with *Mahagonny*: the big difference between hearing the actors of the Berliner Ensemble sing *Mahagonny* and hearing opera singers sing it. You cannot hear what the opera singers are singing because of their way of using their voices.

4   In the songs there is always the problem of translation. It is difficult to write good poetry if you are bound to music written for another language. The music for the Brecht songs is written for the German language and every language which is not very close to German makes translation difficult. You have to make big compromises in order to use the music. I think it is a very bad solution that many Brecht plays for copyright reasons are connected with an "obligatory" music: by Weill, Eisler, Dessau.

One example is *The Caucasian Chalk Circle* with the music of Dessau, which I think was a mistake from the very beginning. The music in the play is supposed to be played by the ensemble of one of the Kolchozes, and Brecht thought it should be a "small" music. But Dessau started to write. He wrote and he wrote, and the music grew bigger and bigger. He invented new instruments and at the end he made a music which is almost impossible to use. I think Dessau's music is one reason that *The Caucasian Chalk Circle* is not performed as much as it should be. I think that Brecht made a bad decision by tying his plays in this copyrighted way to a special music. It is not a question of the music being good or bad, it is just that this music many times prevents the use of Brecht's plays. And the holders of his copyrights have been very rigid. At least in Europe.

* * * * * * * *

Staying Ahead of Brecht

Paul Binnerts

There are many reasons to take Brecht seriously today. But even before the Berlin Wall came down in 1989, I was puzzled by most of what are considered to be his major plays: *Mother Courage, Galileo, Puntila, The Good Person of Szechwan,* and *The Caucasian Chalk Circle.* At the same time I kept being attracted to them, especially since I had directed quite a few of his plays: almost all his *Lehrstücke,* but also *Saint Joan of the Stockyards, The Threepenny Opera, Drums in the Night,* and *Man equals Man.*

Brecht's plays are beautifully written and full of surprises. They are of a dramaturgical concept different from most modern plays, with unexpected plots and unusual story lines. They are witty, sharp, satirical, poetical, and in general have a very powerful and imaginative language. Above all his plays are highly political. In the late sixties I discovered Brecht as a young scholar. In the seventies and the eighties I worked with his plays as a director. Committing myself to social and political change, I found in his plays what I was looking for: not so much the ways and means to bring that social change about but a way of looking at the mechanisms in society that made this wish so urgent. Brecht called this way of thinking, of analyzing the problems of the world "the great (dialectical) method."

Later, when society changed, when many of us became disappointed, and when we all became more realistic about our ideals, I still was attracted to Brecht's plays. Wasn't he asking questions without providing the answers? Didn't he show the dilemmas, paradoxes and contradictions of people who try to live under the general rule of capitalist society? Didn't he reveal the greater impersonal mechanisms of that society and the smaller personal mechanisms of human behavior and human relations? The only problem was, and still is, that the questions Brecht asked in his plays, the paradoxes and contradictions he showed, the mechanisms he revealed, however true or relevant, always seemed to be a little too explicit, a little too explanatory, a little too obvious. Some would say: a little too didactic. Others would say: a little too preoccupied with the unstated but implied answers pointing towards another form of society, towards communism. Leaving the preoccupation of this last opinion for what it is, the fact is that now the idea of communism has died. Having seen the failures and deadly mistakes of communism, many of us feel ashamed and embarrassed. The reading of Brecht's plays causes, understandably, an uneasy feeling. They still are beautifully written, witty, and poetical. And they still ask relevant questions for a society that appears to be more capitalistic than ever. But we know that the unstated yet implied answers are not the right answers. That is why it is so difficult to put on any of Brecht's plays today. Now in 1994, we are stuck. And not only with Brecht.

In 1974 I started to work with a combined group of West German actors, dramaturgs, drama teachers, and one musician. They had committed themselves to the political education of young apprentices who attended the theater courses they organized for that purpose, a very common thing in those days. It was their aim to make their "worker-students" conscious of who they were, the dilemmas, paradoxes, and contradictions in their daily lives, at work, and at home. They did that through play. By acting out scenes of their lives, they hoped to articulate the problems with which these youngsters were confronted and to make them better prepared for them. After a while they found out that they never got more out of these courses than the confirmation of what they and the youngsters already knew. They also found that this had to do with the dramatic and theatrical forms through which they acted out their problems. Since verbal improvisation and role play were the main ways of expression, the results came very close to what we know as realism. They had a lot of fun, but nobody became wiser or, for that matter, more conscious about his situation than he already was. Nobody "learned" anything.

In search of the answer to this problem, the group of theater makers and drama teachers hit upon Brecht. More specifically they found his *Lehrstücke* and the theory that goes along with them. These small plays not only seemed to provide the right material for "political and social education" but also the right form. It was Reiner Steinweg who put them on the right track. In an article in the political magazine *Alternative* (no. 78/79, 1971) and in his dissertation (*Das Lehrstück*, 1972) he pointed out that the word "Lehrstück" had long been misinterpreted. It did not mean "teaching" but "learning." One could also say that Brecht used the wrong word: it should have been "Lernstück." According to Brecht himself, who did not say too much about the *Lehrstücke* in his theoretical work, these plays were not meant to be a learning experience for an audience but for the makers themselves. In that sense they were to be understood as *educational* plays rather than as *didactic* plays. He also said that these plays therefore did not really need an audience. He designed them for special groups of people, for those who worked in the big institutions of our time: for Party members (i.e. the Communist Party), for trade union members, radio workers, for engineers, for students etc. The plays should function as sociological models. As in a laboratory, attitudes (*Haltungen*) and "gests" (*Gestus*) as found in reality should be investigated, tried out, imitated, and applied to the play, in order to define the position or the changing positions of the characters. By using one's own body, one's own voice and ability to express oneself, the expectation was that the participants in such a learning process would learn about themselves and their own position in society, about the dilemmas, the paradoxes and contradictions they lived in. The use of the "V-effect," though, was indispensable, Brecht said. Which meant that although no audience was required for these plays, we still had to see them as theater.

Trying to find an answer for themselves and to apply Steinweg's new interpretation of the *Lehrstücke*, the German group started in 1972 to work on *The Measures Taken*. A little earlier I myself started to work on the same play with a group of students of the directors' and drama teachers' department of the Amsterdam Theater School. In a later phase of the work we asked composer Louis Andriessen to join us. I wanted to use the *Lehrstücke* in order to find out about the practical and theoretical meaning of Brecht's work. I wanted to know how far the content and form of his plays were still valuable and actual for theater makers and audiences of that time and how we could use them. This meant that we also had to investigate the role of theater in society and our position as (future) theater makers. I chose this play because in my eyes *The Measures Taken* was the most complete one.

The play has been called "the only communist tragedy ever written," which is not only a gross exaggeration but also a misjudgment. Another common misjudgment of the play is that it is about rigid party discipline. Since Brecht's plays were political, they caused a lot of dispute and political controversy. There is no dispute about the central theme in this play however, which is also the main question in Brecht's work throughout: *how to do the right thing, how to be good*. The controversy is about what sort of good and what sort of bad, showing only that these are not objective categories. In this case there is the Young Comrade who wants to do the right thing in terms of social justice, but who does the wrong thing in terms of party strategies. The Four Agitators do not know whether they did the right thing by killing him for endangering the revolution, whereas those who should know, represented by the Control Choir (which is the Central Committee of the Party, or more specifically the Executive Board of the Comintern), are not really

interested in right or wrong, as long as the revolution "marches."
That is not of great help if you have a life-and-death problem.

In its dramaturgical form the play is very clear. The action takes
place on two levels: the justification of the actions of the Four
Agitators to the Control Choir and their actual revolutionary actions
in China. Because of this the play has a clear demonstrative and
exemplary character. Between the scenes through which the Four
Agitators show the Control Choir what has happened, there are
songs that comment on these things. They give the actions a more
general political-philosophical meaning and they show the quite
opinionated standpoint of the Control Choir. *The Measures Taken*
is not a political tragedy; on the contrary, the play shows in an
exemplary way different sorts of revolutionary behavior.

Fortunately, working on it we found out more about the theater
of Brecht and how he might have intended it than about how we
could become "real revolutionaries." However, it did raise our
political and social consciousness. After a long and thorough
structural analysis of the text (which also implied a historical study
of background information), trying to find words (literally verbs and
adjectives) for the dramatic action of the characters in the play, their
motives and intentions in each scene, and most of all the way they
expressed themselves (their "attitudes" or *Haltungen*), in order to
define the *Grundgestus* of the scenes and the play as a whole, we
found ourselves at a loss when we tried to act out our findings on
the stage. At that time we simply did not have the acting technique
to play and "demonstrate" instead of to play and "be the character."
In other words, this technique, as we found out, was not available.
Not in the current theater practice nor in the school where I was
teaching and the students were taught. What was taught was
basically an interpretation of Stanislavsky's psychological realism. So
when we started to play, even after we read about the "sociological
experiment" Steinweg was writing about, we started to improvise in
a traditional manner (putting the scenes in our own words) and
arranging the space by making some sort of mise-en-scene. Soon we
found that everything we did was random and interchangeable. We
stayed far behind our interpretation of the play, we could not make
it visible. As Brecht demanded, we changed roles continuously, but
we still walked around like blind horses in a treadmill. When we
tried to speak the text in a rhythmical manner, or when we created
a pattern of steps on the stage, forward, backward, sideways, it was
just an empty form. What we needed was a stylistic principle, an
aesthetic principle for the form the play should take on stage, which
also included a style of acting. The key for this stylistic principle
had to be found in the play itself. It was evident that we had to find

this in the *Grundgestus* of the play. This was: "the reality of revolutionary action is the yardstick of revolutionary change (and not the theory about it)." This is the lesson the Control Choir learns from the Four Agitators (and a severe criticism on Brecht's part of the dogmatic and dictatorial Marxist-Leninist party line, for that matter). Therefore the Four Agitators and the Control Choir were the main characters and not the Young Comrade, who is only used as an "example."

For this reason we decided that the play should take the form of a lesson. This was appropriate because of the context in which we carried out our experiments. It was logical, then, that we chose the classroom as our theatrical space. Everything in that classroom could be used to make our point. We only added a piano for the music (which in a theater school is a normal presence in a classroom) and a long piece of rope as the only prop. Within the context of the lesson though, every scene demanded its own style and form. At the basis was the idea that the Agitators demonstrated to the Control Choir what happened in Mukden and how it came that they had to kill the Young Comrade. This meant that they had to "quote" the situations they acted out, rather than playing them by fully identifying themselves with the characters. Thus they became "reporters," who told their story to the Control Choir, which in its turn sang revolutionary songs, rather than playing the full burden of the Central Committee of the party. The Agitators told their stories about the things that happened, by introducing and describing the general situation and by acting out the crucial moments in which they could show what the Young Comrade did, why it was wrong, and how they tried to remedy his faults. Since they made this distinction openly they did what Brecht requires: they "showed that they showed."

The actors did this, of course, through the text but also with clear attitudes (*Haltungen*) and gests, including the emotions that go along with the story. But these attitudes, gestures, and emotions were "quoted," just like the different theatrical forms we used. This created the "distance" between the actor and his role that Brecht demands for the epic theater, as he describes in his famous "Street Scene" in the *Messingkauf*. By doing so we could refrain from realistic impersonation and scenery. We could even refrain from using masks for the Agitators, otherwise maybe a useful V-effect. It was enough that they demonstrated the situation in which it became clear that they had to make themselves invisible, in order to carry out their revolutionary tasks. The reality of the play always remained the relationship between the Agitators and the Choir. The greatest discovery was, that we did not really need an actor who played the

Young Comrade. He was always played by one of the Four Agitators. The Agitators were only four when they were talking with the Control Choir, but they were never four in the demonstrated scenes. Through the device of role-changing everyone played the Young Comrade. The role-changing took place from scene to scene and every time the actor who introduced the scene would also play the Young Comrade, and told the audience this. Furthermore we made two versions of the performance, so that the other three participants who did the Choir in one version could play the scenes in the other. In this way everybody had a chance to play the Agitators and the Young Comrade (and to sing in the Choir). Through this role-changing principle we really created a possibility to "imitate" each other: what we had found in terms of "attitudes" and gests, emotions and movements in space all had to be copied, so that everybody would go through this experience and understand it. Since we were quoting "historical images" anyway, everyone could fill it with his or her very own intensity of expression. The "signals" were the same, but the intensity of expression was different for every actor.

There is much more to say about this very intense working process: about the solutions we found in terms of theatrical style for every single scene; about the acting; about the use of the music; about the effect on the previously selected small audiences; about the effect on ourselves. But since it was the first time I carried out an experiment like this, it is perhaps better to point out that we also made many mistakes. I now wish for instance that when we found that the Agitators were "reporters" who told a story, we would also have been able to apply this device to the actors themselves. We considered the possibility but we found it too explicit and explanatory to present ourselves as "students of the theater school." Everybody knew what we were anyway. We did not understand yet that this would not be a role we would play but a reality, just as the classroom was reality. We thought wrongly, that we had to do something extra for it, in terms of acting, whereas we only had to *be there* as who we were. It was some time later that I found out that this would have enabled us to create not only a distance between the Agitators reporting to the Control Choir but also between the actors and the roles of Agitators and Choir. This distance would have taken away the relative rigidity of the performance and would have enabled us to look critically at the Agitators, just as we did at the Young Comrade and the Choir. Now I realize that our lack of experience and the time in which we lived prevented that. After all, we admired Che Guevara, who told about similar situations during the revolution in Cuba, and we were on the side of the Agitators.

The next step I took to understand Brecht better was my cooperation with the German group of drama teachers and theater makers I mentioned above. Working on *The Measures Taken* and later on *The Exception and the Rule*, they had come across the same problems as I had met with my students. They had a brilliant understanding of the text, but as soon as they started to try things out on the stage, they stayed far behind their own interpretation. Worse, they could not make it visible. Following Brecht's and Steinweg's instructions for empathy (*Einfühlung*), they produced untraceable "private" expressions, which they could not imitate or copy from each other, except into the ridiculous. They found that by doing so, they *denounced* the Young Comrade in *The Measures Taken* and the Coolie in *The Exception and the Rule*, instead of seriously investigating their behavior. The first outcome of their work was psychological realism and parody, exactly what they had accomplished with their young apprentices. Like us in our project in Amsterdam, they lacked the acting and theatrical technique to meet Brecht's demands. Like us they were running around like blind horses in a treadmill.

When we started to work together, in 1974, the first thing we did was to make a thorough structural analysis of *The Exception and the Rule*, which included the analysis of the dramatic action of the play and the form of the play as it was written. This constituted what I called the *dramatic metaphor* of the play. It was the most extreme situation of a Merchant, a Guide and a Coolie traveling through a desert in order to get an oil concession. In these bare circumstances their relationships are stripped to the bone, which enabled Brecht to tell his story about the basic capitalist relationship between employer (i.e. exploiter) and employee (i.e. exploited) showing their *mutual dependency*, which is the *Grundgestus* of the play. Added to this is an ending which shows the justification of this relationship by means of a court session.

This strong dramatic metaphor needed an equally extreme theatrical metaphor and stylistic principle for the acting, in order to avoid showing something everybody already knew. This play does not want to show how *bad* the Merchant is, nor how *stupid* and *pitiful* the Coolie, nor how *clever* and *biased* the Judge; it wants to show the "class character" of these relationships, on the basis of which a change would be conceivable. The Coolie is not just a weak character in the play, a loser who does not understand his own situation and therefore becomes a victim. On the contrary, he is aware of it and tries to use the Merchant for his own purposes, which is to survive under the given circumstances. He tries to use the givens of the situation, knowing that he has no power and that the Merchant does. In a way, at least for the sake of the demonstration, the Merchant needs the Coolie just as much as the Coolie needs the Merchant.

Because of the totally unrealistic conditions of the trip through the desert, we had to look for an equally unrealistic, purely theatrical metaphor. It was in the classical "clowning principle" that we found the theatrical equivalent of the almost primitive master-servant relationship of the play. In our research we watched Fellini's film *Clowns* several times and were confirmed in our assumption that the classical white clown is the authoritarian master and the *Dumme August*, the clown with the red nose, is the servant, and that in order to do their acts in the circus, they need each other. They are as fully dependent on each other as the Merchant and the Coolie. We also came across the clown without a mask, the "mediator," who represents the middle class. That is where the Guide fitted in. Finally we found the *Sprechstallmeister*, the Master of Ceremonies, who announces the numbers and is often teased by all the clowns, who at the same time are afraid of him, because he is everybody's boss. With these clowns we finally had found something that really was theatrical, that seemed to fit, could be funny (if we were good enough) and at the same time could be the acting vehicle par excellence for "attitudes" and gests. First we tried to make the characters of the play into clowns. We worked on gags, on timing, on ways of walking, gestures, ways of talking, and even tics. Then we turned to the text itself and looked for the mutual dependency of the characters. Between every change of initiative, from one character to the other, we looked for the "hinge." At these moments a gag would be played out that in the previous action would have been prepared or just come out of the blue. Thus we found "long burns" and "short burns" (surprise gags), for which the text proved to be extremely helpful. It was as if the play was written with this theatrical principle in mind. We did not have to leave out or change a single word. The final result was a wild and funny spectacle. At the end there was a court scene as anarchistic and absurd as in a Marx Brothers movie, with the Master of Ceremonies as Judge. We built a circus ring, used Felliniesque costumes, and the musician, as a musical clown, took care of the songs. Most important, we made it perfectly clear that the Coolie was not just a pitiful victim but a clever (and funny) guy who understood his situation very well and acted accordingly. It was evident that while he was being carried to his grave during a hilarious funeral procession, he cried over his own death and that during the court scene he played his own widow. He only had to add a lot of water to his performance and to put two balloons under his dress.

The clowning principle did not allow the actors yet to present themselves as who they were, but it enabled them to make a direct contact with the audience. They were acting out a story, which the audience watched with "cheerful astonishment and curiosity." *How* these clowns were doing their tricks became at least just as important as the text that led to them, with which we met another one of Brecht's devices for the epic theater. By using the clowning principle we also found out what Brecht had meant with his famous "V-effect": it is every theatrical device that will make "normal things" "look strange" (*fremd*).

We suddenly understood that Brecht's own plays could be ruined by the wrong assumption that he himself already had provided the V-effect in his texts. We saw this at the celebrated Berliner Schaubühne, which performed *The Exception and the Rule* at the same time as we made our investigations into that play. Within the context of a symbolically reproduced desert, the acting was throughout realistic and did not add anything to what we already knew. In the former GDR, on the other hand, we saw that the songs, the titles, the half-curtain, all the usual attributes for the V-effect of the Brechtian theater, and most of all the codified gestures and attitudes of Brechtian acting, which were copied from the *Modell-Buch*, had gradually turned into mannerisms without meaning and effect. The conclusion was clear: one had and still has to invent one's own V-effects, according to the interpretation of the play itself and the theatrical metaphors one wants to apply, in order to make the interpretation work.

This experiment with *The Exception and the Rule* was followed by many others. I went on experimenting with plays by Brecht and other playwrights: Euripides, Shakespeare, Molière, Pirandello, and Büchner. I found out that the same principles for the theatrical form (the stylistic principle) and the method of acting could be applied to any play by any author. It was a way of approaching theater in general. In the course of this work as a director I discovered much about the traditional ways of acting as opposed to the Brechtian way. I understood that in search of the truth on stage, the imitation of reality through psychological realism or naturalism leads to what Brecht called the "deadly fate" of many a character. An audience can "consume" this as if it is tasting a "culinary specialty," without really being affected by it. It makes the audience lazy and the actor all too easy-going. By using theatrical metaphors, I learned what it meant not to create the "illusion of reality," but quite the contrary, the "reality of the illusion," which means that it is the actor who creates, knowingly and openly, the illusion on stage. It is he who creates the images. It also means that the only reality is that of the stage, the actor on it and the audience in front of it. Actors can create any illusion they like within the limits of the interpretation of the play and the chosen stylistic principle, leaving the text intact. By putting the actor in the position of a story-teller, the actor had to "disclose" his actions to the audience as if he is just "demonstrating" or "quoting" from the play or trying out possibilities for interpretation. I also discovered that the proscenium arch of the traditional theater is an enormous obstacle. The "open space," as Peter Brook demanded, is really the only way to make visible that the actor creates the "reality of the illusion." It also enables him or her to communicate directly with the audience.

At last I was able to take the final step and to ask the actor to be on the stage as himself, looking freely into the audience, talking with them as it were (using the text of the play), going into any illusion we decided that he would create, using any possible theatrical form that we found fit, from exuberant to intimate, from comical to tragic, coming out of the illusion again, making the story of the play into a *personal* story he had to tell, *especially tonight to this audience*. This is the consciousness of the actor I had been looking for from the beginning. Many times I used existing plays for this way of acting, on other occasions I created my own plays, sometimes by adopting a novel for the stage, sometimes by improvising on themes by using literary material, poetry, documents, newspaper clippings etc. Since "telling a story" is the basis of the epic theater, I developed in the course of the years a training that gives the actor access to himself as the major tool he is using. He tells a story and, by acting and creating images, he makes theater of it.

This process is not simple. It demands a good deal of "deconditioning," before an actor is able to look at the audience in a relaxed and confident manner. It takes courage for an actor not to draw back behind the proscenium arch and admit openly that he is not the character but that he just plays him. The rewards are enormous though. The actor does not have to give up any of his talents or abilities. What he gains is that he can use his skills and talents without losing himself. The epic theater demands a clear form, but it also demands that the actor commands this form, of which he himself is a part. Epic theater is not a trick, it is a technique that demands a special state of mind of the actor. He needs an awareness about the position he is in when he acts and the possibilities he has. Thus the epic theater indeed changes the way theater is produced and therefore also the working relations in the theater. If the means of production are in this sense given into the hands of "those who really make it," the theater loses its hierarchical organizational structure, as many groups who broke away from the "system" have proven in the past. Perhaps it is the most "political" can ever be.

It is because of all these ideas, formulated in his big theoretical works and so often misunderstood, misinterpreted, and underestimated, that I still take Brecht seriously today. His concern was to make a theater that asks questions; not just to entertain, but also to make the audience think, to make the audience actively part of it, and finally, to give it back to those who make it. His importance lies in his ideas: how to make theater and communicate with it. The questions he asked in his own plays, the unstated but implied answers, might not be so relevant today. But if we still want to perform *Mother Courage* or *Puntila*, we must ask ourselves the same questions about content and form and ways of acting as he did in order to "stay ahead" of him. Playing Brecht is using him for the needs of the times.

* * * * * * * *

Brecht Today: An Australian Perspective

Robyn Archer

The picture for Brecht in Australia at present is a familiar one. The plays are very little performed, the poetry is not widely known, and the lyrics are a secondary adjunct to Kurt Weill's music, now better known in serious music circles. But the legacy of Bertolt Brecht's stage theory and methodology pervades everything we see on the stage: from opera to musicals, drama to cabaret, and I suspect, is invading the world of film and video too. I have a particularly good opportunity through my current roles as artistic director of the National Festival of Australian Theater and as a member of the Australia Council to observe widespread theatrical activity throughout the Australian continent, which is vast, isolated and diverse. I believe that there is only one planned production of a play by Brecht (*Mother Courage*) over the next twelve months.

In terms of actual texts by Brecht, the greatest exposure comes from those which have been set to music, and largely to music by

Kurt Weill. Weill's music has been undergoing a certain popularizing process within respectable music circles. *The Seven Deadly Sins* was performed two years ago with the Queensland Symphony Orchestra, and I am singing the work with the Adelaide Chamber Orchestra in May 1993. Such concerts normally tend to place Weill's music at the forefront, and scant attention is given to the texts. It is particularly easy for audiences if they are sung in German which is not a widely held second language in Australia. When such works are presented in the context of "high" music, they very often lose the very thing that made them so great — the marvelous contradiction of difficult gritty words with infectious melodious tunes and jazzy arrangements. Clearly the effect is not always lost. When I have the opportunity to perform these works, I always take up the original challenge — to sing the composer's music well, and to make the pungent contradictions of the texts as clear as possible.

As for other musical collaborators, Eisler's music is known, again with texts secondary, to the small coterie of specialized classical music people who are devoted to twentieth-century music. My feeling is that in the future staging of any of the plays, it will be more likely for theater companies to commission new musical settings rather than use those of Eisler, or of Dessau, who is almost completely unknown. In the concert world, I imagine that Weill will continue to be presented from time to time on the larger conservative stages, and Eisler on the smaller contemporary ones. Clearly some in those audiences *will* have an ear for the texts. As far as the plays are concerned, I believe that they are now relegated to the classification of "classics," and that as such, they will continue to move in and out of waves of fashion and favor as long as theater exists. At present the fashionable classics are Shakespeare, anything of the ancient Greeks, Molière, Chekhov and Ibsen, though these flavors tend to last only a few years, and it would not surprise me to see a resurgence of interest in Brecht as "classic" in the near future. Until then, the plays will be staged according to the individual desires of particular directors.

Australia is going through profound socio-political change. We are, by force of an economic situation and a rediscovered geographical situation, in the process of partition from our colonizers, and the talk of a Republic is now widespread. In that process there are many imperatives, economic and cultural, from the Federal government, to align ourselves with the Asian-Pacific rim, our immediate neighbors — and therein is perceived our main hope for economic stability in the future. At this kind of conference in Australia, for instance, it would be impossible to think of such a convocation without significant representation from Japan, Malaysia,

Indonesia, or the Philippines, and this comes from a long overdue understanding of our real place in the world. Such is the power of colonization, that it has taken us over two hundred years to realize that our nearest neighbor, Indonesia, is very close indeed, and has a population of 180 million people almost all of whom are Muslim — these are the kinds of things that Australia is now trying very hard to come to grips with, and they are the kinds of things which are destined to change the cultural profile of the country.

This preoccupation is naturally reflected in the theater, where a new kind of Australian performance medium is being forged from more physical/visual, and less verbal, elements. Though there are writers of drama in Australia, the real energy at present comes from a strange concoction of spectacle, movement, dance, circus, comedy, vaudeville, satire, cabaret — a kind of deliberate move away from what are perceived to be inherited European forms of the straight dramatic tradition. These new forms have much more in common with the collaborations in Paris earlier this century, when visual artists, choreographers, writers, and composers combined their talents to produce the most exciting work.

These forms are also testament to Brecht's enduring legacy of the freeing up of forms. Many of these new forms of Australian theater show all the signs of those popular entertainment forms which Brecht brought to the theater. And of course it is also true of these forms that they show their debt to Brecht in terms of staging, lighting, attitudes towards non-realism, and so on. And this is the universal legacy: that Brecht's revolutionary ideas, methods, and theories of theater practically govern our whole attitude towards the theater now. Precisely because of the kind of opening up that Brecht achieved, it is much easier for the new theatrical creators to draw from popular entertainment forms, from South East Asian music and pageants, from Japanese epic and dance forms.

In a way, Brecht's legacy is also that of "giving license" to anyone with ideas to express them in the most effective, popular, and non-realist ways they can. I would also venture to say that a lot of that theory and methodology are also starting to show up on film and video, where realism is starting to become passé, and there is a much greater tendency towards episodic, objective, V-effect kind of film-making, certainly in the avant garde, but also sneaking into the mainstream.

In terms of the material written by Brecht, opportunities can still be found — if not in larger theater companies, then in all kinds of other concert and cabaret formats. This requires the use of what Stuart Hood has called "cunning." I believe, along with John Willett, that it is possible to remain faithful to the original intentions of both author and composer, yet at the same time present the repertoire to a new audience in ways that make the material perfectly intelligible and accessible. In a concert tour I did earlier in 1992 in Australia, one of the solutions was to use those songs which are difficult for a contemporary audience, in juxtaposition with more familiar songs. In that way I was doing a concert where I was singing country and western music (yodelling and all), political Australian songs that I'd written myself, and some of the more difficult Brecht/Eisler songs, with success. Michael Morley and I did a concert in a packed pub in Tasmania, and as long as I hooked my audience with more familiar material I was then able to do the Hollywood Elegies in a pub, to an audience who listened, appreciated and understood. In this context, even the most difficult texts still seem to have enormous power. If you confine yourself to doing the songs straight, in a concert platform setting, then you run the risk of restricting your audience to a small group of specialists or serious music fans.

My experience of singing in translation at first in Australia, and then in the U.K. was that the audience would have preferred it in German so they could not understand what the words were saying. They had grown used to hearing a song like "Surabaya Johnny," and its seductive tune, and did not really want to hear the harshness of the text. It is an interesting contrast to the things we have been hearing about Bangladesh, for instance, where it would seem an absurdity for the audience not to understand the texts, and where there is a clear demand for translation to the local language. And yet when I came to this material considerably later than many of you, the music and text in German had already established themselves as something more akin to classical repertoire, with beautiful sounds and a classical approach to singing so it would sound lovely, but with little regard for meaning. So singing them in English came as something of a shock and an affront, because I suppose the audience had grown comfortable with the material as some romantic idea of Weimar. In many ways I think the repertoire is still in danger of being romanticized.

Once you have your audience, you have no problems selling them the material in the most uncompromising way — the songs remain the greatest performance challenge I know, and on those rare occasions when I manage to get both the notes and the words to my satisfaction, I know I am wielding a very powerful theatrical weapon. The trick these days is seducing that audience inside in the first place, and trying to ensure that they leave their romantic and nostalgic preconceptions at home.

* * * * * * * *

Bourges Resolution on the Copyright of Music to Brecht's Work

Dear———

Between 22-24 October I chaired a discussion at the Maison de la Culture in Bourges on the theme of "Brecht Aujourd'hui." There were some forty-five participants — theatre directors, actors, musicians, writers, adminstrators and teachers — from twenty-four different countries, who had been asked to speak spontaneously (without presenting formal papers) about Brecht's theatre and its role today, about his poetry and songs, and the impact of his work on film, TV and the other media.

This meeting and the associated performances had been organised by the city of Bourges and its twin-city Augsburg, with the aid of the International Theatre Institute (UNESCO) and the French Ministry of Culture. It was presided over by Bernard Dort.

On the last day it passed an unopposed resolution calling for the removal of a number of constraints on the performance of Brecht's plays and songs. This was expressed in general terms, and I am writing now to comment and explain them further.

The first constraint was the banning by the Brecht heirs of performances of the *Lehrstück, Die Maßnahme* (by Brecht and Hanns Eisler) over most, if not all, of the European continent. This masterly work was withdrawn in the 1950s by Brecht, with Eisler's agreement, when a Swedish theatre was planning to stage it on Cold War lines as an anti-communist piece. His pretext was that it was a didactic play, intended to teach the performers, and not to be played to an audience. Moreover, he said, every actor must have played all the parts, and also sung in the chorus.

Understandable as it was that Brecht should want no performances in the Cold War climate, his pretext was unconvincing. During the 1930s the play was performed to audiences, and there is no record (and little probability) of it ever having conformed to his new conditions. At the same time it was being staged in the United States with impunity in an anti-Communist sense without the permission of the Brechts and without Eisler's all-important music.

Today the old Cold War is over. Manfred Wekwerth has reported Brecht saying at the end of his life that *Die Maßnahme* was formally the most important of all his plays for the theatre of the future. The ban has been maintained for thirty-six years after its writer's death. Pirated productions without the music still seem to take place. Only in Britain has it been possible to stage the full work so as to communicate its power.

Hence the Bourges resolution says that the pretext for the ban cannot have any validity beyond the rigid and unthinking loyalty of the Brecht heirs. Legally, it seems, they can suppress one of Brecht's greatest works for so long as it remains in copyright. Morally and artistically their duty is to make it accessible now to those who have never heard anything like it.

The second constraint is due to the Kurt Weill Foundation, which maintains a watchdog-like attitude to any deviation from the key, pitch, tempo and orchestration prescribed by Weill in his lifetime, irrespective what degree of latitude he himself may have allowed in particular instances. Irksome as this strictness may be, it is legitimate under the rules of copyright. But this is not at all the case when the Foundation intervene to ban a spoken text. There is a speech in scene 9 of *The Threepenny Opera* which was added to Brecht's script (along with other passages) before its publication in 1931 as one of his plays, and this is regarded as unacceptable by the Foundation despite the fact that it has no music and is not even known to have been objected to by Weill.

To the National Theatre they called it a "Marxist diatribe" and ordered its omission. Later, when licensing the Banff/Toronto production of 1989, they put forward the new argument that because the speech was not included in the libretto published in 1928, it was not part of the Brecht-Weill work. That work however was not an opera, but a "play with music" which the dramatist(s) could add to as wanted; moreover the 1928 libretto lacked at least two songs and other material now integral to most productions. The National Theatre obeyed orders without querying the Weill Foundation's authority. Banff insisted on including the "diatribe" because it is rhetorically effective (if politically undisturbing). Later it mysteriously slipped out till the Brecht lawyer had it restored.

In fact, of course, the original scripts and drafts for *The Three-penny Opera* contain much good material which can be dramaturgically useful, and like other work by Brecht call out for cuts and changes to avoid the risk of boredom. The point here is that such cuts cannot be dictated by outsiders, particularly when the motive is so clearly a political one.

For to see the thrust of the Foundation's interference one has only to collate the pretended sanctity of the 1928 libretto with the growing myth of a great enmity between Weill and Brecht from 1930 on. This myth too is being promoted by some supporters of the Foundation who are anxious to dissociate the composer from his Marxist collaborator. But surely there is no longer all that much need to bother about being considered un-American; while the rehabilitation of Weill's Broadway works (as implied thirty-five years ago in *The Theatre of Bertolt Brecht*) should not mean belittling Brecht's musicaltheatrical contribution.

The third element in the Bourges resolution was the revelation by the director of an amateur company that in France there are only two Brecht plays that can be performed by such groups unless they have a professional director to speak for them. Those plays are *Fear and Misery of the Third Reich* and *Senora Carrar's Rifles* — the two Brecht works whose world premiere was given in Paris in 1937/38. However common or uncommon such restrictive measures actually are, the suggestion of them prompted the meeting to call for their removal.

I hope that the above will explain the meeting's concern that the work of Brecht and his collaborators should be liberated from its chains, whoever may be imposing them. Few of us seemed to feel that it is dying, but there was a general longing to see it given a new lease of life.

John Willett
Le Thil-Manneville,
76730 Bacqueville-en-Caux, 9 November 1992

Bertolt-Brecht-Erben; The Kurt Weill Foundation; SuhrkampVerlag; Editions de l'Arche; ITI (UNESCO); Universal-Edition (Vienna); Albrecht Dümling; Georg Eisler; Michael Gilbert; Michael Morley; ICB; PRS; Jerold Couture; Donald Mitchell; David Drew; Pierre Sallet; Albert Botbol; Bernard Dort; Ralf Långbacka; Ernst Schumacher; Paul Binnerts; the National Theatre; The Banff Centre.

Das Arena-Teater und die Brechtsche Tradition: Indonesisches *Grassroots*-Theater

Die meisten indonesischen Theatergruppen, die sich mit Brecht auseinandergesetzt haben, führten dessen Stücke in verschiedensten kontextualisierten Formen auf. Die Zentral-Javanische Gruppe, das Arena-Teater, unterscheidet sich von den anderen Gruppen dadurch, daß ihre Kenntnis Brechts nicht aus der direkten Bekanntschaft mit seinen Stücken oder seinen theoretischen Schriften herrührt, sondern vielmehr aus der Arbeit mit Schülern Brechts, wie Augusto Boal und dem *Philippine Educational Theater Association* (PETA). Die Weiterentwicklung des Arena-Teaters führte zu einem Nicht-Betonen der Bühnenaufführung für das städtische Publikum. Statt dessen konzentrierte man sich darauf, das Theater für die Bewuβtseinsvermittlung und Mobilisierung der Bevölkerung für *Grassroots*-Bewegungen zu nutzen. Die Inszenierungen und Werkstattgespräche des Arena-Teaters zeigen jedoch auch interessante Verbindungen sowohl zu Brecht wie auch zu anderen, bekannteren indonesischen Theatergruppen auf.

Arena Teater et la Tradition Brechtienne: le Théatre rural Indonesien.

Les troupes de théâtre indonésiennes qui ont représenté des pièces de Brecht l'ont généralement fait sous diverses formes contextualisées. La troupe du centre de Java, Arena Teater, se différencie de celles-ci car sa connaissance de Brecht ne provient pas directement de l' étude de ses pièces ou de ses textes théoriques, mais plutôt du travail d' autres auteurs inspirés de Brecht, tels que Augusto Boal et l'Association du Théâtre Educatif Philippin (PETA). Par ailleurs, l'évolution d'Arena l'a conduite a donner moins d'importance aux représentations destinées au public indonésien urbain, et à mettre au contraire l'accent sur l'utilisation du théâtre comme moyen de prise de conscience et de mobilisation des populations rurales. En définitive, les pièces et les ateliers d' Arena révèlent cependant des liens intéressants à la fois avec Brecht et avec d'autres troupes de théâtre se trouvant davantage dans la mouvance dominante.

Arena Teater y la tradición brechtiana: el teatro popular de Indonesia

La mayor parte de los grupos teatrales de Indonesia que están comprometidos con el teatro brechtiano, interpretan las obras teatrales de Bertolt Brecht de diversas formas contextualizadas. El grupo Central Javanese Arena Teater difiere de otros grupos debido a que su conocimiento de Brecht no proviene de una directa familiaridad con sus obras teatrales, ni se deriva tampoco de sus escritos teóricos, sino que por contra están influenciados por las versiones de otros grupos brechtianos tales como Augusto Boal y el Philippine Educational Theater Association (PETA). Además, pensando en una audiencia urbana indonesia, el desarrollo teatral de Arena hace desenfatizar la actuación en el escenario y lleva a concentrarse en un uso del teatro con un fin de *concienciación* y movilización popular. Por último, sin embargo, las obras y talleres teatrales de Arena destacan puntos de contacto con Brecht y también con otros grupos de la tendencia principal del teatro indonesio.

Arena Teater and the Brechtian Tradition: Indonesian Grassroots Theater

Michael Bodden

Brecht reception has a long history in Indonesia, a history of active response, reinterpretation, and recombination of Brechtian theater and ideas with local forms and projects. In this respect, the efforts of Arena Teater, based in the Central Javanese city of Yogyakarta, are similar to other Indonesian responses to Brecht's work. Yet the process by which Arena appropriates elements of a Brechtian theater for its own specific uses — for example, its 1986 play, *Tumbal*, and its grassroots theater projects of the 1980s and 1990s — is also radically different from the way in which most other groups in Indonesia come to terms with Brecht. Furthermore, one of the most fascinating aspects of Arena's relationship to Brecht is the fact that until very recently, it did not involve much direct knowledge of Brecht and his ideas. Rather, the members of Arena Teater selected elements of the work of several individuals and groups who had already appropriated features of Brechtian theater for their own practices (Augusto Boal, Ross Kidd, The Philippine Educational Theater Association), and combined them with Indonesian regional theater traditions and Freirian pedagogy in order to create a distinctive theater practice which addressed significant local needs for social change. Arena Teater's engagement with the Brechtian tradition is equally concerned with grassroots development strategies and initiatives, social and cultural democracy, and the mechanics of staging a performance.

In order to situate Arena properly as both similar to and different than other Indonesian appropriators of Brecht, a brief review of Indonesian Brecht reception will be helpful. Indonesian cultural workers had begun to be aware of Brecht's work by at least 1957,[1] although none of his plays were probably staged before 1967. And although Brecht's *Kleines Organon für das Theater* was translated into Indonesian in 1976 by Boen S. Oemarjati,[2] much of the recent Indonesian interest in Brecht has been devoted to staging his plays rather than to conceptual or theoretical discussion. Early productions centered around three scenes taken from *Furcht und Elend des Drittes Reiches*: "Informan" ("Der Spitzel"), "Mencari Keadilan"

Brecht Then and Now / Brecht damals und heute
Eds. Marc Silberman et al. *The Brecht Yearbook / Das Brecht-Jahrbuch*,
Volume 20 (Madison: The International Brecht Society, 1995)

("Rechtsfindung"), and "Isteri Yahudi" ("Die Jüdische Frau"). Several of the major figures of contemporary Indonesian theater mounted productions featuring one or more of these scenes, including Rendra (1967), Arifin C. Noer (1969), and the Padang, West Sumatra-based Wisran Hadi (early 1970s?).[3] The selection of these specific scenes from one of Brecht's most "realistic" plays suggests the concern of Indonesian cultural workers of the time with concepts of justice, ideological manipulation, and political coercion — problems which were felt to be acute during the waning years of the Sukarno era and which persisted and may have actually intensified, much to the alarm of many urban intellectuals hoping for democratic reform, under the new dispensation begun during the years 1966-67.[4]

Similar concerns contributed to a renewed interest in Brecht's work in the mid-1970s. First, increasing disillusionment with the lack of "democratization" under General Suharto's New Order government led many cultural workers to protest or make statements against what was perceived to be the brutal, materialistic path of development being pursued by government and economic leaders. In 1976 Teguh Karya's Teater Populer, under the direction of Slamet Rahardjo, performed Brecht's *Perempuan Pilihan Dewa* (*Der Gute Mensch von Sezuan*), a play whose central themes could certainly find resonances in the perceptions of Indonesian society held by dissident Indonesian intellectuals. Teater Populer attempted, according to one reviewer, to offer the play much as Brecht might have, with costumes, names, and props designed to distance the action from the audience.[5]

This effort, however, stood in contrast to the majority of Indonesian performances of Brecht from the seventies to the nineties. These latter performances drew on the widespread experimentation with traditional forms then in vogue. Such experimentation was mainly aimed at developing a modern, nationally-rooted, broadly communicative theater.[6] In addition, many cultural workers of the time felt a special need to make plays immediately relevant. Under such circumstances, a number of groups began to "indigenize" Brecht's plays stylistically and to adapt the scripts to fit local circumstances. I will mention only three representative examples here.

Rendra's 1976 staging of *Lingkaran Kapur Putih* (*Der kaukasische Kreidekreis*) is indicative of this trend. Though Rendra kept the original names of the characters in Brecht's play, the costumes were changed, and the scenes demonstrating Azdak's brand of justice referred exclusively to Indonesian circumstances. In addition, Rendra used the script to question the apparent unwillingness of the Indonesian Armed Forces to dialogue with dissident groups.[7] The same play was staged again in 1980 by the Surabaya-based Bengkel

Muda and Grup Teater Surabaya under the direction of Basuki Rachmat. Rachmat's production used a combination of folk theater forms, such as the East Javanese urban melodrama/comedy theater, *ludruk*, and the Central Javanese semi-historical theater, *ketoprak*, to bring the play's material closer to regional audiences. The performance on the Gajah Mada campus in Yogyakarta, Central Java, also included the improvisational use of local graffiti slogans which commented negatively on the government's attempts to neutralize campus political activities.[8]

One of the more controversial of contemporary stage directors, N. Riantiarno, who attained a high degree of commercial success in Jakarta with a style which combines elements of the Broadway musical, folk theater, and pointed social criticism, admits that in his own work, Brecht has also been a central source of study and appropriation.[9] In 1983, Riantiarno and his group, Teater Koma, staged an adaptation of Brecht's *Die Dreigroschenoper* (*Opera Ikan Asin* or "The Salted-Fish Opera"). This adaptation was set in a rundown section of Jakarta's rough Pasar Senen area during the colonial era, yet the production emphasized contemporary issues of government corruption, crony capitalism, and lack of human rights. Through slight alterations to the text, Riantiarno and his collaborators were able to provide a number of humorous allusions to local incidents of corruption and government coercion, and the play was enormously popular.[10]

In contrast to these appropriations of Brecht, which emphasized adapting his plays for local stage production, Arena's development led it to engage with more radical notions of theater as a tool for social change. Arena Teater was formed in the mid-sixties, initially staging European and American plays as well as Indonesian plays which corresponded roughly to notions of theatrical psychological realism. It, too, experimented with folk forms in the late 1960s and early 1970s much as other Indonesian groups of the times. In 1971 Arena affiliated itself with a Yogyakarta-based Catholic media production center, PUSKAT. This move gave Arena an institutional base, helped the group to crystallize its commitment to social activism, and provided access to equipment and funds that would eventually aid them in many of their projects.

At about this same time, the thinking of Arena's young leader, Fred Wibowo, and of other group members, was being stimulated by the rise of activist-oriented, non-government development organizations (NGOs).[11] Many of these organizations, involved in community development projects, criticized the Indonesian New Order government's development strategy, arguing that it was designed chiefly to satisfy the resource needs of Japan and the Western countries as well as the desire of the local Indonesian elite for luxury consumer items. Such policies, they felt, benefitted foreign corporations and a local alliance of military bureaucrats and their Chinese-Indonesian business partners. At the same time, the economic position of small-scale entrepreneurs eroded, as did that of the great majority of Indonesian peasants, who derived few benefits as extra state revenues were used to modernize the major urban areas.[12] National events caused Wibowo and his Arena/ PUSKAT colleagues to agree with the analysis put forward by the NGOs, and to sympathize with those left out of New Order development plans:

> After the Malari incident (1974 riots protesting perceived Japanese encroachment on the Indonesian economy) and the events of 1978 (student protests about government corruption which were met with rather severe repression), people within Arena began to feel that development wasn't really reaching a large part of the people. Arena works with Puskat, and they wanted to use their media for the people. As a voice for the people. The main impediment is that there is no means for horizontal communication. We are trying to become a means for creating solidarity in a certain sector. A media for the lower classes.[13]

Members of Arena and PUSKAT, which was headed by Father Rudi Hoffmann, a Swiss Jesuit, spent much of the late 1970s studying liberation theology and the works of radical educator, Paulo Freire, who advocated creating a more egalitarian, co-educational relationship between teacher and student. Freire's method was to begin the educational process with the students' own day-to-day experiences and codes for understanding the world. Such codes were then to be posed as a problem for the students. The method was aimed at helping peasants and others become more critically aware of the conditions of their own oppression as well as at giving them the self-confidence and analytical abilities that would enable them to become active participants in the struggle for their own "liberation."[14]

In 1979, Wibowo and several members of Arena Theater were invited to attend one of the Philippine Educational Theater Association's (PETA) summer workshops in the Philippines. During the period 1979-81, PETA was engaged, through its Asia Theater Forum Partnership program, in training cultural workers from South and Southeast Asia in the techniques of the grassroots theater which PETA and other Philippine groups had been developing for almost a decade.[15] Staging grassroots theater workshops, these Philippine groups helped peasants, workers, and students to develop and produce plays based on their own life experiences. Grounded in Freirian pedagogy, children's and improvisational theater techniques, and a Brechtian notion of the role of theater in educating people for social change[16], this approach used theater as a tool for creating community solidarity, for breaking the "culture of silence" so common to marginalized groups by drawing out people's stories of personal and social oppression, and for helping communities to analyze and organize against the conditions which allow those oppressions to exist. During the process, the participants' confidence and creativity are built and strengthened. In this kind of theater, the focus is not on an actor or director but on what PETA calls ATORS (artist-trainer-organizer-researcher), whose main role is to facilitate the process of others' cultural production, as well as their *conscientization* (awakening of one's critical consciousness).[17] The Indonesian participants of 1979 spent one month undergoing workshop training and then were sent to separate Philippine villages to immerse themselves in the daily lives of ordinary Filipinos, gather data, and create theater-related projects.[18]

At about the same time that Wibowo and the other Arena members returned from the Philippines, Father Hoffmann was also returning from a year in Latin America. While there, Hoffmann had participated in the founding of a Basic Christian Community in Colombia, and he had brought back books by Freire and the Brazilian theater activist and playwright, Augusto Boal, who had attempted to apply Freire's pedagogy to theater work.[19]

In his book, *Theatre of the Oppressed*, Boal attempts to outline the ways in which theater can be used to "conscientize" the poor and the oppressed by offering them a new "language" with which to express themselves that will at the same time help them discover new concepts.[20] Like Freire, Boal felt that the oppressed must take control of their own lives, become the agents of their own history. While drawing on the concepts of Brecht, Boal also attempts to go beyond what he sees as the limitations of Brecht's ideas and practice. In essence, Boal feels that Brecht distinguishes his theater from Aristotelian concepts of theater by creating a situation in which spectators do not completely yield their power to act and think about the character. In Brechtian theater, according to Boal, the spectator reserves the right to "think for himself, often in opposition to the character." This promotes the awakening of critical consciousness. Boal wants to create a kind of theater in which the spectator does not even delegate the power to act to the dramatic character, but instead becomes an active subject capable of transforming the dramatic action. Assuming the protagonistic role, the spectator changes the dramatic action, discusses plans for change, tries out

157

solutions. Boal sees this as training for real action, as "a rehearsal for revolution" (121-22).

Boal stresses furthermore that the grassroots theater he proposes, the "Theater of the Oppressed," should not show the "correct path," but rather offer "the means by which all possible paths may be examined" (141-142). Similarly, Boal suggests that grassroots "Theater of the Oppressed" practices should "create an uneasy sense of incompleteness that seeks fulfillment through real action" (142). These formulations certainly bring to mind Brecht's idea of a theater attuned to the "scientific age" in which all of a society's actions would be treated as "experiments" using the "great productive method," the critical approach. As outlined in *A Short Organum for the Theater* of 1948, Brecht hoped that he would eventually be able to construct this type of theater so that the new thoughts and feelings which it produced among the spectators might encourage them to transform the existing "historical field of human relations."[21] However, despite Brecht's pedagogical experiments with turning the audience into active learner/participants in his *Lehrstücke* of the 1928-33 period, his arguments in *A Short Organum for the Theater* do indeed posit an audience which is separated from, though responding critically to, the events on the stage. Boal is much more intent on using theater to prepare the performer/spectators for real action, while Brecht is primarily concerned with creating a radically new consciousness.

Building on the experiences and techniques brought back from the Philippines and beginning to incorporate slowly lessons from Freire and Boal, the Arena group constructed their own grassroots theater methodology over the course of the ensuing years, though it remained rather similar to that developed by PETA. As has been documented by van Erven, one of Arena's first grassroots projects was the use of theater in integrating previously shunned lepers of the Lewoleba colony in Lembata, Flores, into the surrounding community.[22] The success of the Lewoleba workshops of 1980 and 1983 gave Arena's facilitators the necessary experience and confidence to conceive of even more ambitious uses for their newly learned techniques.

In 1981, the year following the first Lewoleba workshop, Arena staged a weekend people's theater workshop for 150 participants, most of whom were students. By conducting the workshop in the rural, coastal area of Parangtritis, which was rapidly being developed as a national tourist site, Arena confronted the workshop participants with the impact of "development from above" on the people of an isolated rural area. Participants were required to undertake research into local conditions as a part of their training. At the end of the weekend, the attendees broke down into three groups and performed for the residents of the surrounding villages, who grasped their own problematic in the plays presented. Wibowo termed the event an "incredible success" based on the enthusiasm and dialogue which the workshop generated between participants and villagers. Yet, as he remarked, there remained the problem of follow-up: "The students returned to the city — what was needed was the participation of someone directly involved in the situation who could help make a movement.[23]

In 1983, Arena conducted another project, using Freirian pedagogical methods in combination with theater to help the residents of an impoverished Central Javanese village, Tanen Pakem, overcome a number of debilitating economic and political problems. Tanen Pakem's village cooperative was dysfunctional, its irrigation systems inadequate, its residents too poor to afford basic necessary tools, while local children were having great difficulties in school. Arena surveyed village residents concerning the fundamental aspects of their life and problems, carefully drawing out the villagers' own codes of understanding. In the next phase of the project, Arena members proposed that they should work together with the villagers to solve their problems. A referendum was held to determine the key issues. With Arena members facilitating the process, the villagers gradually came to a decision about how to tackle each problem. A contributing factor to the overall situation of the village was its neglect by the local village chief, the local government liaison official, who was influential in determining where government development money was channeled. With workshop training from Arena facilitators, village residents put on two plays addressing the situation. Both plays were based on traditional theater forms.

The play which the village adults produced told the story of a village suffering because of the inattention of an irresponsible *demang* or district administrator. The *demang* is primarily concerned with his own family's affairs, and he demands the villagers provide help in preparing for his daughter's wedding. The villagers refuse, insisting that they must first solve the problem of obtaining sufficient water supplies for their rice fields. The village youths then plan to form a cooperative to begin tackling their problems. In anger, the *demang* refuses to allow his daughter to marry the village youth whom she loves. She runs to him with the news, and the *demang's* men pursue her, initiating a fight with the villagers. Finally, the village elder brings the two sides together to talk things out and settle their problems peacefully, stressing that the *demang* has to be willing to listen to those living under his jurisdiction.[24]

The play obviously intended to criticize the current village chief, and Wibowo and the Arena facilitators had worried that he would try to stop the entire project.[25] The chief, who had been present, admitted after the show that he had been made more aware of existing problems, and he requested that similar workshops be held in the other villages under his jurisdiction. He seemed to realize, now, that dealing with the current problems successfully required the mobilization of — and a willingness to listen to — the ordinary people rather than a "top down," bureaucratic, centralistic approach. Inspired by their success with the performance, the villagers went on to solve the other problems in a variety of ways, using available resources and services. Throughout the process the villagers continued to make all the decisions themselves.[26]

A little over two years later Arena performed *Tumbal* (The Sacrificial Victim), an original play written by Fred Wibowo. If judged simply by the venue of the performance (the performing arts center of Gajah Mada University in the city of Yogyakarta) and the fact that the play was performed by a theater group for an urban middle-class audience whose members were not necessarily directly involved in the creation or the staging of the piece, *Tumbal* would seem to be more closely related to the kind of urban, elite-focused theater with which Arena had begun in the early sixties and which it had continued to perform even while pursuing the development of a grassroots theater practice. Yet a brief synopsis of the play indicates that *Tumbal* was closely linked to Arena's grassroots theater work both thematically and conceptually.

As the play opens, a number of angry peasants, carrying the dead body of a village youth, waylay a student and request that he preside as judge in a trial which they plan to hold in order to determine who is responsible for the youth's death. The student doubts that he is qualified, but the peasants respond by declaring:

JALI: This is the people's court, sir. Its judges are chosen by the highest authority in the country.
BOYING: Good God! Are all of you government officials charged with appointing judges?
OLA: What d'ya mean! In a democratic country, the highest authority is the people. And we here are the people.[27]

Thus *Tumbal* begins with a two-fold gesture. On the one hand, through the peasants' assertions the play attempts to give Indonesia's poor and disempowered their voice, their claim to a share of social power based on the government's own careful efforts to cultivate Indonesia's image as a "democratic country." On the other hand, the opening scene lays the groundwork for the play's courtroom frame, a frame in which the "people's" justice will be sought. The trial which follows will invite the audience to become judges: hearing the testimony of witnesses, weighing the evidence, listening to summary arguments.

Performed for an urban audience consisting mainly of intellectuals, students, and members of Indonesia's small but increasingly important middle class, *Tumbal* indeed suggests that such an audience must also become judges, must educate themselves about conditions of the rural peasants. To make the point doubly clear the ex-student is given a number of co-judges to help him reach a verdict: an academic, a businessman, a promoter, and a model. All profess a lack of time for such affairs, but are eventually shamed into participating by a village doctor who has become the peasants' spokesperson and advocate. They agree to hear the case after the doctor suggests that they are selfishly over-concerned with their own affairs while a large group of fellow citizens are in dire need of assistance.

The courtroom testimony relates the story of Wasa, a youth from an average Indonesian village who leaves his home for lack of economic opportunity. On his way to the big city the dilapidated bridge he must cross collapses, and he is thrown into the ravine below. The villagers attempt to save him, but at every turn their efforts are thwarted by a lack of necessary facilities: the only automobile in the village has no headlights, so their departure is delayed until the following morning; the bridge is impassable, and the resulting detour leads them over muddy and rutted roads; the phones in the nearest small town do not work, so an ambulance can not be summoned to meet them. By the time they finally arrive at a hospital in the capital, the village youth can no longer be saved.

Following this account, the heads of several government departments are called to give testimony. One after another they all deny responsibility for the lack of facilities in the village which has led to Wasa's death. Finally, two social researchers appear to help clarify the situation. Using statistical data, the two throw into sharp relief the "urban bias" of current national development programs. The villagers are forced to realize that the individual neglect of any particular functionary does not explain why the village is lacking in facilities, infrastructure and opportunities — the reason for Wasa's decision to leave and his death. Rather, the structure and logic of the entire social system is to blame. The play ends with a call for all Indonesians to recognize their responsibility to solve these pressing problems.

Tumbal is, of course, the product of a fundamental transformation the group was undergoing as it increasingly turned from the urban stage to grassroots theater. As such, it is closely connected to Arena's other projects, particularly to the Parangtritis workshop and the Tanen Pakem project. After all, the play's material is drawn predominantly from the conditions with which Wibowo and his co-workers became familiar in the course of their 1980s grassroots theater work. For example, just as in the Tanen Pakem project, issues such as the existence of bad or incompetent village chiefs, a lack of job opportunities forcing the out-migration of local youth to the cities, poor rural education facilities, corrupt cooperatives, broken machinery without means to repair it, and a lack of financial resources in general, all figure prominently in the action and arguments of *Tumbal*. Problems of tourism and the ideological hegemony of urban, capitalist, consumer culture, such as those encountered by workshop participants at Parangtritis, are also treated.

Even more crucial here is the fact that Wibowo and Arena attempted to duplicate some of the techniques of their grassroots theater and development projects in the play. Their strategy for accomplishing this was to implicate psychologically the members of their mostly middle-class, urban audience in the plot, thereby involving the audience in an emotionally direct way in a problem-posing, educational situation roughly similar to Freirian pedagogical methods. The problems posed — why is the village in such a dire situation? and who is responsible? — are presented within a framework in which several symbolic representatives of the majority of audience members are shamed, partly through an appeal to nationalism, into taking time to consider the problems of their fellow citizens — to sit as judges and thus to weigh the evidence. And, like Boal's notions of theater, *Tumbal* offers no specific solution to the problems it represents. It attempts to put forward evidence which defines the problems and leaves the construction of a solution to the audience.

The purpose of the performance is to engage the audience both viscerally and critically in the issues it presents with the hope that they will be moved to discuss these issues as well as to work to resolve them in the world outside the performance space. Such an orientation marks clearly the "Brechtian tradition" in theater as Arena found it in the works and writings of PETA, Boal, and the Canadian theater activist, Ross Kidd, with whom Wibowo began to correspond in the early 1980s.[28] Thus, though Wibowo stated in 1991 that he was only then beginning to read Brecht's plays and theories, well after the writing and staging of *Tumbal*, the play nonetheless contains several features which bear a striking similarity to those found in Brecht's dramas which indeed seem aimed at engaging the audience's critical consciousness and prompting them to act.

First and foremost among these is the courtroom frame, a device which appears repeatedly in Brecht's plays, particularly in *Lehrstücke* such as *Die Maßnahme* (1930) and *Die Ausnahme und die Regel* (1930), but also in his later works such as *Das Verhör des Lukullus* (1938-39) and *Der kaukasische Kreidekreis* (1943-45). The importance of the courtroom frame for both Brecht and Arena as well as for other appropriators of Brechtian notions lies, of course, in placing the performers and/or the audience in a position in which they may hear a number of different arguments and witness the presentation of various bits of evidence. The audience is urged to deliberate; it must weigh the evidence critically and ultimately decide the case.

Another technique that parallels Brechtian theater is the specific way in which the chorus of peasants defines the socially constructed personae of its members during the scene in which Wasa decides to leave the village.

MAYA: Why are conditions in our village so very different than those in the city?
WASA: I can't say. Perhaps some of our friends know?
THE WHOLE GROUP: (chorus)
   No, we don't know
   We're just ordinary farmers after all
   Loyal and obedient
   To the authorities
   We continue striving
   To cope with our fate
   Without too much resentment
   Though our suffering hasn't ended.[29]

The exchange continues through two more sets of question and response. The series of choral statements is reminiscent of two aspects of Brechtian theater. The terse summary of who the peasants are and how they fit into the social structure is very similar to the way in which characters introduce themselves in Brecht's *Die Massnahme*. Secondly, the way in which Maya and Wasa pose questions which the *Koor* then refute through argumentation resembles the debates involving choruses in *Das Badener Lehrstück vom Einverständnis* and *Die Massnahme*. In these plays by Brecht and in *Tumbal* these devices present characters and basic social situations in a spare, condensed, non-melodramatic form and facilitate a critical approach to the issues by modelling concise modes of argumentation.

Music is also used at least once in *Tumbal* in order to offer ironic commentary on the relationships between different characters. This is most evident in the scenes in which the government officials appear to testify. Each official's entrance is accompanied by a Javanese song, "Dayohe Teko" (A Guest Comes), which relates with bitter humor a poor family's embarrassment at having nothing to offer worthy guests who visit them. Every time an official enters, the existing power relations are thus underscored by a verse of the song which narrates the impoverished peasants' feelings of humiliation and social inferiority. A final similarity with Brechtian theater is the use of a screen and projected slides during both the recounting of Wasa's death and the final summation of Indonesia's rural development problems by the "experts." The use of such technology underscores the gap between theater and "reality," distancing the audience from too close an emotional identification with the characters in the play and inviting reflection on the relationship between the play and the world it attempts to problematize.

Yet for all this, Arena's play is quite different from those of Brecht. It draws on local theater forms such as *Ketoprak* for some of its sets and adapts the comic, clown-figure conventions of a number of Javanese stage genres from the classical shadow theater to the contemporary populist theater style *sampakan*. Such clowns usually represent the "common people" and have often been used to voice commentary and criticism relating to current conditions. Arena's clowns, however, are much more bitter than usual, their criticism sharper and more aimed at the need to change the system, than at the foibles of individual excess and the need for simple reform — the typical themes of traditional critical clowns. In addition, the Government Functionaries' Chorus in the closing scenes of the trial is reminiscent of Yogyakartan playwright Rendra's chorus in his most famous satirical play, *Kisah Perjuangan Suku Naga* (1974). Typically, and in marked contrast to Brecht's work, this chorus baldly parodies the parties it claims to represent on stage, allowing popular audiences to laugh at their oppressors. In *Tumbal* the chorus also involves moments of parody but has been altered slightly to allow the Functionaries to present a defense of their own position that is not completely specious or motivated solely by self-interest. As such, this chorus calls for a serious response from the village doctor and the experts testifying about government development priorities. Yet the Chorus is not allowed to respond in turn to this rebuttal of its arguments, thus awarding the "last word" in the debate to the critics of government policy.

These elements point to the importance of evolving local conventions of signification and social criticism in order to engage the audience's critical faculties and at the same time to channel its sympathies to certain characters and drive home some of the arguments presented. As such, they run counter to Brechtian practice which stresses distanciation. Along these same lines, the very setting for *Tumbal*'s action — contemporary Indonesia — and the final plea to the audience to help solve the concrete problems which the play has represented also help to distinguish the play from the dominant tendencies in Brecht's own work.

An instructive comparison can be made with two of Brecht's plays. *Das Badener Lehrstück von Einverständnis* literally gives the audience "marching orders" in its closing scene, which on the surface seems similar to the appeal to the audience in *Tumbal*. The chief difference is in the kind of appeal being made: Brecht's play is concerned with learning specific attitudes towards the self and the collective, and it urges the audience/performers to accept the idea of sacrificing ego in service to the group. The ending of *Tumbal* is designed, on the other hand, to prompt the audience to undertake a specific strategic task — solving the inequities of New Order development policy. Only one of Brecht's plays, *Die Mutter*, approximates this kind of orientation through its combination of experimental techniques, designed to engage and develop the audience's critical consciousness, with an attempt to channel the audience's emotions into general action on a particular social problem. *Tumbal*, on the other hand, is not an isolated example that presents issues of immediate relevance to its society. Such a choice, indeed, demonstrates the play's linkages to Arena's own grassroots strategy, as well as to broader discourses in contemporary Indonesian Theater (as seen in the ways Brecht's plays are "contextualized" by other Indonesian theater groups) and to the common practice of much progressive theater throughout the "developing" world.

In this way, *Tumbal* can be viewed as a supplement to Arena's grassroots activity. Still a difficulty exists in so far as the play's function is clearly also to create a bridge, a way of building an intellectual and emotional alliance between the rural poor and the small, urban middle class composed of business people, intellectuals, students, and professionals. Despite the fact that the means of constituting that alliance in political practice, as well as its specific goals, are not explicitly stated — apparently leaving these "details" as issues for all concerned parties to deal with once the performance has ended — the play's structure and the perspective which that structure contains suggest an unequal relationship between the potential allies. Part of this difficulty can be attributed to the fact that the attempt to simulate some of the grassroots theater methods in the performance and text of *Tumbal* was doomed to failure, or at least, was only a partial success.

To begin with, the play was performed on an arena stage in an auditorium where more conventional contemporary theater performances often occurred. Through an implicit identification of the audience with the five "judges" the performance attempted to break down only symbolically the audience/performer barriers existing in such conventional venues by appointing the audience as "judge." Secondly, in contrast to the Tanen Pakem project, though the play's themes are immediately relevant in so far as middle-class Indonesians are concerned with "national development" policies, this play does not present the everyday problems of the urban audiences for which it was performed. These factors distort and subvert the Freirian co-intentional educational methods which characterized Arena Teater's grassroots practice. Thirdly, in the performance of *Tumbal* before urban audiences, egalitarian relationships of co-educational dialogue are replaced by a hierarchy in which the urban, middle-class audience can see itself as the judge of the peasants' problems and as teacher to peasant students.

Acting as a voice for the concerns of the rural populations, Arena took its case to the middle class, the professionals, and the intellectuals, writing them into the play as judges, but also as spokespeople for the villagers and experts who clarify the common people's confusion. In so doing, *Tumbal* makes it possible for the middle-class audience members to visualize themselves as patrons and benefactors rather than as someone whose own situation is in question, as would be common in the grassroots theater projects. Indeed, the critical consciousness of the villagers, as found in characters such as Kewa, Igo, and the wisecracking Gopil, completely disappears in the final pages of the script when the expert testimony is presented by Engineer Banda and Professor Darma. Ironically, even Dr. Juha, the professional who acts as spokesperson for the villagers, ultimately bows to the analysis of these progressive-minded experts, shifting the play even farther in the direction of promoting a "vanguard" group's analysis and solutions. To be sure, *Tumbal* remains a remarkable and lively play precisely because of what it attempted to accomplish. Still, the problems generated by this attempt to build an emotional and critical alliance between two distinct social groups as well as to synthesize several distinctive theatrical practices into a new stage approach, necessitated further work. Between 1986 and 1991, Arena began to search for the means to transcend those problems.

The appeal to the nationalistically-oriented urban middle class contained in *Tumbal* implicitly posed once more, but on a larger scale, the issue raised by the Parangtritis workshop: how to create with theater a sustained development effort nationwide? Arena's work in Tanen Pakem had shown that sustained efforts were possible and productive, but Arena did not have the resources to undertake such efforts nationally. Drawing on the arguments of Ross Kidd, a theater activist from Canada who acknowledged Brecht as one source of inspiration for his own work[30] and who had been involved with grassroots theater projects in Botswana and Bangladesh, Wibowo and Arena determined that theater, as a rehearsal for social change (to alter Boal's phrase), needed to be tied to organizational activity which could provide an ongoing framework for actual material improvements.[31]

Arena had already begun to alter the format of its 1984 and 1985 workshops before taking a decisive step in 1987, a year after the performance of *Tumbal*. For the 1987 workshop held in the coastal village of Pantai Baron, the invited participants consisted entirely of NGO field workers. These participants were trained in Arena's grassroots theater techniques with the hope that NGOs would gain both the necessary skills and interest in combining their sustained, grassroots development efforts throughout Indonesia with cultural and theatrical tools for *conscientization*. Since such training would eventually be given by the NGO field workers, in turn, to the groups with whom they worked, it was assumed that peasants, workers, and others would themselves increasingly gain the skills to become more critically conscious, as well as the confidence to articulate that knowledge. This approach was continued in subsequent annual workshops.

The dissemination of such techniques has resulted in a large number of grassroots theater projects. Arena and other grassroots theater activists even convinced a government agency, BAPPENAS (The National Planning Board), to use grassroots theater techniques as one component of its 1990 program to promote integrated pest management.[32] Eventually, these activities became the central focus for Arena, and its original thrust, producing performances for the stage, declined in significance. In 1991, Wibowo temporarily stepped down as leader of Arena in order to devote himself more exclusively to his work at PUSKAT and to community animation and grassroots theater projects. In line with this decision, Wibowo was preparing three short books covering the orientation, methodology, and performance of "people's theater." Based on pre-publication manuscripts available in August of 1991, Wibowo's approach can be summarized as follows.

Wibowo asserts that people-oriented theater can not be separate from the contexts of daily life. Secondly, he insists that the basis of such cultural activity is not some dogmatic notion of aesthetics, but rather originality and honesty of expression. Borrowing from Boal's reading of "Aristotle's Coercive System of Tragedy," which holds that Aristotle's theory, when put into practice, converts the viewers into passive observers who surrender authority to the characters on the stage, Wibowo criticizes modern theater, television, and film.[33] Not only are viewers rendered passive by such productions, they are "alienated" from their normal surroundings, drawn into a culture that is not their own. This is particularly true in Indonesia where most films and television serials are about the lives of the well-to-do or upper middle-class Indonesians. Modern plays, while often concerned about the plight of the poor, present such themes in relation to issues and clothed in styles more familiar to the urban intelligentsia. Viewers, especially the poor for whom such entertainments seem so alluringly alien, can never become "creators" in these situations. For Wibowo, becoming a creator is crucial — it means becoming critical (3).

According to Wibowo, people's theater should allow the broad masses of people an opportunity to express themselves; it should take the side of the people's interests and be the voice of conscience and reason; and it should not differentiate between the protagonist and the audience. In such a way, it will become a true "pesta rakyat" (people's festival). Theater which does not serve the interests of the people for whom it is performed will have little relation to the primary concerns of the audience. It will form one more part of the "culture of silence" in which the poor have to depend on the culture and the sympathy of the rich. In such a culture, drama will mainly convey messages from above. There is no opportunity for the people to become creators (10-12). For Wibowo this is inhuman because the essence of life is change and development. Those who are not allowed to become creators are eventually unable to change and develop. They are denied life, are virtually dead (15).

Wibowo lists six essential characteristics of People's Theater summarized as follows (16-18):

1. *The story must have its origins in local social conditions.* It should be based upon research and open dialogue among the performers and the community with which they work or in which they themselves live. It should touch on awareness of history and should raise critical consciousness and a discussion of the issues presented.

2. *The script should be created and arranged by the people*

themselves. The people must be involved in the performance from the very beginning. They should write the story and thereby begin to take charge of their own history.

3. *Performance should be kept simple.* It should be interesting enough to get everyone involved and should make use of resources which are easily accessible, locally available. This is a chance for the people to show and develop their creativity.

4. *Break down the barriers between audience and performers.* Create a dialogue between performers and the audience. No professional performers should be used.

5. *No catharsis.* The performance should make participants more aware of the problem and instill in them a desire to deal with the problem. This begins with discussions during and after the performance.

6. *Build a dialogue.* Dialogue occurs between two (or more) people in the same life circumstances; it is intended to change conditions, to create a better, more just, harmonious, and peaceful world.

As with Boal and Kidd, Wibowo perceives people's theater to be but a part of a larger cultural process aiming at complete social change. One or two performances are not enough. Continuous, directed activities are needed. Yet, and here Wibowo borrows a term often used by Kidd, "animateurs" (people who help form, train and motivate locally-based theater groups) should not tell people what to do.[34] According to Wibowo, they are present in any given situation to help discover and utilize people's talents to analyze and solve their own problems (18, 20-21).

Arena had already tried to realize a number of the elements of this approach in an earlier play, *Ombak-Ombak*, written in stages by Endro Gunawan and other members of Arena and finished by Fred Wibowo.[35] Based on Arena's research into the conditions of Parangtritis and other coastal villages in 1981, *Ombak-Ombak* was originally performed at the 1981 workshop at Parangtritis. Subsequently, it was revived and performed several times during the late 1980s and early 1990s, becoming more integral to Arena's efforts as Arena devoted itself increasingly to grassroots theater activities and deemphasized middle-class-oriented urban stage theater. The play's 1991 performance at the grassroots theater workshop at Pantai Sundak, Central Java, coincided with a growing awareness among the members of Arena, fostered by the experiences of the integrated pest management program, that grassroots theater training skills could not become the exclusive domain of middle-class NGO workers. One way in which Arena adjusted its practices accordingly was to have local villagers create and perform plays along with the NGO workshop participants at Pantai Sundak. This was done in order to begin breaking down the barriers between the young activists and ordinary villagers as well as to increase the confidence of the villagers in dealing with urban, educated Indonesians.[36] *Ombak-Ombak*, with its focus on villagers rather than on urban, university-educated intellectuals, was another component in Arena's strategy to shift the thinking of the participants and local villagers alike in regard to the existing relations of power within the development process.

The Sundak performance of *Ombak-Ombak*, staged for an audience of local villagers and NGO theater workshop participants, also shows how Arena's performance strategy had changed in response to the problems illustrated by the structure and performance venue of *Tumbal*, which, in turn, suggested the existing gap between middle-class NGO activists and ordinary villagers that was becoming apparent to Arena members. Using cultural images, forms, and language taken from the villagers' daily life, *Ombak-Ombak* was designed to stimulate dialogue with local villagers about their economic problems, and thereby model the techniques of the *pesta rakyat* for both the villagers and the NGO workshop participants. As in *Tumbal*, the play concludes by suggesting the need to work together to overcome the desperate economic situation in which the village finds itself. Here too there is no specific solution given, leaving the audience to construct its own methods of solving the problems. Yet unlike *Tumbal*, no "experts" are summoned during the course of the drama to provide a well-articulated critique of the current program of development. In a related change, the peasants, particularly the village youth such as Pardi and Isah, are constituted as the critical, reasoning subjects in *Ombak-Ombak*. The play thus suggests that ultimately only the villagers will be able to determine the best ways to address their own needs. Used in such a fashion, Arena's new approach attempted to initiate critical discussion among the direct subjects of its material, while endeavoring to minimize the amount of "vanguard" guidance which middle-class voices provided in *Tumbal*. Here the Brechtian tradition in theater was appropriated, developed, and opened up to entirely new audiences and performers.

NOTES

[1] Bintang Suradi, "Meperingati: Bertolt Brecht," *Zaman Baru* (20-30 Agustus 1957): 5, 9-10.

[2] Bertolt Brecht, *Organon Kecil untuk Teater*, Budaya Jaya 102 (Nopember 1976): 665-704.

[3] Based on two references it is clear that Rendra performed one or more of these scenes. The first is "Mengapa Rendra? Mengapa Bukan Rendra?" *Tempo* (23 Agustus 1975): 50. This article discusses Rendra's 1967 staging of an "anti-Nazi Brecht play" but does not give the title. At least one of the three scenes mentioned above, and possibly all three were performed. Rendra's translation of "Der Spitzel," published as "Informan," in *Budaya Jaya* 1.6 (Nopember 1968): 373-83, suggests that this piece at least was performed by his *Bengkel Teater* group. Arifin C. Noer staged "Mencari Keadilan" in late March 1969 as reported in *Horison* 4.5 (Mei 1969): 158. Wisran Hadi's production of "Isteri Yahudi" probably occurred in the early 1970s, but I have been able to find only a reference to the staging without a specific date in Darman Moenir, "Wisran Hadi, Seorang Penggerak Kesenian yang Gigih di Padang," *Kompas* 28 (Maret 1978): 5.

[4] See Harold Crouch, *The Army and Politics in Indonesia* (Ithaca: Cornell University Press, 1988), 255-72, and Julie Southwood and Patrick Flanagan, *Indonesia: Law, Propaganda and Terror* (London: Zed Press, 1983).

[5] Goenawan Mohamad, "Pelacur Baik Dari Setzuan," *Tempo* (1 Mei 1976): 41-43.

[6] Two theoretical statements of this desire, which existed to varying degrees among leading Indonesian theater workers, can be found in Arifin C. Noer, "Teater Indonesia Masa Depan," *Horison* 3 (1983): 428-34, and Wisran Hadi, "Sebuah Konsep Kerja Teater: Dari Yang Telah Ada," *Pertemuan Teater 1980* (Jakarta, 1981), 125-29.

[7] Bambang Bujono, "Astaga! Kurang Ajar!" *Tempo* (28 Februari 1976): 15.

[8] Bambang Bujono, "Brecht yang Penuh Tawa," *Tempo* (29 Maret 1980): 24.

[9] N. Riantiarno, Personal Interview, 8 August 1991.

[10] Jakob Sumarjo, "Teater Koma dan Penontonnya," *Kompas* (15 Februari 1987).

[11] Fred Wibowo, Personal Interview, 15 August 1991.

[12] Philip Eldridge, "NGOs and the State in Indonesia," in Arief Budiman, ed., *State and Civil Society in Indonesia* (Victoria, Australia: Monash University Centre of Southeast Asian Studies, 1990), 506-7.

[13] Fred Wibowo, Personal Interview, 14 November 1987.

[14] Paulo Freire, *Pedagogy of the Oppressed* (New York: Continuum, 1989). See especially Chapters 1 and 3.

[15] Lutgardo Labad, "Philippine People's Culture Across the Seas: The Values of Internationalism in our People's Cultural Work," *Makiisa* 1.1 (1988): 4; Jules Dasmarinas, "Artists From Other Lands Came and Sang Our Songs," *Makiisa* 1.1 (1988): 19.

[16] Michael H. Bodden, "Imagining the Audience as Agent of its Own History: Brecht, Grassroots Theater, and Representations of Inter-Class Alliance in the Philippines and Indonesia," diss., U of Wisconsin, 1993, Chapter 2.

[17] Eugène van Erven, *Stages of People Power: The Philippines Educational Theater Association* (The Hague: Centre for the Study of Education in Developing Countries [CESO], 1989), 26-43.

[18] Fred Wibowo, Personal Interview, 15 August 1991.

[19] Eugène van Erven, *The Playful Revolution* (Bloomington: Indiana University Press, 1992), 187; Wibowo, Personal Interview, 15 August 1991.

[20] Augusto Boal, *Theatre of the Oppressed* (New York: Theatre Communications Group, 1985), 121 (subsequent references in text in parentheses).

[21] Brecht, *Brecht on Theatre* (New York: Hill and Wang, 1986), 185-195. These ideas are articulated as part of Brecht's *Kleines Organon für das Theater*, sections 20-25 and 35-52.

[22] Eugène van Erven, "Beyond the Shadows of Wayang: Liberation Theatre in Indonesia," *New Theatre Quarterly* 5.17 (February 1989): 38-40.

[23] Wibowo, Personal Interview, 14 November 1987.

[24] *Motivating the Village*, video recording of the Tanen Pakem project, produced by Studio Audiovisual Puskat, 1984.

[25] van Erven, "Beyond the Shadows of Wayang...," 40.

²⁶ Wibowo, Personal Interview, 14 November 1987. Wibowo and Arena materials are main sources for this information on the Tanen Pakem project. It would be worthwhile to solicit firsthand accounts from the villagers involved to gain their impressions of the workshop and related events, since the project aims at empowering the community in which it occurs. Due to time constraints I was unable to undertake such interviews. This fact certainly influences my narrative of the project and should be taken into account.

²⁷ Wibowo, *Tumbal*, xeroxed manuscript, 3-4.

²⁸ This information is based on personal conversations with Fred Wibowo and with a number of his associates from Arena Teater and from PUSKAT as well as on three pre-publication manuscripts given to me by Wibowo which contain both theoretical justification and practical instructions for the kind of theatrical practice which Arena seeks to create in its grassroots activities, i.e., the "Pesta Rakyat" (People's Festival).

²⁹ Wibowo, *Tumbal*, 11.

³⁰ Ross Kidd and Mamunar Rashid, "From Outside In to Inside Out: People's Theatre and Landless Organizing in Bangladesh," *Theaterwork* (January/February 1983): 31.

³¹ Ross Kidd, "Liberation or Domestication: Popular Theatre and Non-Formal Education in Africa," *Educational Broadcasting International* (March 1979): 7. Kidd sent this article to Wibowo in the course of their correspondence.

³² Fred Wibowo, "Teater Rakyat (Sebagai Alternatif Penyuluhan Internal)," Xeroxed copy of paper, 1.

³³ Fred Wibowo, "Tiga Buah Buku Teater Rakyat," ts. 1991 (Volume 1: Orientasi), 2, 6, 8-9 (subsequent references in text in parentheses).

³⁴ Ross Kidd, "Reclaiming Culture: Indigenous Performers Take Back Their Show," *Fuse* (January/February 1983): 271; Kidd, "Liberation or Domestication...," 7.

³⁵ Endro Gunawan, Personal Interview, 13 July 1994.

³⁶ Fred Wibowo, Personal Interview, 14 July 1994.

Dilemmas: Brecht's Fragment *Der Untergang des Egoisten Fatzer*

The *Fatzer* fragment assumes a central position in Brecht's path to the *Lehrstück*. He attempts to stage the fragile (and hence modern) identity of the Fatzer figure as a change in perspectives. Functioning according to various rules, the decentered figure is too big for the isolated group of four deserters. Brecht failed in his efforts to free the historical material from the pressure of illegality by designing alternative scenes. Integrating commentary loosens the connection to the figures and works toward the conversion of the dramatic play into the *Lehrstück*. Emphasizing the materiality of language, the *Fatzer* verse asserts itself against the characters and against the claim to individuality on the part of the actors. In these ways the play still throws into question the dominant practice in today's theater institution.

Dilemmes: le Fragment *Der Untergang des Egoisten Fatzer* de Brecht

Le fragment *Fatzer* occupe une position centrale dans l'itinéraire de Brecht vers le *Lehrstück*. Il tente de représenter l'identité fragile (et de là, moderne) de Fatzer à partir de points de vues changeants. Obéissant à de multiples lois, le personnage décentré est trop imposant par rapport au groupe isolé des quatres déserteurs. Brecht a échoué dans ses efforts pour libérer le matériau historique de la pression de l'illégalite en élaborant des scènes alternatives. L'intégration du commentaire affaiblit le contact avec les personnages et joue en faveur de la transformation de la pièce dramatique en *Lehrstück*. En insistant sur la matérialité du langage, le fragment en vers *Fatzer* s'établit contre les personnages et la revendication à l'individualité des acteurs. En ce sens, la pièce remet malgré tout en question les pratiques dominantes au sein des institutions théâtrales de nos jours.

Dilemas: El fragmento de Brecht *Der Untergang des Egoisten Fatzer*

El fragmento de *Fatzer* representa un momento central en la evolución de Brecht hacia el *Lehrstück*. El trata de escenificar la identidad frágil (y por ende, moderna) de la figura de *Fatzer* así como un cambio de perspectiva. Al funcionar según varias reglas, la figura descentrada es demasiado grande para el grupo aislado de los cuatro desertores. Diseñando escenas alternativas, Brecht falló en sus esfuerzos de liberar la materia histórica de la presión de la ilegalidad. El comentario integrador destensa la conexión de las figuras y tiende hacia la conversión de la obra dramática en el *Lehrstück*. Enfatizando la materialidad del lenguaje, el verso de *Fatzer* se impone contra los personajes y contra la afirmación de individualidad por parte de los actores. De esta forma la obra todavía hace cuestionar la práctica dominante en la institución teatral de hoy en día.

Zwangslagen: Brechts Fragment *Der Untergang des Egoisten Fatzer*

Stefan Mahlke

da war mein name aus aller mund
meine geste vergessen mein wort gefälscht.
  da sagte ich:
ich bin nichts wert noch mein werk noch meine zeit
und nicht dein name noch dein werk noch deine zeit
sondern nur daß ich den mann fatzer gesehen habe gehen
und umkommen zu seiner zeit.[1]

Wie der ganze Textkörper des *Fatzer* bleibt auch das Gedicht fragmentarisch. Die Datierung ist unsicher, Lenze ordnet den Entwurf in die Textstufe XIV.1 (1930) ein. Prüfend sein Werk und anderer, betrachtet als von Kommendem vergessen und gefälscht, bleibt Brecht, den Fatzer gesehen zu haben. Die faschistische Diktatur wirft ihre Schatten voraus, der Sturm naht. *Fatzer* also als kleinste Größe, als Rest, der bleibt. Dieser türmt sich für die Nachwelt zum Gebirge auf. Das "ganze stück, da ja unmöglich" (Brecht) erzeugt ein "dramaturgisches Geraune" (Mittenzwei, in Berliner Ensemble 114), das den Zugang eher versperrt denn öffnet. Das Produkt des Scheiterns wird für die Wissenschaft zu einem Leuchten: das Fragmentarische an sich wird schon für Qualität genommen. Selten genug wird gefragt, warum Brecht aus dem *Fatzer*-Material kein bühnenfertiges Stück zusammenbekommt. Auch die bisherigen Inszenierungen blieben hinter den hochgespannten Erwartungen zurück. Offensichtlich stellt sich der *Fatzer* quer zum herrschenden Theaterbetrieb.

Im folgenden soll angedeutet werden, warum Brecht am *Fatzer*-Projekt scheitert; inwiefern er hier auf Zwangslagen stößt, die Dramatik auf neue Weise in Frage stellen. In diesem Raum ist die Genese der Lehrstückkonzeption anzusiedeln. Gerade die neuere Diskussion insistiert auf der zentralen Stellung der Lehrstücke im Gesamtschaffen Brechts, auch hinsichtlich dessen, was bleiben wird. Innerhalb dieses Komplexes ist es das *Fatzer*-Fragment, dem eine strukturierende Funktion zugesprochen werden muß. Entwickelt wird die Darstellung in der Auseinandersetzung sowohl mit kano-

Brecht Then and Now / Brecht damals und heute
Eds. Marc Silberman et al. *The Brecht Yearbook / Das Brecht-Jahrbuch*,
Volume 20 (Madison: The International Brecht Society, 1995)

nischen Positionen der Brecht-Forschung als auch mit eher dekonstruktivistisch inspirierten Lektüren.

1

In einem Aufsatz zur "doppelten Polarität des Lehrstücks" gehen Hans-Thies Lehmann und Helmut Lethen einer für sie unauflöslichen Spannung nach. Sie insistieren auf einen "Rest," der im Lehrstück von der Maschine der Dialektik nicht wegdisputiert werde. Ihre Kritik richtet sich gegen eine "logifizierende Lesart," die aus den Stücken Brechts Gedanken extrahiert, die dann argumentativ durchbuchstabiert werden und schließlich zu erkenntnistheoretischen bzw. politischen Einsichten führen. Die "linken" Lesarten (von Steinweg, Brenner u.a.) würden so die Stücke jedesmal als Vehikel einer Theorie nehmen. Lehmann und Lethen setzen dagegen eine Interpretation, die der spezifischen Leistung der Lehrstücke, d.h. poetischer Texte, gerecht zu werden versucht. Sie öffnen den Blick für die Vergegenwärtigung von Momenten, die an den Körper gebunden sind und somit von Theorie nicht eingeholt werden können. Damit wird das zwischen den Instanzen Diskutierte (z.B. politisch richtiges Handeln) prinzipiell in Frage gestellt. Aufgabe der Lehrstücke (poetischer Texte überhaupt) kann es nicht sein, in einem philosophischen oder politischen Diskurs aufzugehen. Die These von Lehmann und Lethen lautet:

> Die begriffliche Antithetik insgesamt (Ebene I) [auf ihr stehen sich zwei Positionen gegenüber, eine "richtige" und eine "falsche"; vgl. 307] wird konfrontiert mit einer zweiten Ebene: Auf ihr werden nicht falsche Gedanken, sondern das Denken in Frage gestellt, nicht eine These, sondern das Thetische, nicht eine gedankliche Ordnung, sondern die Ordnung des Gedankens. (Lehmann und Lethen 306)

Auf die *Maßnahme* bezogen heißt das für die Autoren:

> Das Einverständnis des Jungen Genossen mit seinem Tod ist Resultat einer politischen Argumentation, die Einsicht in die Notwendigkeit, Spuren zu verwischen. Aber umso schmerzlicher bleibt die ungelöste Widersprüchlichkeit, die in der Vernichtung der Spontaneität, der individuellen Lebenszeit besteht. (Lehmann und Lethen 307)

Während der Konflikt auf der ersten Ebene im Prinzip lösbar sei, bleibe der auf der zweiten Ebene (im Prinzip) unlösbar. Weil er einer sei "zwischen Begriff und dem, was dieser nicht erreicht" (ebd.). Das ist die Spannung, in der Adorno sein in der *Negativen Dialektik* entwickeltes Programm von Philosophie ansiedelt: es geht auf das Begriffslose im Begriff. "Die Utopie der Erkenntnis wäre, das Begriffslose mit Begriffen aufzutun, ohne es ihnen gleichzumachen" (Adorno 21). Die Anstrengung einer solchen Arbeit ist bei Lehmann und Lethen nicht auszumachen. Sie sprechen von "begreiflichen menschlichen Regungen" (303), von der "unmittelbaren Spontaneität" (303, eine Tautologie), von einem "Moment stummen Protestes der Körperlichkeit" (306), eben vom "'tragischen' Konflikt von Spontaneität und Rationalität" (304). Dieser folge aus einer "radikalen Heterogenität im Subjekt dem Begriff gegenüber" (309). Damit greifen sie auf jenes Begriffsarsenal zurück, das die Munition für die Verteidigung des "autonomen Individuums" liefert. Ebene II fällt auf Ebene I zurück. Auf letzterer zeigt sich in seiner ganzen Pracht "der Mensch, der lebendige, [der] brüllt, und sein Elend zerreißt alle Dämme der Lehre" (*Die Maßnahme*, GBA III: 92). In der unterschwelligen Affirmation des unmittelbaren Individuums, des "von Einsichten unbelehrbaren Impulses" (Lehmann und Lethen 309) aber wäre man wieder dort, "was hier mit aller Vorsicht als bürgerliche Ideologie bezeichnet sei" (305-306).

Der ideologische Sprengstoff lagert schon im Wort "Spontaneität" selbst. Es suggeriert, es könne ein Tun ohne Überlegung geben. Sein alltagssprachlicher Gebrauch im Sinne von Natürlichkeit, Direktheit verdeckt die Unmöglichkeit, zu handeln ohne zu denken. Die Wörterbuch-Definition berücksichtigt dies, indem sie vom Handeln "ohne *langes* Überlegen" spricht (Hervorhebung von S.M.). Dem Denken (und damit der Sprache) ist nicht zu entkommen.

Berechtigung hat Lehmann und Lethens Vorschlag da, wo er politisch "richtiges" Handeln nicht nur als Hort der Wahrheit, sondern als vermeintliches Zentrum der Lehrstücke überhaupt in Frage stellt. Und positiv zu wenden wäre jene Beobachtung der Autoren, wonach die "sinnliche Qualität" der Lehrsätze die "Kälte gegenüber den dramatis personae" sei. Nur ist der andere Pol nicht der des Unmittelbaren, Kreatürlichen. "Hilfe erhalten, Ansprüche anmelden, Grausamkeit meiden" (Lehmann und Lethen 311) sind keineswegs spontane Wünsche des Menschen. Sie sind nicht allein der "Negativität" des Körpers zuzurechnen, sondern mindestens ebenso kulturell determiniert. Oder wie Nägele sagt: "Spontaneität ist codiert, nichts stereotyper, als was aus dem Herzen fließt" (Nägele 315).

Nägeles Hinweis ist umso bemerkenswerter, als er seine Lehrstück-Interpretation auf einem Weg sieht, den Lehmann und Lethen eingeschlagen haben. Seine Lektüre versteht sich als Spurenauf-

nahme der "unaufhebbaren Reste des Todes, der Gewalt, des Lei-
dens" (Nägele 303) in den Lehrstücken selbst. Darin sich vom
Programm Lehmann und Lethens kaum unterscheidend, kommt
Nägele zu leicht modifizierten Ergebnissen. Wie für Lehmann und
Lethen ist da ein Rest, ein "Stück Überschuß an Negativität, die an
der Ökonomie der Dialektik keinen Anteil hat" (309). So stellt sich
der Junge Genosse in der *Maßnahme* als beschriebenes Blatt vor
("Mein Herz schlägt für die Revolution"). Mit der Auslöschung
seines Gesichtes wird er zum "leeren Blatt," auf das die Revolution
ihre Anweisung schreibt. Nägele nun versteht dieses Einschreiben
der Schrift der Revolution als ein "Wieder-Einschreiben der ausge-
löschten Schrift" (315), und zwar indem jedem Satz des Jungen
Genossen eine Szene entspreche. Bis dahin reiche die Dialektik. In
der Verschiebung gehe etwas "unwiederholbar verloren. Das ist das
Jenseits der Dialektik" (316). Dieser Konflikt schlage sich nieder in
der Form: als Bruchstücke, als die Fertigen, die in Brechts Augen
nicht fertig sind.

Das jenseits der "Ökonomie der Dialektik" sei das Negative, vor
dem nicht verweilt wird. Dennoch ist es da. Weil Lindbergh in den
USA "als Faschist eine dunkle Rolle gespielt" hat, nimmt Brecht
Änderungen vor. Die "Ausmerzung des Namens" wird namhaft
gemacht in jenem Prolog, der von nun an (1950) für jede Aufführung des *Ozeanflugs* obligatorisch ist. Der Auftritt des Fliegers —
"Mein Name tut nichts zur Sache" — meint nicht, was er sagt.
Brecht hätte ihn durchaus auch mit "Ich bin der Pilot" oder "Ich bin
der Flieger" einführen können. So aber wird man erst auf den
fehlenden, "nichts zur Sache" tuenden Namen aufmerksam. Das
"Ich bin Derundder" zitiert die gewöhnliche Redewendung, d.h.
verfremdet sie, indem eine erste Person ("Ich") sie sich als Prädikat
zuschreibt. Das erheischt genau die Fragen, die nach Nägele ins
Dunkle abgeschoben werden. Eine "implizite Verdeckung" stellt
dies nur insofern dar, als die Rede etwas anderes behauptet als sie
praktiziert. Auch Lindberghs "natürliche Schwäche" ist anwesend,
indem sie erwähnt wird. Nicht "der Text," sondern Lindbergh geht
darüber hinweg: "Ihre Arbeit war ohne Fehler." Die makellose
Arbeit, ist das nicht die "stählerne Einfalt" (*Der Flug der Lindberghs*,
GBA III: 24) im "Bericht über das Unerreichbare?" Wo über die
natürliche Schwäche nicht mehr geredet wird und sie dennoch
anwesend ist, diesseits des "Unerreichbaren," "aufzeigend das
Mögliche," d.h. auch das Unmögliche.

Die Entgegensetzung von "Ökonomie der Dialektik" und ihrem
Jenseits funktioniert nur, wenn erstere als Maschine der Auflösung
von Widersprüchen gesehen wird. Wenn Nägele in den Lehrstücken
ihren "todsicheren Blick fürs Antagonistische und nicht Integrier-

bare" (Nägele 316) sieht, macht er nichts anderes, als eine (neue) Totalität aufzusuchen, von einem Ganzen auszugehen. In dieser Totalität ist das Antagonistische, nicht Integrierbare anwesend als das Negative. Indem dieses Ausschließen *gezeigt* wird, gewinnt die Reflexion ihre Negativität selbst zum Inhalte, wie Hegel sagen würde. Die Leistung von Nägeles Untersuchung besteht darin, daß er (eher mit als gegen Steinweg und Knopf) die Bewegung der Widersprüche als ihr Eindringen in die Form aufzeigt. Vor allem die Gewichtsverlagerung vom Signifikat hin zum Signifikanten ist für unsere Zwecke von Interesse. In der Konstruktion des Lehrstück-Typus setze Brecht eine

> Zäsur, die eine andere des 18. Jahrhunderts rückgängig macht. Wenn das 18.Jahrhundert Rhetorik, Poetik und Auswendiglernen verwirft zugunsten des freien, schöpferischen, eigenen Ausdrucks des Innern, konstituiert Brecht den Sinn wieder in der Körperlichkeit der materiellen Signifikanten und in der Mechanik der symbolischen Maschinerie. (Nägele 307-308)

Der Charakter als Substanz fällt weg; das Zeichen/die Geste emanzipieren sich, indem sie nicht nur Resultat von "stimmungen und gedankenreihen" sind, sondern ihrerseits zum Produzenten von jenen werden. Aus der Differenz von Zeigen und Gezeigtem, von Bezeichnen und Bezeichnetem speist sich die Spannung der dramatischen Darstellung (vgl. Weimann 18).

2

> Wer sagt nicht einmal so, einmal so? Wer weiß, was er sagt? Ein ganz mittelmäßiger Mensch.
> (GBA 21: 283)

Mit Hartnäckigkeit hält sich in der Brecht-Forschung die antithetische Gegenüberstellung von Individuum und Gesellschaft. Verdichtet in der Diskussion der Lehrstücke, produzierte sie Gegensatzpaare wie abstrakt-konkret, Verstand-Gefühl, Individuum-Masse, Individuum-Kollektiv (vgl. Nägele 302). Das ist in den meisten Interpretationen des *Fatzer* nicht anders. Ralf Schnell und Florian Vaßen sehen den Widerspruch zwischen Kollektiv und Individuum als strukturellen Konflikt an. Für Reiner Lenze wird der "Typus Fatzer" in der Entwicklung der verschiedenen Entwürfe "zunehmend als Vertreter eines Individualismus kenntlich, dem als überlebter bürgerlicher Kategorie der Untergang bevorsteht" (Lenze 336). "Die Problematisierung dieses Verhältnisses von individuellen und kollektiven Bedürfnissen" lasse sich als zentrales Interesse Brechts am *Fatzer*-Projekt begreifen (ebd.). Im *Fatzer* habe Brecht eine "neue und groß angelegte Figur des jetzt negativ bewerteten anarchischen Individualismus" begonnen, behauptet Manfred Voigts (Voigts 183). Als Regie-Assistent der Berliner Aufführung (Premiere Juni 1987) stellt Holger Teschke Fatzer mit seinen extrem egoistischen Haltungen gegen Koch, "der einzig in der kollektiven Moral der Vernunft einen Ausweg sieht" (Berliner Ensemble 70).

Diese Sichtweisen behaupten zweierlei: Zum einen wird Fatzers Egoismus tendenziell gleichgesetzt mit einem Individualismus, der sich jeder Kollektivität verweigert. Zum anderen werden Kollektiv/ Kollektivität mit der Gruppe (und darin Kochs/Keuners Ansichten) zur Deckung gebracht.

Auch wenn beide Positionen problematisiert werden — wie es etwa Teschke tut, indem er ihnen jede Unschuld abspricht —, so wird hier der Treibsatz des Stückes aus jener Konstellation gewonnen. Dabei scheint man sich auf den Meister selbst berufen zu können:

> ihre odyssee beginnt mit ihrem durch den individualisten fatzer gegebenen irrtum, sie könnten, einzeln, den krieg abbrechen. hierdurch wo sie um zu leben sich von der masse scheiden verlieren sie ihr leben von vornherein. sie kommen nie mehr zur masse zurück. (Lenze 199 [VII. 10])

So schreibt Brecht in einem eher als Selbstverständigung zu verstehenden Kommentar. In ihm ist ebenfalls die Rede von Fatzers "Schädlichkeit" und davon, "niemals den anschluß an morgen zu verlieren, nie zu vergessen was gewollt wird, alles andere als hindernis zu sehen nicht als hauptsächlich zu bewältigendes, was dann ziel wird" (Lenze 200 [VII. 10]). Damit scheint Fatzer derjenige zu sein, der den Anschluß an morgen blockiert. Eben der Einzelgänger, das "anarchische Individuum," das Kollektivität verhindert.

Produktiver ist ein anderer Ansatz. Wolfgang Engler geht in modernetheoretischer Perspektive der Frage nach, wie sich Kollektivität und von daher Individualität bei Brecht bilden.[2] Zum einen gibt es den Substanzverlust des Individuums, das seine Identität nur über andere gewinnt und seine Totalität nur in seiner Zugehörigkeit zu mehreren Kollektiven erfährt. Zum anderen bedeutet Kollektivität, "daß der Zusammenhang der einzelnen im Kollektiv und die Integration der Kollektive untereinander selbst Gegenstand kollektiver (geistig-praktischer) Handlungen wird" (Engler 283). Wichtig für uns ist, daß beide Phänomene erst im Makrosozialen Kontur gewinnen. Indem sie wesentlich als (nicht abzuschließende) Produktion verstanden werden, als ein In-Verhältnissen-Sein, verdampft das Substantialische an ihnen.

In seinen Anläufen auf das Fragment versucht Brecht immer wieder, sich seiner Figuren zu versichern. In mehreren Entwürfen legt er Figurencharakteristiken an: Mit "einer ist gerecht, einer gleichgültig, einer subjektiv" (Lenze 94 [IV.4]) werden schon in einem frühen Entwurf Koch, Büsching, Kaumann skizziert. Etwas ausführlicher dann ist Koch

ein fanatiker
er wird krank wenn er
die gleichgültigkeit des
büsching riecht. (Lenze 130 [V.6])

Büsching ist "ein kaltschnäuziger materialist" (Lenze 162 [V.8]), in einem späten Entwurf dann "revolutioniert" — von dem inzwischen zur Keuner-Figur transformierten Koch als "dummkopf" bezeichnet (Lenze 250 [VIII.11.2]). Auch wenn die Attribute die Figuren keineswegs abdecken, so zeigen sie immerhin eine gewisse Stabilität ihrer Anlage an.

Anders als Koch, Kaumann und Büsching kann Brecht seinen Fatzer so nicht festmachen. Fatzer ist den anderen voraus. Seine Spaziergänge sind die Abenteuerreisen desjenigen, der sich in die weite Welt wagt.[3] Er, der die Gruppe überredet hat, im trauten Heim zu warten, hält es dort selbst nicht aus. Er muß den feuchten Finger in die Luft halten, um zu wissen, woher der Wind weht. Er beansprucht, "frei zu gehen im strom der verkehrenden." Situationen verschafft er sich, "die mütter der menschen":

und nicht so
verschieden ist die
schlachtluft voll
von einem sommertag
als dieser fatzer von jenem ist
also sind die situationen
die mütter der menschen. (Lenze 153)

Auf seinen Unternehmungen erkundet er, wie es dem Krieg geht. Er zeigt sich listig, wenn es darum geht, Fleisch zu besorgen. Einfallsreich verführt er die Kaumann. Er will Proviant besorgen, und er will kämpfen, Frauen will er haben und die Freundschaft zu seinen Kameraden nicht verlieren. Anders als Odysseus, der alle seine Handlungen rationalisiert im Hinblick auf den Sieg gegen Troja und seine Heimkehr, geht Fatzer ein solcher Zielpunkt ab. Er denkt nicht

strategisch,[4] seine Handlungen sind eher laufende Perspektiven-
wechsel, die seine Absicht, nicht in den Städten zu verschwinden,
permanent in Frage stellen. Sein ausgeprägtes Aneignungsverhalten
läßt ihn seine Fühler immer wieder ausstrecken. Er bewegt sich in
verschiedenen Diskursen. Diese besitzen jeweils eigene Regeln, die
nicht so ohne weiteres unter ein Metasystem subsumierbar sind.
Fatzers Lust auf die Kaumann kollidiert mit dem Besitzanspruch
Kaumanns wie auch mit dem Anspruch, die Gruppe zusammen-
zuhalten. Er will einerseits Fleisch besorgen und andererseits seine
"Ehre" gegenüber den Fleischern wiederherstellen. Fatzer kann
Versprechen abgeben und in einer neuen, anderen Situation dieselben brechen. Es ist ihm unerträglich, nach nur einer Regel zu
handeln, Zukunft auszurechnen:

> ich geb euch zu bedenken
> daß nicht immer alles so nach plan geht
> auf der welt. (Lenze 179 [V.8])

> ihr aber rechnet auf den bruchteil aus
> was mir zu tun bleibt und setzts in die rechnung.
> aber ich tus nicht! rechnet!
> ...
> behaltet von allem was an mir ist
> nur das euch nützliche.
> der rest ist fatzer. (Lenze 238 [VIII.11.1])

In der Ablehnung seiner Ausrechenbarkeit scheint Fatzer auf
einem unveräußerlichen Kern seiner Person zu bestehen, auf einen
Mittelpunkt zu insistieren, der dem neuen Menschen, dem "massen-
menschen" fehle. Dessen Geist war ihm in einer Vision erschienen:

> seine art ist mechanisch
>   einzig durch bewegung zeigt er sich
> jedes glied auswechselbar selbst die person
> mittelpunktlos. (Lenze 152 [V.7.3])

Der vermeintlich substantielle Rest "fatzer" gerät jedoch durch den
Namen in Zweifel. Wie Lenze vermerkt (386), bedeutet der Name
Schwätzer, Aufschneider (nach Grimm), das Verb "fatzen" jemanden
foppen, zum besten halten. Das Substantielle entpuppt sich als
Unsicherheit par excellence. Fatzers Bild von sich selbst korreliert
mit seiner Unzuverlässigkeit den anderen gegenüber. Daß er das
reflektiert — einem Arbeiter zusehend, der mit seinem Kran spricht,
sagt er zu sich: "die sind in ordnung aber ich/ bin in unordnung"

(Lenze 188 [V.8]) —, macht ihn zum Intellektuellen. Ordnung (Arbeiter und Kran scheinen eins zu sein) vor Augen, ahnt er: wenn auch vielleicht gewünscht, so kann die Alternative nicht aussehen. Seine Positionswechsel sind auf der Ebene der kleinen isolierten Gruppe nicht vermittelbar. Sein Egoismus ist der notwendige Widerstand, um sich nicht an eine Instanz zu delegieren. Zudem weiß er, daß ihre Isoliertheit die Gruppe gefährdet: Mit Hilfe der Kaumann (als Hure) versucht er, Kontakt mit der Außenwelt (hier Arbeiter) herzustellen.

Kaumann, Büsching und Koch geben sich ab, mit Fatzer. Für sie ist er ein "großes ich das / reicht / für uns 4" (Lenze 175), wie Koch meint. Büsching denkt, die drei könnten Fatzer gebrauchen:

das ist das gute an dem fatzer dass er
so viel appetit hat dass es
für uns mitlangt, und dass er ein solcher egoist ist
dass es für uns noch mitlangt. (Lenze 180)

Die drei setzen ein Vertrauen in Fatzer und in ihre eigenen Möglichkeiten, ihn zu steuern, über das dieser längst hinaus ist. Das kulminiert in der Szene, in der Koch meint, wenn er Fatzer ihre Pässe und ihr Geld gebe, würde das als Vertrauensbeweis verstanden werden und Fatzer würde damit sorgsam umgehen, denn schließlich sei einer sicherer als vier und Fatzer wäre immer der sicherste gewesen. Darüber kann Fatzer nur noch lachen; er wird die Pässe wegwerfen. Seine Unzuverlässigkeiten verletzen das aufgestellte Gesetz des Zusammenhaltens, der Solidarität. Deshalb muß er "hin sein." Fatzer gerät in diese Mühle, weil eine seiner Perspektiven ist, daß er nicht allein sein kann. Immer wieder kehrt er zurück zur Gruppe; selbst zu seiner Hinrichtung geht er ohne zu zögern, obwohl er ahnt, was kommt. Auch das Mädchen kann ihn nicht halten; er hat sie schon besessen. Er kehrt zurück zur "Familie," die der Tank geboren hatte. Mit großem Pathos versucht er, mit den Kameraden eins zu werden. Doch solcherart Identitätsbildung ist für einen, der schon weiter war, nicht mehr zu haben. Sein Tod zieht auch die anderen mit in den Abgrund: Sie hatten sich an ihn gekettet.

Nicht so die Kaumann. In einer Figurencharakteristik will Brecht die Figur der Kaumann in eine den anderen ähnliche Lage bringen:

sie verdächtigt ihn zuerst
da sie ihn erkennt.
dann vögelt er sie und sie
wird wie eine hündin.

noch bei seinem prozeß ver-
teidigt sie ihn — aber es
ist nur mehr eine klage
um "das schöne tier fatzer". —
sie erhebt ihren arm zu
seiner verurteilung. (Lenze 162)

Realisiert davon werden nur das Mißtrauen der Kaumann gegenüber
Fatzer (sie warnt die anderen drei vor ihm) und der Geschlechtsakt.
Die Kaumann bindet sich keineswegs an Fatzer wie dessen Kame-
raden. Vielmehr benutzt sie ihn wie er sie, indem sie ihrer ge-
schlechtlichen Lust Befriedigung verschafft. Fatzer kommt dabei die
Leistung zu, daß er sie von einem Treueverständnis befreit, das sie
durch die Unlust (aus Schwäche) ihres Mannes unbefriedigt ließ.
Fatzer lehrt sie, was Brecht später in einem Sonett wieder aufnimmt:

Das Neunte Sonett

Als du das Vögeln lerntest, lehrt ich dich
So vögeln, daß du mich dabei vergaßest
Und liebe Lust von meinem Teller aßest
Als liebtest du die Liebe und nicht mich.

Ich sagte: tut nichts, wenn du mich vergißt
Als freutest du dich eines andern Manns!
Ich geb nicht mich, ich geb dir einen Schwanz
Er tut dir nicht nur gut, weil's meiner ist.

Wenn ich so wollte, daß du untertauchst
In deinem eigenem Fleische, wollt ich nie
Daß du mir eine wirst, die da gleich schwimmt
Wenn einer aus Versehn hinkommt an sie.
Ich wollte, daß du nicht viel Männer brauchst
Um einzusehn, was dir vom Mann bestimmt. (GBA 11: 188)

Der anschließende Verrat der Kaumann zeigt: mit ihr haben wir
eine, auf die können wir nicht bauen. Darin wie Fatzer, bindet sie
sich nicht an die vier. Im Fortgang der weiteren Handlung ver-
schwindet sie aus dem Blickfeld; sie geht nicht mit unter.
    Fatzer selbst bindet und distanziert sich (Wärme/Kälte). Er
bewegt sich in einem Feld von Progressionen und Regressionen, die
sich gegenseitig in Frage stellen und in dem er sich nicht endgültig
entscheiden kann. Seine erotische Ambivalenz korreliert damit. Er
will Frauen, und er sucht die Wärme der Kameradschaft (welche

allerdings in Hitze umschlägt und die Gruppe verbrennt). Er trifft keine grundsätzliche Entscheidung, die immer auch ein Ausschliessen des anderen bedeuten würde. Fatzers Rückkehr zu seinen Kameraden, die ihn dann hinrichten, kann gelesen werden als Reaktion auf die als unerträglich empfundene Unsicherheit seiner eigenen Identität. Sein Tod soll die Sache beenden. Doch selbst hier ist seine Unverläßlichkeit stärker: eingetroffen bei der Gruppe, will er nicht mehr sterben.

Das Fehlen der Autoriät, die zu stürzen wäre, geht einher mit der Dynamisierung von Identitätsbildung. Das "menschliche Wesen ist kein dem einzelnen Individuum inwohnendes Abstraktum. In seiner Wirklichkeit ist es das Ensemble der gesellschaftlichen Verhältnisse," heißt es in der sechsten Feuerbachthese (Marx und Engels 3: 6). Die moderne bürgerliche Gesellschaft in ihrer ungeheuren Dynamik setzt voraus und produziert zugleich ein neues Individuum. Marx im *Kapital*:

Die moderne Industrie betrachtet und behandelt die vorhandne Form eines Produktionsprozesses nie als definitiv. Ihre technische Basis ist daher revolutionär, während die aller früheren Produktionsweisen wesentlich konservativ war.... Die Natur der großen Industrie bedingt daher Wechsel der Arbeit, Fluß der Funktion, allseitige Beweglichkeit des Arbeiters.
(Marx und Engels 23: 510-511)

Einerseits produziere sie die "alte Teilung der Arbeit mit ihren knöchernen Partikularitäten" (511), andererseits "macht die große Industrie durch ihre Katastrophen es selbst zur Frage von Leben und Tod, den Wechsel der Arbeiten und daher möglichste Vielseitigkeit der Arbeiter als allgemeines gesellschaftliches Produktionsgesetz anzuerkennen" (511-512). Zu ersetzen ist "das Teilindividuum, der bloße Träger einer gesellschaftlichen Detailfunktion, durch das total entwickelte Individuum, für welches verschiedne gesellschaftliche Funktionen einander ablösende Betätigungsweisen sind" (512).

Fatzers Dezentrierungen sind der Versuch, "die Knochen seiner Ich-Identität aus seinem Dasein in verschiedenen Praktiken zusammen[zu]suchen" (Engler 281). Indem Fatzers Anstrengungen, sich der Komplexität der Welt zu stellen, von ihm selbst gebremst werden (die Konstituierung der Gruppe mit dem Zwang der Illegalität ist das Abschneiden der Kontakte nach draußen), gerät, so Engler, die Repräsentation dieser Komplexität in die Krise. Die Negation des Krieges bleibt stecken: ihr fehlt fortan das makrosoziale Feld, auf dem sie ihre Energie wirken lassen könnte. So "wendet sich der negative Impuls der Gruppe nach innen. Bei dieser Binnenhitze zerfällt sie und speit Fatzer aus" (Engler 286).

Gleichzeitig wird die Schwierigkeit Brechts deutlich, diesen Substanzverlust des Individuums ins Dramatische zu transformieren. Ihm droht die dramatische Figur des Fatzer zu zerfließen. In *Mann ist Mann* wird Identität gewechselt. Der Packer Galy Gay wird in eine andere Funktion gebracht: Er wird zum Soldaten Jeraiah Jip. Fatzer zerfällt in mehrere Identitäten, oder anders gesagt: Identität wird fortlaufend neugebildet.

3

Die Zwischenkriegszeit zwischen dem ersten wirklich modernen Krieg und seiner Wiederaufnahme mit Tempoerhöhung ("Blitzkrieg") ist der Ort, an dem Brecht an die Grenzen der Repräsentierbarkeit stößt. Während die "stärksten Erleber" schilderten, "wie schrecklich es war, vier Jahre lang keine Persönlichkeit gewesen zu sein" (GBA 21: 306), ist für Brecht die Persönlichkeit verschwunden. Der erstmalige Einsatz von Tanks und Gas, der flächendeckende Beschuß durch die Artillerie, der Stellungskrieg in Gräben, ohne den Feind zu sehen, waren Phänomene der Maschinisierung, der Anonymisierung, die nun auch den Krieg erreicht hatten. Der Umbau Galy Gays findet im Vorfeld eines Krieges statt. Sein Widerstand dagegen ist eher gering wie die Verwunderung seiner Frau von kurzer Dauer. Die Reduktion Galy Gays auf seine kleinste Größe läßt ihn eine neue Identität gewinnen. Damit nimmt *Mann ist Mann* Momente der Lehrstücke vorweg. Da Galy Gay in ein (schlechtes) Kollektiv wechselt, bleibt jedoch die Berücksichtigung der Zugehörigkeit zu vielen Kollektiven ein ungelöstes Problem. Mit dieser "Last" steigt Brecht in die Arbeit am *Fatzer* ein.

In der ersten Arbeitsphase (1927; vgl. Lenze 334ff.) bringt Brecht die Desertion in Varianten aufs Papier. Fatzer wird als der Aktive gezeichnet, dem sich die anderen anschließen. Zugleich ist er ansatzweise schon der Unzuverlässige, der am Ende exekutiert wird (vgl. Stückplan Lenze 98 [V.5]). Für Lenze wird er damit zunehmend zum Vertreter eines überlebten Individualismus (Lenze 336). Fatzer wehre sich "schon früh gegen seinen 'Umbau' nach Maßgabe gemeinschaftlicher Bedürfnisse" (338) in einem — nun nicht mehr schlechten — Kollektiv. Bei Lenze (wie bei anderen) bilden die Desertierenden ein Kollektiv, welches dann für Kollektivität überhaupt genommen wird.

In der zweiten Arbeitsphase (1927-1929) führt Brecht, nachdem er eine Reihe von Szenen entworfen hat (Lenze [V.6]), erstmals einen Chor ein (Lenze 142 [V.7.1]). Wer damit eine Instanz erwartet, die Sätze liefert, an denen man sich festhalten könnte, wird

sogleich enttäuscht. Nach einer ersten Kommentierung der Desertion (142-143) stellt der Chor im nächsten Auftritt seine eigene
Autorität in Frage:

>   w e r   i s t   d e r   c h o r ?
>   vor dem schluß:
>   aber auch er ist doch
>   ein mensch wie ihr!
>   unbestimmt von ausdruck
>   frühzeitig verhärtet, vieles
>   versuchend
>   äußerte er viel:
>   haltet ihn doch
>   nicht bei dem was er sagte bald
>   ändert ers...
>   nichts endgültiges saht ihr und alles
>   alles ändert sich vor es einging
>   warum
>   nehmt ihr ihn beim wort?
>   w e n   i h r   b e i m   w o r t   n e h m t   d e r
>   i s t s   d e r   e u c h   e n t t ä u s c h t !
>   x
>   a b e r   s i e   b r a u c h e n   d o c h   a u c h
>   o b d a c h + w a s s e r + f l e i s c h! (Lenze 142 [V.7.1])

Die Rede stürzt sich ins Dilemma jeglichen Sprechens. Einerseits ist
auf das Wort kein Verlaß. Ein naives Vertrauen auf seine Gültigkeit
mißachtet jene Unbestimmtheit im Ausdruck und endet in Enttäu-
schung und Katastrophe (die drei gehen mit Fatzer unter). Andererseits ist das Wort unverzichtbarer Bestandteil, um die Befriedigung
der Elementarbedürfnisse (Trinken, Essen, Wärme) zu organisie-
ren/zu verabreden. Diese scheinbare Trivialität ist höchst folgenreich
für das Problem der Autorität. Marx faßt in der *Deutschen Ideologie*
(Marx und Engels 3) den Menschen als natürliches und gesellschaftliches Wesen. Das heißt, daß auf jeder Entwicklungsstufe von
Gesellschaft (auch in der hochkomplexen der Gegenwart) die Notwendigkeit der Befriedigung elementarer Bedürfnisse besteht. In der
Spannung von diskursiver und nichtdiskursiver Praxis, also im
Bezugnehmen in der Rede auf ein außerhalb ihrer Liegendes kon-
stituiert sich Autorität. Der Einspruch, daß doch auch "obdach +
wasser + fleisch" gebraucht wird, steht für die Einsicht in die prag-
matische Dimension der Sprache. Gleichzeitig scheint Brecht zu
bemerken, daß er mit der fast archaischen Situation (es geht die
ganze Zeit um Fressen und um das Besitzen der Frau) auch stark

vereinfacht. Der unmittelbar(!) anschließende Entwurf (Lenze [V.7.2])
— die vier kehren aus dem Krieg heim ins besetzte Ruhrgebiet
(März 1923) — könnte so als der Versuch gelesen werden, die Konstellation von dieser Vereinfachung zu befreien. Damit aber droht
die Linse zu beschlagen, durch die Brecht überhaupt sein Material
verorten kann. Fatzers Rede "über die / unbeurteilbarkeit menschlicher / handlungen" stellt das aus:

> ganz unbeurteilbar
> ist der mensch dem menschen.
> so wie gegangen durch
> ungeheuren magen
> der jeden knochen + haut durch
> saft einschmilzt
> so daß du aus dem kot nicht
> fisch noch apfel auskennst
> so liegt im trüben brei des menschen
> leben
> ist es genossen vor dem aug der welt. (Lenze 149-50 [V.7.2])

Das untergräbt die Möglichkeiten von Dramatik überhaupt. Aus
dem "trüben brei des menschen" ist kein Stück mehr rauszuholen.
Das Wühlen in der Scheiße zaubert uns Fisch und Apfel nicht
hervor — unten schwimmt nichts anderes als oben.

So kehrt Brecht zur vorigen Konstellation zurück. Vorerst führt
er einzelne Szenen weiter aus. Die Textstufe V.8 wird neben V.6
zum textreichsten (szenischen) Teilkomplex. Die Konzeption von
Chören kommt vorerst über Ansätze nicht hinaus. Parallel dazu
(Ende 1928) beginnt Brecht mit der Arbeit am Lindhberg-Stoff.
Ursprünglich nicht als Lehrstück geplant, wird es Brechts erster
Versuch mit dem neuen Stücktypus. Im Frühjahr 1929 arbeitet er
mit Paul Hindemith am *Badener Lehrstück vom Einverständnis.* Die
Genese einer neuen Theaterkonzeption fällt also mitten in die
Produktionszeit des *Fatzer.*

In der dritten Arbeitsphase (1929/30) beginnt der Umbau vom
Schaustück zum Lehrstück. Die Konstruktion wird jetzt "aufgebaut,"
damit

> ihr entscheiden sollt
> durch das sprechen der wörter + das anhören der chöre
> was eigentlich los war denn
> wir waren uneinig. (Lenze 202 [VII.10])

Brecht unterteilt das Fragment in "Fatzerdokument" und "Fatzerkommentar." Das Dokument besteht aus den szenischen Teilen. An ihm hat Brecht bis hierhin hauptsächlich gearbeitet und — gelernt:

> der zweck wofür eine arbeit gemacht wird ist nicht mit jenem zweck identisch zu dem sie verwertet wird. so ist das fatzerdokument zunächst hauptsächlich zum lernen des schreibenden gemacht.... ich der schreibende muß nichts fertig machen. (Berliner Ensemble 72)

Mit dem Einbau des "Fatzerkommentars" versucht Brecht, sich herauszukatapultieren aus dem Dilemma zwischen Komplexität von Welt und ihrer Darstellbarkeit. "Das Kommentar" enthält: "zweierlei anleitungen für die spieler: solche, die die darstellung und solche, die den sinn und die anwendung des dokuments betreffen" (Berliner Ensemble 73).

Dabei ist das Studium der letzteren vor dem Darstellen (dem Spielen also) gefährlich. An den Sinn ist nur durch das Spiel zu gelangen (vgl. ebd.). Aus Zuschauern werden Spieler — wir sollen die Wörter sprechen. Die "Basisregel" (Steinweg, *Lehrstück*) des Lehrstücks: "das lehrstück lehrt dadurch, daß es gespielt, nicht dadurch, daß es gesehen wird" (1937; Berliner Ensemble 164), wird so vorweggenommen.

Im *Fatzer* als Schaustück können sich die Dezentrierungen Fatzers nicht voll entfalten. Vor den Augen der Zuschauer agieren Schauspieler, die den Figuren einen Rest von Konsistenz geben. Die sinnlich-wahrnehmbaren Gestalten der Akteure evozieren die Vorstellung, so etwas wie "ganze Menschen" vor sich zu haben. Dezentrierungen laufen so Gefahr, für Aufspaltungen genommen zu werden: Aufspaltungen von etwas als Ganzes Gedachtem. Der epische Schauspieler "muß imstande sein, seinen Typus trotz oder besser vermittels der Brechungen und Sprünge als einen einheitlichen vorzuführen," notiert Brecht im Frühjahr 1931 (GBA 24: 49). Die Aufführung vor Zuschauern bildet diesen gegenüber einen relativ geschlossenen Raum. Von dieser anderen Realität wird dann erwartet, sie nehme die außertheatralische Wirklichkeit der vor der Rampe Sitzenden auf und repräsentiere sie. Das bedeutet keineswegs plattes Abspiegeln; Repräsentieren schließt die Veränderung ein (Reproduktion und Produktion). Der Kitt, mit dem die Teile der Figuren zusammengefügt werden, wird im *Fatzer* immer wieder als das Anarchische, das Vitalistisch-Egoistische wahrgenommen und stiftet — ob der Autor will oder nicht — Identifikation. In Heiner Müllers Bemerkung über die nun einsetzende "Materialschlacht Brecht gegen Brecht (= Nietzsche gegen Marx, Marx gegen Nietzsche)" (Hörnigk 36) ist Brecht selbst davon betroffen. Doch Müllers

Behauptung, mit der Umwandlung der Koch-Figur in Keuner beginne der Entwurf zur Moralität auszutrocknen (vgl. ebd.), übersieht den Gewinn.

Aus dem Eigennamen Koch (d.h. einem Ausweis seiner Identität) wird der paradoxe Name Keuner. Er transportiert "das Allgemeine" (von griechisch "keunos") wie auch "Keiner" (vgl. Benjamin 11 und 21). Der Name stellt die Identität seines Trägers permanent in Frage. Odysseus hatte seine Identität zeitweilig verleugnet, um als "Niemand" den Kyklopen zu foppen. Wir wissen, daß Niemand eigentlich Odysseus ist. Dagegen ist Keuner Keuner.

Die Tendenz zur Auflösung der relativ ganzheitlichen Gestalten schlägt voll durch erst im Übergang zum Lehrstück. Aus Bühnenraum und Zuschauerraum macht Brecht jetzt einen. Aus der Not, daß sich doch immer wieder Identifikation einstellt, macht er eine Tugend: "Als ich für das Theater mit der Einfühlung mit dem besten Willen nichts mehr anfangen konnte, baute ich für die Einfühlung noch das Lehrstück" (GBA 22: 447). Identifikation im Lehrstück-Spielen bedeutet nicht, sich in eine imaginäre (ganze) Gestalt hineinzuversetzen, sondern durch ständigen Positionswechsel der Spieler zwischen den einzelnen Figurenreden sowie den Chören "ein sich Zerstückeln in die Verhaltensweisen des Stückes...: ein sich ausfalten in die Verkettung der gestischen Rhetorik" (Nägele 318).

Dieser Gewinn macht Vereinfachungen möglich, ja sogar nötig. Brecht schickt Keuner ins Rennen, um Fatzers Dominanz zu relativieren. Der Aufstieg Keuners soll ein Korrektiv schaffen. Zugleich frißt die Tendenz zum Lehrstück an der Konsistenz der dramatischen Figuren. Denn "ästhetische maßstäbe für die gestaltung von personen, die für die schaustücke gelten, sind beim lehrstück außer funktion gesetzt. besonders eigenzügige, einmalige karaktere fallen aus" (Berliner Ensemble 164). Die Herstellung strenger Muster für die Spielenden verlangt nach Abbau dramatischer Figuren überhaupt. Sowohl Fatzer als auch Keuner stellen Übergänge dar. Tragen sie nicht mehr "normale," sondern paradoxe Namen, so sind es immer noch Namen. In der *Maßnahme* haben wir nur noch Instanzen (ohne Eigennamen) vor uns: die vier Agitatoren, der junge Genosse, der Leiter des Parteihauses usw.

Zudem erfordern strenge Muster eine relative Freiheit von konkret-historischem Handlungsraum: um das Spielen/Üben freizuhalten von der Gefahr, vor dem Sprechen eine mit Bedeutung angereicherte Totalität vor Augen zu haben. Zu derart starken Schnitten am *Fatzer*-Material kann Brecht sich nicht entschließen. Lieber legt er es beiseite, denn mit einer solchen Reduzierung droht Brecht auf der Stoffebene das Fundament zu zerbrechen, von dem

aus er gegen Kapitalismus und aufkommenden Faschismus an-
schreiben kann.[5]

4

Stimme gegen Körper lautet eine gängige Beschreibung des Kampf-
feldes, auf dem sich die modernen Theaterauffassungen tummeln.
Rationalität gegen Irrationalität ist ein anderer Name dafür: Brecht
und Artaud gelten weithin als die Anführer der Parteien. Rainer
Nägele hat in seinem Aufsatz über "Brechts Theater der Grausamkeit" diese Opposition einer Kritik unterzogen. Nicht zuletzt die
Tatsache, daß der *Fatzer*-Text diese Opposition radikal in Frage
stellt, macht seine Bedeutung aus. Das Theater der Körperlichkeit
evoziert gelegentlich die Vorstellung von größerer Freiheit der
Spieler gegenüber dem Text. Der Herrschaft des Textes zu entkommen, gilt als Devise. Die Freiheit des Spiels wähnt sich als die
Freiheit der Schauspieler, die sich mithin als autonome Individuen
zu verwirklichen meinen. Zusammen mit den Lehrstücken gehört
der *Fatzer* zu den Spielvorlagen, die gerade an diesem Punkt ihre
Grenze ziehen. Als Körper sind sie abgedichtet gegenüber dem
Verlangen, das einem Genehme herauszulesen oder hineinzulegen.
Die "Aufladung" führt zur Zerstörung.

Auf der Frankfurter "Experimenta 6" (1990) war Heiner Müllers
synthetisches Fragment *Germania Tod in Berlin* in Inszenierungen
von Frank-Patrick Steckel (Schauspielhaus Bochum) und Fritz Marquardt (Berliner Ensemble) zu sehen. Im Vergleich der Aufführungen
wurden verschiedene Konzepte im Umgang mit dem Text sichtbar.
Steckel stattete seine Inszenierung mit Slapstick-Elementen aus.
Wollte er damit die Komik des Stückes herausspielen, so über-
formte/verdeckte er damit die Gewalt der Müllerschen Sprache.
Marquardt dagegen stellte den Text heraus, indem er die Versenden
demonstrativ sprechen ließ. Der Schauspieler als "Textablieferer"
(Rischbieter). Darin Brecht nahe, war die Komik der Berliner
Aufführung eine andere als die der Bochumer. Durch eine Ver-
flüssigung des Sprechens und fast hektische Bewegungen geriet die
Szene "Hommage a Stalin 1" (die Nibelungen "rächen" Siegfried)
bei Steckel zur Kabarett-Nummer (mit entsprechend reagierendem
Publikum). Die Verwischung der Konturen der Körper durch die
Kostüme verstärkte diese Tendenz noch. Marquardts asketische
Inszenierung ließ die Sprache ganz ohne Beiwerk zur Geltung
kommen. Die Komik der Berliner Aufführung war so von eher böse-
gespenstischer Natur — eine Qualität, die Müllers Sprache prägt
und deren Quelle nicht zuletzt Brecht ist. Bei Steckel war die
"inszenierte Komik" (Heiner Goebbels) eine entschärfte.

Inszenierungspraxis, wie sie ansatzweise in Marquardts Aufführung gegeben ist, stellt Schauspieler noch immer vor große Schwierigkeiten.[6] Wenn Heiner Müller davon spricht, daß es sehr schwer ist, "Schauspieler dazu zu überreden, daß sie z.B. mal einen Block herstellen und da mit einer Wirkung auskommen über zehn Zeilen" (Marquardt et al. 49), so ist das ein Problem, mit dem sich schon Brecht herumschlug: Der Schauspieler, "ganz abhängig vom Zuschauer, ihm blind unterworfen" (GBA 21: 28), versetzt sich selbst und das Publikum in Trance, unter Zuhilfenahme der Suggestion.[7] Aufschlußreich ist die positive Beschreibung des Problems, die Brecht mit einem Beispiel gibt:

> Als eine Schauspielerin dieser neuen Art die Magd im *Ödipus* spielte, rief sie, den Tod ihrer Herrin berichtend, ihr "tot, tot" mit ganz gefühlloser, durchdringender Stimme, ihr "Jokaste ist gestorben" ohne jede Klage, aber so bestimmt und unaufhaltsam, daß die nackte Tatsache ihres Todes gerade in diesem Augenblick mehr Wirkung ausübte, als jeder eigene Schmerz zustandegebracht hätte. (GBA 21: 281-282)

Das gefühllose, durchdringende Sprechen schafft die Distanz, indem es den Text als Körper akzeptiert. Das suggestive Spielen dagegen nimmt den Text nicht in seiner Gestalthaftigkeit/Konturiertheit wahr; vielmehr benutzt es ihn als Medium, als Transportmittel einer Idee vom Text. Der *Fatzer* läßt das nicht zu. Müllers Satz: "Der Text ist präideologisch, die Sprache formuliert nicht Denkresultate, sondern skandiert den Denkprozeß" (Hörnigk 35), benennt jene Autonomie, die ihn für das Theater so sperrig macht. Ausklammerungen und Anschlüsse mit "und" sowie häufiges Weglassen von Satzzeichen lösen hypotaktische Strukturen auf. Der Übergang zu Parataxe ermöglicht immer weitere Anschlüsse. Das Resultat ist ein Gedanken nachholendes Reden:

> FATZER: ...aber ich hab die
> augen offen gehabt und gesehn daß
> eine neue zeit anfängt und
> mit dem volk
> etwas und was noch nie war
> und man sieht leut herumgehen die
> man sonst nie gesehen hat, das
> kommt
> weil alles, was unten ist,
> heraufkommt. (Lenze 112 [V.6])

Der Fatzervers arbeitet am Verschwinden der Schauspieler. Werden die Versgrenzen auch als solche kenntlich gemacht (d.h. durch Pausen), geraten die Schauspieler zu Sprechmaschinen. Deren Qualität besteht darin, das sprachliche Material vor "privatem Expressionismus" (Heiner Goebbels) zu schützen. Der beste Beamte gibt den Staat heraus (vgl. "Fatzer, Komm", Lenze 267-269 [VIII.- 12]), der beste Schauspieler liefert den Text ab. Man achte auf den Zeilensprung:

> wollt ihrs wirklich wissen? jetzt
> fordre ich euch auf einzu-
> treten in diesen kampf den ich
> da hab und heute abend
> zur gleichen stund an diese stell
> zu kommen, wo ihr versagt habt, damit
> wir
> uns wieder in die augen sehen können und
> daß ich die umleg die mich
> umgelegt haben! (Lenze 178 [V.8])

Die dramatische Rede ist dem gewohnten Sprachfluß nicht einzuverleiben, der Sprung erfolgt fast immer "zu spät." Immer wieder setzt Brecht das "und" ans Versende, ein signifikanter Bruch mit der Alltagssprache (kein normaler Satz darf auf "und" enden). Unterstützt von Ausklammerungen, wird so der Redefluß gestaut. Das auf die Nuance gehende Spiel ignoriert diese Stauung, es verflüssigt den Text. Damit versucht es, Herrschaft über den Text zu gewinnen. Derart starkes Eingreifen hat als Hintergrund die Vorstellung, die (bestehende!) Institution Theater habe Priorität. Herrschaft der Rede über die Figur wirkt noch immer abschreckend auf das zeitgenössische Theater.

Die *Fatzer*-Aufführung von Wekwehrt am Berliner Ensemble krankte daran, daß sie sich nicht konsequent zu einer solchen Sprechweise durchringen konnte; zu sehr wurde auf "kräftige Figuren" orientiert. Wird die "fremde" Rede nicht auch so gesprochen, sondern in einen gegebenen Theaterbetrieb eingetaktet, geht die Sache daneben. Die Kritiken der Aufführung hatten recht in ihrem Unbehagen: allerdings nicht weil zu zuwenig, sondern zuviel "fesselndes" Theater geboten wurde (vgl. Berliner Ensemble 146-161).

Überzeugen kann dagegen die Hörspielfassung in der Regie von Heiner Müller. Das monotone, im Tonumfang reduzierte Deklamieren durch die Sprecher (bis auf zwei Berufsschauspieler waren nur Amateure beteiligt) erzeugt hier ein parataktisches Nebeneinander

zwischen den und innerhalb der Figurenreden, das die Zuord-
nungen aufbricht und die Bildung von Identität über Ausdruck
verhindert.[8] Die Textblöcke werden so fremd, daß ihre sinnliche
Qualität abgelöst erscheint von der Individualität der Spieler. Die
Sprechkunst Heiner Müllers ist es, die diesem Ideal nahe kommt.
Wann ist Müller Brecht am nächsten? Beim Rezitieren![9]

Der *Fatzer* ist der Traum von einem neuen Theater in einer
anderen Zeit. In einer Zeit, in der die Texte nicht vom Apparat
geschluckt werden, sondern ihre Sinnlichkeit behalten. In der der
Rhythmus der Verse seine affektierende Wirkung (neu) gewinnt —
als "Unfähigkeit/Unmöglichkeit, die Konstitution semantischer
Formen vom Empfinden des eigenen Körpers abzusetzen" (Gumbrecht 722).[10] Der *Fatzer*-Text transportiert den Anspruch, als
musikalisches Material behandelt zu werden. Dieser mag für viele
Texte gelten; nur ist er beim *Fatzer* so radikal, daß jede Aufführung
bei Nichteinhaltung dieser Forderung zur "Hinrichtung des Textes"
(Müller) gerät. Die Rede selbst übt die ordnende Funktion aus.

THEATER

...

wenn einer am abend eine rede zu halten hat, geht er am
morgen in das pädagogium und redet die 3 reden des johann
fatzer. dadurch ordnet er seine bewegungen, seine bewegungen, seine gedanken und seine wünsche. (Lenze 286 [XIV.2])[11]

ANMERKUNGEN

[1] Lenze 276 [XIV/1]. Im folgenden verweisen die im Text in eckigen Klam-
mern gesetzten Zahlen auf die *Fatzer*-Ausgabe von Reiner Lenze. Dabei gibt
die römische Zahl die Textschicht an, die arabische den Skriptenkomplex.
Nähere Ausführungen zur zeitlichen Zuordnung des Materials in Lenze 334-
370. Eine Fotokopie dieser Magisterarbeit von der Universität Münster liegt
im Bertolt-Brecht-Archiv vor und stellt den einzigen Versuch dar, Brechts
Prozeß der Arbeit am *Fatzer* auch nur andeutungsweise zu rekonstruieren
und bewerten. Die 1994 in Suhrkamp Verlag erschiene Taschenbuchaus-
gabe ist lediglich die Veröffentlichung in Buchform des Bühnenmanuskripts
von Heiner Müller, der 1978 eine Textmontage für das Deutsche Schauspielhaus Hamburg erstellte.

[2] Engler greift hier eine Formulierung Brechts von 1929 auf:

Unser Massebegriff ist vom Individuum her gefaßt. Die Masse ist so ein Kompositum; ihre Teilbarkeit ist kein Hauptmerkmal mehr, sie wird aus einem Dividuum mehr und mehr selber ein Individuum. Zum Begriff "einzelner" kommt man von dieser Masse her nicht durch Teilung, sondern durch Einteilung. Und am einzelnen ist gerade seine Teilbarkeit zu betonen (als Zugehörigkeit zu mehreren Kollektiven). (GBA 21: 359)

1944 versteht Brecht den einzelnen als "Mitglied *eines* riesigen, notgedrungen in sich selbst widerspruchsvollen Kollektivs" (GBA 23: 41; Hervorhebung von S.M.).

[3] Welche Bedeutung die Spaziergänge haben, kann man daran ermessen, daß Brecht beim Versuch, Keuner zu etablieren, ihn auf die Reise schickt:

stehe auf keuner und gehe
durch die stadt und
untersuche [...]
betrachte alle die dir begegnen und
prüfe jeden! (Lenze 249 [VIII.11.2.]).

[4] Interessant scheint mir eine Entdeckung Lorenz Jägers zu sein. Auf den Augsburger Brechttagen 1991 berichtete er von einem Projekt Brechts zu einem Kriminalroman Anfang der dreißiger Jahre. Protagonist des geplanten Romans ist der pensionierte Richter Lexer. Dessen Überlegenheit (als Detektiv) über die Polizei besteht darin, daß er nicht mehr von der Annahme einer moralischen Kohärenz ausgeht und somit nicht mehr nach langfristigen Motiven sucht. Dies könne — so Jäger — als Anweisung zum Verhalten in Krisenzeiten gesehen werden. Unbetroffen von der Krise sei hier einzig die Vernunft selbst. Diese letzte Mächtigkeit (der Perspektive) des Detektivs kann m.E. Fatzer angesichts dessen eigener Instabilität nicht zugesprochen werden.

[5] Vgl. auch Steinwegs von Brechts eigener Deutung abweichende These:

Der Grund für das Scheitern der Lehrstückfolge *Der böse Baal der asoziale* wird weniger in einer Verkennung der Bedeutung asozialer Triebe zu suchen sein als in der Schwierigkeit, das mit dem Schaustück *Baal* gegebene Sprachmaterial in eine Folge strenge Muster zu "transformieren.... Baal war zu sehr als besondere Persönlichkeit angelegt" (Steinweg, *Lehrstück*, 155).

[6] In dieser Perspektive sind Marquardt und Robert Wilson Verwandte. Müller beschreibt die Qualität von Wilsons Theater so:

Das Wesentliche an Wilsons Theater ist die Trennung der Elemente, ein Traum von Brecht. *Hamletmaschine* hat er, entsprechend der fünfaktigen Struktur, in fünf Segmente zerlegt: Er sah das Stück als Uhrwerk.... Der Text wird nie interpretiert, er ist ein Material wie das Licht oder der Ton oder wie das Dekor oder ein Stuhl. Er läßt die Texte in Ruhe, und wenn die Texte gut sind, ist das gut für die Texte. (Müller, *Krieg*, 331)

Bezogen auf die Arbeit der Schauspieler: "Was ein Text sagt, darf ein Schauspieler nicht bedienen. Es ist langweilig, wenn ein trauriger Text traurig gesprochen wird" (ebd.). Wilsons Theater ist eine Maschine der Freiheit:

Bedingung dieser Freiheit ist die Mechanisierung der Schauspieler, die totale Disziplin. Die *Hamletmaschine* 1986 in New York war strenger, präziser als in Hamburg, weil die Studenten in New York einen härteren Arbeitsmarkt vor sich haben. Die sind disziplinierter und kommen nicht auf die Idee, daß sie eine Persönlichkeit sind. (Müller, *Krieg*, 334)

[7] Bemerkenswert die Parallele bis ins Detail: In einer Diskussion über die Inszenierung von *Macbeth* (1982) beschreibt der Schauspieler Ulrich Mühe die Probenarbeit:

Für Heiner war es immer am schönsten, wenn wir nur dastanden in einem bestimmten Arrangement und einfach den Text nur sagten. Und wenn man über Wochen miteinander arbeitet, dann erwischen die Schauspieler auch Stunden, wo Heiner nicht "auf dem Posten" ist und dann können sie was spielen. Und wenn sie stark genug sind, können sie das bis zur Premiere durchhalten. Und dann ist es raus. (Marquardt et al. 49)

Brecht 1929:

Je mehr die Aufführung herannahte, desto mehr entfernte er sich davon [von einer Spielweise für den Zuschauertypus des wissenschaftlichen Zeitalters], er wurde zusehends anders; denn er fühlte wohl, daß er den nunmehr zu erwartenden anderen Zuschauern so nicht gefallen würde. (GBA 21: 281).

[8] Mittenzwei berichtet, daß schon 1967 von Schauspielern des Berliner Ensembles beklagt wurde, die Figuren des Stückes seien zu "kurzatmig." Er meint, diese tatsächliche Schwäche sollte nicht "mit dem Hinweis auf einen neuen Figurentypus weggeredet werden" (Berliner Ensemble 18). Diese Schwäche lobte schon der Dramaturg im *Messingkauf*:

Der Star von Shakespeares Globetheater war aber ein breiter, kurzatmiger Mann, so daß eine Zeitlang die Helden alle breit und kurzatmig sind, Macbeth sowohl als Lear.... Es wurden Stromschnellen eingebaut. Das Stück [*Hamlet*] wurde so viel interessanter. (GBA 22: 749)

Die Kurzatmigkeit der Figuren ist ihr Widerstand gegen Vereinnahmung (Einfühlung) von Seiten der Schauspieler. Die Schwäche ist eine des Theaterbetriebs.

[9] Ein Mitproduzent des Hörspiels berichtete, daß Müller solches Sprechen jederzeit reproduzieren konnte. Der Sprecher des Koch hätte dagegen zum Ende Probleme damit bekommen.

[10] Eine derartige Wirkung ist gebunden ans Sprechen, nicht zuletzt an dessen Dauer. Es scheint, daß Ermüdung durch das Spielen/Sprechen einen Widerstand bricht, der durch vorgegebene Bedeutungen gespeist wird. Reiner Steinweg erlebte diesen Vorgang bei der Arbeit des TheaterAngelus-Novus am *Fatzer*-Material und der *Ilias* von Homer. Er berichtet:

> Erst als ich mich 16 Stunden dieser Sprache und Situation ausgesetzt hatte, zerbrach die Abwehr — dieser mit den Sinnen, mit den Ohren und mit den Stimmbändern wahrgenommenen Sprache, die keinen Unterschied macht zwischen solchen "scheußlichen" Details [Schlachtszene aus dem 20. Gesang der *Ilias*] und "schönen" Stellen, sondern gleichmäßig dahinrollend alles hochspült, was da ist. (FatzerMaterial 26)

[11] Die ordnende Funktion gesprochener rhythmischer Sprache erreicht auch scheinbar entfernte Gebiete. Ihre erotische Qualität ist nicht nur Produkt eines abgebildeten Tuns, sondern Sprechen kann seinerseits den Genuß körperlicher Liebe steigern. Brecht macht dies zum Gegenstand im "Dritten Sonett" (1933, an Margarete Steffin). Die Genußsteigerung wird erzeugt durch Erschrecken: durch Erkennen des Gekannten.

LITERATURVERZEICHNIS

Adorno, Theodor W. *Negative Dialektik.* Frankfurt/M. 1975.

Benjamin, Walter. *Versuche über Brecht.* Frankfurt/M. 1978.

Berliner Ensemble. *Bertolt Brecht: Untergang des Egoisten Fatzer. Fassung Heiner Müller. Eine Dokumentation der Aufführung des Berliner Ensemble.* Berlin 1987.

Brecht, Bertolt. *Werke* (= GBA). Werner Hecht, Jan Knopf, Werner Mittenzwei, Klaus-Detlef Müller, Hrsg. Berlin und Frankfurt/M. 1988 ff.

Brenner, Hildegard. "Heiner Müllers *Mauser*-Entwurf: Fortschreibung des brechtschen Lehrstücks?" *Alternative* 110/111 (1976).

Engler, Wolfgang. "Kollektivität und Distanzierung: Stichworte zur Dialektik von Einverständnis und Negation in der Dramatik Brechts." In *Brecht 85. Zur Ästhetik Brechts.* Berlin 1986. 279-292.

"FatzerMaterial." *Maske und Kothurn* 34.1-4 (1988).

Gumbrecht, Hans Ulrich. "Rhythmus und Sinn." Hans Ulrich Gumbrecht und K. Ludwig Pfeiffer, Hrsg., *Materialität der Kommunikation.* Frankfurt/M. 1988. 714-729.

Hörnigk, Frank, Hrsg. *Heiner Müller Material.* Leipzig 1989.

Jäger, Lorenz. "Mord im Fahrstuhl: Benjamin, Brecht und der Kriminalroman." *The Other Brecht II / Der andere Brecht II, The Brecht Yearbook / Das Brecht-Jahrbuch* 18. Madison 1993. 25-40.

Knopf, Jan. "*Die Maßnahme,*" *Brecht-Handbuch: Theater.* Stuttgart 1980. 92-105

Lehmann, Hans-Thies und Helmut Lethen. "Ein Vorschlag zur Güte: Zur doppelten Polarität des Lehrstücks." Reiner Steinweg, Hrsg., *Auf Anregung Bertolt Brechts: Lehrstücke mit Schülern, Arbeitern, Theaterleuten.* Frankfurt/M. 1978. 302-318.

Lenze, Reiner. "*Untergang des Egoisten Johann Fatzer* von Bertolt Brecht: Kritische Ausgabe." Magisterarbeit. Münster 1986.

Marquardt, Fritz, Ulrich Mühe und Heiner Müller. "Der Rhythmus, die Arie und der Leim. Über Heiner Müllers Herausforderung an die Schauspieler." Wolfgang Storch, Hrsg., *Explosion of a Memory Heiner Müller DDR: Ein Arbeitsbuch.* Berlin 1988. 49-52.

Marx, Karl und Friedrich Engels. *Werke* (= MEW). Berlin 1958ff.

Müller, Heiner. *Krieg ohne Schlacht. Leben in zwei Diktaturen.* Köln 1992.

____. "Notate zu Fatzer." *Die Zeit* 12 (27.3.1978): 9/10.

Nägele, Reiner. "Brechts Theater der Grausamkeit: Lehrstücke und Stückwerke." Walter Hinderer, Hrsg., *Brechts Dramen. Neue Interpretationen.* Stuttgart 1984. 300-320.

Schnell, Ralf und Florian Vaßen, "Ästhetische Erfahrung als Widerstandsform. Zur gestischen Interpretation des *Fatzer*-Fragments." Gerd Koch, Reiner Steinweg und Florian Vaßen, Hrsg., *Asoziales Theater.* Köln 1983. 158-174.

Steinweg, Reiner, Hrsg. *Brechts Modell der Lehrstücke. Zeugnisse, Diskussion, Erfahrungen.* Frankfurt/M. 1976.

_____. *Das Lehrstück. Brechts Theorie einer politisch-ästhetischen Erziehung*. 2, verbesserte Auflage. Stuttgart, 1976.

Voigts, Manfred. *Brechts Theaterkonzeptionen. Entstehung und Entfaltung bis 1931*. München 1977.

Weimann, Robert. *Shakespeare und die Macht der Mimesis*. Berlin und Weimar 1988.

Bertolt Brecht's Learning Play: Genesis and Validity of the "Lehrstück"

Based on the *Lehrstück* theory that was (re-) constructed after the mid-sixties and on the discussions concerning the relations between the *Lehrstück* (teaching-play), and "Lern-Spiel," (learning-play) the author introduces the central categories of body, psyche, and art as "islands of disorder" in the *Lehrstück*. The goal is to counter a reductive tendency to rationality and enlightenment in the *Lehrstück* discussion by drawing attention to issues of attitude and bodily destruction, of forms and fantasies of violence, and of the contradiction between asociality and society. The author insists on the *Lehrstücke* as vehicles of aesthetic experience that result from artistically constructed texts. They also problematize the concept of the dialectic. The article concludes by rejecting the notion of a "pure" *Lehrstück* theory in favor of Brecht's heterogenous and spirited "art for the producers."

La Pièce didactique de Bertolt Brecht: Genèse et Validité du *Lehrstück*

Se fondant sur la théorie du *Lehrstück*, qui fut (ré-)élaborée dans la deuxième moitié des années soixante et sur les discussions concernant le rapport entre le *Lehrstück* (pièce d'enseignement) et le *Lern-Spiel* (pièce d'apprentissage), l'auteur introduit les catégories centrales du corps, de la psyché et de l'art comme "îlots de désordre" dans le *Lehrstück*. Le but est de freiner une tendance réductrice à la rationalité et aux lumières dans le débat autour du Lehrstück en attirant l'attention sur des questions d'attitude et de destruction du corps, de formes et de fantasmes de violence, et de contradiction entre l'asocialité et la société. L'auteur met l'accent sur les *Lehrstücke* en tant que véhicules d'une expérience esthétique résultant de textes composés artistiquement. Ceux-ci problématisent également le concept de dialectique. L'article conclut en rejetant la notion d'une théorie "pure" du *Lehrstück* en faveur de la conception hétérogène et animée de Brecht "d'art pour les producteurs."

La obra teatral didáctica de Bertolt Brecht: Génesis y validez de "Lehrstück"

Basándose en la teoría de *Lehrstück* que fue (re-)construida después de mediados de los sesenta y basándose también en las discusiones sobre las relaciones entre el *Lehrstück*, la obra teatral didáctica y "Lern-Spiel," el autor presenta las categorías principales de cuerpo, psique y arte como "islas de desorden" en el *Lehrstück*. El objetivo es de oponerse a la tendencia de simplificación de la racionalidad y la ilustración en la discusión del *Lehrstück* por medio de atraer la atención a temas de actitud y destrucción corporal, de formas y fantasías de violencia, y de la contradicción entre la indiferencia social y la sociedad. El autor insiste en *Lehrstücke* no sólo como camino hacia la experiencia estética resultante de textos construidos artísticamente, sino que también "Lehrstücke" problematiza el concepto de la dialéctica. El artículo en su conclusión, rechaza la noción de una teoría *Lehrstück* pura basada en el concepto heterogéneo y enérgico de Brecht de "arte para los creadores."

Bertolt Brechts "learning-play": Genesis und Geltung des Lehrstücks

Florian Vaßen

1

Als Brecht 1929 zum erstenmal den Titel "Lehrstück" verwendete und *Das Badener Lehrstück* am 28.7.1929 im Rahmen der Baden-Badener Musikfestwochen aufgeführt wurde, hatte er einen Theater-Typus geschaffen, der in einem zentralen Punkt deutlich über seine Experimente mit einem neuen Theater, mit "einer antimetaphysischen dialektischen nichtaristotelischen dramatik",[1] eben mit dem *Thaeter* hinausging: Die Kommunikation von Bühne und Publikum, das Spielen *für* ein Publikum war abgeschafft oder war zumindest nebensächlich geworden: "das lehrstück lehrt dadurch, daß es gespielt, nicht dadurch daß es gesehen wird. prinzipiell ist für das lehrstück kein zuschauer nötig, jedoch kann er natürlich verwertet werden."[2] Brecht "führt eine...Kette von Versuchen" durch, "die sich zwar theatralischer Mittel bedienten, aber die eigentlichen Theater nicht benötigten."[3] Stattdessen initiierte er einen selbstreflexiven politisch-pädagogischen Spiel-Prozeß, in dem die "tätigen und betrachtenden" nicht mehr voneinander getrennt sind, so wie im Marxschen Sinne die gesellschaftliche Trennung zwischen "filosofen" und "politikern" aufzuheben ist.[4]

Diese im politischen und kulturellen Umfeld der kommunistischen Arbeiterbewegung am Ende der Weimarer Republik entstandene, politische Theater-Pädagogik war nicht nur den bekannten Verleumdungen und Beschimpfungen von Links und Rechts ausgesetzt;[5] vor allem auch die Bezeichnung "Lehrstück" führte im allgemeinen Sprachverständnis und sogar in der Literaturwissenschaft zu vielfältigen Mißverständnissen im Sinne von Stück mit einer Lehre, politischem Zeitstück, Agitprop, d.h. Indoktrination und Kunstfeindlichkeit. Auch Brecht selbst stellte sich zumindest die Frage, "ob nicht die bezeichnung lehrstück eine sehr unglückliche" wäre.[6] Die englische Übersetzung "learning-play," die er höchstwahrscheinlich mitformuliert hat, drückt dagegen in ihrer Betonung des Lernens gegenüber der Lehre und des Spiels gegenüber dem Stück viel stärker Brechts Intention aus.[7] Das "Lern-Spiel," wie die

Brecht Then and Now / Brecht damals und heute
Eds. Marc Silberman et al. *The Brecht Yearbook / Das Brecht-Jahrbuch*,
Volume 20 (Madison: The International Brecht Society, 1995)

deutsche Rückübersetzung heißen könnte, verweist jedenfalls auf Aspekte, die die Bezeichnung "Lehrstück" allzuoft verdeckt hat.

Als sich Reiner Steinweg 1963/64 in einer Seminararbeit erstmals mit dem Lehrstück beschäftigte, auf die 1965 eine weiterführende Examensarbeit und einige Jahre später die Dissertation folgte, begann es ihm klar zu werden, daß nicht Theaterfiguren eine "fertige" Lehre vortrugen, sondern daß die Spielenden als Lernende die eigentlichen Protagonisten waren. Damit aber wird die sprachlich fixierte Lehre ersetzt durch äußere körperliche und innere emotionale, rationale, psychische *Haltungen* der Spielenden. Gleichfalls erkannte Steinweg schon den zentralen Widerspruch "von sozialer Verantwortung und einem erfüllten Eigenleben," wie er damals formulierte, d.h. den von Sozietät und Glücksverlangen/-Asozialität, und er verteidigte Brechts Betonung eines "positiven Individuums," eingebunden in ein Kollektiv, gegen die Auffassung von der Auslöschung des Persönlichen im Lehrstück.[8] Etwas später, im Kontext der Studentenbewegung, stellte sich dann — nicht nur für das Lehrstück — besonders prägnant die Frage nach der Gewalt. Es entstand die Diskussion um Gewalt als Widerstand, um das Verhältnis von gesellschaftlicher und persönlicher Gewalt. Die Re-Konstruktion von Brechts Lehrstücktheorie auf der Grundlage langjähriger Forschungen im Bertolt-Brecht-Archiv, der Versuch ein "Begriffsgeflecht" zu entwickeln und es in Verbindung mit den Lehrstück-Texten zu sehen, hieß auch, wie Steinweg selbst betont, "*Konstruktion der Lehrstücktheorie*" (8). Nicht zufällig spielte dabei die Arbeit an den beiden wichtigsten, sehr unterschiedlichen Lehrstück-Texten, an der *Maßnahme* und dem Fragment *Der Untergang des Egoisten Johann Fatzer*, eine zentrale Rolle. Ein Desiderat der Forschung dagegen blieb über Jahre die Analyse des "ästhetischen Typus Lehrstück" (9), dessen artistisches Prinzip und poetische Struktur sowie allgemein der Kunst-Aspekt erst neuerdings wieder ins Blickfeld geraten sind (siehe weiter unten).

Auf eine intensive, theoretische Kontroverse um Ahistorizität und Überbetonung des Lehrstücks gegenüber dem epischen Theater (Haarmann, Wallach, Baumgarten 1973; Berenberg-Gosler, Müller, Stosch 1974; Mittenzwei 1976)[9] folgte Ende der 70er Jahre eine neue, vielfältige, in sich heterogene Lehrstück-Praxis in der Bundesrepublik, vor allem in den Bereichen Schule, Universität und politische Bildung, aber auch im Theater.[10] 1981 wurde die Gesellschaft für Theaterpädagogik gegründet. Sie bot einen organisatorischen Rahmen für die praktische Lehrstück-Arbeit, betreut seit 1984 das Lehrstück-Archiv-Hannover (LAH), das vor allem die sogenannte "graue Literatur" sammelt, und gibt seit demselben Jahr die theaterpädagogische Zeitschrift *Korrespondenzen* heraus, die bis vor kurzem den programmatischen Untertitel "Lehrstück...Theater...Pädagogik..." trug. Die praktischen Spiel-Versuche, dargestellt u.a. in dem schon zitierten Band *Asoziales Theater* (1984), und das empirische Forschungsprojekt "Jugend und Gewalt" konzentrierten sich mit unterschiedlichen Methoden vor allem auf die Lehrstück-Erfahrungen und Bewußtseinsprozesse heutiger, junger Erwachsener bzw. Jugendlicher in einer deutlich gegenüber den 30er Jahren differenten gesellschaftlichen Situation.[11] Die Frage war: was und wie wird *heute* mit Brechts Lehrstücken gelernt? Beide Ansätze haben sich in den 90er Jahren fortgesetzt: das Lehrstück-Spielen als theatraler Lernprozeß und als ästhetische Erfahrung, aber auch als "'Erhebungsinstrument' in der Sozialwissenschaft, Lehrstück eben als Lern-Spiel.'"[12]

2

In dem Maße, in dem die gesellschaftlichen Verhältnisse in den Industrieländern und zugleich die globalen Strukturen immer komplexer und bedrohlicher werden, offenbart sich auch eine zunehmende Hilflosigkeit gesellschaftlich "eingreifender" Modelle, eine Unzulänglichkeit politisch-pädagogischer Methoden, ein Versagen aufklärerischer Konzepte, zumal in der Dialektik der Aufklärung, deren immanente Widersprüche und Grenzen allemal sichtbar geworden sind. Die utopielose Zeit der sogenannten Postmoderne scheint angebrochen.

Gleichwohl bestehen und entstehen allenthalben "Inseln der Unordnung", die ohne Totalitätsanspruch gleichsam als "Furchtzentrum", wie Brecht es im *Untergang des Egoisten Johann Fatzer* nennt, als utopischer Focus, wirken.[13] Zu nennen sind hier vor allem: der Körper, die Psyche, die Kunst oder auf einer anderen Ebene: das Fremde, das Andere, der Tod. Die Erinnerung an diese "vergessenen," ausgegrenzten und verdrängten Bereiche scheint lebens- und überlebensnotwendig in einer Zeit, in der Rationalität als instrumentelle Vernunft zur Destruktionskraft wird, wie Brecht es schon im *Galilei* beschreibt. Dabei besteht jedoch die Gefahr, daß jeweils neue Totalitätsansprüche entstehen und aus einer punktuellen Gegenbewegung, z.B. eine neue "umfassende" Ideologie des Körpers, der Psyche oder der Ästhetik wird. Die "Inseln der Unordnung" sind demnach keine rettenden Inseln inmitten allgegenwärtiger Herrschaftszusammenhänge, sie sind kein sicheres Terrain. Der heile Körper, die gesunde Psyche und das versöhnende Kunstwerk existieren ebensowenig wie der völlig aufgeklärte Mensch.[14]

Auch der "folgenlose Klassiker" Brecht unterliegt bekanntlich dem oben beschriebenen Verdikt aufklärerischer Gesellschaftsentwürfe. Zwar ist er gar nicht so folgenlos wie immer behauptet wird, wenn man sich z.b. genauer zum einen die Schauspiel-, Regie- und Inszenierungspraxis, sprich das Theater, und zum anderen die Dramen-, Lyrik- und Prosaproduktion, d.h. die Literatur der letzten 50 Jahre in Europa, aber auch weltweit und besonders in den letzten Jahrzehnten in der Dritten Welt ansieht. Das Theater des 20. Jahrhunderts und das Drama der ästhetischen Moderne sind jedenfalls ohne Brecht nicht denkbar. Dennoch aber zeigt Brechts episches Theater als Modell eines politisch wirksamen, "eingreifenden" Theaters mit seiner komödienhaft "überlegenen" Parabelform, mit seinen am Wissenschaftsbegriff[15] orientierten ästhetischen "Versuchen,"[16] eine spezifische Begrenztheit in seiner historischen Situierung, zumal die zugrundeliegende Gesellschaftstheorie, der Marxismus, zumindest in ihrer deformierten Realisierung als gescheitert anzusehen ist.

All diese genannten Probleme müßten noch verstärkt für Brechts Lehrstücke Geltung haben, da hier die in Frage gestellten gesellschaftlich eingreifenden Methoden Pädagogik und Politik in besonderer Weise ins Zentrum rücken. Es mag deshalb überraschen, daß ich gerade diese beiden Begriffe in Verbindung setzen möchte mit den drei oben genannten, mit Körper, Psyche, Kunst, aber auch mit dem Fremden, Anderen und dem Tod.

Der bedrohte, versehrte, zerstückelte Körper und dessen Auslöschung im Tod spielt in unterschiedlicher Weise in allen Lehrstücken eine zentrale Rolle.[17] Die Akzeptanz der "kleinsten Grösse," das "Einverständnis" mit dem Tod und die clowneske Körperzerstückelung im *Badener Lehrstück vom Einverständnis* sind z.B. — neben der "Auslöschung" des Knaben in *Der Jasager* und des jungen Genossen in *Die Maßnahme* sowie der tödlichen Gewalt in den Fragmenten vom *Bösen Baal dem asozialen* und vom *Fatzer* — besonders radikale Ausdrucksformen dieser Körperlichkeit. Entsprechend der Lehrstück-Konzeption findet diese Auseinandersetzung jedoch nicht nur und nicht einmal primär auf der Textebene statt. Vielmehr realisieren die Lehrstück-Spielenden diese destruktive Körperintensität im Spielprozeß. In quasi rituellen Gegenentwürfen wird die reale Zerstörung menschlicher Körperlichkeit so zugespitzt, daß deren Negation aufscheint. Tendenziell gelingt es so, den "Körperpanzer" aufzubrechen.[18] Dabei geht es aber weder um Ekstase und Rausch (Brechts Gestus bedeutet vielmehr Unterbrechung und beinhaltet eine gewisse Strenge und Kontrolliertheit) noch um das Streben nach neuer Ganzheit des Körpers, also um einen therapeutischen Prozeß, in dem der "kranke" Körper geheilt wird.

Eine gewisse Nähe zu therapeutischen Ansätzen, wie z.B. dem Psychodrama,[19] läßt sich jedoch auf einer anderen Ebene feststellen: Die Auseinandersetzung mit Gewalt als gesellschaftliche Gewaltform (*Badener Lehrstück*), als kollektive Gewaltform (*Der Jasager, Die Maßnahme*), als individuelle Gewalttätigkeit (*Der böse Baal der asoziale*) ist prägend für die Struktur der Lehrstück-Texte ebenso wie für die Lehrstück-Praxis.[20] Im Lehrstück-Spiel können internalisierte Gewaltformen ausagiert werden; Gewaltphantasien werden im "Schutz" der Lehrstückfigur zugelassen, ja hervorgeholt:

> ...gerade die darstellung des asozialen durch den werdenden bürger des staates ist dem staate sehr nützlich besonders wenn sie nach genauen und großartigen mustern ausgeführt wird. der staat kann die asozialen triebe der menschen am besten dadurch verbessern, daß sie, die von der furcht und unkenntnis kommen, in einer möglichst vollendeten und dem einzelnen selbständig beinah unerreichbaren form von jedem erzwingt.[21]

Abgesehen von Brechts sonderbarer Fixierung auf den Staat ist hier eine starke Betonung der kathartischen Wirkung des Lehrstück-Spielens sichtbar, verstanden — nicht im Sinne des klassischen deutschen Theaters, sondern in der Art der Antike — als lustvolle, durchaus auch körperliche "Erleichterung von Schrecken und Rührung."[22]

Dieser Ansatz wird mit unterschiedlicher Akzentuierung schon seit den 80er Jahren von Ingo Scheller, Reiner Steinweg und anderen vertreten und praktisch erprobt.[23] In der Publikation *Asoziales Theater* finden sich verschiedene Spielversuche mit dieser Tendenz, am deutlichsten wohl wiederum bei Scheller, bei dem es heißt:

> Im Mittelpunkt...stand das Thema Gewalt: Wie verhalten wir uns in Situationen, in denen wir Gewalt ausüben [müssen], wie gehen wir mit unseren Aggressionen um, welches Bewußtsein haben wir davon, wie wir auf andere [unterdrückend] wirken, welche Haltungen nehmen wir ein in einer gewaltförmig organisierten Gesellschaft und ihren Institutionen?[24]

Eine Folge der Gewalt, selbst ausgeübter oder erlittener, ist das Erschrecken vor sich selbst und vor anderen; der Schrecken aber ist Ausgangspunkt für Erkenntnis und für Veränderung, der "Schrecken die erste Erscheinung des Neuen."[25] Steinweg hat diesen Ansatz in dem schon erwähnten theaterpädagogischen Forschungsprojekt zur politischen Bildung aufgegriffen (siehe Anmerkung 10), ihn in der praktischen Arbeit der Friedenserziehung weiterentwickelt und zuletzt in einem vierjährigen Projekt des Grazer Büros für Frieden und Entwicklung über "Gewalt in der Stadt" verwendet.[26] Diese sehr produktive Vorgehensweise ist freilich nicht unwidersprochen geblieben. Bernhard Gaul z.B. kritisiert, indem er weniger den psychologischen Aspekt betont als den politischen, daß mit dieser Methode Gewalt als Widerstandsform weitgehend ausgegrenzt wird; zurecht weist er darauf hin, daß sich in Brechts Lehrstücken auch ein klassenkämpferisch positives Verhältnis zur Gewalt artikuliert.[27]

Noch auf einer anderen Ebene ist die Diskussion über das Verhältnis von Psychologie/Psychoanalyse und Lehrstück-Theorie eröffnet worden.[28] In dem Widerspruch von Asozialität und Moral, wie er besonders in Brechts Lehrstückfragmenten *Der böse Baal der asoziale* und *Der Untergang des Egoisten Johann Fatzer*, aber auch sonst in der Versuchsreihe der Lehrstücke zum Ausdruck kommt, wird eine der wichtigsten gesellschaftlichen und ästhetischen Problemstellungen des 20. Jahrhunderts sichtbar: "der unversöhnliche Antagonismus zwischen den Triebforderungen und den von der Zivilisation auferlegten Einschränkungen," wie es im Kontext von Sigmund Freud heißt.[29] Brecht hat sich offensichtlich gerade in den Lehrstücken intensiver als andere Schriftsteller seiner Zeit mit dem Widerspruch von Asozialität und Sozietät auseinandergesetzt und versucht, das Glücksverlangen der Menschen und ihre Bedürfnisse als Ausgangspunkt bzw. als Basis gesellschaftlicher Veränderungen zu nutzen. Brecht stößt dabei auf das gleiche Problem, man könnte es auch Aporie nennen, das Freud in seiner Untersuchung *Das Unbehagen in der Kultur* formuliert: Die beiden "Strebungen," die "des Strebens nach Glück, das wir gewöhnlich 'egoistisch' nennen, und des Strebens nach Vereinigung mit anderen in der Gemeinschaft," diese "Prozesse der individuellen und der Kulturentwicklung" sind, weil sie sich "einander feindlich begegnen und sich gegenseitig den Boden bestreiten", nur schwer zusammenzufügen und kaum miteinander zu versöhnen (265f.). Eben dies aber hat Brecht mit seinen Lehrstück-Experimenten versucht und ist daran in einer "Materialschlacht Brecht gegen Brecht" (Heiner Müller) politisch und ästhetisch "gescheitert." In den z.T. fragmentarischen Lehrstück-Texten mit ihren (ungelösten) politischen Widersprüchen haben die Lehrstück-SpielerInnen jedoch Raum für Erfahrungen, Raum, um äußere und verinnerlichte Asozialität und Sozietät als gesellschaftliche Muster an sich und anderen wahrzunehmen, im Spiel zu untersuchen, sie auszustellen, sie demnach öffentlich zu machen und so zu lernen, damit umzugehen.

Die Kunst scheint im Vergleich zu den offensichtlich zusammengehörigen Aspekten des Körpers und der Gewalt in der Lehrstück-Theorie und -Praxis auf den ersten Blick eher ein nachgeordneter Gesichtspunkt. So schreibt Brecht auch in dem Text "Zur

Theorie des Lehrstücks": "ästhetische maßstäbe für die gestaltung von personen, die für die schaustücke gelten, sind beim lehrstück außer funktion gesetzt"; aber es heißt dort ebenfalls: "für die spielweise gelten anweisungen des *epischen theaters*. das studium des V-effekts ist unerläßlich." Schließlich formuliert Brecht: "die form der lehrstücke ist streng, jedoch nur, damit teile eigener erfindung und aktueller art desto leichter eingefügt werden können."[30] In eine poetische Form, die jedoch sehr karg und sparsam in ihren Mitteln ist, eben streng — diese Texte befinden sich sozusagen auf einer mittleren Abstraktionsebene — können also eigene Erfahrungen, alltagssprachlich formuliert, eingefügt werden. Immerhin basiert der Spielprozeß anders als beim Rollenspiel und Psychodrama aber auf kunstvoll gebauten, poetischen Texten, in denen nicht nur die gesellschaftlichen Muster "hochqualifiziert" sind, sondern auch die sprachlichen, denn es geht Brecht um "die durchführung bestimmter handlungsweisen, einnahme bestimmter haltungen, wiedergabe bestimmter reden" (ebenda).

Mit dem Begriff der ästhetischen Erfahrung, "gewonnen im gestischen Umgang mit literarischen Texten," die ihre politische Qualität in dem Widerstand gegen die "Deformationen des Alltags" besitzen, haben Ralf Schnell und ich schon Anfang der 80er Jahre eine Dimension der Lehrstück-Konzeption angesprochen, die in vielen anderen Spiel-Versuchen marginal blieb. Uns ging es um die ästhetische Konkretion von historischen Erfahrungen in den Lehrstücken, um die Komplexität und Unausdeutbarkeit der Texte, die in Gesten, Haltungen und Reden materialisiert waren und in szenischen Bildern ihre Ausdrucksform fanden:

> Der Prozeß der Visualisierung verdeutlicht außerdem den Prozeß der literarischen Produktion, die Produziertheit des Textmaterials.... Angelegt ist diese Arbeitsweise auf eine ästhetische Sensibilisierung, die in ihrer intellektuellen wie körperlichen Fundierung neue Wahrnehmungsmöglichkeiten und Produktionsformen gegen Zurichtung und Instrumentalisierung entwickelt, Wahrnehmungsmöglichkeiten, die nicht aus der sinnlichen Produktion und Reproduktion des Alltags (Spiel, Tanz etc.) entstehen, sondern aus der Destruktion von ästhetischem Text *und* Geschichte.[31]

Von einem anderen Ansatzpunkt aus wurde 10 Jahre später erneut die poetische Intensität der Lehrstücke, speziell ihrer Sprache, in den Mittelpunkt gestellt und dem "spröde[n] sich verweigernde[n] Textkorpus," in dem "das dichterische Wort" funktionalisiert wird, da es sich "zur didaktischen Metapher" erniedrigt, "höchste künstlerische Strenge" zuerkannt.[32] Mit Adorno sieht Susanne Winnacker "das Lehrstück als artistisches Prinzip" und konzentriert sich auf die Aufdeckung der "poetische[n] Schichten."[33] Einerseits betont sie ausdrücklich die Notwendigkeit, auch gegen die "so vertrauten 'Inhalte'", den Text genau zu lesen, andererseits zeigt sie, daß die Lehrstücke, hier speziell *Die Maßnahme*, weder "*nur* als Spielvorlage" noch "*nur* als Text" zu verstehen sind.[34] Ausgehend von einer genauen sprachlichen Analyse des Wortes "Maßnahme" wird die Abwesenheit, insbesondere die des Jungen Genossen, der als selbständige Figur weder im Text noch im Spiel existent ist, sondern immer nur von den anderen dargestellt wird, als zentrale Kategorie von Brechts "Theater der Verhandlung" gedeutet. Gegen die Illusion vom Subjekt konzipiert schon Brecht die "Zertrümmerung der Person": "Sie fällt in Teile, sie verliert ihren Atem. Sie geht über in anderes, sie ist namenlos, sie hat kein Antlitz mehr, sie flieht aus ihrer Ausdehnung in ihre kleinste Größe."[35] Der junge Genosse ist "das andere des Einverständnisses," er bleibt noch in seinem Tod der "Fremde".[36]

Mit dieser Akzentuierung von Körper, Psyche/Asozialität und Kunst ist nicht beabsichtigt, die politische Pädagogik der Lehrstücke zu negieren, im Gegenteil. Ich stelle vielmehr die These auf, daß sich das Handlungsmodell der Pädagogik mit seiner Zielgerichtetheit durch die theatrale Orientierung in Richtung Sinnlichkeit und Subjektivität öffnet und daß die politische Dimension sich in Körper, Psyche und Kunst vervielfältigt. Walter Benjamins früher Hinweis, daß die "pädagogische Wirkung...zuerst" komme, "ihre politische dann und ihre poetische ganz zuletzt," zeigt nicht nur eben diese Verbindung, sondern betont auch eine gewisse zeitliche Reihenfolge, mit der er u.U. sogar eine Steigerung ausdrücken will.[37]

Ein zentraler Begriff der Lehrstück-Theorie ist mit der bisher skizzierten Entwicklung jedoch zunehmend problematisch geworden, ein Begriff, der in der Lehrstück-Praxis den Spielenden immer schon Kopfzerbrechen bereitet hat; ich spreche von der Dialektik. Immer schon wurde gefragt, wie lerne ich beim Lehrstück-Spielen dialektisches Denken, wie hat Brecht das gemeint? Oft wurde bezweifelt, daß das überhaupt möglich sei. Brecht, für den Dialektik bekanntlich kein Naturprinzip, sondern eine Denkmethode ist, hat immer die Widersprüche stärker betont als die Synthese oder gar die Totalität: "Die materialistische Dialektik...behandelt...die gesellschaftlichen Zustände als Prozesse und verfolgt diese in ihrer Widersprüchlichkeit. Ihr existiert alles nur, indem es sich wandelt, also in Uneinigkeit mit sich selbst ist."[38] In diesem Sinne ist auch der bekannte Lehrstück-Satz zu verstehen: "einverstanden sein heißt auch: *nicht* einverstanden sein."[39] In einem Gespräch mit Pierre

Abraham betont Brecht, daß es ihm im Lehrstück nicht um "Argumente für oder gegen...Meinungen" geht, "sondern ausschließlich um Geschmeidigkeitsübungen, die für jene Art Geistes-Athleten bestimmt sind, wie es gute Dialektiker sein müssen."[40] Zwar bringt der Dialektiker nach Brecht "in seinem Denken die Erscheinungen in die Krise, um sie fassen zu können,"[41] aber diese Krisen führen heute immer seltener zu dialektischen Lösungen, vielmehr entstehen, indem die Widersprüche gegeneinander stehenbleiben, eher Paradoxa oder Aporien und nur bedingt eine "praktische Kenntnis — von dem..., was Dialektik ist."[42] Dialektisches Denken scheint "zur Zerstörung von Ideologien" nicht mehr ausreichend.[43] Nicht nur die Wirklichkeit, wie Heiner Müller meint, sondern auch Brechts Lehrstücke sind offensichtlich "mit den klassischen marxistischen Kategorien nicht zu greifen." Sie "schneiden ins Fleisch."[44]

3

Die "reine Lehre" des Lehrstücks gibt es nicht mehr und hat es sicherlich auch nie gegeben, selbst bei Steinweg nicht, der in seinen frühen Untersuchungen den Versuch unternahm, Brechts Lehrstücktheorie zu rekonstruieren.[45] Auch die jüngste Bemühung in dieser Richtung, Krabiels verdienstvolle Analyse der Genese des Lehrstücks liefert zwar eine Fülle interessanten Materials, bleibt aber in ihrer Fixierung auf das Lehrstück als musikalisches Genre letztlich doch eine historische Reduktion auf die reine Lehre vom Lehrstück.[46]

Die Praxis sah schon zu Brechts Zeit anders aus, die einzelnen Lehrstücke und Lehrstück-Fragmente waren durchaus unterschiedlich strukturiert, und auch die Theorie — im Prozeß von Kooperation und Kritik — war immer in sich widersprüchlich, wie Tatlow in seiner Kritik an Krabiel nochmals verdeutlicht.[47] Diese Tendenz hat sich verstärkt, die Praxis ist bunt, gemischt, "unrein," die Theorie-Diskussion produktiv und lebendig und das Lehrstück ist allgemein stärker in die Theaterpädagogik integriert, wie 65 Jahre nach Brechts Anfängen und 30 Jahre nach Steinwegs Neuanfang das 140 Seiten dicke Heft "Brecht Lehrstücke" der theaterpädagogischen Zeitschrift *Korrespondenzen* (1994), insbesondere die umfangreiche Bibliographie, erneut belegt.

Da gibt es Vermischungen mit Alexander Kluge[48] und wichtige Weiterentwicklungen mit und bei Heiner Müller; da existieren z.B. die Performance-Experimente mit *Fatzer* von Andrzej Wirth in Berlin, Los Angeles und Sydney, widerspruchsvolle und nicht unproblematische Lehrstück-Experimente mit *Fatzer* und der *Maßnahme* durch Josef Szeiler[49] oder die "multiästhetische und -technische Aufführung" des *Badener Lehrstücks vom Einverständnis* von Joachim Lucchesi und Gerd Koch.[50] Verbindungen zur Theorie des Alltagsbewußtseins (Steinweg, Heidefuß, Petsch), zur interpretativen Soziologie mit ihrem Akteurs-Konzept (Windeler, Koch) und zum symbolischen Interaktionismus (Czipke), zu Bourdieus Habitus-Theorie (Scheller, Gipser) und zum Kommunitarismus (Koch), zum Psychodrama (Scheller, Steinweg, Weiß) und zu Freuds Kulturanalyse (Vaßen) werden hergestellt; praktische Erprobungen finden statt im Unterricht — in den verschiedensten Schulstufen und -typen (z.B. Höllfritsch, Nündel, Ritter, Schremmer) —, im deutsch-französischen Jugendaustausch (Liebe), in der Lehrerausbildung (Bätz) und -fortbildung[51] und besonders in der Ausbildung von SozialarbeiterInnen und SozialpädagogInnen (Koch, Streisand, Lucchesi); weiterhin in der Hochschuldidaktik (Gipser) und in der politischen Bildung (Heidefuß, Petsch, Steinweg), in der Arbeit mit Strafgefangenen (Thielicke, Thirslund) und mit städtischen Angestellten (Steinweg); vor allem aber in der Friedenserziehung (Steinweg).[52] Lehrstück-Theorie und -Praxis werden verwendet im politikwissenschaftlichen (Gantzel) und literaturwissenschaftlichen Studium (Vaßen), um Haltungen und Verhaltensweisen bzw. die Ästhetik von Texten nicht nur diskursiv zu bearbeiten. Nicht zuletzt im Theater wird immer wieder mit dem Lehrstück gearbeitet, vor allem das Kinder- und Jugendtheater, aber auch z.B. Zadeks Inszenierung von *Der Jasager und der Neinsager* am Berliner Ensemble, die auch in Kneipen und Versammlungsräumen brandenburgischer Dörfer aufgeführt wird.

Lehrstück-Versuche mit Arbeitern in Terni (Besson) und mit Partnerbetrieben der Volksbühne in der DDR (Tasche) blieben dagegen offensichtlich einmalige Ereignisse und sind im Gesamtzusammenhang der Lehrstück-Praxis eher marginal. Auch der Kontext des Sozialismus/Kommunismus ist abgesehen von einer kurzen Zeitspanne im Gefolge der Studentenbewegung zunehmend zurückgetreten hinter einer Lehre vom Verhalten, hinter Haltungen wie Zweifel, Staunen, Querdenken, hinter Körperlichkeit, Emotionalität und ästhetischer Erfahrung. Diese neuen Akzentuierungen verweisen auf die gegenüber den 30er Jahren veränderte soziologische Basis, auf differente kulturelle Zusammenhänge, auf unterschiedliche gesellschaftliche Formationen und neue politische Funktionen.

Das Brüchige und Disparate, gerade auch in seiner poetischen Form, tritt im Lehrstück verstärkt an die Stelle von praktischen Anweisungen und von oft verkürzter Dialektik. Gemeinsam ist dabei den meisten Versuchen Handlungsorientiertheit, Themenzentrierung, vergleichbar durchaus mit Brechts "dritter Sache," und ästhetische Konzentration. Lehrstück-Spielen bietet immer wieder die Möglichkeit, erstarrtes Alltagsbewußtsein aufzulösen und sich neuen

Erfahrungen, zumeist auch ästhetischen auszusetzen. Selber agieren und spielen — und sei es nur im Modell des Lehr-Stücks/"Lern-Spiels" — sowie darüber — sich selbst und andere beobachtend — reflektieren kann entgegen der anfangs geäußerten Zweifel immer noch zu eingreifendem Verhalten führen.

Lehrstück-Spielen im Sinne von Selbstverständigung als politisch-pädagogischem und zugleich sinnlich-genußvollem Prozeß und im Sinne einer kollektiven Kunstübung fände letztlich wohl auch Brechts Billigung. Manches würde ihn sicherlich irritieren, ließe ihn mißtrauisch den Kopf schütteln. Eine Formulierung von Heiner Müller variierend ist jedoch festzuhalten: Brecht gebrauchen, ohne ihn zu verändern, ist Verrat. Letztlich würde Brecht die Historizität auch seiner Theorie akzeptieren und ihre Veränderungen begrüßen, dann nämlich wenn die Spielenden im Probehandeln ihre Realität verarbeiten und sie politisch reflektiert und ästhetisch theatral gestaltet im Lehrstück-Spielprozeß mit der Spielvorlage montieren; denn Lehrstücke sind Texte, Verfahren, Spiele, sind "Kunst für Produzenten."[53]

ANMERKUNGEN

[1] Brecht, "Mißverständnisse über das Lehrstück," Reiner Steinweg, Hrsg., *Brechts Modell der Lehrstücke. Zeugnisse, Diskussion, Erfahrung* (Frankfurt/M: 1976) 129.

[2] Brecht, "Zur Theorie des Lehrstücks," ebenda, 164.

[3] Brecht, [Das deutsche Theater der zwanziger Jahre], *Gesammelte Werke* (Frankfurt 1967) 15: 239.

[4] Brecht, "Theorie der Pädagogien," Steinweg, *Brechts Modell*, 71.

[5] Vgl. die Zeugnisse der Rezeption der *Maßnahme* in Brecht, *Die Maßnahme. Kritische Ausgabe mit einer Spielanleitung*. Reiner Steinweg, Hrsg. (Frankfurt/M. 1976) 319-468.

[6] Brecht, "Mißverständnisse über das Lehrstück," 129.

[7] Brecht, "The German Drama: pre-Hitler," Steinweg, *Brechts Modell*, 150.

[8] Steinweg, "Die (Wieder-)Entdeckung des Lehrstücks. Geschichte einer Reise," *Korrespondenzen* 10.19-21 (1994): 6. Steinwegs Artikel dient z.T. als Grundlage dieses ersten Abschnitts.

[9] Siehe die Lehrstück-Bibliographie in Gerd Koch, Reiner Steinweg, Florian Vaßen, Hrsg., *Asoziales Theater. Spielversuche mit Lehrstücken und Anstiftung zur Praxis* (Köln 1984) 286-299. Steinweg setzt sich mit dieser Kritik auseinander in "Begriff und Erfahrung. Anmerkungen zur Lehrstück-diskussion," Steinweg, *Brechts Modell*, 427-452.

[10] Vgl. Reiner Steinweg, Hrsg., *Auf Anregung Bertolt Brechts: Lehrstücke mit Schülern, Arbeitern, Theaterleuten* (Frankfurt/M. 1978).

[11] Reiner Steinweg, Wolfgang Heidefuß, Peter Petsch, *Weil wir ohne Waffen sind: Ein theaterpädagogisches Forschungsprojekt zur Politischen Bildung. Nach einem Vorschlag von Bertolt Brecht* (Frankfurt 1986).

[12] Steinweg, "Die (Wieder-)Entdeckung des Lehrstücks," 12.

[13] Heiner Müller, "Mich interessiert der Fall Althusser...," Müller, *Rotwelsch* (Berlin 1982) 178.

[14] Vgl. Florian Vaßen, "Der ganze und der zerstückelte Körper. Stichworte zum Verhältnis von Körper-Therapie und Körper-Theater," *Korrespondenzen* 9.17-18 (1993): 15-21.

[15] Fang Wang, "*Man experimentiert auch an Menschen...*": Zur Thematik der Einheit von Wissenschaft und Kunst bei Bertolt Brecht (Würzburg 1992).

[16] Vgl. Florian Vaßen "Bertolt Brechts Experimente: Zur ästhetischen Autonomie und sozialen Funktion von Brechts literarischen und theatralen Modellen und Versuchen," Hans Joachim Piechotta, Ralph-Rainer Wutenow, Sabine Rothemann, Hrsg., *Die literarische Moderne in Europa* (Opladen 1994) 3: 146-174.

[17] Vgl. Rainer Nägele, "Brechts Theater der Grausamkeit: Lehrstück und Stückwerke," Walter Hinderer, Hrsg., *Brechts Dramen. Neue Interpretationen* (Stuttgart 1984) 300-320; Florian Vaßen, "Das Lachen und der Schrei oder Herr Schmitt, die Clowns und die Puppe," Gerd Koch, Florian Vaßen, Hrsg., *Lach- und Clownstheater: Die Vielfalt des Komischen in Musik, Literatur, Film und Schauspiel* (Frankfurt/M. 1991) 158-183.

[18] Vgl. z.B. Otto Clemens und Peter Rautenberg, "Die Wiedergewinnung körperlich-sinnlicher Ausdrucksformen als ein Element des Lehrstückspiels," Gerd Koch u.a., Hrsg, *Asoziales Theater*, 14-23.

[19] Vgl. Silvia Losacco und Reiner Steinweg, "Psychodrama und Lehrstück," *Korrespondenzen* 10.19-21 (1994): 64-68; ausführlicher in Steinweg, *Lehrstück und episches Theater: Brechts Theorie und die theaterpädagogische Praxis* (Frankfurt 1995) 133-148; vgl. auch Steinweg, "Gewalt, Krieg und Alltagserfahrung," *Dialog. Beiträge zur Friedensforschung* 2 (1985): 38-64.

[20] Vgl. aber auch Florian Vaßen und Jörg Golke, "Von der Freundlichkeit: Erfahrungen mit gewaltfreiem Lehrstück-Spiel," *Korrespondenzen* 6.7-8 (1990): 34-37.

[21] Brecht, "Theorie der Pädagogien," 71.

[22] Wolfgang Schadewaldt, "Furcht und Mitleid? Zur Deutung des Aristotelischen Tragödienansatzes," Schadewaldt, *Antike und Gegenwart: Über die Tragödie* (München 1965) 53.

[23] Vgl. z.B. Florian Vaßen, "Lehrstück und Gewalt. Die Wiederkehr des jungen Genossen aus der Kalkgrube," Paul-Gerhard Klussmann und Heinrich Mohr, Hrsg., *Spiele und Spiegelungen von Schrecken und Tod: Zum Werk von Heiner Müller* (Bonn 1990) 189-200.

[24] Scheller, "Arbeit an asozialen Haltungen und Lehrstückpraxis mit Lehrern und Studenten," Gerd Koch u.a., Hrsg., *Asoziales Theater*, 63.

[25] Heiner Müller, "Der Schrecken die erste Erscheinung des Neuen: Zu einer Diskussion über Postmodernismus in New York," Müller, *Rotwelsch* (Berlin 1982) 94.

[26] Steinweg, *Gewalt in der Stadt: Wahrnehmungen und Eingriffe. Das Grazer Modell* (Münster 1994).

[27] Bernhard Gaul und Reiner Steinweg, "Eine Brief-Kontroverse über den Gewaltbegriff, das Zeitmaß und die Stellung des Spielleiters," *Korrespondenzen* 10.19-21 (1994): 41-48.

[28] Vgl. hierzu ausführlicher Florian Vaßen, "Die Vertreibung des *Glücksgotts*: Brechts asoziale Lehrstück-Muster und Freuds *Unbehagen in der Kultur* — der Versuch eines Vergleichs," *Korrespondenzen* 10.1-21 (1994): 52-63.

[29] Editorische Notiz zu Freud, *Das Unbehagen in der Kultur*, Studienausgabe (Frankfurt/M. 1974) 9: 193.

[30] Brecht, "Zur Theorie des Lehrstücks," 164; daß die Relevanz des Kunst-Aspekts von dem jeweiligen Kunst-Begriff abhängig ist, zeigt Steinweg in seinem neuen Buch *Lehrstück und episches Theater*, 93-103.

[31] Ralf Schnell und Florian Vaßen, "Ästhetische Erfahrung als Widerstandsform. Zur gestischen Interpretation des *Fatzer*-Fragments," Gerd Koch u.a., Hrsg., *Asoziales Theater*, 170.

[32] Susanne Winnacker, "Wer immer es ist, den ihr sucht, ich bin es nicht": Gedankensplitter zur Dramaturgie der Abwesenheit in Bertolt Brechts Lehrstück *Die Maßnahme*," *Korrespondenzen* 10.19-21 (1994): 71.

[33] Theodor W. Adorno: "Engagement," Adorno, *Noten zur Literatur* (Frankfurt/M. 1981) 419.

[34] Winnacker 72-74.

[35] Brecht: "[Notizen über] Individuum und Masse," *Gesammelte Werke* 20: 61.

[36] Winnacker 72 und 74.

[37] Benjamin, *Versuche über Brecht* (Frankfurt/M. 1981) 10; zit. nach Winnacker 74.

[38] Brecht, *Kleines Organon für das Theater, Gesammelte Werke* 16: 682.

[39] Brecht, [Einverständnis und Widerspruch], Steinweg, *Brechts Modell*, 62.

[40] Brecht referiert von Pierre Abraham, Steinweg, *Brechts Modell*, 198.

[41] Brecht, "*Katzgraben*-Notate," *Gesammelte Werke*, 16: 794.

[42] Brecht referiert nach Pierre Abraham, Steinweg, *Brechts Modell*, 198.

[43] Brecht, [Notizen über Dialektik], *Gesammelte Werke*, 20: 157.

[44] Heiner Müller, "Brecht gebrauchen, ohne ihn zu kritisieren, ist Verrat," *Theater heute* (Jahrbuch 1980): 134.

[45] Vgl. Steinweg, *Das Lehrstück: Brechts politisch-ästhetische Erziehung* (Stuttgart 1972).

[46] Klaus-Dieter Krabiel, *Brechts Lehrstücke: Entstehung und Entwicklung eines Spieltyps* (Stuttgart und Weimar 1993).

[47] Antony Tatlow, "Landkarten für Maulwürfe oder Eine rückwärtsgewandte Zukunftswissenschaft," *Korrespondenzen* 10.19-21 (1994): 23-30.

[48] Siehe Alke Bauer: "Wer hat Angst vor Manfred Schmidt: Versuche über widerständige Theater-Spielereien," Bernd Ruping, Florian Vaßen, Gerd Koch, Hrsg., *Widerwort und Widerspiel: Theater zwischen Eigensinn und Anpassung. Situationen, Proben, Erfahrungen* (Lingen/Hannover 1991) 273-281.

[49] Szeiler, "FatzerMaterial," *Maske und Kothurn* 1-4 (1988); Aziza Haas, Josef Szeiler, Barbara Wallburg, Hrsg., *MenschenMaterial 1 Die Maßnahme: Eine Theaterarbeit mit Josef Szeiler* (Berlin 1991).

[50] Siehe "Spiel-Versuch 1991: *Das Badener Lehrstück vom Einverständnis* (1929)," *Korrespondenzen* 8.11-13 (1992): 3-30.

[51] Siehe Daniela Michaelis, *Asoziales Theater und Friedenserziehung in der LehrerInnenbildung? Eine theoretische und praktische Grundlegung zu einer ganzheitlichen Form der Friedens- und Konfliktarbeit* (Frankfurt/M: 1994).

[52] Soweit nicht anders vermerkt, finden sich genauere Darstellungen bzw. bibliographische Angaben dieser verschiedenen Bereiche in *Korrespondenzen* 10.19-21 (1994); siehe dort besonders die umfangreiche Lehrstück-Bibliographie (115-126); für bibliographische Angaben bis 1983 siehe Gerd Koch u.a., Hrsg., *Asoziales Theater* (vergriffen, noch zu erhalten über den Verfasser). In Steinwegs "Lob der Vielfalt" (11), Vorwort zu seinem neuen Buch *Lehrstück und episches Theater*, findet sich eine vergleichbare, aber unabhängig entstandene Auflistung von Anwendungsfeldern und Arbeitsbereichen. Steinweg untersucht in diesem Buch erneut das "Lehrstück 30 Jahre nach der (Wieder-)Entdeckung" und unterzieht seine eigene Re-Konstruktion unter dem Einfluß vielfältiger Praxis-Erfahrungen, insbesondere seiner Lehrstück-Arbeit in Brasilien, einer genauen Analyse und partiellen Revision.

[53] Brecht, "Das deutsche Theater der zwanziger Jahre," *Gesammelte Werke* 15: 239.

Re-Construction, Error, Improvement, or Thinking for the Museum: A Response to Klaus Krabiel

In his extended 1993 study of Brecht's learning plays Klaus Krabiel believes that he can disprove almost all of my 1972 learning play theory. My reply sets out a list of the points with which I agree; my critique follows. I show that Krabiel uses concepts and definitions arbitrarily and contradictorily. In particular I criticize his exclusion of the "Theory of Pedagogies," "The Grand Pedagogy," and the fragments of "Der böse Baal der Asoziale" from the *Lehrstück* material because they do not reflect on their contexts. If we include this material, however, then it is impossible to ignore the social experience of the learning play actors. This Krabiel refuses to acknowledge. Hence he unintentionally imputes to Brecht an authoritarian, doctrinaire conception of pedagogy. Although Krabiel fails with his methodologically naive demand for *absolute* historicity, he does in my opinion bring our understanding an essential step further, especially with regard to the genesis of Brecht's first learning plays.

Constructions, Erreurs et Améliorations, ou Comment Penser pour le Musée: Réponse à Klaus Krabiel

Dans son étude exhaustive des pièces didactiques de Brecht, Klaus Krabiel pense qu'il peut parvenir à invalider presque la totalité de ma théorie sur les pièces didactiques de 1972. Ma réponse est constituée d'une liste des points avec lesquels je suis d'accord , puis d'une présentation de mes critiques. Je montre que Krabiel utilise les concepts et les définitions de manière arbitraire et contradictoire. Je critique en particulier son exclusion de la "Théorie des Pédagogies," "La Grande Pédagogie," et des fragments de *Der Böse Baal der Asoziale* du corpus des textes concernant les pièces didactiques parcequ'ils ne comportent aucune réflexion sur leur contexte. Cependant, si nous incluons ces textes, il est impossible d'ignorer l'expérience sociale des acteurs des pièces didactiques, ce que Krabiel refuse de reconnaître. C'est pourquoi il impute involontairement à Brecht une conception autoritaire et doctrinaire de la pédagogie. Bien que Krabiel échoue dans son exigence d'historicité absolue, méthodologiquement naïve, selon moi, il fait franchir un pas essentiel a notre compréhension, particulièrement en ce qui concerne la genèse des premières pièces didactiques de Brecht.

Re-construcción, error, mejora, o pensar para el museo: una respuesta a Klaus Krabiel

En su estudio sobre las obras de teatro didácticas de Brecht, Krabiel piensa que puede desacreditar mi teoría sobre el teatro didáctico desarrollada en 1972. Mi replica enumera una lista de los puntos con los cuales estoy de acuerdo, para exponer mi crítica. Muestro que Krabiel usa conceptos de manera arbitraria y contradictoria. En particular critico que de la obra completa que reune todo el teatro didáctico, él excluye "Theory of Pedagogies," "The Grand Pedagogy," y fragmentos de "Der böse Baal der Asoziale" porque no reflejan sus contextos. En cambio si incluimos estos escritos, es imposible hacer caso omiso de la experiencia social de los actores del teatro didáctico de quienes Kriebel se niega a hacer mención. De esta forma, atribuye a Brecht un concepto de la pedagogía doctrinario y autoritario. Aunque Krabiel decepciona con su demanda de una historicidad absoluta, metodológicamente ingenua, él avanza un paso nuestra comprensión con respecto al surgimiento de las primeras obras teatrales didácticas.

Re-Konstruktion, Irrtum, Entwicklung oder Denken fürs Museum: Eine Antwort auf Klaus Krabiel

Reiner Steinweg

1993 erschien — im gleichen Verlag wie 1972 meine Arbeit *Das Lehrstück* — Klaus Krabiels noch umfangreicheres Werk *Brechts Lehrstücke*. Vom Singular zum Plural — die Untertitel machen es noch klarer. Meine Absicht war es, *Brechts Theorie einer politisch-ästhetischen Erziehung* zu erschließen, von der ich Bruchstücke in den Äußerungen zu den Lehrstücken wahrnahm; Krabiel beschreibt *Entstehung und Entwicklung eines Spieltyps*. Er löst damit eine Forderung ein, die die Kritik an meinem Buch schon früh vorgetragen hat: die *Veränderung* des Lehrstückgedankens bei Brecht in den sich verändernden historischen Situationen und im Hinblick auf verschiedenartige Stücke herauszuarbeiten (Berenberg-Gossler, Müller, Stosch 1974). Nach zwei Jahrzehnten war es wirklich an der Zeit, daß meine Ergebnisse einer genauen Prüfung unterzogen wurden.

Krabiel hat in gewisser Hinsicht dort fortgesetzt, wo ich 1969 aufgehört habe (es hat damals drei Jahre gedauert, bis mein Buch auf dem Markt war; Steinweg 1994). Krabiel hat mit großer Zähigkeit Zeitzeugen angeschrieben und Archive durchforscht, die damals entweder noch nicht zugänglich waren (z.B. das Hindemith-Archiv) oder die ich unter dem Zeitdruck, in den ich beim Schreiben durch meine Beteiligung an der Kampagne gegen die Notstandsgesetze geraten war, nicht mehr bereisen konnte. Krabiel hat dabei vor allem die Beziehung Brechts zur Bewegung für Gebrauchsmusik (Fritz Jöde usw.) und zu den Kammermusiktagen für Neue Musik (Donau-Eschingen, Baden-Baden, Berlin) durchleuchtet bzw. die Geschichte dieser Bewegungen geschrieben, und er hat dabei einige bis dahin unbekannte Texte von Brecht sowie zahlreiche interessante Zeitzeugnisse entdeckt. Die überaus detaillierte Nachzeichnung der Entstehung von *Lindberghflug*, *Badener Lehrstück* und *Jasager* als Text wie als Komposition (wenn auch ohne musikwissenschaftliche Analyse) ist hervorragend, ebenso die Dokumentation der Aufführungspraxis und der Rezeption, ferner die differenzierte und kenntnisreiche Darlegung der unterschiedlichen Haltungen von Adorno, Hindemith und Brecht/Weill zur Bewegung für Gebrauchsmusik (Krabiel 128-32).

Brecht Then and Now / Brecht damals und heute
Eds. Marc Silberman et al. *The Brecht Yearbook / Das Brecht-Jahrbuch,*
Volume 20 (Madison: The International Brecht Society, 1995)

Das Buch ist über große Strecken als "Anti-Steinweg" angelegt.[1] Ich halte es gleichwohl für einen Meilenstein der Lehrstückforschung und möchte daher in Krabiels polemischen Ton nicht einstimmen, zumal ich allen Grund habe, mich bei ihm zu bedanken: Beschäftigt mit ganz anderen Dingen (Zweitstudium der Sozialwissenschaften, seit 1974 Mitarbeit an einem der größten europäischen Institute für Friedensforschung, seit 1979 Entwicklung einer Lehrstück*praxis* und empirische Untersuchungen dazu) hatte ich gar nicht registriert, in welchem Ausmaß die Literaturwissenschaft weltweit meine Grundpositionen akzeptiert hat. Dies ist mir erst durch Krabiels Arbeit deutlich geworden. Indem er gegen diese Rezeption antrat, hat er ein neues Kapitel der Lehrstückforschung aufgeschlagen, das, soviel läßt sich voraussagen, die Wissenschaft noch eine Weile beschäftigen wird. Die "zahlreichen Widersprüche" in Krabiels Arbeit, die Tatlow 1994 in einer ersten Rezension konstatiert, ohne sie im einzelnen zu benennen, sind zu prüfen und abzuarbeiten. Das kann hier nur in beschränktem Umfang geschehen, zumal ich als "Betroffener" wahrscheinlich nicht über hinreichend Distanz verfüge, um die unterschiedlichen Positionen so leidenschaftslos abzuwägen, wie es nötig wäre. Meine Bemerkungen haben also vorläufigen Charakter.

In den Darstellungen von Krabiel und mir prallen zwei Sicht- und Vorgangsweisen aufeinander: eine historisch-genetische und eine systematische, die zugleich vor allem an verändernder gesellschaftlicher *Praxis* orientiert ist. Die Äußerungen Brechts zum Lehrstück und die einzelnen Lehrstücke selbst erscheinen aus diesen Blickwinkeln in jeweils anderem Licht. Welche Interpretation, von einer dritten Warte gesehen, am ehesten zutrifft, werden andere zu entscheiden haben.

Fehler und Fehleinschätzungen

1. Der größte Irrtum meiner Arbeit von 1972 scheint mir nach der Lektüre von Krabiels Buch gewesen zu sein, daß ich aufgrund von Brechts später "Theorie des Lehrstücks" und den darauf folgenden Äußerungen einerseits und seinen *allgemeinen* theatertheoretischen Äußerungen um 1930 andererseits angenommen hatte, Grundtyp und Theorie des Lehrstücks seien bereits 1929/30 *der Idee nach* mit den ersten Lehrstücktexten vollständig ausgeprägt gewesen, sozusagen fertig aus Brechts Gehirn entsprungen wie Pallas Athene aus dem Haupt des Zeus. Krabiels Rekonstruktion der Entstehungsgeschichte, sehr viel detaillierter als mir damals bei allem Bemühen möglich war, ist im wesentlichen überzeugend. Sie zeigt, daß die "Theorie" des Lehrstücks sich nicht ohne Wider-

sprüche, Schwenks und Akzentverlagerungen entwickelte. Von daher ist auch meine These, daß die erste, noch mit dem "großen Brauch" argumentierende Fassung des *Jasagers* als *Provokation* gedacht war, wahrscheinlich hinfällig. Das gilt auch für meine Vermutung, Brecht habe im Text Nr. 52 (GW 8: 329) zum *Lindberghflug* Selbstkritik eher zum Schein geübt ("erschien mir der Plan undurchführbar").[2] Die Bedeutung Hindemiths für die Anfänge habe ich unterschätzt.

2. Den Ausdruck "Muster" in den Texten Nr. 53 und 145 habe ich mangels lexikalischer Überprüfung fälschlich im Sinne von "pattern" interpretiert. Es scheint nun, daß Brecht diese Wortbedeutung 1930 nicht gemeint hat. Offenbar sind (gestische) *Vorbilder* gemeint.

3. Der Versuch, Lehrstückspiel theoretisch analog zum streng *natur*wissenschaftlich organisierten psychologischen bzw. physiologischen Experiment zu konstruieren, war überzogen und in sich nicht schlüssig. (Ich halte jedoch in meinem neuen Buch, Steinweg 1995, an einem am *Dreigroschenprozeß* orientierten *sozial*wissenschaftlich revidierten Experiment-Ansatz für das Lehrstückspiel fest.)[3]

4. Überzogen war auch der Versuch, die Reihe der Lehrstücke als Versuchskette im *engeren* Sinne zu interpretieren (Steinweg 1971b). Nach der entstehungsgeschichtlichen Rekonstruktion von Krabiel ist einleuchtend, daß ein Plan zu einer solchen Versuchsreihe vorab nicht bestanden haben kann.

5. Die Annahme, daß Brecht auch in der ästhetischen Konstruktion der Lehrstücktexte *dialektische* Gesichtspunkte verfolgt habe, ist durch meine damaligen Ausführungen nur schwach belegt. Diese Vermutung war ein Vorgriff auf geplante Untersuchungen, die anzustellen ich keine Gelegenheit mehr hatte (Steinweg 1994).

6. Einleuchtend ist schließlich die Kritik, daß meine Versuche, die *Maßnahme* (1971a) und das *Badener Lehrstück vom Einverständnis* (1973) zu interpretieren, in einer Hinsicht in Widerspruch zu einem Kernpunkt meiner Lehrstückauffassung stehen: Wenn das Lehrstückspiel offen für die sozialen Erfahrungen der Teilnehmer bleiben soll, darf der "Sinn," die "Aussage" der Lehrstücktexte nicht vorab ausdefiniert sein.

7. Darüber hinaus korrigiert Krabiel auf der Basis weitergehender Recherchen zu Recht eine Anzahl von kleineren, weniger weit ins Grundsätzliche reichenden Fehlern: Die "Einführungsrede" zur konzertanten Aufführung des *Lindberghflugs* (Text Nr. 11) ist doch gehalten worden, und zwar von Brecht; die "Protokolle" aus der Karl-Marx-Schule bezogen sich nicht auf die *Aufführung* des *Jasagers*, sondern auf vorangehende Diskussionen über den *Text*, usw.

Insgesamt und in vielen weiteren Details seiner Fußnoten erscheint mir Krabiels Kritik soweit als nützliche Korrektur und als bedeutender Schritt in Richtung einer genaueren Erkenntnis des *historischen* Lehrstücks.

Fragliches

Es folgen einige Punkte, bei denen ich nicht ganz so sicher bin, daß Krabiel mit seiner Kritik Recht hat.

1. *Textänderungen*: Aus einigen Äußerungen Brechts habe ich damals geschlossen, daß er es prinzipiell für denkbar hielt, daß die Lehrstückspieler, *nach intensiven Auseinandersetzungen*, an seiner Textvorlage nicht nur Kritik üben, sondern sie auch aufgrund von Einsichten, die *im Spielprozeß* gewonnen werden, partiell abändern könnten. Das läge in der Logik einer entschiedenen Autonomisierung des Zuschauers. Krabiel führt gegen diese Position mehrere mir damals unbekannte Briefe an, in denen Brecht und Eisler Kürzungen nicht zuließen; damit sei eindeutig bewiesen, daß Änderungen nur durch die Autoren in Frage kamen. Nicht einmal die Einfügung von "Szenen eigener Erfindung" mag Krabiel den Lehrstückspielern, sondern allenfalls einem "Übungsleiter" überantworten (290), was immer "eigener" dann heißen mag. Diese Briefe beziehen sich aber erstens alle auf *öffentliche Vorführungen*, also nicht auf den intendierten Interaktionstyp "Spielen ohne Zuschauer," und zweitens auf potentielle Änderungen zu *Lebzeiten* der Autoren. Wenn Textänderungen von der Logik der Lehrstücktheorie her als Element besonders flexibler Reaktion auf Entwicklungen der Wirklichkeit erforderlich sind, dann wären die Autoren davon ausgegangen, daß das ganze Modell nach ihrem Tod ad acta zu legen wäre. Ist das wahrscheinlich? Auf *eine* Textstelle geht Krabiel im übrigen nicht ein, wenn ich es in der Flut der extrem unübersichtlich angeordneten Anmerkungen (125 eng bedruckte Seiten ohne Kopfzeilen) nicht übersehen habe: "Auf diese Weise ['Vorschläge für Abänderungen...sollen schriftlich gemacht werden'] können auch die Anweisungen des Kommentars jederzeit geändert werden. Sie sind voller Fehler, was unsere Zeit und seine Tugenden, sie sind unverwertbar, was andere Zeiten betrifft" (Text Nr. 56). Unter "Kommentar" ist zwar nicht der gesamte Stücktext zu verstehen, sondern die Teile, die — wie z.B. im *Badener Lehrstück* die Geschichte vom Denkenden, der den Sturm überwand — gewissermaßen *neben* der Fabel stehen, aber jedenfalls ein wichtiger Teil des Stücks. Vielleicht würde Krabiel einwenden, diese Textstelle sei nicht relevant, weil aus dem *Fatzer*-Material stammend, das nirgends ausdrücklich als "Lehrstück" bezeichnet wird (dazu unten).

Dann müßten aber auch viele andere Argumente aus der Lehrstück-Debatte ausgeschlossen werden. Im übrigen ist der Stellenwert von Textänderungen in der von mir mitentwickelten Lehrstückpraxis marginal (s. Steinweg 1986 und 1995); die Frage hat sich also nachträglich als eher akademisch erwiesen.

2. *Arbeit mit einzelnen Lehrstückszenen* (399, Anm. 36): Die Konzentration auf eine Szene kommt selbstverständlich für öffentliche *Vorführungen* nicht in Frage. Insofern ist Krabiel Recht zu geben. Aber warum sollten Gruppen *für sich* nicht mit einzelnen Szenen arbeiten, wenn der zeitliche Rahmen eine Bearbeitung des ganzen Stücks nicht erlaubt? Viele — nicht alle — Lehrstückszenen sind nach dem epischen Prinzip so gebaut, daß sie problemlos für sich stehen können und unabhängig voneinander Sinn ergeben. Es wird ja niemand gehindert, den ganzen Text zu *lesen*.

3. *Zum Ideologiebegriff*: Krabiel nimmt die Verwendung des Begriffs "Idsek" (Ideologischer Sekretär) in frühen Texten zu einzelnen Lehrstücken als Beleg dafür, daß Brecht vor 1931 den Ideologiebegriff noch nicht in dem von Karl Korsch wiederhergestellten kritischen Sinn von Karl Marx verwendet habe (363, Anm. 9). Das könnte insofern stimmen, als Brecht erst Anfang der 30er Jahre, möglicherweise im Wintersemester 1930/31, Vorlesungen bei Karl Korsch gehört hat. Ich sehe mich derzeit zeitlich außerstande, philologisch nachzuprüfen, ob das Wort Ideologie tatsächlich bis dahin immer im "positiven," unkritischen Sinne von Brecht verwendet wird, habe aber Zweifel: Es wäre zwar in der Tat grammatisch und semantisch merkwürdig, wenn ausgerechnet der "Denkende" bzw. "Herr Keuner" als "ideologisch" (-er Sekretär) im Sinne des *Marxschen Ideologiebegriffs* bezeichnet würde. Es kann aber kein Zweifel sein, daß sowohl die epischen Opern als auch der Abschnitt "Ideologie" im *Flug der Lindberghs* der Sache nach Ideologie*kritik* intendieren, unabhängig davon, wie das *Wort* "Ideologie" im *Lindberghflug* von 1930 gemeint ist (siehe u.a. Hartung 1959): die "Zertrümmerung der Anschauungen durch die Verhältnisse" (Text Nr. 16). Der *Begriff* war vorhanden, das *Wort* könnte im schon damals gängigen heruntergekommenen Sinn verwendet worden sein. Allerdings ist durchaus vorstellbar, daß die zeitweise vorgesehene Rolle des "Idsek" (Text Nr. 44) gerade deshalb so genannt wurde, weil er die ideologie*kritischen* Teile des "Kommentars" vortragen sollte (vgl. auch Text Nr. 57 über die Funktion des "Kommentars").

4. *Der "tragische Rest"*: Meine Interpretation der *Maßnahme* von 1971 ist in der Sprache der Studentenbewegung geschrieben und etwas zu forsch gewesen, was die *vollständige* Abwesenheit des tragischen Elements betrifft. Beim *Spielen* dieses und anderer

Lehrstücke wird in bezug auf die strukturell korrespondierenden Realitätserfahrungen der TeilnehmerInnen vorübergehend Tragik durchaus stark empfunden, z.B. hinsichtlich des mit den Vorgängen in der *Maßnahme* assoziierten "Schicksals" der kommunistischen Weltbewegung als Ganzes. Aber der Schicksalsbegriff ist auch hier nicht angemessen. Zu Krabiels Formulierung an anderer Stelle sehe ich keine Differenz: "Wobei das Ziel des Kampfes — dies hat weniger mit Paradoxie als mit Dialektik zu tun — die Überwindung des [kapitalistischen] Regelsystems selbst wäre" (252; ähnlich 406, Anm. 59: "'Dialektik' ist bei Brecht keine menschenvernichtende Maschine, sondern ein Instrumentarium, das den verändernden Eingriff in deren tödlichen Mechanismus ermöglichen soll").

Was also meint Krabiel mit "tragischem Rest"? Daß das ethisch gesehen in der Tat "absolut inakzeptable" Tötungsmotiv in der *Maßnahme* eine *didaktisch-provokative* Funktion hat, räumt Krabiel selbst ein (197). Seine *Trennung* der "Fragen politischer Taktik" als eigentlicher Lehraufgabe der *Maßnahme* von der Frage des Umgangs mit Menschen seitens der jeweiligen Parteiführungen und von der notwendigen permanenten selbstkritischen Überprüfung auf Ideologiemomente im eigenen Denken ist zumindest für den *Spielprozeß* undurchführbar. Sie ist aus meiner Sicht auch politisch völlig verfehlt. Im Spielprozeß, das haben unsere Versuche hinlänglich bewiesen, werden die TeilnehmerInnen durch den Text der *Maßnahme* keineswegs "fehlgeleitet." Das räumt Krabiel in Bezug auf den *Jasager* mit vergleichbarer Problematik (mythischer Rest der Selbstopferung) auch halb ein: "Es ist dies ein Problem, dessen Lösung — wenn überhaupt — nur im Übungszusammenhang befriedigend gelingen kann" (154). Krabiel bietet aber keine Erklärung, was das bedeuten soll, wenn er gleichzeitig darauf besteht, daß der Kern des Übens im "Nachvollzug" und in "Zustimmung" besteht (297, dazu unten); und noch unklarer ist, wie Krabiel sich den "Mitvollzug" der "Übung" durch *Zuschauer* (270) vorstellt.

Die Frage, die Krabiel in diesem Zusammenhang an mich richtet, kann ich dagegen teilweise beantworten: "Waren denn 'tragisch' endende Situationen vergleichbarer Art damals in der politischen Realität ein der Lösung bedürfendes Problem?" (217) Natürlich waren — außer im illegalen Kampf — tragische Situationen mit physisch tödlichem Ausgang nicht Bestandteil der Alltagsproblematik, die die Adressaten der *Maßnahme* erlebten. Aber im übertragenen Sinne werden ähnlich strukturierte Konflikte damals ebenso vorgekommen sein wie heute; es fällt den TeilnehmerInnen meiner Lehrstückseminare meist nicht schwer, strukturell verwandte Alltagsszenen zu assoziieren, in denen entweder der Tod als Möglichkeit latent enthalten oder *psychische* Opfer verlangt oder gebracht werden, die dem *sozialen* Tod gleich- oder nahekommen.

Widersprüche und Widerspruch

1. *Was macht ein Lehrstück zum Lehrstück?* Krabiel zufolge
sind Lehrstücke "keine Theaterstücke. Sondern vokalmusikalische
Gebrauchskunst für Laienmusiker und Laienspieler" (225, ähnlich
an vielen anderen Stellen des Buches, z.B. 263, 269, 288, 303). Da
diese Definition auf *Die Ausnahme und die Regel* nicht anwendbar
ist, heißt es dann plötzlich: "*Die Ausnahme und die Regel* ist daher
weniger für Laienchöre als für Laienspieler geeignet und stellt somit
eine neue Variante im Lehrstückkomplex dar. *An der Zugehörigkeit
am Spieltypus ändert dies insofern nichts, als es sich um Kunst für
Laien handelt und das Lernen durch Selberspielen Übungszweck
bleibt*" (242, Hervorh. R. St.). Wenn dem so ist, warum werden
dann "die kleinen Lehrstücke" ohne Musik vom *Bösen Baal dem
Asozialen* (bis auf in dieser Hinsicht nichtssagende Anmerkungen,
z.B. 407 und 420) aus der Untersuchung ausgeklammert?

In bezug auf *Die Ausnahme und die Regel* heißt es wenige
Zeilen vorher: "Erst durch den Chor, der die Einbeziehung einer
größeren Anzahl von Laienspielern bzw. -sängern in die Produktion
im Sinne des Gebrauchskunstkonzeptes ermöglichte, wird das Stück
zum Lehrstück!" (242) Warum werden dann die späten Bearbei-
tungsstufen von *Fatzer* mit ihren Chören ausgeklammert? Zu *Die
Horatier und die Kuratier* heißt es wenig später: "Obwohl sich das
Stück, da unvertont, von einem kleinen *Theater*stück allenfalls durch
den erheblichen Anteil der Chöre am Spielvorgang unterscheidet,
hielt Brecht an der Typusbezeichnung 'Lehrstück' fest" (269). Das
hätte er nach Krabiel eigentlich nicht tun dürfen. Aber da Brecht das
Wort "Lehrstück" verwendet, wagt er nicht zu widersprechen.

Krabiels Begründung für diese Ungereimtheiten müßte wohl
sein: Es gibt eben nicht *das* Lehrstück (290). Aber einen von
anderen Unternehmungen deutlich abgrenzbaren "Spieltyp" Lehrstück (ein Begriff, der m.W. nirgends genauer definiert wird) soll es
schon geben! Damit wird das Problem aber nur semantisch ver-
schoben. Denn nicht einmal das "Spielen für sich selber" (Text Nr.
146, die von mir so genannte "Basisregel" für das Gesamt von
Lehrstücktext, Lehrstückmusik und Spielprozeß) gilt nach Krabiel für
alle Lehrstücke, egal wie oft Brecht es so definiert: Wenn Brecht am
Ende seines Lebens (wieder einmal) darauf insistiert, so kann das
Krabiel zufolge nur politisch-opportunistische Gründe haben, um
eine Rechtfertigung dafür zu finden, *Die Maßnahme* mit ihrem
irreführenden "tragischen Rest" weiterhin aus dem Verkehr zu
ziehen (205). Krabiel macht sich über Brechts Äußerung im Inter-

view mit Pierre Abraham (Text Nr. 179) geradezu lustig: Der Satz stehe im Widerspruch zur ursprünglichen Werkintention, die auf nichts Geringeres als die

> ...Revolutionierung der Arbeitersänger, eine agitatorische Massenwirkung und die Umfunktionierung des Konzerts in ein politisches Meeting abzielte! Massenchor, Orchester und vier Spieler sollten nun lediglich aufgeboten werden, damit ein einziger Darsteller, verschiedene Parts ausführend, etwas lernen könne? Welch ein Mißverhältnis zwischen Aufwand und Gebrauchswert! (204)

Das Argument wird durch die Ausrufezeichen nicht schlüssiger. Brecht spricht nirgends von einer beabsichtigten "agitatorischen Massenwirkung," und selbstverständlich bedeutet der zitierte, von Abraham wiedergegebene Satz nicht, daß nur eine Person aus dem Stück lernen kann. Viele Personen können nacheinander im Verlauf schon weniger Tage den Jungen Genossen darstellen, und *weil* er von den Agitatoren lediglich referiert bzw. sein Verhalten gezeigt wird, ist jeder, der den Jungen Genossen zeigt, zugleich Agitator und kann immer wieder auch in die Rolle des Chors zurücktreten.

Meine umgekehrte Vermutung, daß Eisler bereits 1930 einen opportunistischen Rückzieher gemacht hat, als er in der *Roten Fahne* zu Protokoll gab, "er habe den politischen Lehrwert der *Maßnahme* für die an ihrer Einstudierung beteiligten Arbeitersänger betonen" wollen, "ohne die *ausschlaggebende* Bedeutung der politischen Massenwirkung zu verkennen" (Text Nr. 73, Hervorh. R. St.) läßt Krabiel dagegen nicht gelten, obwohl Eisler der Kommunistischen Partei viel enger verbunden und damit ihren Sanktionsmechanismen viel stärker preisgegeben war als Brecht. Krabiel betont: "Seine [Eislers] Klarstellung befindet sich im Einklang mit allen überlieferten Äußerungen zum Lehrstück" (393, Anm. 23). Wie das mit dem "Lernen durch selber spielen" als "Übungszweck" (242) vereinbar sein soll, verrät uns Krabiel nicht. Stattdessen wiederholt er später ohne Rückbezug auf diese Stelle: Brecht und seine musikalischen Mitarbeiter "stimmten weitgehend darin überein, daß sich der primäre Zweck des Lehrstücks in der Realisierung durch die Spielenden/Singenden selbst erfüllt" (289).

Auch ich hatte 1972 verschiedene Lehrstückformen unterschieden, nämlich nach dem jeweils bevorzugten Medium: Filmlehrstück, Musiklehrstück, Theaterlehrstück, Radiolehrstück (Steinweg 1972, 93). Davon läßt Krabiel nur letzteres gelten, weil dies das einzige ist, für das Brecht den *Ausdruck* selbst benutzt (426, Anm. 7). Eine Erklärung für den folgenden Satz im *Dreigroschenprozeß* gibt Krabiel aber nicht: "...wobei noch gar nicht die Rede sein soll vom eigentlichen Lehrstück, das sogar die Auslieferung der Filmapparate an die einzeln Übenden verlangt" (Text Nr. 99). Der Satz ist nur schwerlich mit seiner häufigsten, auf "vokalmusikalische Gebrauchsmusik" abhebenden Lehrstückdefinition vereinbar. Den Satz aus der "Theorie des Lehrstücks," es sei "für Musiker lehrreich, zu mechanischen Vorstellungen die Musik zu erstellen," zitiert er dagegen, aber wie dies mit seinen Vorstellungen vom Lehrstück vereinbar sein soll, erläutert er ebenfalls nicht (291; Text Nr. 145).

Auch daß in diesem Text die Musik "eine vergleichsweise geringe Beachtung" erfährt, hindert Krabiel nicht, an seinem vorwiegend auf vokale Gebrauchskunst ausgerichteten Lehrstückverständnis festzuhalten. Er führt die Tatsache der "bescheidenen" Rolle der Musik in der "Theorie des Lehrstücks" ("Begleitmusik") auf die geringen Möglichkeiten zurück, die im Fall der *Maßnahme* aufwendige Musik im Exil zu realisieren (291). Dabei gibt es auch Lehrstückmusiken, die mit Schulchor und -orchester auskommen (Weills *Jasager*). Daß Brecht das Lehrstück im Text Nr. 148 über die "Avantgarde" ein Jahr später, ebenfalls im Exil, in einer Reihe mit Massenlied und Gebrauchsmusik nennt, hatte er dagegen kurz zuvor als besonders bemerkenswert hervorgehoben (288).

2. Was und wie lehrt das Lehrstück? Leider sind Krabiels Antworten auf diese Fragen ebenfalls widersprüchlich. Einerseits soll "am Text gelernt" werden. Gemeint ist offensichtlich: Die "Aussagen" des Textes sollen mit Hilfe der Musik angeeignet, übernommen, internalisiert werden. Der Spieler soll, wie im alten Jesuitentheater, mit der Methode der Darstellung zu einer besonders nachhaltigen "Zustimmung" (299) gebracht werden. "Es ging Brecht durchaus um die Vermittlung einer inhaltlich-spezifischen *Lehre*" (55, in bezug auf das *Badener Lehrstück*). Eine solche Lehre extrahiert Krabiel z.B. den ersten Fassungen der *Maßnahme*: "Von emotionalen Antrieben...geleitetes Handeln verfehlt immer wieder sein Ziel." Allerdings war der Text Krabiel zufolge mißverständlich, weil der Eindruck entstehen konnte, "die abstrakte Grundsatzentscheidung 'politische Rationalität oder Gefühl'" sei das "Kernproblem politischen Handelns" (179). Vielmehr sei es "die erklärte Absicht der Autoren" gewesen, "*konkrete* Fragen politischer Strategie und Taktik in den Arbeitergesang einzuführen" (205, Hervorh. R. St.). Die Texte Brechts leisten selbst "die fällige Kritik," der Zuschauer braucht sie sich nur zu eigen zu machen, und schon ist das Lehrziel erreicht (302, ähnlich 297). Krabiel polemisiert zwar (zu Recht) gegen die zahlreichen Interpretationen, die die *Maßnahme* als Vorwegnahme der Moskauer Prozesse mit ihren unfaßlichen tödlichen Selbstbeschuldigungen "im Dienste der Partei" deuten. Und er stimmt mir ausdrücklich zu, daß "politische Indoktrination" nicht Ziel der Lehrstücke sei (199). Aber wodurch *unterscheidet* sich das von ihm definierte Lehrverfahren von den Praktiken der ideologischen Indoktrination stalinistischer Provenienz? Und wie sind diese Bestimmungen mit der Aussage vereinbar, daß die Autoren der *Maßnahme* "textimmanent wie organisatorisch alle erdenklichen Vorkehrungen [getroffen hatten], um *Diskussionen* in Gang zu setzen. Nicht vorbehaltloses Einverständnis sollte zelebriert, sondern die politische Auseinandersetzung provoziert werden"? (224).

Wenn auch die Inszenierung von Auseinandersetzung und Diskussion letztlich "allemal" auf "Zustimmung" aus ist (299), unterstellt Krabiel Brecht (wie einige Kritiker dessen spätere Stücke), er habe Denken nur zum Schein befördern wollen, nämlich nur soweit, als und bis die jeweilige Fabelkonstruktion und die daraus zu extrapolierende Lehre angenommen sei. Der Denkende wäre ein notorischer Immer-Jasager, Eigenständigkeit wäre nicht gefragt, die Differenz zu den hundertfältigen Lehren der Gebrauchsmusikbewegung bestünde nur in anderen (politischen) Vorzeichen; kurz, Brecht würde selbst einer reaktionären Haltung Vorschub leisten, die er an den vordergründig klassenkämpferischen Inszenierungen seiner Zeit so deutlich kritisiert hat (u.a. in den Anmerkungen zur *Mutter*). An anderer Stelle heißt es bei Krabiel: "Gelernt wird durch den übenden Vollzug der im Lehrstücktext fixierten Haltungen." Hier fehlt nur noch der Vollzugsbeamte, jemand, der die "Belehrung" vornimmt, wie Krabiel an anderer Stelle konsequenterweise aus Text 145 schließt (290). Der autoritäre Duktus dieser lerntheoretischen Annahmen wird durch den Zusatz, Brecht habe dann, wenn die Zustimmung mit überzeugenden Argumenten verweigert wurde, die beanstandete Fassung in jedem Fall kassiert, nur geringfügig gemildert (298): Spätestens nach seinem Tod war ja Krabiel zufolge eine solche Reaktion auf die soziale Wirklichkeit nicht mehr möglich.

Im Kapitel "Holzwege [sic]. Positionen der Lehrstückforschung" verschwendet Krabiel an meine Zweckbestimmung des Lehrstücks von 1972 ("Negation der mit dem Text vorgegebenen Muster durch das bewußte bzw. daran bewußtwerdende Subjekt") eine ganze Batterie von rhetorischen Fragen, die beweisen sollen, daß meine Position unhaltbar sei, z.B.: "Hat Brecht in pädagogischer Absicht *Fehler* in die Texte einmontiert, falsches Verhalten als richtig, asoziale Verhaltensweisen als positive 'Muster' vorgestellt?" (297).

Alle diese Fragen sparen den lebendigen Spieler mit seinen sozialen und politischen Erfahrungen, die er in das Spiel mitbringt, aus. Daß Brecht den "Muster"-Begriff, wie er uns heute aus der amerikanischen Psychologie geläufig ist, noch nicht gebrauchte, besagt ja nicht, daß er die zugrundeliegende soziale Wirklichkeit (beim Sprechen, Schreiben, Handeln und vor allem in den Gesten und Haltungen) nicht gekannt hätte. Der Lehrstücktext, so möchte ich meine Position noch einmal umreißen, muß geeignet sein, die in Haltungen sedimentierten Erfahrungen hervorzulocken, sie zugänglich zu machen, sich mit ihnen auseinanderzusetzen. Meine Formulierung "Negation der mit dem Text vorgegebenen Muster" (Steinweg 1972, 142) war offensichtlich zu unpräzise, sonst hätte Krabiel mich nicht so gründlich mißverstehen können. Die "Negation" — in der Sprache der Dialektiker etwas hochtrabend ausgedrückt, Psychoanalytiker würden dafür andere Begriffe verwenden — bezieht sich nicht auf die Texte, sondern auf die von ihnen aufgerufenen *Haltungen, Gesten, Rede- und Verhaltensweisen*, sofern sie ihnen bei der Verfolgung ihrer Ziele und Interessen im Wege stehen. Der Autor der Spielvorlagen muß Sorge tragen, daß sie diese Evokation leisten. Die vielfältigen Bearbeitungen der Lehrstücktexte durch Brecht haben (auch) hierin einen Sinn. Der Abstand zu den sozialen Erfahrungen darf einerseits nicht zu groß sein, andererseits muß das Provokatorische erhalten bleiben.

Krabiel wird einwerfen: Aber das steht nirgends bei Brecht. Das ist richtig. Aber es ist *völlig unmöglich*, auch nur eine Lehrstückszene dreimal hintereinander zu spielen, ohne eigene soziale Erfahrungen aus formal ähnlich strukturierten Alltagskonflikten, wie sie der Text vorgibt, zumindest in Fragmenten zu assoziieren. Selbst wenn man die gestische Vorgabe bzw. die Haltungen, an denen die Spieler sich abarbeiten sollen, von verfremdungsfähigen Schauspielern, den "ersten Künstlern ihrer Zeit" (Text Nr. 56) im Lehrstückspiel vorgeben läßt, so blieben doch auch diese an ihre konkreten sozialen und politischen Erfahrungen gebunden und würden entsprechende Assoziationen in den Spielern wachrufen. Damit beantwortet sich auch die von Krabiel wiederholt gestellte Frage, wozu man denn für die von mir beschriebenen Zwecke Lehrstücke brauche, sie könnten doch mit jeder *beliebigen* dramatischen Szene (278) oder auch mit freiem Rollenspiel erreicht werden. Dem ist keineswegs so. Wir haben mit allen möglichen Texten, selbstverständlich auch mit Rollenspiel, experimentiert. Die Funktion der Evokation tiefliegender sozialer Erfahrungen über die mit ihnen verbundenen *körperlichen Haltungen* wird durch kein anderes Medium so intensiv und vielschichtig bewirkt wie gerade durch Lehrstücktexte von Brecht. Es ist wenig wahrscheinlich, daß dies Zufall ist; dafür unterscheiden sich diese Texte, und zwar auch die nicht vertonten, zu sehr von denjenigen, die Brecht für die Schaubühne bestimmt hat.

Man kommt also in keinem Fall um die Kategorie der sozialen Erfahrung herum, die von Krabiel systematisch ausgespart wird.

Selbst dann, wenn man das autoritäre Lernmodell, das Krabiel unterstellt, akzeptieren würde, wäre das nicht der möglich. Auch noch so geschickte Indoktrination kann auf Dauer nicht die eigenen sozialen Erfahrungen überspielen oder unterdrücken, wie die Geschichte der Indoktrination in den ehemals realsozialistischen Ländern zeigt. In dieser Beziehung möchte ich an meiner Position festhalten, obwohl ich sie mit keinem wörtlichen Zitat belegen kann: Entweder man nimmt Brecht beim Wort, daß er das "Nachdenken" befördern wollte (Text Nr. 175), oder man unterstellt ihm, daß er das in *Wirklichkeit* gar nicht beabsichtigte. Entschließt man sich zu ersterem, so muß man die tatsächlichen sozialen Erfahrungen als Substrat und Gegenstand des Nachdenkens über angemessenes Verhalten in Konfliktsituationen in Rechnung stellen.

3. *Welche theoretischen Äußerungen Brechts beziehen sich auf das Lehrstück und welche nicht?* Die Frage nach der Rolle der sozialen Erfahrungen der Spieler auszuklammern, gelingt Krabiel, indem er die Texte über die "Pädagogien" aus dem Lehrstückkorpus ausgrenzt. (Dazu zählt er offensichtlich auch das Fragment Nr. 33, wo im Hinblick auf das zukünftige "klassenlose Gemeinwesen" von einem "aktiven Lehrtheater, einem neuartigen Institut ohne Zuschauer" die Rede ist, ohne daß der Begriff "Pädagogium" benützt würde, 422 Anm. 26). Bei dem dazu erforderlichen Interpretationsakt unterlaufen ihm, der sonst ein so genauer Leser ist, einige erstaunliche Fehler.

Entgegen seiner eigenen definitorischen Konzession gegenüber dem Lehrstück *Die Ausnahme und die Regel* nennt er als Grund für die Ausgrenzung die Tatsache, daß in der "Theorie der Pädagogien" "musikalische Aspekte keinerlei Rolle spielen, dagegen darstellerische, gestische, mimische Mittel in den Vordergrund treten" (277). Im Text Nr. 54 über das Pädagogium vermag Krabiel, der sonst so auf Wortlaut pocht, die Aussage zu erkennen: "Das Theater-Pädagogium soll das existierende Theater nicht ersetzen, es stellt keine Alternative, gar progressivere *Theaterform* dar..." (288). Daraus, daß in dem einen Fall junge Leute (Text Nr. 53), im anderen eher Erwachsene angesprochen sind (Text Nr. 54), schließt er, "daß die Theorie der Pädagogien selbst durchaus kein in sich einheitliches Konzept darstellt" (281f.). Aber auch *Das Badener Lehrstück* und *Die Maßnahme* sind nicht oder jedenfalls nicht ausschließlich für junge Leute geschrieben, im Gegensatz zu *Lindberghflug* und *Jasager*; trotzdem werden sie von Krabiel *einem* "Spieltypus" Lehrstück zugeordnet.

Aus der Tatsache, daß in Text Nr. 54 die zwei *Worte* "asoziale Muster" nicht vorkommen (im Gegensatz zu Text Nr. 53), schließt er, daß es hier *nicht* darum gehe, "soziales Verhalten zu erlernen." Weil nur von *einem* Denkenden die Rede ist, stellt Krabiel sich die soziale Situation im "Pädagogium" für Erwachsene so vor, daß dort einzelne *"allein*, nicht in der Gruppe, gemeinsam mit anderen" spielen (282). Das ist natürlich absurd. Das "Pädagogium" ergibt nur einen Sinn, wenn es ein Ort ist, an dem man zu bestimmten Zeiten genügend andere Personen findet, die ebenfalls Zeit und ein Interesse daran haben, bevorstehende, schwierige soziale Situationen durchzuspielen, um sich ihrer eigenen, für diese Situation optimalen Haltungen zu vergewissern bzw. "spontan" im Hinblick auf diese Situation aus dem Körpergedächtnis auftauchende, eigene Haltungen ideologiekritisch auf ihre Angemessenheit zu prüfen. Dazu braucht man das Gegenüber, Mitspieler, die bereit sind, die Rollen der erwarteten Gesprächspartner zu übernehmen (im Rollenspiel) oder die entsprechenden Rollen in analogen Lehrstückszenen darzustellen. Daß "Essen" in Gemeinschaft ein meist in gewichtige Rituale, bestimmte "Sitten und Gebräuche" (Text Nr. 30) eingebundener Vorgang ist, der nicht selten (z.B. beim sogenannten Arbeitsessen oder in Konflikten) mit vielschichtigen sozialen Bedeutungen hoch aufgeladen ist, kommt Krabiel nicht in den Sinn: "Auch die Einübung eines Abendessens dürfte in einer sozialistischen Gesellschaft keine vordringliche Aufgabe sein!" (282).

Den Zweck der Übung in einem solchen "Pädagogium" für Denkende kann Krabiel nur in der "Erlangung einer gewissen Sicherheit, Routine, Perfektion im körperlich-gestischen und rhetorischen Vollzug bestimmter Handlungen, Verhaltens- und Redeweisen" erkennen (282). Dies zeigt — wie im übrigen sein ganzes Schlußkapitel "Anmerkungen zur neueren Spielpraxis" —, daß er von den tatsächlichen Vorgängen bei einem selbstreflexiven, also nicht nach außen gerichteten und auf ästhetische Wirkung bedachten Theaterspiel im allgemeinen und beim Lehrstückspiel im besonderen nicht die geringste Ahnung hat. Weder um die Erlangung von Routine noch um Perfektion geht es, sondern um Distanzgewinnung, immer neue (selbst-)kritische Überprüfung des eigenen Denkens auf ideologisch gewordene Elemente sowie um die Erprobung und Untersuchung möglicher grundsätzlicher Alternativen *gegen* Routine und eine gelackte "Perfektion" — was immer dieser bei Brecht nicht vorzufindende Ausdruck in bezug auf Verhaltens- und Redeweisen bedeuten soll (den für die Lehrstückarbeit zentralen Begriff der *Haltung* läßt Krabiel an dieser Stelle vorsichtshalber gleich beiseite). Das ist mit beiden Texten über die Pädagogien absolut vereinbar.

Weil das Wort Lehrstück im Zusammenhang mit der "Theorie der Pädagogien" nur einmal vorkommt (Text Nr. 41) und weil umgekehrt von den "Pädagogien" als Austragungsorten des Lehrstückspiels später nicht mehr die Rede ist, glaubt Krabiel, daß es sich bei beiden um voneinander abgrenzbare, allenfalls miteinander "verbindbare" (285), aber dann doch nicht verbundene Konzepte gehandelt habe, wobei das Konzept der "Pädagogien" im Gegensatz zum Lehrstück bald wieder "fallen gelassen" wurde. Der Grund dafür sei sein "äußerst geringer Realitätsgehalt" gewesen. Das hindert Krabiel aber nicht, einige Seiten später die implizit in der "Theorie des Lehrstücks" von 1937 (Text Nr. 145) formulierten Annahmen über die Art und Weise, *wie* theaterspielend gelernt werden kann, unter Rückgriff auf die Texte zur "Theorie der Pädagogien" zu erklären (289). Da aber diese Aussagen das Zentrum jener Texte ausmachen, werden sie auf diese Weise hinterrücks doch wieder zum Bestandteil der Lehrstücktheorie.

Während Krabiel sonst mit politisch-historischen Erklärungen für Brüche und Akzentverlagerungen in der Entwicklung von Brechts Denken über das Lehrstück rasch bei der Hand ist, kommt er an dieser Stelle nicht auf die Idee, daß die konkreten politischen Entwicklungen in Deutschland *und* in der Sowjetunion (Hitler ante portas, Stalin an der weit über die Grenzen der Sowjetunion hinausreichenden Macht, deren brutale Handhabung deutlich zu werden beginnt) die "guten [bösen] Gründe" gewesen sein könnten, warum Brecht die "Gesetze des Lehrstücks" (Text Nr. 41) *im Rahmen* einer umfassenderen "Theorie der Pädagogien" 1931/32 nicht mehr weiter ausformuliert hat. Daß die Situation des Exils wegen der inzwischen noch erheblich zugespitzten Situation kurz vor den Moskauer Prozessen noch weniger geeignet war, gelassen grundsätzliche Überlegungen für eine *wirklich* klassenlose Gesellschaft anzustellen und zu veröffentlichen, wird ebenfalls nicht reflektiert. (Möglicherweise steht die Niederschrift des Textes Nr. 155 "Zur(!) Theorie des Lehrstücks" im Zusammenhang mit der Vorbereitung des Drucks von *Die Ausnahme und die Regel* in einer Moskauer Emigrantenzeitschrift, in einer Fassung, die, um angenommen werden zu können, um fast alle Chöre gekürzt werden mußte und auch dann noch nur mit einem abwertenden Vorspann seitens der Redaktion möglich war. Solche öffentlichen Abwertungen konnten sich damals rasch in Todesurteile verwandeln.) Unter solchen Bedingungen wären in der Tat weitreichende Überlegungen dieser Art bloße "Gedankenspiele" (282) gewesen. Daraus zu schließen, daß sie auch über diese sehr speziellen historischen Situationen hinaus und ein für allemal einen "äußerst geringen Realitätsgehalt" hatten, ist eine reine Setzung des Autors.

Noch weniger überzeugend als Krabiels Interpretation der Texte zum "Pädagogium" (bzw. zu den nach Altersstufe verschiedenartigen "Pädagogien") ist seine Deutung des Textes über die "Große" und die "Kleine Pädagogik" (Text Nr. 29). Völlig kontextlos ordnet er den Begriff "Pädagogik" der "Institution Schule" zu und "nicht (dem) *Theater!*" (283) Dabei laufen alle theoretischen Überlegungen zum Theater, die Brecht seit spätestens 1929 anstellt, auf die Formulierung zu: "Der neue Zweck [des Theaters] heißt Pädagogik" (GW 15: 198). Brechts Pädagogikbegriff ist erheblich weiter als der von Krabiel unterstellte. Er schließt die Schule selbstverständlich ein, aber das weite Feld der politischen Erwachsenenbildung nicht aus. Warum sollte das in diesem Text plötzlich der Fall sein? Die "Große Pädagogik" als eine besonders hohe Form von Theater ist mit der Zweckbestimmung der "Pädagogien" nicht nur vereinbar; diese dürften vielmehr ihr integraler Bestandteil sein; die Aufhebung des "Systems Spieler und Zuschauer" ist mit der Beschreibung, die Brecht im Text Nr. 54 über das "Pädagogium" für "Denkende" gibt, problemlos vereinbar. Krabiels Einwand, daß in diesem Text ein klassenloses Gemeinwesen nicht gemeint sein könne, weil in einem solchen "Verrat" nicht mehr vorkäme, ist irrig, wenn man mit Brecht davon ausgeht, daß die "Oberbaudinge" (Text Nr. 30), denen Brecht Kultur sowie die Sitten und Gebräuche (ebenda) und damit zweifellos auch die Haltungen zurechnet (Text Nr. 25), sich in gewisser Hinsicht verselbständigen und über lange Zeiträume halten können, u.U. viel länger als die ökonomischen Verhältnisse bzw. die Form der privaten oder gesellschaftlichen Verfügung über die Produktionsmittel, aus denen sie einmal hervorgegangen sind.

Etwas schwieriger ist dagegen die Zuordnung des Textes "Theorie der Pädagogien" zur "Großen Pädagogik" und damit zur klassenlosen Gesellschaft, weil dort in der Tat "irritierend" (Krabiel 279) davon die Rede ist, daß der Staat die "asozialen Triebe der Menschen" in einer "möglichst vollendeten...Form" von jedem *erzwingen* müsse, um sie so zu "verbessern." Staatliche wie jede andere Zwangsausübung zu pädagogischen Zwecken ist grundsätzlich problematisch, erst recht in einer klassenlosen Gesellschaft. Allerdings könnten hier auch Formen *sanften* Drucks gemeint sein, die sich aus Erwartungen einer vom Educandus *positiv* besetzten sozialen Umwelt bzw. aus sozialer Anerkennung ergeben. Gezwungen soll ja lediglich zu etwas werden, was Genuß verschafft, so heißt es in den ersten Texten zu den Lehrstücken und im Kontext der letzten Äußerung Brechts zur *Maßnahme*, wie Krabiel jenes Gespräch mit Manfred Wekwerth kurz vor Brechts Tod plausibel deutet. (*Die Maßnahme.* Kritische Ausgabe 262-66; allerdings wäre das keine neue Stufe bzw. Akzentverschiebung, wie Krabiel meint, 294, sondern allenfalls eine Rückkehr zu den Ursprüngen). Das Ausmaß des Zwangs dürfte also eher gering anzusetzen sein.

4. *Interpretationsprämissen, Methode, Historizität:* Krabiels Umgang mit Texten, die ihm zu seiner Hauptdefinition von Lehr-

stück nicht zu passen scheinen, nämlich Ausgrenzung oder Abwer-
tung ("Gedankenspiele"), macht deutlich, was Hermeneutiker und
nominalistisch orientierte Wissenschaftstheoretiker nicht überraschen
wird: Er ist, so wenig wie ich es war und bin (dazu Steinweg 1994),
von den Präkonzepten und "mitgebrachten" Fragen unabhängig, mit
denen er sich ans Interpretieren macht (Ihwe 1985), von den spezifischen Filtern also, die er aufgrund seiner persönlichen und wissenschaftlichen Sozialisation vor Augen hat.

Das möchte ich an einem Beispiel verdeutlichen: Die Zeilen
aus der *Versuche*-Fassung des *Lindberghflugs*: "Laßt uns bekämpfen
die Natur / Bis wir selber natürlich geworden sind" kommentiert
Krabiel so:

> [D]ie Lösung der mit der Technisierung entstandenen Probleme
> kann nicht in der (völlig illusorischen) Rücknahme fortgeschrit-
> tener Technik bestehen, sondern allein in ihrer Weiterentwick-
> lung zur "Natürlichkeit" — in moderner Terminologie: in der
> Weiterentwicklung zu ökologischer Verträglichkeit. (104)

Bei diesem Satz handelt es sich keineswegs nur um eine "Moderni-
sierung" der "Terminologie"; vielmehr wird dem Text aus heutiger
Problemsicht eine Aussage unterlegt, die Brecht um 1930 unmöglich intendiert haben kann (die wenigen umweltbewußten Prophe-
ten in der Weimarer Zeit wie z.B. der Begründer der Anthroposo-
phie, Rudolf Steiner, fanden damals außer bei ihren Jüngern damit
keinerlei Resonanz). Der Wortlaut "die Natur bekämpfen" ist ganz
offenkundig mit heutigen ökologischen Einsichten und Kenntnissen
nicht vereinbar. "Bis wir selber natürlich geworden sind" könnte
viel eher eine Aussage über die "unnatürliche" soziale Ungleichheit
sein als eine Aussage über ein bescheidenes Sich-Einfügen in ökologische Kreisläufe, denn Brecht fordert in der Fortsetzung dieses
Textes nicht eine "ökologische Verträglichkeit" der Technik, sondern
beschreibt im Interesse der Ideologiezerstörung eine (heute selbst
ideologisch gewordene) Haltung der hemmungslosen Expansion der
Technik und der durch sie ermöglichten Infrastruktur bis in die
letzten Winkel der Erde.

Es gibt keine *letztlich* objektive Wahrnehmung und Interpretation historischer Phänomene und Texte, sondern nur immer neue
Annäherungen und hin und wieder auch Entfernungen oder, wenn
man will, Rückfälle. (Noch einmal: Für mich steht trotz meiner
Gegenkritik außer Frage, daß Krabiel in mancher Hinsicht der
historischen Wahrheit ein großes Stück näher gekommen ist als ich
— aber die "Quelle" wird *niemand* erreichen, um ein Bild aus der
Maßnahme umzudrehen.) Ich habe diesen Sachverhalt 1972 aus-

drücklich thematisiert und von "(Re)-Konstruktion" gesprochen, wobei im terminus "Konstruktion" der Aspekt des eigenen unbewußten Hinzufügens liegt, was bei allem Bemühen um Objektivität aufgrund eigener, nur in Kritik und Gegenkritik nach und nach abzuarbeitender Wahrnehmungsfilter unvermeidlich ist. Das hat Krabiel mir als "wissenschaftstheoretische Unschuld" angekreidet und einen *absoluten* Anspruch auf "Historizität" dagegengestellt (304).

Auch die Interpretation der Lehrstücktexte von Lehmann/Lethen 1978 verfällt dem Verdikt mangelnder Historizität (235). Wenn die Nachgeborenen in früher entstandenen Texten nichts anderes entdecken dürften als das, was den Autoren und Zeitgenossen seinerzeit bewußt zugänglich war, dann kann man vermutlich den größten Teil der wissenschaftlichen wie der praktischen (theatralen etc.) Interpretationen dramatischer und anderer Kunstwerke der Müllabfuhr anvertrauen. Die Verabsolutierung des gleichwohl richtigen Strebens nach Historizität kann nur in Aporien enden.

Krabiel grenzt nicht nur relativ willkürlich theoretische Texte aus und behandelt sie, wenn sie ihm quer liegen, als nicht ernst zu nehmende "Gedankenspiele" oder wertet sie als fadenscheinige Verschleierungen ab. (Letzteres wäre, wenn nachweisbar, allemal legitim, gegenüber *jedem* Autor; der Versuch an sich ist notwendig und lobenswert, falls er von eigenen Beweisinteressen frei ist.) Auch poetische Texte, die Brecht eindeutig als Lehrstücke gekennzeichnet hat, werden ausgegrenzt, wenn sie nicht ins einmal fixierte Bild passen. Und wenn es gar nicht anders geht wie bei *Die Ausnahme und die Regel* wird flugs die Definition geändert.

Noch gravierender scheint mir die Ausblendung von Zusammenhängen und Kontexten zu sein (siehe oben). Damit gerät Krabiel, der Adorno-Kenner, ungewollt in die Nähe eines platten, buchstabenhörigen Positivismus. Das geht so weit, daß dann, wenn Brecht (pars pro toto) von *einem* "Denkenden" spricht, dieser auch allein Theater spielen muß, oder daß ein Gegensatz zwischen Nachahmung und Wiedergabe von Handlungen und Haltungen behauptet wird (422, Anm. 22), der ganz unsinnig ist: Menschen sind im Gegensatz zu technischen Apparaten nur zu Annäherungen, eben zu Nachahmungen, in der Lage (s. dazu auch Gebauer/Wulf 1992, 432f.). Und wenn Krabiel Äußerungen, die Brecht ausdrücklich als "Theorie" kennzeichnet, als "höchst abstrakt und *theoretisch*" geißelt und postuliert, sie "dürfen vor allem nicht generalisiert werden" (290), dann kann man nur mit Morgenstern/Palmström fragen: Ja, *durfte* dann Brecht überhaupt eine "Theorie" des Lehrstücks schreiben? Theorien müssen nun einmal generalisieren oder sie sind keine.

Einverständnis

Mein "re-konstruierendes" Verfahren, das ich als solches vor niemandem verborgen habe, hat zu einer Reihe von Fehlern geführt. Im Bewußtsein dieser Möglichkeit habe ich damals mit großem Aufwand versucht, jede einzelne Aussage überprüfbar *und kritisierbar* zu machen (Steinweg 1972, 73). Krabiels Nachweis, daß die von mir vermutete Homogenität der Äußerungen Brechts zum Lehrstück in der 1972 dargestellten Spannbreite überdehnt war, hat auch etwas Entlastendes. Einige Annahmen müssen revidiert werden (was in Steinweg 1995 geschehen ist), und die Zufriedenheit über die verbesserte Einsicht ist stärker als der Schmerz über den Irrtum. Den nächsten möchte ich, Brecht/Keuner nicht nur zitierend, mit folgendem Vorschlag vorbereiten, ein erster Versuch, eine Art Resultante der beiden Herangehensweisen und ihrer Widersprüche zu zeichnen:

1. Die Merkmale des Lehrstücktypus entstanden zunächst nacheinander, teilweise als Reaktion auf bestehende kulturelle Strömungen, Bestrebungen und Krisen insbesondere im musikalischen Sektor, teilweise aufgrund eigenständiger theoretischer Überlegungen Brechts, dem jene Strömungen durchaus zupaß kamen, obwohl er sich von Anfang an — die ideologiekritische *Dreigroschenoper* war schon geschrieben — intentional und im Niveau des gesellschaftskritischen Denkens stark von ihnen unterschied. Die Entwicklung der einzelnen Lehrstückformen und der Etappen der Lehrstücktheorie erfolgte nicht geradlinig, sondern durchaus mit Brüchen und Kehrtwendungen. Insofern kann auf der konkreten Ebene der *Oberflächengestalt* der Lehrstücke nicht von einem einheitlichen Typus gesprochen werden. In jedes einzelne Lehrstück gehen sowohl konkrete "Anforderungen" der jeweiligen gesellschaftlichen und kulturellen Situation sowie neuer theoretischer und politischer Kontexte ein als auch Brechts Verarbeitung der Reaktionen, die das jeweils vorangehende Lehrstück hervorgerufen hatte.

2. Gleichwohl machte Brecht später den Versuch, ihm wesentlich erscheinende Elemente in verallgemeinerter Form festzuhalten, wobei die politischen Zeitumstände eine gelassene und differenzierte Ausformulierung der Theorie nicht mehr zuließen, weder vor noch nach Krieg und Exil. Der Versuch, die 1937 nicht geschriebenen Teile dieser Theorie gewissermaßen wiederherzustellen, ist auf eine Analyse der Gesamtentwicklung seines Denkens über die Funktionen von Bühne, Theaterapparat, Zuschauer- und Schauspielkunst sowie Theatermusik einerseits (dazu Steinweg 1995, 34-56) und eine vorsichtige Einbeziehung der frühen Ansätze zu einer Theoriebildung im unmittelbaren Umfeld der Lehrstücke anderer-

seits angewiesen. Zu diesem Umfeld gehören auch die Überlegungen zu einem umfassenderen, die schon vorhandenen Lehrstücke einschließenden, sich darin aber nicht erschöpfenden theaterpädagogischen Gesamtkonzept ("Theorie der Pädagogien").

3. Mein philologischer Irrtum, die "Muster" betreffend, war ausgesprochen fruchtbar: Er hat sensibel gemacht für die real existierenden Sprachmuster in den Lehrstücktexten, ohne die auch "die ersten Künstler ihrer Zeit" kaum produktive, zur Auseinandersetzung geeignete Muster von Gesten und Haltungen liefern könnten. Der konkrete, körperlich-geistige *Haltungen* provozierende Charakter dieser Muster erlaubt es, die Lehrstücke auch dann zu nutzen, wenn verfremdungsfähige, in der epischen Spielweise ausgebildete Schauspieler nicht zur Verfügung stehen.

4. Auch wenn die praktischen Verfahren, die aus den Versuchen zu einer didaktischen "Umsetzung" der Lehrstücktheorie und einer Verwendung der Lehrstücktexte in einem politisch fast vollständig veränderten Umfeld hervorgegangen sind, sich in vielerlei Hinsicht von dem unterscheiden, was Brecht sich vorgestellt zu haben scheint; auch wenn insofern die heutige Lehrstückpraxis mit der von Brecht zunächst ins Auge gefaßten (aber in den Texten zur Theorie der "Pädagogien" schon auf das Erfahrungsfeld der Spieler hin erweiterten) Spielpraxis eher weniger als mehr gemein haben, so wäre doch auch diese Praxis ohne Brechts theoretische Grundüberlegungen und ohne seine Lehrstücktexte nicht möglich. Noch im Widerspruch gegen einzelne seiner Vorstellungen (Steinweg 1995, 106-11) bleiben wir ihm bzw. seinen übergreifenden Einsichten verpflichtet:

> Das Denken des Denkenden bedeutet verändern. Der Denkende ist für die *Änderung*. Ihn hält von keinem Gedankengang der Wunsch ab, daß etwas bleiben soll. Er ist einverstanden damit, daß durch sein Denken die Welt verändert wird. Sein Denken ist ein Wenigdenken, es ist beschränkt durch die Verpflichtung der Nützlichkeit. Wählt man von allen Dingen nur aus, die nützlich sind, so wählt man wenige aus. Geht man vom Zweck aus, dann verliert man sich nicht in Gedankengängen, die nichts ändern. (Text Nr. 87)

Das gilt uneingeschränkt auch für unseren heutigen Gebrauch des Lehrstückmodells und der einzelnen, nach Entstehungskontext und Form unterschiedlichen Lehrstücke. Ich habe nicht für das Brechtmuseum gedacht und gearbeitet, sondern in *Brechts Sinne* für eine Veränderung der Welt, auch wenn diese Welt zunächst nur der Mikrokosmos zahlloser kleiner Gruppen ist, die ihre soziale Wahr nehmungsfähigkeit, ihr Denken und ihre soziale Kompetenz mit Hilfe der Lehrstücke genußvoll erweitern.

Mein Verfahren — Klaus Krabiel möge diesen Satz bitte nicht als Zynismus oder Schlimmeres mißverstehen — hat seine Gegenreaktion hervorgerufen. Die "Schnur der alten / Aufgerollten chinesischen Leinwand" mit dem Zweifler wurde erneut herabgelassen.[4] Gut so.

ANMERKUNGEN

[1] Schon 1973 hat Krabiel in seinem Seminar an der Universität Frankfurt mündlich Einzelheiten meiner Arbeit leidenschaftlich kritisiert.

[2] Die Text-Nummern beziehen sich auf meine kritische Ausgabe der Texte zur Lehrstücktheorie, soweit sie mir damals zugänglich waren (Steinweg 1976).

[3] Brechts Formulierung in Text Nr. 32 "die Lehrstücke...untersuchen auch" mag so gemeint sein, wie Krabiel schreibt: "Lehrstücke sollen nicht lediglich fertige Antworten," sondern 'daneben' (!) "die Probleme und Fragestellungen szenisch-dialogisch sich entfalten lassen" wie in den "Untersuchungen" des *Badener Lehrstücks* (S. 298). Allerdings bleibt die Formulierung, daß "die Lehrstücke" (Texte) selbst etwas "untersuchen," problematisch, auch wenn diese Lesart syntaktisch korrekt ist. Texte sind keine Subjekte, semantisch gesehen können sie nichts untersuchen. Es kommt darauf an, ob man den Ausdruck "Lehrstück" als "Text" oder als Veranstaltungstyp liest.

[4] Siehe Hartung 1992 und korrespondierend Steinweg 1992.

ZITIERTE LITERATUR

Berenberg-Gossler, Heinrich, Hans-Harald Müller und Joachim Stosch, 1974: "Das Lehrstück: Rekonstruktion einer Theorie oder Fortsetzung eines Lernprozesses? Eine Auseinandersetzung mit Reiner Steinweg," Joachim Dyck u.a., Hrsg., *Brechtdiskussion*. Kronberg/Ts.: Athenäum, 121-71.

Gebauer, Gunter, und Christoph Wulf, 1992: *Mimesis, Kultur, Kunst, Gesellschaft*. Reinbek: Rowohlt.

Hartung, Günter, 1959: "Zur epischen Oper Brechts und Weills," *Wissenschaftliche Zeitschrift der Martin-Luther Universität Halle-Wittenberg*, Gesellschafts- und sprachwissenschaftliche Reihe 8, 659-73.

____, 1992: "Brechts unvollendetes Gedicht 'Der Zweifler,'" Ulrike C.

Wasmuht, Hrsg., *Ist Wissen Macht? Zur aktuellen Funktion von Friedensforschung*. Baden-Baden: Nomos, 19-32.

Ihwe, Jens, 1985: *Konversationen über Literatur*. Braunschweig-Wiesbaden.

Koch, Gerd, Reiner Steinweg, und Florian Vaßen, Hrsg., 1984: *Asoziales Theater. Spielversuche mit Lehrstücken und Anstiftung zur Praxis*. Köln: Prometh.

Krabiel, Klaus-Dieter, 1993: *Brechts Lehrstücke: Entstehung und Entwicklung eines Spieltyps*. Stuttgart und Weimar: Metzler.

Lehmann, Hans-Thies und Helmut Lethen, 1978: "Ein Vorschlag zur Güte: Zur doppelten Polarität des Lehrstücks," Reiner Steinweg, Hrsg., *Auf Anregung Bertolt Brechts: Lehrstücke mit Schülern, Arbeitern, Theaterleuten*. Frankfurt/M.: Suhrkamp, 302-18.

Steinweg, Reiner, 1971a: "Brechts *Die Maßnahme*: Übungstext, nicht Tragödie," *Alternative* 78/79, 133-43; auch in Manfred Brauneck, Hrsg., *Das deutsche Drama vom Expressionismus bis zur Gegenwart: Interpretationen*, 2. erweiterte Auflage. Bamberg 1972, 145-58.

_____, 1971b: "Die Lehrstücke als Versuchsreihe," wie 1971a, 121-24.

_____, 1972: *Das Lehrstück: Brechts Theorie einer politisch-ästhetischen Erziehung*. Stuttgart: Metzler. 2. ergänzte Auflage 1976.

_____, 1973: "*Das Badener Lehrstück vom Einverständnis*: Mystik, Religionsersatz oder Parodie?" *Text und Kritik*, Sonderheft "Bertolt Brecht II," 109-30.

_____, 1976: "Kritische Ausgabe der theoretischen Äußerungen von Brecht und seinen MitarbeiterInnen zum Lehrstück," Steinweg, Hrsg., *Brechts Modell der Lehrstücke: Zeugnisse, Diskussion, Erfahrungen*. Frankfurt/M.: Suhrkamp, 31-221.

_____, 1986: "Streng am Text und ganz bei sich: Wahrnehmung und Erprobung von Haltungen in Konfliktsituationen," Reiner Steinweg, Wolfgang Heidefuß und Peter Petsch, *Weil wir ohne Waffen sind: Ein theaterpädagogisches Forschungsprojekt zur Politischen Bildung. Nach einem Vorschlag von Bertolt Brecht*. Frankfurt/M.: Brandes und Apsel, 320-88.

_____, 1992: "'Der Zweifler' von Bertolt Brecht: Assoziationen eines (selbst-)kritischen Friedensforschers," Ulrike Wasmuht, Hrsg., *Ist Wissen Macht? Zur aktuellen Funktion von Friedensforschung*. Baden-Baden: Nomos, 33-47.

_____, 1994: "Die (Wieder-)Entdeckung des Lehrstücks: Geschichte einer Reise," *Korrespondenzen* 10.19-21, Sonderheft "Brecht Lehrstücke," Hannover: 5-14.

_____, 1995: "Lehrstück und episches Theater: Brechts Theorie und die theaterpädagogische Praxis." Mit einem Nachwort von Ingrid Kundela: *Brecht in Brasilien*. Frankfurt/M.: Brandes & Apsel.

Tatlow, Anthony, 1994: "Landkarten für Maulwürfe oder: Eine rückwärts gewandte Zukunftswissenschaft," [Rezension von Krabiel 1993], *Korrespondenzen* 10.19-21, Sonderheft "Brecht Lehrstücke," 23-31.

Brecht and Company: Ein kritischer Essay

John Fuegis neue Biographie hätte die erste sein können, die Brechts Leben ohne die Voreingenommenheiten durch den Kalten Krieg, früher von rechts wie links vorgetragen, neu studierte. Statt dessen konzentriert er sich, wie andere vor ihm, auf die weniger attraktiven Seiten von Brechts Persönlichkeit (er hätte nicht eine einzige gute Tat vollbracht) sowie auf die autoritären Aspekte seiner Politik (in ihm habe sich sowohl Hitler als auch Stalin gespiegelt). Fuegi behauptet, sein neues Material beweist, daß die Mitarbeiterinnen die eigentlichen Autoren der Stücke gewesen seien. Dabei vernachlässigt er die Analyse der Texte selber, um seine Behauptungen beweisen zu können. Fuegis mutmaßlicher Feminismus dient allenfalls dazu, seine politisch und ästhetisch konservativen Angriffe auf Brechts Leben und Werk, die noch dazu schlecht und sensationell geschrieben sind, zu tarnen. Das Buch hat eine neue Brecht-Debatte ausgelöst, allerdings nur mittels eines faktisch brüchigen und philosophisch inkohärenten Textes.

Brecht et Compagnie: Essai Critique

La nouvelle biographie de Brecht par John Fuegi aurait pu être la première à étudier sa vie sans porter le fardeau d'attitudes héritées de la guerre froide, qu'elles soient de gauche ou de droite. Malheureusement, elle est centrée sur le côté peu reluisant de la personnalité de Brecht (Brecht n'a jamais commis une bonne action) et sur les aspects autoritaristes de ses positions politiques (Brecht était un miroir à la fois d'Hitler et de Staline). La nouvelle documentation constituée par Fuegi est axée sur le rôle des collaboratrices féminines de Brecht, dont Fuegi prétend qu'elles sont les véritables auteurs de ses pièces. Mais il n'examine jamais l'œuvre afin de fonder ses accusations, et son féminisme putatif sert surtout à masquer une attaque politiquement et esthétiquement conservatrice, mal écrite et sensationnaliste, contre chaque aspect de la vie de Brecht. Le livre de Fuegi a lancé un nouveau débat sur Brecht, mais au moyen d'un texte incertain sur le plan des faits et incohérent sur le plan philosophique.

Brecht y Compañía: una reseña

La nueva biografía de John Fuegi sobre Brecht podría haber sido la primera en estudiar su vida sin estar bajo la influencia de actitudes, de izquierdas o de derechas propias de la Guerra Fría. Sin embargo, desafortunadamente, tal y como muchos escritores anteriores, esta nueva biografía se centra en el aspecto más feo del carácter de Brecht (Brecht nunca cometió ningún acto bueno) así como en los aspectos autoritarios de su política (Brecht era un espejo de Hitler y Stalin). La información de Fuegi se centra en el papel de las colaboradoras de Brecht, que según Fuegi son las verdaderas autoras de su obra. Pero él nunca analiza el trabajo para de probar su argumento y su supuesto feminismo sirve principalmente para enmascarar un ataque politicamente y esteticamente conservador sobre cada uno delos aspectos de la vida de Brecht, escrito malamente y de una forma sensacionalista. El libro de Fuegi motivo un nuevo debate sobre Brecht pero lo hace a través de un texto poco sólido según los hechos y incoherente filosóficamente.

Brecht & Company: A Review Essay

Erika Munk

John Fuegi. *Brecht and Company: Sex, Politics, and the Making of the Modern Drama*. New York: Grove Press, 1994. 732 pages

John Fuegi's *Brecht and Company* is the first Brecht biography to appear in English since the Wall came down. It could have been the very first to study Brecht and his work without the burden of Cold War attitudinizing. Instead, Fuegi's book reflects every American conservative accusation against Brecht from Ruth Fischer's 1944 "Bert Brecht, Minstrel of the GPU" through Ronald Hayman's hostile 1983 life, while identifying Brecht with Hitler as well as Stalin (perhaps this is a post-Wall touch), and claiming that Brecht is not Brecht at all but "Brecht," the creation of exploited female lover-collaborators. This claim, in its apparent feminism, has made *Brecht and Company* an object of furious debate and the subject of an astonishing number of mainstream reviews; the book has become important not so much as Brecht scholarship, but in its effect on our general cultural understanding of Brecht's influence on theater professionals and playgoers.

In his preface, Fuegi describes a visit Maxim Gorki made to a Soviet prison camp in the 1920s. The camp had been prettied up for Gorki and the inmates given newspapers to read so they would look well treated. They held the papers upside down to alert him that he was being deceived, but he ignored them and wrote glowingly about the place. "Under the aegis of the Gorky report began the cancerous growth of a system where, according to some estimates, more people died than in Hitler's camps" (xiii). Thus Fuegi lets us know from the start that, unlike Gorki (and Brecht), he is neither fooled by Bolshevism, insensible to victims, nor a prop to tyranny. And unlike most Brechtians, he is not fooled by BB either: he can tell us the truth behind Brecht's stage-set, for he has seen the signals of the prisoners of the Brecht Collective, those playwriting collaborators—particularly Elisabeth Hauptmann, Margarete Steffin, and Ruth Berlau — whose tiny bylines in the published work have been visible from the beginning, yet never taken seriously enough.

Brecht Then and Now / Brecht damals und heute
Eds. Marc Silberman et al. *The Brecht Yearbook / Das Brecht-Jahrbuch*,
Volume 20 (Madison: The International Brecht Society, 1995)

He has heard their cries, too: "Their voices are from Arctic Circle death camps, from the ashes of Treblinka and Auschwitz, and from cemetaries from Berlin to Beverly Hills" (xix). Though Fuegi himself describes Steffin's death in a Moscow hospital (where she was treated as a member of the priviligentsia), and quotes Hauptmann and Berlau when they were growing old in Berlin, the notion of Brecht as a one-man Gulag runs straight through all Fuegi's 700-plus pages. (So does his taste for portentous, clumsy, tabloid prose.)

What is Fuegi's vision of this "Brecht" who did not write? The first page describes a photo taken when Brecht was two years old, standing "with a tiny hobbyhorse, and a whip big enough for a real horse" (1). This Nietzschean whip turns into a veritable Leitmotif (after its fourth appearance [74], 90% of the book still ahead of me, I stopped tracking it); so does the horse — we are endlessly told that Brecht thought of women as beasts to be ridden, tamed, exploited, and put out to pasture.

Though Fuegi includes anecdotes which most people would find endearing — it's hard not to like the Augsburg schoolboy who, asked for a brief essay on the quintessentially German romantic subject, "What draws us to the mountains?" curtly writes, "a ski lift"? (11) — nothing Brecht does from infancy on can be any good in Fuegi's eyes. (This is odd for someone who has made Brecht his life's work, though perhaps not so odd for someone apparently uninterested in Brecht's art.) If Brecht compares himself unfavorably to Goethe, he's "making a virtue of intellectual limitations" (73). If he studies economics, it is because unless it "can be understood and controlled, all his other systems of control and subjugation can be rendered worthless" (86). Does Brecht become a Marxist because he was a radical artist in a Weimar Berlin swarming with Nazi thugs? No. "At the level of Brecht's deepest psychic economy, his need always to feel in control...Marx provided a cosmic answer" (178). What does Brecht read? "Mostly one detective story after another" (223). (Even a quick look through Brecht's *Journals* shows how absurd this is.) What defines his character? "The pleasure he had always taken in seeing people in pain" (177). (Both the *Journals* and the *Letters* contradict this; cool perhaps, and selfish — not sadistic.)

Brecht's financial slipperiness, sexual duplicity, and political temporizing are certainly not news. He was a misogynist in his youth and always a deceiver; he sold his political soul for a theater; he was sometimes a terrible man. All of this has been told and re-told, in and out of the academy. This made sense when Brecht was being mythologized from the Left, and, done with an eye for contradiction, correcting that hagiography might still be useful. But Fuegi's portrait of Brecht is so obsessively one-dimensional it's just another kind of mythologizing.

Fuegi's Brecht could never have sat through, let alone written, Brecht's plays. Of course, this is Fuegi's point. He constructs someone unimaginable as the playwright Brecht, the better to frame his statement that Hauptmann, Steffin, and Berlau *were* that playwright. That they were collaborators has always been recognized; so were a number of men — Neher, Weill, Feuchtwanger, Eisler, many others. Theater is a collective enterprise, and left-wing theater often makes a principle out of Brecht's production practices that are always to some degree inescapable. However, though Fuegi's emphasis on the women seems in great part to be his way of getting feminist credentials and attention, he is right that they played a different role from the male collaborators. They worked harder, typing as well as thinking. They were emotionally, physically, and sometimes financially bound to Brecht in a period when it was almost impossible for a woman to make her way as a writer; so they were infinitely more vulnerable. Marieluise Fleisser, who had the greatest gifts of all his writing collaborators, broke with Brecht and produced a wonderfully mean play about him, but she is the rule-proving exception. The men who worked with Brecht had their own careers; these women dissolved into him. What they would have accomplished on their own is anyone's guess.

What does Fuegi actually claim about the authorship of individual works? He says Hauptmann wrote *Mahagonny*'s songs in English; *A Man's A Man* is "overwhelmingly" her work (154; in fact, Brecht credited five collaborators, including her); she provided the translations for the *Lehrstücke* — as well as, with Paul Hindemith, devising the form itself — and much of *The Mother* and *St. Joan of the Stockyards*. After the war she and Benno Besson did the adaptation of Molière's *Don Juan*. Much of this information has been published before. Fuegi's most detailed charges concern *The Threepenny Opera*: adapting John Gay's *Beggar's Opera* was Hauptmann's idea, and, he says, she wrote "at least 80% of the fabric of the work" (196). Brecht credited both Hauptmann and Weill as collaborators, so if you take into account whatever (outside the score) Weill contributed and the six songs plagiarized from Ammer's translation of Villon, Brecht, according to Fuegi, did not write much of anything except the Moritat.

Fuegi does not break *Threepenny*'s plot or dialogue down into Brecht's work and Hauptmann's. He simply states that "Hauptmann may speak in what we choose to recognize as 'his' voice, but what she says in that voice is very much hers," (180) and that "the surviving manuscripts, and the tone of the works themselves indicate that Hauptmann was responsible for the songs that tell a story from a woman's point of view" (198). He never explains how he deduced authorship from "tone" if she uses Brecht's voice (to reach 80%, she *must* have written quite a bit in what amounts to stylistic drag), and he does not describe the evidence of the manuscripts themselves. What weird essentialist code is needed to sort out *Threepenny*'s "male" and "female" lyrics? A seminar he took with Carol Gilligan helped Fuegi hear "different" voices (624); he assumes that nurturing, relationship-oriented, unaggressive tones are Hauptmann's, their opposites are Brecht's "voice," or even really Brecht's. When this leads to hearing the Cannon Song as a reflection of Brecht's private macho-colonialism, Fuegi is hamhandedly simplifying a rage and satire that could be gendered either way or not at all. The women's-point-of-view songs include not only a vengeful victim's fantasy but a how-I-love-bad-guys ballad and a silly-women's-jealousy duet. It is impossible to know, on the evidence Fuegi presents, what difference Hauptmann's femaleness made in their form or content. Yet this is in the long run a much more important question than how much money and professional credit she was cheated of, and it is the question Fuegi claims to be addressing.

This muddle is complicated by, no surprise, politics. Hauptmann is painted as both more (femininely) humane and more (communistically) hardline than Brecht, but Fuegi describes *Threepenny* as "deeply reactionary," because its beggars are not really poor (irony is not his strong point), and backs himself up, despite his anti-Stalinism, with a hostile *Threepenny* critique from the official German communist newspaper. If *Threepenny* was both Hauptmann's idea and her text, what explains this neither humane nor communist outcome? Fuegi is forever getting himself into a bind because he wants us to deplore Brecht's work while admiring the women who, he says, actually wrote it.

When Brecht went into exile, he and Hauptmann parted ways; Margarete Steffin accompanied him, his wife Helene Weigel, and their two children, to Scandinavia and then Moscow, where she died of TB while the rest travelled on to America. Steffin apparently worked on Brecht's only conventional, "realist" anti-Fascist plays, *Fear and Misery of the Third Reich* and *Señora Carrar's Rifles*, as well as everything else done from 1933-41. That she was a collaborator in these plays has been noted in English criticism at least as far back as John Willett in 1959. Again, Fuegi credits her with an enormous creative contribution without any examination of exactly what she wrote. She seems to have been an influence towards Party conformity. Ruth Berlau, who joined the entourage in Denmark and went with them to Hollywood, wrote in her memoir that Steffin "wanted to ensure that even the workers would understand Brecht's poetry. She insisted he rephrase formulations she considered 'twisted'" (*Living for Brecht: The Memoirs of Ruth Berlau* [New York: Fromm International, 1987], 80). Steffin's children's plays have been published, and Fuegi quotes a remarkable erotic poem she wrote for Brecht, but she died too young for anyone to predict what kind of writer she would have become and whether she would have declared independence.

Berlau — another party activist, who convinced Brecht to versify the *Communist Manifesto* — wrote more, lived longer, and made her feelings clear. She worked, says Fuegi, on *Puntila* (which Brecht swiped from the Finnish writer Hella Wuolijoki in the first place), *Mother Courage*, *The Caucasian Chalk Circle*, *Galileo*, and *The Good Person of Szechwan*. Again, Fuegi never says what characters, scenes, or lines are hers. On the evidence of her own soft and histrionic prose, it is hard to believe Berlau wrote much, however profound her contribution as editor, researcher, and soundingboard. Her great work is the photographs in the *Model Books*.

Though taking the anti-victim-feminism stance has become a way sneakily to deny feminism's basic point that women are, as a group, exploited by men and powerless compared to them, thinking about Berlau makes me wonder about Fuegi's own posture as gallant knight rescuing the helpless. She had lovers, left Brecht behind to go to Spain during the Civil War, spied a bit, took to drink. Her furious and sentimental book about Brecht can be interestingly at odds with Fuegi's portrait: speaking of her novel *Every Animal Can Do It* — which Fuegi calls "daringly feminist and very lively" — she says, "I provided the material, Brecht the wording. This collaboration taught me a great deal" (Berlau, *Living for Brecht*, 25). The warm stories Berlau interweaves with her anger, Hauptmann's postwar descriptions of the intellectual pleasures of working with Brecht, Steffin's sexy poems, may be prideful or defensive self-justifications. But they also help answer an inevitable question: why would three intelligent, gifted communist women let Brecht bed, bully, and overwork them for such a long time when they had no chance of replacing his gifted, intelligent communist wife? (And why would the wife put up with it? Eventually she got great parts and a large, well-financed theater to run, but for years she made dinner.)

Fuegi's own answers have nothing to do with sex, intellect, or comradeship. The first is that Hauptmann's "commitment, like that of Berlau and Steffin, was not to Brecht but to the success of communism and to a world of equality and peace" (513). (Fuegi on and off falls into an unmediated Stalinoid rhetoric that certainly would have made Hauptmann, if not the other two, wince.) This analysis conflicts not only with his description of the plays he says they wrote, but with his descriptions of the women's overwhelming emotional commitment to Brecht himself — breakdowns, attempted suicides, pregnancies, jealousies. Instead, they are suddenly in a new role, manipulatively using Brecht.

Never mind. This is a minor theme compared to Fuegi's real obsession with the second reason he gives for their attraction to Brecht: Brecht's overwhelming magnetism and lust for power, which Fuegi sees as a mirror of twentieth-century European totalitarianism. Fuegi has cooked up a *Reader's Digest* version of Wilhelm Reich, sauced with a ridiculously inflated notion of the-personal-is-the-political. As an academic, Fuegi must have noticed over the decades that quite uncharismatic male professors routinely sleep with their student assistants and use their work. He is so busy making Brecht evil, he refuses to acknowledge how banal Brecht's sexism was.

Sexual politics do not really interest Fuegi. Hauptmann, Steffin, and Berlau are not his main concern. He barely discusses their own writings and makes only superficial attempts to place their lives within the history of communist attitudes towards women or the development of feminist thought. Patronizingly, he calls Berlau "Ruth," though other people go by their surnames, and he thinks the only reason women have sex with women is that their husbands have strayed (183, 186).

Yes, Brecht's sexism in his teens and 20s was dreadful; after all, it reflected his time and culture. Before he was 30 it had almost disappeared from his work (certainly not from the culture). If his women collaborators influenced this change — which I do not doubt for a second — at least he listened to them. When Americans first really became aware of Brecht, in the late 1950s and early 1960s, our other hip writers were Mailer, who stabbed his wife; Burroughs, who shot and killed his wife; and Artaud, who imagined scorpions coming out of vaginas. Fuegi ignores this context and the many feminist analyses of and reactions to it. For him, "feminism" exists to serve another, quite conservative, agenda.

Conservative, but confused. Brecht's politics are denounced from every side. Not properly communist ("[he] helped strengthen the hand of his inquisitors," states Fuegi, referring to the fact that Brecht, when called to testify before HUAC, said he was not in the Party rather than, like the Americans, refusing to answer under the First Amendment), not really anti-Nazi ("he did not directly confront the Nazis, he did not support the Jewish cause"), he was no anti-Stalinist ("he did not defend people like Bukharin"), so he ends up a genuine Red Fascist, "among the millions whose tacit complicity helped turn the tide toward Hitler, Stalin, and McCarthy." All in one paragraph (483). Bizarre. Brecht's sly HUAC testimony hurt no one, his writing was anti-Fascist by any possible definition, and unfortunately there was nothing tacit about his complicity with Stalinism.

The crucial fact, according to Fuegi, is that Brecht was "a master in the microcosm of his personal circle, [who] saw nothing odd in Stalin's mastery over those around him...in the same way that Hitler ruthlessly divided the world into masters and subjects" (332). Fuegi's basic, totally gaga trope is "Hitler, Stalin, or Brecht," as in, "the wholly irrational power these figures — whether Hitler, Stalin, or Brecht — exerted when they were encountered in person" (128). The reader is forced to remind herself that Brecht had no political power, did not wage war, did not build prison camps. The reader is also forced to remind herself of the work: that poetic, critical, ironic, smart, moving, witty body of theater art which is the reason Fuegi had something to debunk in the first place. Certainly Fuegi himself is useless about Brecht's writing; his taste is more psychological, more conventional, perhaps Stanislavskian — though he himself calls Stanislavski Stalin's "sycophant," which is worse than anything one could say in that line about poor BB.

In *Brecht and Company*'s penultimate paragraph, answering his own rhetorical question, "Where were the women dramatists of world rank in the first half of the twentieth century?" Fuegi says we should look "under the mask of the brutal male 'lover' Shui Ta, at the hidden face of the woman who loves him despite his brutality, Shen Te in *The Good Woman of Setzuan*" (621). But of course Shui Ta is not Shen Te's lover. He is the male persona, the gender mask, she takes on when she has to be ruthless, a disguise assumed not out of love — despite brutality — but from economic necessity. Shui Ta and Shen Te are enacted by one female performer: the audience sees her put on her male costume. Shen Te does have a lover, Yang Sun, a vain, deceitful but affectionate fellow who wears no mask and gets her pregnant. That Fuegi gets something so basic wrong about one of Brecht's most popular, most written-about, and most potentially feminist plays is astounding. He even uses Eric Bentley's version of the title, so that *Mensch* becomes "woman," not "person."

Eric Bentley has pointed out to me that in America, the positive and negative reviews do not line up in any neat right-left configuration with conservatives defending Fuegi's point of view, liberals and radicals deploring it. Instead, conservatives seem to praise the book for its generic Brecht-bashing or condemn it as "feminist," while more leftish types praise it for its "feminism" or condemn it for its political and aesthetic anti-radicalism. John Simon, a public anti-feminist, lauded the book in the *Wall Street Journal*. Former liberal, now neo-conservative Robert Brustein, allowing Brecht a scoundrel soul but great art, denounces Fuegi for "political correctness," using the Shui Ta sentence as a revelation of Fuegi's "[u]nderlying feminist theme" without noticing its inaccuracy (*New Republic*, October 10, 1994, 35). Similarly, Donald Lyons writing in the *National Review* (November 21, 1994) accuses Fuegi of Vulgar Feminism (his caps) and reflects on "the resemblances between new feminism and old Stalinism" (66). Michael Meyer in *The New York Review of Books* (December 1, 1994) ignores political questions, accepts Fuegi's "facts" whether true or false, and defends Brecht only as a master who has never been properly translated into English.

Well, at least Brecht is suddenly alive again as a subject for discussion in the non-academic world, so some good has been done. But by an exceedingly ill wind. For me, the worst crime committed by this mean-spirited, mushy-minded, overwrought tome has less to do with its facts and factoids than with the disingenuousness of the entire enterprise and the calamitous effect it will have on the general reader's understanding of Brecht. Above all, its devious, phoney "feminism," deployed to disguise its basic rightwingness will discourage women and other dissenters from any serious consideration of Brecht's useful dramaturgy and beautiful texts.

NOTE: This is a somewhat revised and expanded version of a review that appeared first in *The Nation*, October 31, 1994; permission granted by the author.

Die Konstruktion des Sexisten und Ausbeuters Bertolt Brecht

In den letzten Jahren sind zahlreiche Publikationen erschienen, die Brecht als Ausbeuter weiblicher Mitarbeiter bezeichnen. Angeblich machte er seine Mitarbeiterinnen sexuell abhängig, um ihre Kreativität zu kontrollieren und ihre Beiträge unter seinem eigenen Namen zu veröffentlichen. Der vorliegende Aufsatz versucht, dieses Bild zu korrigieren. Es ist grundfalsch, Brechts weibliche Mitarbeiter als Opfer männlicher Intrige zu charakterisieren. Zu einer Zeit, in der es für Frauen schwierig war, beruflich anerkannt zu werden, bot Brecht ihnen Gelegenheit, ihre Fähigkeiten zu erproben. Brechts kollektive Arbeitsweise ermunterte zur gleichberechtigten Teilnahme. Seine Arbeit hing ab von der intensiven Zusammenarbeit aller seiner Mitarbeiter. Der Einzelne fühlte sich nicht ausgebeutet, sondern angespornt, seine Kreativität voll auszuschöpfen, eine Tatsache, die heute oft übersehen wird.

La Construction d'un Bertolt Brecht Sexiste et Exploiteur

Les publications donnant à Brecht l'étiquette d'un exploiteur de ses collaboratrices se sont amassées au cours des dernières années. Il les aurait prétenduement assujetties de façon patriarcale afin de contrôler leur créativité et de publier leurs contributions sous son propre nom. Cet essai a pour but de rectifier cette image. Il est radicalement faux de présenter les collaboratrices de Brecht comme des victimes d'intrigues masculines. À une époque où il était difficile pour une femme d'atteindre la reconnaissance professionnelle, Brecht leur a donné l'occasion d'éprouver leurs capacités. La méthode de travail collective de Brecht encourageait une participation égale. Ses travaux dépendaient de la collaboration intensive de tous ses collaborateurs. Les individus ne se sentaient pas exploités mais poussés à leur plus haut niveau de créativité, une réalité qu'on oublie souvent aujourd'hui.

La construcción del Bertolt Brecht sexista y explotador

En los últimos años se han acumulado publicaciones que nombran a Brecht un explotador de sus colaboradoras. Según cabe presumir, él las subyugó sexualmente de una forma patriarcal con el objeto de controlar su creatividad y de publicar sus contribuciones bajo su propio nombre. Este ensayo pretende corregir esta imagen. Es basicamente erróneo caracterizar a las colaboradoras de Brecht como víctimas de una intriga masculina. En un momento histórico cuando para las mujeres era difícil obtener un reconocimiento profesional, Brecht les ofrecía la oportunidad de poner a prueba sus habilidades creativas. El proceso de trabajo colectivo fomentado por Brecht estimulaba una participación igualitaria. Sus obras dependían de la participación intensa de todas sus colaboradoras. Los individuos no se sentían explotados sino por el contrario estimulados para alcanzar su mayor creatividad, una percepción esta que a menudo hoy en día es olvidada.

The Construction of the Sexist and Exploiter Bertolt Brecht

Gudrun Tabbert-Jones

In recent years Brecht, his "productive" relationships with female collaborators, and his literary images of women have been at the center of heated debates. Critics have argued that Brecht, who presented himself as an advocate of social justice and an opponent of exploitation and oppression, conducted himself in a very different manner in private life. The author who considered art a means to enlighten audiences about the exploitative nature of human relationships in capitalist societies is said to have exploited ruthlessly his friends and most of all his female associates. The current emphasis on women's roles relative to men has led some critics to scrutinize closely the lives of male authors who presumably owed much of their fame and fortune to selflessly devoted women. Brecht's "use" of female collaborators is widely known and has made him a target of criticism. Theorists consider him an example of male exploitation of women and have not tired of stealing a glance at his private life to find proof of wrong-doing on his part. Discussions of where, when, with whom, and to what extent, Brecht conducted his dubious affairs have led to speculations about psychological, philosophical, and ethical issues. This has caused critics to ask the wrong questions and to loose sight of the real issues: what is Brecht's contribution to modern drama and what does authorship mean in Brecht's case?

Personal letters, memos, and notes exchanged between Brecht and some of his collaborators seem to support the claim that he cleverly manipulated his partners emotionally in order to extract services from them. Margarete Steffin's letters from Russia, for example, give us the impression that love in conjunction with loyalty and blind devotion drove her to endure physical hardship and isolation, which ultimately proved to be fatal. In his sonnets Brecht stylized her as the valiant soldier, indicating that he expected her to fight his battles at distant frontiers. She, on the other hand, stylized herself as the lover whose main motivation for remaining in an inhospitable environment was her personal feelings for Brecht who, according to her letters, all too often failed to respond to her

Brecht Then and Now / Brecht damals und heute
Eds. Marc Silberman et al. *The Brecht Yearbook / Das Brecht-Jahrbuch*,
Volume 20 (Madison: The International Brecht Society, 1995)

pleas for signs of affection. Critics have speculated that Brecht may have rendered women like Steffin emotionally dependent in order to foster their willingness to serve him, causing them to subordinate their self-interest to his. No wonder some American critics view Brecht as fitting the mold of the stereotypical male oppressor who exploited women by emotionally manipulating them, causing them to see themselves as objects of pleasure as well as a means of production.

John Fuegi's recently published book, *Brecht and Company. Sex, Politics, and the Making of the Modern Drama*, is the most striking example of a biased interpretation of biographical data. Fuegi charges that, typically, Brecht played on his lovers' desires to get what he wanted from them. Arnolt Bronnen, a male collaborator and "lover," according to John Fuegi, is cited as saying that Brecht "seemed to be a monstrous sucking organ that could envelop any material with its many arms" (Fuegi 105). While undermining his lovers' egos, he allegedly used their talents and achieved fame and fortune at their expense. John Fuegi is not the first to express such extremely negative views of the author who for decades was considered the dramatic genius of the twentieth century, the "don" of modern European drama. Participating in the deconstruction of a genius has been a favorite sport among American critics for a long time. They have eagerly tried to focus on the dark side of the author. John Fuegi goes so far as to discover similarities between Stalin, Brecht, and Hitler, a comparison which demonstrates how irresponsible some of the so-called research has been.

Some German critics have followed the current discourse on Brecht with surprise and disbelief. The recent reviews of John Fuegi's book published in *Der Spiegel* and *Die Zeit* poke fun at the "Gartenzwergperspektive amerikanischer Germanisten" who have constructed a Brecht that fits their theories. Close examination of the biographical materials and of witnesses' reports, however, reveals a large gap between fact and fiction, between reality and the theoretical pronouncements of critics. Because of their geographical distance from authentic material, speculations and preconceived notions rather than careful research have dominated the critical discourse on Brecht, particularly in the United States. Outrage about Brecht's exploitative strategies as well as charges of intellectual "thievery" (Brown) and fraud have been a considerable obstacle to recognizing Brecht's real achievements, his contribution to modern art and artistic production.

Brecht's literary images of women have been equally misunderstood. Rather than examining these characters in conjunction with his theories, the majority of American critics have viewed them as figures who are representative of the author's convictions. In her article, "A Feminist Reading of Pirate Jenny," Renate Fischetti asserts that Brecht uses stereotypes to endorse "patriarchal ideology with all its consequences," a practice which, according to this critic, is "totally unacceptable from the feminist point of view" (Fischetti 32). Her comments are indicative of the problems American scholars and theater practitioners typically have had with Brecht. Accustomed to psychological realism and naturalistic acting, they have had great difficulties understanding the concept of *Verfremdung* and *Gestus*. They have mistakenly assumed that Brecht's female characters are "realistic" and reflect his own attitudes and beliefs. The failure to grasp the "distancing" function of plot and character design has played a major role in the ongoing debates of Brecht's "sexism" and his "sexist" depiction of female characters.

Not all critics have been unaware of the implications of Brecht's use of stereotypes. Sara Lennox proposes to examine in her article, "Women in Brecht's Works" (1978), Brecht's dramatic characters in light of his own dramaturgy. Although Brecht's early works seem to suggest that he "took himself and his characters seriously as men and portrayed the contradictions and dilemmas of real sensual human relationships," Lennox prefers to use his dramatic theories as a frame of reference (Lennox 85). In view of his theoretical pronouncements it becomes clear that the dramatic characters were not intended "to function as mirrors of existing reality but instead to encourage the transformation of that reality" (Lennox 90). Unlike Lennox, the majority of American critics in the seventies and eighties dismissed Brecht and his notions about gender roles as outdated and politically incorrect.

Ironically, a female scholar in Germany was one of the first to come to the defense of Bertolt Brecht. Although she presents her book, *Ein akzeptabler Mann?*, in a less-than-scholarly fashion, Sabine Kebir contends convincingly that, contrary to widespread belief, Brecht "liberated" women. According to Kebir, Brecht offered his female collaborators the unique opportunity to function as intelligent and creative human beings at a time when such practices were virtually unknown (Kebir 50). She cites Elisabeth Hauptmann, who considered working with Brecht an overall rewarding experience. Personal and not professional disappointments may have been responsible for Hauptmann's conflicting remarks about the author and her relationship with him at different times. Kebir shifts the blame for the sense of betrayal women experienced after their intimate relationships with Brecht ended. She charges that their own conventional expectations and not Brecht's unconventional arrangements with them were the cause of their disenchantment. Kebir argues that male and female "feminists" who condemn Brecht for his shabby treatment of women judge him on the basis of their own petit-bourgeois morality. While her arguments remain controversial, Kebir's positive view of Brecht's personal and professional relationships offers an alternative to the largely negative assessments that have dominated the discourse on this aspect of Brecht in the United States.

Brecht's great contributions to modern theater, especially his concept of collaborative production, have often been ignored or dismissed by critics who have been fascinated and distracted by his sex life or by his alleged sexism. As a theater practitioner who worked with actors, technicians, and support staff, Brecht knew that collaboration was essential to stage production. Not only staging a play, which typically results from drawing on the various talents of each team member, but actually writing and re-writing a play became a collaborative effort under Brecht's direction. He reportedly used his actors' ideas to redesign their roles; he integrated his collaborators' input with the constantly changing versions of the manuscripts. Literary scholars apply theoretical ideas about what constitutes authorship to Brecht's theatrical practice, which often results in discrediting his real achievements. Accustomed to the tradition of the autonomous artist who writes poems or novels, they misjudge the practical aspects of stage production and the issues involved in collaborative efforts. Thus, literary critics have expressed dismay upon discovering that Brecht did not create his plays "on his own," without the assistance of others. John Fuegi certainly disapproves of Brecht's use of collaborators for the purpose of writing his plays. He charges him with having fraudulently presented himself as the single author of his plays, which Brecht never did. A glance at the "Kommentare" in the *Berliner und Frankfurter Ausgabe* establishes that the names of those who contributed to particular plays were acknowledged. As Brecht saw it, "Brecht" was a company label, which stood for a new concept of dramatic art. Elisabeth Hauptmann, Brecht's first collaborator, recognized that selling a piece under the "Brecht" label was more successful and profitable than insisting on signing her own name. In view of the status of women in the society of that time, Hauptmann's decision was sensible. Not Brecht but his heirs ultimately are responsible for fabricating the myth of single authorship, a myth which was in their own financial interest.

By all accounts Brecht never concealed the fact that his collaborators were vital to his creativity. He needed them as sounding boards, as partners, as resource persons, as researchers, as editors. Collaboration with others was the soil out of which artistic projects grew. Brecht used the term "love" to describe human relationships which fostered productivity. In one of the *Stories of Mr. Keuner* Brecht writes: "Liebe ist die Kunst, etwas zu produzieren mit den Fähigkeiten des andern. Dazu braucht man von dem andern Achtung und Zuneigung" (Brecht 407). Contrary to what some American critics would have us believe, Brecht's close associates eagerly cooperated because they believed in Brecht. Arnold Bronnen recalls: "Er [Bronnen] liebte Brecht, und selbst im Zorn, in der Verzweiflung hörte er jenen zu lieben nicht auf." And elsewhere: "Er [Bronnen] versuchte Brecht zu helfen, denn es war diese Magie um Brecht, daß man ihm helfen mußte. Jeder fühlte sogleich, dies war der Bessere, der Kommende, der Endgültige, beug dich vor ihm, wenn er dich braucht" (quoted in Horst 33). Elisabeth Hauptmann expressed similar feelings. She insisted that she did not feel exploited because Brecht "knew" so much more than any of the members of his team. Ultimately all of them benefitted from collaborating with him: "...damit es nicht so aussieht, als ob die Mitarbeiter ausgebeutet wurden. Wir hatten ja unendlich viel davon...er hat einem ja auch geholfen.... Wir wußten alle, daß er viel mehr wußte und verstand als wir — selbstverständlich" (Hanssen 200). Other contributors to the "Brecht" enterprise made similar remarks. Interestingly, most of Brecht's female collaborators continued working with him in spite of rumors about exploitation and abuse. This tends to cause us to dismiss John Fuegi's thesis according to which Brecht enjoyed a parasitic existence at the expense of others.

When discussing the productive relationships within the Brecht team we must consider as well what the term "collaboration" means. By definition, collaboration is "working together with others on artistic or literary endeavors" (Webster's *New English Dictionary*). Typically one person is "federführend," meaning that he or she takes responsibility for the project at hand and coordinates and directs the efforts of others. This is exactly how Brecht viewed his role in a dramatic production. While all members of his team, both men and women, contributed to the best of their abilities, it was Brecht who had the final word.

Consistent with the charges of intellectual thievery and sexual exploitation is the widespread belief that Brecht predominantly relied on women because it was easier for him to dominate them. Peter Georgen claims: "Die Frauen sind bei ihm (untergeordnete) Mitarbeiterinnen, Schülerinnen — das enthält immer noch das Moment der Unterlegenheit" (Georgen 258). This again is a difficult assertion to substantiate. According to Brecht's writings, he selected the members of his team on the basis of their talents, the only requirement being that each person be committed to be "productive." As the composition of his team at any given time shows, Brecht liked to "work" with women and typically maintained lasting working relationships with them long after any personal involvement had ceased. Elisabeth Hauptmann, Margarete Steffin, and Ruth Berlau are good examples. This is also true in the case of his wife Helene Weigel, whom he respected and trusted as a friend long after their intimate relationship had ceased.

Contrary to charges made by many American critics, Brecht's work-related behavior showed that he was quite progressive for his time. Obviously he did not reduce women to the status of sex objects whose personal identity and worth were solely defined in terms of his sexual needs. In fact, sexual attraction played a minor part in the selection of female collaborators. Commitment and "productivity" were of far greater importance to him and determined his assessment of women. This is particularly striking in the case of Margarete Steffin, whose human qualities and professional abilities he did not cease to admire long after he had lost interest in her as a woman. According to Carl Weber, a one-time collaborator himself, the working atmosphere in the Brecht team was such that each member, regardless of gender, felt inspired and stimulated to excel (Weber, ix). By current standards Brecht was an "equal opportunity employer" at a time when such an attitude was uncommon. By contrast, few of his contemporaries were inclined to acknowledge women's talents and creativity. Many men from that period perceived women to be mentally and intellectually inferior, unsuitable to work at challenging tasks. Otto Weininger (1880-1903), an Austrian psychologist and an advocate of widespread beliefs about women's inferiority in the early part of this century, attempted to prove that women were biologically unequal to men. When we consider Brecht's trust in his female collaborators, we must conclude that he did not share his contemporaries' biases.

Charges that Brecht's female figures reflect his own sexist view of women are also unfounded. As noted earlier, Brecht's literary characters were not intended to be images of real people. They function to elicit criticism, to draw attention to different and often conflicting aspects of human behavior. Such characters were intended to raise among the audience questions about motivations for human behavior and the social and political forces that conditioned such behavior. The female figures in Brecht's early plays, for example, are designed to show how bourgeois society constructs women's sense of identity, to what extent their lack of self-esteem and feeling of powerlessness can be traced to early socialization. These female characters were intended not to confirm but to "question" the existing female stereotypes and to examine critically human relations in bourgeois, capitalist societies. In later plays the function of Brecht's female stereotypes changes. They often metaphorically describe issues relating to class struggle. In *Die heilige Johanna der Schlachthöfe* the relationship between the working class and the capitalists is likened to the ongoing struggle between the sexes. The behavior of Joan Dark, for example, causes workers to identify attitudes that lead to failure. Joan's blindness to Mauler's dissembling alerts the workers to their own weaknesses and teaches them to see through capitalist strategies of deception, a process Brecht termed "Verfremdung" (distanciation). While one might object to Brecht's use of negative "female attitudes" for didactic purposes, one should also admit that his model is positive in the sense that he demonstrates how such attitudes are not "natural." In the course of the play it becomes obvious that Joan's feminine propensity to yield to emotions is "discursively constructed" and not a natural trait.

The notion that Brecht's gender stereotypes are realistic and reflect his own prejudices is based on the wrong assumption that he created characters which reflected his own convictions. In his theories Brecht explicitly and repeatedly explained that his dramatic figures represent "types" and not "characters" as portrayed in conventional, illusionist theater. By focusing on certain types of behavior rather than on psychologically convincing individuals, Brecht "distances" audiences and causes them to observe critically and to seek alternatives to existing modes of thinking. By demonstrating "how" Joan weakens and forgets her political tasks when exposed to Mauler's rhetoric, Brecht alerts the oppressed to the forces standing in the way of gaining political influence and power. Similarly, in the earlier play, *Im Dickicht der Städte*, human relationships are shown to be responsible for reducing women to objects of barter, rather than enabling them to become agents of their fate. The characters focus our attention on the alienation and dehumanization experienced in the urban jungle. All of Brecht's characters are designed to elicit criticism and to initiate change.

While much has been said about Brecht's "sexist" view of women in life and literature, few critics have acknowledged that their own concerns and biases have affected their objectivity and their sound judgement. Rather than focusing on the positive aspects of Brecht's collaborative working style, they have imposed their own notions about what constitutes authorship and they view Brecht through the lens of their own biases. The prejudices of critics which have emerged from the contemporary discourse on the oppression of women may have been largely responsible for ignoring that, in his own time, Brecht was progressive and anticipated the move toward equality in the latter part of this century.

WORKS CITED

Brecht, Bertolt. *Gesammelte Werke 12*. Frankfurt am Main: Suhrkamp Verlag, 1967.

Berlau, Ruth. *Brecht's Lai-Tu. Erinnerungen und Notate von Ruth Berlau*. Ed. Hans Bunge. Berlin: Eulenspiegel Verlag, 1985.

Brown, Thomas K. "Brecht's Thievery." *Perspectives and Personalities*. Heidelberg: Carl Winter, 1978. 70-88.

Fischetti, Renate. "A Feminist Reading of Brecht's *Pirate Jenny*." *Communications of the International Brecht Society* 14 (1985): 29-33.

Fuegi, John. *Brecht and Company. Sex, Politics, and the Making of the Modern Drama*. New York: Grove Press, 1994.

Goergen, Peter. *"Produktion" als Grundbegriff der Anthropologie Bertolt Brechts und seine Bedeutung für die Theologie*. Frankfurt am Main: R.G. Fischer Verlag, 1982.

Hanssen, Paula. "Brecht's and Elisabeth Hauptmann's Chinese Poems." *Focus Margarete Steffin. The Brecht Yearbook / Das Brecht-Jahrbuch* 19. Madison: International Brecht Society, 1994. 187-201.

Horst, Astrid. *Prima inter pares. Elisabeth Hauptmann. Die Mitarbeiterin Bertolt Brechts*. Würzburg: Verlag Königshausen & Neumann, 1992.

Kebir, Sabine. *Ein akzeptabler Mann? Streit um Bertolt Brechts Partnerbeziehungen*. Berlin: Buchverlag Der Morgen, 1987.

Lennox, Sara. "Women in Brecht's Works." *New German Critique* 14 (1978): 83-96.

Steffin, Margarete. *Konfutse versteht nichts von Frauen. Nachgelassene Texte*. Ed. Inge Gellert. Berlin: Rowohlt Verlag, 1991.

Weber, Carl. "The Life and Times of Mr. K." Introduction to Völker, Klaus. *Brecht Chronicle*. New York: The Seabury Press, 1975. vii-x.

John Fuegis *Brecht and Company*: Vier kritische Reaktionen und eine Zusammenfassung der Probleme und Fehler

In Reaktion auf die Herausforderung durch Fuegis Brecht-Biographie beginnen vier Brecht-Spezialisten, die wissenschaftlichen Fehler zusammenzutragen, die Zuverlässigkeit des Buches unterminieren. Zu den aufgelisteten Fehlern gehören: faktische Ungenauigkeiten; inkorrekte und fehlerhafte Nachweise; unbelegte Annahmen und Behauptungen; Fehlübersetzungen und Fehlinterpretationen; falsche Zitate; ungenaue und falsche Darstellungen; Wiederholung fehlerhafter oder unbelegter Argumente, die anfänglich als Behauptung auftauchen und später als Fakt zitiert werden; sowie methodologische Probleme beim Zusammenstellen und Darlegen des Beweismaterials. Die Autoren schließen daraus, daß die Art und Weise, in der Fuegi sein Material benutzt, und nicht seine Intention, die gesamte Argumentationsführung zweifelhaft erscheinen läßt, so daß es unmöglich wird, seinen Auf- und Entdeckungen den geringsten Glauben zu schenken.

Brecht and Company de John Fuegi: Quatre Réponses Critiques et un Résumé de Problèmes et d' Erreurs.

Les quatre auteurs souhaitent commencer a répertorier les déficiences scientifiques qui, à leurs yeux, empêchent de prendre au sérieux le livre de Fuegi comme travail documentaire fiable. Les déficiences dont ils dressent la liste comprennent, mais ne se limitent pas à: des erreurs concernant les faits, des citations et des références inexactes ou fausses, des théories et des affirmations non argumentées et non documentées, de mauvaises traductions et des erreurs de lecture évidentes, des erreurs de citation, des distorsions, des représentations imprécises ou fausses, une récurrence d'arguments mal fondés ou injustifiés qui commencent en affirmations et finissent par devenir des faits, et des problèmes méthodologiques dans la réunion et la présentation de preuves appuyant les arguments de l'auteur. C'est la façon dont Fuegi utilise ses documents, et non quoi que ce soit d'inacceptable dans ses intentions, qui rend ce long livre si peu fiable qu'il est impossible d'accorder crédit à n'importe laquelle de ses révélations.

El Brecht y compañía de John Fuegi: Cuatro respuestas críticas y un resumen de problemas y errores

En respuesta al desafio que presenta la nueva biografía sobre Brecht escrita por Fuegi, cuatro especialistas brechtianos empezaron a catalogar deficiencias de erudición que en su opinión socavan la fiabilidad del libro. Las faltas que ellos enumeran incluyen: errores de hechos; citas y referencias descuidadas o erróneas; declaraciones y afirmaciones que carecen de base firme y de documentación; malas traducciones y malas lecturas explícitas; citaciones incorrectas; distorsiones; representaciones inexactas o equivocadas; repetición de argumentos insustanciales o de base errónea que empiezan siendo declaraciones y más tarde se citan como hechos; y problemas metodológicos en reunir y presentar las pruebas. Los autores concluyen que la manera en que Fuegi emplea sus datos, no sus intenciones, quitan valor a todo su argumento, hasta que llega a ser imposible confiar en las revelaciones de cualquier punto.

A Brechtbuster Goes Bust: Scholarly Mistakes, Misquotes, and Malpractices in John Fuegi's *Brecht and Company*

John Willett, James K. Lyon, Siegfried Mews,
Hans Christian Nørregaard

Introduction

James K. Lyon

When I first read John Fuegi's book *Brecht and Company*, it disturbed me. My reaction had nothing to do with the book's essential arguments, most of which were well known. In fact, Fuegi acknowledges that John Willett and I had gone in print before he did with information about Elisabeth Hauptmann's having written parts of works attributed to Brecht. And in 1973, when many feminists were celebrating Brecht as one of their champions, I delivered a paper on his outrageous treatment of his female collaborators which anticipated some of what Fuegi argues in his book. That paper angered some of my listeners who did not know the unpleasant facts which have since emerged. Attempts to demonize Brecht, as some reviewers claim Fuegi's book does, also never upset me. I was familiar with other works that tried to do this and could look beyond (or see through) personally motivated attacks. Besides, I knew enough about Brecht's personal life to have concluded that despite his writings, which I greatly admired, as a human being he was far from admirable.

Why, then, did this new book trouble me? I am a long-time admirer of Fuegi's work; I have participated with him in a number of conferences of the International Brecht Society and other scholarly meetings and know him well; I contributed to the *Brecht Yearbook* while he was a co-editor; I corresponded with him frequently, and we have shared material on Brecht; and I had discussed with him some of his findings long before they appeared in this book. So it was with considerable sympathy, not to say interest, that I began reading. What alarmed me by the time I finished was

Brecht Then and Now / Brecht damals und heute
Eds. Marc Silberman et al. *The Brecht Yearbook / Das Brecht-Jahrbuch*
Volume 20 (Madison: The International Brecht Society, 1995)

the degree of carelessness, inaccuracy, wild speculation, distortion of evidence, and the striking number of factual errors, mistranslations, misrepresentations, careless or irresponsible use of sources, and claims not supported by any sources at all. In over 30 years in the profession I have not read an allegedly scholarly book on any subject I knew well that fell so short of minimum standards of serious scholarship. The evidence it presents is, for the most part, so flawed or unsustainable and the presentation of that evidence violates basic standards of accuracy and responsibility so egregiously that the book cannot stand up to careful scrutiny. After examining it carefully, the four reviewers whose names appear together here believe that *Brecht and Company* fails to provide reliable evidence or firm proof for most of the major points it attempts to make about the role Brecht's women collaborators played in contributing to his works. This struck me as especially unfortunate in the light of Fuegi's unique access to so many unpublished sources, among them Margarete Steffin's posthumous papers, previously unknown publishers' contracts with Brecht, unpublished Brecht letters, etc. Many of us looked forward to his findings on these sources. If, however, the way he drew on these documents reflects the care he displayed, for example, in citing Brecht's FBI file, which is not widely accessible (see my account below of his citations from FBI documents), then the distortions, speculations, omissions, misreadings, and errors in the former case raise serious questions about his reliability in presenting information from other less accessible sources.

Soon after finishing the book, Siegfried Mews shared with me his concerns. Mews, who began publishing on Brecht more than 20 years ago, counts as one of the major Brecht scholars in this country. His reservations about Fuegi's book paralleled my own. I had already begun compiling a systematic list of what I saw as serious errors, flaws, and problems when I learned that John Willett had also begun work on a list of what he called "scholarly mistakes, misquotes, and malpractices" in the Fuegi book. Willett, who over the years had access to vast amounts of archival material on and about Brecht as he edited numerous editions of Brecht in English, was as appalled as we were at the carelessness of Fuegi's book. He states that "it is the way he uses his material, not anything unacceptable about his intentions...that makes his huge book so untrustworthy that one cannot have confidence in its revelations at any point."

After some discussion the three of us agreed to compile a list of the inadequacies in this work for those readers who might mistakenly view its argumentation and conclusions as having arisen from well-grounded, careful scholarship. What follows is a compendium of what we see as major problems or weaknesses. It is neither exhaustive nor comprehensive. One German reviewer, for example, noted that Fuegi renders over fifty names or book titles incorrectly. We made no attempt to catalog all incorrect names, titles, typos, grammatical or other relatively superficial errors, though we did mention a few in the context of other issues we raised. Nor did we address in detail matters such as the incomplete, and therefore unreliable index, which encumbers all serious attempts to locate references. Even first-rate scholarly books sometimes suffer from such defects. And our goal was not to enter into a debate or to attack the author's motives. The German press, and some reviewers in the USA, have done that with varying degrees of vehemence.

Shortly before our deadline, we learned that Erdmut Wizisla at the Bertolt Brecht Archives in Berlin was also compiling his own list of inaccuracies based on archival sources at his disposal. It was too late to integrate his findings with ours, but we assume there will be other reports from informed scholars that expand on what we have discovered. Our sole purpose was to begin to catalog scholarly deficiencies which, in our view, prevent *Brecht and Company* in its present form from being taken seriously as a reliable source work. These deficiencies include, but are not limited to, factual errors; careless or erroneous citations and references; unsupported or undocumented claims and assertions; mistranslations and misreadings; misquotations, distortions, inaccurate representations, or misrepresentations; repetitiveness of ill-founded or unsubstantiated arguments that begin as assertions and end up as fact; and methodological problems in assembling and presenting evidence in support of the author's arguments. When we have finished, we intend to present our findings to Professor Fuegi in order that he might use or respond to them as he deems appropriate. We understand he will be invited to do so in the pages of the *Brecht Yearbook*.

The contributions (and their authors) appear in the following sequence:

1. "Brecht, Hitler, Stalin": Siegfried Mews
2. "John Fuegi's *Brecht and Company*: A Summary of Problems and Errors"
       a. Prefatory Notes: John Willett, H.C. Nørregaard
       b. Text: John Willett, James K. Lyon, and H. C. Nørregaard
3. "Fuegi's (Mis-)Use of Brecht's FBI File" — James K. Lyon
4. "Final Comments" — John Willett

While these contributions resisted integration into a single format, each addresses similar problems and weaknesses. Siegfried Mews focuses on one leitmotif in the book, the frequent and extensive passages in which Fuegi equates Brecht with Hitler and Stalin. From this single topic he develops an array of methodological, factual, and source problems that continue throughout.

The next section, as John Willett's prefatory note indicates, is based on his initial responses, edited and expanded by me. It follows the book's chronology and pagination. A paragraph not followed by the author's initials represents Willett's response. Where my comments or information could amplify his original findings, I integrated them into his entries. I have identified such joint contributions by our initials in parentheses at the end of the relevant entry (JW,JKL). Comments and observations originating solely with me have been designated by my initials in parentheses (JKL).

For a reasonably quick summary of the long and dense section on "Scholarly Mistakes, Misquotes, and Malpractices," readers might first wish to read Willett's "Final Comments." Like so many concluding remarks, they could serve equally well as an introduction to and summary of what follows.

[NOTE: After James Lyon completed his work, Hans Christian Nørregaard in Copenhagen sent us the English version of his article, "The Strange Tale of the Butcher's Wife in Svendborg, and Other Fairy Tales from Far-away Denmark," published in *Weekend Avisen* (25 November 1994), and over thirty pages of his own notes and corrections. I have edited these and integrated them into the text, marked (HCN) at the end of each paragraph. Limitations of time and space unfortunately prevented the publication of the full article, and some of the material kindly sent by Rudy Hassing, also from Copenhagen. Special thanks also to Siegfried Mews for extra editorial assistance. *Maarten van Dijk*]

* * * * * * * *

1. Brecht, Stalin, and Hitler

Siegfried Mews

One of the questionable aspects of John Fuegi's biography is his use of two political figures who decisively shaped the course of history in our century. Needless to say, no biographer writing about Brecht and the perilous times during which he lived can do without references to Hitler and Stalin, but Fuegi adds a new dimension to the debate in that he seeks to cast Brecht in a role that invites the comparison of the playwright with the two dictators. In the Preface Fuegi establishes his basic pattern of interpretation that rests on the dichotomous pattern of victims, such as Brecht's women collaborators on the one hand, and oppressors/exploiters such as Hitler and Stalin (to whom Fuegi later adds Brecht) on the other (xiii). Although the troika Brecht/Stalin/Hitler may appear as a most unlikely construct, it is useful to review some of Fuegi's arguments and test their validity on the basis of the factual evidence he has to offer.

Hitler makes his first appearance in the narrative when Fuegi describes a photograph of a Munich mass rally by an unknown photographer at the beginning of World War I. The photo shows Hitler's "eyes glowing with enthusiasm" at the prospect of war (15; photo #6). That enthusiasm, Fuegi correctly observes, was shared by young Brecht, whose 1915 poem "Der Kaiser" (*Werke* 13: 76) he cites as evidence. Innocuous as this juxtaposition may be, it serves as the starting point for the common bond between Hitler and Brecht that Fuegi wants the reader to perceive. In the following chapters, Hitler's presence is pervasive — although at the cost of what appear to be gratuitous references (e.g., Hitler's serving in Caspar Neher's regiment — 18). Yet Fuegi's suggestion that Brecht and Hitler's paths might actually have converged would, if supported by incontrovertible proof, cause a minor sensation.

Fuegi writes that Brecht became a "frequent visitor" in Hanns Johst's house on the Starnberger See. Johst's house, he tells us, citing a personal communication from Hitler biographer Joachim Fest, "was also becoming a haven for Adolf Hitler" (39; 630, n. 25). The uninitiated reader may conclude that, even if no personal encounters between Hitler and Brecht took place, Johst must have facilitated communications between them. Brecht visited Johst, Fuegi implies, because Brecht was an unprincipled opportunist who not only remained in personal contact with a man whose work he loathed and whose play *Der Einsame* had initially provoked the

Gegenentwurf of *Baal*, but who also wanted to retain the support of two opposite groups of people who might be important for his career, that is, those who disagreed with Johst on artistic grounds as well as those who agreed with Johst, the "extremely dangerous and influential supporter of nationalist causes" (39).

What appears to be a plausible argument is, in fact, poorly substantiated and rests largely on conjecture. We are never told when Hitler began frequenting Johst's house. The contacts between Brecht and Johst date from 1918 to 1920, a period when "Hitler was not much more than a local Munich agitator" (Fest 132). According to Werner Mittenzwei, Johst was then considered a leftist rather than a right-winger (1: 65-66). Furthermore, Fuegi does not provide any indication as to the frequency of Brecht's visits at Johst's house; the published correspondence, which consists of merely three letters (*Letters/Briefe* #43-45), is inconclusive in this respect. Brecht's friend Hedda Kuhn (whose first name Brecht abbreviated to "He" — hardly an "English" form; 56) reported in a 1969 interview that Brecht dissuaded her from accompanying him when he visited Johst on the grounds that the latter was "'ein Völkischer, da wird es heiß hergehen, das ist nichts für dich'" (qtd. in Frisch/Obermeier 119). Even if Mittenzwei's biography should be read with caution because of its official or semi-official status, one should not ignore his implied warning against the pitfalls of "Rückerinnerung" (65) that may have resulted in Kuhn's projecting later developments onto the period of 1918-20. At any rate, Kuhn's statement also indicates that Brecht was willing to engage Johst in debate about his political ideas — a combative attitude that does not correspond to the "sycophantic tone" that Fuegi detects in Brecht's letters to Johst (39).

Fuegi maintains that Johst continued to function as a connecting link between Brecht and Hitler. In 1932, when Johst had actually begun to support the Nazis actively (Pfanner 303), he is declared to be "a playwright friend of Hitler and Brecht" (285). But Hitler's Munich putsch of 9 November 1923 serves Fuegi as a vehicle to suggest that Brecht sought Hitler's proximity — a move that suggests ideological kinship. There are several inaccuracies in Fuegi's account of the putsch. Fest, Fuegi's chief source concerning Hitler, clearly states that the shooting between the loyalists and the putschists started at the Odeonsplatz (Fest 198) rather than at the Rathaus, as Fuegi has it (127). In any event, the exchange of gunfire caused Hitler to flee unheroically and to hide in the house of his aide Ernst Hanfstaengl in Uffing am Staffelsee (Fest 199), *not* in Utting am Ammersee (Fuegi 127). Both locations are in the vicinity of Munich; hence confusing them may seem insignificant — in fact, this confusion did escape the immediate notice of unsuspecting critics (Winkler; Mews 25) — and is not comparable to other geographical blunders such as calling "the Black Forest area ...Bavaria's small mountains" (41). Yet it is Utting that is used by Fuegi to charge Brecht with a form of political incorrectness. After reporting Brecht's purchase of what Mittenzwei calls a "kleinen Landsitz" (1: 310) near Utting, Fuegi states: "It seems odd for a self-declared Marxist to be buying a country estate practically next door to Hitler while blood ran in the streets of Germany" (280). Odd indeed. The oddity consists of Fuegi's attempt to indict Brecht for being oblivious to — if not callously ignoring — the struggle between the right and the left during the last phase of the Weimar Republic while seeking the vicinity of Hitler. At best, this attempt may be described as a fanciful fabrication that completely disregards chronology and geography.

Fuegi's idiosyncratic use of sources is evident in other instances as well. In citing Arnolt Bronnen, Fuegi gives the impression that a specific passage in Bronnen's *Tage mit Bertolt Brecht*, in which Bronnen indicates Brecht's ambivalence towards the phenomenon of Hitler in 1923, expresses Brecht's unqualified approval of Hitler's histrionic talent (Bronnen 140-44; Fuegi 117). Actually, it is Bronnen who admits to "die Anfänge der Verstrickung" (141) that eventually led him to become an adherent of the Nazis. Klaus Völker, in commenting on Bronnen's passage, remarks that Brecht, despite his interest in Hitler's "bombastic theatrical effects," gradually "became more keenly aware of the danger foreshadowed" by Hitler and his followers (65). For Fuegi it is precisely the "power that either Hitler or Brecht exerted on audiences in Munich in the early 1920s" (128) that is the common cause of their affinity — regardless of the ends to which this power was ultimately exerted. For good measure, Fuegi adds Stalin and speaks of the "wholly irrational power" (128) that the troika held over their respective followers. It does not seem to make the slightest difference to Fuegi that in the case of Hitler and Stalin "tens of millions" were affected, whereas the "mesmeric performer" Brecht was only able to "seduce" a limited number of "both men and women at will" (128).

Hitler was apparently unaware that, according to Fuegi, he had a kindred soul in Brecht. This spiritual kinship was not, if we follow Fuegi, affected by Brecht's turning to Marxism. On the contrary, he continued to practice his unprincipled opportunism and "moved between the political fronts, maintaining friendly contacts on both the left and the radical right" (243). If Hitler was unappreciative of modernist artists, Joseph Goebbels, who had become a friend of Brecht's former collaborator Bronnen, was more attuned to accommodating those artists even after Hitler had assumed the office of Reichskanzler. Hence, Fuegi argues, Brecht's return to Germany after he had left Berlin upon the burning of the Reichstag on 28 February 1933 was "not inconceivable" (290). He supports his contention by referring to texts by Fritz Sternberg as well as by Klaus and Erika Mann. True, Sternberg writes: "Er [Brecht] hätte nicht zu gehen brauchen," but he adds: "Aber Brecht zögerte keinen Augenblick: er emigrierte" (37-38) — surely not a sign of the political fence-straddling of which Fuegi accuses Brecht (290). Conversely, Klaus and Erika Mann make it quite clear that Brecht's return from exile was virtually inconceivable:

> [Brecht] hat man im Jahre 1933 von Berlin aus freundliche Angebote gemacht, ob er nicht vielleicht doch lieber zurückkehren wolle: man würde versuchen, manches zu vergessen, was er in früheren Jahren an Anstößigem geäußert habe. In der Tat, da hätte es gar viel zu vergessen gegeben. Denn es existiert kaum eine Zeile in dem Werk von Bert Brecht, die nicht anstößig für einen guten Nazi wäre (78).

In a similar vein, Völker states unambiguously: "Brecht did not leave Germany of his own free will but because of his political convictions." Referring to the well-known poem from the exile period "Über die Bezeichnung Emigranten/Concerning the Label Emigrant" (*Werke* 12: 81; *Poems* 301) — a poem that cannot be dismissed as a self-serving stylization — Völker continues: "He was not an emigrant, he was a refugee" (173). Apart from his political convictions and his anti-Nazi writings, Brecht was surely aware of the threat that the Nazis' racial theories and policies posed to his Jewish wife Helene Weigel. All of these factors militated against Brecht's return and undermine Fuegi's hypothesis that such a return would have been unproblematic or even possible.

There is an additional twist to Fuegi's argument, however. He agrees with post-Brechtian Heiner Müller's observation: "Ohne Hitler wäre aus Brecht nicht Brecht geworden, sondern ein Erfolgsautor" (Müller 187; Fuegi 279) — a remark suggesting that Brecht's susceptibility to the corrupting influence of commercial success after *The Threepenny Opera* was halted by the political intervention of Hitler and that only the harsh experience of exile enabled Brecht to find his true voice. Whatever the merits of Müller's statement, Fuegi's endorsing it appears to invalidate his own (unfounded) assumption that Brecht could have safely returned to Germany presumably to become a conformist, opportunistic, but commercially successful writer. To be sure, in a psychologizing vein

Müller speaks of the "ungeheure Affinität" between Brecht and Hitler, an affinity rooted in "die gleiche Art von Bosheit" (227). Fuegi, who quotes Müller (395), neglects to mention the latter's view of other aspects of the Hitler-Brecht affinity, that is, the importance for Brecht of "Hitler als Gegner...[als] Idealfeind" (227). It goes without saying that with Hitler as "Idealfeind" Brecht's prospects in Nazi Germany would have been dim indeed.

Fuegi's selective use of sources and his tendency to advance mutually exclusive readings with the aim of discrediting Brecht is in evidence elsewhere. Brecht, the "Erfolgsautor" who violates his Marxist beliefs, does not find his approval; Brecht, the politically committed playwright who shuns commercial success, does not fare much better either. For example, in briefly commenting on *Round Heads and Pointed Heads*, Fuegi does not primarily blame Brecht for writing a political play that exhibits — as several critics think — a limited, Marxist-inspired grasp of the racial question. Rather, he faults Brecht for writing a political play which had little chance to be staged in the politically charged atmosphere in the fall of 1932, instead of the commercially viable, "fairly innocuous Shakespeare adaptation" (281) that his publisher had expected. Similarly, there is an undercurrent of disapproval and the suggestion of improper behavior when Fuegi reports that, in order to secure a Danish residence permit for himself and his family, Brecht declared his abstinence from political activities in general and anti-Nazi activities in particular (301). If we follow Fuegi's curious logic, Brecht should have jeopardized his chances for obtaining a safe haven by confessing to political activities that he, according to Fuegi, did not engage in at all or engaged in to an insufficient degree.

Suffice it to cite one more example of Fuegi's willful interpretations. In a radical departure from generally accepted Brecht criticism he posits that the persona's plea for "Nachsicht" in Brecht's famous Svendborg poem "An die Nachgeborenen/To Those Born Later" (*Werke* 12: 85-87; *Poems* 318-20) — Fuegi refers to it as the "'Dark times' poem" — merely serves to transfer Brecht's "reason for coldness and ruthlessness [in treating his female collaborators] away from self to the convenient 'other,' the 'dark times'" (356). The reduction of the historical context that the "dark times" of Nazi domination signify to a trifling inconvenience and the implication that Hitler's ascendancy apparently did not affect the exiled Brecht is an astounding revelation. Far from depicting Brecht as a potential victim of both Hitler and Stalin, Fuegi implicates him as one of the originators of the "dark times" that are indicative of the "universe according to Brecht, Hitler, and Stalin" (357). Such assertions pertain to the realm of sensationalist speculation rather than to that of serious scholarship. Instead of offering new insights supported by documentary evidence, Fuegi himself engages in and surpasses the "kind of scholarly carelessness" he finds to be "ubiquitous in the Brecht literature in virtually all countries" (670-71, n. 1).

Works Cited

Brecht, Bertolt. *Briefe*. 2 vols. Ed. Günter Glaeser. Frankfurt am Main: Suhrkamp, 1981. Trans. as *Letters 1913-1956*. Trans. Ralph Manheim, ed. John Willett. New York: Routledge, 1990.

_____. *Werke*. Große kommentierte Berliner und Frankfurter Ausgabe. 30 vols. Ed. Werner Hecht et al. Frankfurt am Main: Suhrkamp/Berlin: Aufbau, 1988-.

_____. *Poems 1913-1956*. Ed. John Willett and Ralph Manheim with the Co-operation of Erich Fried. New York: Methuen, 1976.

Bronnen, Arnolt. *Tage mit Bertolt Brecht*. Munich: Desch, 1960.

Fest, Joachim C. *Hitler: Eine Biographie*. Berlin: Propyläen, 1973. Trans. as *Hitler*. Trans. Richard and Clara Winston. New York: Harcourt, 1974.

Frisch, Werner, and K. W. Obermeier. *Brecht in Augsburg: Erinnerungen, Texte, Fotos*. Frankfurt am Main: Suhrkamp, 1987.

Mann, Klaus, and Erika Mann. *Escape to Life: Deutsche Kultur im Exil*. 1939. Munich: Spangenberg, 1991.

Mews, Siegfried. "Nicht gerade zimperlich." Review of *Brecht and Company*. *Dreigroschenheft* 2/1994: 24-27.

Mittenzwei, Werner. *Das Leben des Bertolt Brecht oder Der Umgang mit Welträtseln*. 2 vols. Frankfurt am Main: Suhrkamp, 1987.

Müller, Heiner. *Krieg ohne Schlacht: Leben in zwei Diktaturen*. Cologne: Kiepenheuer, 1992.

Pfanner, Helmut F. *Hanns Johst: Vom Expressionismus zum Nationalsozialismus*. The Hague: Mouton, 1970.

Sternberg, Fritz. *Der Dichter und die Ratio: Erinnerungen an Bertolt Brecht*. Göttingen: Sachse & Pohl, 1963.

Völker, Klaus. *Bertolt Brecht: Eine Biographie*. Munich: Hanser, 1976. Trans. as *Brecht: A Biography*. Trans. John Nowell. New York: Seabury/Continuum, 1978.

Winkler, Willi. "Vom armen B.B." Review of *The Life and Lies of Bertolt Brecht*, by John Fuegi. *Die Zeit* (overseas ed.) 19 Aug. 1994: 14.

* * * * * * * *

2. John Fuegi's *Brecht and Company*: A Summary of Problems and Errors

John Willett, James K. Lyon, and Hans Christian Nørregaard

a. Prefatory Notes

John Willett

In reviewing *The Life and Lies of Bertolt Brecht*, as *Brecht and Company* was titled in the UK edition, I found myself having to look up a number of citations from my own writings that puzzled me. So many of them turned out to be misquoted, or tacitly shortened (so as to alter the sense) or misunderstood, that I decided to make a list of all references which seemed scholarly in presentation but unconvincing when checked. In the process I have also drawn attention to needless repetitions of the more recurrent arguments or assertions, and queried various of John Fuegi's unsupported statements. I have not tried to enter into debate or to attack (or even to understand) the author's motives, but rather to show some of the weak joints in the book's structure. I leave comment for later.

Hans Christian Nørregaard

I read Fuegi's Brecht biography in late September in a hotel room in Madrid with no other books by or about Brecht within reach. I had only a pencil in my hand and made countless dots in the margin. I have now checked these dots, referring not only to Brecht but to a lot of different themes touched on by Fuegi in his book: German history, visual art, even religion and much more. I dedicated most space to Brecht in Denmark, a connection I have studied in particular and published about in both Danish and German. I have only had time to read the entire Fuegi production once, and these are my Spanish dots and their interpretation. Unforgettable but nevertheless uncommented on in my list are the following words of Fuegi on 68:

> It was cold in late February in Berlin. The address of his admirer Frank Warschauer, 13 Eislebenstrasse (ice life street), helped reinforce the poetically useful idea of Berlin as a cold place.

When I hear the word "Eisleben," I think of a rather well-known town to the west of Halle. Brecht did too, I imagine. Fuegi thinks of the Ice Age; perhaps he does not know of this town's existence, although it is quite important to the career of Martin Luther.

b. Text

Preface

xiv. F. claims that Brecht's work is cited to support policies that led to the building of the Berlin Wall. Which work, what policies, where cited? No documentation.

F. mentions that he managed to talk to Helene Weigel, Elizabeth Hauptmann, and Marieluise Fleißer while they were still alive in 1965. Why did he never contact Ruth Berlau, who did not die until 1974? F. never says he did not speak to her, but throughout the book avoids commenting on this interesting point. (HCN)

xv. F. says that Ottwalt's name is only "cautiously mentioned." This was not the case by 1971, when Reclam published the Gersch/Hecht paperback on *Kuhle Wampe*.

xv-xvi. F. claims that dangerous implications prevented him from mentioning the "strongly suspected" collaboration of Hauptmann and Berlau on *Don Juan* in his thesis, 1967. Their names had actually been printed as "Mitarbeiter" (collaborators) in *Stücke XII*, eight years earlier.

xviii. According to F., Brecht's work often was "primarily the work of others." F. claims that to argue this way at the time was a "deadly labyrinth," which he chose to avoid. Deadly? In the early 70s? Really?

xix. F. refers to records of "top-level secret meetings." Are these identified anywhere? No source given.

Chapter 1

1. F. refers to a photo of Brecht as a one-year-old child with a "whip big enough for a real horse." It is lying on the floor and looks more like a cane to me. The child shows no awareness of it. But the description prepares readers for the references to whips in chapters two and three, and the implication that Brecht's sadistic tendencies,

which the author emphasizes repeatedly throughout the book, were already evident at this tender age.

4. F. makes note of "the sexual demands of the master of the house," i.e., Brecht's father. The note reference given here does nothing to support this claim, but refers instead to various meanings attached to the word "mother."

F. says that "Eugen claimed later" that Marie hid an eraser between her breasts or thighs. It was *not* the young Eugen who made this claim, but the fictitious character Ziffel in the *Flüchtlingsgespräche* (c. 1941) where Brecht has him recall this episode involving an unnamed maidservant. Though F. repeatedly reminds the reader of Brecht's tendency to use hyperbole, and though he warns that Brecht's division between fact and fiction is often arbitrary (71), here and elsewhere F. freely cites a fictional account as literal biography. (JW,JKL)

F. further states that in Brecht's family the boys were left in Marie's "care." The quotation marks and the Freudian reference suggests that this was for sexual initiation. But it remains a prurient guess.

7. F. speaks of the "violent tone" of the Moritat "The Heiress of the Rhine." This is true in the earlier "Ballade of June 30th," where it is parodied to refer to Hitler's violence against Röhm and other SA leaders. It is *not* true of the traditional version of the same song as sung by the two girls in Brecht's *Schweyk* (1943-44).

8. F. mentions Brecht's play with lead soldiers. The note about his always winning at these games draws a parallel to Emperor Wilhelm II, bolstering the "friend's" description of the child Brecht as "lordly and imperious."

Chapter 2

10. F. offers no documentation in support of his unequivocal claim that Brecht's mother was diagnosed as having breast cancer. Available evidence suggests it was not breast cancer, but perhaps uterine cancer. (JKL)

13. F. makes the unsupported claim that early poems Brecht wrote about the murder of young boys by older men are typical of a perversity that pervades his personal poems for the rest of his life. All his personal poems? And did he write poems on this perverse topic ever again? And what is meant by "perversity?" (JKL)

19. F. reports how Brecht met an eager young lady at an ice rink. Again, this story comes from a fictive work, the *Flüchtlingsgespräche,* and not from explicit recollection. F. gives it the status of a strict biographical statement.

F. speaks of Brecht's "omnivorous sexuality." This and "the homosexuality that had so preoccupied him earlier" are treated by F. as givens. The argument is insistent but unconfirmed and undocumented.

F. claims that Brecht borrowed creative work from his friends and assimilated it into his own. While this is not improbable, F. makes the claim without giving specific evidence or examples. (JKL)

25. F. writes how in 1916, Brecht would often be seen walking along "slapping a whip against a handsome pair of riding boots" (see 1 and 35). Friede Held, a schoolfriend of Bie Banholzer, reported this of Brecht just after the Armistice and recalls that he quoted Nietzsche's saying. But how could one consider Nietzsche "his favorite," as F. does here? He is *once* mentioned in Brecht's early *Diaries 1920-1922.*

Chapter 3

31. F. attributes Wedekind's "homoerotic" songs to his 53 *Lautenlieder,* but otherwise fails to specify them.

F. says Wedekind was imprisoned "for insulting the Wittelsbachs." From June 1899 to March 1900 he was imprisoned for his poem "Im heiligen Land," mocking the visit of Kaiser Wilhelm to Palestine. Kaiser Wilhelm belonged to the Prussian house of Hohenzollern, not to the Bavarian Wittelsbachs. (HCN)

33. F. mistranslates the phrase "die den Steiß schwenkt" to read "whose ass twitches." (JKL)

35. F. seriously misreads and mistranslates an unidentified poem ("Orges Antwort"). The poem does *not* say that Orge defecates in his own hand. It reads:

Jedoch seine letzte Realie
Gibt ein Mann nur ungern auf
Ja, auf seine letzte Fäkalie
Legt er seine Hand darauf.

(JKL)

35. Münsterer is given as the source for the description of Brecht's attic room where F. claims that, in keeping with Nietzsche's admonishment, "a whip hung on the bedframe." This is *not* in Münsterer's account, nor does Münsterer say that the "ten commandments" were *by* Nietzsche, merely "redolent of Lichtenberg's or Zarathustra's spirit." As for the "Evelyn Roe" poem which follows, it does *not* say that her body "will be eaten by fish large and small," rather that "She gave herself to the dark waves, and they/ Washed her white and fair."

Klaus Völker is quoted as saying, in what F. takes to be a veiled reference to homosexuality, that Brecht liked "dandified men of the Oscar Wilde and Rimbaud type." This was specifically with reference to Brecht's epigram on Münsterer, a nice man who was not one of his closest friends, and certainly not a generalization which he applied to his close friends.

Using a poem as basis for biographical fact, F. describes how Brecht "sometimes pissed in the baskets of clean laundry upstairs." This is a misreading and mistranslation of the poem cited, "Auslassungen eines Märtyrers." In the second line, "Wo die Wäsche zum Trocknen aufgehängt ist und pißt," it is the laundry that is dripping, *not* the poet relieving himself. And again F. takes a poem as a literal biographical statement. (JW,JKL)

For F.'s criticism of the editing of Brecht's *Letters*, expressed in a note to this page, see 629.

37. F. reports how Brecht "would stamp his foot" and yell to emphasize that he was right. Habitually? The source cited, one Richard Ringenberg, reports this happening only *once*. Nor does Ringenberg suggest that "Orge" was homosexual, or objected to Brecht's spending time with women, as F. suggests.

Notes 20 and 21 do not support F.'s references. The former is indeed a letter to Neher, but it does *not* speak of Rosemarie Aman. The second source cites two letters to Münsterer, *not* to Neher as F. states, on different topics altogether. The letter to Neher of 18 December 1917 is correctly quoted but wrongly numbered (26/27 in lieu of 15).

What F. calls an "explicitly loving" poem to Neher ("About a Painter," c.1917) is nothing of the kind. This is a severe distortion. Neher is mockingly shown as drunk; he paints, curses, and is "eaten up by the sun."

38. F. speaks of a 1918 collection of poems as a "group composition." For actual contents of "Songs for the Guitar" see my notes to *Poems 1913-1956*, 488.

39. F. calls Baal "a masculine vamp." What does the German say? No source is given. The "Urbild Baals," actually written by Hauptmann in winter 1925-26, describes this "Josef K." rather as the "illegitimate son of a washerwoman," not a "masculine vamp."

40. F.'s account of events in the plot of *Baal* is grotesquely erroneous. Baal does *not* declare his love for the character Johann. It is *not* Johann(es), but the much more important character Ekart (unmentioned in F.'s résumé) who is the "best friend" murdered by Baal in the bar. By that time Johannes has reappeared, totally gone to seed, as a looker-on. *Nor* does the play end with Baal feigning death and eating a vulture — a poetic image from no.10 of the 13 verses of the introductory "Hymn of Baal the Great." On the contrary, he dies alone, "still listening to the rain," in a forest hut.

41. F. speaks of "the travels of Baal with Johann." Another error. There were *none*. Again, it was Ekart, not Johann.

F. reports that Brecht spent time with Bie at Lake Starnberg, "near" Ludwig II's castle Neuschwanstein. Lake Starnberg is over 50 km distant (as the crow flies) from Neuschwanstein castle. In another geographical error on the same page, Brecht and a friend hike through the Black Forest, where they greet the dawn on the top of a Bavarian mountain. The Black Forest is *not* in Bavaria. (JKL)

43. To reinforce his claim of a homosexual relationship between Brecht and Neher, F. cites an ambiguous statement in Brecht's *Diaries* that says it was "better with a friend than with women." Brecht and Neher had been swimming at Possenhofen. F. omits this point, and cites Brecht's entry (16 July 1920) as if he were referring to sex rather than a swim. But Max Högel's reminiscences of Neher, which F. recommends as the "best account" in note 34, nowhere suggest that Neher was homosexual. Neher's mother, according to the passage referred to, "viewed her Rudolf's growing friendship with the young Brecht with considerable distaste," *not* because of what F. terms their "closeness," but partly because of its encouragement of unprofitable art, and partly because of the appeal of Brecht's subversive songs.

The ensuing description of Brecht's room with its "stains of sperm and blood" being cleaned up by three maids is not documented, but see 35. Again F. repeats that a whip was hanging from the bedframe, while on 44 we have Brecht wearing sporty jodhpurs, with riding boots and a horsewhip.

Chapter 4

48. F. reports that Bie was sent to the "nearby" village of Kimratshofen. Another geographical inaccuracy. Kimratshofen is over 80 km distant from Augsburg. (JKL)

49. F. claims that Brecht's 1919 "Song of the Soldier of the Red Army" was an accurate reflection of his true feelings at the time. Again F. takes a poem as an valid, unmediated biographical statement. (JKL)

50. According to F., Brecht's play *Drums in the Night* suggests that Spartacists were murderers. This can only refer (rather misleadingly) to Babusch's concluding phrases in Act 2: "The masses are stirring. Spartacus is rising. The slaughter continues." As for the "several songs" woven into the play, these consist of "The Legend of the Dead Soldier" and the round "A Dog Went to the Kitchen." *No* evidence is given for F.'s assertion that this play "relied heavily" on the poetry his friends were continually writing.

52. In spring 1919, Brecht is said to have given Neher a private recital of his best pornographic songs, many of which were explicitly homosexual. *No* source is given, and Max Högel, the authority cited, says nothing of this.

53. Based on a letter by Marta Feuchtwanger, F. has Hitler trying to interest her husband in "a portfolio of sketches" at a café in the Hofgarten. In this way F. stages a competition between Brecht and Hitler for Lion Feuchtwanger's recognition of their respective arts, as if the world would have been saved from the politician and dictator Hitler had he been given a chance for a career as a stage designer at the Munich Kammerspiele. In Marta Feuchtwanger's memoirs, *Nur eine Frau* there is nothing about this incidental meeting, although the book covers this period. But among the material F. presented to various TV companies, promoting a semi-fictional Brecht project, there is a letter from her to F., dated 11 April 1981, which mentions this meeting; it says nothing about a portfolio of sketches. There is every reason to doubt that Hitler ever wanted to be a stage designer. His paintings and drawings mostly copy already existing art: architectural photographs, for instance, or even postcards. He even once copied a poster by Käthe Kollwitz. All extant material by Hitler has been published in a book on him as an artist (*Adolf Hitler als Maler und Zeichner*, Zug, Switzerland 1983). There are only a few rough sketches for the stage: one is for

Julius Caesar, and the rest are for operas. This material does not in any way support F.'s theories which seem to me invented out of nothing. (HCN)

Chapter 5

55. Once again, as on 44, F. portrays Brecht wearing his jodhpurs and riding boots, slapping his whip against his boot, and quoting Nietzsche: "Wenn du zum Weibe gehst, vergiß die Peitsche nicht" (when you go to a woman, don't forget to take a whip). A few lines later, on 56, F. asserts that whip-bearing, ruthless, black-booted males, often stimulated by murder, rape, and other forms of sadomasochism, parade through Brecht's poems, short stories, letters, and diaries. Where does this all take place? F. gives *no* sources for these overstated allegations.

56. "Hedda Kuhn (addressed by Brecht in English as 'He')." In German "He" would be a rather ordinary abbreviation of "Hedda," having nothing to do with confusing the sexes. (HCN)

57. Brecht is not the only person to have been known as B.B. He shares this distinction, for instance, with Bernard Berenson, Brigitte Bardot, and Boris Becker. But to call him "Bébé," a term by which he was neither known nor called during his lifetime, is special to F., who is then able to refer to Brecht as "this perpetual 'bébé'" and situate "Cas and his Bébé" titillatingly in the privacy of covered swings. Further, the term "Bébé" makes no sense to a German reader, for it does not mean "baby" as F. implies. It is F.'s highly questionable technique to reiterate such unfounded assertions so often that they lodge in the innocent reader's mind.

58. F. again refers to Hitler's attempt at becoming a theatrical designer having failed (see 53). (HCN)

59. In F.'s version, the episode in which Brecht offers Münsterer his friendship and the familiar form of address represents a serious misreading (see Münsterer 82, or 64 of the English edition, Libris, 1992). F. mistranslates the term "zerzausen" as what Brecht does vis-a-vis Münsterer. It is not "to make an awful mess of [the younger man's] clothes," as F. has it, but to demolish him verbally. Hence the right meaning is "Brecht had just been berating me and had reproached me with my middle-class respectability." Gradually Brecht softens his tone and finally offers him the "du" form of address. It is at this point that Münsterer reports how *he* clasped

Brecht's hand in his for a long time. The reason for Münsterer's happiness is not what F. sees as the ambiguity of this relationship, but the knowledge "that now I truly belonged to that happy band of outcasts," as Münsterer says. (JW,JKL)

F. then gives Brecht's first priority as "emptying his gonads in various paid and unpaid ways." This disgusting formulation seems to mean, if anything, that Brecht got paid for sexual services. It is *not* supported by any evidence provided by F. (or known to myself).

60. Again Hitler's failed attempt to become a designer is mentioned (see 53, 58). This is a special technique with F.: gradually, through repetition, changing a theory into a fact. (HCN)

64. F. refers to a perpetual cycle of sex for text and vice versa. He give no evidence or sources for this claim.

65. F. calls Berlin "the old imperial capital" and "the center of German cultural life." The German empire was not founded until 1871, therefore Berlin was the *young* imperial capital. (HCN)

Chapter 6

66. The misleading chapter heading is of questionable relevance to what follows. It may suggest to the casual reader that Brecht wanted the Jews disposed of, but if one looks up the cited passage in Brecht's *Diaries* (26 February 1921), one will see that the thought is more complicated.

67. F. cites me as saying that the Anna of the Brecht poem may be a real person called Ann Gewölke. This is a misreading. My note did *not* suggest that "Gewölke" was a real name, rather that Anna G. was probably a real individual.

68. In his reading of the poem about the whore Evelyn Roe, F. claims that male sinners are well received in heaven, whereas Evelyn Roe is rejected, meaning that God maintains a double standard. But F. fails to point out that the Devil, too, rejects her in the next stanza in almost the same words. As for male sinners, the same poem says nothing about their being well-received in heaven. In fact, the contrary is usually the case in poems of this period. The pirates (in the ballad of that name) "hurtle to perdition"; Villon "got no glimpse of Heaven's sweet rewards"; in "Model of a Nasty Fellow" Brecht prays for "such swine's" admission; but the "heaven for disenchanted men" is hardly attractive; and the idea of Brecht

himself being well received (see "Mounted on the Fairground's Magic Horses") is patently ironic. None of this is mentioned by F. (JW,JKL)

71. F. repeats his mistranslation and again has Brecht pissing in the laundry (see 36).

72. F. repeats 56 in referring to Brecht as a poor, oft-abandoned "Bébé."

F. reports on Brecht's descriptions of a public coupling of his dog, Ina, and his own couplings, which he conducted "like horses." In the *Diaries*, from which F. derives all this, Brecht writes a short, vivid, and amusing description of the two dogs getting stuck (28 August 1920) as he watched from an Augsburg window, terming it "a little tragicomedy." Then 72 pages later he reports having made love with Marianne "like horses" (26 April 1921). F. gives one reference for the two unconnected entries, so that they appear consecutive.

74. Again F. refers to Brecht with a whip, this time as a "colonial master" (see 55 and earlier references).

75. F.'s claim that Brecht reflects on the world as body and the Jews as the entity that constipates and poisons the body appears to be his own invention. In the passage from Brecht's *Diaries* (26 February 1921) which F. cites, the images of poison and constipation have no relationship to Jews. To read it as an anti-Semitic statement by Brecht is a glaring misreading. (JKL)

77. Based on reports he has heard about photos of the Brechts' servant, Mari Hold, "in drag," F. claims that the 18-year-old Brecht had her put on his clothes while he took photos of her. But Marie Hold Ohm told me (F.'s cited Danish informant) in 1971, that Brecht had been playing billiards with his friends, who were "like a bunch of schoolboys." As Brecht had a camera within reach he suddenly got the idea that she should wear his shirt, trousers, vest, and cap, whereupon he would take a snapshot. "Well, I didn't really feel like it but they talked me into it and then he took the photograph." Later Brecht had given her the picture. I joked, "Maybe we should reconstruct it?" "Oh, no," Mrs. Ohm shuddered, "that was back then when one looked different from today." Apparently the "special things" F. thinks "the young master" had "in mind" were far from being on her mind. This is totally removed from F's context, and his implied sultry photo series (see 138 for a

further refinement of this approach and the comment on the caption to photo 21, between 268 and 269). (HCN)

F. reports that a total of eight people attended an "orgy of sorts" at Otto Müllereisert's place. According to Brecht's *Diaries*, which is F.'s source, nine were there. (JKL)

Chapter 7

79. In the chapter heading and line 3, F. refers to Brecht as "Führer" without translating the term. "Führer" is the normal German term for "leader," though F. must be well aware that most non-German readers associate it with Adolf Hitler. Högel, whom F. is quoting, calls Brecht "the leader of this community." F.'s version in the heading, repeated on alternate pages of this chapter, each time *omits* the last three words "of this community."

81. Again F. cites a poem (in Brecht's *Diaries*) about Pfanzelt and Müllereisert as a valid biographical statement, without allowing for the least exaggeration or poetic fantasy. (JKL)

82. "Bébé." See 56, 72.

83. "Dog whip." See 74, etc.

84. F. uncritically accepts Brecht's reasons for his father's not wanting to raise his illegitimate son Frank. A letter from Brecht's father, which F. does not mention, gives entirely different reasons. (JKL)

"Galgei," the future Galy Gay, is described by F. as bisexual. This is contrary to the rather more extensive notes on this early version in the Methuen edition of *A Man's a Man*, where it appears that Galgei had a wife and a love affair with the landlady Ma Col, but *no* marked interest in men. F. points out that the name would be pronounced "gal/guy," but then doubts if Brecht would yet have known enough "colloquial English" to realize this. The Methuen notes say nothing about "a crew of 'niggers,'" and F. gives no source for this statement.

85. The "abandoned 'Führer'" (see 79).

89. F. says Brecht is "violent and still sexually ambiguous" (see 18).

92. F. cites Brecht's *Diaries* for 7 January 1922. His reference is to the German edition, but in fact the passage quoted (next 12 lines) is my translation from the Methuen English edition. I have not checked other *Diaries* quotes to see if the Methuen translation has been used but not acknowledged.

93. F.'s undocumented assertions have Brecht "moving briskly from bed to bed" and landing in a hospital, where the homosexual Bronnen, who "was a veteran of all-male wards and knew what could be done there," visits him. Sources?

97-99. More repetitions of phrases about the "helpless Bébé"; the famous poem "Of Poor BB" (pronounced "bébé", according to F.); the then twenty-seven-year-old "Bébé" is "now seen as an adult," and "all are expected to care for" him. These phrases are wreathed prettily around the poor translation, to culminate in the statement that "Bébé, like Nero, will survive to observe [the world's] passing" (see 56, 72, 82).

Chapter 8

100. The chapter headings are not attributed, but careless readers might think that the slogan "Down with the Goddamned Jewish Sow, Murder Walther Rathenau" came from Brecht. It did *not*.

101. F. has Hitler again being turned down as set designer for Feuchtwanger (see 53, 58, 60). (HCN)
F. states that Brecht showed no understanding of the Zionism of his Jewish friends. F. might as well have asked Brecht to convert to catholicism. Judging everything in the light of Auschwitz is unhistoric and vulgar. Apart from that, a lot of Jewish Germans were anti-Zionists. How can F. ask of Brecht, who was not Jewish, that he be pro-Zionist? Then he would not have been Brecht. One of F.'s projects is to demonstrate that Brecht was an anti-Semite. He should have compared him with Thomas Mann, and many others. (HCN)

103-4. F. cites a passage of how Brecht allowed himself to be taken into Caspar Neher's arms following the performance of Bronnen's *Vatermord*. F.'s truncated citation *omits* the words "und bestätigt"; the real sense, therefore, is that "he allowed himself to be hugged and reassured" following this controversial performance. Not an uncommon event after the opening night of a play. But this would spoil F.'s next lines, with their picture of the two men being

Willett / Lyon / Mews / Nørregaard

unable "to spend more time in one another's arms" — on the evident supposition that they would have liked to conclude the night in some such way.

For Neher's drawing of Brecht and Bronnen together, see my *Caspar Neher* (Methuen, 1986), where it is reproduced on 116. It does not correspond to F.'s description ("hostility," "savagely drawn," "a sense of Neher's horror"), and what he sees as a whip (yet again) appears to me to be a scroll bearing the title of Bronnen's play.

105. As far as I know, Blandine Ebinger is still alive. Nothing in her book, *Blandine* (Zürich 1985) indicates that she ever shared the "casting couch" with Brecht. How does F. know? (HCN)

107. F. refers to Bronnen's own lowercase style as the model for Brecht's letter. It was not uncommon in the twenties, and can be traced back at least to the typography of Stefan George's poems two decades earlier.

Chapter 9

112. Again F. refers to Bronnen's own lowercase style as though it were uniquely Bronnen's. It was not (see 107).

116. F. mentions "anishole" as a ribald term for Bronnen in a letter. A careless reader might read the "anis" bit as "anus," but in Manheim's translation it is "anise," or absinthe.

117. F. refers to Brecht working on "a very wooden adaptation of Selma Lagerlöf's play, *Gösta Berling*." This is not a play but the most famous novel by the Swedish Nobel prize winner. (HCN)

118. F. refers to Neher's "treasonous" marriage with no attribution to a source. The "treason," however, had nothing to do with a sexual relationship. The source of this citation, Högel, whom F. quotes elsewhere, says Brecht saw a "Verrat" or betrayal in Neher's working with the director Jürgen Fehling, but that "the lost son had been forgiven" by the time of *In the Jungle of Cities*'s première in May 1923 — six months before the marriage.

F. chooses to translate "Befruchtung" as "impregnation" rather than as "fertilization" or "cross-pollination." Bronnen used the term to describe the intellectual stimulation his work with Brecht produced, a testimonial repeated by others who collaborated with Brecht.

119. F. says the director of Helene Weigel's Vienna school "brought a stream of successful professional women...for her pupils to emulate." The school's director, Genia Schwarzwald (whose name F. does not mention), brought remarkable scholars and artists of both sexes to her school — Oskar Kokoschka among others. When F. advocates women's rights he turns to stereotypes in the same way as he does in connection with people of Jewish origin. (HCN)

120-21. Friedrich Gnass was *not* "an obscure actor," as F. states. He was in Piscator's company in 1929 and in Pabst's *Kameradschaft* and many other films, before joining the Berliner Ensemble in 1949. Contrast the "famous" Arthur Rundt. Famous how?

121. F. states that Granach, like Helene Weigel and Bronnen, was an "assimilated Jew who had come to Berlin from the former Austro-Hungarian empire." He forces people together who have very little in common. Weigel and Bronnen belonged to the emancipated Jewish bourgeoisie in Vienna, with few — if any — connections to Jewish tradition. Granach was born in East Galicia as Jessajah Ben Aron. He was in command of both Yiddish and Hebrew. Weigel and Bronnen were born emancipated; Granach had to emancipate himself. That is quite a difference. Making them three of a kind is, in fact, a Nazi view. (HCN)

Chapter 10

127. F. incorrectly states that after Hitler's failed coup in 1923, he left Munich and went to the "nearby village of Utting" on the Ammersee. In fact he went to another village called Uffing, which is on the Staffelsee, about 35 km south of Utting. Regarding proximity to Munich: Utting was approximately 25 kilometers distant, Uffing more than 50 km away. (JKL)

132-33. F. claims that both personally and professionally, Brecht began, publicly at least, "to distance himself from the homoerotic." It is not stated how or why this sudden change occurs, and no evidence is given.

133. F. has Leopold Jessner eating his dish of Bavarian swine's head with "great relish." Is not this the quite ordinary dish of "Sülze" — known in Denmark as "sylte" — rather old-fashioned but very delicate? Oh, this exotic, barbaric Germany! (HCN)

135. F. claims that Brecht now adopted Bronnen's "orthography." It was not only Bronnen's (see 107, 113), and the term "orthography" normally refers to spelling.

F. erroneously refers to a man with the name of Brown who appeared in *Galgei* "together with beasts of prey." Here he misreads my editorial note on an early scheme for the Galgei project, where scene 5 is headed "Bar. Brown. Beasts of prey. Schnaps." Brown here is the dominant color, *not* a person, let alone a reference to Father Brown in the Chesterton stories, as F. appears to suggest. The "he" throughout is quite plainly Galgei, and it is he, not the imagined Brown, who "murders Matthi" (*not* Matti as in *Puntila*). The quote "God left for Chicago" is F.'s reading of a jotting for scene 8: "Today God is in Chicago."

F.'s "character called bak" has already been explained in the same editorial note as being a shorthand version of Baker, the Polly Baker of the final play.

This early material was included in the leather-bound script of winter 1925-26 (see 143).

136. Again F. refers to "the explicit excitement of the homoerotic" which he sees in early versions of *Galgei* (see 84). Brecht called the play "a sex murder story" in a *Diaries* note of 1920, but this phrase was hardly serious, and by 1924 the project was far from explicit.

Chapter 11

138. Story of Marie Hold's drag repeated (see 77), but now there is no camera; instead, we have ritual and age of consent, and she has been "pepped up" with a nickname, "Mari 'Peppi' Hold." Peppi was not *her* name but that of her sister, Josefine. (HCN)

139. F. claims Brecht slighted his collaborator's role in the writing of *Edward II* by crediting Feuchtwanger's name in "small letters that might easily be overlooked." The inscription is (I reckon) in 10-point small capitals, and has a page to itself facing the reverse title. F. does *not* mention the reciprocal inscription on 110 of Feuchtwanger's *Drei angelsächsische Stücke* (1927) where his *Kalkutta, 4. Mai* is prefaced "I wrote this play with Bertolt Brecht" in 10-point italics. This was the play about Warren Hastings that Brecht helped Feuchtwanger to revise in 1925. Premiered in November 1927, it was to have included a performance of "Surabaya-Johnny."

140-41. For some reason F. does not explain how Hauptmann came to work with Brecht. As I understand it (and I think I knew Hauptmann better than F. did), she was a part-time translator and publishers' reader for Kiepenheuer when Brecht moved to Berlin in 1924. Kiepenheuer had an agreement with Brecht to publish three of his books — *In the Jungle of Cities*, the incomplete *Galgei* project, and a first book of poems, the *Devotions*, which had been due since 1922. When he heard that Hauptmann had met Brecht, he gave her the semi-secretarial, semi-editorial job of getting these out of him. This lasted until Brecht got Ullstein to take over the Kiepenheuer agreement in mid-1925. It was Kiepenheuer thereafter who published the *Versuche* booklets, starting in 1930.

143. F. quotes me as saying that from late 1924 on "it is often difficult to know who wrote exactly what." Checking this, I see he has *omitted* the parenthetical " — in this context — " (between "who" and "wrote"). The context makes it clear that I was referring specifically to the English-based works, and not the work in general.

The bound typescript of *A Man's a Man*, with Brecht's inscription to Hauptmann saying that "piecing the manuscript together... was the only part I did on my own," is interpreted by F. to mean that Brecht's "own work had mainly been editorial." On the contrary, the point was that they worked together throughout, until he thought of preparing this gift for her. If that dedication "characteristically...was not published" it could be because the gift to which it applied was not published either. For F. seems not to have realized that this was far from being a final text, even for the productions of 1926; moreover it included all kinds of extra riches — two Hong Kong scenes, to start with, and the whole of the *Elephant Calf* one-acter (as a scene in the play), as well as notes on the early *Galgei* schemes (see 135). The *one* point which Hauptmann told me was a significant contribution by her (and had marked as such on the script) was Polly Baker's introduction of the word "elephant" in scene 8.

F. also attributes to me the report that the English-language "Alabama" and "Benares" songs had been written by Hauptmann and marked by her as such on the scripts "at the time." But the reference he gives specifies only that this notation was "marked...on the Brecht-Archive photocopies." These copies were of course made some thirty years later, as was the notation. I don't think I ever saw the originals.

144. F. cites me correctly on the possibility that Hauptmann *may* have borne the major responsibility for the Berlin short stories;

and I named four of those stories whose typescripts show *no* corrections or marks by Brecht. But he is confused in suggesting that I think "it likely that at least seven of the eleven short stories that comprise...'Brecht's Berlin stories' are Hauptmann's." What I wrote (again in the article cited on 143) was that seven stories known to be Hauptmann's and published under *her* name around that time seemed thematically and stylistically indistinguishable from eleven of Brecht's.

145. F. claims that the "final form" of *A Man's a Man* (and many other plays) was "unthinkable" without Hauptmann's work (see 143). Once again, the final form was *not* unthinkable without her, since she did not have a hand in it. That play underwent further transformations in 1928, 1931, 1938, and 1954 before reaching its "final form."

F. quotes Hauptmann as saying she "either wrote or wrote down" most of the poems before 1933. The German is "geschrieben oder abgeschrieben," which in my view means "either typed or retyped" — i.e., from Brecht's dictation or his rough copies. She is saying how hard she had to work, and she resents his reported remark that they only used to work before lunch; "I know I often had to stay up very late making copies — again and again it all had to be recopied." In this phrase, at least, she is *not* claiming the authorship of what she was writing for him.

For the first time, F. claims here for Hauptmann that *The Threepenny Opera* was "overwhelmingly her work" and that Brecht's participation was "marginal at best." By 196 he claims more precisely that "*at least* 80% of the fabric of the work...was hers." But nowhere in his book does F. offer adequate evidence from primary or secondary sources to document his claim. His citation of Shull and Lucchesi (196 and note 15) as saying that the original typescript "relied heavily on Gay's original piece" fails to acknowledge how Shull and Lucchesi go on to document the enormous transformations the play undergoes after this original version. It is also significant that Hauptmann herself would later claim publicly that her contribution to *He Who Says Yes* was as high as 80%, but make no such public claim for the more important *Threepenny Opera*. (JKL)

146. F. refers to Kipling's "Mary, Pity Women" in Hauptmann's translation. This was the basis of "Surabaya Johnny," on whose typescript there are marks by both Brecht and Hauptmann. In 1927 he worked on it with the singer Kate Kühl; later it was included in *Happy End*.

Using Lyon as his source, F. cites Hauptmann as stating that she "intentionally omitted her name [from collaborative writings] because Brecht's alone carried more weight." Lyon's book carries this as a paraphrase. F. turns it into a direct quote from Hauptmann. (JKL)

F. claims that soon after Brecht's arrival in Berlin in autumn 1924, when he moved there permanently, the plays, poems and short stories on which Hauptmann worked with him finally "did get finished." Yet only ten lines above, F. had stated that "for the first four years in Berlin, no really new Brecht plays would get completed." This contradictory statement is true of *The Breadshop, Joe Fleischhacker, Karl der Kühne* and *Fatzer.* Hauptmann was involved with him on all these unfinished works. Even *Saint Joan of the Stockyards,* on which she also collaborated, never reached performance (except on the radio). In other words, she did *not* solve his problem of getting the job finished.

Here and on 141 F. speaks of Hauptmann's excellent English. While it was probably adequate for translations from English into German at this point, to call her written English "beautiful" (141) or "superb" as F. does is not an accurate assessment. Letters she wrote in English to Ferdinand Reyher in 1928-29 reveal strong German syntax, limited vocabulary, and a complete lack of command of English idioms. The "Mahagonny" songs she wrote in English for Brecht at this time (and she did write those) reveal her relative command of the language, e.g., in the Benares song, as originally written: "Where is the telephone? Is here no telephone?" etc. This might better be termed "quaint." It is *not* English as spoken by native speakers. (JW,JKL)

149. Presumably by the "novelist" Egon Kisch F. means "der rasende Reporter," Egon Erwin Kisch, who wrote only one novel, *Der Mädchenhirt* (1914); his fame was based on journalistic reports from all over the world, collected in a series of books. (HCN)

The "Fat Ham" story. The reference to 89 of Völker's Brecht biography appears to be wrong, and F.'s notion of Brecht in the mid-1920s making a feeble American pun about donkeys and bottoms via the German word for "ass" is, by any count, slightly crazy.

F. claims that documents from the archives of Kiepenheuer publishers reveal that Brecht's story about wanting to leave them because of censorship attempts against his poetry is a lie, but he gives no citation or sources to corroborate his claim. What documents? Can he cite them? (JKL)

Chapter 12

153. F. speaks of the change in the title of *Galgei* to *Mann ist Mann* (hereafter referred to as *A Man's a Man*). In the bound script (see 143) the central character is referred to variously as Galgei or Galy Gay. But the most recent version of the play can hardly be said to "center" on the business dealings of Widow Begbick, who originated as Ma Col in the first scheme. I cited Private Baker's flippant remark about "the impressions one can pick up in gents' urinals" acknowledgedly from that script, but it cannot stand being made into the general statement that *Galgei* "had turned around homoerotic encounters in urinals" before Hauptmann began working with Brecht. For the supposed homoeroticism that had marked the earlier version, see also 84, 136.

The title emerging from Brecht's summer 1924 rewrite was *Galy Gay or Man = Man*. The gist was interchangeability, not cannibalism.

F.'s phrase that *A Man's a Man* is seen "from the point of view of a woman" is attributed to a quote from me. It plainly referred, however, *not* to this play, but to Hauptmann's cooperation "if only as a copyist" on another work altogether — the "Reader for Those Who Live in Cities" poems, which "for the first time" (I said) clearly voiced "a woman's point of view."

154. For F.'s claim that the leather-bound typescript and its covering letter prove that Brecht only assembled *A Man's a Man* and that Hauptmann really wrote it, see yet again 143. He claims these were suppressed when Brecht's letters were published, but they were *not* part of Brecht's letters. Nor does F. ever explain what is meant by more than a thousand "similarly revealing items" allegedly omitted from the collection of published letters. Contrary to F.'s claim, the names of Hauptmann and other collaborators, while omitted from the first publication, were in fact listed in the 1938 edition.

F. claims that *A Man's a Man* would not be performed until early 1928. Yet ten pages further on he describes the Darmstadt production of 1926.

F. refers to an "ecstatic though anonymous reviewer" of a radio broadcast of *A Man's a Man* in 1927. The reference given is to my foreword to the play, which makes it perfectly clear that the review was by Kurt Weill.

Regarding the claim that *A Man's a Man* is "overwhelmingly" the work of Elisabeth Hauptmann, see 143 to 145. These points appear to constitute F.'s only "evidence" so far for this sweeping supposition.

For the reference to Joseph K. see 39, concerning *Baal*.

156. "Bronnen's *Battle of Catalonia*" (*Katalaunische Schlacht*, 1924) takes its name from the Battle of the *Catalaunian* Fields, where Attila and his Huns were defeated near Troyes in 431 AD. The events of the play take place during and after the First World War. Weill wrote incidental music for Hilpert's Staatstheater production of 1928.

157. F. describes Bronnen dropping in on a Jessner rehearsal and seeing "provocatively and opportunistically, a huge nationalist flag of old Imperial Germany." Bronnen in fact describes the opposite: "Bei der Generalprobe hatte ich zum ersten Mal die riesige schwartz-rot-goldene Fahne (the flag of the Weimar Republic) gesehen." The whole of bourgeois Germany flew the "schwartz-weiß-rot (the Imperial flag)," says Bronnen, and the workers flew the red flag. He therefore had to ask what sort of flag Jessner's was. Bronnen's point, which F. misses, is that he did not know the democratic flag at all. (HCN)

158. F. calls Carola Neher "one of Brecht's current mistresses." According to gossip — but to what other authority?

161-62. I am credited with saying that the "manuscript" (more precisely, typescript) of the short story "North Sea Crabs" (or, in our edition, "Shrimps"), "is mainly Hauptmann's work." What I actually *said* was that it bears few marks of revision by Brecht.

165-68. This section quite rightly contradicts F.'s statement on 154 that there was no performance of *A Man's a Man* till 1928. All the same, his description here of the 1926 version, as staged in Darmstadt, is odd. Thus he has the soldiers shoot up the pagoda of scene 2 while speaking "Hauptmann's brilliant rendering of Kipling." The dialogue is in fact highly comic, but not at all like Kipling and is probably Brecht's own. The pagoda, which is some kind of Indian temple looked after by a Bonze, or Buddhist priest called Wang, is "a place run for profit by a mysterious Mr. Wang." At the end of the play the newly assimilated soldier Galy Gay, in his one-man assault on the Tibetan defenses, achieves a gigantic "public orgasm of brutality" on stage before announcing his "desire to sink my teeth into the enemy's throat...to carry out the conqueror's mission." These words were *not* in the 1926 text or production, but come from a closing verse speech added in 1938.

One scene, according to F., is headed "The Demonstrability of

Any Conceivable Assertion." It is *not* a scene in any printed text of this play, but the one-act play, *The Elephant Calf,* which became an optional appendage in the 1926 version.

F. notices that some editions of Kipling bear a swastika symbol (whose Indian significance dates from long before Hitler) and reminds us of this in concluding that it was necessary for Hauptmann only to render Kipling into accurate German in order to have the new text (become) "drenched in casual murder and outright racism." How much casual murder exists in this text? The description "Comedy" on the title page of the 1926 edition is *not* mentioned.

Chapter 13

170. F. claims that in 1926-27 one sees an explicit homophobic undercurrent emerge in Brecht's poetry. The cited reference is to the three notes on a 1927 poetry competition run by the *Literarische Welt,* for which Brecht was a judge that year. Here he complains about the younger (bourgeois) poets and their chosen models — Rilke, Stefan George and Werfel (an old dislike of his). Brecht's ascription elsewhere of one of his own "priapic" poems to Thomas Mann is primarily a flippant insult to that revered figure, and, despite F.'s claim, nothing particularly homophobic emerges from it.

171. F. talks about "the now largely forgotten artist Rudolf Schlichter, whose rather wooden portraits..." Schlichter is still considered one of the most important portraitists of "die neue Sachlichkeit." His portrait of Brecht was included in one of the earliest "degenerate art" exhibitions in Nazi Germany, 8-30 April 1933, in Karlsruhe. (HCN)

172. "Hauptmann as 'Ham.'" *No* fresh evidence since 149, where the identification is ascribed to a guess by Klaus Völker. Now it is treated as fact.

173. F. maintains that Brecht continued his "ties with Bronnen and the circle of nationalist friends with whom his former lover was now involved." "Former lover" remains unproven, see 93, 103. By contrast, Bronnen in his own memoir *Tage mit Bertolt Brecht* (1960, subtitled "The history of an unfulfilled friendship"), stops the story in autumn 1923, saying "A bond had ended...."

"A poem written in his fifties." This erroneous dating refers to the "Ballad of Knowledge," written in Brecht's late thirties and put into his last play *Turandot.*

174. F.'s claim that *The Measures Taken* and *Mother* are both based on Hauptmann's "dramaturgy and beliefs" is an assertion that remains to be shown.

F. speaks of the "Kipling-fathered *Galgei.*" Galgei's first appearance in Brecht's work was unrelated to Kipling (see 84, 135).

175. F. reads the poem "Cover your tracks" (which he calls "Wipe Out Your tracks!") as an admonition for communist agents to go underground. It belongs to the collection "Reader for Those Who Live in the Cities" and is addressed to the inhabitants of the modern metropolis. This poem is about self-preservation in the big city and has nothing to do with undercover agents and the other ideas F. puts forth.

"To Chronos" in the same group of poems. F. has clearly overlooked the final parenthesis ("That is how we speak to our fathers"), which undercuts his meaning. See also 176, where F. links this poem with *Mein Kampf,* and 177, where its attitude to "enemies" is compared with those of Hitler, Eichmann, and Beria. The word "enemies" is *not* mentioned in Brecht's poem.

His reference to "the murderous Garga" makes the reader ask if F. knows the play in which Garga appears (*In the Jungle of Cities*). Garga a murderer?

When talking of *Die Hauspostille* F. does not mention the great poem "Of the Infanticide Marie Farrar," perhaps because it is difficult to make it fit into his conception of Brecht as a woman hater. (HCN)

179. The "Alabama" and "Benares" songs as written by Hauptmann. See 143 for an elaboration of this claim. F. is repeating, (a) what he said there about the songs, (b) his reference to me, and (c) his error in calling the photocopies on which Hauptmann thirty years later pencilled her comments the "archival copies." They are not.

180. F. refers to the poet Hannes Küpper as a "bicycle racer." Küpper's poem "He, He! The Iron Man!" was about an Australian cyclist called Reggie MacNamara. I doubt if Küpper was known as a cyclist himself. Brecht knew him as a dramaturg at the Essen Stadttheater, and editor of its program/journal, *Der Scheinwerfer,* in which Hauptmann's Noh-play versions appeared.

185. F. claims (without supporting evidence) that Lenya had

"apparently worked part-time as a teenage prostitute" while studying ballet. Seven lines later she is a "homely gentile woman with a past." Two pages further on, "circus performer and teenage prostitute" has become her real-life history.

186. F. reports that Weill turned to the "Mahagonny" poems from the *Hauspostille* as a base for a loosely constructed "Song-spiel." This was actually in response to the demands of the 1927 Festival for "short operas" and comprised the *Mahagonny* Songs 1, 2 and 3, the two English-language songs, and the Finale ("Aber dieses ganze Mahagonny"). Two of the six, *not* "at least half," as F. claims, were Hauptmann's work; *none* was based on Villon and Kipling, as F. further asserts. In addition, says F. (188), Madame Begbick was taken over from *A Man's a Man* to give "bilingual foreplay instructions" to men entering the bordello, an element cited from my editorial notes. But these are notes *not* to the "Songspiel," but to scene 14 of the full opera (where the "foreplay instructions" of the script were suppressed on the insistence of Weill's publishers). Begbick does *not* figure in the "Songspiel."

187. F. says that tunes for a number of the individual poems had "already been provided by Krauss-Elka and Bruinier." Brecht has suddenly disappeared as a composer of his own songs, although F. has told us about his singing from his earliest youth. Then who provided the music before Brecht met Bruinier? (HCN)

188. "...a barely clothed Lenya." This is a misquotation of Ronald Sanders, who is cited for this description. He reports the women as dressed "for an evening out...rakishly in straw hats." (JKL)

Chapter 14

190. F. reports that Hauptmann was aware of Carola Neher's having an intense affair with Brecht in mid-1927. Did Hauptmann ever say this? Where is the evidence? By 193 their affair has "heated up." Again, what is the source?

191. F. reports how Brecht still maintains "his connections with the increasingly right-wing Bronnen and his nationalist friends," though Bronnen reports their friendship ended in 1923. This repeats the suggestion on 173, where much the same words were used.

192. According to F., Brecht blames Upton Sinclair for his failure to translate one of Sinclair's ballads, though he has started on

it seven or eight times. In the letter F. cites, what Brecht says is that he has given up because the ballad is not revolutionary enough for him. (JKL)

193. F. asserts that Hauptmann was fascinated by Gay's two operas, *The Beggar's Opera* and *Polly*. Brecht never alludes to *Polly*, nor do we know whether Hauptmann was aware of it. F. speaks of "Gay's bold heroine," who is *not* the figure of the same name portrayed in *The Beggar's Opera*.

F. describes how Hauptmann begins preparing a new "version" of *The Beggar's Opera* "designed to fit Berlin." This phrasing begs the question of Hauptmann's responsibility, which most knowledgeable commentators consider began as that of a translator, working with a view to an adaptation by Brecht rather than by herself. "Version" of course is a slippery word, and opinions differ about the degree of interest Brecht showed in her project before speaking of it to Aufricht, its eventual producer. As there is *no* original script, there is uncertainty from the start with regard to the changes which Hauptmann may have made in translating Gay's English; as also to the preliminary work which Brecht is said to have done on the first two scenes, the wording of the original script seen and accepted by Aufricht in March or April 1928, and the degree of revision it underwent before being duplicated by the agents Bloch-Erben to make the earliest text we now have. Certainly F. provides *no* evidence to show that Hauptmann had done more before its acceptance than to make a straight translation of Gay's original, and from the duplication onwards the revisions, additions, cuts, and story changes by the various collaborators came thick and fast, until finally *only* Peachum's "Morning Hymn" remained of Gay's songs and almost nothing of his dialogue. Much of this was collective work, and F. has discovered *no* means of distinguishing the individual contributions, let alone quantifying the different degrees of final responsibility as he pretends to do. See 145.

194. F. has Brecht working with Piscator on "ambitious plays." *Rasputin, The Romanovs, The War* and *The People That Stood up against Them* sound like four separate titles, but in reality this was one play, *Rasputin*, with a long subtitle. F. does not mention Lania's *Konjunktur*, which was more interesting to Brecht; it included Weill's "Shell Song" and provoked intervention by the Communist Party in defense of Soviet oil interests.

196. F. now states as fact ("the fact remains") that Hauptmann was the almost exclusive author of *The Threepenny Opera* text sold

to Aufricht. Even if Völker agrees with this view in his reported remark to F. on this topic, this is still an opinion, *not* a fact. Nor is it made more factual by repeating "despite the fact" (that it was Hauptmann's work) three lines later.

F. speaks of Weill's projects with playwrights like Ivan Goll and Georg Kaiser. These works, *Royal Palace, Der Protagonist,* and *Der Zar läßt sich fotographieren,* are all operas, as against *The Threepenny Opera,* which is a "play with music."

197. "The expanded version of Mahagonny." See David Drew's *Kurt Weill. A Handbook* (171), which says that "the opera was the first to be conceived and also the first to be started" — despite the fact that the much shorter and simpler "Songspiel" was performed in July 1927, some two and a half years before the main work. Yet again the use of Hauptmann's two English-language songs is mentioned (see 143, 179, and 186). But in the opera they constitute less than a tenth of the total. Throughout F.'s book, *all* references to both the main and the secondary versions are indexed indiscriminately as "Mahagonny Songspiel" and counted as Hauptmann's work. *No* further evidence for this attribution is given.

198. F. mentions how Brecht spends two weeks looking in on *Warren Hastings,* a play in which he had a "financial interest" with Lion Feuchtwanger. See 139 for the echo of their cooperation on *Edward II* — a factor that F. ignores. And Brecht had more than a financial interest in the play. In 1927 he helped Feuchtwanger rework it. It had since been renamed *Kalkutta, den 4. Mai* and was being staged at the Berlin Staatstheater by Engel, with sets by Neher. It opened there on 12 June. Both these men were also crucially involved in *The Threepenny Opera.*

F. speaks of "Hauptmann's free renderings of Kipling ballads" for *The Threepenny Opera.* The earliest extant scripts contained versions of Kipling's "The Ladies" and "Mary, Pity Women," but both were eventually cut. Then Hauptmann and Weill secured the retention of the four-line refrain of the latter as "Polly's Song" at the end of scene 4. This remains the only Kipling item, despite the program's mention of his "ballads" (plural).

The "Cannon Song" parodies the Kipling spirit, but is in *no* sense a translation or free rendering of any Kipling poem, as F. claims. Moreover, there is *no* evidence for ascribing it to Hauptmann. Its refrain was added to the 1928 *A Man's a Man,* where the music was by Meisel, but was not used in Brecht's 1931 production of that play.

199. F. claims that "Pirate Jenny" reveals Hauptmann's knowledge of Gay's later play, *Polly*. Even if she knew this play, and there is no evidence she did (see 193), it is *not* proof that Brecht could not have written this song. There are scripts in both his hand and Hauptmann's.

F. also gives no evidence for his assertion that the "Barbara Song" can be ascribed to Hauptmann.

The "four" Villon ballads F. mentions as being used in *The Threepenny Opera* were the "Ballade de Villon et de la grosse Margot," the ballade "Il n'est trésor que de vivre à son aise," the "Épitaphe en forme de ballade" (combined with the "Ballade par laquelle Villon crie merci à chacun"), the "Double Ballade," and the epistle "en forme de ballade à ses amis" from his Codicil, making *six* in all. Acknowledgement was made in the program to Villon, but not to the original German translator Karl Klammer, whose versions Brecht had taken and improved without asking permission.

F. makes the erroneous claim that "several scenes and songs familiar to [Lenya] from *A Man's a Man*, which had been revised in *Mahagonny*, were recycled" for the 1928 *Threepenny Opera* production (see 186). According to Drew, Weill wrote *no* music for the former play before Brecht's 1931 production (and *not* exactly a "song" even then). And there seems to be *no* record of Lenya ever appearing in it at all.

F. calls Elias Canetti a protégé of Karl Kraus. The two men never worked together.

200. F. asserts that Brecht was "much taken" with the attractive young widow Carola Neher. This is surely rather a backward step in his supposed affair with her, which he claims had already "heated up" some time before (see 159, 190, and 193).

201. F. erroneously states that Weigel was "replaced" in *The Threepenny Opera* production "by the cabaret artist Rosa Valetti." Weigel was to have played Gay's Mrs. Coaxer, and when she dropped out, the part was cut. Valetti was *already* playing Mrs. Peachum, a marginally more respectable figure.

202. What are F.'s "dance elements of the blues tradition" being interwoven into "Mac the Knife?" Blues are a black American *song* tradition without dance elements. (HCN)

203. The claim that "other Kipling" was reworked into the final text of *The Threepenny Opera* is an error. None was. See 198.

Chapter 15

204-6. F. erroneously has the "chambermaid Jenny" singing the song about the ship with eight sails and fifty cannon. It is Polly who sings it. (JKL)

The "Cannon Song," contrary to F.'s claim, is *not* done to a foxtrot tempo. It is a march. (JKL)

See 199 for F.'s unsupported assumption that Hauptmann wrote the song of "Pirate Jenny." Again he fails to state that it was to be sung by Polly Peachum, *not* Low-Dive Jenny. Thus he characterizes the *singer* as "the chambermaid Jenny, one of Hauptmann's many abandoned women in this work" (204), who is "at first sight another typical maid-prostitute" in Brecht's world (206). F. also describes her again as one of "Hauptmann's women who is tired of being kicked around by ruthless and egocentric men" and mentions Jenny's dream of "turning the cannon on her foes." F. does nothing to reconcile these fantasies of violence in women with his claim that it is the men in Brecht's works who dream of and carry out violence. More ambiguously (13 lines earlier) "Polly and Jenny dream..." of such violence. It was Lenya who, in the popular mind, established this song as Low-Dive Jenny's a year or two later, notably via her performances of it in Pabst's film version and the early recordings. (JW,JKL)

205. In another of his vague characterizations F. calls Count Kessler a "man-about-town and playwright-librettist." Kessler was one of the prominent liberal aristocrats of the Weimar Republic. A diplomat and politician, he inspired Hugo von Hofmannsthal to write the libretto for *Der Rosenkavalier* which Hofmannsthal dedicated to him. He was a patron of artists, ranging from Edvard Munch and Aristide Maillol to the young Johannes R. Becher, George Grosz, and John Heartfield. (HCN)

207. This is the first of F.'s numerous undocumented assertions about or references to the "flood" of Brecht's foreign income, in this case deposited in a Swiss bank account, but without evidence and without amounts. Note 6 on this page gives as its source a letter allegedly not published in the Brecht *Letters*. This is an error. It *is* published in both the German and the English editions as number 130. But the letter says nothing about Brecht's having money deposited in Switzerland.

208. F.'s claim that the story "Barbara" is almost certainly by Hauptmann is very possibly valid, though the script does bear a few

marks by Brecht. But it is perfectly clear that it is the narrator (a *man*) who is "almost killed," *not* Barbara, who (in the words of the story) "only comes into it right at the beginning."

213. F. calls Brecht "enormously wealthy." Given that F. had access to Brecht's business papers, it seems regrettable that he cannot give figures for this enormous wealth.

214. F. cites a letter from Brecht to Hauptmann which mentions a possible business deal with Fritzi Massary. F.'s comment on this incomplete letter, given in his note 26, suggests that Brecht was trying to claim the idea of *Happy End* as his own. If so, his "attempt" is surprising in view of his later insistence on dissociating himself from the entire work. Aufricht, its producer, thinks that Brecht had "constructed" the story. Hauptmann herself headed the first script "Happy End by Elisabeth Hauptmann/Songs by Bert Brecht and Kurt Weill" before withdrawing behind a pretence that she was once again the translator, this time from an American story by a (non-existent) "Dorothy Lane." Erich Engel, Caspar Neher, Theo Mackeben and the Lewis Ruth Band, too, were involved as previously.

215. F. has "The Communist paramilitary group, the Red Fighting Front" of Berlin "planning its annual May Day rally." Of course it was not only the uniformed RFF but the entire KPD, members and sympathizers, who rallied. (HCN)

217. Again "a torrent of income" and a Swiss bank account, but no evidence or further information (see 213).
F. reports how Aufricht nagged Brecht to complete *Happy End*. Brecht had not sent the script of the third act.

Chapter 16

219. Again a reference to the *Mahagonny* opera as "an expansion of the original, rather short *Mahagonny*." It was *not* (see 197).
Note 2 alludes to an interview, proving that Brecht was not working on *He Who Says Yes*. With whom? No name given.

220. F. claims that *He Who Says Yes* was published with Brecht as the primary author. This was in 1931 in the *Versuche* series, all issues of which bore Brecht's name. A small footnote to the title *He Who Says Yes* says, "After the Japanese play Taniko in the English translation by Arthur Waley." *He Who Says No* is coupled with this;

then come the names "Brecht. Hauptmann. Weill." The previous year Hauptmann had published the play in the Essen theater magazine *Der Scheinwerfer,* edited by Hannes Küpper (see 180).

222. F. claims that Brecht took over Hauptmann's versions of the Japanese plays she had translated. He took over this one play only. There were three others which she translated for her radio program on Seami. Waley's book included nineteen plays in all, of which ten (including *Taniko)* are not by Seami.

F. suggests that for mercenary reasons "Brecht declared his commitment to *Lehrstücke.*" But it would have been much more profitable to make another success of *Happy End,* which he was neglecting.

223. "The film maker Slatan Dudow" had not made any films before 1929, the year in question. His and Brecht's first collaboration was the play *Die Maßnahme.* Until then the Bulgarian Dudow had mostly been a theater student in Berlin and Moscow. (HCN)

224. Again F.'s claim for Hauptmann's "grasp of several foreign languages" is not substantiated. Her English was moderately good (see 146), her French less so.

F. claims the *Lindberghflug* receives its formal structure from the Japanese models with which Hauptmann was working, but he says nothing about Claudel, whose *Christophe Colomb* with Darius Milhaud surely reflects his actual experience of Japanese theater and has a related theme.

226. Though "*Happy End* was only partly done," the difference with the previous summer's last-minute panic lay in the fact that Brecht was now concentrating on the *Lehrstücke.* It is not clear what is meant by Weill's having to "create new songs," rather than having to wait for new song texts from Brecht. Brecht did in fact supply fourteen songs for *Happy End,* of which the most successful, the Kipling-derived "Surabaya Johnny," had been written at least two years before.

227. Valeska Gert was not "the sex sensation of the German dance scene" but rather a grotesque dancer. (HCN)

228. F. refers to "the theme of agreeing to be killed" as something Brecht had "played with" in *Baal, In the Jungle of Cities,* and *A Man's a Man.* What does this mean? This theme is *not* a feature in the earlier plays mentioned, but is evidently F.'s way of consider-

ing "Einverständnis," whose treatment was Brecht's particular contribution to the *Lehrstücke*.

230. F. claims that Weill's music for *Happy End*, "as now appears likely," was based on new lyrics by Hauptmann and older poems by Brecht and Hauptmann. My supposition (not a statement of fact), on which F. bases the first point, related to the Salvation Army songs, the Prologue, the "Sailors' Song," "Obacht, gebt Obacht," and the "Tough Nut" song. I did *not* credit her with the "Bilbao Song," as F. now does ("almost certainly by Hauptmann"), a claim he also makes for "Surabaya Johnny." Though *none* of this is proven with any documentary evidence, F. speaks unreservedly of "six of Hauptmann's and Weill's most brilliant songs."

231. In note 27 F. again claims without any evidence that the "Cannon Song" derives from Kipling (it did *not*, unless F. has a source unknown to Brecht scholarship) and seems to imply that it was included in this play. It was *not*.

"With six of Hauptmann's and Weill's most brilliant songs in hand..." As is the case on 187 when Brecht's name disappears from his own original music, it has now disappeared from the songs of *Happy End*. (HCN)

Chapter 17

232. The chapter title is neither by Brecht nor about him.

Without giving a source, F. also writes that at the end of *Happy End*, Weigel came on stage and read aloud from a Communist party brochure. Other documented accounts (e.g., Aufricht's) have her speaking lines given to Macheath in some versions of *The Three-penny Opera*. F. fails to mention this conflicting account.

233. F. erroneously dates the "Ballad of Hell's Lily" in 1919 and attempts to relate it to Lilli Krause Prem, whom Brecht knew in Augsburg in 1919. A brief comment in *Brecht in Augsburg* seems to be all there is to connect the song with her. In Hauptmann's play, the Lily is Lilian Holiday, the Salvationist heroine. A note in the Berlin and Frankfurt edition of Brecht's works states that the song was written during rehearsals in 1929. Clearly it was not written in 1919.

F. makes another error when he refers to the "same refrain" heard in the original "Mac the Knife." That song has *no* refrain.

234. F., referring to one of Brecht's "poem-weapons" in which

he lashes out against Hauptmann, cites Völker's biography as his source. F. carelessly accepts Völker's claim that Brecht wrote the poem after Hauptmann's suicide attempt and the failure of *Happy End*. He locates it in 1929. It belongs, however, to the "Poems Belonging to the Reader for Those Who Live in the Cities" written two years earlier. F. has failed to consult basic secondary sources which, since 1986, have given a firmly established date of 1927 for the poem's origin, i.e., two years before the events he claims triggered them. This misdating not only negates the circumstances he says prompted it but raises questions as to whether it was addressed to Hauptmann at all, as he claims. There is no evidence that it was. (JKL)

In the same poem, F. mistranslates the phrase "die nicht abreißende Liste" as "the never-to-be-torn-up list" of those who have fallen away. A more accurate rendering would be the "ongoing" or "unending" list. (JKL)

240. F. says very little about Hauptmann's collaboration on *Mahagonny*, perhaps because there was so little. She was heavily involved in her own writing and translation at the time. Her limited participation, however, raises questions about F.'s thesis that Brecht was unable to finish works without her help. (JKL)

241. F. claims that for Weill Brecht was no pleasure to work with because of his capricious behavior concerning his song texts. His reference is to 160 of my book *Brecht in Context*. I say nothing about the matter there and cannot see the relevance.

243. F. has Brecht maintaining friendly contact with the radical right, but he gives no details or evidence other than anecdotes about Bronnen's efforts to cultivate Goebbels. But by Bronnen's own account, his friendship with Brecht had ended earlier. See 191, 173 ("a bond had ended"), etc.

244. For an account of what F. calls *Happy End*'s "engineered collapse," see 232.

F. translates "Mitarbeiter(in)" as "co-worker." The more common rendering is "collaborator."

Chapter 18

245. F. speaks of Waley's version of a Japanese play called "The Valley Hurling." More accurately, its title was "Taniko/(The Valley-Hurling)," as given in Waley's original 1921 edition.

Again, F. refers to my *Brecht in Context* (160), as he does on 241, note 22, and again I cannot find that this is relevant as a source to corroborate his remarks.

F. informs his readers that the first draft of *The Measures Taken* was actually called *Der Jasager*. If F. is referring to BBA 826/27-28, it is more interesting than that, as it is in Brecht's handwriting and is headed "Der Jasager (Konkretisierung)." Hauptmann is nowhere evident here. This version is two pages long and bears only on the first two scenes.

246. F. says Eisler was born to "Jewish university professors in Austria." Just like Kurt Weill, Hanns Eisler is given the wrong place of birth. *He*, not Weill, was born in Leipzig, his mother being a non-Jewish butcher's daughter with the maiden name Fischer, later used by Eisler's sister, Elfriede (Ruth Fischer). Because the father was Jewish he was never allowed a position as a "university professor in Austria." In Vienna he could only practise as a "Privatgelehrter." It is remarkable that F. misses this point: "Jewish university professors in Austria" were a non-existent category until after WWII. F. is also wrong when he says that Eisler went to Holland and Berlin where he studied with Schönberg and Webern. Eisler went to Holland for only six months in 1920 as Schönberg's assistant and then returned to Austria. And of course he had studied with these "giants of the avant-garde" in Vienna, not Berlin. (HCN)

As usual F. is vague when he says that Ruth Fischer rose "to extremely high rank in the CPG after Rosa Luxemburg's death." During the "Bolschewisierung" of the KPD 1924-25, Ruth Fischer led the party together with Arkadij Maslow. (HCN)

F. annotates a statement about Hanns Eisler's being ready to commit himself to the Communist Party of Germany with a reference to Eisler's *Musik und Politik. Schriften 1924-4* [sic](misprint for -48?). As those three volumes contain about 1500 pages and no page reference is given, the reader has little chance of discovering what, if anything, Eisler said about this supposed decision.

247. F. commits another error by stating that the Young Comrade is sent to ask for arms and money from a wealthy "woman" rice dealer. The Merchant (der Händler) is on the contrary a *man*, a tenor.

In the original Universal-Edition piano score, the first chorus of the work is marked *fortissimo, not* the "ear-drum bursting triple fortissimo" claimed by F.

248. "Führung." This is the normal German word for "leader-

ship," and if it is unnecessarily repeated, the point can only be to suggest an association with the Führer, Adolf Hitler, which F. relentlessly pushes. See 79.

249. F. mentions "a strong woman character very like those found in Hauptmann's *Happy End*" whom Brecht added to the film script of *The Threepenny Opera*. I cannot recognize her; which character was it?

Leo Lania was not Piscator's "colleague," as F. has it. Lania was a playwright; he wrote *Konjunktur* for Piscator, and together with the latter, and Brecht and Felix Gasbarra, he had adapted Hašek's *Schweyk* novel for the stage. (HCN)

249. F. calls *Die Weltbühne* "widely read." The importance of *Die Weltbühne* had nothing to do with the hypothesis that it was "widely read" (compared with what? *Uhu? Die Dame?*). What mattered was the quality of its contributors (Ossietzky, Tucholsky). Today you might say that *Bild Zeitung* is widely read. (HCN)

250. F. writes that the writers of *He Who Says Yes* had introduced "one small modification." This is not correct. Other *major* changes he does not mention were the insertion of the opening chorus (linking this to the two *Lehrstücke* of the previous year) and the addition of roughly one out of its ten pages (in Szondi's first "Fassung") introducing the teacher's question and the ensuing dialogue.

There is faulty documentation when F. cites "the critic Edward Cole" and refers to Mittenzwei's biography (1:345) as its source. This cited page says nothing about such a critic and his views.

251. Brecht allegedly "dragooned" a reticent Weill into pressing a lawsuit against Nero Films relating to the film version of *The Threepenny Opera*. This may well be, but F. gives no source about Brecht's coercion or Weill's reluctance. (JKL)

252. In reference to the birth of "Mari Barbara Brecht," F. claims he has hunted vainly for her birth certificate in order to establish whether she was the child of the family maid, Mari Hold, which he clearly wants to do. Besides this first name (by which she was never known), "when the barbaric appeared," according to Brecht's poem of 5 October 1934, she had Hold's eyes (again F. equates poetic license with biographical fact), and "soon had two mothers." From this point on F. repeatedly reminds the reader of the possible relationship by using the name Mari every time Barbara

Brecht is referred to. To my knowledge, F. is the only writer, of any nationality, to call her Mari Barbara. Throughout her life she has been known only as Barbara.

F. uses the "uncommon first name" to support his innuendo, but police records in Denmark have her full name as "Marie Barbara Brecht," and "Mari" Hold was then still called by the name, extremely common in Catholic Bavaria, of "Maria." F.'s trump card in his insinuation that Barbara was Mari's child is Brecht's occasional poem, written as a thank-you and a tribute for her indispensable help around the house, in honor of Maria Hold's marriage to Jørgen Henrik Ohm, the Svendborg butcher, in 1934. If Brecht's wording is anything but a joking compliment it would be a bizarre code to smuggle into a wedding poem which actually might have been recited or handed out around the festive table where both Helene Weigel and Karin Michaelis were seated. Brecht himself was excused as he was in London. I read this wedding poem aloud to Maria Ohm in 1971 while the camera and the tape recorder were running to capture her spontaneous reactions (these recordings still exist). She had either forgotten about the poem or never received it. She even asked if Brecht had written it himself, which F. eagerly notes. Neither Mrs. Ohm nor myself showed any signs while we listened to the lines about the "barbaric" Barbara, of grasping the unsuspected possibilities of interpretation these might be holding. She spoke to me with unadulterated devotion about the two generations of Brechts she had served as a maid. (HCN)

253. F. cites Mittenzwei as a source for Brecht's call to Kurella announcing he was no longer Kurella's friend. Mittenzwei does *not* say that "Brecht was furious at this," as F. claims.

Chapter 19

255. F. reports that Hauptmann published a story in early 1931 under her real name. This is one of the seven such stories referred to by me (see 144), and the second of them to be published in the Ullstein magazine, *Uhu*.

256. F. claims that the Soviets sent György von Lukács (Georg Lukács) to "promote" the Berlin journal *Linkskurve*. This was the journal of the BPRS or Proletarian-Revolutionary Writers' League, and Lukács's mission was *not* to "promote" the journal but rather to keep it on the new Socialist Realist line, and to check the influence of innovators like Tretyakov.

In describing the Staatstheater production of *A Man's a Man*,

1931, F. has seemingly based his descriptions of the production on photographs, some of which were not taken at the production: the bobbed Helene Weigel as Begbick in Legal's 1928 production, and Lorre in a posed picture from 1931, as reproduced in my book *The Theater of Bertolt Brecht*. Stage photos do not show Lorre wearing all that ironmongery in the play.

258. F. claims that the existence of a translation/adaptation of Tretyakov's *I Want a Child* is often ignored. Ernst Hube's translation, adapted by Brecht (1930), is published in Fritz Mierau's *Erfindung und Korrektur* (East Berlin, 1976). Mierau's own translation was one of the *Zwei Stücke* published by Henschel (East Berlin, the same year). The play had been scheduled for one of Meyerhold's last avant-garde productions in 1928, in a theater space designed by Lissitzky, but was stopped during rehearsals.

259. Again the use of the word "Führer." See 79, 86, 248
In stating that Brecht complained about the service at his Riviera hotel, F. gives a note that has nothing to do with the poor service and talks instead about unrelated gossip concerning Brecht and Lenya.

260. It is not entirely remarkable, as F. implies, that Brecht's letter to Hauptmann's sister as to why he counseled her against going home when her mother died is not included in Brecht's *Letters*. The Hauptmann family apparently had their reasons for keeping it private before communicating it to F.

261. F. describes Slatan Dudow as a Hungarian director. Dudow was born in Bulgaria.
F. mentions how characters in *The Mother* come to the stage apron, as though it occurred in every scene. This happens in four out of the thirteen scenes.

262. The editor of the volume *Die Säuberung*, which F. cites, seems to accept that Ernst Ottwalt, whom F. describes as a "strutting Freikorps member," left the Freikorps soon after he joined, and that those accusations against him which cause F. to call him "a shadowy, ex-right-wing spy" came from a confusion of names. F. mentions none of this. F. further states that a script of *Kuhle Wampe* was published "as though Brecht were mainly responsible for it," which is yet another example of Brecht's perfidy. This is an error. The script for *Kuhle Wampe* was *not* published till 1971, when it bore both Ottwalt's and Brecht's names, in spite of Ottwalt's saying

that he had been "chucked out." He died in a Soviet camp in 1943.

263. Again F. insists that Brecht's own male characters are consistently arrogant, egocentric, and ruthless. Leading male characters who are *not* so consistent include Edward II, Ackermann, Kragler, Galy Gay, the Young Comrade, Pavel, Galileo, and Schweyk.

Again F. mentions poor "Bébé" (see 56, 72, 82, 97). *Nowhere* does Brecht himself use this name spelled thus.

264. In an attempt to equate Steffin with the heroine of the play *Saint Joan,* F. imprecisely says that Joan dies from "something wrong with her lungs." More precisely, its German text says she dies of "Lungenentzündung" — the usual word for pneumonia. Steffin had tuberculosis.

Chapter 20

265. F. claims that Hauptmann would have been "happy with equal billing" for the works on which she collaborated. Did she *ever* say this? What is F.'s source?

Regarding Hauptmann's role in *The Measures Taken,* the Versuche edition of *Die Maßnahme* (published in 1931 in one of the first volumes edited by Hauptmann) lists the collaborators as "Brecht. Dudow. Eisler." If she edited the volume, why did she not list herself as a collaborator?

F. states that the relationship between Brecht and Hauptmann would now "more or less peter out." But work on the *Measure for Measure* adaptation was just starting. According to personal statements made by Hauptmann to James K. Lyon, she was involved with Brecht as a collaborator on his works until he fled Germany more than a year later in 1933. (JW, JKL)

F. calls Streicher "one of Berlin's most prominent Nazis." The perverted anti-Semite Julius Streicher was known as "der Frankenführer" and resided in Nuremberg where he published *Der Stürmer.* (HCN)

266. F. makes a great deal of Bronnen's experiences as a Nazi in 1932-33. These are relevant after the mid-1920s only if his former friendship with Brecht is still treated as significant.

267. Again F. claims that Weigel had sabotaged the production of *Happy End.* For a different account, see 232, 244.

268. F. paints a dismal picture of Steffin's birthplace in Berlin, calling it "a loud, filthy, smelly, tiny, damp...slum flat." Rudy Hassing says that in interviews he conducted in 1987 and 1989 with a very close friend of Steffin, Herta Reinecke, she told him that the Steffin's flat was in a well-built house with nice big rooms, compared to her place. Neither did Steffin's sister, Herta Hanish, describe the flat in F.'s way in another interview, and a photograph of the flat does not back up F.'s Dickensian description.

268-69. The caption to photograph 21 between these pages: Jørgen Henrik Ohm, Mari Hold's husband, the Svendborg butcher, died unexpectedly of a heart attack aged only 63, while visiting his daughter in Copenhagen, *not* after a shocked rummaging through his wife's old photos of her posed in drag by Brecht. And it was she who subsequently burned them when in a state of severe shock and grief before moving into a much smaller house (see 77). (HCN) Rudy Hassing comments that the photo was not taken by Nørregaard but by a local Svendborg photographer, from whom he acquired it in 1978, and passed it on to F.

Photo 44's caption reads, in part: "In the proletarian milieu in which Steffin lived, she reports it was widely believed at the time that Brecht's work such as *The Threepenny Opera* were 'stolen from A to Z.'" This was a common opinion since the attacks by Kerr and Tucholsky and had nothing to do with any "proletarian milieu." In 1938 in a book *Die Juden in Deutschland*, published in Munich by the "Institut zum Studium der Judenfrage," you can read about Brecht in connection with Kurt Weill: "Daß...dem findigen Autor, dessen eigener 'dichterischer' Anteil sich hauptsächlich auf die freigebig eingestreuten Zynismen beschränkt, eine ganze Reihe ausgewachsener Plagiate nachgewiesen wurden, darf wohl als bekannt vorausgesetzt werden." (HCN)

269-70. Twice F. says that in the 1931 production of *The Mother* the song "In Praise of Communism" was sung "in triple fortissimo." In the score the first is marked *ff*, the second moves from piano to pianissimo (see 247).

The Mother was performed at "the progressive Volksbühne," according to F. It was not. Apart from being performed in various places *The Mother* was produced by "die junge Volksbühne." The Volksbühne (without the adjective) was not progressive in that sense. In 1927 it had already broken with Piscator, accusing him of "Kulturbolschewismus." *The Mother* was no less communist than Piscator's work. (HCN)

F. says that Weigel, as a Communist party member and Jewish

woman had to "face the anti-Semitic thugs outside the theater who constituted a threat to her very life." It is important to F. that everybody but Brecht himself was in life-threatening danger at some time or other. I think he has seen Fosse's *Cabaret* too many times. I know of no violent attacks on Jewish or communist performing artists before Hitler's take-over. It is known that performances of *The Mother* were forbidden or interrupted by the Prussian police — a different matter. Nazi papers could raise a campaign against "typically Jewish" actors like Fritz Kortner and other prominent scapegoats in the theater and film. Helene Weigel was hardly known to these propagandists, and the Nazis did not care about an off-off-Kurfürstendamm enterprise like *The Mother*. (HCN)

Chapter 21

275. F. states that Eisenstein was summoned back to Moscow "in disgrace for his decadence and formalism." More accurately, he had been forced to return to Russia as a result of the delays and differences that had put a stop to his work on the Mexican project, exacerbated by the hostility of Shumyatzky, the new head of the Soviet film industry.

276. F. claims that in the USSR, experimentalists "would be dead or in the gulag." Not true of Tatlin, Rodchenko, Stepanova, Lissitzky, the Vesnins, Melnikov, Shostakovitch, Okhlopkhov, Tairov, Olyesha, Ehrenburg, Pasternak for a start, though it was true of Mayakovsky, Tretyakov, Koltsov, Meyerhold.

278. Bronnen again. See 266.
F. says that the Feuchtwangers, "despairing of Communist party chances" cast their votes for Hindenburg as "an anti-Hitler measure." As far as I can see, F. is confusing the Reichstag election (31 July 1932) with the Presidential election (13 March). In the Reichstag election which F. is discussing, the Feuchtwangers could not vote for Hindenburg but had to decide on a party. (HCN)

279. F. describes "large ovens" on the Reiss estate. This is probably a mistranslation referring to stoves (*Öfen* in German).

280. F. mentions a "Comrade H. Diamond." Probably Heinrich Diament, an official concerned with the International League of Revolutionary Theaters and its journal.

282. F. fails to be specific about contacts with right-wing

persons that Brecht is maintaining in 1931. Names, sources? See 173, 191, 243.

Elisabeth Hauptmann, according to F., had taken "as flat-mates the fine Russian poet Lily Brik and her husband, a Red Army general." I know of only one Lily Brik who was living together with Vladimir Mayakovsky and her husband Ossip Brik in — what F. might call — a ménage-à-trois. This Lily Brik was no poet, and Ossip Brik to my knowledge was no Red Army general. Lily Brik has published her memoirs of Mayakovsky's life and death. She herself died in 1978. (HCN)

283. F. writes that after Hitler came to power, Brecht would "rewrite his own history...and declare how early he had become a prominent anti-Nazi." No sources are given to document this.

284. F. does not identify Carola Neher's "Communist function-ary husband." This was Anatol Becker, formerly a teacher of Russian at the MASch, who was attacked by Wangenheim and Ottwalt in the Moscow inquiry reported in *Die Säuberung*; in 1936 he was arrested and shot.

285. F. refers to Hanns Johst as a very popular "playwright friend of Hitler and Brecht." Brecht is not known to have had any contact with him since leaving Munich, nor was Johst prominent in the theater of the Weimar Republic. He joined the Nazi party on 1 November 1932 and became a leading dramatist and writer of the Third Reich.

289. F. says the Garrison Church at Potsdam was the "scene in the past of Germany's greatest imperial triumphs." He keeps con-fusing the kingdom of Prussia with the German empire. (HCN)

Chapter 22

290. F. finds it notable that Brecht's name was not on a list of authors Goebbels put out (no date given, but presumably early 1933). There were various lists, it seems. Brecht was not the only person who failed to make this one; neither did Anna Seghers, Ludwig Renn, J.R. Becher and other leading (but not best-selling) communist authors. Brecht was, however, on a longer list of "books deserving to be burned" compiled by the Berlin *Nachtausgabe* on 26 March 1933. This was before the Berlin book-burning.

Many of these lists seem chaotic: a lot of writers are simply forgotten in this early phase, like Johannes R. Becher, which does not mean that he was accepted by the Nazis. (HCN)

F. characterizes Herbert Ihering as "well regarded" within Goebbels's ministry. On the contrary, he was expelled from the Chamber of Writers and forbidden to write, before (against Rosenberg's opposition) being made "Artistic Adviser" to the Vienna Burgtheater after the Anschluß.

In referring to Neher and laws against homosexuals, F. still assumes without clear evidence that he was one. See 37, 43, 52.

291. Mari Barbara. See 252, 259, 287.

"Nor had Brecht burnt his bridges behind him." The "nor" refers to the film director G.W. Pabst, who returned to Germany after the Austrian Anschluß. The Pabst case is without parallel and has never been fully explained. There are no documents supporting F.'s theory that Brecht had not "burnt his bridges"; on the contrary. That he and his family were registered as "Germans living abroad" had nothing to do with the idea of returning. This was the normal way to handle things for German refugees, especially during the first years of the Third Reich. Or — to put it without any possibility of being misunderstood — Brecht had burnt every bridge to the Nazis, but during the first years of exile he did not know how long their regime would last. In that respect he was ready to return "tomorrow" — after the overthrow of the government. (HCN)

F. finds it a mystery that Mari Hold decided to leave her language and her country. But nobody knew it was going to be for good. It was not the Brecht family that caused her permanent absence but her marriage to a Dane in November 1934. (HCN)

292. F. states that Brecht sent a number of incomplete sonnets to Steffin and asked her to finish them because he could not find suitable rhymes. No source is given. (JKL)

Again F. refers again to a Swiss bank account into which Brecht had been depositing money for years. No evidence or details are given.

F. finds Brecht's signing his letters with the "old south German expression," "Grüß Gott!" "oddly inconsistent with his Marxist beliefs." As a Berlin girl Steffin might have been fascinated by this Bavarian standard greeting. "Grüß Gott!" simply means "Guten Tag" and "Auf Wiedersehen" in Bavaria, just like the short, jargon-like "Tschüß!" which originally derived from the French "Adieu". The name of God is included but the significance forgotten. (HCN)

293. F. claims that both "Weill and Neher had decided to avoid Brecht." There is no evidence for this, and the order of Weill's work

which F. gives here is wrong. *Die Bürgschaft* was composed first, on a script by Neher — see my Neher catalogue for a remarkably Brecht-like passage. It was finished in October 1931 and first performed on 10 March 1932. *Der Silbersee* (usually translated as *The Silver Lake*) was composed between August 1932 and January 1933, and performed on 18 February 1933.

Two women characters are central to *The Seven Deadly Sins.* This seems to contradict F.'s claim that Brecht was incapable of creating women characters without women collaborators. (JKL)

F. says the ballet was "built around the biblical seven deadly sins." Where in the Bible can one find the seven deadly sins? (HCN)

294. F. mentions that in Paris Caspar Neher was introduced into a homosexual circle. Presumably all the visiting Germans were, as this was the ambience of the Paris production of *The Seven Deadly Sins.* See 37, 43, 52, 290. According to F., Weill had originally "proposed Jean Cocteau for the libretto."

F. reports that Weill was upset because he believed Brecht was "involved in some shady business." According to F.'s undocumented claim, Weill "proposed a musical version of *Round Heads, Peak Heads* to Brecht." It seems more likely that at the beginning of 1933, Brecht had shown Weill an early script of the *Measure for Measure* adaptation and was already trying to interest Eisler in the same work (which ended up as *The Round Heads and the Pointed Heads,* with songs set by Eisler).

F. should not mock Brecht for misspelling Mr. Wreede. Among his own misspellings so far are Harold Paulsen and Ernst von Salamon. In these cases he anglicizes German names while he does not respect the intentional anglicizing by Georg Grosz of his name to George. The Berlin police president was called Zörgiebel, not Zörrgiebel. (HCN)

295. F. refers to an attempt by Aufricht to mount a Paris charity production of *The Threepenny Opera* to aid Jews driven from Germany. This is not mentioned in Aufricht's memoirs, and according to his own letter, Brecht heard it only as a rumor. F. reports it as fact, and without further documentation.

F. refers to an unidentified "book of some earlier songs written with Hanns Eisler." This was *Songs Poems Choruses,* Brecht's second collection of poems. Beside those ten songs (with their Eisler settings) from *Die Mutter* and *Die Maßnahme,* it contained six quasi-Lutheran anti-Hitler hymns (new), nine anti-Nazi poems (mainly new) and twelve other poems or songs from before 1933.

297. F. erroneously refers to the "annexation" of the Saar region by Germany. The Saar had been under a League of Nations mandate from 1920 until the plebiscite of January 1935, which decided that it would be returned to Germany. In winter 1934-35 Brecht and Eisler wrote a "Saar Song" and a "United Front Song" at the request of the Comintern. These and other poems which he was now writing, along with his brief involvement in the preparation of the "Brown Books," conflict with F.'s view that Brecht "consistently maintained a low anti-Nazi profile."

298. F. cites and references a poem allegedly located in the "SA," the "Steffin Archive." He intends to deposit all this material in a public library. From this statement, one assumes that the poem is unpublished. It appears, however, to be a loosely translated version of the easily accessible "The Sixth Sonnet," (538 of the 1967 edition *Gesammelte Werke in 20 Bänden*, abbreviated hereafter as *GW*), whose draft is dated "Svendborg 1933."

Rudy Hassing reports that these "Steffin Archive" papers are deposited with Kurt Groenewold, a lawyer in Hamburg, who has a Generalvollmacht" from Herta and Herbert Hanish, and is in charge of Steffin's rights (see 655, note 29).

299. F. again refers to lines from "a still unpublished version of Sonnet 10" by Steffin and situates them among the unpublished materials in the SA. They look, however, very much like Brecht's "The Tenth Sonnet" in *Poems 1913-1956*, i.e., a different English version of *GW* 8:164, ending with:

The fact that I of all men should look down
On those in trouble hurts me to report.

Here translated by Edith Roseveare, this was published in Aufricht's program-journal *Das Stichwort* in April 1929, well before Brecht met Steffin.

Chapter 23

300. F. gives an address, 36, Avenue Morère, but what is the name of the town/city?

"Mari Barbara" repeated, as on 252, 259, 287, 291.

F. speaks of the Union of German Writers. Is this Goebbels's *Reichsschrifttumskammer*?

301. Talking of the Brechts' Danish residence papers F. says

that Weigel was "listed simply as Helene Brecht rather than Helene Weigel." Helene Brecht was her legal name; for instance, in her passport; she seems to have dropped Weigel after her marriage although she still used it as her artistic name. (HCN)

The Threepenny Opera was not produced at the Royal Theater of Denmark but at Det ny Teater (1930). There were a lot of other theaters in Copenhagen in those days, and still are. (HCN)

I am sorry to say that the problem with F. and others originally started when Hans Bunge brought out his Ruth Berlau book *Brechts Lai-tu* in 1986. It is wrong to say that Berlau is lying but she arranges the truth and neglects details and chronology in such a way that she is almost impossible to rely upon if not double-checked with other witnesses. But F., thinking that Berlau is too modest in some of her claims, actually inflates them. During his many visits to Copenhagen he has been told the truth and even shown written evidence (manuscripts) from the collection of Berlau's close friend, the architect Mogens Voltelen. He also met Berlau's proletarian star actress Dagmar Andreasen. They are both mentioned in the acknowledgments on 623, but F. never listened to them. In some way it is terrible to put down this dead woman: she must have had qualities — but as an artist, actress, director, writer, she was mediocre. When Bunge's book was published and translated, she was almost forgotten and to this very day in this country (Denmark) she is known only as Brecht's Danish mistress. (HCN)

F. asserts that Berlau founded the Revolutionary Theater group in Copenhagen." This is not true. The RT was formed on the initiative of the Danish communist party in late 1932. The professional theater people involved were Per Knutzon (actor, director), his wife Lulu Ziegler (actress) and Ruth Berlau (actress). Knutzon was without question the brain and the inspiration of RT's early period. In fact, Berlau had got her first training as a pupil of the "Forsøgsscenen" (experimental) drama school led by Per Knutzon around 1930. "Forsøgsscenen" had been an experimental left-wing theater organization, mostly attended by university students and intellectuals. Most of its actors had been unemployed professionals. "Forsøgsscenen" was a very poor enterprise, of course, without its own house and the productions were only shown a few times. Per Knutzon got the idea to direct and produce Brecht's *Trommeln in der Nacht*. It was only shown once, on 17 May 1930, at midnight on the stage of the "Folketeatret," and for the part of Anna Balicke he chose one of his pupils in the "Forsørgsscenen" drama school, namely Ruth Berlau. Nobody knows how long this drama school existed and how it was run. I only know about it from the many newspaper reviews of *Trommeln in der Nacht*. After this single midnight performance Berlau seems to disappear from the "Forsøgs-scenen." Knutzon continued, and in November 1930 he directed the more sensational *Cyankali* by Friedrich Wolf which was repeated several times. Friedrich Wolf attended one of the performances and gave a lot of interviews. Knutzon even had a new female star, called Banne Dütsch. Whatever happened to Ruth Berlau? Just like today there were a lot of starlets, making headlines one day, forgotten the next — even in little Copenhagen. But in the summer of 1930 — after her theater debut with the "Forsøgsscenen" — Berlau headed for the Soviet Union on her bicycle. Back home again in the fall, she started a new period of study — now at the drama school of the Royal Theater where she was employed as an actress from 1931 on. All this is confirmed by newspapers of the time. Berlau met up again with Per Knutzon, her former teacher and director, when the Revolutionary Theater was founded in late 1932. We know very little about the material performed by this agitprop group but all the actors involved — working class people, mostly communists — agree that Knutzon was the dynamic leader of RT. He also seems to have picked up the German agitprop style during his studies abroad. (HCN)

F. says that Berlau was known in "Copenhagen as Red Ruth." Because she was hardly known in public at all, this is an exaggeration. I do not know who might have called her by this nickname. Again F. is relying too much on her own version in the Bunge book. (HCN)

302. F. discusses Berlau writing articles on her Paris trip which she sent back to the paper *Ektrabladet* published under her byline with accompanying photos. When she got back "she found she was famous and recognized everywhere." The story about her 1928 trip to Paris is basically true. She wrote letters (not articles) to *Ekstrabladet*, a Copenhagen boulevard paper — rather childish letters about Ruth and "Fut" (her bicycle). Of course she was neither famous nor recognized everywhere after this adventure. *Ekstrabladet* was not the only paper in Copenhagen, and this kind of "Guinness Book of Records" stunt was very popular and widespread in the twenties and thirties. (HCN)

Rudy Hassing comments that Berlau did not act in *The Jungle of Cities*, which was not performed in Denmark in Brecht's lifetime, nor did she ever play the lead in *Miss Julie*. She included extracts from the play in a recital she gave in the "Odd Fellow Pallæet" concert hall Monday, 26 February 1934, hired by herself. She was assisted by two other actors, and also read from works by Gelsted,

Bull, Jensen, and Whitman. There were even two musicians playing music by Kulau and Roussel. This information is on the poster in the possession of Hassing, who showed it to F. The frontispiece photo which F. dates wrongly to 1930, also shows her as Miss Julie, according to him. Incorrectly attributed in the photo credits to the Berlau collection, Berlin, it was taken by the well-known Danish woman photographer, Rie Nissen, when Berlau had just started as a student at the Royal Theater School. Rie Nissen's signature is on the left bottom of the original picture, but has been "left out" here.

303. "Kongens Have" is not "the garden of the king," but a public park with the official name "Rosenborg Have." It has been public for at least 150 years and for centuries no king or queen has lived in the small castle of Rosenborg in it. (HCN)

F. says that early in 1933 "Red Ruth" (sic) was invited to bring her theater group to Moscow. No, she was not. The group was invited via its director Per Knutzon, Berlau was only part of the gang. On F.'s "own" photo 50 you can see the group exercising on board the ship to Leningrad. Per Knutzon is the man on the left — inspecting his troops. Next to him — marching on the left in the front row — his wife, the actress Lulu Ziegler. In the middle of the second row you see Berlau. This might reflect the hierarchy among the professional artists in this proletarian theater group in those days. We cannot prove that the group "won a prize"; it might be a legend. The French "Groupe Octobre" won a first prize, performing sketches by Jacques Prévert who was present. (He wrote a poem about the trip, found in the Hanns Eisler-Sonderheft of *Sinn und Form*.) F. also claims that Berlau had "become well known both in Denmark and in international theater circles." How could she? As one among thousands from all over the world? F. is building up his Berlau myth, step by step. (HCN) Rudy Hassing comments that the credit to photo 50 is incorrectly given as the Berlau Collection, Berlin; it belongs to the collection of Mogens Voltelen.

304. F. states that Berlau immediately used "the familiar 'Du' that only a handful of people were allowed to use with Brecht." In Denmark we have "du" and "De" corresponding to the German "du" and "Sie" but all Danish party communists said "du" to each other — and mostly addressed Brecht in the same way — Per Knutzon, Lulu Ziegler, the party leader Aksel Larsen and others. In fact Lulu Ziegler addressed Brecht with "Genosse" and "Du" in German in a letter before Berlau ever met him. (HCN)

305. "German émigré Comintern functionaries." Otto Katz had

been the business manager of Piscator's companies in 1927-29. Münzenberg made him a director of Mezhrabpom-Film in Moscow in winter 1931-32, then brought him to Paris to work on the "Brown Books." He was thought to be reporting back to Moscow.

307. F. states that Brecht borrows money from Walter Benjamin but gives no source.

308. F. cites a letter Brecht wrote from Sanary to Denmark. This is letter 184, which, however, contains nothing about "excessive emphasis...on the anti-Semitic part of Hitler's policy," or indeed about antisemitism at all. Brecht complains about Zionism as a sign that Hitler "has fascized not only the Germans but the Jews as well." This was not an unknown argument among Jewish opponents of Zionism.

309. Another mention of Brecht's Swiss bank account and again, no details.
F. states that Steffin had "several" "psychologically and physically draining abortions" because she and Brecht did not practice birth-control. Rudy Hassing states that Steffin had two abortions in 1928 and 1930 during her relationship with Herbert Dymke. She had another in 1932 according to records obtained by Hassing's family doctor, Morten Nielsen. F.'s later "abortions" are contradicted by Steffin's diary, where she carefully noted her periods.

310. F. states that Tretyakov wrote to complain about Brecht's lack of real antifascist work. F. does not quote the letter, so Tretyakov may merely have spoken to Weigel about it when she was in Moscow. Brecht's words, in a letter thanking the Tretyakovs for their hospitality to her, were "You ask why I don't take a prominent part in Antifa[scist] action."
F. says Brecht wrote against the Nazis but mostly this would not be published "until decades later when it was safe." F. never mentions the large number of poems against the Nazis Brecht published in the various exile magazines, plus those in translation and under his own name in Danish left-wing magazines, although he was forbidden by the Danish government to attack any foreign government in public. (HCN)

311-12. F. refers to a Comintern volume Brecht would bring out with Hanns Eisler. Already discussed on 295.
F. mentions that Hauptmann invested some time on the song volume that Steffin was assembling for Editions du Carrefour. This

is the same book as in the previous reference.

F. speaks of Steffin and Berlau working on a Copenhagen production of *Mahagonny*. David Drew says the last production of that work in Weill's lifetime was the Vienna version directed by Heinsheimer in 1932. This may explain the absence of royalty payments to Weill for which F. faults Brecht — there was no production.

313. F. mentions how Brecht's contracts with Moscow and Western agencies were paying him well. Again, no amounts are given. The crucial question with Moscow payments was whether they were transferable into Western currencies.

F. makes Brecht's house at Skovsbostrand seem rather luxurious. In fact, his house on Funen was a normal fisherman's, smallholder's, or even worker's house. The Danish Nazis, who would have enjoyed F.'s description, just called it "a smallholder's cottage" in their propaganda against Brecht. Ruth Berlau took pictures, published by Hecht and others, which show modest, not to say spartan, interiors. (HCN)

F. states that Brecht's toilet at Skovsbostrand was so primitive it had to be emptied daily, but that "fortunately, for tasks like this Mari Hold was with the family." In the material F. received from me, Mrs. Ohm says: "He (Brecht) made sure that I didn't work too much. It was he who saw to it that there was somebody else to wash up the dishes and do the hard work. I wasn't allowed to. No, sir, I wasn't supposed to do that." "There was no guile in him," Mrs. Ohm said further, but this statement F. also chooses to ignore. (HCN)

F. unfairly parallels Steffin's and Berlau's writing and translating skills. Which of these skills were at Berlau's command? In fact, the only Danish translation of Brecht, published as if it were done by her, *Fru Carrars Geværer*, was ghost-translated by Mogens Voltelen. He has admitted this himself; he spent several hours telling F. about Berlau's general lack of "translating skills." (HCN)

Chapter 24

314. The cryptic description of Steffin's involvement in a "less savory" project for Brecht presumably refers to the proposed *Mahagonny* production reported on 312, which apparently never materialized.

F. insists that "the important plays of the period were written only with Steffin's daily work." This does *not* say, however, that the work was creative. Cf. Ruth Berlau's judgment on Steffin in *Brechts*

Lai-Tu (108): "she did not share in the writing of the plays as did Elisabeth Hauptmann, but she was a relentless critic." Note also the report of Steffin's landlord's on 315 of how she carried out secretarial assignments or read proofs for Brecht.

315. F. refers to a first version of *The Caucasian Chalk Circle*. These earliest sketches can hardly be termed a "version." Brecht marked "first script" and "first version" on the typescript dated 5 June 1944, three years and a day after Steffin's death. F. fails to mention her translation of Martin Andersen Nexø's *Die Kindheit*, with which Brecht is jointly credited (he is named second).

316. F. again mentions a Brecht-Eisler song volume for Münzenberg's communist press. This is the same book referred to on 295 and 311.

F. mentions remarks by Zhdanov at an unidentified conference. Presumably this was the 1934 Congress of Soviet Writers, which has not been mentioned.

319. F. writes of a joint Hauptmann-Brecht script of *The Round Heads and the Pointed Heads*. This is F.'s attribution. So far he has *not* discussed any evidence for, or the nature of, Hauptmann's involvement. She was named with Brecht and Burri at the end of the unpublished 1932 version of the play and with Brecht, Eisler, Burri, and Steffin at the start of the 1938 Malik-Verlag version.

"Brecht was in Copenhagen to talk with the director Per Knutzon, a close friend of Berlau." This is the first and last time Knutzon, Berlau's teacher, the founder and now former leader of the Revolutionary Theater is mentioned. He had left the RT c. 1934. Berlau then took over with scenes from Brecht's *The Mother*. The proletarian actors — especially Dagmar Andreasen, Berlau's favorite, her Mother and Carrar — always claimed Knutzon to be the better director, compared with Berlau. (Andreasen has written several books.) (HCN)

F. says Berlau's production of *The Mother* was "remarkable...for its fine worker actors, who are still very much remembered in Denmark...." Of course these productions and workers were completely forgotten until the late 1960s when suddenly the left-wing movement dominated the universities with its interest in working-class culture of the 1930s and the actual political possibilities of Brecht's dramas. Very little is known about the Berlau production of a selection of scenes from *The Mother*. (HCN)

F. says that Berlau's work on *The Mother* for the Revolutionary Theater was important as the "virtual beginning" of a new way of recording theatrical history, because she made an extensive photographic record of the production. Not true; we have only a few snapshots. But Mogens Voltelen, who had a Leica, later took about 60 pictures of the Carrar guest version with Helene Weigel, at Borups Højskole, 18 February 1938, with the "Arbejdernes Teater" (Workers' Theater). According to Rudy Hassing that should be the correct caption to photo 62. Perhaps Voltelen's work was the inspiration when Berlau recorded Laughton's *Galileo*. Until then she had not done this kind of work, whatever F. may say. "From now until Brecht's death, she would photograph every production with which he and she were involved." (See comments on photo 62, 492-93.) (HCN)

320. F. mentions Brecht's "double dealings over the rights" to *The Threepenny Novel* but gives *no* details or evidence.

The unnamed poem for Steffin which F. cites is "Questions." Compare the translation by Naomi Replansky in *Poems 1913-1956*, 231. The rhymes in F.'s translation are the same.

321. F. speaks of Mari Hold, "with whom he [Brecht] had now lived...." A suggestive phrase for the fact that she had worked for him and his family.

Again F. mentions a volume for Carrefour. This is still the same book as on 295 (note on its contents), 311 and 316. *None* of its contents (contrary to F.'s claim) appears to be modelled on Kipling.

322. F. sees Brecht's invitation to Moscow in 1935 as a chance for him to resume relations with Carola Neher. F. further claims that in hopes of this, Brecht sent a poem and note to her via Bernhard Reich. This is an error. The fragmentary note was never sent, nor is it clear what poem is meant. See 159, 190, 193, 200.

324. F. again speaks of Brecht's efforts to resume his old affair with Carola Neher (see 322, etc.).

F. attributes to Carola Neher a "sexy rendition" (how does he know?) of a song entitled "Johnny, Take That Cigar out of Your Mouth" from *Happy End* — in other words, the "Surabaya Johnny" song.

F. incorrectly states that Arthur Pieck was Wilhelm Pieck's brother. He was *not* his brother, but his son.

325. F. states that Brecht began an affair with Maria Osten. Again he gives no evidence.

328. While in Moscow, Brecht had been dubbed "the great master." This title was given Brecht by an evidently ill-informed writer in the Moscow paper *Krasnaya Nov.*

Chapter 25

331. The title of Berlau's novel, *Videre*— (with a dash in the original), does not mean "Forward." The word is the same as the German "weiter" (further); there is a dimension of resignation in it too. (HCN)

"Berlau showed sections of the novel to Brecht, but his suggestions surprised her." Maybe she should have followed them, since it is a rather dull book. It was not recognized in Denmark when it appeared, and soon it was completely forgotten to this very day. Of course, F. has not read it either, but he is trying to build up Berlau as a gifted Danish novelist, which she was not. His reiterated "women's rights in a male-dominated society" is just a cliché and an expression of a faked solidarity. (HCN)

332. F. states that Bie wrote to Brecht and asked that he help pay for his son Frank's education as a dental assistant. No source is given for the request. (JKL)

"Her next novel..." She never wrote another novel. *Ethvert Dyr kan det* (published 1940) is a collection of short stories. (HCN)

F. says the young Danish journalist, Fredrik Martner (his pre-1945 name was Knud Rasmussen who often signed his articles "Crassus," a sophisticated abbreviation of this — it had nothing to do with ancient Rome, and was *not* a nickname), got so friendly with Brecht whom he interviewed in New York, that he "wrote some" of the Herr Keuner aphorisms, later collected in Brecht's collected works. Not true. Writing on purely Danish themes, Rasmussen sometimes borrowed the Keuner signature from Brecht. These polemic articles were printed in *Fyns Socialdemokrat*; they have nothing to do with Brecht's Keuner series and were hardly inspired by Brecht. Rasmussen/Martner was one of those people who liked to copy elements from Brecht, even at times his handwriting. As a Danish provincial journalist, Rasmussen was highly flattered to be accepted by the Brecht household, and Brecht seems to have treated him in a friendly and polite way. Comparing the Brecht-Rasmussen relationship with that of Stalin and his terrified followers is F. at his worst. (HCN)

F. claims that Brecht saw nothing odd in Stalin's mastery over those around him. Contrast this statement with Brecht's remarks about Ni-en (Stalin) in his *Me-Ti* aphorisms.

333. F. mentions a poem written by Steffin before Brecht left Denmark for the USA, but erroneously ascribed to Brecht and published in various editions of his works over the years. Steffin's authorship of this poem has been known to Brecht scholars for years. F. himself makes an error when he states that it is included in the newest Brecht edition of poems. It is *not* listed anywhere in this Berlin and Frankfurt edition (1993).

F. again notes that the Soviets called Brecht "the great master." *Not* "the Soviets," but an unnamed Soviet journalist (see 328).

F. says that Brecht did not publish the "Hold poem" during his lifetime (see 252). F. never tells us that only a minor part of Brecht's poems were published during his lifetime. And where should he have published this personal poem to his former maid, a matter of no public interest? In *Fyns Socialdemokrat*? (HCN)

335. F. states that Brecht attacked Hauptmann in a letter. He does not quote or date the letter in question and he gives no archival source number, though he complains in note 32 that this "enormously important interchange" is not published in the Brecht *Letters*.

337. F. dates Blitzstein's *The Cradle Will Rock* as 1936. Standard reference works give the date as 1937. (JKL)

338. F. cites a statement Brecht made to Lee Strasberg and attributes it (in note 43) to a "private source." The remarks quoted, however, are found in a very public source, Letter 287 in both German and English editions of the *Letters*. A pity that the same source could not have told us more about this contact between the two men.

339. F. mistakenly has Brecht depart from the USA for Denmark in January, 1936. Brecht's actual departure date was 5 February 1936.

Chapter 26

341. F. mentions a Berthold Fles. Who was he?

343. F. says Solveig Hansen "handled wood for the stoves and emptied the ashes." Rudy Hassing reports that this Solveig, who played with Steff and Barabara Brecht, was only five years old — the daughter of the Brechts' neighbors at Skovsbostrand, the Rasmussens, who lived opposite. Her father indeed helped in the

Brecht household, but his name was not "Lazar." F. confuses him with Maria Lazar, Helene Weigel's school friend from Vienna, who rented the ground floor of the Rasmussen's house, where she lived with her daughter.

F. states that Weigel's Jewish family in Austria could not readily obtain travel documents. Why should they have found these hard to obtain before the Anschluß of 1938? Not clear.

F. speaks of Caspar Neher's "intimate friend" Wagner-Regény and cites Högel, who, he claims, is frank about the closeness of the two. F. takes the relationship to be sexual. What Högel *says* is that the two men "had become friends, and in 1933 swore to link their fates and join in a creative working partnership for ten years." See 37, 43, 52, 56, 290.

344. F. misreports information obtained from a printed source. He writes that Gustav von Wangenheim and Neher's husband, Anatol Becker, denounced her to the NKVD. In *Die Säuberung* (1991), which F. cites as his reference, there is a report from the KGB archives of von Wangenheim's interrogation on 1 June 1936, when *he* denounced both Becker and Carola Neher as being anti-Soviet and sympathizing with Erich Wollenberg, a supposed Trotskyist. Becker had been arrested that April and was shot. She, too, would be shot some six years later.

346. F. cites a poem by Steffin and translates it in a way that makes it unrecognizable as a sonnet, which it is in the original. The poem is dated 8 July 1933, well before the events recounted in this chapter, which occur in 1936-37.

349. F. gives fragmentary quotations as though they were of whole cloth. He quotes seven lines from the section of *GW* 20 entitled "On the Moscow trials," which the editors appear to have put together from various notes made, partly for his own clarification, at the time. The passage starts with "Underlying the actions of the accused we have to bring out a political conception that is within their grasp, such as led them into contemptible crimes." Then it leaps some twenty lines of print, to pick up at "All the scum both domestic and foreign..." and on to the end of the quotation. There is *no* indication that those twenty lines have been omitted.

Chapter 27

350. F. mentions tens of thousands of rubles going to Feuchtwanger's bank account from royalties on a Russian edition of

200,000 copies of his report on the Moscow show trials. He gives a reference to David Pike's *German Writers in Soviet Exile* (179), but this (imprecise) detail is *not* given there. On the other hand, Pike cites the restriction of the Russian version of Feuchtwanger's book to one edition and its alleged removal from the libraries as evidence that it was not simply "a propaganda bonanza for Stalin," as F. calls it. Of such a double-edged effect F. says nothing.

351. By referring to a Steffin-Brecht version of *Riders to the Sea,* F. is begging the question, not yet having argued the case for Steffin's joint authorship (and indeed priority). But the scripts in the Brecht-Archive do not bear many marks of Brecht's involvement in this work which he termed "Aristotelian (empathy) drama."

352. F. speaks of the Brechts' neighbor, Mie Andersen. F. seems to be conflating Mrs. Andersen with her niece, Mie. (Both are mentioned in Brecht's letters to Weigel — Letters 341 and 342).
While arguing that Weigel was trying to leave Brecht and become financially independent, F. claims that Brecht gave her various tasks, among them to check *his* Swiss bank account. Letter 340 shows that they had a *joint* deposit account with the Crédit Suisse in Zurich. Letter 342 inquires about an account there in the name of a Mrs. Mary Fränkel (see 309).

353. F. mistranslates a key word in the final line of the poem "To Be Read Morning and Evening." The German "erschlagen" does not mean "to hit," but "to kill" or "to slay." F.'s rendering misses the point of the poem. A note in the Berlin and Frankfurt edition (1993) says that Brecht's covering letter has been lost, and that Berlau transcribed the poem from memory. There is also a notebook version with four more lines. (JW,JKL)

354. F. speaks of "Hauptmann's and Brecht's *The Measures Taken.*" Regarding F.'s argument for Hauptmann's primary authorship, see 220, 222, 245, 265. It is now being assumed to be fact. F. says that "writers who had previously been willing to work closely with the Comintern and their publisher Willi Münzenberg would be driven out or murdered by the NKVD." This is not clear. Whom does "their" refer to? Driven out of what? One person who was expelled from the KPD and is thought to have been murdered *was* Münzenberg himself.

355. F. now has Brecht calling himself the "great master." See 328, 333.

356. F. claims to be citing a "Dark Times" poem by Brecht, which he calls one of his most famous. Brecht wrote two poems with this title, but F. is citing yet a third, "An die Nachgeborenen," ("To those born later"). He mistranslates the last line, "Mit Nachsicht," to read "with pity." In German it means "with indulgence" or "with understanding."

359. F. has Stalin asking Koltsov if he had a gun with which he could commit suicide. As a source he cites a passage in David Pike. The reference there does *not* mention this incident.

360. F. claims that every available copy of Feuchtwanger's book on the Moscow show trials "were [sic] now collected and pulped." See 350 for a summary of Pike's slightly different account. F. asserts that three poems addressed to Steffin as the "Soldier of the Revolution" were obviously written by her, not Brecht, but he produces no convincing evidence beyond the text of the poem itself and gives a flawed reading of the poems in support of his claim. The fact that a copy of one of the poems (*not* the original manuscript) is dated in Steffin's hand means nothing. In her role as secretary/archivist, she did this with numerous poems and plays. And the statement in the "Standing Orders" poem that the soldier's rifle has a girl's name likewise offers no convincing proof; this practice was not uncommon among soldiers in war. To infer that this soldier is a woman on the apparent assumption that *Gewand* is used of women's clothing only is also flawed; the terms refers to any garment. And to conclude that it is Steffin's voice because these poems capture a sense of the muck of the trenches, which was unknown to a "Führer" who stayed behind the lines in his "Gemütliche Hauptquartier" (which has an incorrect gender in German), raises the question of how Steffin had come to know the "muck of the trenches." Had she been in a combat zone? For "Führer" see 79, 86, 248, 259. F. ignores the evidence that the accepted attribution might be correct: e.g., Brecht's dedication of the five "Songs" to "the good comrade MS," and the prevalence of Brecht's own handwriting and typing, to say nothing of the verdict of Brecht's various editors. (JW,JKL)

361. F. claims that Brecht ignored Steffin's firsthand account of the murder of the "Formalists." To this point there has been no reference to this account and no clue in the book's index.

F. lists an "additional abortion." (See 309.)

F. claims that Brecht "rarely" responded to letters. From this poor correspondent we have over 6,000 extant letters. (JKL)

Chapter 28

362. Attempting to show that Brecht was falsely pleading poverty, F. mentions Wieland Herzfelde paying him for a two-volume edition of his Collected Works that Herzfelde brought out in London in 1938. But for this Brecht received the total sum of £5! The Malik-Verlag had no money, and Brecht agreed with Herzfelde upon this symbolic payment. (HCN)

363. To reinforce his oft-repeated equation of Brecht with Hitler, F. uses a truncated and poorly translated citation from Benjamin. In Anya Bostock's standard translation (as against F.'s) from Benjamin's *Understanding Brecht*, it reads: "I felt a power being exercised over me which was equal in strength to the power of fascism — I mean a power that sprang from the depths of history no less deep than the power of the fascists." This, like the original German, *cannot* be interpreted as a comparison of Brecht with Hitler. Benjamin was an audience of *one*, and an exceptional one at that.

F. refers to "Brecht's (Steffin's) *Round Heads.*" Again, he presents *no* argument or evidence for this oblique attribution. See 319, 351, 354.

364. F. asks why Brecht refused to help defend his old friend Ottwalt. But he gives no source. Ottwalt had been arrested in the USSR in November 1936. The following February Brecht wrote to Brentano (Letter 305) that as soon as he had "authentic information" he could tell his Moscow colleagues that "you never received any pro-Hitler letter from Ottwalt..." This was not exactly a refusal, and it seems to have been Brentano who was asking to be defended.

F. refers to an unnamed poem Brecht had showed to Benjamin, which he claims praised Stalin. This is "The Peasant's Address to his Ox," which is subtitled "after an Egyptian peasant's song of 1400 BC." Brecht's remark to Benjamin may not have been entirely serious.

365. F. writes how, after Steffin's death, Brecht "ransacked" her translations of Nordahl Grieg's play, *The Defeat*. But Brecht did not use her translation for several more years. Grieg, the author, died in 1943. Writing to Piscator in 1948 to encourage him, too, to return to Berlin, Brecht suggested one or two plays Piscator might direct, "best of all, *The Defeat* by Nordahl Grieg." Then after some three weeks he told Weigel he had just read the play and found it "astonishingly bad." In Zurich over the next two months he wrote

a new version under the title *The Days of the Commune*, and Caspar Neher made many drawings. But all plans to stage it with the Berliner Ensemble fell through.

Citing unpublished papers by Paula Hanssen, F. further claims that six "Chinese Poems" allegedly translated and published by Brecht were in fact rendered into German by Hauptmann, but published under Brecht's name. Hanssen's research, which has since been published in the *Brecht Yearbook 19* (1994): 187-201, gives a somewhat different account. Hauptmann did in fact produce original German translations of the poems from Waley's English versions. But with the exception of one poem, which appeared under Brecht's name almost exactly as she translated it, he worked with her in adapting and rewriting her renderings, a process in which Hauptmann, according to Hanssen, played a "major role" because her work was the basis for the reworkings. Hanssen's evidence shows how Hauptmann's translations were subsumed in the reworkings before being published. She believes that Hauptmann is entitled to be considered coauthor with Brecht on all but one of the poems, which is almost solely hers, and she notes that most manuscripts bear both their names as co-translators/adaptors. Contrary to F.'s assertion, Hanssen never claims sole authorship of these poems for Hauptmann. F. claims elsewhere (225, note 10) that after Hauptmann stopped working and Brecht and his collaborators again tackled questions of these Chinese poems in translation in the late 1930s, Steffin would do most of the work on them, thus weakening his claim here for Hauptmann as sole author of the published versions. (JKL)

368. Brecht's reaction to a book of stories Berlau had written says nothing about "despising women," as F. states. His Letter 445 of mid-1942 tells her that it "might be acceptable for a women's magazine, if at all."

369. F. states that *Galileo* is constructed in the "prescribed Aristotelian manner." This might suggest that it observed the unities, which it does not.

F. cites Brecht's view of *Galileo* as "technically...a great step backwards." The reference given is to an unpublished item in the Brecht Archive, but this view is also stated in the *Journals* entry for 25 February 1939. It refers to the progress of Brecht's own dramaturgical technique, *not* to chronology, and goes on to contrast *Galileo* with two earlier fragments where he felt he had achieved "the highest technical standard."

370. F. speaks of Steffin's "intense work" on *Galileo*. He does not say what work this was other than secretarial. But a few lines later the authors have become "Steffin and Brecht." See 319, 351, 354, 363.

F. states that Brecht asked Berlau to arrange for him to meet Dr. Møller because he wanted to know more about the work of Niels Bohr. Brecht's meeting with Dr. Møller took place *before* Otto Hahn's and Fritz Strassmann's splitting of the atom in Berlin and Dr. Møller's participation in the Danish radio program. Some of this information F. had from me but, again, he does not use it correctly. (HCN)

371. Taking Brecht literally, F. states that during a visit by his brother Walter to Denmark, Brecht told him to join the Nazi party and work his way up in it "if possible to the rank of gauleiter within it." Brecht could be ironic, sarcastic, even nasty. (HCN)

372. F. cites George Grosz's view of Brecht's driving and claims it came from 1934. This verdict was retrospective (1955) and actually reads "Brecht was a brilliant driver, one of the fastest and least careful I've known." F. omits the phrase "a brilliant driver."

374. F. notes that after World War II, Hauptmann learned how Brecht had stolen her rights to the *Happy End* film project and sold them for 50,000 marks ($15,000). Is there any documentary evidence that Brecht actually got paid this amount? We need to know before accusing him of stealing. (JW,JKL)

F. accuses Brecht of lying when he writes to Weill saying, "They do not give us our royalties." Weill had been asking about money owed by Bloch-Erben, the Berlin agents, on performances in Stockholm, Paris, and elsewhere. It is possible that "they" referred specifically to these agents, not to Brecht's lawyer Domke who had got him some money from Paris. If so, then Brecht was not "lying" so much as lying low.

F. asserts that *The Good Person of Szechwan* revolves around a woman. But its title is *Der gute Mensch* — The good *person*. The difference is essential to the story. F. further says that in its 1941 version it was "written for America." What does this mean? Brecht wrote a version for American audiences in 1943, which F. nowhere discusses.

Chapter 29

377. F. claims that neither Steffin nor Berlau thought to put any reference to themselves in the Svendborg collection of Brecht poems. But Brecht did. It contained the three-part poem "Appell" which clearly refers to Steffin's illness, as well as two of the "Soldier of the Revolution" poems later dedicated to her (see 360). Berlau financed the book's separate publication (as a "Vorabdruck" from vol. IV of the Malik edition), and later regretted that she had not named herself as publisher. Not as a contributor, however.

F. cites from Brecht's "Dark Times" poem. As on 356, this is "To Those Born Later"; the translation now ends more accurately.

F. refers to *Galileo* as a "Steffin-Brecht" play, though earlier he gave no concrete evidence for her purported role in helping write it. Assertion now has become fact. And despite his claim that Brecht's career as a world-class dramatist died when Steffin did (407), he fails to note that the *Galileo* play he wrote in American exile and revised yet again in Germany is a new, essentially different play from the one written in Denmark while Steffin was still alive. F. himself views *Galileo* as one of Brecht's two greatest plays (369).

F. claims that problems arise with reading a poem like "Chased Out With Good Reason" if one reads them only in a biographical context, for, as he notes, they involve a good deal of sheer fantasy. Yet this is precisely the method he uses in interpreting many of the earlier poems. (JKL)

F. again states, with a snide turn, that Brecht had works "produced even at the elitist" Danish Royal Theater. As mentioned already (see 346), Brecht was produced for only two evenings at the Royal Theater (*The Seven Deadly Sins*) in November 1936. The Royal Theater had originally bought the rights for *Saint Joan of the Stockyards* with the leading lady Bodil Ipsen in mind, but did not dare to produce it. With the Weill ballet they chose the most harmless Brecht work they could lay their hands on. And again, before Brecht's Danish exile the Royal Theatre had *neither* produced *The Threepenny Opera* (Det ny Teater) *nor Drums in the Night* (Forsøgsscenen); in fact, nothing at all. (HCN)

F. has Berlau performing at the Royal Theater in Copenhagen, writing "feminist works," and directing "her Revolutionary Theater group in antifascist plays." The first point is correct — she stayed an actress at the Royal Theater. The two other points are not so certain. In F.'s book she writes and writes but apart from *Videre—*, *Ethvert Dyr kan det* and *Alle véd alt* (the two last titles in collaboration with Brecht), one should like to know *what* she wrote. She did not publish anything about the Spanish Civil War in papers or magazines; in fact, we only know a few articles from her hand, nothing of great importance. The Revolutionary Theater did not exist any more. She had directed the Danish *Señora Carrar's Rifles* with Dagmar Andreasen for Arbejdernes Teater (the Workers' Theatre), an amateur organization with Social Democratic roots, which she (Berlau) had revived together with others, among them the painter Else Alfelt, bringing some of her own actors from RT like Dagmar Andreasen into this enterprise. In November 1938 she directed two scenes from *Fear and Misery of the Third Reich* with actors from Arbejdernes Teater. Since then I have not come across any newspaper — Communist or Social Democratic — of Berlau's Antifascist work as a director or performer, and nobody remembers anything of that kind. The only witness is Berlau herself in her talks with Bunge and, of course, she might have read or recited this or that poem or monologue at a Party or union meeting, but it has never been verified in print or by other witnesses. (HCN)

379. F. states that Brecht was rewriting scenes from *Macbeth* and *Romeo and Juliet* for Naima Wifstrand. He was *not* rewriting so much as devising supplementary scenes.

F. attributes the unfinished fragment, *The True Life of Jakob Geherda* wholly to Steffin, though the typescripts show evidence of Brecht's handwriting and typing as well as hers. F. gives no grounds, and it is *not* true, as his note 12 says, that her name is not even mentioned in the *GW* edition. An editorial note about this work in the *GW* edition begins: "Brecht and his collaborator Margarete Steffin began writing [it] around 1935-36. They wanted to show...." The *GW* editor who wrote this was Elisabeth Hauptmann.

F. writes that Brecht only occasionally looked in on a production of two plays he had written with Berlau. The incorrect source F. gives, note 14, does not even refer to this. (JKL)

Berlau's adaptation of Flaubert, called *The Case of Madame Bovary*, exists. It combines the trial against Flaubert with quotations from the novel. It is completely unknown to the public in Sweden and Denmark. (HCN)

380. The earliest extant version of *Mother Courage*, as F. states, does indeed have large numbers of handwritten notes by both Steffin and Brecht (in F.'s order of naming them). More significantly, it is typed by Brecht, and (at the time of cataloguing) was the only complete script not to have come out of a duplicator. There is thus *no* objective evidence to support F.'s view that whereas Courage

herself was Brecht's creation (on the basis of Grimmelshausen and other models), Dumb Kattrin reflects the values of Steffin and Berlau.

383. F. makes another attribution without discussion or evidence when he speaks of "the Steffin-Brecht antiwar play, *The Trial of Lucullus.*" See 319, 351, 354, 363, 370.

384. F. claims that Brecht's *Journals* condone the Soviet invasion of Finland. The evidence in his *Journals* leads to an opposite conclusion. See entries speaking of the Soviets on 24 December 1940 ("are they really toying with the idea of conquering the world at Hitler's side?"); 1 January 1940 ("thoughtless opportunism") or 29 January 1940 ("the USSR could find itself...having to support the Nazi regime") as well as the earlier entries about the Russian invasion of Poland. None of this is taken into account by F.

Referring to Steffin's trip to Copenhagen for her appendectomy F. writes dramatically: "Despite the war and the constant threat of a Nazi occupation of Denmark...she made the sea journey south." According to Rudy Hassing this "sea journey" takes a maximum of 30 minutes by ferry. The rest of the journey was by train.

Chapter 30

387. F. again refers to Brecht as "the great master." See 328, 333, 355.

The Danish Communist party officials, F. states, told Berlau to leave because her work with the Revolutionary Theater "had been so public that she was in immediate danger of arrest or murder." Not true. From the German invasion of Denmark (9 April 1940) until Hitler's attack on the Soviet Union (22 June 1941), there were communists in the Danish parliament. Formal democracy still existed in Denmark. Nobody was arrested or murdered because he or she had been active antifascists. Nobody — Jew or communist — was persecuted during the period in question. In the Nazi propaganda of 1933-39 I have not seen Ruth Berlau's name once, but certainly those of Brecht, Per Knutzon and Lulu Ziegler. The story about her apartment having been "smashed by Nazis," told to Bunge, repeated by F., has never been confirmed. Which Nazis? The Wehrmacht? The SS? Danish Nazis? Danish history at that time cannot be compared to that of any other country in Europe. (HCN)

388. F. speaks of Steffin's involvement on *The Good Person of Szechwan* as absorbing most of her energy. It is clear that Brecht kept her continually at work analyzing and revising the play but this does not mean she wrote it. The evidence is that the creative force was Brecht's. Both she and Berlau would be credited as collaborators.

389. F. states that in 1932 the NKVD had seized Brecht's papers. He gives no evidence for this, nor is it mentioned earlier in the book.

Late in *The Good Person of Szechwan*, according to F., it is revealed that Shui Ta is really Shen Te in disguise. "Revealed" to the characters, that is. The audience has known all along.

Now the Walter Brecht Gauleiter episode has become a serious fact, not a typical Brecht joke or provocation. (HCN)

391. F. has Wuolijoki telling Brecht the story of Puntila. It may not have been this oral transmission that triggered Brecht's play. Wuolijoki had written a story where the landlord was called Punttila (with two t's); then it became an unfinished play called "The Sawdust Princess." Wuolijoki dictated a version of this to Steffin in German, after which the adaptation process started.

F. states Berlau could not return to her home in Denmark because she would be arrested "on sight" by the Nazis. Of course she could return home. Formally, Finland, Sweden, and Denmark were all still neutral countries. The only authority that could arrest people in Copenhagen was the Danish Police. Nobody would arrest Berlau "on sight" because her face was not known. (HCN)

393. F. misreads and mistranslates Brecht's *Journals* entry of 5 November 1940, which reads: "heute wählt amerika." F.'s rendering reads: "today chose america," which he interprets as Brecht's decision finally to go to America. The accurate rendering about an event on the first Tuesday in November when the American electorate chose Roosevelt for a third term is "today America goes to the polls."

394. F. maintains that it was Hauptmann who got H.R. Hays involved in doing Brecht translations. By his own account, Hays began translating Brecht's works — which he learned about through his acquaintance with Hanns Eisler — long before he ever met Hauptmann. (JKL)

395. In the context of work on *The Resistible Rise of Arturo Ui*, F. cites Heiner Müller as saying that "there is an extraordinary affinity" between Brecht and Hitler. See F.'s persistent build-up of Brecht as a "Führer" (79, 86, 248, 289, 360).

A statement by Steffin in Brecht's *Journals* reads: "und der schwankende boden unter mir öffnet sich." F. mistranslates it to read: "The swaying bottom opens under me." A more accurate rendering might be "and the quaking ground beneath me opens."

396. F. reports that Brecht asked the Soviets to pay for past work done, especially the Nexø translations. He was doing this on behalf of Steffin, since they were overwhelmingly hers.

F. claims that Brecht asked William Dieterle and Luise Rainer to provide a financial guarantee for Steffin so she could obtain a tourist visa. F. gives no documentation to support this statement. Documents confirm that Dieterle did in fact sponsor Brecht, but there appears to be no record of Brecht's approaching Rainer on this matter. (JKL)

Chapter 31

399. As Koltsov's assistant in 1935, Apletin is first described by F. as "a man of considerable power in the hierarchy" (325). Now he is a "second-level bureaucrat."

401. Again F. erroneously states that Arthur Pieck is the brother of Wilhelm Pieck, instead of his son (see 324). And Wilhelm Pieck was *not*, as F. states here, the "future premier" of the GDR, but its President, as he correctly states later. (JW,JKL)

In support of a claim which Brecht allegedly made years later, viz. that Apletin offered to employ him in the Moscow Art Theater, F. cites Lyon. In the source cited, Lyon says nothing about this offer coming from Apletin. (JW,JKL)

403. F. reports that Weigel and Brecht took copies of all the plays Steffin had worked on and controlled access to them "for decades." Did they have them copied, or simply take what appeared to be Brecht's scripts? Did she object? Was F. denied access? This account is not clear.

In note 29, F. claims that Marta Feuchtwanger told him how Brecht received 18,000 rubles from her husband's account while in Moscow. She also told Lyon the same story, but it has never been documented from any other source. By contrast, Weigel, who was with Brecht and who allegedly received an expensive coat from this money, claimed she knew nothing about receiving such a sum. Unless this can be documented from at least one more source, the story remains hearsay. (JKL)

405. F. reports that, according to Berlau, Brecht recovered very quickly from the loss of Steffin. The question is whether the highly emotional Berlau is reliable enough to be quoted as an authoritative source on this. Journal entries Brecht wrote after this suggest he did not recover quickly at all.

406. F. repeats the claim that Brecht did not try to help Ottwalt. If this refers to the suggestion on 364, it is untenable.

407. F. claims that with Steffin's death, the career of Brecht the world-class dramatist died." Some "world-class" plays still to come in which Steffin had no hand included *The Caucasian Chalk Circle*, the 1943 *The Good Person of Szechwan*, the American *Galileo*, and *Antigone*. Arguably, *Schweyk*, *The Visions of Simone Machard*, and *The Days of the Commune* were in the second rank.

Chapter 32

413. Mari Barbara. See 252, 259, 287, 291, 300.
F. notes that when Brecht attended his first Hollywood cocktail party, he was asked to spell his name. No source is given. (JKL)

415. Noting that Brecht quickly resumed his polygynous sex life in the USA, F. implies an affair by saying that Brecht took "a particular interest" in Valeska Gert. He gives no evidence or documentation for any contact, much less an affair. (JKL)
F. states that Brecht's thoughts turned to times when much of the writing had been done by Steffin. Certainly much of the typing and secretarial assistance was by her, but this is not the same as the starting of new plays or film projects. That Brecht felt paralyzed by her loss is clear from the *Journals*.
Again F. cites the use of the word "Führer," but this time — since it refers to Steffin — he translates it as "leader" in the sense of a guide. See 79, 86, 248, 249, 360, 395.

416. F. speaks of Brecht's often "stylized" *Journals*. It is not clear what this epithet means. He refers to a fairly short but vivid entry, including the image: "A giant nation was rising, still half-asleep, to go to war."

Note 13 on this page, referring to the arrest of a few Nazi sympathizers in the US after the outbreak of World War II is an incorrect reference. The source cited (Brecht's *Journals*), says nothing about the claim made.

417. F. speaks, without being specific, of the somewhat nebulous role Ruth Berlau played in the creation of *The Visions of Simone Machard*. But there is no manuscript evidence of her contribution. Was it Brecht's wish to see her provided for that caused her to be written in for a rather surprising 20% of the royalties? There is no mention of her or of the play in Marta Feuchtwanger's memoirs, which end just before then.

418. F. incorrectly calls the film actress Lupe Velez by the nickname "The Mexican bombshell." She was featured by Hollywood publicists as "The Mexican spitfire." (JKL)

F. claims that Neher was designing almost thirty productions a year. My count in *Caspar Neher, Brecht's Designer* (London 1986) was fourteen productions in 1941, eight in 1942, six in 1943, five in 1944 till the German theaters were closed: totalling thirty-three over four years.

F. calls Herbert Ihering "head of one of the crown jewels of the Third Reich." See 290 for his appointment as an advisor to the Burgtheater. Brecht read in a newspaper that he had become "Intendant" in 1942, but this seems doubtful.

F. talks of the "newest films of Pabst, Riefenstahl, and Ernst Salomon." After Riefenstahl's two Olympic films of 1938 she had no new film in the cinema until 1954 (*Tiefland*). Pabst had only two films released during the Third Reich. Ernst von Salomon has nothing important to do with Brecht. The only person of importance to the big German audience did not produce any films at all: Pabst never re-established his fame from the Weimar republic, and von Salomon was hardly known to anyone and had no top billing. Only the very relevant Erich Engel made a lot of film comedies, sometimes two in one year, but is not mentioned by F. (HCN)

419. F.'s claim that by January 1942, mass killings were taking place at "Auschwitz, Dachau, Mauthausen, Bergen-Belsen, Buchenwald, Theresienstadt, and in Poland" suggests, erroneously, that Auschwitz was *not* in Poland. And at this point, all but Auschwitz were concentration camps and had not been set up as death camps, which had the specific goal of exterminating as quickly as possible all deportees who arrived there, not holding them prisoner. (JKL)

421. F. mentions "The List of the Lost." "Die Verlustliste" is a poem about those whose loss Brecht feels most: a piece of paper (as its fourth line says) bearing "the names of those/Who are no longer around me." Steffin and Benjamin are followed by Karl Koch (the film-maker, an assistant to Pabst) and Caspar Neher. These, he says, "were taken away by death." (He was wrong, in that both Koch and Neher survived the war.) The poem F. cites as having been written on the death of his mother (*GW* 8: 79) says nothing about her abandoning him, as F. claims, only about her departure ("Abschied") from the world. The unfinished poem where he speaks of himself dying "like a dog" has an entirely different tone. F. gives no reference, but it is in the notes to the *Poems 1913-1956* (528).

"Bébé." See 56, 73, 82, 97-99, 263.

422. After Berlau left for New York City, F. states that Brecht now felt abandoned. Letter 446 and the entry in the *Journals* for 20 June 1942 could be read as suggesting that he at first felt relieved. F. does not mention either of them.

423. Clearly the two phrases in the unidentified poem cited are from "And the dark times now continue," *GW* 10: 862. This *is* the poem originally called "Ruth," and it is given under this title in the Berlin and Frankfurt edition. There is no explanation of the change, and no indication who made it. The smooth (*glatt*) forehead is hers, *not* Brecht's, as F. claims.

Chapter 33

425. F. incorrectly reports that Stefan Brecht by this time, i.e., 1943, had left to study philosophy at Harvard. Stefan at this time was a student at UCLA. He did not go to Harvard until 1946. (JKL)

Again, Mari Barbara, as on 252, 259, 287, 291, 300, 413.

426. Can F. give us more information about Gerhart Eisler's alleged short-wave radio hookup? It is not clear whether this was for broadcasting or for secret communication. Or both. See 430 note 20.

F. claims Eisler's music for the film *Hangmen Also Die* received an Academy Award in 1944. This is incorrect. It was nominated but did not receive an Oscar.

F. states that Brecht told Berlau he earned only $250 on the *Hangmen* film but gives no source. (JKL)

427. F. inaccurately states that Brecht's move to a new house increased his monthly rent. Since Brecht bought the home into which he moved, he no longer paid rent, though his monthly payments were more than his previous rent. (JKL)

Mari Barbara. See 425. This makes eight instances so far where F. uses the first name to reinforce his unsupported suggestion that she was the daughter of Mari Hold.

429. F. calls Brecht's work in preparing antifascist broadcasts for the OWI a propaganda failure. This and his citation from Houseman suggest that the broadcasts were not sent. Archival material from the OWI makes it clear that at least one program Brecht helped prepare was broadcast by OWI. (JKL)

H. R. Hays was not exactly a "little-known poet" in America, as F. states. He had written *A Song about America* (theme song, "Sweet Liberty Land") for the American Communist Party in 1938, followed by the "living newspaper play" *Medicine Show,* which Joseph Losey directed in New York in 1940. Both had music by Eisler. And he was *not* "given" to Brecht as a partner to work on *The Duchess of Malfi,* a word which suggests that a third party arranged it. It seems that Brecht, whose works Hays had already been translating, approached Hays and asked him if he would collaborate. (JW,JKL)

430. F. states that Brecht let H. R. Hays know he was no longer needed on the *Malfi* project. By Hays's own account, he resigned on learning that Auden had been brought in. Much of the dramaturgical work had by then been done by him with Brecht. (JKL)

F. notes that Steffin's name does not appear in Hays's English translation of *The Trial of Lucullus.* This was surely due in part to Hays and New Directions, the publishers, who may well have been unaware of her involvement. In *Fear and Misery of the Third Reich* the same would have been true of Eric Bentley, New Directions again, and (for England) Gollancz. In the *GW* edition many years later under Hauptmann's editorship, Steffin was named as the sole collaborator on both plays.

F. writes of Piscator and his attempt to interest Brecht in a musical play for a pro-Jewish cause. The letter cited by F. actually speaks of a "revue" which Piscator had asked Brecht to write, and he complains that Brecht had not telephoned about it. Brecht says nothing about having refused. See 295 for a rather similar suggestion.

431. F. has Brecht and Berlau planning a *Schweyk* adaptation, followed seventeen lines later by Brecht and Berlau returning to *The Good Person of Szechwan*. The suggestion is of a partnership, but once again it is unsupported. Compare other question-begging attributions on 319, 351, 354, 363, 370, 383 and 417.

433. F.'s account of Brecht's *Journals* entry for 27 May 1943 is confusing and inaccurate. Brecht told his son Stefan about the *Schweyk* idea the day *after* he arrived back in Los Angeles from New York, having reread "the old *Schweyk*" on the train. F. erroneously situates their conversation in Chicago, where he claims that Brecht stopped briefly to visit Stefan, who was in military training. Two years after this *Journals* entry (in 1945) Stefan did in fact enter the U.S. army and ended up in Chicago, where Brecht visited him. In 1943, however, Stefan was not in the army and not in Chicago, but a student at UCLA. He lived in Los Angeles and had this conversation with his father there. When Stefan criticizes Schweyk's attitude (as in the entry), F. says Brecht was unwilling to change "his and Berlau's conception." In Brecht's immediately preceding *Journals* entry it is not Berlau, but he and Weill of whom he says "we plan a *Schweyk*." F. fails to provide any evidence for Berlau's purported role in creating *Schweyk*. (JW,JKL)

F. also states incorrectly that the same *Journals* entry contains a "dream of millions of Schweyks busily undermining Hitler." The entry says nothing about this. F. is confusing events in the actual *Schweyk* play with Brecht's brief description of the play given in the *Journals* entry. (JW,JKL)

Chapter 34

436. F. states that Brecht put aside his hostility toward Thomas Mann and urged him to attend a meeting at the Viertel home. He gives no evidence, and since the two were barely on speaking terms, this seems unlikely. Other participants claim that it was Salka Viertel who invited Mann. (JKL)

437. It seems unlikely that Hans Bendix, a Franco sympathizer, according to F., would have fired Ruth Berlau from the Office of War Information on account of her not being on the "right side" in Spain — i.e., the fascist one. Bendix was a famous Danish artist, a social democrat, and already in 1933 the editor of a magazine banned by the Danish government after three issues for its attacks on the Third Reich, and Bendix's own aggressive drawings of Hitler and Goebbels (HCN)

438. F. writes that Berlau helped Brecht with problems of character or scenes in *Schweyk*, but he makes no attempt to analyze or substantiate this.

F. further observes that when *Schweyk* was published, Brecht gave Berlau no acknowledgement. Perhaps this was because it was first published in 1957, the year after his death.

Though F. states that Brecht earned a "substantial sum" for writing an unidentified film script with Lorre, he gives no amount, nor does he document his assertion. What is the source?

F. cites Brecht as instructing Berlau to look after his "business interests." What Brecht said in Letter 472 (as referred to by F.) was to look after "meine Sachen," "my affairs," including theatrical matters — e.g., of casting, production, and translation that were not strictly financial.

440. "Bébé." See 56, 73, 82, 97-99, 263, 421.

F. refers to the "latest update" of the "*Good Woman of Setzuan.*" Is this the important 1943 "Santa Monica version"? Not clear.

441. F. describes how Brecht "attacked Isherwood's motives." This is *not* what the relevant *Journals* entry of 20 September 1943, says to which F. refers in note 17. It reads: "the conversation turned to english upper-class writers, himself, AUDEN, HUXLEY." Viertel (the "Bergmann" of Isherwood's *Prater Violet)* and Brecht tell him that India has "infected you" — the "you" (*euch*) is plural. The "he" who Brecht says has been "bought" is clearly Huxley, *not* Isherwood himself, as F. claims.

442. F. refers to a pledge Brecht allegedly made to Apletin in Moscow. See 399, 401.

445. Contrary to F.'s statement, *The Caucasian Chalk Circle* was not just a "new title," but a new start on a project which is traceable back through Klabund's *Kreidekreis* to the medieval Chinese story which Klabund dramatized. F. gives no evidence for his claim that Brecht started writing the play with Steffin and Wuolijoki in Finland. He did write a short story, "The Augsburg Chalk Circle," in Sweden in 1940, but F. offers no proof of Steffin's alleged role in the play, and available evidence suggests that work on it did not begin until several years after her death. In the 1957 *Stücke* edition, Ruth Berlau is named as the sole collaborator. F.'s claim that Brecht and Berlau had begun work on it together *before* they approached Luise Rainer is also unsubstantiated and contradicts Rainer's story that

Brecht began it *after* he spoke with her; then she had agreed to arrange a Broadway production and perform in it. (JW,JKL)

F. mistakenly claims that Azdak sexually "harrasses" (sic) a woman who had brought a charge of sexual harassment before him. It is not the girl, Ludovica, but her elderly father-in-law who brings the case, which is one not of "harassment," but of rape. And Azdak concludes it by finding that the seductive Ludovica has committed the rape and then inviting her to "come with me to the stable so that the Court may investigate the scene of the crime," which is not exactly harassment either.

446. F. mistakenly claims that the prologue and epilogue of *The Caucasian Chalk Circle* were later additions to the play. Manuscripts verify that they were written early on and existed as part of the play from the outset. (JKL)

"Bébé." See 56, 73, 82, 97-99, 263, 421, 440.

After intimating that Brecht had a sexual relationship with Elisabeth Bergner, F. speaks of "another woman" entering the picture (Naomi Replansky). Hardly; she is twice briefly mentioned, and F. presents nothing more than innuendo to support his intimations.

447. F. notes that Feuchtwanger would have to "kick back" half the proceeds on *The Visions of Simone Machard* to Brecht. Is there any evidence that Feuchtwanger's sharing the money was not a voluntary act of generosity? Marta Feuchtwanger reported it this way to James Lyon. (JW,JKL)

449. F. reports that beginning in June 1944, Berlau and Brecht (in that order) worked daily on *The Caucasian Chalk Circle*. Yet in his *Journals* for 6 June 1944, Brecht reports he had "finished [the play] yesterday and sent it to Luise Rainer." F., however, says that Brecht's *Journals* give 1 September 1944 as the date of completion. The entry for that day actually reads "write a new version of the prologue and of the (optional) epilogue."

Chapter 35

451. F. refers to the "plays that Berlau had written with Brecht." See 417, 431, 438, 449 for the development of this unsubstantiated assumption.

452. Again, the short-story collection, *Every Animal Can Do It*, turns into a novel. (HCN)

454. Again F. calls Margarete Steffin "the coauthor" of *The Private Life of the Master Race* (the New York title of *Fear and Misery of the Third Reich*). Since he cannot cite any attempt to analyze the authorship of the thirty or so scenes, the attribution of any share of it to Steffin has to be hypothetical.

457. F. recalls a pledge Brecht gave to Knorin and Apletin. For Apletin see 442. References to Brecht's meeting with Knorin in 1935 do not mention any "pledge."

458. Accusingly F. notes that for the young Brecht the world was female and filthy. In German the word for world (*Welt)* is in fact feminine, and the metaphor of the world as female is not limited to Brecht or German literature. (JKL)

F. speaks of the "brilliant use of language" in a 1945 poem about Germany. This is not reflected in F.'s stilted translation.

459. F. mistakenly claims that in 1945 Brecht was negotiating with Wieland Herzfelde's "Malik Press." This press no longer existed. It came to an end with the publication of Brecht's *Svendborg Poems* in 1939. Herzfelde's New York enterprise, the Aurora Verlag, lasted from 1945 to 1947. It had no successor.

461. F. quotes Leopold Lindtberg (the director of the 1941 Zurich *Mother Courage*) who reported that Brecht said, "The Jews have now had their six million deaths, now they should give [us] some peace." F. even makes the first part of the sentence his chapter heading and presents it as if it reflected Brecht's own sentiments. In fact, the context makes it clear that Brecht was speaking about the attitude of the Allies and the peoples of the occupied territories towards the thousands of Jews recently liberated from the camps. Nobody wanted them, they were seen as a nuisance, and they were not even given permission to go to Palestine. F. quotes only Brecht's (bitterly ironic) comment and ignores the rest of the conversation with Lindtberg.

461-62. Again F. refers to "the Steffin-Brecht *Private Life of the Master Race*." See 454.

In writing of Brecht's response to Ruth Berlau's infidelity, F. has him railing in his *Journals* about "deceptions." He mistranslates the word "Enttäuschungen" in the *Journals*, which means "disappointments," not "deceptions."

466. F. accuses Brecht of making no "mention of Steffin or provision for her heirs" in a business letter he writes to Suhrkamp. Steffin had no formal rights; she had made no claim to share the authorship of any Brecht work; and F. has still *not* shown that she really has one. It remains a generous assumption.

Chapter 36

467. F. speaks of how Brecht was "pushing Auden to finish up a translation of *The Caucasian Chalk Circle*." The dialogue was being translated by Auden's friends, the Sterns. Auden was responsible only for the verse.

Why, as F. claims, was Auden "at the end of his tether?" Not clear.

470. F. claims Brecht used Berlau's New York apartment for assignations with wives of various émigrés and other young women. Who? And what are his sources? The only example he gives is of one woman who rejected his advances. (JKL)

472. F. speaks of the Hauptmann/Bentley English edition of Brecht's plays, which was "about to appear." It never did. What materialized was Bentley's edition of *Seven Plays* in 1960.

Mari Barbara. See 252, 259, 287, 291, 300, 413, 425, 427.

F. gives no source for his statement that "Brecht told Piscator the Soviets had approached him" to take over the old Schiffbauerdamm Theater. It is not in the Brecht *Letters*. But in December, 1946 he told Caspar Neher (Letter 532) in confidence that he had "offers from Berlin to use the Theater am Schiffbauerdamm for certain things." Is this F.'s source?

474. F. states that Brecht put Rhoda Riker and Naomi Replansky on the payroll for the *Galileo* production. Source? Both parties told Lyon of Brecht's attempts to get money out of Laughton for their assistance with the play because Brecht had failed to get them on the payroll. (JKL)

Chapter 37

478. F. states that Brecht appeared at a rally for the Hollywood Nineteen in the Shrine Auditorium on 15 October 1948. Though his name appeared on the program, Brecht (according to statements by two members of the Hollywood Ten and two of their attorneys) did *not* attend. (JKL)

481. F. refers to Mr. Baumgardt, Brecht's interpreter. This was David Baumgardt, a friend of the poet Georg Heym in pre-1914 Berlin.

482. Before HUAC, F. claims that Brecht "knowingly or un-knowingly" switches to the description of "a quite different play of the same period, *He Who Says Yes*" (see 245). An early (1931) sketch for *The Measures Taken* was in fact marked as deriving from *Der Jasager* (1930), and at one time they were to have been staged one after the other to make a double bill.

"Ost und West" was not a Soviet but a German bi-zonal maga-zine, edited by Alfred Kantorowicz. (HCN)

483-84. F. asserts that Brecht's cooperative answers before HUAC "strengthened the hand of his inquisitors," just as his failure to confront the Nazis directly, or to support the Jewish cause, or to defend Bukharin and Tretyakov made him a tacit accomplice who "helped turn the tide toward Hitler, Stalin, and McCarthy." Repeat-edly in his writings Brecht did confront the Nazis, though F. ignores or downplays this; and though indifferent to Zionism, his record of support for Jewish friends was known.

F. cites Lester Cole as claiming that Brecht was in tears as he rode back to the hotel with him in the same taxi. Brecht, he claims, apologized for taking a different position, thereby betraying the other witnesses who had appeared before HUAC. Lyon, whose account F. terms "useful," gives a rather different version based on interviews with three of the Hollywood Ten and two of their attorneys. Not only had the eighteen agreed in advance that Brecht was free to differ in his testimony; according to their attorneys, they also knew and accepted that Brecht would answer the Committee's questions because he was the only non-citizen among them. Lyon further cites statements from both Lawson and Trumbo who approved Brecht's "outsmarting of the Committee." To speak of this as "betrayal" seriously distorts the testimony of at least five partici-pants. To assess the reliability of Cole's account, one needs to ask how many examples are known of Brecht apologizing or Brecht in tears? (JW,JKL)

Hanns Eisler also answered the same question: "I am not now a member of the Communist party." (HCN)

Again Brecht's bad joke about his brother taken literally. (HCN)

485. F. accusingly speaks of Brecht's "self-exculpating" version of his hearing before HUAC because his *Journals* stated that they were "very satisfied" with his testimony. Statements by three of the

Hollywood Ten and two of their attorneys confirm Brecht's view. See Lyon, *Brecht in America*, 335. (JKL)

Chapter 38

487. F. identifies Anna Seghers only as an acquaintance from prewar days. She was an outstanding communist novelist, whose *The Seventh Cross* (1942) was extremely successful in the USA, both as book and as film. Like Brecht, she would settle in East Germany. Her Hungarian husband had taught at the pre-1933 MASch in Berlin.

F. incorrectly states that Berlau "supervised" the opening of *Galileo* in New York with Laughton. In fact, Laughton and Losey prevented her from having any involvement except to take photos and film the production. Even these activities annoyed Laughton, who could not stand her. (JKL)

488. F. mentions Neher, "who had exchanged so many loving letters" with Brecht thirty years before. Affectionate, certainly, but F.'s implication is that they were homoerotic. Neher's Zurich drawings for *Puntila*, *The Days of the Commune*, and the *Ares's Chariot* project are evidence of his sense of relief and renewal, which would first come to a head in the two friends' joint production of *Antigone*.

489. Mari Barbara. See 252, 259, 287, 291, 300, 413, 425, 427, 472.

F. states that Berlau faced "anger on the right and left" for Brecht's behavior before HUAC. Examples? Sources? (JKL)

490. F. notes that for Caspar Neher, the *Antigone* production "was small potatoes." Financially perhaps. But it was a landmark in the Brechts' return and a link (through Hans Curjel) with the avant-garde opera of the 1920s.

492. F.'s note that Brecht wrote to Otto Katz implies that this pertained to his settling in Czechoslovakia. It did not, but only to passing through the country.

Pertaining to F.'s statement about the rights of Steffin's heirs, see 466.

The "Swiss" actor Leonard Steckel, whom F. mentions, was born in Hungary. He had been in Piscator's first company in Berlin in 1927-28.

Austria, says F. "had just gained a large measure of independence from the East and the West." What does that mean? Austria was divided into an American, a British, a French, and a Soviet zone, just like Germany and stayed so until the mid-fifties.

Brecht's daughter, Hanne Hiob, F. states, was in a Nazi film. Klaus Völker pointed out that the film in question was based on the Paul Lincke operetta, *Frau Luna*, directed by Hiob's step-father, Theo Lingen, and so was no Nazi film. (HCN)

492-93. Of photo 62 F. asks us to note "this scene of a woman viewing her dead son, a clear anticipation of the use of the same image in *Mother Courage...*" How do you look into the face of someone lying on the floor when you are standing yourself? F. does not ask this simple question and so the Berlau myth as a director rises from this tableau-like situation in the Copenhagen *Señora Carrar's Rifles* (see 319). (HCN) According to Rudy Hassing many of the photographs between these pages are wrongly credited.

493. F. writes that Brecht lied to Bentley when he claimed that he was not entitled to plead the first or fifth amendments before HUAC. It is true that attorneys for the Hollywood Nineteen informed him of his constitutional rights as an alien, and that he could have invoked the first amendment as ten of the nineteen did (the fifth amendment was never raised in these hearings). But Brecht, with his European background, was skeptical. It was probably this skepticism, not duplicity, which prompted his statement to Bentley. (JW,JKL)

F. mentions Paul Dessau, "who had now left Hauptmann for Brecht." Is this meant to sound odd?

494. In mentioning "the many brilliant works that Brecht & Co. had completed," F. omits *The Round Heads and the Pointed Heads*, *Arturo Ui*, *Schweyk*, *The Visions of Simone Machard* and *The Good Person of Szechwan*.

F. speaks of the phrase "playing one segment against another" as one of Brecht's old theatrical ideas. Does this perhaps mean *Trennung der Elemente* ("separation of the elements"), as in his notes to *Mahagonny*?

495. F. cites Bentley as saying that for Brecht, "the heart of drama is plot." Is this not a misunderstanding of Brecht's term *Fabel*, the fabula or story, which in *Brecht on Theater* ("Organum," section 12) is translated as "narrative"? Thus "narrative is the soul of drama."

496. F. cites a passage from Brecht's *Journals* incorrectly by translating "monuments to bourgeois culture in this decade." The original reads *dieser Jahrzehnte,* a plural meaning "in these decades." Rorrison's translation of the *Journals* renders this phrase as "monuments of bourgeois culture in our time."

497. F. describes how Brecht, rather than Piscator, was invited to Berlin because Piscator had become a *persona non grata.* The correspondence, however, suggests that both men might have gone to Berlin, with Wolf and Ihering as their sponsors.

Cultural power in the Eastern zone of Germany was not, as F. states, solely in the hands of Lukács, Kurella, and Ulbricht. To these should be added Erpenbeck, Becher, and Abusch.

499. Mari Barbara. See 252, 259, 287, 291, 300, 413, 425, 427, 472, 489.

Chapter 39

501. F. misquotes a *Journals* entry by Brecht on distributing rations according to "a strictly hierarchical scheme." The entry to which F. refers does not say this, but that "the Russian view was that unequal rations improved production."

F. refers to a "Cultural Relations Club." This is an unfamiliar term for the Kulturbund, then operating in both halves of Berlin. Becher was its president until 1947.

503. F. mentions two actors in his production of *Mother Courage* whom one critic had labeled "Hitler's most spoiled children." The reference given in Mittenzwei's biography attributes this view to the journalist Curt Riess. F. does not mention that Mittenzwei himself disagreed with this characterization.

F. speaks of Gerda Müller, a "lover from prewar days." Müller, a leading Expressionist actress, had been a friend of the young Bronnen. She married the conductor Hermann Scherchen. This is the first reference to her as one of Brecht's lovers.

F. states that Erich "Engel had worked in the German theater throughout the Third Reich." But only under handicaps. Heinz Hilpert, for instance, was not allowed to make him head of productions at the Deutsches Theater; Engel and Neher were only able to collaborate on one play there per year. It was easier for him to work in the cinema.

F. refers to Berlau as "one of the directors" of *Mother Courage,* "now rehearsing segments of the play, just as she had done in

Scandinavia." But where is the evidence she had done that there for Brecht, and in German? Such a role is not indicated in the literature, not even in the volume *Theaterarbeit*, which she helped to compile.

507. F.'s citation about "a position-seeking artist who overrated himself" gives an incorrect reference for this remark. F. states that "Brecht and Harich seemed to prevail" in their dispute with East German authorities over formalism, decadence, and cosmopolitanism. Curious, since Harich, according to Pike, "otherwise found formalism, decadence and cosmopolitanism singularly disgusting."

508. F. claims that "Hauptmann would get small fees from Suhrkamp for her work." How small?

Chapter 40

509. F. again notes that Hauptmann agreed to edit Brecht's work for a "small salary." How small?

510. F. accuses Brecht of excluding Steffin from any credit for her role in shaping *The Days of the Commune* (see 365). Steffin was the translator; it is not clear what she added to the play to justify joint credit. What Brecht claimed to be writing was a "counter-play."

F. claims that *The Days of the Commune* was dropped because of Bentley's reservations or questions about the copyright. He says nothing of a third reason, the lack of support from the Party and its Repertoire Commission.

511. Mari Barbara (three times). See 499 for previous appearances, making twelve times so far. Here, however, F. quotes a use of the name by Barbara Brecht herself, reminding us of her "second mother," Brecht's old servant Mari Hold, i.e., to refresh our memory about her possible origins.

F. says that Barbara Brecht was not at home in English or German. From her attendance at junior high and high school in America, from numerous letters she wrote (in English) to Ferdinand Reyher, and from a number of personal conversations Lyon conducted with her in English, Lyon has come to the opposite conclusion. Her English is excellent. (JKL)

512. F. gives an incorrect title to a poem ("Driving through the Rubble"). The poem is "Ein neues Haus" ("A New House"). Besides a grammatical error ("give" is plural, not singular), he also mistrans-

lates the quoted passage. The poet's privileges gave *him* the house, *not* vice versa as F. writes.

513. F. refers to the model books which Berlau helped produce. There seem to have been three categories: first, the published albums (starting with *Antigone*, then *Señora Carrar's Rifles, Galileo,* etc.); then secondly, the bigger pasted-up albums kept for loan to producers and directors; and finally the volume *Theaterarbeit*, with many photographs, drawings, essays, and descriptions by various hands, covering the first six productions of the Berliner Ensemble. Which of these appeared "in a constant stream" is not clear.

Based on Willett's and Lyon's conversations with Hauptmann, F.'s claim that her commitment at this point was "not to Brecht" but to the success of communism, is surely untrue. (JW,JKL)

514. In his reference to Hauptmann as "sole author" of Brecht's Chinese Poems, F. does *not* mention Arthur Waley, nor Po Chü-yi and the other Chinese poets (cf. 225, 365).

515. Regarding Brecht's alleged shabby treatment of the Steffin family, F. seems to dismiss or ignore certain evidence. He says nothing of the letter supposedly written by Brecht from Vladivostok after Steffin's death, to which he might have had access. Brecht's long letter to Steffin's sister (no. 541) from Santa Monica spoke of another letter to a Berlin address and two food parcels, and enclosed a letter for their mother. In it Brecht said he had not been able to get the mother's address. F. mentions none of this.

In claiming that Steffin's family had no idea of "their rightful share of the income" from *Mother Courage*, F. provides no calculation and no clue to Steffin's share of the authorship.

F. writes about a time when annual earnings from the Steffin-Brecht works were "in six figures." Where and in what currency? Not specified. See 351, 383, 461 for F.'s establishment of the "Steffin-Brecht" label and claim, without any attempt to work out a detailed case. A paragraph later, Hauptmann and Berlau are brought in to join Steffin "as writers of 'Brecht' texts."

517. The grammatically awkward claim that Brecht "now collected royalties from...plays he both in fact and claimed to own" appears to summarize F.'s thinking on matters he has never substantiated.

Chapter 41

518. F. mentions Hans Albers's "personal charisma." Aufricht described him at the end of the Weimar Republic as "the heart-throb of the time to come: big, blond, blue-eyed, with a walk like a beast of prey."

F. now refers to Orge Pfanzelt as Brecht's "boyhood lover." Hypothetical (see 37).

519. F. cites a letter from Brecht to Arnold Zweig, which he claims is not published in Brecht's *Letters*. It *is* there as Letter 607, with a probable date, June 1949.

520. F. refers to a long poem that Brecht "really did apparently write." How was this apparent, and why is it presented as exceptional? F. does not explain the "really."

After returning to East Germany, F. states, Brecht completed no significant new plays and very few poems. In fact, from 1948 until his death in 1956, he completed nearly 250 poems, including the brilliant *Bukow Elegies* and some beautiful love poems. (JKL)

F. claims that in his last years, Brecht published mainly Hauptmann's works or work completed during the exile years with Steffin or Berlau. F. seems to forget how much was not published until after Brecht's death. (Nearly two-thirds of *Poems 1913-1956*, for instance.)

521. F. speaks of several "Brecht" works which were on the assembly line, implying that they were works by his collaborators issued under his name. The first edition to contain these was the Suhrkamp/Aufbau *Stücke*, which was edited by Hauptmann herself. Vols. 11 and 12 were published as Bertolt Brecht: *Bearbeitungen* three years after Brecht's death in 1956. Before each play the "Mitarbeiter" are named. On the other hand, the illustrated volume *Theaterarbeit*, published by Dresdner Verlag in 1952, attributes *Vasa Shelesnova*, *The Tutor*, and *Biberpelz und Roter Hahn* to their respective authors (Gorki, Lenz, and Gerhart Hauptmann) "in der Bearbeitung des Berliner Ensembles," i.e., in the BE's adaptation, followed by the names of those members most involved.

522. "Bébé." See 56, 73, 82, 97-99, 263, 421, 440, 446.

523. F. claims that Berlau's work as director was "still essential." This is not proven. The value of the model books and often brilliant photos, however, is indisputable.

524. F. states that Berlau needed to get credit for her directing and contributions to numerous plays. See the preceding entry. For the model books, see 513.

525. Mari Barbara. See 511 and *eleven* previous appearances.

F. states that Brecht was being turned into an "icon of socialist culture." To make sure this characterization lodges in his readers' minds, he will repeat it four more times in subsequent pages.

526. F. cites Bentley, who calls Brecht's shouting at stage personnel his "Hitler imitation." See 363, 395, and five "Führer" references listed there.

F.'s account of Brecht's anger over an anti-Semitic song he heard at the Oktoberfest should be set against the suggestion on 483 that he "did not support the Jewish cause."

527. F. erroneously gives the name of "Kurt Wendt." He means Erich Wendt, who was Brecht's editor at Aufbau, the firm set up by the Kulturbund. Before 1936 he had helped direct the Soviet foreign-language publishers Vegaar, but was arrested in the purges.

Chapter 42

530. F. describes *The Trial of Lucullus* as "an antiwar opera [Brecht] had created with Steffin." This was *not* created as an opera but as a radio play. Four lines later F. calls it "the play (with music by Paul Dessau)." In California Dessau had been involved in a scheme of Brecht's to get Stravinsky to make an opera of it, and then got Brecht to let him do so himself. Brecht made some modifications in the text (notably the ending). It was composed between 1949 and 1951. The nature of Steffin's involvement still has to be precisely established.

F. mistakenly states that *The Trial of Lucullus* officially opened on 17 March 1951. This was an open dress rehearsal ("Probeaufführung") to which special guests, including party officials, were invited. Because of what the party officials saw and heard, it had to be reworked, and then opened later. (JKL)

531. What does "archly" mean? Curious in this context (see 370).

Speaking of Brecht's *Herrenburg Report* (which he misspells as "Herrenberger"), F. implies that it was hack work because Brecht did it "for cash." Brecht was a professional writer.

F. claims that the *Herrenburg Report* was well received. On the contrary, according to Brecht's account, it "was supposed to be played each day but was then suppressed, and finally taken off the repertoire by decree" (*Journals*, 17 August 1951).

F. claims that "the United States" leaked information about Brecht's Austrian passport in order to damage Brecht. To whom? How? The "United States" is somewhat broad. (JKL)

532. F. describes how Brecht's theoretical arguments gravitated not to the "new," e.g., *Madame Bovary, Lady Chatterly's Lover,* etc., but back toward the nineteenth century. *Madame Bovary* was published in 1856-57.

Contrary to F.'s claim, Brecht never staged Schiller, nor either part of the full *Faust*.

533. F. repeats Hauptmann's words about how, up until 1933, she "either wrote or wrote down" most of his poems. See the note on 145, where this passage was already quoted as evidence of Hauptmann's authorship.

534. F. incorrectly speaks of "the Ulbricht government" of 1951-53. Pieck was president, Grotewohl premier. Ulbricht as party secretary was outside it until 1960.

The word "Marckian" seems to be F.'s invention. *Märkisch* means part of the *Mark*, i.e., Mark Brandenburg, the most important of the medieval marks or marches that would become the kingdom of Prussia.

537. F. has misread my *Caspar Neher* with his citation about a kind of art being pushed by the East German government just like "in Goebbels's day." Neher's letter to Brecht, which I cite, complains of being bothered with inquiries as to his views about Realism, "letters that have to go straight into the wastepaper basket, just like in Goebbels's day."

538. F. claims that "two dazzling sonnets" written by Martin Pohl have since "been published repeatedly as Brecht's work." Neither here nor in the long note does F. identify these. They are "Lieschen und Gretchen am Brunnen" and "Ach, neige, du Schmerzensreiche." How "dazzling" they are is a matter of judgment, but neither is a sonnet (the first has eighteen lines, the second sixteen) and they do *not* appear in the most recent Frankfurt and Berlin edition of Brecht's poems. (JKL)

540. F. describes the death of Otto Katz (André Simone) and Brecht's lack of concern for a friend (see 305). In the *Letters* there are only two from Brecht to him, and they hardly qualify him as a "friend" in any close sense.

541. Which performing artists went to prison or "disappeared" in the GDR because they were Jewish? Was Helene Weigel — or Brecht on her behalf — aware of this danger? Another variation of the theme of the brave women risking their lives while Brecht is hiding. (HCN)

542. In describing the events of 16 June 1953, F. claims that Brecht's main concern was to send off a letter he had drafted the day before about getting his own theater. This is Letter 724, which is actually *dated* 15 June. It seems very possible that it was written and sent off after the demonstrations became threatening, but F. cites no evidence.

543. F. translates Brecht's letter to Walter Ulbricht to say that large-scale discussions with the masses "would lead to recognition-...and consolidation of socialist achievements." The German sentence is *not* in the conditional. See *Letters*, no. 725: "The great debate with the masses...will...". (But the *Letters* version is wrong where F.'s is right. It should read "revolutionary impatience," *not* "patience.")

544. F. speaks of "the Soviet tanks." Can we not know approximate numbers?

F. says Manfred Wekwerth was Brecht's "assistant and later a politburo member." Wekwerth was never a Politbüro member, of course; many years after Brecht's death, as President of the Akademie der Künste of the GDR, he became a member of the ZK (central committee) of the SED. (HCN)

Chapter 43

547. The poem called "Nasty Morning" is only quoted in part. This is not made clear. Citing this poem, F. mistranslates a passage to read: "The nails were broken." There is *no* mention of nails. It should be "they," the fingers.

548. Citing Brecht's *Journals*, F. claims the writer's "whole existence 'had been soured.'" Not quite what he said (*Journals* entry of

20 August 1953). Rather: "17 june has alienated the whole of existence."

Citing a Brecht letter, F. claims Brecht said: "I stand at its [the government's] side." No: "it" refers to the party, not the government.

550. F. writes of conversations Brecht had with old comrades whom Ulbricht later removed from the party. The order of these events is not clear.

To claim, as F. does, that Brecht's best writing days were long since over at this point is to ignore, among other superb poems, his *Buckow Elegies* — some of the most remarkable German verse in the twentieth century. (JKL)

552. After Berlau went back to Denmark, F. says, she found her "former colleagues at Copenhagen's Royal Theater were now stars with the leading Scandinavian film company, Nordisk." There were a lot of "leading" film companies in Copenhagen in those days and everybody filmed everywhere without exclusive contracts with one firm. Some of Berlau's colleagues had started filming already in the 1930s and continued doing so. While writing this I came across a minor sensation. These days the most obscure feature films are released on video tapes. A few days ago I bought such a curiosity, *Det gyldne Smil* (The Golden Smile), produced by Nordisk Film in 1935. It is directed by the internationally known, Hungarian-born Paul Fejos and is based on a script by the famous Danish playwright Kaj Munk (who was killed by the Gestapo in 1944 although he had Fascist sympathies in the 1930s). The star of this long-forgotten film is Bodil Ipsen, the greatest actress of 20th century Danish theatre. Ipsen plays an operetta diva in the film and in its opening sequence her door is answered by her maid played by — Ruth Berlau. Berlau has a 90-second dialogue with a young poet (played by Sam Besekow who is still alive) and Ipsen herself, and is not seen again after that. Berlau is not credited among the actors. The Danish film scholar Björn Rasmussen who wrote the standard encyclopedia on Danish sound film in 1968 tried to identify all uncredited actors in every film. In connection with *Det gyldne Smil* he identified Sam Besekow and others who are not credited either, but not Ruth Berlau. The only reason must be that he did not know who she was. Until now this is the only film sequence with Berlau — fiction or documentary — that I have ever seen or heard of. The year 1935 is vital to her relationship with Brecht and you get an impression of how she moves and talks which is a unique addition to the many descriptions, especially the lyrical ones, by F. Berlau was working

together with Bodil Ipsen at the Royal Theatre (the two of them were even photographed together with Brecht and Weigel in 1938 when Ipsen had recited Brecht's poem "Die Schauspielerin im Exil" after Weigel's guest appearance as Carrar in Copenhagen), and it might have been Ipsen who had recommended Berlau for the small part of the maid to Fejos or Nordisk Film. The possibility that Berlau appeared in similar roles in other films cannot be excluded although the chances are few. (HCN)

555. F. fails to mention that the Vienna Scala theater (*not* La Scala, as he has it) was communist-run and situated in the Soviet sector of Vienna.

556. Again F. has the chorus in *Mother* singing in triple fortissimo. See 247, 269.

F. again refers to "his [Brecht's] and Berlau's *Caucasian Chalk Circle*." See 438, 449.

560. F.'s word "Essays" in the Hauptmann letter is presumably a way of translating "Versuche," the grey, paperbound series of Brecht's assorted writings begun in 1930.

F.'s English title for the poem "Millet for the Outlaws" is a mistranslation based on a misreading. This is the Chinese play "Hirse für die Achte" ("Millet for the Eighth [Army]") and has nothing to do with outlawry.

561. Again F. calls Brecht a "socialist icon" (see 525).

Chapter 44

563. F. credits Berlau and Steffin with having helped on the early stages of *The Mother*. Yet Brecht names neither of them as "Mitarbeiter" in the *Versuche*, *Stücke*, or *GW* editions of *Mother Courage*, though he freely credits their "Mitarbeit" on other works. F. has provided no evidence for doing so on this play.

564. F. calls Brecht "the quintessential casting-couch director" with a "growing number of sex partners available" to him. I should like to know *who* got roles at the Berliner Ensemble because Brecht fucked them. According to F. there must have been a lot of them, but Brecht did not engage actresses because of their sex appeal. (HCN)

568. F. cites Andrzej Wirth's 1957 essay, which, he states, describes the "stereoscopic nature" of Brecht's work. Wirth's essay

was *not* about stereoscopy, or giving an illusion of solidity as through a stereoscope, but about the work's "stereometric structure," its combination of different levels — practical, poetic, dialectical, dramatic, philosophical and so on — all intersecting with one another, and each with its own time-scale.

570. F. again states that Berlau's contribution to *The Caucasian Chalk Circle* was ignored, but he has not yet defined it.

Chapter 45

575. F. notes Brecht would get 5% on *Trumpets and Drums*. But 5% plus twice 2.5% for Besson and Hauptmann makes 10%, and the original play was in the public domain. The basis of calculation is not the same as with earlier examples. The same page refers to a "six-figure sale," and "earnings...in the mid-six-figure range." Again, no currency is specified.

F. states that after this time, the disaffected Caspar Neher was "never again to be won back to East Berlin." He *did*, however, design the setting for Brecht's intended Berliner Ensemble production of *Galileo*, which was taken over and realized in 1957 by Erich Engel.

576. F. again emphasizes that Brecht is a socialist icon. See 525, 561.

577-78. F. reprints what he calls Brecht's "last testament," but he fails to mention the source where he found it.

579. F. mentions "the Serapion brotherhood," which he calls "a group of experimental poets." Founded in Petrograd in 1921, it did *not* consist primarily of poets. Other members besides Tikhonov included Fedin, Zamyatin, Zoshchenko, and Shklovsky.

For F.'s repeated (and unsubstantiated) claim that Knorin had "personally recruited" Brecht for a Comintern assignment, see 457.

582. F. cites a passage by Lotte Lenya's husband, George Davis, in which he allegedly described Brecht and Weigel as "two shady con artists." F. draws this from Donald Spoto's biography of Lenya. The extract from Davis's letter given there actually reads: "Together Brecht and Weigel look like a pair of shrewd and hardbitten peasants — with at times another atmosphere coming through, of two shady con artists...and so, for me...overwhelming charm."

With a slight variation, F. now calls Brecht a "Communist icon." See 525, 561, 576.

F. now calls Berlau a "coauthor" of *The Caucasian Chalk Circle.* See 438, 449, 556, 570.

583. F. infers that the name "Wu" in Weber's and Palitzsch's version of the Chinese farce, *The Day of the Great Intellectual Wu*, clearly means Walter Ulbricht. It is unbelievable that Weber and Palitzsch would have intended anything so pointlessly silly, or potentially dangerous.

Mari Barbara. See 252, 259, 287, 291, 300, 413, 425, 427, 472, 489, 499, 511, 525.

Hurwicz, Giehse, and Berlau, according to F., sometimes were not credited for their work, but "they did get to direct at a time when women directors were few and far between." I should like to quote Erwin Geschonneck on this one: "Brecht schätzte die Münchner Schauspielerin Therese Giehse sehr und hatte sie für einige Rollen ans Berliner Ensemble geholt und bot ihr an, Regie zu führen, was sie auch tat. Aber sie konnte nicht richtig inszenieren. Brecht saß immer neben ihr und half. Im Grunde genommen hat er die Inszenierung gemacht." (*Meine unruhigen Jahre*, 1984) Geschonneck writes about *Der zerbrochene Krug* in which he played the main role as the village Judge, Adam. There were many occasions when Brecht credited others but did much of the work himself. And why does F. in his 700-page book not mention major actors of the Berliner Ensemble like Geschonneck, Regine Lutz, Curt Bois and others? (HCN)

584. Again F. decries "the enormity" of what Brecht had done to his women collaborators. This has still *not* been established, merely asserted.

585. F. cites a letter Brecht wrote Berlau on 31 December 1955 but makes *no* reference at all to the long, exasperated, unfinished letter dated 20 January 1956, which deals severely with all her complaints and claims. This was published by Mittenzwei in his biography (556 ff.) and is included in *Letters 1913-1956* (Letter 848x). It was presumably not sent. Its most telling lines, which contradict F.'s entire argument about Berlau's alleged co-authorship of plays, read: "We are not two playwrights who have collaborated in writing plays."

According to F., Brecht told Steffin earlier and Käthe Reichel now that *Galileo* was intended as a commentary on Bukharin's behavior at the Moscow show trials. F. fails to document this claim.

591. F. mentions a batch of poems Brecht sent to Pasternak. Pasternak did not respond.

592. Mari Barbara. As on 583, making fourteen instances in all.

593. In choosing the Charité Hospital for his treatment, Brecht, according to F., was returning to his own and Germany's past. It was, however, more than sentimentality that dictated his choice. The hospital was close to his flat, to the Academy, and to the theater.

Chapter 46

597. Here F. repeats for the third time the same citation from Brecht about his allegedly poor memory. This pattern of repeating the same citations verbatim at various points in the book is common (and tiresome). (JKL)

602. Mari Barbara. Twice more.

606. Based on an unspecified note he found in Piscator's papers, F. reports that Piscator's main reaction upon hearing of Brecht's death was anger. F. cites him as saying, "He stole my legacy." F. ignores the thoughts jotted down by Piscator when he was asked to the memorial ceremony. This response, published by Herbert Knust in 1974, includes the acknowledgement: "then he was the greater one after all," and the conclusion, "one can only appreciate him."

608. According to F. Ernst Busch sang "The Song of Praise" at Brecht's funeral. There is no song with this title and it would have been absurd if there had been. "The Song of Praise" — of what? From Hans Mayer I remember that Busch sang the "Einheitsfront-lied" accompanied by Eisler, who was so emotionally taken by Brecht's death that he had his piano stool placed off the stage so that he could not be seen by the public. In that sense F. is wrong too, reporting how Eisler "strode to the piano." (HCN)

Chapter 47

613. F. now refers to Hauptmann as *The Threepenny Opera's* "principal author." See 193. Except for this sort of repetitive assertion, there is nothing in F.'s book after that point which even tries to reinforce his case.

F. again refers to Berlau as "coauthor" of *The Caucasian Chalk Circle*. First named by F. as such on 582.

F.'s suggestion that Otto Müllereisert was "one of Brecht's lovers from his teenage years" seems to grow from Müllereisert's having been one of the "Brecht circle" in Augsburg, mentioned in a poem among the others drunkenly hugging one another under a table (*Diaries 1920-1922*, entry for 26 August 1920).

614. Mari Barbara. Again.

Again F. ascribes "iconic status" to the socialist Brecht. See 525, 561, 576, 582.

615. F. claims that in 1994, Suhrkamp published an edition of Brecht's works that makes no effort to identify which writings emanated from Steffin, Hauptmann, Berlau, Ottwalt, Pohl, and several others, or to acknowledge their contributions. In the case of Ottwalt and Pohl it looks as if *no* such effort can have been made by F. either. In that of the three others named, F. has nothing but his sweeping conclusions to add to what scholars knew already. The edition to which F. refers began to appear in 1988, not 1994.

F. refers to "Mari Barbara" (three more times).

616. F. repeats his earlier claim and again misquotes me to the effect that at least seven of Brecht's eleven so-called Berlin stories are probably by Hauptmann. See my note to 144. F. has misread what I wrote, which concerned seven stories published under *Hauptmann's* name. It is possible that she also wrote some of the stories we attribute to Brecht, but hunches are not enough to change what publishers' editors have decided, and in this case the general editor for the *GW* was Hauptmann herself.

616-17. Shull and Lucchesi do *not* claim, as F. asserts, that the "original text" of *The Threepenny Opera* is overwhelmingly Hauptmann's work. (JKL)

For F. to say that Willett has acknowledged Hauptmann's role in the creation of the *Lehrstücke* is also not accurate. In the creation of the form and the translation of *He Who Says Yes*, yes, but not necessarily the writing of the other texts.

F. claims that Paula Hanssen, who examined the manuscripts for Brecht's "Chinese Poems," attributes them "overwhelmingly" to Hauptmann. Hanssen does not say this. She states rather that Hauptmann played a "major role" in working on them with Brecht and that she should be listed as coauthor. For further information on F.'s wrongly citing Hanssen, see 365. (JKL)

According to F., Hauptmann told him that she had often done "almost entire poems" that were later published under Brecht's name. Which ones? Naming titles would be more useful than making unsupported assertions. (JKL)

For Brecht's assessment of what F. calls Berlau's "fine feminist book," see 368. (JKL)

617. F. looks for excuses in Berlau's health problems for her not returning to the Royal Danish Theater, and in the obscurity of the Danish language for not resuming her writing career. Of course there was no place left open for Ruth Berlau at the Royal Theater. At various times she started writing something in Danish — a mixture of diary and letter — but could not manage it. After Brecht's death she even had a printer design the logo, "Ruth Berlau publishing house," but this was nothing but imagination. All this reflects her lack of capacity. (HCN)

618. F. says that Hans Bunge's book on Berlau was "long-delayed and heavily censored in the GDR." The Brecht heirs did not allow Bunge to use original Brecht material (the Lai-tu stories, poems, and letters) in his book. This decision is open to question but it has nothing to do with "heavy censorship." (HCN)

Mari Barbara. See 252, 259, 287, 291, 300, 413, 425, 427, 472, 489, 499, 511, 525, 583, 592, 602, 614, 615.

620. Though he has taken pains to show what has long been known, viz. that *Happy End* is *not* by Brecht, F. lists it here among the "best of the texts" Brecht wrote.

F. refers to Jenny of *The Threepenny Opera*. Is this Pirate Jenny or Low-Dive Jenny?

F. now claims that these women collaborators "wrote more of the work than Brecht himself." Wrote or translated? If the latter, then in Hauptmann's case, yes. But elsewhere the question has barely been argued, and overstating the assertion this way does nothing to prove it.

621. Speaking of *The Good Person of Szechwan*, F. incorrectly speaks of Shen Teh's brutal male "lover" Shui Ta. Does he mean the

flier Yang Sun? Brecht's Shui Ta "loves" nobody; he *is* Shen Teh. The idea that Shen Teh loves him is a serious misreading of the play.

From the Notes

629. F. states that the volumes of published *Letters* contain less than one-third of Brecht's known letters. Günter Glaeser's edition of the Brecht *Briefe* originally appeared in 1981 in the Federal Republic and 1983 in the GDR. It appears to be the same in both versions and contains 887 items. F. complains elsewhere that "well over nine hundred other known Brecht letters and notes to Berlau" are not included. In the course of the present book he quotes a few of these and also some important letters to Hauptmann. He promises "in future notes" to say how "in hundreds of instances" he is drawing on letters that have been deliberately excluded from this "shamelessly manipulated volume." The "hundreds" turn out, in a quick count, to consist of thirty-six items marked "*Not* in BL" (by which F. means *Letters*).

Glaeser's introductory note says at the outset that his edition is provisional. He has left out purely "business correspondence" except where an item has "special relevance," likewise "letters which touch on legally established personal rights, deal mainly with private matters, or are still being withheld by the rights holders." Decisions of this cramping kind are not unknown to editors of such papers. On top of this Margarete Steffin's letters from Brecht were apparently produced too late for inclusion by the Moscow archives where she had left them. Much of the over-copious Berlau material consists of Brecht's short (sometimes daily) attempts to keep in touch and show affection. One or two other items *were* in the *Briefe* all along.

The English (Methuen) edition of 1990 was contractually supposed to be based on that of the Federal Republic. The editors supplied some 35 pages of general background and over 220 pages of notes on the separate items. They left out a number of tedious, obscure, petty, or parochial letters, particularly from 1950 on, and at the same time added short summarizing notes about some of the more important letters that the *Briefe* had omitted in cases where they had become available for study. Some of Steffin's letters brought from Moscow, for instance, and those of Kurt Weill whose publication was still reserved by the Kurt Weill Foundation, were covered in this rather makeshift way. Among them was an important unfinished letter of January 1956 from Brecht to Berlau summing up her contribution to his work and his theater. This deflates many of her claims as a "coauthor," which the present book takes at their face value. We numbered it Letter 848x. F. never mentions it.

635 n.59. F. gives an inaccurate title for Michael Morley's book. The English edition F. cites is not entitled *A Study* but *A Student's Guide to Brecht.* (JKL)

656 n.5. F. notes that despite years of battling with alcoholism, Berlau's knowledge of things relating to Brecht of which she had direct knowledge was "amazingly reliable." In my experience with her, I found her knowledge to be so distorted by personal considerations that it was difficult to sort out truth from fantasy. She told me, for example, that she and Brecht had named the child in *The Caucasian Chalk Circle* after the child she bore Brecht in September, 1944. Manuscripts reveal that the child in *The Caucasian Chalk Circle* had its name long before she gave birth, probably before she knew she was pregnant. (JKL)

661 n.22. I met Mrs. Hold Ohm in the summer of 1971 and not, as F. writes, in October 1986 because by then she had been dead for six years. (HCN)

693 n.13. F. says that *Any Animal Can Do It* is "Berlau's best sustained long piece of writing." I am sure that he has nothing to compare it with. Nevertheless, here he knows at least that it is "a linked set of short stories," not a novel. (HCN)

697. Throughout the notes, one looks in vain for a reference to the only other book-length study devoted to the topic of Brecht's women collaborators — Sabine Kebir's *Ein akzeptabler Mann? Brecht und die Frauen*, which appeared in 1987. By the end of the notes, F. has still not cited it. One wonders why he neglects to mention or make use of widely reviewed and well-known work that addresses many of the same matters he explores. (JKL)

* * * * * * *

3. Use and Misuse of Brecht's FBI File

James K. Lyon

John Fuegi's remarkable access to unpublished material from archives and private sources, e.g., the Brecht Archives, Margarete Steffin's private papers, publishing house files, etc., gave promise that his research on this book would reveal considerable new information and insights about Brecht and his collaborators. Only a few scholars have seen one or the other of these unpublished sources, and none has seen all of them.

My own access to Brecht's FBI file (I obtained it before F. did and wrote lengthy articles on it, which appeared in the USA and Germany more than a decade ago) gave me a chance to examine how he dealt with information from that relatively inaccessible source. My findings were not encouraging. If his use of materials from the FBI file is a paradigm for the manner in which he analyzes and reports on other unpublished sources, it results in a depressingly low reliability quotient.

As a source of information, FBI files themselves are not always reliable. Facts are interwoven with hearsay information, and no attempt is made to resolve discrepancies or contradictions which exist between and among sources. Masses of uncorroborated data, some based on rumor and in many cases error, are indiscriminately interwoven with allegedly factual information. This, of course, suggests extreme caution in drawing conclusions. F. not only fails to exercise the necessary caution, he misreads, misunderstands, and misquotes these documents while drawing speculative, unwarranted conclusions from them which seriously undermine a knowledgeable reader's confidence in his work with other inaccessible sources. The following list represents the most conspicuous misuses of the FBI file.

On 449 F. states that during the summer of 1944 Brecht and Berlau were "never out of the sight or the hearing of the FBI," which suggests constant surveillance and telephone monitoring. FBI reports speak of neither. According to their file, Brecht was *not* under daily or hourly surveillance at this time, and his phone was not being tapped. The FBI did in fact tap Brecht's telephone a few months later when Berlau was no longer there but not at this time.

On 452 F. writes that FBI files report how their agents boarded a train which took Ruth Berlau to New York, went to the baggage car, and searched her suitcases without warrant. By his account they found developed and undeveloped microfilm scattered "haphazardly through the various bags" along with unpaid medical bills, papers, etc. This is a careless misreading, for the FBI file says something quite different. It reports in detail on the contents of four boxes which Berlau took on the train with her but it says nothing about the contents of her suitcases. Further, according to the file, it did not learn about their contents by searching the boxes in the train's baggage car but by inquiring about them with the owner of a "packing service" in Santa Monica which had packed Berlau's papers and photographic equipment for shipment by train. The owner cooperated by providing FBI agents with a complete list of contents, and he is clearly identified as their source.

In 1945 the Los Angeles office of the FBI requested and received permission from its Washington headquarters to install a microphone in the Los Angeles motel where Berlau would stay when she returned from New York. A "bug" was in fact installed. F. then states, "the trap was set to be sprung" (453). The FBI file says no such thing. The "bug" was not set as a trap to be sprung, i.e., they had no plans to burst in and arrest Brecht or Berlau. The file gives no hint that the FBI ever intended to arrest either Brecht or Berlau at this or any other time. The purpose of the bug was to gather enough information to incriminate Brecht, but the FBI never succeeded in this. In fact, two different times before he left the USA in 1947, the FBI closed his file for lack of evidence. Neither he nor Berlau was ever in imminent danger of having a "trap sprung."

By F.'s account on 457 the FBI reports that Brecht was "horrified" to hear that postwar Germany would be divided and "dismayed" that the greatest part was going to "the Soviet." The actual FBI report reads quite differently. After calling Germany's loss of cultural unity "very bad news," the report quotes Brecht as telling a friend (without horror or dismay) that "the greatest part is going to the Soviet." From his friend's response that this would quicken the development of the new state, and from Brecht's subsequent positive remarks, it seems clear that he welcomed the notion of a Soviet-supported state on German soil.

F.'s most striking misuse of the FBI files occurs in his repeated attempts to link Brecht to Soviet infiltration of the atomic bomb project being carried out by Robert Oppenheimer and others in Berkeley. He claims (428) that FBI files assumed Brecht's involvement in three important cases — one concerning emigrés who were trying to shape the government of postwar Germany; another investigation known as the MOCASE; and the so-called COMRAP case. F. is correct in the first instance, but the FBI file never mentions the MOCASE or anything about it, and while names associated with the COMRAP case do appear in his file, the acronym itself never does, nor is any linkage firmly established. F., however, desperately attempts to make the case that the FBI saw Brecht as part of an atomic spy network. Both his arguments and his evidence are flawed.

He begins by making an error in identifying Grigori Kheifetz, an NKVD agent whom the FBI suspected of efforts to penetrate the atomic bomb project at Lawrence Radiation Labs in Berkeley. At several points the FBI file clearly states that Kheifetz was a vice-consul in the Soviet consulate in San Francisco, a logical base for meeting scientists working at the Lawrence Radiation Labs. F., however, mistakenly claims he was attached to the Soviet consulate in Los Angeles, which he was not. Kheifetz did, however, come to Los Angeles frequently, for reasons explained below. FBI files show records of his meeting with Brecht five different times between April 1943 and January 1944, either in Brecht's home or in the Soviet consulate.

F. uses this guilt by association to link Brecht to the Soviet espionage effort directed by Kheifetz against the atomic bomb project nearly 400 miles away in Berkeley, though he bases his assertions on speculations in the FBI file that produce no evidence or conclusions. F. claims that FBI suspicions increased after Brecht met Vladimir Pozner, a friend of Oppenheimer's, who also may have been a Soviet operative. With an almost paranoid sense of universal conspiracy, the FBI employed a *modus operandi* of connecting names of suspicious types with those of other suspicious types, as they did with Pozner and Brecht. But even when their files mention names of parties who had no contact with each other, as they frequently do, this hardly constitutes an established "link." Thus the FBI file twice reports that Horst Bärensprung, an acquaintance of Brecht's (but by no means a good friend) who lived in New York City, was "an acquaintance" of Haakon Chevalier, an assistant professor of French at Berkeley, who in turn was a leftist friend of Oppenheimer's. From this tenuous "link" ("an acquaintance of an acquaintance") F. goes on to claim (486) that FBI files had "repeatedly" and "directly" linked Brecht to Kheifetz and "to Haakon Chevalier, who in turn was directly linked to J. Robert Oppenheimer, head of the Los Alamos laboratory." This is patently wrong. The FBI file establishes no such "direct" link. Almost everything in the file is conjecture or speculation. Further, Brecht had never met Chevalier and probably did not know who he was. The same can be said of his knowledge of Oppenheimer and the Soviet espionage effort targeted against him. Even if he did, no firm evidence made its way into Brecht's FBI file to substantiate such claims. Yet on 485 F. elevates what began as speculation and then became assertion to the level of fact by stating that when Brecht left the USA in 1947, he took with him "whatever secrets he may or may not have possessed concerning Kheifetz, Eisler, Stern, Chevalier, Pozner, Oppenheimer, and Soviet networks."

A section of the FBI file shows how seriously F. misreads this file and explains Brecht's frequent contact with Kheifetz. Apparently Kheifetz was in charge of *all* Soviet espionage activities in the state of California, which explains his frequent trips to Los Angeles. Doubtless he was cultivating Brecht as a source of information about the movie industry. The file states clearly that the FBI was not watching Brecht and his meetings with Kheifetz and the Soviet vice consuls who succeeded him after 1944 out of suspicion over his connection with espionage efforts directed against Oppenheimer and the atomic bomb project in Berkeley. Instead, it reports, they engaged in the surveillance of his activities in order "to develop information relative to Soviet espionage activities in the Los Angeles area and communist infiltration of the movie industry." Where the FBI failed in an attempt to link Brecht to any sort of espionage, much less to make him out to be an atomic spy connected to Chevalier and Oppenheimer, F., using the same documents, appears to have succeeded.

* * * * * * * *

4. Final Comments

John Willett

At the time of writing (13 November 1994), my list of questionable points and passages in Fuegi's book has been completed and now has to be merged with those of others who have been worried by similar flaws. Roughly speaking, this first installment consists of some 450 comments, corrections or queries on the 621 pages of text and eight pages of preface, an average roughly of two comments to every three pages. Fuegi's notes are also considered, but as part of the pages to which they refer. (The ninety-eight contentiously captioned illustrations might be mentioned in connection with the book's production and publication.)

My reading is based on the UK edition and an unbound set of the US proofs. Page references are given to the former, which appears to all intents and purposes to be the same book.

Those 450 or so points fall into several categories. There are mistranslations from the German, some of them surprising in anybody of this author's qualifications. For instance, on 560, where the Chinese play *Hirse für die Achte* (or *Millet for the Eighth Army,* a play in the Berliner Ensemble repertory) is called "Millet for the Outlaws," presumably because in another, less common usage "Acht" (normally "eight") can mean banishment. There are misquotations and unacknowledged omissions, sometimes radically changing a meaning. Thus on 582 a New York visitor is said to describe the Brechts as "shady con artists," when his primary impression of two "shrewd and hardbitten peasants" has been tacitly omitted. There are important conclusions from no evidence or supported by doubtful references which do not provide any. There are vague exaggerations, as on 448, "a stream of young male lovers," or on 515, earnings "in six figures." There are plain mistakes and misstatements, due perhaps to ignorance. There are some radical misreadings of Brecht's best-known plays (Baal killing Johannes: 40; Shui Ta and Shen Teh as lovers: 621).

Such things might be unremarkable in a work of lesser pretensions, ignored by the media, and lacking the imprimatur of any academic bodies. But what makes them extraordinary in a work of supposed scholarship is that all of them are geared to the dominant thrust of the book, which is to blacken and discredit a hated figure. The object of the present list is not to dispute them so much as to set them down.

A revealing aspect of the list is its series of repetitions. This author is not one of those who can state something and leave it at that. Certain facts, hints or suggestions recur over different chapters or even the whole of the book, rather as in the kind of advertising, public relations or propaganda campaign which hammers away at a few significant points. Far the most conspicuous of these has to do with Brecht's daughter Barbara, against whom Fuegi turns the (oddly-translated) words used by herself of Ruth Berlau, that she was "in no way capable with any kind of contribution of earning a living." Here, on 615, he calls her MARI BARBARA for the nineteenth time in order to remind us, as he puts it, of her "second mother," Brecht's old servant Mari, who he thinks (but cannot prove) might have given birth to her. These are names which in thirty-eight years of intermittent friendship with the Brechts I have never heard used, and their reiteration every eighteen pages or so (on average) from 252 on says more about Fuegi's resentments than about Brecht's work.

The list does not comment on these recurrent items other than to mention them each time with the relevant page number and let such references pile up. There is Fuegi's image of Brecht as "Bébé" from 56 to 522, his supposed association with WHIPS from 1 to 104 (with the odd whiff of Nietzsche thrown in), then the over-stressed HOMOSEXUALITY linking Brecht forcibly to Bronnen and virtually all his Augsburg friends other than the girls, from the misquoted "Psalm" to Caspar Neher (37) to Müllereisert's appearance at his deathbed (613). Such shaky pillars of the book's structure come to suggest, much more clearly than any vague aura of hatred, what the author is trying to build. Thus BRONNEN's recruitment to right-wing politics in the mid-twenties leads into references associating Brecht with his new friends (such as Joseph Goebbels), while any mention of the actual word "lead" in connection with Brecht is used to introduce the normal German word for "lead" or "leader," and so to remind us of the FÜHRER Adolf Hitler (this from 79 to 526). Correspondingly, it is more than once claimed that Brecht failed to help in some Jewish cause, and even that he was not opposed to antisemitism. Towards the end of the book Fuegi picks a phrase from the second page of the preface, Brecht as a "socialist icon." It comes back four more times in the last hundred pages, rising to "Communist icon" on 582. All these pillars are pointers to what is being put across.

Fuegi's technique, conscious or not, is to make a guess or an allegation, and then by gradually pushing and petting it, to present it to his readers as true. Much the same is done on a larger scale with the three main weight-bearing columns of his whole edifice, his presentation of Elisabeth Hauptmann, Margarete Steffin, and Ruth Berlau as the coauthors, who, according to his peroration (620), "wrote more of the work than Brecht himself." One problem here is that the book never makes it entirely clear what he means by "wrote." Does it cover the retyping of a draft, such as both Hauptmann and Steffin often enough had to do in their secretarial capacity, something nobody would deny? Or do we use it of the translation of a foreign original which was later added to, adapted, and altered by Brecht's and other hands? This is how Fuegi applies it in Hauptmann's case, most notably to *The Threepenny Opera* and the *Lehrstück He Who Says Yes*, both of which she translated most stimulatingly from the English for Brecht to work on later. In pressing what he sees as her claims, it is Fuegi who ignores the original authors, the Englishman John Gay and the Japanese Zenchiku, as well as Arthur Waley, whose English verse was closely followed by Hauptmann. Admittedly they were not women, but Brecht's producers and editors gave them more acknowledgement before 1933 than Fuegi does in the present book.

The argument here involves a more complex form of reiteration, but we can still see how it grows in the course of the list. For Hauptmann's work on the earlier plays, see the references under 140-45, then 193 on the development of *The Threepenny Opera*. By the last reference on 613 she has come through as its "principal author." For *He Who Says Yes* starting on 220, Brecht's additions to her translation are played down (see 250), and Hauptmann's pioneering of the *Lehrstück* form overstated; while her contribution to the two *Mahagonnys* is asserted on the basis of two carelessly read songs (197). Yet of the three columns of Fuegi's structure, hers is much the strongest. She knew what to translate, she was in tune with Brecht's imagination and prejudices, and she understood the theater and its collective approach to the most confusing and unpredictable tasks. He was extraordinarily lucky to have her, but the driving genius was always his.

Steffin appears about halfway through the book, editing Brecht's second collection of poems at the start of the emigration. By 314 her "daily work" is essential to the writing of the main new plays. So *Señora Carrar's Rifles* is termed a "Steffin-Brecht version" (of the Synge original), followed by "Brecht's (Steffin's) *Roundheads*." It is quite possible, too, that she contributed creatively to *Fear and Misery of the Third Reich*, though nobody has established exactly how. But to say that "with *Galileo*, Brecht and Steffin have returned to the world of the classic drama" is to suggest a joint authorship that has not been critically argued. And this remains so right up to the rather weak case of *Mother Courage* on 563, where "Berlau, of course, had helped...(as had the forgotten Steffin)."

While Fuegi fails notably to cite Berlau's view that Steffin "did not share in the writing of the plays" (314), the evidence of the book itself is that her strength lay in her conscientiousness as a secretary, her status as a communist, and her invaluable role in dealing with the Russians. The cumulative effect of these things can be seen in the sense of paralysis felt by Brecht after her death. His difficulty in working without her, however much it put him morally in her debt, is no proof of a significant creative factor such as Fuegi asserts.

As for Ruth Berlau, except in her talents as a photographer, she was less qualified as a collaborator than either of the others. Her secretarial skills were minimal, her aptitude for research slight, her knowledge of German erratic, her temperament for working with other people uneven. She was ready enough to provide Brecht with comments and suggestions, and he seems to have been anxious not to rebuff her; but it is difficult to identify signs of the "collaboration" which the playwright acknowledged in the cases of *The Good*

Person of Szechwan and *The Caucasian Chalk Circle*. In that of the Brecht/Feuchtwanger *The Visions of Simone Machard*, where Brecht did not do this, Fuegi thinks (417) that the others involved can confirm "the role Ruth Berlau played in its creation," and he shows that for a time she was written into the contract for 20%. Much the same, however, occurred with Marta Feuchtwanger, who claimed no such role. And there is the unfinished letter of January 1956 (585) where Brecht's patience seems to have gone and he tells her bluntly that, "We are not two playwrights who have collaborated in writing plays." The book nowhere refers to it.

Such is the way Fuegi sets about pulling down Brecht. As far as its "scholarship" goes, the book would have been every bit as flawed if he had applied it to doing the exact opposite. It is the way he uses his material, not anything unacceptable about his intentions — shabby as some of us may think them — that makes his huge book so untrustworthy that one cannot have confidence in its new revelations at any point. The *appearance* of diligent research and scrupulous reference provided by his many acknowledgements and his seventy pages of notes has been able to convince even senior critics that the result is a work of "massive scholarship." No sooner does one start looking up those references, however, than one begins to see how this kind of apparatus can be a beautiful facade: push it at any point, and something is liable to give. The number of mistakes he makes is inexcusable by any recognized standards — this quite aside from cases of bad writing or unnecessary delvings beneath the bedsheets, to which the list deliberately draws no attention — and it is shocking that neither publisher took steps to weed them out. Together he and they provide a great demonstration of the modern use of academic posture. Scholars of varying opinions can suspect it, but an amazing number of bodies that should have known better appear to have been taken in.

Whatever the real scale of its "scholarship" (which is not something to be reckoned by numbers of pages or notes), the public launching of this book has been a massive operation, which it might be illuminating to follow up. But this aspect of the business is perhaps less disturbing than the author's final acknowledgements, where he lists the eminently respectable institutions which must have felt so convinced by the first plans of his edifice as to underwrite various aspects of its construction. They include (he says) the NDEA (for grants in Comparative Literature and Russian Studies), the Fulbright Commission, the Germanistic Society of America, the Humanities Center (Wesleyan), the Center for Twentieth Century Studies (Milwaukee), the West Berlin Academy of Arts (for a residency), the American Council of Learned Societies (grant for East European Studies), Harvard, Wesleyan, and the Free University in Berlin (all for Visiting Professorships), the Guggenheim, Rockefeller, and Kurt Weill Foundations (all for awards), and the University of Maryland where he is a professor, for further grants.

Many of these bodies are devoted to a great tradition of support for scholarly research in literature, history and the arts. They are particularly strong in the United States, where they have a great record. How disillusioning it must be for them now to see the way their decisions have turned out in the case of the sensationally-named *The Life and Lies of Bertolt Brecht*. What were your referees up to? Who were the publishers' readers who approved this icon-busting work? Why were some of its critics so gullible? Why did reputable papers and broadcasting organizations give so much space to it, its syndication, and its author's opinions? And why at the present time, when socialist ideas and ideals are not exactly flourishing in the developed world? These are only some of the many questions which you should be asking yourselves. We all make mistakes, but other people are liable to judge us by them. Do you think the results in this case can be reconciled with the purposes your institutions were set up to serve?

Book Reviews

Bertolt Brecht. *Poesie.* A cura di Guido Davico Bonino. Nota introduttiva di Cesare Cases. Traduzioni di Emilio Castellani, Roberto Fertonani, Cesare Cases, Mario Carpitella, Ruth Leiser, Franco Fortini. Note di Giuseppina Oneto. Torino: Einaudi, 1992. xxiv + 341 pages.

Italien hat sich für Bertolt Brecht von Anfang an als besonders aufgeschlossen erwiesen, sowohl was die italienische Kritik und Forschung als auch was das italienische Theater betrifft. Und für Brechts Lyrik, die, anders als seine Dramatik und Dramentheorie, im Ausland immer noch weithin unterschätzt oder zuwenig beachtet ist, und erst recht für deren Übersetzung gilt dies nicht minder. Das Erscheinen einer umfangreichen Auswahl von Brechtschen Gedichten im Jahre 1992 — und zudem einer zweisprachigen, was gleichfalls eher eine Ausnahme darstellt und besonders hervorgehoben zu werden verdient — könnte daher auf den ersten Blick zu dem erfreulichen Schluß verleiten, daß die Italiener, im Gegensatz etwa zu den Franzosen und Spaniern, den Engländern und Amerikanern und nicht zuletzt, nein zuvörderst auch den Deutschen, von der inzwischen ja sprichwörtlichen "Brechtmüdigkeit" bisher verschont geblieben sind. Doch ein solcher Schluß würde trügen oder wäre zumindest voreilig. Bei genauerem Hinsehen nämlich ergibt sich, daß auch in Italien der allgemeine Schrumpfungsprozeß, der seit Jahren, wenn nicht gar Jahrzehnten, an Wirkung und Ansehen des Augsburgers zehrt, längst schon stattgefunden hat — jedenfalls zu einem gewissen Grad.

Denn es handelt sich bei dem vorliegenden Auswahlband keineswegs um eine wirkliche Neuerscheinung; er beruht vielmehr seinerseits auf einer Auswahl, und zwar auf der zweibändigen, ebenfalls bei Einaudi in Turin erschienenen Ausgabe der Brechtschen Gedichte von 1968 und 1977. (Die beiden Jahreszahlen sind so aufschlußreich wie die schlichte Tatsache, daß beispielsweise die entsprechende englische Ausgabe von 1976, die man zum Vergleich heranziehen könnte, lediglich einen Band umfaßt und auf die Wiedergabe der deutschen Originaltexte durchweg verzichtet.) Eine nähere Betrachtung jener scheinbar so neuen *Poesie* enthüllt aber außerdem noch in anderer Hinsicht einiges recht Bemerkenswerte. Nicht allein *daß* hier aus einer bereits vorhandenen Auswahl wiederum ausgewählt wurde, sondern *wie* man dabei verfuhr, ist für den Wandel der Zeiten auch in Italien bezeichnend. Schon das Vorwort des Herausgebers läßt daran nicht den geringsten Zweifel. Bonino nimmt kein Blatt vor den Mund: Brechts Lyrik, erklärt er so knapp wie entschieden, soll von den Zwängen oder "Banden" (*vincoli*) ihrer "ideologischen Programmatik" (*programmaticità ideologica*) befreit werden. Was statt dessen — unter höchst einseitiger Berufung auf eine schmale Broschüre von Furio Jesi — in den Vordergrund gerückt werden soll, sind etwa, neben dem Brechtschen Naturverhältnis, Themen wie "Weisheit, Mut, Stoizismus" (*saggezza, coraggio, stoicismo*) und schließlich Brechts "Streben nach echter Klassizität" (*aspirazione ad un'autentica classicità*). Diese rigorose Doppelpurgierung hat unter anderem zur Folge, daß, rein quantitativ gesehen, vom Textmaterial der einstigen zwei Bände nur noch ein mageres Fünftel übriggeblieben ist — was der Herausgeber auch freimütig eingesteht — und daß zugleich, qualitativ gesehen, zum Beispiel eine beinah schon läppische Nichtigkeit wie "Kleines Lied" ("Es war einmal ein Mann/Der fing das Trinken an...") geradezu programmatisch aufgenommen wurde, nicht hingegen das dichterisch wie weltanschaulich so bedeutsame (doch im übrigen alles andere als politische) "Schlußkapitel" aus der *Hauspostille*, "Gegen Verführung."

Indes, solche Fehlgriffe sind trotz Boninos Umorientierung vergleichsweise selten; und daß das bloße Faktum, sich heutigentags für den armen B.B. einzusetzen, überaus löblich und zu begrüßen ist, versteht sich wohl ohnehin von selbst — von der historisch-ästhetischen Berechtigung des Umgangs mit Brecht und Brechts Schaffen einmal zu schweigen. Ganz und gar nicht selbstverständlich dagegen und darum vollends rühmenswert ist aber die durchgehend hohe Qualität der ausgewählten Gedichtübertragungen, deren Treue und Sorgfalt immer wieder bestechen. Wer auch nur die leiseste Ahnung davon hat, wie schlimm es vor allem hierzulande mit dem Übersetzen von deutscher Literatur und namentlich eben von deutscher Lyrik steht, wird derlei desto mehr zu schätzen und zu würdigen wissen. Zusammenfassend darf man deshalb getrost sagen, daß es Carpitella, Cases, Castellani, Fertonani, Fortini und Leiser gelungen ist, ihr einheimisches Verdikt, wonach Übersetzer stets notgedrungen "Verräter" seien, auf weite Strecken Lügen zu strafen. Von *traduttore* gleich *traditore* kann in diesem Band wahrlich nicht die Rede sein. Jedenfalls sind mir ausgesprochene Fehlübersetzungen (von sprachlicher Unkenntnis oder einfach von Nachlässigkeit herrührend) auf keiner Seite begegnet — und auch die Druckfehler, um dies vorwegnehmend anzumerken, halten sich durchaus in Grenzen (entstellend wirkt höchstens das Versehen, das einem unaufmerksamen Setzer in mehreren Zeilen des deutschen Textes von Brechts "Brief an den Schauspieler Charles Laughton" [238] unterlaufen ist; im Italieni-schen finden sich solches Mißgriffe natürlich nicht).

Vollkommenheit gibt es halt nirgends, und am allerwenigsten dort, wo es um das Übertragen von Lyrik geht. Ein paar einschlägige Fälle — nicht so sehr Fehler als vielmehr Probleme — seien daher trotz meiner allgemeinen Rühmung kurz verzeichnet. Ob zum Beispiel "senza timori" für "unbesorgt" (vgl. 22/23) oder "deve fare in modo/che" für "wird dafür sorgen/Daß" (vgl. 46/47) die jeweils beste Übersetzung ist, scheint mir immerhin fraglich zu sein; schwerlich einzusehen vermag ich aber, warum man Titel wie "Lied der Staren-schwärme," "Mein Bruder war ein Flieger" und "Der Zettel des Brau-chens" mit "Gli uccelli migrano" (wörtlich: "Die Vögel ziehen" [im Sinne von "Zugvögel"; vgl. 150/151]), bzw. "Mio fratello aviatore" (das bedeutungsschwangere "war" fällt weg [154/155]), bzw. "Il foglietto degli acquisti" (also der "Käufe" oder "Erwerbungen" [194/195]) zu übersetzen hätte. Weniger gravierend und darum einigermaßen verzeihlich ist hingegen wieder die ja im Sinngehalt abweichende Übersetzung von "'s ist keine Red davon" mit "ma non servono parole" (152/153); denn hier handelt es sich, wie aus dem Zusammenhang eindeutig hervorgeht, um einen Fall von leidiger Reimnot. Sogar wenn einmal ein ganzer (freilich nur aus drei Wörtern bestehender) Satz wie in "Fragen eines lesenden Arbeiters" gänzlich ausfällt, wird man — zumindest sofern man sich selber in Gedicht-übertragungen versucht hat — geneigt sein, Nachsicht zu üben, weil gegen solche Pannen auch der gewissenhafteste Übersetzer auf die Dauer kaum gefeit ist. Es darf demnach (vgl. 156/157) nicht heißen:

Roma la grande
è piena d'archi di trionfo. Su chi
trionfarono i Cesari?

Der entsprechende deutsche Text lautet nämlich, wie bekannt:

Das große Rom
Ist voll von Triumphbögen. *Wer errichtete sie?* Über wen
Triumphierten die Cäsaren?

Doch das sind, wie gesagt, bloße Kleinigkeiten.

Ich erlaube mir, noch zwei weitere und, wie ich meine, beson-ders erhellende Belege anzufügen. Man vergleiche zunächst die berühmte zweizeilige Schlußstrophe des Gedichts "Wahrnehmung" (hier unnötig frei durch "Constatazione" ["Feststellung"] wiedergege-ben) in ihrer deutschen und italienischen Fassung (250/251):

Brecht Then and Now / Brecht damals und heute

Die Mühen der Gebirge liegen hinter uns
Vor uns liegen die Mühen der Ebenen.

Le fatiche delle montagne sono alle nostre spalle
davanti a noi le fatiche delle pianure.

Brechts "liegen hinter uns" durch "sono alle nostre spalle" (wörtlich: "sind in unserem Rücken") wiederzugeben ist natürlich nicht falsch; nicht minder offenkundig ist jedoch, was dadurch an rhetorischer Schärfe und Prägnanz wie an dichterischer Wucht und Gedrängtheit verlorengeht. Und nicht nur hat der Übersetzer — in diesem Falle Roberto Fertonani — den ursprünglichen Chiasmus "hinter uns/Vor uns" in beträchtlichem Maße abgeschwächt, ja verwischt, sondern er hat darüber hinaus, indem er auf die insistierende Wiederholung des Verbums "liegen" verzichtete, die Lakonik der Brechtschen Aussage noch zusätzlich aufgeweicht. Daß man das alles aber ohne jede Schwierigkeit völlig wortgetreu übertragen kann und mithin muß, lehrt beispielsweise die englische Fassung von Martin Esslin aus dem eingangs erwähnten Band *Poems 1913-1956* von 1976. In ihr, die auch den richtigen Titel (nämlich "Observation") trägt, lauten die betreffenden Zeilen:

The travails of the mountains lie behind us.
Before us lie the travails of the plains.

Sollte dergleichen nicht auch im Italienischen möglich sein?
Meinen zweiten Beleg — die Übersetzung stammt abermals von Fertonani — liefert Brechts "Lied vom kleinen Wind" aus seinem Stück *Schweyk im zweiten Weltkrieg*. Wie sich alsbald zeigen wird, ist es diesmal allerdings notwendig, beide Fassungen in ihrer Gesamtheit zu zitieren. Bei Brecht heißt es:

Eil, Liebster, zu mir, teurer Gast
Wie ich kein teurern find
Doch wenn du mich im Arme hast
Dann sei nicht zu geschwind.
　　Nimm's von den Pflaumen im Herbste
　　Wo reif zum Pflücken sind
　　Und haben Furcht vorm mächtigen Sturm
　　Und Lust aufn kleinen Wind.
　　So'n kleiner Wind, du spürst ihn kaum
　　's ist wie ein sanftes Wiegen.
　　Die Pflaumen wolln ja so vom Baum
　　Wolln aufm Boden liegen.

Ach, Schnitter, laß es sein genug
Laß, Schnitter, ein Halm stehn!
Trink nicht dein Wein auf einen Zug
Und küß mich nicht im Gehn.
[Refrain]

In Fertonanis "Canzone della brezza" (wörtlich: "Lied von der Brise")
haben dieselben Brechtschen Verse folgenden Wortlaut:

Corri da me, amante mio caro,
un'altro piú caro non ho sulla terra,
ma quando mi terrai fra le braccia
non avere tanta fretta.
　　Fa' come le susine d'autunno, quando
sono mature e della bufera
furiosa hanno paura, e voglia
di una brezza leggera.
　　Una simile brezza quasi non senti,
è come un soave cullarsi.
Le susine vogliono staccarsi cosí
dall'albero e a terra posarsi.

Ah, falciatore, lasciane quanto basta,
falciatore, lasciane un gambo,
non bere il tuo vino in una sorsata,
e mentre te ne vai non voglio il tuo bacio.
　　[Refrain]

Die Probleme, die eine Übersetzung dieses Gedichts — und zwar in
jede beliebige Sprache — aufwirft, erwachsen sowohl aus dem spezifischen Grundton der Brechtschen Verse samt den darin unüberhörbar
mitschwingenden Untertönen als auch, kaum weniger gewichtig, aus
Gehalt und Struktur einiger Einzelzeilen. Was die letzteren anbelangt,
so müßten, zumindest bei sorgfältiger und mehrfacher Lektüre, vor
allem zwei davon ins Auge fallen. Fertonani schreibt nämlich im
Kehrreim für "Die Pflaumen wolln ja *so* vom Baum" beidemal
ziemlich genau "Le susine vogliono staccarsi [sich loslösen] *cosí*": er
hat mithin Brechts "so" (und zunächst offenbar durchaus einleuchtend)
im allereinfachsten und buchstäblichsten Sinne aufgefaßt. Mir scheint
indes nach reiflicher Überlegung außer Frage zu stehen, daß der
Dichter hier dieses Wort als — übrigens im *Duden* verzeichnete —
umgangssprachliche Nebenform für das gängigere "sowieso" oder
"ohnehin" gebraucht, wofür man dann im Italienischen wohl kaum
"cosí," sondern eher "lo stesso," oder "anche senza questo" zu sagen

373

hätte. Ganz ähnlich, obschon nicht ebenso eindeutig, so scheint mir ferner, verhält es sich auch mit der Schlußzeile der zweiten Gedichtstrophe, bei der es der Übersetzer vorgezogen hat, das schlichte deutsche "Und küß mich nicht *im Gehn*" durch ein arg weitschweifiges "*e mentre te ne vai* non voglio il tuo bacio" (wörtlich: "und während [wenn] du weggehst, will ich nicht deinen Kuß") wiederzugeben. Denn die heikle Frage, die sich hier erhebt, ist ja, ob Brechts "im Gehn" tatsächlich "beim Weg- oder Fortgehen" im Sinne von "Abschiednehmen" meint und damit eine Situation bezeichnet, in der bekanntlich — jedenfalls in der Regel — gerade besonders gern und viel geküßt wird, oder ob jene Wendung nicht vielmehr wirklich und wortwörtlich "im Gehen" im Sinne von "während des Gehens" bedeuten und damit in der Tat eine für den Austausch von Küssen und sonstigen Zärtlichkeiten nicht übermäßig geeignete oder bequeme Stellung bezeichnen soll.

Doch ich möchte diese Frage (wie auch andere, die zum Beispiel das Verhältnis von Titel und Text beträfen) lieber offenlassen und mich statt dessen in aller gebotenen Kürze noch dem zuwenden, was ich vorhin den Grundton des Brechtschen Gedichts samt seinen Untertönen genannt habe. Zweierlei dürfte nämlich bereits beim flüchtigsten Durchlesen unverkennbar sein: zum einen, deutlich für jedermann, das nicht bloß bewußt Volksliedhafte, sondern zugleich vielfach Umgangssprachliche bis geradezu Dialektale von Brechts Versen; zum zweiten, ebenfalls deutlich genug zumindest für den mit Brecht Vertrauten, das bewußt Erotische, ja unverblümt Sexuelle, das untergründig in ihnen mitschwingt (denn "Das Lied vom kleinen Wind" ist schließlich ein handfestes Liebesgedicht). Freilich, wie soll man jene besondere Sprachfärbung oder gar jene bald leisen, bald lauteren Untertöne in einer fremden Sprache treffen und wiedergeben? Oder fänden sich in dem an Dialekten bekanntlich nicht armen Italienischen am Ende doch überzeugende Entsprechungen für — um bloß drei Proben allein aus der ersten Strophe herauszugreifen — Brechts "kein teurern" statt "keinen teureren," für sein "wo" statt "die" und sein "so'n" statt "so ein"? Ich dächte eigentlich schon. Noch weitaus schwieriger, zugegeben, ist allerdings das den Kehrreim durchdringende Erotisch-Sexuelle zu fassen. Was es mit "Pflaumen" in einem Brechtschen Liebeslied auf sich hat, bedarf zwar keiner Erörterung: "Die Pflaume ist in Brechts Lyrik ein häufig verwendetes Sexualsymbol." So Klaus-Detlef Müller, mit Bezug auf das sogenannte "Pflaumenlied" aus *Herr Puntila und sein Knecht Matti*, in der *Großen kommentierten Berliner und Frankfurter Ausgabe* (6: 476). Und dieser Symbolgehalt gilt selbstverständlich nicht nur für Brecht, sondern fürs derb umgangssprachliche Deutsch allgemein. ("Vulva. Wegen der Formähnlichkeit," heißt es im *Wörterbuch der deutschen Umgangs-*

sprache [607] unzweideutig.) Ob dieselbe oder eine ähnliche Symbolik auch im Italienischen vorkommt, weiß ich, wie ich gestehen muß, leider nicht; falls es sie jedoch gibt, so hat Fertonani sie — und erst recht ihre drastischen, deftigen Weiterungen — vielleicht nicht hier, wohl aber anderswo aufs gründlichste verfehlt. Denn in dem besagten, von ihm gleichfalls übertragenen und in den *Poesie* unmittelbar vor dem "Lied vom kleinen Wind" erscheinenden "Pflaumenlied" ("La canzone delle susine") singen die Mädchen bzw. Frauen in der dritten Strophe (vgl. 306/307) nun weiß der Himmel unmißverständlich:

> Als wir eingekocht die Pflaumen
> Macht er gnädig manchen Spaß
> Und er steckte seinen Daumen
> Lächelnd in so manches Faß.

Doch wie lautet dies in Fertonanis Fassung? Es lautet so:

> Mentre la caldaia delle susine bolliva
> fece qualche scherzo indulgente
> e metteva le sue dita
> in un fusto o nell'altro, sorridendo.

Brechts "er" ist selbstredend, wie es in der ersten Strophe heißt, "ein schöner junger Mann"; und was dessen "Daumen" (wie vollends sein Stecken "in so manches Faß") in solch einem Pflaumenzusammenhang bedeutet, brauche ich nunmehr ja schwerlich noch breitzutreten. Fertonani aber setzt — von anderen Mißgriffen nicht zu reden — für dieses metaphorische Glied den absurden Plural "le sue dita," also "seine Finger"! Woraus wir nachträglich, denke ich, guten Gewissens schließen dürfen, daß es jene spezifisch deutsche und insbesondere Brechtsche Symbolik im Italienischen offenbar doch nicht oder jedenfalls nicht im selben Maße, nicht in derselben Weise gibt und daß folglich der Übersetzer sich hier einem schier unlösbaren Problem gegenübersah.

Insgesamt jedoch, ich möchte das nochmals betonen, sind die Übertragungen der *Poesie* durchaus brauchbar und zuverlässig. Gleiches gilt auch für die "Nota introduttiva" von Cesare Cases, obwohl sie bereits über zwanzig Jahre alt ist. Hingegen scheinen die (ebenfalls nützlichen) "Note" aus der Feder von Giuseppina Oneto eigens für Boninos Neuausgabe geschrieben zu sein. Gewiß, diese Onetoschen Anmerkungen beschränken sich auf ein Minimum an Informationen; doch bin ich der Meinung, daß die Verfasserin dazu im Rahmen einer derart gesiebten Auswahl und zudem eines (obschon recht umfangreichen) Taschenbuchs auch ohne weiteres berechtigt war. Desto weniger vertretbar, ja schlechthin unentschuldbar ist aber dafür, so meine ich, der immer wieder festzustellende Mangel an Informationen bei gleichzeitigem Überschuß an Fehlinformationen in einer Ausgabe, die sich ausdrücklich, laut ihres bereits im Titel erhobenen Anspruchs, als eine "kommentierende" verstanden wissen will. Ich spreche beileibe nicht von dem von Müller betreuten Band der *Stücke*, aus dem ich soeben erst beifällig zitiert habe und der nur höchst selten zu wünschen übrigläßt; nein, was ich im Auge habe, ist jene anspruchsvolle Werkedition im allgemeinen wie deren Bände der *Gedichte* im besonderen. Um hierzu bloß einen einzigen Beleg zu bieten: Brechts biblische Bezüge in "Gegen Verführung" — dem schon zu Beginn von mir beigezogenen, weil in den *Poesie* bedauerlicherweise ausgelassenen "Schlußkapitel" der *Hauspostille* — werden von den zuständigen Bandbearbeitern Jan und Gabriele Knopf (vgl. 11: 323) mit keiner Silbe erwähnt, geschweige denn erläutert, so wichtig, ja unumgänglich nötig gerade bei diesem Schlüsseltext solche erklärenden Hinweise wären. Aber all das — und mehr — steht im wahrsten und konkretesten Sinne auf einem anderen Blatt...nämlich in meinem zusammenfassenden Bericht über die ersten zehn Bände der *Großen kommentierten Berliner und Frankfurter Ausgabe*, der vielleicht nicht ganz zufällig, so will mir jetzt rückblickend scheinen, von einer italienischen Zeitschrift (vgl. *Studi tedeschi*, N.S. I.1/2 [1991]: 269-88) veröffentlicht wurde.

Reinhold Grimm
University of California, Riverside

Bertold Brecht. *Journals 1934-1955*. Translated by Hugh Rorrison. Edited by John Willett. New York: Routledge, 1993. 556 pages.

Brecht has warned us that he was a person not to be trusted. He also pointed out that he did not set great store by the idea of "intellectual property," although he did use the concept of intellectual property to his own advantage, when it suited him. Therefore, the Brecht researcher should be the last one to be surprised to find out that not everything which goes under the name of Brecht has actually been written by Brecht, and John Fuegi's *The Life and Lies of Bertolt Brecht* (Harper Collins 1994; US title *Brecht and Company*) should come as no surprise to the serious researcher of Brecht's life and work. Perhaps "Brecht" himself has to be treated as a dividuum, or a name of convenience. I will make no attempt, therefore, to apportion this text to the various authors who go under that name.

Except for the first four pages, the English edition is based on the Suhrkamp edition of the *Arbeitsjournal*. Even less than the letters of Brecht do the journals allow us great insight into the life of the author. Although it is not one Brecht himself used, the German title *Arbeitsjournal*, or literally "Work Journal," indicates more clearly than the English title that the journals were a repository for ideas and for work in progress rather than for biographical or autobiographical jottings. The journals are arranged in six periods: Denmark 1934-1939; Sweden 1939-1940; Finland 1940-1941; America 1941-1947; Switzerland 1947-1948; and Berlin 1948-1955. Excluded are the recently discovered handwritten diary of 1913, when Brecht was an adolescent, and the diary for the years 1920-1922 which appeared in the Methuen edition in 1979. The editors have included a number of autobiographical notes originally collected in the Suhrkamp edition of the *Tagebücher* (1975), along with the earlier *Diary*. This accounts for the first four entries of the English edition dated 1934, 1935, 1936 and 1938. This addition gave me the great pleasure of rereading the short text "i am a playwright," which not only has a very personal meaning to me (my father was a woodcarver and cabinetmaker) but shows Brecht's typical aesthetic pleasure in beautiful and well-crafted objects, a pleasure which always informed his selection of theatre props:

> i would actually like to have been a cabinetmaker, but of course you don't earn enough doing that. i would have enjoyed working with wood. beautiful panelling and balustrades of the old days, those pale, maplewood tabletops as thick as the span of your hand that we found in our grandparents' rooms, worn smooth by the hands of whole generations.

The "Work Journal" proper starts with an entry dated July 1938. In contrast to the first adult diary of 1920, the "Work Journal" is much less spontaneous and, as Brecht himself remarked, "quite distorted for fear of unwelcome readers" (vii). John Willett points out in this introduction that "Brecht was spurred on to write his journals by the fact that after the purges and show trials in the years 1936 to 1938 he could not dare to make a public input into leftist cultural politics any longer." The journals are essentially a product of the dark times, that is, Brecht's period of exile: the period of the Second World War and the Stalinist Period in Russia. Neither could Brecht discuss his modernist views much more openly after his return to the German Democratic Republic in 1949. Not only does this journal say very little about Brecht's private life, but also large areas of his work on such important plays as *Mother Courage*, *Lucullus*, and *Fear and Misery of the Third Reich*, are hardly covered at all. Nevertheless, the journals are not merely a must for the serious Brecht scholar — a collection of theoretical jottings, insights into the psyche of his fellow exiles and the countries of exile, descriptions of mundane everyday events — but they contain as well gems like the text of classical simplicity and wonderfully Brechtian dialectics "Love of Clarity":

> my love of clarity comes from the unclear way i think. i become a little doctrinaire because i was in pressing need of instruction. my thoughts readily become confused, and i don't at all mind saying so. it's the confusion i mind. when i discover something, i immediately contradict it passionately and to my dismay call everything into question again, when a moment before i had been happy as a sandboy, because at least something had, in some measure, been established for my, as i told myself, modest requirements. such statements as that the proof of the pudding is in the eating, or life is a protein condition, console me uncommonly, until i run into further inconveniences. and scenes that take place between people i write down simply because i can't imagine them clearly unless i do.

The journals also contain a collection of often bitingly sarcastic references to fellow exiles, comments on the Second World War and on Californian life and landscape. The scrapbook effect is enhanced by the insertion of photographs (public and personal) and newspaper cuttings from different sources. It is not quite clear why some of the newspaper cuttings and other collected material shown in the German edition have been left out in the English translation. Sometimes, as in the case of the entry for the 17 October 1942, which refers to the letter of Ruth from NY (259), the text does not make sense without either printing the facsimile or giving a translation of that letter.

Translations can never be perfect, but an attempt to translate the sense should not be an excuse for inaccuracies. The sarcastic reference to "Kulturgüter" [cultural assets] with its overtone of [consumer] goods becomes toned down in the translation as "works of art" (255). Brecht's "die realismusdebatte blockiert die produktion" becomes a more slangy: "the realism debate will gum up production" (15). On the whole, however, the translation is adequate.

The German original (Bertolt Brecht, *Arbeitsjournal*. Herausgegeben von Werner Hecht. Frankfurt am Main: Suhrkamp Verlag, 1973) has no notes or index, so the Editorial Notes and the index in the English version add much needed background information and referencing not only for the non-German-speaking reader. The English version, of course, needs to explain references to figures and places well-known to German readers, such as Goethe's Tasso, Alfred Döblin, Erich Maria Remarque, Theodor Wiesengrund-Adorno, Ernst Bloch, Potsdam, and Schwabing. There are, however, a host of helpful notes which explain otherwise obscure allusions in the text and which assist even the informed Brecht reader in navigating the varied personnel of Brecht's days in exile. Most readers, for example, will find an explanation about Julius Hay and his connections to Brecht (2 jul 38) most helpful in order to understand Brecht's immense irritation with his success among the "Moscow clique" (11, 463). A useful addition is also the "Chronology" of Brecht's works and times from 1933 to 1956, allowing the reader to place the individual entries within a wider framework not mentioned or only alluded to in the *Journals*.

This volume was translated by Hugh Rorrison (while the veteran Brecht translator Ralph Manheim could still assist with his advice, he died during the preparation of the volume) and edited by the dean of Brecht translation, John Willett. Notwithstanding some quibbles one may have with the translation and edition, the present volume of Brecht's *Journals* is a valuable addition to the growing collection of Brecht in English, making more of Brecht accessible to the English-speaking audience.

Peter Horn
University of Cape Town

Axel Schnell. *"Virtuelle Revolutionäre" und "Verkommene Götter":*
Brechts "Baal" und die Menschwerdung des Widersachers.
Bielefeld: Aisthesis Verlag, 1993. 152 Seiten.

Baal ist der Böse, der Asoziale. Brechtsche Dialektik vorausgesetzt,
wird damit nicht er selber negiert, sondern das, was um ihn ist: die
bürgerliche Gesellschaft. So sind uns das Stück und gängige Inter-
pretationsmuster zum Baal bekannt. Die Kritik Brechts richtet sich
zuallererst gegen die kapitalistische Gesellschaft, die mittels der
Asozialität der Hauptfigur als an sich asozial entblößt wird. Genauso
— zieht man die Benjaminsche Faszination für den "virtuellen
Revolutionär" in der Figur des Brechtschen Baal in Betracht — kann
man den Text auch als mehr oder minder offene Anklage gegen den
Sozialismus der Brecht vertrauten, frühen fünfziger Jahre lesen: die als
"große Ordnung" wahrgenommene Realität DDR scheint die "permanente Revolution" nicht fortführen zu wollen — oder können. Gegen
beide gesellschaftlichen Ordnungen also, beide "asozial" trotz
gegensätzlicher Programmatik, rennt nunmehr der lebenshungrige wie
lebensmüde Baal an. Soweit der Stand unter den Brecht-Hermeneuti-
kern.

Doch wesentlich mehr steckt hinter dem Image der Figur Baal: er
ist Gott, er ist Ur-Tier, vielmehr Medium eines Mythos. Angenommen
und bisweilen nur angedeutet wurde dies in der Interpretation des
Stückes/Textes vor überraschend langer Zeit. Bewiesen oder hergelei-
tet konnte es bisher nicht werden. Nun steht Baal vor uns als die
mythische Gottheit. Nun taucht es auf aus den Untiefen, das dem
alttestamentarischen Leviathan verwandte Untier des Ichthyosaurus.
Axel Schnell hat die Schichten freigelegt, hat den Ursprung ausgegra-
ben, ist mit dem Leser in die Tiefen, in den "Untergrund," gegangen
— dorthin, wo das Böse lebt und nach Negation drängt. Negation ist
Revolution. Revolution ist Bewegung. Und damit sind wir dann bei
Brecht, dem geistigen Vater des Gedankens, der in seiner magisch-
mythischen Retorte jenen dionysisch-fordernden Homunkulus aus
"virtuellem" (sprich ewigem) Revolutionär und antichristlichem
Fruchtbarkeitsgott geschaffen hat.

Der Autor dieser neuerlichen Baal-Analyse geht aus von frühen
Brecht-Studien und erweitert deren Horizont um Beachtliches. Vor
drei Jahrzehnten bereits entdeckten Eric Bentley (1964) sowie Dieter
Schmidt (1966) mythische Ansätze in der Anlage der Figur des Baal.
Damals endeten deren Ausgrabungen allerdings in Sackgassen der
Inkonsequenz. Erst Schnell gelingt es, mit Hilfe von religionswissen-
schaftlichem, ethnologischem und psychologischem Handwerkszeug
den Stollen weiterzutreiben: in Richtung Mythologie. Dort wird er
fündig. Der "gute Bibelkenner Brecht," der sich mit diesem Text

absichtsvoll auch in der Tradition der *poètes maudits* bewegt, kannte seine Götter zu gut, um beim Entwurf der Figur jenen Gegenspieler Jahwes aus dem Alten Testament nicht mitgedacht zu haben: Baal, Gott und Abtrünnigen, verbannten "Beelzebub," den Erzfeind der asketischen, christlich-jüdischen Tradition — den Fruchtbarkeitsgott.

Neben der Suche nach dem *Woher* der Figur Baal, der sich zwei Drittel der Analyse widmen, ist es auch die (viel wichtigere) Frage nach dem *Wohin* des Baal, des *Wohin* mit dem Baal heute. Was ist/wird nach der Selbstauflösung des Sozialismus von Interesse am Baal? Kann man auch diesen Text anders lesen — oder *Was bleibt* uns Heutigen am Baal? Der Autor sieht drei prinzipielle Kritikpotentiale in der Figur wie im Stück. Da ist zum einen die altbekannte, mythisch-mythologisch verkleidete Revolte gegen die bürgerlich-kapitalistische Gesellschaft. Zum zweiten gelangt die in der Figur des Baal eindeutig gezeichnete antichristliche Haltung auf die Bühne: sich hier auf Nietzsche berufend, behauptet Schnell, das mit der Verurteilung des einst positiv bewertetem Eros durch das Verdikt der Kirche, ausgelebtes "Laster" bestrafen zu müssen, der natürliche Umgang mit dem eigenen, dem menschlichen, Körper verwehrt wurde. Den dritten Kritikkomplex, den hedonistischen Gegenentwurf zum realexistieren*den Sozialismus der frühen 50er Jahre, hatte Benjamin bereits erkannt. Warum sollte es uns nun aber nicht freigestellt bleiben, so Schnell, die Figur Baal als permanente Provokation gegen die "große Ordnung" — unter welchem gesellschaftstheoretischen Namen auch immer — zu lesen. In dem Konzept vom "virtuellen Revolutionär" sieht der Autor Brechts Versuch einer Brauchbarmachung der Dialektik des Bösen. Nicht das Böse an sich ist interessant, sondern die Spirale das Schlimmeren; so wird mit Jean Baudrillard argumentiert, um im nächsten Atemzug zu folgern: "Die Repräsentanz des Bösen ist gleichzeitig die Repräsentanz des Glücksverlangens" (28). Baal ist somit lesbar als die Inkarnation der Revolte von *unten* — auch und vor allem aus der Brechtisch sozialen Perspektive gesehen — die in der heutigen Gesellschaft nur allzuselten zu verspüren ist. Ein weiteres, wesentliches Positivum der Figur des Baal realisiert sich durch ein neues Bewußtsein zur Natur: durch ein ins nahezu Unangenehme getriebene Ausleben der Verkommenheit unserer zivilisatorischen Beziehungen zum (eigenen) Körper und zur Sinnlichkeit.

Auch dort, wo die Revolte auf Negation beruht, wo die Bewegung aus der Zerstörung (des Individuums) hervorgeht, bleibt Raum für Utopie: trotz des Verschleißens an gesellschaftlichen Utopien — und das Böse/Asoziale ist dabei nur Mittel zum Zweck und nicht schon Ziel an sich — zeigt sich im Aufbegehren des Subjekts ein vorwärts-gewandtes Prinzip des Lebens. Das utopische Element liegt ganz darin, "daß eine völlig andere Möglichkeit menschlichen Daseins im

Stück enthalten ist. Der Entwurf ist dionysisch, und er gilt letztlich der Versöhnung von Mensch und Natur" (127).

Dieses kleine Buch liest sich wie eine große Archäologie des Bösen und ist dabei ein Plädoyer für die Revolte des Dionysisch-Archaischen gegen die "große Ordnung," liefernd Wissen für Gegenwärtiges wie Zukünftiges. Auch ist es — und dies ist vom Autor der Studie an die Kollegen gerichtet — ein Plädoyer für die Subjektivität unserer (Literatur-) Wissenschaft: für eine Subjekt-Subjekt-Beziehung zwischen Literaturwissenschaft und zu untersuchendem Text.

Um der straff organisierten Argumentationsfolge des Textes folgen zu können, ist beste Text-/Stückkenntnis vorausgesetzt. Der Autor verschwendet kein Wort auf die Wiedergabe des Handlungs- und Konfliktsfadens. Dagegen ist die Vertrautheit des Autors mit dem biografischen Material Bertolt Brecht (Tagebücher, Briefe, Selbstkommentare) durch eine ausgewogene Anzahl von Zitaten nachvollziehbar. Von kleineren Exkursen abgesehen (z.B. Heiner Müller als folgerichtiger Um-Weg von *Baal* über *Die Maßnahme* zu *Der Auftrag*) und einem meines Erachtens deplazierten vierten Kapitel zur Mythologie der Figur Baal an sich, die man gewiß wesentlich früher im Text hätte einbauen können, bleibt ein Lese- und Denkerlebnis, das in der heutigen postmodernen Interpretationsvielfalt seinesgleichen sucht. Ein wissenschaftlich klarer, harter, zuweilen etwas apodiktischer Duktus führt von einem kurz gefaßten und dafür präzise ausformulierten Kapitel zum nächsten. Des Autors Liebe zur gezielt gesetzten verblosen Apposition läßt vereinzelte Druckfehler vergessen.

Thomas Jung
University of Wisconsin, Madison

Peter Thomson and Glendyr Sacks, eds. *The Cambridge Companion to Brecht*. Cambridge: Cambridge University Press, 1994. xxxii + 302 pages.

Brecht has been dead for nearly forty years, but Brecht scholarship is thriving despite the cataclysmic changes that, beginning in 1989, have radically changed the political map of Europe and have fundamentally altered the post-World-War-II world as Brecht knew it. It seems that the disappearance of communism in Eastern Europe has not completely outmoded the theater theory and practice of one of the proponents of societal change and foes of apparently victorious capitalism. Yet it may be argued that devoting a *Cambridge Companion* to Brecht is tantamount to enshrining him in the pantheon of illustrious, but very dead white male writers such as Dante, Chaucer, Shakespeare, Milton, and their modern equivalents Joyce, Beckett, and Ibsen — all of whom appear in the *Cambridge Companion* series. Actually, it was Max Frisch who, as early as 1964, spoke of Brecht as an ineffectual classic, and for quite some time it has been *de rigueur* in the (West) German *Feuilleton* to consider Brecht's theater as essentially *passé*.

It is not necessarily a given, however, that handbooks and reference works are bound to further the process of canonization of a writer, as is evident from the two volumes of Jan Knopf's *Brecht Handbuch* (1980, 1984) that combine the results of painstaking research with a deliberately engaged pro-Brechtian stance. In contrast to Knopf, the present volume does not promote a unified partisan view. Rather, it attempts to offer "crucial guidance on virtually every aspect of the works of this complex and controversial writer" ([i]). Hence the volume reflects the differing approaches and emphases of the twenty contributors, the majority of whom hail from Great Britain, although Australia and the USA are also represented. *The Cambridge Companion* is, then, clearly intended for an English-speaking public for whom it provides a fairly comprehensive guide and reference work of Brecht scholarship in English.

The volume opens with a useful "Brecht Calendar" by Glendyr Sacks, while the main body of the text is divided into three parts that deal with "Context and Life," "The Plays," and "Theories and Practices," respectively. The emphasis is clearly on Brecht's "theatrical eminence" (xxxii) inasmuch as only the essay by Eve Rosenhaft on the social and political conditions prevailing in Germany from 1898 to 1933 and that by Peter Thomson on the major phases of Brecht's life establish the framework for the discussion of the plays, from *Baal* to *The Caucasian Chalk Circle*, that forms the major section of the volume.

Because of space constraints, a summary review of the ten essays that deal with individual plays or groups of plays may suffice. Tony Meech posits that perhaps the "most extraordinary feature" of Brecht's early plays *Baal, Drums in the Night,* and *In the Jungle (of the Cities),* which are not linked by any "coherent line of thought" (54), "is their originality" (53) and continuing "theatrical appeal" (54). In his essay on *The Threepenny Opera,* in which he indulges in pointedly witty, parenthetical remarks, Stephen McNeff emphasizes the musical aspects of this "unique" (56) work by concentrating on the Brecht/-Weill collaboration.

The following essay by Joel Schechter, in a departure from the generally observed chronological sequence according to the origin of the plays, draws attention to the clownesque elements in *A Man's a Man* but presents debatable conclusions. For example, the assertion that young Brecht "witnessed terrible acts of brutality when he was a medical orderly in the First World War" (76) clearly pertains to the realm of fable rather than fact. Furthermore, the claim that the play "conveys some of Brecht's fiercest opposition to war and militarism" (76) is not convincing, and the analogy Schechter establishes between "The Legend of the Dead Soldier" and *A Man's a Man* is dubious. In her previously published essay Roswitha Mueller distinguishes perhaps too rigidly between the *Lehrstück* and the epic *Schaustück* and ascribes to the former a utopian potential; however, she does not indicate how this utopian potential might be realized in the late 1990s. In a somewhat different vein Christopher McCullough argues that *Saint Joan of the Stockyards* "is best read as part of the *Lehrstück* experiment, a planned transition to socialist art" (98) and polemicizes against Martin Esslin and Eric Bentley's concept of the "lone authorial genius" (102) who was led astray by ideology.

The most controversial piece is, without doubt, John Fuegi's "The Zelda Syndrome: Brecht and Elisabeth Hauptmann," the condensation of arguments he has developed more fully in *Brecht and Company: Sex, Politics, and the Making of the Modern Drama* (New York: Grove, 1994; the title of the British edition is *The Life and Lies of Bertolt Brecht*). Briefly put, Fuegi attempts a wholesale dismantling of Brecht's stature as a playwright and poet by portraying him as an unscrupulous exploiter and scoundrel. He describes Brecht's well-known habit of working in a collective — this method is referred to by several contributors who do not share Fuegi's opinion — as a process during which "Brecht overwhelmingly collected and where others contributed to his fame and financial welfare" (114). Elisabeth Hauptmann in particular, Fuegi suggests, suffered from the "Zelda syndrome," named after F. Scott Fitzgerald's wife, whose literary contributions to her husband's career were not acknowledged.

Although it surely is a *desideratum* to ascertain and acknowledge the contributions of Brecht's female collaborators to his work, Fuegi overshoots the mark by advancing claims based on his mistaken assumption that all Brecht scholarship is hagiographic and that Brecht's collaborators have remained completely unacknowledged. The latter assumption is contradicted, for example, by *Focus: Margarete Steffin* (*Brecht Yearbook* 19 [1994]). As has been pointed out by several critics, underlying Fuegi's reasoning is a misconception of the nature of collective work that comes to the fore especially in the theater and makes it difficult to establish the exact proportion of each contribution to the total work.

Elizabeth Wright offers a Lacanian *cum* feminist reading of *The Good Person of Szechwan* by pointing out that, while Brecht criticizes the institution of "bourgeois marriage [as] a form of legalised prostitution," he neglects to explore the "relation of class oppression to sexual oppression" (121). In his republished essay on *The Life of Galileo* — hardly Brecht's "most popular single work" (139) — Darko Suvin elegantly focuses on the metaphors of seeing and eating and analyzes the play's "unresolved oscillation[s]" (151). Maria Shevtsova's essay on *The Caucasian Chalk Circle* concludes the discussion of the plays and refers to the presence of the Bakhtinian carnivalesque, particularly in the figure of Azdak. She states the fairly obvious by writing that the play is not "an allegory...from a Chinese or Caucasian perspective" (162), but her argument becomes highly speculative and hard to follow when she likens the present countries of Europe to Grusha and Michael who are presumably to serve as an inspirational model for European integration.

As the foregoing remarks have shown, the essays do not cover all the plays. Perhaps the major omission — and one the editors readily acknowledge — is *Mr. Puntila and His Man Matti*, a work that after some initial neglect now has assumed its rightful place among the major plays. All in all, despite their comparative brevity, these essays do provide access to the Brecht canon, even if several of them have been published before or are based on their authors' previous work. At their best, they introduce the reader to new readings as well as unresolved problems of Brecht scholarship.

The lack of inclusiveness is also evident in the seven essays that deal with theoretical and practical issues. As the editors explain, because of space limitations no essays on Brecht's prose had been commissioned. In view of the fact that a considerable part of Brecht's novels, short stories, letters, journals (see the recent translation of *Journals 1934-1955*, published in Great Britain in 1993, in the USA in 1994), and diaries are now available in English, the missing treatment of the prose is regrettable. It is a somewhat different matter with Brecht's work on film, an area that has received increasing attention; because of the paucity of extant translations, the lack of essays on Brecht and film tends to be less conspicuous.

Despite these omissions, the pieces on Brechtian theory and practice, mostly penned by scholars affiliated with departments of theater, do provide a good overview of Brecht's creativity. Carl Weber's historical eye-witness account of the Berliner Ensemble during Brecht's lifetime, which stresses the practical aspects of work in the theater, may serve as a refutation of some of Fuegi's claims, discussed above. Peter Brooker elucidates Brechtian "key terms" such as dialectics, epic theater, *Verfremdung*, and *Gestus*. As Brooker and other contributors mention, owing primarily to John Willett's rendering of the term as "alienation" in his authoritative *Brecht on Theatre*, the translation of *Verfremdung* still poses problems. "Alienation" seems to be inadequate in that it is the "equivalent of the Hegelian/-Marxist *Entfremdung*" (Michael Patterson 274) rather than that of *Verfremdung*. The essay by Philip Thomson on Brecht's poetry is rather incongruously placed among the pieces on the theory and practice of the Brechtian theater. Although it succinctly traces the major stages of Brecht's development as a poet, its comparative brevity poses some limitations. For example, the famed "Of Poor B.B." merits hardly any comment at all, and the note on "house painter" Hitler in "Bad Time for Poetry" refers to the trade Hitler occasionally engaged in but neglects to mention Hitler's ambition to become an artist and, in a different vein, to give Nazi Germany a more pleasant appearance by literal and figurative whitewashing. Kim H. Kowalke deals with Brecht's musical collaborators; he is virtually the only contributor who provides a brief survey of pertinent secondary sources. Stage design, especially Brecht's collaboration with Caspar Neher, and actors' and playwrights' opinions on Brecht are the respective topics of Christopher Baugh and Margaret Eddershaw. Michael Patterson's essay on Brecht's legacy in the theater fittingly concludes the handsomely illustrated volume. Patterson refrains from advancing grandiloquent claims; he takes note of the wide currency of the adjective Brechtian in the English-speaking countries and posits that "[p]erhaps the most truly revolutionary legacy of Brecht is his effect on our understanding of the relationship between performer and spectator" (283-84). Not the ideological Brecht, but Brecht the theater practitioner who insists on seeing "the world with fresh eyes" (285) is in demand at the end of our millenium, it appears.

Restrictive as some may consider such a view, the variety of approaches represented and the fairly encompassing discussion of important aspects of Brecht's work make *The Cambridge Companion* a reliable guide. The volume has been carefully edited; there are few errata (e.g., recte: Berliner Illustrierte [xix], omission of Umlaute [94-95, nn.1, 4, 9]). There is, however, one error of howler format: Der Dreigroschenoper (62). A select, annotated bibliography that is essentially confined to titles in English provides useful information and offers guidance by alerting the reader to the regrettable "unresolved disparities" (288) between the English and American editions of Brecht's Collected Plays. Both editions are still incomplete — the English edition is further advanced — and there seems to be little prospect that eventually a complete English-language standard edition, analogous to the Große kommentierte Berliner und Frankfurter Ausgabe, will emerge. The situation has become further confused by the reissue of translations of both individual plays and groups of plays from the English Collected Plays that are currently being marketed in the USA by the Arcade publishing company. Even if the textual basis for Brecht studies in English is in slight disarray, volumes such as the present one may help readers chart their course through the wide expanse covered by Brecht and his work.

Siegfried Mews
University of North Carolina at Chapel Hill

Bertolt Brecht. **The Arcade Edition of Brecht's Complete Dramatic Work.** (New York: Arcade Publishing, 1993ff.)

The New York Arcade publishing company is currently advertising and marketing a "definitive edition of Brecht's complete dramatic work." Without doubt, such an edition is very desirable; but, as the following discussion will reveal, the claims made by Arcade should be viewed with caution.

The list of currently available Arcade paperback titles of both individual plays and "anthologies" of three plays each published in 1993 and 1994 includes: The Threepenny Opera (Threepenny), Life of Galileo (Galileo), Mother Courage and Her Children (Mother Courage), The Good Person of Szechwan (Good Person), and The Caucasian Chalk Circle (Chalk Circle). Forthcoming in 1995 will be The Rise and Fall of the City of Mahagonny and The Seven Deadly Sins as well as Mr. Puntila and His Man Matti. The "anthologies," which are designated on their respective back covers as the first, second, and third volume of "Arcade's definitive edition," are comprised of the following: The Threepenny Opera, Baal, and The Mother

(Arcade 1), *The Good Person of Szechwan, Mother Courage and Her Children,* and *Fear and Misery of the Third Reich* (Arcade 2), and *Life of Galileo, The Resistible Rise of Arturo Ui,* and *The Caucasian Chalk Circle* (Arcade 3).

While one may applaud the comparative speed with which the volumes have appeared on the American market, the strategy behind issuing individual texts in both single-play editions and "anthologies" remains puzzling. It certainly makes good commercial sense to introduce a new edition (for an elaboration of the term "new," see below) that is not primarily intended for literary scholars and the academic community via plays with an established reputation such as *Threepenny* or *Mother Courage* and to let these plays pave the way for less well-known texts. The sad fate of the American *Collected Plays* (ACP; translated by Ralph Manheim and John Willett, Random House/Vintage) of which only volumes 1-2, 5-7, and 9 have appeared — all of which are now out of print — should serve as a warning. Begun with great hopes in the early 1970s, the editors' initial purpose was to publish all of Brecht's works, as the general title of the series, *Bertolt Brecht: Plays, Poetry, & Prose,* suggests. Yet the goal of publishing the entire body of texts "over a five-year period," announced at the appearance of the first volume of ACP in 1971, proved to be illusory. In contrast to the ACP, the British *Collected Plays* (BCP; also translated by Manheim and Willett) continues to do well in that virtually all published volumes are still in print, some of them in revised translations. After the appearance of *Poems 1913-1956* (1976), two other major publications during the 1990s have considerably enlarged the body of texts of Brecht in English, that is, *Letters 1913-1956* (1990) and *Journals 1934-1955* (1993).

In contrast to both ACP and BCP, which adopt an encompassing and a strictly chronological approach, there is no indication in the Arcade project as to the guiding editorial principle that determines the criteria of selection and the sequence of the plays' publication. In the random order of appearance the Arcade volumes resemble those issued by Grove Press under the general editorship of Eric Bentley since the 1970s and based on Bentley's early translations of the 1940s and 1950s. However, whereas Bentley does not tend to identify the original text or version on which the translation (or adaptation) is based, the Arcade edition of single plays retains the editorial notes and critical apparatus of the Manheim/Willett editions found in both ACP and BCP. For example, the back cover of the Arcade *Mother Courage* (with minor variations, similar comments can be found in other single-play editions) reads:

Commissioned and authorized by the Brecht estate, Arcade's

definitive edition contains a new translation by John Willett and an introduction by the joint editors of Brecht's complete work in English, John Willett and Ralph Manheim. The extensive appendix provides variants and Brecht's own notes and working plan, as well as commentary by the editors on the genesis of the play.

So far, so good. It is one of the distinct advantages of both ACP and BCP that they include commentary, notes, variants, and so on in the same volume that contains the play to which they pertain, unlike the *Gesammelte Werke* of 1967, the authoritative German edition when ACP and BCP began to be published. The flourishing of BCP necessitated reissues of various volumes; hence the critical apparatus in the Arcade single-play volumes, which is that of BCP, tends to be more recent than that of ACP. Introduction and notes in volume 6 of the ACP version of *Good Person*, for instance, date from 1976; the same material in BCP and the Arcade edition was copyrighted in 1985.

Whereas retaining the BCP critical apparatus in the Arcade editions does not seem to pose a problem, one should perhaps be less sanguine about the choice of translations — one major area in which ACP and BCP do not agree. The fact that these translations are derived from BCP rather than from ACP raises the legitimate question of their appropriateness for an American audience. It is to be assumed that one of the reasons for offering two different versions of Brecht's plays in English was the editors' recognition of the linguistic, idiomatic, and other differences between American and British English. Ironically, these differences are disregarded in that the Arcade edition uses the BCP translations — with the exception of *Threepenny* (Manheim and Willett are listed as translators in both ACP and BCP), *The Mother* (not included in ACP), and *The Resistible Rise of Arturo Ui* (Manheim is the translator in both cases). Perhaps owing to the death of Manheim in 1992 at age eighty-five — Willett acknowledged his collaborator's contributions to "Englishing the German from Hitler to Grass" in a tribute (*Guardian* 29 Sept. 1992) — and resulting copyright restrictions, recourse to the translations of BCP was the only possibility. One certainly could have done worse than to use the translations by Willett, now the unchallenged chief mediator of Brecht in the English-speaking world, and others.

But there are obvious drawbacks in Arcade's use of the BCP translations for the American market. For example, in the introduction to the Arcade *Mother Courage* Willett writes:

> Our translation [i.e., Willett's] therefore sets out to tackle this key problem [of how to render adequately the "untranslatable" speech in the play] by using a somewhat analogous artificial diction,

based this time on those north English cadences which can reflect a similarly dry, gloomily, humorous approach to great events. (xxi)

It is not the place here to engage in a detailed analysis of various translations; suffice it to cite the beginning passage of *Mother Courage*, in which the Recruiter is addressing a Sergeant, to illustrate the considerable differences between ACP and BCP/Arcade:

How can you muster a unit in a place like this? I've been thinking about suicide, Sergeant [sic]. Here am I, got to find our commander four companies before the twelfth of the month, and people round here are so nasty I can't sleep nights. S'pose I get hold of some bloke and shut my eyes to his pigeon chest and varicose veins, I get him proper drunk, he signs on the line, I'm just settling up, he goes for a piss, I follow him to the door because I smell a rat; bob's your uncle, he's off like a flea with the itch. No notion of word of honour, loyalty, faith, sense of duty. This place has shattered my confidence in the human race, sergeant [sic]. (Willett, Arcade 3: 3)

How can anybody get a company together in a place like this? Sergeant, sometimes I feel like committing suicide. The general wants me to recruit four platoons by the twelfth, and the people around here are so depraved I can't sleep at night. I finally get hold of a man, I close my eyes and pretend not to see that he's chicken-breasted and he's got varicose veins, I get him good and drunk and he signs up. While I am paying for the drinks, he steps out, I follow him to the door because I smell a rat: Sure enough, he's gone, like a fart out of a goose. A man's word doesn't mean a thing, there's no honor, no loyalty. This place has undermined my faith in humanity, sergeant. (Manheim, ACP 5: 135)

The problems of how effectively to communicate Brecht to the American public are exacerbated in Arcade 1-3 that dispense with the critical apparatus of the single-play volumes and substitute a chronology of Brecht's life and work as well as a general introduction by Hugh Rorrison. Rorrison's introductory material was copyrighted by Methuen in London in 1987. Apart from being clearly geared to "Britain in the eighties" (Arcade 3: xxxviii), no attempt has been made to take recent, post-Wall developments into account. In discussing *Galileo*, for example, Rorrison refers to "[s]cientific ethics in the USSR" and cites as a reason for the topicality of the play "Chernobyl and the Reagan Star Wars programme" (Arcade 3: xxix). Similarly, the now defunct "German Democratic Republic" is mentioned as a country that "still silently groans today" under its special form of "information management" (Arcade 3: xxxiii). It goes without saying, general introductions that — unlike the ACP/BCP editorial comments on textual genesis and the like — seek to demonstrate the relevance of Brecht's plays by alluding to current affairs need to be reasonably up-to-date.

The Arcade volumes 1-3 also raise the question as to which criteria governed the inclusion of specific plays in specific volumes. It is probably not too far-fetched to assume that commercial considerations were the motivating factor for combining renowned plays such as *Threepenny*, which would sell well independently, with plays that lack such stature (e.g., *Baal* and *The Mother* in Arcade 1). Such an assumption does not adequately explain, however, why precisely these three plays were incorporated in one volume. Surely, Rorrison's remark that in "the three plays in [Arcade 1] Brecht travels from absolute sensual anarchism [in *Baal*] to absolute intellectual socialism [in *The Mother*]" (Arcade 1: xxxviii) hardly qualifies as a convincing explanation, particularly in view of the fact that no reasons are given for the selections in Arcade 2-3. Although Rorrison's statement, "The volumes that follow [Arcade 1] show how the position he [Brecht] reached at the end of the Weimar Republic was refined and elaborated in the years of exile that were to follow" (Arcade 1: xxxviii) appears to point in the direction of non-inclusive, chronological selection, adherence to chronology would virtually preclude issuing further "anthologies" inasmuch as Arcade 3 includes *Chalk Circle*, Brecht's last major play.

As the foregoing remarks have shown, the claims of "Arcade's definitive edition of the complete dramatic work" that offers "new" translations should be perceived with considerable caution. While the editorial comments and critical apparatus of the Manheim/Willett ACP and BCP continue to be an important tool for gaining informed access to the texts, the choice of the BCP translations and introductory materials in the three "anthologies" are puzzling indeed. True, the handsomely designed Arcade paperbacks may take their place alongside the editions of the Grove Press plays and contribute to enriching the extant body of Brecht texts in the United States. But a clear editorial concept of the Arcade project's purpose as well as an explanation of this concept might have gone a long way in facilitating the general acceptance of the "new" Arcade edition. It remains to be seen whether Brecht's *Plays* in the Continuum German Library, edited by Reinhold Grimm and, according to the publisher, scheduled to appear in May 1995, may compensate for what is lacking in the present "definitive" edition.

Siegfried Mews
University of North Carolina at Chapel Hill

Herbert Frenken. *Das Frauenbild in Brechts Lyrik*. **Frankfurt: Peter Lang, 1993. 250 pages.**

In the present study, a well laid-out doctoral dissertation, the term *Bild* (image) encompasses both metaphor and simile/comparison (18). Frenken posits that so far only feminists have analyzed the image of woman in Brecht's work and that these scholars have mainly focused on female figures in Brecht's theatrical work, while the imagery of the feminine in his poetry has gone largely unexplored. Therefore, Frenken sets out to examine the metaphoric changes to which Brecht subjects the embodiment of the feminine in his poetry, expecting that the insights gained by this inquiry will add to the appreciation of Brecht's lyrical work (14ff.).

In the first part of his study, entitled "Leit-Bilder und Leit-Motive," constituting more than half of the book, Frenken succeeds particularly well in his purpose. Under the heading of "Aquamorphismus" he demonstrates good judgment and sound skills in his analysis of poems like "Beuteltier mit Weinkrampf" (27ff.), while in a later subsection he gives a sensitive reading of "Das Schiff" (63ff.), associating these and other poems and ballads of the *Baal* years with Brecht's unscrupulous vitalism and his male bravado (passim). In the section "Der Körper der Frau," Frenken examines closely the erotic function of words like "knee," "eyes and face," "skin," and "hair" in Brecht's poetry. He comes to the conclusion that, despite Brecht's relentless criticism of bourgeois society, his early poetry abounds with examples of conventional male chauvinism (106). In the last section of part I, "Die Erotik des Essens," Frenken surveys how in Brecht's early lyrical work pirates and other male figures show a tremendous appetite for both food and women as a way of appropriating the world. What follows is quick saturation on the one hand and eventual poetic production on the other (119ff.).

The second half of Frenken's study offers fewer new insights. In the chapter "Mutterbild" Frenken analyzes early poems dealing with Brecht's contradictory relationship to his mother: his closeness to her, his love and respect for her, and his rebellion against her. Frenken devotes a subsection to the political implications of Brecht's mother image in which he dwells briefly on Pelagea Vlassova of *The Mother*. However, by overlooking poems of the poet's middle period in praise of resolute women, like "Ballade von der alten Frau" and "Mutter Beimlen," Frenken misses a link between Brecht's early poetry devoted to the special mother-son relationship and the lyrics he bestows in his late plays on spirited mother figures like Shen-Te and Grusha. In fact, these lyrics are totally ignored in Frenken's study.

The third and last chapter, "Frauen um Brecht," focuses first on the lyrical precipitates of the young poet's relationship with the pliable "Bittersweet," Paula Banholzer, which Frenken pits against poems concerning Brecht's simultaneous love affair with the more independent-minded Hedda Kuhn. Frenken calls attention to the young Brecht's anxieties in "An Bittersweet," pointing to a vulnerability covered up in most of his love poetry by the male's cool bravado (184f.). While it is a joy to follow Frenken's careful and sensitive analyses of even the shortest poem, like the late, twelve-word "Gleichklang" also devoted to Banholzer (186f.), there is not much new here.

The same holds true for the discussion of poetry devoted to three of the four most important women in Brecht's later life: Helene Weigel, Margarete Steffin, and Ruth Berlau. From the poems available, Frenken draws perceptive conclusions concerning Brecht's relationship to his actress-wife. Undoubtedly, the great mother roles in Brecht's plays (Pelagea Vlassova, Teresa Carrar, Mother Courage) were inspired by Weigel (197). Yet, speaking of the poems Brecht dedicated to this formidable actress, it appears unfair to call her a "demonstration object" (203) rather than a demonstrator of Brecht's (and her own) political ideas. Turning to Brecht's lyrical production for Steffin, Frenken observes rightly that the love poetry of 1933/34 is closely connected with the erotic verses of the *Baal* years, whereas in the poetry written for or about Steffin in 1937/41, he celebrates a new equality between a male and a female partner (222). In the writings directed to Berlau there is just one poem, "Kin-jeh sagte von seiner Schwester," in which Brecht expresses a similar sense of equality. Frenken is correct in pointing out that this is a case of spurious sameness, since Brecht envied Berlau's courage when she ventured into the Spanish Civil War, leaving her frightened lover behind (228f.). A perceptive analysis of Brecht's resigned poem of 1953, "Veränderung aber zum Schlechten" (234f.), adds to what is already known from Lyon and Bunge about the Brecht-Berlau relationship.

Frenken seems unaware of the two poems in which Brecht apparently addressed Elisabeth Hauptmann, his closest and foremost *Mitarbeiter* (see Klaus Völker's *Brecht: Biographie*, 144, and John Willett, "Bacon ohne Shakespeare? The Problem of Mitarbeit," *The Brecht Yearbook* 12, 122). The latter is not included in Frenken's otherwise excellent bibliography that will do much to acquaint German readers with secondary literature in English. The book has a helpful index of the more than 200 Brecht poems discussed. It is a good introductory text, written in clear prose.

Laureen Nussbaum
Portland State University

Susan A. Manning. *Ecstasy and the Demon. Feminism and Nationalism in the Dances of Mary Wigman.* Berkeley: University of California Press, 1993. 353 pages.

Ein Buch über ein Kapitel der deutschen Tanzgeschichte, dem Ausdruckstanz und seiner Verquickung mit dem Faschismus im Deutschland der dreißiger und vierziger Jahre, von einer amerikanischen Autorin, auch als Spiegel zur ideologischen Selbstreflexion des amerikanischen Modern Dance geschrieben — und nun von einer deutschen Autorin für eine amerikanische Fachzeitschrift, ausgerechnet einem Brecht-Jahrbuch, rezensiert.

Welche Blickwinkel, welche Blickvielfalt, treffen da aufeinander? Sicherlich kann ich nicht umhin mit dem Blick eines deutschen Lesers, einer deutschen Tanzforscherin, diesem Buch zu begegnen; freudig, wo es endlich die Lücken der deutschen modernen Tanzgeschichtsschreibung füllt; nachdenklich, wo mich der amerikanische Blick auf das jüngere Tanzgeschehen in Deutschland befremdet; beunruhigt, wo jener Blick diese mißinterpretiert, vorschnell etikettiert und zu vieles auf einen Nenner, in den Blick-Gestus des Buches drängen will. Liebend gerne würde ich den Kern des Buches — die Auseinandersetzung mit dem Werk Mary Wigmans und dessen schleichender ästhetischen wie kontextuellen Angleichung an die faschistische Ästhetik und Ideologie sowie ihrer nachträglichen Selbst-Mystifizierung zum Opfer im Nachkriegsdeutschland — der deutschsprachigen Tanzliteratur als Bereicherung zugesellen. Aber ebenso liebend gerne würde ich in den verkürzenden bis verzerrenden Darstellungen Susan Mannings über die Beziehungen zwischen Ausdruckstanz, Tanztheater und dem Tanz im geteilten Deutschland für den amerikanischen Leser die Lücken und Auslassungen auffüllen.

Doch zuerst zur Faszination des Buches: Susan Manning entwirft in ihrer anti-biographischen Lesart des Lebenswerkes der ebenso bewunderten wie mystifizierten Protagonisten des deutschen Ausdruckstanzes ein Szenarium, in dem die Verwobenheit von professionellen Arbeitsbedingungen, den sich verändernden Strukturen zur Förderung des modernen Tanzes in Deutschland und dem schleichenden Wechsel des ideologischen Bedeutungsgehaltes in Wigmans Werk deutlich und klar wie nie zuvor zu Tage tritt. Manning entwirrt Paradoxa im Werk und künstlerischen, pädagogischen und persönlichen Wirken Mary Wigmans ohne anzuklagen, ohne die Person Wigmans politisch abzustempeln oder abzuurteilen. Vielmehr zeichnet sie behutsam den stufenweisen Wandel in Wigmans Werk von einer modernistischen Ästhetik in den zwanziger Jahren zur faschistischen Ästhetik und nationalistischen Rhetorik in den dreißiger Jahren nach. Darüberhinaus entdeckt sie einen weiteren Bruch im

Bedeutungsgehalt der Stücke nach 1936, der Zeit der Negierung Wigmans durch die nationalsozialistische Kulturpolitik, hin zu einer ambivalenten Reflexion über die Rolle des Individuums, des Künstlers und der Frau in der deutschen "Volksgemeinschaft." Begrenzter Widerstand oder Verdrängung der eigenen Einlassung? Das, so die Autorin, bleibe die aufregende Frage in Wigmans Karriere.

Unabhängig davon, ob man jeder Spur ihrer Lesart zustimmen mag, ist es faszinierend, der Autorin in ihrer facettenreichen "Rekonstruktion" der Solo- wie Gruppenchoreographien Wigmans zu folgen. *Celebration* von 1928, die letzte Ensemblearbeit der ersten und berühmtesten Tanzgruppe Wigmans, versteht Manning als Kulmination des Paradoxon der utopischen Versöhnung von Gemeinschaft und Individuum, von Autorität der Choreographin (Führerin) und Autonomie des Ensembles (einer weiblichen Gemeinschaft). Die Choreographie markiert das Ende einer Ära. Susan Manning widerspricht, wie an vielen anderen Stellen auch, mit ihrer werkimmanenten Lesart von Tanzgeschichte eindimensionalen Erklärungen, hier z.B. der bekannten Version von der Auflösung der Tanzgruppe Wigman aus finanziellen Gründen. Die Individualität ihrer Tänzer, die Wigman trotz ihrer Utopie von einer weiblichen Gemeinschaft und des "collective body" herausforderte, sprengte letzlich die Idee einer utopischen Tanzgemeinschaft. Am Beispiel ihres nächsten Gruppenwerkes, des Tanzspektakels *Totenmal* von 1930, verdeutlicht die Autorin ein Miß- oder politisches Unverständnis, mit dem viele Künstler dieser Zeit indirekt der nationalsozialistischen Ästhetik Vorschub leisteten: Im Streben nach einem Theater jenseits aller Politik kreierten sie ein Theater der ambivalenten politischen Stellungnahme. *Totenmal* gerät zum protofaschistischen Theater und liefert als choreographisches Massenspektakel das dramaturgische Modell der späteren Nazi-Inszenierungen. Trotz klarer Position zieht Manning auch hier feine Linien, verweist auf unseren Vorsprung der retrospektiven Interpretation.

Aus der additiven, zeitgenössischen wie retrospektiven, Lesart der Stücke kristallisieren sich typologische Widersprüchlichkeiten und Kategorien heraus, die der Autorin als Gradmesser für ästhetische wie ideologische Veränderungen der Werke im Verlauf der Jahrzehnte dienen. Dem bereits erwähnten Verhältnis von Gruppe und Individuum, artikuliert im Verhältnis von Gemeinschaft und Autorität bzw. charismatischer Führerschaft der Choreographin, kommt dabei besonderer Stellenwert zu. Manning demonstriert, wie die utopische Versöhnung von Autorität und Autonomie, offenkundig in den frühen Werken, dem dystopischen Kontrapunkt zwischen Führer und Masse in den dreißiger Jahren weicht: "It is this shift — and Wigman's choreographic realization of the Führerprinzip (leadership principle) — that I term fascist." Das Ideal einer weiblichen Gemeinschaft — für

Manning zweifelsfrei der zentrale Gehalt der Arbeiten Wigmans bis 1928 — weicht dem faschistischen Vorbild der Volksgemeinschaft. Widersetzten sich Wigmans Choreographien bis Ende der zwanziger Jahre dem vereinnahmenden "männlichen Blick" — u.a. durch die geschlechts- und nationalitäts-unspezifische "Gestalt im Raum" und den neutralisierenden Gebrauch der Maske — so greifen die Choreographien der dreißiger Jahre auf vormals abgelehnte Repräsentationen des tanzenden Körpers zurück: Autobiographie, weibliche Archetypen, Musik-Visualisierung. Mit der klaren Artikulation von traditionellen (und von den Nationalsozialisten wieder propagierten) Frauenbildern in Gruppen- wie Solostücken — die Frau als Ehefrau und Mutter, als Trauernde und als heroische, aufopferungsvolle Märtyrerin — tritt Wigman nicht nur hinter ihre eigene Position der "Gestalt im Raum" der zwanziger Jahren zurück, sondern, eine weitere Lesart Mannings, auch hinter Isadora Duncans autobiographische Bühnen-Repräsentationen einer neuen weiblichen Erfahrung und eines teil-emanzipierten Frauenbildes.

Immer wieder zeigt Manning neben der internen Sicht (aus dem Werk heraus gelesen) die äußeren Umstände als mitwirkend auf. Nie zuvor wurden für mich in einer Darstellung über den Ausdruckstanz und seine Involvierung mit dem Faschismus die alltäglichen Gleise in die Anpassung so deutlich: zum Beispiel das Faktum der Sättigung des Bedarfs an Laientanz-Schulen Ende der zwanziger Jahre, das die jungen Tänzer sich den Opernhäusern als neue Betätigungsfelder nähern ließ und somit den Konflikt um die Professionalisierung des modernen Tanzes nur noch schürte. Oder die Direktheit, mit der die Kulturpolitik der Nationalsozialisten die ökonomische wie künstlerische Krise des Ausdruckstanz in ihrem Sinne nutzte, "löste," u.a. indem das Kulturministerium Forderungen der Tänzerkongresse aus der Weimarer Zeit aufgriff und (seiner Politik gemäß modifiziert) realisierte. Die Aufteilung der Verantwortlichkeit zwischen Kulturministerium für den Bühnentanz und Alfred Rosenbergs Kampfbund für deutsche Kultur für die mehr der körperlichen Erziehung zugeordneten Laientanz- und Gymnastikbewegung vertiefte, so die Autorin, den Konflikt zwischen populistischer (Laientanz-) Fraktion und den Befürwortern einer autonomen (Bühnen-) Tanzkunst. Die kunsttheoretische Zuordnung von avantgardistisch versus modernistisch, die Manning hier für die beiden Lager vornimmt, erhellt die oft widersprüchlichen Positionen im Ausdruckstanz zusätzlich.

Mary Wigman als Fallstudie für die Auseinandersetzung mit dem Ausdruckstanz bildet den Kern des Buches. Eingerahmt wird dieser Kern durch tanzhistorische Lesarten zur deutschen wie amerikanischen Tanzmoderne, für die Wigman lediglich als Aufhänger dient. In diesen Rahmenkapiteln wird der Demonstrationscharakter des Buches deutlich spürbar: die Fallstudie soll auf eine "Revision" der westlichen Theatertanzgeschichte vermittels neuer interdisziplinärer, ideologie-kritischer Forschungsmethoden im Tanz verweisen. Die beiden letzten Kapitel — über das zeitgenössische Tanztheater in beiden deutschen Staaten bzw. über den Amerika-Mythos im frühen amerikanischen Modern Dance — wirken dabei wie angehängt, die Zusammenhänge zum Kern des Buches konstruiert. Nun könnte man auf den Informationscharakter dieser Kapitel verweisen. Doch dieser Gedanke bereitet mir hinsichtlich der sehr interpretativen und z.t. fehlerhaften Ausführungen Susan Mannings zum Tanzgeschehen in Deutschland seit 1945 Unwohlsein. Geschichte wird hier den Hypothesen des Buches angepaßt. Manning beschreibt beispielsweise die personelle wie ästhetische Kontinuität im Bühnentanz über die Schwelle 1945 hinaus, hinterläßt dabei jedoch den Eindruck, daß diese Entwicklung tanzspezifisch gewesen sei. Dem ist mit vielfältigen Beispielen aus dem Sprechtheater oder Musikbereich zu widersprechen. Die sensiblen Ohren der zurückgekehrten Emigranten konstatierten sehr wohl auf den deutschen Sprechtheaterbühnen der Nachkriegszeit die Kontinuität von "Reichskanzleistil" und "Rhetorik der Nazizeit." 1945 als "Stunde Null" wird heute für viele Bereiche der künstlerischen Produktion in der Rückschau in Frage gestellt. Ebenso wird die in der Literatur oft zitierte Bruchstelle von 1933 hier in einer zu eindimensionalen Blickweise kritisiert. In meinem Verständnis der geschichtlichen Lesart hat genau der von der Autorin an Hand von Mary Wigman beschriebene, schleichende Veränderungsprozeß dazu geführt, das Datum 1933 (und nicht 1945) als die wesentliche Bruchstelle (in Sinne einer historischen Marke) für die anschließende Kontinuität der nationalsozialistisch verbrämten Weimarer Kunstästhetik über 1945 hinaus zu benennen. Dies nicht zu erkennen, darin bestand das große Mißverständnis des Kulturlebens im Nachkriegsdeutschland.

Unverständlich ist mir, wie Manning den Eindruck gewinnen konnte, das Ausdruckstanz-Erbe hätte in der DDR offizielle Pflege erfahren und sei integrativer Bestandteil des ost-deutschen Tanztheaters geworden. Künstlerisch widersprechen dem Ästhetik und Formensprache des DDR-Tanztheaters; ideologisch suspekt waren subjektiver Ausdruckswille und die Betonung des Individuums des Modernen Tanzes. Bereits Ende der vierziger Jahre begannen in der DDR die hitzigen Debatten über sozialistischen Realismus und Ausdruckstanz, die u.a. Wigman, Hoyer und Vogelsang zum Übersiedeln in den West-Teil veranlaßten. Die Abteilung Neuer Künstlerischer Tanz (die offizielle Bezeichnung in der DDR für Ausdruckstanz) an der staatlichen (Ost-) Berliner Ballettschule wurde 1958 abgeschafft. Die Duldung der Präsenz von Gret Palucca in ihrer 1949 verstaatlichten Dresdner "Fachschule für Tanz" gäbe sicherlich Anlaß zu einer vergleichbaren Recherche wie Manning sie zu Wigman und dem Dritten Reich unternahm. Wie Wigman, so hat wohl auch Palucca ihren Schülern etwas vom Geist des Ausdruckstanzes — neben oder trotz der offiziellen Linie — vermitteln können. In dieser personenbezogenen Vermittlung konnte die junge Generation in Osten wie Westen Deutschlands in den Nachkriegsjahrzehnten die eigene moderne Tanzvergangenheit erahnen.

Innerhalb der deutschsprachigen Literatur müßte Susan Mannings Lesart der Geschichte des deutschen Tanztheaters von den verfügbaren Primär-Quellen oder auch der Sekundärliteratur kommentiert und korrigiert werden. Schade, daß diese Möglichkeit für den amerikanischen Leser kaum besteht.

Susanne Schlicher
Universität Bremen

Seung Jin Lee, *Aus dem Lesebuch für Städtebewohner. Schallplattenlyrik zum "Einverständnis."* Frankfurt/M.: Peter Lang, 1993. 190 Seiten.

Originally a University of Karlsruhe dissertation supervised by Jan Knopf, Seung Jin Lee's book on Brecht's poetry reader *Aus einem/dem Lesebuch fur Städtebewohner* undertakes an exhaustive reassesment of the existing textual variants, drafts, and other sources contained in the Bertolt-Brecht-Archiv, the Akademie der Künste, and the estates of collaborator Elisabeth Hauptmann, publisher Wieland Herzfelde, and Walter Benjamin. On the basis of his research, the author argues that the *Lesebuch* is in fact two "books," a more expansive, planned but uncompleted compilation dating from 1926/27, which is related to dramatic fragments like *Weizen/Joe Fleischhacker*, and the largely autonomous collection reconceived as "Schallplattenlyrik" for volume two of the media-experimental *Versuche* published in 1930.

The book's first twenty-odd pages recount the text's travails proceeding from the first mention of the title in 1927 to the first publication in 1930, the hindered *Malik-Ausgabe*, and ending with the recent GBFA edition. In this chapter Lee corrects the view that the 1930 *Lesebuch* represents the belated realization of Brecht's earlier plans for the collection and in fact no longer corresponded to his aesthetic and political interests at the time of its publication. Without questioning the so-called *Phasen-Theorie* in a fundamental way, the author goes on to challenge the notion that the *Lesebuch* is a transitional work in Brecht's political and aesthetic development, arguing here and elsewhere in the book that the text is very much in keeping with the "Marxist" Brecht. In contradistinction to the practice of GBFA and earlier editions, in which the final verses are enclosed in parenthesis and are thus not distinguished from other parenthetics in the poems, Lee plausibly recommends the differentiating square brackets that Brecht introduced for the *Versuche* edition in the interest of accentuating their media-aesthetic dimension.

The second, and longest, chapter provides a text-critical apparatus and stemmic representations of the development of each of the collection's ten poems. Without claiming to be a historical-critical edition, the author's meticulous work complements and extends the notes and commentary in the 1988 GBFA edition and illustrates the changes made for the 1930 collection which included the rearrangement, editing, and new selection of poems.

In Chapter 3, the author treats the *Lesebuch* with regard to the context and composition of the second volume of the *Versuche*, dealing with the theme of urbanity, the text's media-experimental character, and the notion of "Einverständnis" as the *Lesebuch's* pedagogical objective. Unfortunately, the author's often suggestive individual observations are impeded by his inattention to the theoretical developments that have occupied literary studies in recent years. The section on the *Lesebuch* as a media experiment suffers particularly in this regard: Lee operates with an unsophisticated concept of media and sorely underestimates the complexity of Brecht's textual practice in the *Lesebuch*, relying too heavily on Brecht's assumed authorial/pedagogical intentions.

Close readings of each of the poems comprise the bulk of Chapter 4. In his somewhat conventional analyses the author affords special attention to the "Redesituation" of the *Lesebuch*, showing how the text stages a complex communicative configuration aimed at productively engaging and "schooling" the reader for the demands of the big city. Less convincing is the author's distinction between a "first" and "second" reading in the chapter's organization. While Lee shows how meaning and structures of address and communication accrue in a chronological reading of the *Lesebuch*, one is left wondering what new aspects might emerge when a more "epic" reading posture is assumed. Moreover, the author suggests that the reader can "know" this text in some comprehensive way and that "Unklares" can be eliminated through repeated readings (152). While one need not appeal to Brecht's authority in this matter (as Lee generously does in other places), Brecht's own concept of reading — and of reading poetry in particular — would seem to allow for more possibilities than this.

The closing discussion in the final chapter, of the sparse scholarly literature on the *Lesebuch* begins with a short methodological prelude that proposes a Knopf-inspired "Objektivierung" of literary studies and introduces the book's second problematic binary with the opposition between "Deutungen" and "Analysen." Whether or not one agrees with the possibility of distinguishing between the "subjektive Beliebigkeit" of the former and the latter's "objektivierbare[n] Daten" in a theoretically rigorous way, this contrivance serves neither author nor reader very well (163). It leads to rather frequent pronouncements of correct and false readings that seem out of place in the treatment of something as subtle as poetic language. Lee's critique of Dieter Wöhrle's *Bertolt Brechts medienästhetische Versuche* in particular seems unnecessarily polemical. Wöhrle's interpretation of the *Lesebuch* as a figuration of the urban "Hörsituation" overlaps to no small degree with Lee's own media-aesthetic approach to the text. The author's brief mention of Walter Benjamin in the history of the *Lesebuch's* reception deserves more attention and does not engage the critic's complex relationship to the text in ways that could open up his own interpretation in productive ways. Instead, Benjamin's notice of the *Lesebuch's* "sadistic element" and his later renunciation an earlier commentary on the text is omitted and the matter relegated to a footnote (165).

Lee's contribution to scholarship on the *Lesebuch* lies above all in his painstaking documentation and detective work. The author describes the convoluted history of the collection in an uncluttered prose that illustrates Brecht's characteristic process of continuous revision and rewriting. In several instances in the book's more interpretive portions Lee points to suggestive connections to dramatic and other lyric projects. The book's weaknesses stem from the author's inattention to pressing theoretical concerns and his tendency to accept Brecht's own political and aesthetic positions uncritically in interpreting the *Lesebuch*.

Stefan Soldovieri
University of Wisconsin-Madison

Chetana Nagavajara. *Brecht and France*. Bern: Peter Lang, 1994. 191 pages.

The latest book of a scholar, who — Professor of German at Silpakom University in Nakom Pathom (Thailand) — is widely known for his monograph *August Wilhelm Schlegel in Frankreich* (Tübingen 1966), concerns a writer whose plays the author has discussed in his native tongue in a study entitled *The Dramatic Works of Bertolt Brecht* (Bangkok 1983). Moreover, as Nagavajara explains, "a shortened version" of *Brecht and France* "was published in Thai in the *Journal of the Faculty of Arts, Silpakom University* 10.2 (1988)" (13). To this bibliographical reference he adds the comment: "Although the present version in English does not depart substantively from the shortened Thai version, I have tried to incorporate into the monograph relevant findings from more recent publications" (ibid.). Indeed, as the perusal of the bibliography shows, the most recent entries date from 1991.

The slim volume here under review is an outgrowth of the author's alertness to a noticeable gap in Brecht scholarship and his desire to fill that gap as best he could. His impulse was surely right; for although, at least in matters artistic, Brecht's French connections were considerably weaker than, say, those with England which, focused on the drama, have been fully explored by specialists like Paul Kussmaul (*Bertolt Brecht und das englische Theater der Renaissance*), their scope and significance must not be underrated. Unfortunately, by producing a fairly eclectic and to a certain extent superficial study on the subject that is basically a Review of Research, Nagavajara has missed an opportunity to map the terra incognita with the help of truly original research.

For "purely practical reasons" (12) *Brecht and France* was written in, or better translated into, English rather than German because, as the author puts it: "I know many scholars, critics and practitioners who know their Brecht very well but who have little German. My experience particularly[...]in my home country and in non-German-speaking countries, has been that non-Germanists have played a very decisive role in keeping Brecht alive." He has a point, but regrettably his command of the English language is far from perfect, and no proper editorial care has been lavished on his manuscript.

As for Nagavajara's method, it is by his own admission factual: "It will[...]appear at times that the present study makes too many concessions to positivism. But I come from a non-Western culture and do not feel committed to any particular research methodology which may happen to be held in high esteem in Western academic circles at a particular time" (12). It is quite in keeping with this credo that he routinely introduces such minor, though not necessarily trivial, evidence as is constituted by unpublished letters and marginal notations in the books from Brecht's personal library now in the Bertolt-Brecht-Archives.

Taken by itself, i.e., lacking an explanatory subheading, the title of Nagavajara's book is ambiguous. In an essay published over three decades ago, Anna Balakian remarked: *and* as well as *in* are "defenseless little words" meant "to protect precarious hypotheses and international literary debts" ("Influence and Literary Fortune: The Equivocal Junction of Two Methods," *Yearbook of Comparative and General Literature* 11 [1962], 25). However, any doubts regarding the author's real intentions are removed in the opening paragraph of his Introduction (1), where a basic distinction between the formulas "Brecht and France" and "Brecht in France" is drawn. According to Nagavajara the latter refers to Brecht's reception in France, already dealt with by Agnes Hüfner and Daniel Mortier, and the former to the central subject of the book under review, the "impact of France on Brecht." Thus, to use the technical terms introduced by the founders of *littérature comparée* as an academic discipline, the matter is being viewed from the receiver's rather than the emitter's standpoint. As it were, Nagavajara's practice is not quite consistent in this respect, for certain portions of Chapter II, being of a biographical cast, invariably lapse into "Brecht *in* France."

Nagavajara has chosen a tripartite structure for the body of his book. Chapter II treats "The Country, the People and Personal Relationship" [sic] and, taking "Brecht in France" at face value, offers a detailed account of the writer's fourteen visits to that country between 1926 and 1955. Chapter III, entitled "French Literature," constitutes a survey of Brecht's responses to various authors, arranged not so much in historical goose-step as chronologically in tandem with Brecht's evolution as a writer and connoisseur of literature, beginning with the triumvirate Verlaine/Rimbaud/Villon and ending with Molière, whose *Dom Juan* Brecht adapted for the Berliner Ensemble. Thematologically and imagologically oriented, Chapter IV ("The Image of France") rounds out the picture by providing information about literary works, mostly of late vintage, in which Brecht's views on the civilization, culture, and society of France lie embedded. The bulk of this chapter is devoted to a discussion of three plays concerned with the *matière de France*, *Die Gesichte der Simone Machard*, *Die Tage der Commune*, and *Der Prozess der Jeanne d'Arc zu Rouen*, whose collective artistic merits the author tends to overestimate. Sandwiched in between are brief summaries/interpretations of three stories penned in the Scandinavian exile and three film scenarios written for Hollywood.

Chapter III offers some food for thought to this reviewer. Brecht's fascination with André Gide — the *romancier*, "playwright," and *zoon politicon* — was considerably greater than might have been expected. Among Gide's novels Brecht was especially taken by *Les Faux-Monnayeurs* and *L'Immoraliste*, an episode from which he considered using as the point of departure for a novel of his own entitled *Stepke*. As regards matters theatrical, the German author strongly disliked Gide's dramatization of Kafka's *Der Prozess* for Jean-Louis Barrault, which he discusses in a letter addressed to Gottfried von Einem, who was then at work on an operatic version. And the politician in Gide roused his ire both on account of his views on the Soviet Union as expounded in the book *Le Retour de l'USSR* and in connection with his performance at the "Congrès international des écrivains pour la défense de la culture," which Brecht, planning to use it for his *Tui-Roman*, ridiculed in a letter to his fellow-satirist George Grosz written in July 1935, as follows: "Bruder Barbussius (= Henri Barbusse) frass gegen Schluss Bruder Andreas Gideus bei offener Bühne mit Haut und Haar auf."

Readers of *Brecht and France* are likely to note the deep impression, both personal and professional, which Paul Claudel's drama *L'Echange* made on the young Brecht and, on the negative side, the latter's apprehensions about Baudelaire, which he vented in conversations with Walter Benjamin during the days they spent together at Skovsbostrand. As for Nagavajara's treatment of the influence exerted by Voltaire, whose *Candide* served as a strong incentive for the *Flüchtlingsgespräche*, and Diderot, little new information is provided.

Given the modest scope of Nagavajara's enterprise, one would hardly expect an all-encompassing panorama. The segment devoted to Emile Zola (116-18), for instance, strikes me as being pitifully short, if one considers that already at age sixteen Brecht had read (which?) works by the great novelist. He discussed Zola's great art in a letter to Caspar Neher dated November 11, 1914: "Ein moderner Maler muss Zola lesen. Denn noch immer ist die Stelle des grossen (Maler-) Naturalisten frei. Die Seele des Volkes ist noch nicht erforscht"; and later he spoke quite warmly about Zola's historical significance in his attacks on Georg Lukács (*Arbeitsjournal* 26, and elsewhere) which form part of the *Realismusdebatte*. There is, furthermore, no single reference to Alexandre Dumas, a performance of whose *Dame aux camélias* Brecht saw in Augsburg and seems to have kept well in mind, for in the twenties he assisted Ferdinand Bruckner, though anonymously, in adapting it as a vehicle for Elisabeth Bergner. We draw equal blanks with regard to Eugène Scribe, whose popular comedy, *Un verre d'eau*, he planned to add to the repertory of the Berliner Ensemble, and to his "French" contemporary Samuel Beckett, to whose "classic" *Waiting for Godot* he thought of opposing a "Gegenversuch." And what about his enthusiasm for detective novels such as Gaston Leroux's *Das gelbe Zimmer* which, in a *Tagebuch* entry for May 15, 1921, he calls "einen vorzüglichen Detektivschmöker"?

In so far as *Brecht and France* is the work of a literary scholar, one cannot expect its author, in our age of increasing specialization, to demonstrate expertise in the other arts, let alone in the Mutual Illumination of the Arts, as well. Nevertheless, it seems strange that in a book which aims at assessing an author's knowledge of and response to the culture of a foreign country this subject has fallen by the wayside. Thus one regrets Nagavajara's failure to explicate the following passage from Brecht's remarks on Julius Meier-Gräfe's book on Delacroix: "Wo ist bei uns [i.e., in Germany] diese ernste, oft nüchterne Hingabe an die Idee und die ebenso oft fanatische an das Handwerk, wie etwa in Frankreich (in dem Werk der van Gogh [sic], Flaubert, Gauguin, Maupassant, Cézanne, Zola, Baudelaire, Stendhal, Delacroix)?" (*Tagebuch*, May 20, 1921). In the case of musico-literary interaction within Brecht's *oeuvre*, Navagajara quotes my contribution to the *Akten des VII. Internationalen Germanistenkongresses Göttingen 1985* ("Brecht und das Musiktheater: Die Epische Oper als Ausdruck des europäischen Avantgardismus") but overlooks its antecedent ("Cocteau, Stravinsky, Brecht and the Birth of Epic Opera" *Modern Drama* 5 [1962]: 142-53), whose *Lektüre* might have prompted him to pay a little more attention to Jean Cocteau, with some of whose works Brecht was quite familiar — *vide* the two pertinent entries in his *Arbeitsjournal* (101 and 985) — but whose name does not figure in the Index.

Other points which could, and probably would, have been raised in a more extensive review of *Brecht and France* include the author's somewhat cloudy views on the nature of Comparative Literature (on the dialectic of "contactological" and "non-contactological" relations, for example), his uncertainty with regard to Brecht's active and passive knowledge of French (was it inadequate, or was Brecht, of whom his daughter Barbara is quoted as stating that he "read Simenon in the original" (66), simply "too lazy" (16) to go to the trouble?), as well as a lack of insight into the *Problematik* of an artistic mind inclined to suppress information relating to certain father figures. In this regard, the positivist Nagavajara, who relies on *rapports de fait* and documentary evidence, is clearly stymied and unable to fathom that, to modify a famous quip by Ludwig Wittgenstein, "worüber man nicht reden will, darüber wird man schweigen."

In sum, a book that would have greatly benefitted from the inclusion of an *index rerum*, primarily of Brecht's own works, *Brecht and France* is a useful compendium which, without offering significant new insights, introduces us to a subfield of Brecht scholarship that had not previously received its due. Thanks to Nagavajara, the relevant information is now readily at hand. What remains to be done accordingly is a critical adumbration of the topic on a higher level of sophistication which places Brecht's affinities with France in the total context of his responses to other foreign cultures and literatures, notably English, American, Scandinavian, Russian, Chinese and Japanese — in other words: an in-depth version of Reinhold Grimm's pioneering *Bertolt Brecht und die Weltliteratur* (1962) in which France is assigned its proper place.

Ulrich Weisstein
Bloomington/Graz

Books Received

Herbert Arlt, ed. *"...mir ist in den 80er Jahren kein DDR-Theater bekannt...": Dokumentationsgespräche, Materialien, Anmerkungen.* Frankfurt/M.: Peter Lang, 1993.

Tamara Berger-Prößdorf. *Heilsarmeegeistlichen in den Dramen Brechts.* New York: Peter Lang, 1993.

Bertolt Brecht. *Journale 1: 1913-1941.* Hrsg. Marianne Conrad und Werner Hecht. Große Berliner und Frankfurter Ausgabe 26. Berlin und Weimar: Aufbau; Frankfurt/M.: Suhrkamp, 1994.

Bertolt Brecht. *Journals 1934-1955.* Trans. Hugh Rorrison. Ed. John Willett. New York: Routledge, 1993.

Bertolt Brecht. *Mother Courage and Her Children.* Trans. John Willett. Eds. John Willett and Ralph Manheim. New York: Arcade, 1994. [Reprint of original 1980 Methuen edition.]

Bertolt Brecht. *Poesie.* Turino: Einaudi, 1992.

Bertolt Brecht. *Schriften 2: 1933-1942.* 2 Bde. Hrsg. Inge Gellert und Werner Hecht. Große Berliner und Frankfurter Ausgabe 22.1 und 22.2. Berlin und Weimar: Aufbau; Frankfurt/M.: Suhrkamp, 1993.

Bertolt Brecht. *Schriften 3: 1942-1956.* Hrsg. Barbara Wallburg. Große Berliner und Frankfurther Ausgabe 23. Berlin und Weimar: Aufbau; Frankfurt/M.: Suhrkamp, 1993.

Bertolt Brecht. *The Threepenny Opera. Baal. The Mother.* Ed. Hugh Rorrison. New York: Arcade, 1993. [Reprint of original Methuen editions.]

Bertolt Brecht. *Der Untergang des Egoisten Johann Fatzer.* Bühnenfassung von Heiner Müller. Frankfurt/M.: Suhrkamp, 1994.

Gay Gibson Cima. *Performing Women: Female Characters, Male Playwrights, and the Modern Stage.* Ithaca and London: Cornell UP, 1993.

Brian Docherty, ed. *Twentieth-Century European Drama*. New York: St. Martin's Press, 1994.

John Fuegi. *Brecht and Company: Sex, Politics, and the Making of the Modern Drama*. New York: Grove Press, 1994.

Marja-Leena Hakkarainen. *Das Turnier der Texte: Stellenwert und Funktion der Intertextualität im Werk Bertolt Brechts*. Frankfurt/M.: Peter Lang, 1994.

Christa Hasche, Traute Schölling and Joachim Fiebach. *Theater in der DDR: Chronik und Positionen*. Mit einem Essay von Ralph Hammerthaler. Berlin: Henschel, 1994.

Peter Jelavich. *Berlin Cabaret*. Cambridge: Harvard UP, 1993.

Horst Jesse. *Brecht in München*. München: Das Freie Buch, 1994.

Horst Jesse. *Die Lyrik Bertolt Brechts von 1914-1956 unter besonderer Berücksichtigung der "ars vivendi" angesichts der Todesbedrohungen*. Frankfurt/M.: Peter Lang, 1993.

Korrespondenzen 10.19-21 (1994), Sonderheft "Brecht Lehrstücke." [Hrsg. Florian Vaßen, Gerd Koch und Bernd Ruping für die Gesellschaft für Theaterpädagogik e.V., Wedekindstr. 14, 30161 Hannover].

Klaus-Dieter Krabiel. *Brechts Lehrstücke: Entstehung und Entwicklung eines Spieltyps*. Stuttgart: Metzler, 1993.

Ursula Käser-Leisibach and Martin Stern, Hrsg. *Kein einig Volk: Fünf schweizerische Zeitstücke 1933-1945*. Bern, Stuttgart und Vienna: Verlag Paul Haupt, 1993.

Karen Ruoff Kramer. *The Politics of Discourse: Third Thoughts on "New Subjectivity"*. Bern: Peter Lang, 1993.

Martin Linzer and Peter Ullrich, Hrsg. *Regie: Heiner Müller. Der Lohndrücker 1988, Hamlet/Maschine 1990, Mauser 1991*. Berlin: Zentrum für Theaterdokumentation und -information, 1993.

Susan A. Manning. *Ecstasy and Demon: Feminism and Nationalism in the Dances of Mary Wigman*. Berkeley: University of California Press, 1993.

Fernando Duque Mesa, Fernando Peñuela Ortiz and Jorge Prada Prada. *Investigacion y Praxis Teatral en Colombia*. Santafé de Bogotá: Instituto Colombiano de Cultura, 1993.

Chetana Nagavajara. *Brecht and France*. Bern: Peter Lang, 1993.

Peter Peters. *"Ich Wer ist das": Aspekte der Subjektdiskussion in Prosa und Drama der DDR*. Frankfurt/M.: Peter Lang, 1993.

Roland Petersohn. *Heiner Müllers Shakespeare-Rezeption*. Frankfurt/M.: Peter Lang, 1993.

Janelle Reinelt. *After Brecht: British Epic Theater*. Ann Arbor: University of Michigan Press, 1994.

Axel Schnell. *"Virtuelle Revolutionäre" und "Verkommene Götter": Brechts "Baal" und die Menschwerdung des Widersachers*. Bielefeld: Aisthesis Verlag, 1993.

Mady Schutzman and Jan Cohen-Cruz. *Playing Boal: Theatre, Therapy, Activism*. London and New York: Routledge, 1994.

Katrin Sieg. *Exiles, Eccentrics, Activists: Women in Contemporary German Theater*. University of Michigan Press, 1994.

Anatoly Smeliansky. *Is Comrade Bulgakov Dead? Mikhail Bulgakov at the Moscow Art Theatre*. Trans. Arch Tait. New York: Routledge, 1993.

Peter Thomson and Glendyr Sacks. *The Cambridge Companion to Brecht*. Cambridge and New York: Cambridge UP, 1994.

Petra Waschescio. *Vernunftkritik und Patriarchatskritik: Mythische Modelle in der deutschen Gegenwartsliteratur*. Bielefeld: Aisthesis Verlag, 1993.

The Brecht Yearbook / Das Brecht-Jahrbuch

Index to Volumes 1 - 20

The following index consists of three parts: a list of the 20 volumes published between 1971 and 1995 with complete bibliographical information; an alphabetical list of authors-titles of articles, book reviews, and books reviewed; and an alphabetical list of works by Brecht mentioned in the articles.

Jost Hermand in Verbindung mit Gisela Bahr, Eric Bentley, Walter Hinck, Hans Mayer, Ulrich Weisstein und der Internationalen Brecht Gesellschaft. Frankfurt/Main: Suhrkamp, 1977). 222 pp.

8   *Brecht-Jahrbuch 1978*. Eds. John Fuegi, Reinhold Grimm und Jost Hermand in Verbindung mit Gisela Bahr, Eric Bentley, Walter Hinck, Hans Mayer, Ulrich Weisstein und der Internationalen Brecht Gesellschaft. Frankfurt/Main: Suhrkamp, 1978. 201 pp.

9   *Brecht-Jahrbuch 1979*. Eds. John Fuegi, Reinhold Grimm und Jost Hermand in Verbindung mit Gisela Bahr, Eric Bentley, Walter Hinck, Hans Mayer, Ulrich Weisstein und der Internationalen Brecht Gesellschaft. Frankfurt/Main: Suhrkamp, 1979. 175 pp.

10 *Brecht-Jahrbuch 1980*. Eds. Reinhold Grimm und Jost Hermand. Frankfurt/Main: Suhrkamp, 1980. 299 pp.

11 *Beyond Brecht / Über Brecht hinaus, The Brecht Yearbook / Das Brecht-Jahrbuch* [1982]. Eds. John Fuegi, Gisela Bahr, and John Willett. Detroit: Wayne State University Press and Munich: edition text + kritik, 1983. 260 pp.

12 *Brecht: Women and Politics / Brecht: Frauen und Politik, The Brecht Yearbook / Das Brecht-Jahrbuch* [1983]. Eds. John Fuegi, Gisela Bahr, and John Willett. Detroit: Wayne State University Press and Munich: edition text + kritik, 1985. 254 pp.

13 *Brecht Performance / Brecht Aufführung, The Brecht Yearbook / Das Brecht-Jahrbuch* [1984]. Eds. John Fuegi, Gisela Bahr, Carl Weber, and John Willett. Detroit: Wayne State University Press and Munich: edition text + kritik, 1987. 160 pp.

14 *Brecht in Asia and Africa / Brecht in Asien und Afrika, The Brecht Yearbook / Das Brecht-Jahrbuch*. Eds. John Fuegi, Renate Voris, Carl Weber, Marc Silberman; Consulting Ed. Antony Tatlow. Hong Kong: The International Brecht Society, 1989. 209 pp.

15 *Essays on Brecht / Versuche über Brecht, The Brecht Yearbook / Das Brecht-Jahrbuch*. Eds. Marc Silberman, John Fuegi, Renate Voris, Carl Weber. Madison: The International Brecht Society,

Author Index
(R = book review/reviewed)

_____, *Briefe*, ed. Günter Glaeser, 11: 233-37 R

_____, *Briefe an Marianne Zoff und Hanne Hiob*, ed. Hanne Hiob, 17: 267-73 R

_____, *Collected Plays*, ed. Ralph Manheim and John Willett, 6: 216-26 R

_____, *Gedichte I. Sammlungen 1918-1938* (GBA 11), eds. Jan Knopf and Gabriele Knopf, 15: 219-22 R

_____, *Gedichte II. Sammlungen 1938-1956* (GBA 12), ed. Jan Knopf, 15: 219-22 R

_____, *Gedichte über die Liebe*, 12: 230-45 R

_____, *Journals 1934-1955*, trans. Hugh Rorrison, ed. John Willett, 20: 377-79 R

_____, *Letters 1913-1956*, trans. Ralph Manheim, ed. John Willett, 17: 263-66 R

_____, *Liebste Bi: Briefe an Paula Banholzer*, ed. Helmut Gier and Jürgen Hillesheim, 18: 220-23 R

_____, *Poesie*, a cura di Guido Davico Bonino, 20: 369-76 R

_____, *Prosa 1* (GBA 16), ed. Wolfgang Jeske, 17: 260-62

_____, *Prosa 2* (GBA 17), ed. Wolfgang Jeske, 17: 260-62

_____, *Prosa IV. Me-ti — Buch der Wendungen*, ed. Werner Mittenzwei, 7: 208-10 R

_____, *Schriften 1 (1914-1933)* (GBA 21), ed. Werner Hecht, Marianne Conrad, Sigmar Gerund and Benno Slupaniek, 18: 217-19 R

_____, *Short Stories 1921-1946*, 12: 245-54 R

_____, *Stücke 2* (GBA 2), ed. Jürgen Schebera, 15: 215-19 R

_____, *Stücke 4* (GBA 4), eds. Johanna Rosenberg and Manfred Nössig, 15: 215-19 R

_____, *Stücke 5* (GBA 5), eds. Bärbel Schrader and Günther Klotz, 15: 215-19 R

_____, *Stücke 6* (GBA 6), ed. Klaus-Detlef Müller, 17: 253-56 R

_____, *Stücke 7* (GBA 7), ed. Michael Voges, 17: 257-59 R

_____, *Tagebücher 1920-1922. Autobiographische Aufzeichnungen 1920-1954*, ed. Herta Ramthun, 7: 211-15 R

Brecht, Stephan, "Prinzipien eines Brechtschen Theaters," 8: 9-12

Breithaupt, Fritz, "Die Inversion der Tautologie: Die Waage und die Gerechtigkeit in *Die Rundköpfe und die Spitzköpfe*," 18: 85-103

Brown, Hilda Meldrun, *Leitmotiv and Drama: Wagner, Brecht, and the Limits of "Epic" Theatre*, 19: 377-81 R

Brüggemann, Heinz, *Literarische Technik und soziale Revolution. Versuche über das Verhältnis von Kunstproduktion, Marxismus und literarischer Tradition in den theoretischen Schriften Bertolt Brechts*, 4: 162-65 R

Bryant-Bertail, Sarah, "Women, Space, Ideology: *Mutter Courage und ihre Kinder*," 12: 43-61

Brynhildsvoll, Knut, *Dokumentarteater*, 10: 297-99 R

Buck, Theo, *Brecht und Diderot oder über die Schwierigkeiten der Rationalität in Deutschland*, 3: 275-76 R

Buckwitz, Harry, "Nekrolog auf einen Schein-toten," 10: 9-13

Bunge, Hans, *Brechts Lai-Tu: Ruth Berlau erzählt*, 12: 226-28 R

____: T. M. Surin, *Stanislawski i Brecht*, 9: 158-62 R

____: Sergej Tretjakov, *Die Arbeit des Schriftstellers*, ed. Heiner Boehncke, 3: 266-70 R

Horn, Peter, "Die Wahrheit ist konkret. Bertolt Brechts *Maßnahme* und die Frage der Parteidisziplin," 8: 39-65

____ "'Doch die am ärgsten brennen/Haben keinen, der drum weint.' Die Verleugnung der Emotion in den frühen Gedichten Brechts," 16: 3-23

____: Bertolt Brecht, *Journals 1934-1955*, 20: 377-79 R

____: Bertolt Brecht, *Letters 1913-1956*, trans. Ralph Manheim, ed. John Willett, 17: 263-66 R

Hrvatin, Emil, "Theater im Kampf mit dem Realen," 17: 181-94

Hsia, Adrian: Antony Tatlow, *The Mask of Evil: Brecht's Response to the Poetry, Theatre and Thought of China and Japan. A Comparative and Critical Evaluation*, 10: 286-91 R

Huang, Zuolin, "A Brief Account of Brechtian Reception in China," 14: 1-3

Huettich, H. G., "Zwischen Klassik und Kommerz. Brecht in Los Angeles," 4:

Innes, C. D., *Erwin Piscator's Political Theatre: The Development of Modern German Drama*, 3: 273-74 R

Ivernel, Philippe, "Vertiges de Brecht," 20: 116-20

Jäger, Lorenz, "Mord im Fahrstuhlschacht: Benjamin, Brecht und der Kriminalroman," 18: 25-40

Jeske, Wolfgang, "'...jetzt habe ich ihm wieder Flöhe ins Ohr gesetzt': Anmerkungen zu Margarete Steffin, 'Hauslektorin' bei Brecht," 19: 119-39

Johns, Marilyn E.: Knut Brynhildsvoll, *Dokumentarteater*, 10: 297-99 R

Jost, Roland, "*Panem et circenses?* Bertolt Brecht und der Sport," 9: 46-66

Jung, Thomas: Axel Schnell. *"Virtuelle Revolutionäre" und "Verkommene Götter": Brechts "Baal" und die Menschwerdung des Widersachers*, 20: 380-82 R

Kaiser, Volker, "Der Phall Brecht: Eine andere Lektüre vom armen B.B.," 19: 203-23

Kao, Shuhsi, "Brecht et l'Autre chinois: Questions préliminaires," 15: 85-97

____: Daniel Frey, *Brecht, un poète politique: Les images, symboles et métaphores dans l'oeuvre de Bertolt Brecht*, 16: 160-61 R

____: Philip Thomson, *The Poetry of Brecht: Seven Studies*, 15: 241-42 R

Karasek, Hellmuth, *Bertolt Brecht. Der jüngste Fall eines Theaterklassikers*, 10: 270-76 R

Kässens, Wend, and Michael Töteberg, "'...fast schon ein Auftrag von Brecht'. Marieluise Fleißers Drama *Pioniere in Ingolstadt*," 6: 101-19

Kebbel, Gerhard, *Geschichtengeneratoren: Lektüren zur Poetik des historischen Romans*, 19: 355-58 R

Kebir, Sabine: Bertolt Brecht, *Briefe an Marianne Zoff und Hanne Hiob*, ed. Hanne Hiob, 17: 267-73 R

____: Bertolt Brecht, *Liebste Bi: Briefe an Paula Banholzer*, ed. Helmut Gier

literarischen Nachlasses, Bd. 3, Prosa, Filmtexte, Schriften, 3: 251-53 R

_____: Werner Zimmermann, *Bertolt Brecht: Leben des Galilei. Dramatik der Widersprüche*, 14: 186-87 R

Kobel, Jan, *Kritik als Genuß: Über die Widersprüche der Brechtschen Theatertheorie und die Unfähigkeit der Literaturewissenschaft, sie zu kritisieren*, 19: 371-74 R

Koerner, Charlotte, "Das Verfahren der Verfremdung in Brechts früher Lyrik," 3: 173-97

Köhn, Eckhardt, "Das *Ruhrepos*. Dokumentation eines gescheiterten Projekts," 7: 52-80

Koliazin, Vladimir, "Brechtian Theater in the Soviet Union. Attempt at an Overview," 16: 39-72

_____, and Boris Zingerman, "The Taganka Theater and the Brechtian Tradition. Iurii Liubimov in Dialogue," 16: 111-23

Kopelew, Lew, "Brecht und die russische Theaterrevolution," 3: 19-38

Korea, Senda, "Greetings from Japan to the International Brecht Society," 14: 5-6

Koreya, Senda, "Directing History (1923-1990)," 19: 323-45

Koreya, Senda, "Meine Brecht-Rezeption," 19:

Kotze, Astrid von, "First World Industry and Third World Workers. The Struggle for a Workers' Theater in South Africa," 14: 155-65

Kruckis, Hans-Martin: Bertolt Brecht, *Prosa 1*, ed. Wolfgang Jeske, 17: 260-62 R

_____: Bertolt Brecht, *Prosa 2*, ed. Wolfgang Jeske, 17: 260-62 R

_____: Gerhard Kebbel, *Geschichtengeneratoren: Lektüren zur Poetik des historischen Romans*, 19: 355-58 R

Kruger, Loren, "Heterophony as Critique. Brecht, Müller and *Radio Fatzer*," 17: 235-50

_____: Werner Hecht, ed., *Brechts Theorie des Theaters*, 14: 190-97 R

Kruschkova, Krassimira, "Die Erotik scheitert am Gestusdiskurs," 17: 53-61

Kunert, Guenter, "Ein Nachwort zur Herausgabe der *Kriegsfibel*," Two Poems, and "Versagen der Gedichte," 20: 29-32

Kussmaul, Paul, *Bertolt Brecht und das englishce Drama der Renaissance*, 7: 195-99 R

Lacis, Asja, *Revolutionär im Beruf*, ed. Hildegard Brenner, 3: 266-70 R

Långbacka, Ralf, "Brecht in Finland," 20: 128-33

Lehmann, Hans-Thies, "Das Subjekt der *Hauspostille*. Eine neue Lektüre des Gedichts 'Vom armen B.B.,'" 10: 22-42

_____, "Schlaglichter auf den anderen Brecht," 17: 1-13

_____, and Helmut Lethen, "Verworfenes Denken. Zu Reinhold Grimms Essay 'Brecht und Nietzsche oder Geständnisse eines Dichters,'" 10: 149-71

Leiser, Erwin, "'Die Wahrheit ist konkret'. Notizen eines Filmemachers über Brecht und Film," 11: 29-39

Lellis, George: Dana B. Polan, *The Political Language of Film and the Avant-Garde*, 14: 188 R

Thiele, Dieter, *Bertolt Brecht. Selbstverständnis, Tui-Kritik und politische Ästhetik*, 11: 254-57 R

Thomas, Emma Lewis, "The Stark-Weisenborn Adaptation of Gorky's *Mutter*: Its Influence on Brecht's Version," 3: 57-105

Thomas, Linda, *Ordnung und Wert der Unordnung bei Bertolt Brecht*, 11: 245-47 R

Thomson, Peter and Glendyr Sacks, eds. *The Cambridge Companion to Brecht*, 20: 383-87 R

Thomson, Philip, *The Poetry of Brecht: Seven Studies*, 15: 241-42 R

Torbruegge, Marilyn K., "*Turandot* in Columbus," 7: 169-73

Torres, Maria Luisa F., "Brecht and the Philippines: Anticipating Freedom in Theatre," 14: 134-51

Töteberg, Michael, and Wend Kässens, "'...fast schon ein Auftrag von Brecht'. Marieluise Fleißers Drama *Pioniere in Ingolstadt*," 6: 101-19

Tretjakov, Sergej, *Die Arbeit des Schriftstellers*, ed. Heiner Boehncke, 3: 266-70 R

Trexler, Roswitha [Mitarbeit F. Hennenberg], "Was der Sänger von Brecht lernen kann oder Meine Auffassung von Kurt Weill," 9: 30-45

Trilse, Christoph, "Über Sprache im Theater oder Drama in der Sprache. Einige kritische Überlegungen, durch Brecht-Aufführungen angeregt," 10: 172-82

Trommler, Frank, "Tom O'Horgan inszeniert *Arturo Ui* für La Mama," 9: 115-17

Trumpener, Katie: Roswitha Mueller, *Bertolt Brecht and the Theory of Media*, 16: 162-65 R

____: Dieter Wöhrle, *Bertolt Brechts medienästhetische Versuche*, 16: 162-65 R

Ullrich, Renate, *Mein Kapital bin ich selber: Gespräche mit Theaterfrauen in Berlin-O 1990/1991*, 18: 232-34 R

Ungvári, Tamás, *Brecht Szinházi Forradalma*, 10: 283-85 R

____, "Brecht und Ungarn," 10: 138-48

____: Reinhold Grimm, *Nach dem Naturalismus. Essay zur modernen Dramatik*, 10: 292-96 R

Unseld, Siegfried, "'Seine Verleger hatten es nicht leicht mit ihm,'" 4: 92-105

Vaßen, Florian: Bertolt Brecht, *Brecht für Anfänger und Fortgeschrittene: Ein Lesebuch*, ed. Siegfried Unseld, 19: 385-86 R

____, "Bertolt Brechts 'learning-play': Genesis und Geltung des Lehrstücks," 20: 210-15

____: Aziza Haas, ed., *MenschenMaterial I: Die Maßnahme. Eine Theater-Arbeit mit Josef Szeiler*, 18: 235-39 R

____: *FatzerMaterial.* Sonderheft *Maske und Kothurn*. Internationale Beiträge zur Theaterwissenschaft 34/1-4, 18: 235-39 R

Voigts, Manfred, and Peter Groth, "Die Entwicklung der Brechtschen Radiotheorie 1927-1932," 6: 9-42

Völker, Klaus: Franco Buono, *Zur Prosa Brechts. Aufsätze*, 4:170-71 R

* * * * *

Bertolt Brecht's Works